P9-AQK-040

UNITED COLLEGE LIBRARY
WINNIPEG 2
MANITOBA, CAN.
DISCARDED

A SURVEY OF ENGLISH LITERATURE

1830-1880

BY

OLIVER ELTON

D.LITT., LL.D., F.B.A.,
EMERITUS PROFESSOR IN THE UNIVERSITY OF LIVERPOOL

IN TWO VOLUMES

VOL. I

LONDON
EDWARD ARNOLD (PUBLISHERS) LTD.

First Published in 1920
Reprinted 1926
Reprinted 1932
Reprinted 1948
Reprinted 1955
Reprinted 1961

Printed in Great Britain by
Lowe and Brydone (Printers) Limited, London, N.W.10

TO

L. M. E.

PREFACE

In a *Survey*, published eight years ago, of the English literature written between 1780 and 1830, the motto was taken from Hazlitt: 'I have endeavoured to feel what is good, and to give a reason for the faith that was in me, when necessary, and when in my power.' The present work is a continuation; the motto and spirit, the plan and arrangement, are the same as before. Here are another fifty years chronicled; that they form a real, not an artificial, period, the book itself must prove. And the aim is still critical, rather than simply historical, although the historical pattern and background have been kept well in mind. I hope at least to have shown that more Victorian prose and verse deserves to live than is sometimes imagined. No doubt, if any one born in the present century reads these pages, and is led back by them to the literature itself, it is he that will be the real judge of my findings. He will turn away, very properly, from whatever seems an unearthing of dead bones. But I have tried to be on guard against the treacherous glow that is felt by the mere excavator, and to admit nothing that has failed to give me pleasure or entertainment, or to inspire a living interest, or at any rate an active distaste.

Another motto, indeed, was suggested by Goethe's[1] remark to Crabb Robinson:—

> I do hate the Egyptians and all that are connected with them. I am glad that I have something to hate, otherwise one is in danger of falling into the dull liberal habit of finding all things tolerable and good in their place, and that is the ruin of all good sentiments.

To-day that sounds too like the wrong kind of morning hymn; nor have I written in such a spirit. Still, those of us who went to college about 1880, who thought that we were beginning to think, and who either found in the Victorian authors our mental food and vital air, or else sharply rejected what they offered us—we cannot speak of them remotely, as if they were three centuries old. Shall we deny our fathers, who begat us? Somebody, within twenty years or less, will rewrite the whole story with exemplary coolness. So the attempt may as well be made, while yet there is time, by any one who remembers those likes and dislikes. I speak of artistic, not of political or doctrinal preferences. Not that the reader will find that these latter are concealed ; if he cares, he will easily see where the writer's bias lies, in the field of 'applied literature.' But I for one would sooner, any time, read a good book on what I think the wrong side, than a bad one on my own. Also the artistic judgement itself, after so many decades, ought to have had time to settle ; and the artistic conscience I have tried to preserve. This, it is to be hoped, is not a 'dull liberal habit of mind.'

As the nineteenth century goes on, our literature is seen to be more and more 'strangled with its waste fertility.' Most of the good authors are disconcertingly copious ; the good things in the lesser ones are buried away ; and there is a huge mass of production lying on the doubtful fringe. No one man can ever read all this, no one will ever try. A syndicate of scholars, however, has done it ; and the proof is in that gallant and fruitful enterprise, the *Cambridge History of English Literature*, the last volumes of which appeared while this book was being made. To them I am naturally deep in debt, not only for information and suggestion but for relief. The Cambridge bibliographies have saved me from overloading the notes, which are only in the nature of 'first aid.' Also I have forborne, save here and there, to enter the field of purely scientific, or educational, writing ; or to record the advance of scholarship, or the literature of travel, or the production of the Empire overseas. All these things will be found in the great syndicate-history, which at many a point is a record of thought and knowledge as well as of letters. At the same time, there is always room for a single-handed venture with a specific aim. What may be done in that kind is evident from a work like Professor Hugh Walker's *Victorian Literature*, which any student of the same period must salute. Mr. Walker's scheme and outlook differ from mine, but I have read him with all the more advantage for that.

Many obligations to other scholars are stated in the notes. To one of these, Professor George Saintsbury, I once more give many thanks for the unremitting kindness with which he has read proofs and made suggestions of price. Dr. John Sampson has been good enough to read several chapters, including the pages on Borrow, and to give valued counsel. Professor C. H. Firth, Professor J. G. Robertson, and other friends have been ready with help in difficulty. Whatever errors may remain are the author's own. O. E.

LIVERPOOL, *July* 1920.

CONTENTS

CHAPTER I

TRANSITION

CHAPTER II

THOMAS CARLYLE

CHAPTER III

PHILOSOPHY AND LETTERS

CHAPTER IV

PHILOSOPHY, SCIENCE, AND LETTERS

CHAPTER V

PHILOSOPHY, HISTORY, AND LETTERS

CHAPTER VI

MACAULAY AND FROUDE

CHAPTER VII

OTHER HISTORIANS

CHAPTER VIII

CHURCH AND LETTERS

CHAPTER IX

JOHN RUSKIN

CHAPTER X

EARLIER CRITICS; AND MATTHEW ARNOLD

CHAPTER XI

WALTER PATER AND OTHER CRITICS

CHAPTER XII

MISCELLANEOUS PROSE

CHAPTER XIII

TENNYSON

CHAPTER XIV

THE BROWNINGS

CHAPTER I

TRANSITION

I

DURING the ten years before the accession of the Queen many of the Old Guard of literature had died, or had fallen silent, or had continued speaking to little purpose. Blake lived on till 1827, noticed only by the few; Hazlitt till 1830, keeping his blade well sharpened, but mostly musing on his old books and his vanished youth. As it chanced, there was a mortality amongst writers in the year of the middle-class Reform Act, 1832. Scott died, still holding the pen; Crabbe died, who had pleased a new generation with his rhymed stories in the older style; Bentham too died, and Mackintosh, who count for less in literature. Coleridge and Lamb followed two years afterwards. Several of the elders remained, including Southey, whose best prose lay behind him and whose verse faded during his lifetime. Wordsworth was to survive, as Laureate, until 1850, watching his countrymen slowly travel towards his own estimate of his poetic merits, and writing more verse, in which flashes of the old character may still be found. De Quincey and Landor, in 1830, are in mid-career; the date is of no mark in their record; *The English Mail-Coach* (1849) and *The Hellenics* (1846) are still to come; but the work of both writers originates in the age of romance, and has been described in a former *Survey*. They are not touched by the art or thought of the period which is called Victorian; nor do they greatly affect it, though the debt of 'the youngest to the oldest singer that England bore' is not to be forgotten (see Ch. XVII.).

The years 1830 to 1835 are, therefore, a real date in English literature. But the new spirit is sooner to be traced, and appears more abruptly, in poetry and fiction than in the fields of speculation, historical writing, and criticism. In poetry the exhaustion of the soil is felt during the years between the death of Byron (1824) and Tennyson's volumes of 1830 and 1833. Darley, Beddoes, and their few peers could not aspire to the position that Tennyson and Browning were presently to deserve. The other poets of the transition are noted below (Ch. XVIII.). These two we can see marching together almost evenly in expansion of power, though not in growth of popularity. In 1842 came *Ulysses* and *Morte d'Arthur*, and also the third volume of *Bells and Pomegranates*, containing *My Last Duchess* and *Cristina* ; *The Lotos-Eaters* and *Paracelsus* appeared long before. Afterwards the new poets multiply ; in 1848 was published *The Strayed Reveller* ; and the next phase begins in 1850 with *The Germ*. With Rossetti and his poetic brethren comes a change. The spiritual and ethical impulse, so markedly dominant in Tennyson, Browning, and Matthew Arnold, takes new forms ; it is still deep and strong, but it becomes freer, and proclaims itself less insistently, being now better harmonised with the requirements of poetic beauty ; and the artistic result is less marred by preaching. This is said, of course, without prejudice to Tennyson's youthful, purely beautiful, and disinterested pieces, which inspired the so-called 'Pre-Raphaelites' themselves. But the nature of this change will appear more fully in the sequel, where the multitude of greater and lesser poets who throw light upon it will also be described (Chs. XV.-XIX.).

In fiction, the point of departure is not less clearly marked by the appearance of Dickens and Thackeray on the eve of the new reign. The transition from the old style of novel to the new will be indicated (Ch. XX.) ; and this chronicle ought to bring home the change which also comes over the spirit of fiction during the second quarter of the century. It is in part a change in the scene and the code of manners which the novelist depicts ; and in part a refining of workmanship, a greater delicacy of nerve, and a lowering of the magnificent hard high spirits that we find in the earlier wits. The difference between *Pickwick* and *Copperfield*, or between *The Yellowplush Papers* and *Esmond*, is not merely that the writers have grown older ; it means that the public has grown different, and wants different wares. The advent of the women novelists hastened this change, though the works of the Haworth sisters, which began to appear in 1847, may seem an exception ; but the roughness and frankness in *Jane Eyre* and *Wuthering Heights* are not those of Marryat and his companions, and are due to other causes. George Eliot did not appear as a novelist until 1858, nor did George Meredith ; but I will not anticipate their story, or that of their contemporary Trollope, except to say that the novel now rapidly overran and revealed one region after another, geographical and social, of the map of

England, filling up many of the blank spaces left by the great eighteenth-century inventors: the north country, the west country, Shakespeare's country, the Thames, the Surrey woods, old London. Put them all together, and the result is a kind of *Poly-Olbion*, or 'description of England.' Local fiction is certainly one of the great products of the time, but the poets also do their part, from Matthew Arnold to William Barnes.

II

This noble body of poetry and fiction has been a rich quarry for the historians of politics, of social movements, of thought, and even of theology. The discontent, the reforming passion, and the intellectual stir of the time overflow, beyond all precedent, into inventive art; they extend the artist's territory; they supply him with scenes, characters, and ideas, and with force and flame and colour; they prompt him to invent new literary forms, like that of *Past and Present*; they may be the mainspring of whole long compositions. They may, and often they do, warp his art, by tempting him to preach and argue; they may seduce the poet into the pride of rhetoric ('by that sin fell the angels'), or the novelist, who is not content to delineate, into disquisition. Yet the 'condition-of-England-question,' as Carlyle uncouthly called it, and the European movement, and the enthusiasm of humanity, are, on the whole, good for literature, and put blood into its veins. Else we should never have had *Sybil*, or *Yeast*, or *North and South*. *Oliver Twist* without the Poor Law, and *Maud* without the Crimean War, what would they have been? The Italian struggle produced *Songs Before Sunrise* and *Vittoria*. Such literature, besides being good in itself, forms an indispensable document, and has been the theme of excellent treatises. Likewise *In Memoriam*, and *Easter Day*, and *The Dream of Gerontius*, and also *Hertha* and *The City of Dreadful Night*, fall into their places, higher or lower, in the chronicle of contemporary thought; they are a reflex in art of the intellectual stir of the time, or rather an overflow from it; and, whatever their substantial value to thought, they are at any rate thought which has become *alive*, because it is quickened by passion and dream and fancy into form. But to so familiar a text, on which it is not the aim of this work to enlarge, one warning may be attached.

If we stand back a little, as it may be high time now to do, and regard the whole mass of poetry and fiction produced during the fifty years, we see, in perspective, that all these excitements, indignations, ideals, and speculations count for less to pure literature than might be expected. Their inspiration is exceptional, and in poetry it is more exceptional than in fiction. Most of Browning, of Rossetti, of Miss Rossetti, even of Matthew Arnold; most of Thackeray, of the Brontës, and of Trollope; and much of the best of Tennyson, of Dickens, of George Meredith, of William Morris, is untouched by any such influences at all, and is the better for being thus untouched. There is, it is true, a good deal of what may be called *perplexed* poetry like Clough's *Dipsychus*, or Browning's *La Saisiaz*; but it is a small fraction of the whole; and how little of it is likely to live! We think first of the lines *To Virgil*, not of *Locksley Hall Twenty Years After*, just as we think first of Pip and Pickwick, not of the Circumlocution Office; of Amyas Leigh rather than of Alton Locke; of Mrs. Poyser, not of 'Felix Holt the Radical'; of Reade's madhouse fights because they are fights, and not as illustrations of the bad old lunacy laws. The truth is that vexed questions only inspire the artist by accident. The attraction may come to him from the Greek world, or from the Middle Ages, or from the Renaissance, or from the age of Anne; or it may come simply from the tragedy and farce of life, or from the wish to paint old corners of England which have never been ruffled by ideas, and whose sorry side has never been noticed by the reformer. And very few, in proportion, out of the vast crowd of characters who live and move in the novel, are touched by the political or religious or philosophic questionings of the time. Some, perhaps, and these mostly dummies, in the pages of Charles Kingsley and George Eliot. That, of course, is true enough to life.

III

These remarks refer to pure literature, or creative art, of which poetry and fiction are the principal species; for the drama, in the period before us, hardly counts. But the scene is different indeed when we step out of that circle into the vaguer and vaster tract of 'applied literature.' I will withdraw this inelegant phrase as soon as a better one can be produced; at any rate it may call for explanation. Pure literature, which includes, besides the species just mentioned, the prose meditation or fantasia and the irresponsible essay, creates, or exhibits, or simply muses and converses; it does not strive, or seek to convince, or to harry us into good behaviour (except by the way), or to give even the most valuable information, or to swell the sum of knowledge, or to make a system. Applied literature does all these things : its chief departments are philosophy, science, theology, history, affairs, and scholarship. Its aim is to establish truth of fact, or truth of law, or to influence action directly. Such a description, it will be seen, covers more ground than De Quincey's 'literature of knowledge,' which he contrasts with that of 'power.' Now applied, like pure literature, can only survive by virtue of its form, and is only literature at all just in so far as it possesses form. But its material and spirit are different from those of pure literature, and more than one factor highly disturbing to the critic is thereby introduced. Disturbing, for one thing, because there is plenty of debateable ground between the two realms, as we see in Plato's dialogues, or in Carlyle's *French Revolution* ; and, for another, because the principle of selection and judgment in this field is especially difficult. A poem or story is good, or less good, or bad, as such—as a piece of art. But an historical or philosophical work may be priceless intellectually, and yet be formless and outside literature altogether. Or again, it may be well shaped and written, and eloquent too, and yet it is rejected of thought, or is of no account to the historian of thought. There is no end to such problems in a survey like the present one ; but they are in the nature of things, and not the fault of the critic. His only safe course is to hold fast to the artistic canon ; not to pretend to be writing a history of thought or of knowledge, still less to figure as expertly judging the conceptions of Darwin or the facts of Macaulay. He may, however, speak of the connexions of these writers and their works with the art of literature : a subject which the professed historian and philosopher commonly slight or shelve in a parenthesis, but the neglect of which is an injustice, seeing that to write well adds to the greatness of the greatest thinker. At the same time, the critic must mark, to the best of his power, the place of each writer in the big complex pattern, by the use of due emphasis, selection, and grouping.

Such, at any rate, is the aim of the twelve chapters that follow. They are mostly occupied with applied literature, which in the nineteenth century, from 1830 onwards, is very ample and variegated. Its medium, as is natural, is commonly prose. But then the pure literature of the time, whereof the medium, save in the case of the novel, is commonly verse, is also very ample and variegated. And this balance between pure and applied literature is the great feature of the period. I will return to this point at the end of the book, when the tale has been told. During the first half of the English Renaissance, down to the death of Shakespeare, poetry, despite the presence of Hooker and Bacon, overweighed prose. During its second half, lasting down to the Restoration, prose, despite the presence of Milton, overweighed poetry. The hundred years that followed the Restoration were an age of secondary verse, of classic fiction, and of magnificent applied prose. After 1780, in spite of the survival of Burke, the applied prose is second-rate, while the poetry and fiction are first-rate. But after 1830 there is an equality and balance, not seen before in our history, between these two great provinces of literature, the applied and the pure. This more even distribution of power may be regarded as some set-off against the great deficiency of the Victorian age, I mean the lack of any poet of the highest order.

IV

In each of these provinces, moreover, and also in the doubtful ground that lies between them, there is another great feature, which is the swift and splendid development of the art of prose. In Scott, in Landor, in De Quincey, and in the early work of Carlyle, the process had already begun. Walter Pater's paper on *Style* (1888) is a retrospective Defence of Prose, written in the light of what the century had achieved. Watching Carlyle and Ruskin, Newman and Froude, Thackeray and the Brontës and Matthew Arnold, we wish that an anniversary could be established, a St. Cecilia's Day, to celebrate the invention, not of a single instrument, but of a whole orchestra of new ones. New, in the sense of being unprepared for, they are not; and the formal development of the modern out of the earlier prose has scarcely yet been analysed, save, indeed, in the great department of rhythm.[1] But after 1830 the change is well marked, and that in the plainer and soberer as well as in the more imaginative and rainbow styles. Its causes, of course, lie outside art, in the fact that the writers have something fresh to say. A more efficient and expressive language is demanded, is cried out for, to perform the intellectual tasks, and to express the new troubles and visions, of the time. As in the age of Anne, philosophy comes down from the desk to speak the language of this world; history has to be made 'as interesting as a novel'; science has to fight for her claims in the market-place, and divinity in the magazines. Foremost among the great executants are the prophets, Carlyle and Ruskin, who are driven to invent new tunes by the apostolic impulse. If the eighteenth century was the 'age of prose and reason,' the nineteenth might be called the age of prose and imagination. Naturally there also arise new vices—a new brassiness, a new foppishness—of which prose had hardly seemed capable before ; they will appear, in due course, in the sequel ; and yet, seen from afar, they are but minor phenomena, like the rhetoric of Junius or Lyly's euphuism. And if we leave aside the distinction between pure and applied literature, and simply weigh the prose of the time against the verse, it would seem that while there is a great and noble body of achievement in verse, the achievement of prose, both in range and quality, is greater still. The reader will find more space given to the prose in these volumes than to the verse ; whether justly so, he must judge if he reaches the end of them. In an epilogue I shall glance again at some of these conclusions, and also at the condition of letters about the year 1880 ; and shall try, meanwhile, to note from point to point some of the links between the period before and the period succeeding 1830, taking in order first the literature of thought and knowledge, and then poetry, and then fiction ; and shall begin with Carlyle, who in some sense is not only the first but the foremost figure in the whole chronicle, at any rate in respect of the influence he exerted.

CHAPTER II

THOMAS CARLYLE

I

WHAT is left of Thomas Carlyle,[1] for those who cannot remember the year 1881? He has taken thirty years to recover from his biographer, James Anthony Froude, who professed to have painted him, scowl and all, in the spirit of the gospel of veracity. But the mischief is that Froude did no such thing, though he wished to do so. An incurable novelist and theorist, and also something of an artist, he built up a finished portrait of Carlyle. It has a likeness; there is no doubt as to who is intended; some of the features are right, but the *expression* is all wrong. Carlyle's political and religious opinions, or rather intuitions, are well indicated. His acrimonies, and also his self-reproaches, being set down in his own hand, have the air of being the best possible evidence against him. But in truth they are not. The biographer, with the longest of faces, made the worst of them in the name of stern candour and pious fidelity, and admired Carlyle hugely all the same, or all the more, and wondered that the world did not do so too. Carlyle, no doubt, said and meant endless sharp and unjust things, and wrote them down, though often not as Froude represents them; Professor Eliot Norton exposed Froude's lack of scholarly conscience as an editor. Still there, in some shape, they are; but they are after-thoughts, not all representing Carlyle's real inner life or the spirit of his behaviour. He was more genial and less selfish than he makes himself out to be. The bitter sallies, when spoken, were frequently explained away by the accompanying guffaw, and by the vernacular Scots habit of using outrageous language which is understood all round, in Scotland, to be half-jocose. Any one who has known Scots of the primitive type will recognise the trait. It may not be endearing, but it is certainly misleading. 'The insolence offensive to you,' wrote George Meredith, 'is part of his humour. He means what he says, but only as far as a humourist can mean what he says.' Moreover, even of Carlyle's truly vicious sallies some are worth saving. It is better to know than not to know what he thought of Charles Lamb. It gives us a fragment of truth, though it ignores all Lamb's virtue and genius. There is a similar note on Carlyle himself, taken down by Varnhagen von Ense from Tieck in 1852, describing him at his very worst, laughing painfully and posing considerably; 'his bearing rustic' (*sein Benehmen bäurisch*), says the Teutonic critic of manners. We would not miss this note, and Carlyle's shade cannot complain of it; yet it is but the record of a bad hour. The truth is that Carlyle's talk, which was the source of his strength and is the true starting-point for understanding him as a writer, was also the source of offence. He *had* to talk, with voice or pen; it was his ruling passion; he must have been one of the most notable talkers in our history. A certain self-echoing, in speech and writing, was his chief penalty, and iteration his worst literary fault. Sometimes it means that he has ceased to think, and for thinking there can be no 'synthetic substitute.'

If we wish to know what Carlyle was, we must get behind Froude, and also behind the *Reminiscences* and the diaries, and look at the whole evidence; and this the public will never do. The public put Carlyle up behind an altar, and then howled when it found out he was a man, and yet it did not and does not see what manner of man he was. Really we know him better than we do any other English author; better even than Johnson. Yet there is nothing for it but to re-travel the whole ground for ourselves. We must read the material that has come to light since Froude's nine volumes on the Carlyles, man and wife, were published: the family records, the notes of travel, the correspondence with strangers, acquaintance, and friends. The shelves have been flooded, but many letters, such as those written to J. S. Mill in 1830-40, are not yet published. Above all, there are witnesses [1] like Caroline Fox, Espinasse, Allingham, and Mr. Frederic Harrison, to name only a few. A shrewd and sane account was given in 1885 by Masson, in a lecture entitled *Carlyle Personally*. To see how such records correct our impressions, it is enough to compare the petulance and gloom displayed in *Reminiscences of My Irish Journey in 1849* with the genial record by Carlyle's companion traveller, Sir Charles Gavan Duffy, of the same trip. Nothing shows better how unsafe a witness a man can be against himself.

Many other things obstruct his fame. He neither produced nor valued a coherent body of teaching; he seemed to welcome the contradictions in his own doctrine. He cut himself off, rejoicingly, from all science, including the science of history ; he often butted at art and letters in a spirit of caprice ; and, in comical contrast to J. S. Mill, he never supposed that he could be wrong. He achieved no moulded and considered masterpiece on a large scale, and he wrote himself out and went on writing. For all this, he is the greatest figure in English letters in his own day, and the last, along with Ruskin, of our major prophets. The mass and range of his total work, its long authority, its idiosyncrasy, its power to disturb, anger, and quicken the English mind remain unique.

We cannot help pretending to put Carlyle's ideas in order for him ; but he never did so himself, and the procedure must not be driven too far. He worked not by reasoning but by impact, sending out rays this way and that, more or less luminous, which set up a disturbance in unexpected places. For one thing, he gave new life to the conception of *authority*. His belief that providence and power are in the long run, inevitably, upon the same side is but one application of it. But the conception works out differently in Ruskin's benevolent dream of a feudal aristocracy, in the Henry-worship of Froude, and in the rigour of Sir James Fitzjames Stephen when he trumpets the rights of the man over the woman. The influence of Carlyle in all these instances is fairly plain. But how different a turn he gives himself to the same idea, when he thinks of a purely spiritual authority like that of Dante or of Johnson ! So, too, with his earlier and sounder thought, and his mystical vision of the social fabric, which is bound together, in one aspect of it, by the continuity of history, 'past and present,' and, in yet another, by the community and brotherhood of workers ; in each case divinely, and by unseen links. No one can measure how far these thoughts, blending with others drawn from physical science or political schools with which Carlyle had little in common, are found colouring the work of the 'dryasdust' historian, or of the 'pedant' sociologist. Again, Carlyle's passion for recovering some precious concrete fact from the darkness, and representing, say, the colour and angry stir of crowds, behold it infecting the vision of Charles Dickens, in his picture of the Terror or of the Gordon riots, or that of Charles Kingsley in *Alton Locke* ! In these unpredictable ways Carlyle operates, for good or otherwise.

II

He wrote for more than forty years. The first phase opens with *The Life of Schiller* (1823-4), which he unwillingly reprinted, and ends with *Sartor Resartus* (1833-4). Both works appeared in instalments; Carlyle's early productions are shaped by the needs and scale of a magazine article; and during these years he lived, as De Quincey and Hazlitt had done, by writing for periodicals. His native dogmatism was not softened by this way of working; the official 'quarterly' style hampered him and for a time delayed the explosion of his true utterance. Until he was about twenty-eight he did job-work, writing in the *Edinburgh Encyclopædia* and translating Legendre. Then he began his task of discovering German thought and letters to the English public. He antiquated most of the labours of Coleridge and De Quincey in that field; he safely founded German studies, it may be said, in this country. He translated *Wilhelm Meister*, not with great accuracy; he poured forth studies of Goethe and the romantic fantasts. He wrote a destructive review, still amusing, of William Taylor's *Historic Survey of German Poëtry*. More than twenty of Carlyle's articles treat of matters German; his exposition of the *Nibelungenlied* is still fresh.

The pages on Novalis, Tieck, Richter, Fouqué and their group seem to-day somewhat out of scale. To ignore Heine and Schopenhauer was as bad an omission as any of those for which Carlyle castigated Taylor. But some of his noblest sallies are found in these early papers. It is true that there is not a little strain and inflation too—the cruder pulpit note is still audible. But in work like *The Death of Goethe* (1832) Carlyle touches the height of his solemn memorial prose. In elegy he is always great. The thought of a departed hero, or of his own private and beloved dead, plays on his heart as on a violin, and his words on the closing hours of Cromwell or Frederick, on his lost wife, or on Sterling's last letter, are music. But he was perfecting his style for many other ends as well; for ethical appeal, rhapsody, diatribe, prophecy, and criticism. He did this in the course of his effort to clear up his own views of life and history; and he received a great impulse to that effort from his German studies. The influence of Goethe[1] upon Carlyle must not be mistaken; it was the influence of Goethe's moral ideas, and of some of his poetic conceptions, not of his science or of his naturalism. It follows that Carlyle's view of Goethe was one-sided. The old poet's final composure of spirit he could only admire from afar off, though he perceived his ethical sagacity. A little of Goethe, after all, went a long way with him. He recurs constantly to a few texts, usually of stoical or pantheistic verse. It was and is the special gift of Goethe to drop a few seeds into the mind, which sprout almost unawares and end by affecting our whole life and vision. Thus Carlyle drew upon Goethe, as he did in his voracious irregular way on Kant and Fichte, for nutriment in his search for a working faith and for some imaginative answer to the riddle of the world which could satisfy his ethical and spiritual passion. And to such a nature Goethe was a liberating power—the sun breaking through the Scotch gloom and east wind. As we know, he recognised and encouraged Carlyle, who was a puritan qualifying to escape from prison; and when, as so often, we come upon some unexpected wide easy glimpse of life in Carlyle, we incline to see the traces of the author of *Meister*; whenever, indeed, it is not due to the aboriginal, incurable, free-spirited Scot in him, with something yet older than John Knox in his bones.

Carlyle drew on the Germans not only for the philosophy in their poetry but for the poetry in their philosophy. He was himself incapable of systematic thinking, and after a while ceased to respect it altogether. He had little of the instinct that seeks to harmonise the truths which beat in upon the mind from different sides. He found no room for the 'hero as philosopher,' and in 1838 he said of the German school:[1]

I studied them once attentively, but found that I got nothing out of them. . . . This study of metaphysics had only the result . . . at last to deliver me altogether out of metaphysics. . . . I resolved for my part on having nothing more to do with metaphysics at all.

He did not give metaphysics much chance; but it is untrue that he got nothing out of them. Carlyle was not, it is to be feared, quite above biting the hands that had fed him. What he gained from metaphysics leavened his whole body of thinking, and determined considerably the form and substance of his 'Everlasting Yea,' as he came in the end to pronounce it. German philosophy and poetry attracted him just about the date of the mental crisis recorded in *Sartor*, deepened his discontent with current British thought, and provided him with other fare. To see, then, what Germany did for Carlyle and how his mind was moulded, we must remember against what he rebelled.

He rebelled against all consecutive reasoning. He could not bear the 'definitioning and hair-splitting' of Plato,[1] whilst acknowledging his 'magnanimous perception, humour, godlike indignation veiled in silence, and other rare gifts.' A man of intuitions, he came to confound clear thinking either with the 'logic-chopping' of the faithless eighteenth century, or else with the cobweb deductions of 'first philosophy.' But it was the 'age of reason' itself, the pretensions of the 'enlightenment,' that disgusted him first of all. It was his business to misconstrue that age worse than any one else. He is louder than Coleridge in his repudiation of it. It shocked at once his imaginative and his moral sense. He read in Hume and Paley a mechanical view of nature and an ignoble conception of mankind. They reduced motive to a balance-sheet of conveniences; they were blind to beauty, mystery, divinity, and also to the unconscious element in man from which the perception of these things wells up. They did not lift the veil, but thought the veil the whole reality. Their explanation was cheaper than the phenomena behind which they could not see. And they could not even see the phenomena; they fell far short of the plain, pious, traditional view of life of which Johnson was the spokesman. Thus Voltaire, Hume, and Gibbon seemed arch-misreaders of life and history. But the German idealists and poets appeared to assign to life more than its face value. *They* went behind appearances, and saw in the human story the progressive embodiments of a divine Idea; they transferred the grounds of impulse from the region of the mere understanding to that of the moral will, the heart, and the unconscious. They saw in human society not the upshot of a bargain or a dog-fight, but a living, mystical fabric whose pattern was for ever being woven, ever more visibly, in the looms of God. These conceptions, which were never to leave him, Carlyle drew from his study of Goethe, and still more from his study of Fichte.

The age of reason could well enough bide its time through all such contumely, and its great work of science and criticism was by no means to be upset. The 'mere understanding' will always have plenty to regulate, and new rubbish to clear away. It was revenged on Carlyle himself, who shut his eyes to the advance of biology in his own lifetime and to its reaction on universal thought. Hegel, during the same period, conceived of idealism itself on a vaster plan; but of Hegel Carlyle took no heed. He himself talks so like a Hebrew, and his thinking is so disorderly, that it is often hard to specify his creditors.

Amongst them may have been Kant, whose conception of duty and the 'categorical imperative,' and whose account of time and space, find analogies in Carlyle, but whom he did not well understand. Time and space are to Kant the forms under which the mind must needs receive the data of sense; to Carlyle, they are the illusions, the 'clothes,' which we must think away before reaching reality. This motion illuminates his view of the historian's task, which is to make the past and the distant a thing of here and now; to portray, as they truly were, things long dead and forgotten. Such is the work, he thought, for 'us who struggle piously, passionately, to behold, if but in glimpses, the faces of our vanished Fathers.' To do that is to outwit time and space. The ideal is a true one, and Carlyle, at his best, attained it. But on Fichte he founded his view both of the makers and of the process of history. To this influence I return in connexion with *Heroes and Hero-Worship*.

III

The use to which Carlyle puts these ideas is plainer seen in *Characteristics* (1831) than in the more intimate but more shapeless confessions of *Sartor*. The philosopher, in this essay, is seen rejecting reason; the intellect saws the branch it sits upon. He appeals to the spiritual emotions and the moral will, not to the intellect; he tries to give an account of the crisis through which he has passed. Such a crisis can often only be expressed in imaginative terms, religiously, lyrically, through incantations and sacred phrases:

> Let the free, reasonable Will, which dwells in us, as in our Holy of Holies, be indeed free, and obeyed like a Divinity, as its right and its effort: the perfect obedience will be the silent one.

This is the old doctrine of the 'inner light,' minus the theology; it is Carlyle's mysticism, in presence of which mere prudential precept and motive-mongering, the weighing of pensions and penalties in this or another world, shrink ashamed. He does not mind the risks of abjuring reason; he throws over science, verification, the arguments of others, and he does not see how such an attitude may end in conceit and anarchy. He strides over such pitfalls, and proceeds to apply similar ideas to the fabric of society. Through the 'communion of souls,' man becomes a 'new collective individual,' and society a 'true region of the supernatural,' and 'the standing wonder of our existence.' It also embodies a divine idea, that of 'united, victorious labour.' Here, then, is the evangel of silent work, preached by Carlyle all his life afterwards.

He tells us what we are *not* to work at ; not at some of the historic activities of mankind : not at law and its reform, not at metaphysic and its applications, not at art or its principles. Life is too serious for all that. Society is a scene of ignorance, famine and poverty, not to be helped by such pursuits. We are to work in silence ; we are to 'summon the Wisest in the Commonwealth' to effect a cure ; who he may be, the *Lectures on Heroes*, and above all the examples of Cromwell and Frederick, will show us afterwards. And he, the Wisest, in whatever field he works, must have *faith*. What Carlyle's own faith is, we hear in a general way. It is that 'no good that is possible but shall one day be real' ; that 'Evil is precisely the dark, disordered material out of which man's Freewill has to create an edifice of order and Good' ; and that it rests on the assurance that 'a God made this Universe, and a Demon not!' Such a premiss, to Carlyle, is as much an axiom, an unprovable basis of all that is certain, as it is to Newman ; an inherited residue, no doubt, of the faith of his fathers, with all the dogmatic superstructure gone. But his practical inference, while in accord with this axiom, is not staked upon it, and gives the key to his sounder notion of history and historical composition :

The true Past departs not, nothing that was worthy in the Past departs ; no Truth or Goodness realised by man ever dies, or can die ; but is all still here, and, recognised or not, lives and works through endless changes.

Once more, time and space are illusions, which the historian, the beckoner-back of the Past in its living image, has to conjure away ; and what thus remains alive is the Good ; and whatever man shall now do that hereafter may show itself worthy of recovery by the historian, that is the Good also. Carlyle preached this true and great evangel ; he rang the changes on its terms as on a peal of bells, with an iteration that mars him as a writer ; but they sank into the general mind confusedly and potently.

Like most great confessions, *Sartor Resartus* [1] describes a long-past experience for which words had been wanting at the time. Carlyle's early letters [2] give us hardly an inkling of the inner struggle that was shaping his soul and character, though they bring vividly before us the figure of the youthful Scot, with his egoism and rhetoric, his friendliness and piety, and his blind consciousness of future power. They open in a cheery schoolboy tone, touched with vague fierce striving, and soon break out into rhapsody. As the years from twenty to twenty-five go by, there is a sharpening of edge and purpose, though as yet of God only knows what purpose. The young Carlyle is seen flinging himself on life and books. He is by no means precocious ; his mind and style develop slowly and painfully. Deep down in him are the memories, with their rainbow fringe, of his home and schooling, of his loves, and of the private passionate conflicts, afterwards to be recorded in the chapters on the Everlasting No and Yea. All this is set down in *Sartor* in Carlyle's faithful ineffaceable way, happily not before he is master of his predestined style, and master also of the discords which enrich the compass of the style and are indispensable for the expression of his experience. But we must go carefully ; for *Sartor* is also charged with the ideas and antipathies which had grown up in him meanwhile and which reflect their hues backward on the story of his youth.

Sartor is not a book that can be drawn out into propositions, and it seems at first a confusion of unharmonised ideas. But its threefold or fourfold origin can be noticed. There are, to begin with, Carlyle's own remembered doubts, and despairs, and illuminations. Next there is the influence of the humourists, like Sterne and Butler, and possibly Richter ; they may answer in some degree (though probably not much) for the whims and tricks of the language, and the pervading atmosphere of fantasy. And thirdly, there are the German thinkers and poets named already, whose conceptions peer out in a somewhat shapeless, also humouristic guise. A fourth element must be added : Carlyle's fervent sympathy with Piers the Ploughman, and his engrossment with the problem of labour—the 'condition-of-England-question.' These four strands are interwoven past unravelling, but the resulting pattern is like nothing else in the world. Out of the mask that recalls the older humourists comes a voice different from theirs altogether. Swift might well have thought of a naked House of Lords, and *A Tale of a Tub* may have actually suggested the notion of a mystical meaning for clothes, and of working out that exorbitant fancy to the bitter end ; but Carlyle's elaboration of it Swift might have judged to be fit only for the ' house for fools and mad ' that he founded. And, in truth, the whole business of the ' clothes-philosophy ' is worried by Carlyle to death. The gods command a lucid irony, but the Titans hatch a splay and clumsy humour. The handi-work often does injustice to the ideas. The name of ' clothes ' is given to the successive coats, wrappages, or disguises—concealing but also symbolic—of the soul of man, proceeding from the soul outwards, and including all his personal attributes (even his name) and surroundings, his circumstance and origin, and all that makes him be or seem what he is. Carry this process far enough, and it is clear that while each man is alone in his inner fastness and must make his own salvation (by means of the 'Everlasting Yea,' which is the assertion against the universe of his own will, freedom and hope)—still, since the surroundings, the *clothes*, invest my brother as well as me, the fates of all individuals are found in the long run to intertwine and overlap essentially; and by such 'organic filaments' one indivisible society of souls is formed. This is the sphere, and this also the warrant, of all the pieties of life and of human brotherhood, especially the brotherhood of those who labour honestly at any worthy end. The noblest of such labourers stand at the two extremes; 'two men I honour and no third'; the thinker or poet (afterwards the 'hero'), and again Piers the Ploughman, the producer, the underpaid, the ignored, without whose toil we perish. At this stage Carlyle muses more on the sufferings and rights of the mass of men than on their imbecility. He declared later that Piers was only fit to be dragooned and obey; but in *Sartor* that dubious twist to the gospel is unapparent.

The central passages of *Sartor* disclose a surprising transformation of the Protestant consciousness. The pages on the Everlasting No and Yea tell the story of Bunyan and Fox and a million more, but in a form sublimed and universalised, and rid of all doctrine but a vague profound Theism which is hardly personal in character. This is the one fixed article that Carlyle retains. It amounts to a belief in good and justice, which he calls God, finally prevailing: a force regarded, however, not as working from without but as immanent in the actual process of the world's history, and as manifested chiefly in the labours of the elect of the world. When he was eighty-three he said to Allingham:

> The evidence to me of God—and the only evidence—is the feeling I have deep down in the very bottom of my heart of right and truth and justice. I believe that all things are governed by Eternal Goodness and Wisdom, and not otherwise; but we cannot see and never shall see *how* it is all managed. . . . Whoever looks into himself must be aware that at the centre of things is a mysterious Demiurgus—who is *God*, and who cannot in the least be adequately spoken of in any human words.

IV

In the next phase, which opens in 1837 with *The French Revolution, a History*, Carlyle commences historian, biographer, and portrait-painter. The story, or rather the scene and the episode, is now the main thing ; but it is enriched, overloaded, and often suffocated by the comment and the chorus. It is represented in the light of the philosophy of life which Carlyle has now matured ; and the philosophy itself becomes modified in the application. The notion of the hero as ruler, of the autocrat by divine appointment, and of the hammer-wielding maker of history, comes to the fore in *Oliver Cromwell's Letters and Speeches, with Elucidations* (1845). Concurrently, Carlyle's gaze is more firmly fixed on the political and social issues of his time, and he prophesies more and more loudly concerning them, and more definitely. *Past and Present* (1843) is half history and half prophecy, and its real theme (the same as William Langland's), namely the destinies, duties, and hopes of labour, is anticipated in the article on *Chartism* (1840) and continued in *Latter-Day Pamphlets* (1850). Carlyle's larger conception of history, thus proved upon both 'past and present,' is further *and* better revealed in the six lectures *On Heroes, Hero-Worship* and *the Heroic in History*, delivered in 1840. His most genial book, *The Life of John Sterling* (1851) closes this period, during which the essays, including that on Lockhart's *Life of Scott*, are thrown off as of old, though more rarely. By this time all Carlyle's gifts are matured except one, namely his skill in the humorous exhibition of life and manners, for which he finds a huge canvas in *Frederick the Great*.

Carlyle, then, had already sowed his ideas broadcast ; and he would have been false to his own rejection of logic had he condescended to argue them out. But he first proceeded to test them upon the 'crowning Phenomenon of our Modern Time.' *The French Revolution* [1] must be read with such attendant studies as *Mirabeau* and *The Diamond Necklace*, which contain some of his best painting. His tone varies considerably : he is now a satirical, denouncing moralist, now a devotee of strength and the accomplished fact, and now a spectator standing back from the greatest flare-up in history and vociferously admiring it. Thus he often does little but reflect the confusion of the events themselves, and his prodigious declamatory emphasis is like the fire of a million rounds of blank cartridge ; so that the mind is but smokily illuminated.

For this and many reasons it is still easy to form false expectations of *The French Revolution*, and to do it wrong.

Carlyle did not use all the material at disposal, and fuller knowledge has corrected him in countless details. He does not always give us a plain tale of what is happening. He is impatient, as ever, by temper and on theory, with constitutional and legal history, and therefore with many vital issues. He had no clear sense of the international aspects of the Revolution. His account of its proximate causes, financial and social, is admittedly most imperfect. He sees, not without sympathy, that the work of demolition was an historic necessity. The work of reconstruction he does not see, nor its lasting effects, nor its value to the world. Nor does he notice the influence of political events upon the history of thought and art. Moreover, he gets tired and breaks off short at an arbitrary point with the advent of Napoleon, leaving unfaced the new problem then arising. In general, Carlyle's account requires confirmation.

But then, and with all allowance made, it again and again receives confirmation. The diggers and historians who came after him have not excelled him when he is right. Many of the famous passages, especially in the early books, such as the death of Marat, or the fighting at Nancy, or the 'Grand Entries,' are pronounced to be, in substance, though often not in minutiæ, proof against the modern verifier. He divined the nature of many of his personages better, we may almost say, than with his information he had a right to do. Moreover, he was a pioneer. The Revolution was not forty years old when he wrote, and Talleyrand was still alive. He was the first, Lord Acton has said, to deliver the English mind from 'the thraldom of Burke,' who saw nothing in the Revolution but a cataclysm of all order and hope. Whigs like Mackintosh had wavered unquietly, now finding the massacres and the Terror indigestible, and now softening when they thought of how much evil had been abolished notwithstanding. None of them had brought home the world-changing character of the event or its human reality. Carlyle is true to his own conception of historical writing, which is an indispensable if not an adequate one. He tries to recover the past in its fume and passion, and the faces of the dead as they were in life. Mill, in his early salutation of the book in the *Westminster Review* (July 1837) fixed on its true praise, and his pale English 'takes gayer colours, like an opal warmed':

In Shakespeare, consequently, we feel we are in a world of realities; we are among such beings as really could exist, as do exist, or have existed, and as we can sympathise with; the faces we see around us are human faces, and not mere rudiments of such, or exaggerations of single features. This quality, so often pointed out as distinctive of Shakespeare's plays, distinguishes Mr. Carlyle's history.

The justice of the parallel, exalted though it be, is beyond question. Much of Carlyle's power is due to his unrivalled sense of the epical-grotesque, which continually puts out its head amidst scenes of blood and fury or in the solemn functions of assemblies. The Revolution is an Iliad where Thersites often sways the event, and the Assembly and the Convention are a quarry for a satirist of 'talking-apparatus'; pathos and futile heroism, the sublime and the bestial, vanity and efficiency, are intermingled, often in the same person. Yet the reader never forgets the presence of vast issues and consequences, however dimly Carlyle may define them.

The method of the book does not fit into any of the regular categories. It is neither that of the strict historian nor that of the free artist. All is verified, at least to the satisfaction of the writer; but then all is selected, not in the sense in which every chronicler is forced to select, but for the service of epical or narrative art. Mr. Thomas Hardy in *The Dynasts* has presented the great sequel to Carlyle's story. He, too, builds faithfully on the document, and reproduces real scenes and speeches as nearly as the medium of verse allows. The result represents one stage further from science, and nearer to pure art, than Carlyle's volumes. Mr. Hardy also provides a chorus of philosophic comment, which is quite alien to Carlyle's and is the mirror of his own changing moods, whether ironic, compassionate, or hopeful. In the same powerful, inconclusive manner, Carlyle uses prose for a running accompaniment. The effect is the exact opposite of the judicial, impersonal treatment used in the 'scientific' histories, where the author gets himself conscientiously out of the way, though his view of life, all the same, is covertly impressed upon his handiwork.

V

In 1838 Carlyle took up again a broken project of his youth to give some account of the Civil Wars; and after much striving it happily took the shape, not of a general history, but of an edition of Cromwell's [1] utterances, his *Letters and Speeches*; with a running comment, mostly biographical, but also introducing many memorable scenes of Parliament and battle. The work, several times burned in despair, appeared in 1845; editions followed, on the heels of instant success, in 1846 and 1849, with new gleanings added, and with the 'Squire' forgeries, which had deceived Carlyle, doubtfully banished to an appendix. In the modern edition of the book, revised by other hands, these impostures disappear, and some errors of Carlyle's, mostly minute, stand corrected. The *Letters and Speeches* produced a revolution in the general opinion concerning Oliver Cromwell, whom Whigs and Radicals, no less than Tories, had with one accord misread. These descendants of the disbelievers in 'enthusiasm' could hardly credit the honesty of Cromwell's scriptural dialect; Macaulay quotes the judicial Hallam's description of Cromwell as 'one who had sucked only the dregs of a besotted fanaticism'; and his actual words, the best witness to his character, had still to be faithfully cleared and presented. Yet even writers like Macaulay, who recognised Cromwell's political greatness, were cut off by temper and faculty from understanding his spiritual side. Carlyle was born to understand Cromwell—not indeed all his policy or procedure, but his essential spirit and its language; and the main lines of his portrait have been accepted by the impartial school of historians, to which he did not himself belong. He is an advocate, but an advocate largely in the right. However, his editorial service must be distinguished from his commentary, which has admittedly many gaps and faults of perspective. He cared not for constitutional questions, and was fairly crazed against parliaments, whether of the nineteenth or the seventeenth century; Cromwell, as the modern scholar demonstrates, being much tenderer of the rights of assemblies [1] than is Carlyle himself.

In the 'Cromwelliad' the accessory figures are, for Carlyle, unusually faint in drawing; this is a penalty of the doctrine of the hero applied to history. Indeed orderly history was even less the aim than it had been in *The French Revolution*. As before, he was preoccupied, first of all, with the artistic recovery of faces, and characters, and scenes, and tumultuous passages; and also with the overarching moral and spiritual issues of the case. To him the story was a great episode, long ill understood, in the conflict between righteousness (which in the last resort is power) and injustice, which comes soon or late to a bad violent end; the axe being wielded by the hero as King, the single-handed maker of history.

But Carlyle's real theme is the impersonal process of which Cromwell was only the agent. It is

> this grand Puritan Revolt, which we may define as an attempt to bring the Divine Law of the Bible into actual practice in men's affairs on the Earth.

Taking the Puritans at this, their own valuation, Carlyle made them intelligible, and disposed of the long-standing cant against the 'fanatics and hypocrites.' His vindication thus goes far beyond Cromwell. In his posture towards the other party he is remarkably grotesque and ignorant. He is as one-sided as Clarendon. We hear hardly a word of the presence of character, genius, literature, learning, wit, eloquence, or sagacity amongst the loyalists. The intellectual and constitutional history of the time and the ties of that history with the past and the future hardly exist for him. It is true, and is also lucky, that his business was different. He did it memorably well; and the accessory pictures of Dunbar, Worcester, the expulsion of the Rump, the death of the Protector, fulfil Carlyle's ideal of recreating great events forgotten or unrealised. Beside such achievements, we forget the small annoyance caused by his comic jeremiads over his 'job of buckwashing,' and against Dryasdust, without whom he could not move an inch; and by his continued chorus of hoots and interjections.

VI

The *History of Friedrich II. of Prussia, commonly called Frederick the Great* (1858-65), is seldom mentioned now amongst the 'authorities' on its subject; the official correspondence of the king and much other material has become available; so that Carlyle's longest history, to himself the cruellest of tasks, the stiffest of all the furrows he set himself to plough, has not held its place like its predecessors. The mere plan of it is a burden; for the main 'Fredericiad' is overlaid with endless digressions and sallies into general history, genealogical, British, Austrian, domestic and what not; and the chapters and tomes on the European embroilment are at once too much and not enough, despite the immense toil spent upon them. But Carlyle was the first in the field; no one had conceived of the same task in the same manner; by German consent, his picture was the earliest and best in its day; his aim was to give a full and living picture of Frederick, and of his operations and achievement, and of his place in the world-drama of that time.

Frederick seemed to him the one great, heroic, and practical figure in the most unheroic of centuries ; the hero performing as king to the last, in a fashion denied to Napoleon afterwards ; the founder of Prussia, which seemed to be the most solid of modern political edifices ; the incarnation of fact and efficiency on the great scale ; the triumphant example of the virtues of one-man rule ; the victor in creative wars that did not barrenly end with themselves or with mere waste. Carlyle and Bismarck, it is well known, recognised each other's qualities ; and 1870, coming as it did five years after *Friedrich* was finished, seemed to lay the last stone of the fabric. Carlyle was the first Englishman to grasp this fact in a living way ; and his bias, of course, was to give it its utmost value and more. In his youth he had helped to reveal spiritual Germany ; he now saluted and made known to his countrymen the founding of the German State. Other English writers of his time may be searched in vain for any such sense of its significance. It was not to be expected that he, or any one else, should prophesy forty years ahead.

Carlyle was sixty-three when the first two volumes of the six appeared, and seventy before the work was complete. His manner has changed considerably. He is now a delineator of life and manners. The Sauerteig part of him, though by no means quenched, is less in evidence ; the invocations, explosions, and displays of shooting stars, diminish ; everything is more measured, and when Frederick is not actually fighting the tone is that of a sardonic, humorous narrator, delighting in the comedy of the business. It is often snuffy and sordid comedy, but it is 'masterly done.' The 'tobacco parliament,' with Grumbkow and Seckendorf ; the whole story of Voltaire ; and, above all, the domestic doings of the king in the interval between the second and third Silesian wars, provide an admirable canvas. There is not a little of Saint-Simon's gift and temper in this latter Carlyle ; there is the same biting, vivid habit of portraiture and recital ; but Carlyle is mellower and easier than Saint-Simon, as befits a man working a century after the event. *Friedrich*, for all its weary ramifications, is the most amusing of his books. It is only a pity that the satire stops short of the hero, for whom he is always straining allowances, not without visible discomfort. Carlyle, as an ethical teacher, here becomes markedly fatigued. Far better simply to have treated Frederick on the great scale as a pirate who had altered the face of history ; to have analysed and shown the results ; and to have thrown over the fiction that there was any display of providence, or of might-on-the-side-of-right, in the whole matter. The experts tell us that on the military and topographic side Carlyle's work held its ground, at any rate, until the acquisition of the new material. Twice he visited the scene of action, and Froude with justice admires his swift grasp and accurate memory of the ground. The 'devouring eye and portraying hand' of which Emerson had spoken were never more active.

In *Friedrich* Carlyle fashioned for himself his final and most efficient style of narrative. It is stripped bare and close; it is the entire opposite of the traditional, periodic, Ciceronian style that had prevailed since Gibbon; it is curt, breathless, telegraphic, with a scornful running undertone of comment, broken into brief clauses by the punctuation. It is an excellent staple for a long work, though not imitable without disaster. We talk of Carlyle's tricks and mannerisms; in *Friedrich* they are by no means painful, though they are present; but here and everywhere, they are his own, they are himself. The mannerism of a school, the trick of the followers of Macaulay, which has passed into a thousand leading articles, is none the more admirable because it gets into the texture of such daily wear, and forms what is called an 'influence.' There is more style, more literature, in an ounce of Carlyle than in a ton of such work. In *Friedrich*, too, the variety of heads and faces is greater than even in *The French Revolution*; and there is more lightness, even more charity, in the drawing. Gellert saying his little fable to the king, and Saldern defying the king, and the face of the king at the last ('wasted, worn, but beautiful in death, with the thin grey hair parted into locks, and slightly powdered') all are sharply cut, with more of the medallion now about them and less of the old savage impressionist brushwork. There is no real exhaustion or faltering of handiwork in *Friedrich*, though the forced hero-worship revolts the judgment. I now return to the books that are interspersed in point of date amongst the three great histories.

VII

Fichte's [1] discourses *On the Nature of the Scholar*, delivered years before at Erlangen, seem to have reached Carlyle as early as 1827. They count for a good deal in the *Lectures on Heroes*, delivered so long afterwards. The uplifter of the youth of Germany saw the presence of the 'divine idea' everywhere, but above all in the leading and shining spirits of the race. Conspicuous amongst these is the scholar (*Gelehrte*), who is the fountain of knowledge, irrigating each generation of fresh minds. When the scholar plans for the order and progress of society, and also wills the means, he assumes the authority of the 'scholar as ruler.' Fichte elsewhere expands this application: by divine right the ruler can and must compel, and the rest must obey. The pedigree of the 'hero as man of letters' and the 'hero as king,' and of the creed of force-worship, thus comes into sight. It is uncertain how far Carlyle knew Fichte's later books and how far he developed the same ideas independently. The point of departure is different. The Teuton professor begins with the cult of study and the seed-ground of the university, the Scottish historian with the cult of power. It may be physical or spiritual power, but it tends to be both at once; and, since it is based on the divinely ordained triumph or righteousness, it also tends to be absolute. It is clear that the latter postulate comes from Scotland rather than from Germany, from Calvinism and Puritanism rather than from philosophy. But the two thinkers converge, in spite of Carlyle's passion for the fact and Fichte's comparative aversion to the concrete. Yet the 'hero' is a more fruitful notion than the 'scholar,' and Carlyle's treatment, as he marshals Odin, Mahomet, Knox, and Johnson, provides a more liberal education than the spectral vicissitudes of the Ego. He fully owns his debt to the 'robust intellect' of Fichte, a 'soul so calm, so lofty, massive, and immovable.'

The word 'hero' is as good as another, and serves to denote and link together the types of energy which Carlyle, judging by the event, finds to have changed the face of the world for the better. They are incommensurable; they are all embodiments of a divine Idea. The thinker and man of science, the saint and martyr, are absent; the types chosen are the god, the prophet, the poet, the priest, the man of letters, and the king. The book is a series of lectures; it is all the better for being the eddyings and iterations of uplifted talk. It is on the whole the sanest and most prescient of Carlyle's works; not a welter like *Sartor*, nor hoarse and harsh like *Latter-Day Pamphlets*, nor deformed by an uneasy and monotonous Cæsarism. The chalk sketch, made up on slender knowledge, of the old Norse religion, is the first well-inspired one of its kind, although the pseudo-romantic haze hangs about it which had come down from Scott and Gray. Carlyle sees that the Icelandic [1] literature is not all 'at one level of distance' from us, but represents many different layers of culture and history. He drew much on the prose *Edda*; much later, in the *Early Kings of Norway* (1875), he was to turn to the sagas, the characteristic flower of the Northern mind. In 'the Hero as King,' as we have seen, he foreshadows his reading of Cromwell; and he is the first, in 'the Hero as Man of Letters,' to exhibit aright the humanity and dignity of Johnson. His fierce sympathy with the churches militant—more because they are militant than because they are churches—appears in his pictures of Mahomet, Knox, and Luther. Some tribute to the Roman faith, of which he is usually contemptuous, is implied in his words on Dante. He speaks soundly, and in the spirit of Coleridge, of Dante's organising power as an artist, and nobly of his style and music. His own style is in accord; for here, as in the pages on Shakespeare, it is at its best, and in the higher tradition of our speech: it is prose doing the work of the *ode*, but without any trespass on the style or forms of verse. The usual discords are absent; and we are glad to miss that hazy handling of grandiose abstractions which often mars Carlyle's prophesying. It is a pity that he did not oftener forget his mission, and simply fling himself on the greatest things in poetry.

But the attraction of history was as great as that of prophecy, and in *Past and Present* the two are united. Jocelin[1] of Brakelond's chronicle of Abbot Samson, the master of St. Edmundsbury in the times of Henry the Second, Richard the First, and John, attracted Carlyle as a scrap of true local history saved from the night of oblivion, and also as a record of a silent, fighting reformer and builder after his own heart. He does not help the story by his excess of diffuse and shouted commentary; and the same vice makes wearisome his chapters on the 'present,' which is ever in his mind while he portrays the 'past.' The day's work well done long ago by the masterful, astute abbot—who was by no means incapable of a little quiet jobbery—became to Carlyle a type of all such work, planned and enforced by a natural aristocracy. And the message, though greatly smothered in declamation, was a timely one. It was the hour of protest against *laissez-faire*, or the theory that the 'laws' of production and distribution were inevitable and beneficent. The later chapters of *Past and Present* are full of prophetic flashes which have since been justified by the event. Carlyle never came nearer to recommending something definite. 'Captains of industry,' who shall see to it that the workers have an 'interest in results'; a Minister of Education, who 'will actually contrive to get us *taught*'; greater permanence of contract; 'a free bridge for Emigrants'; repeal of the corn laws; these are some of the proposals flung out. Then, in his impatience of mere talking machinery and parliamentary wisdom, he declaims against 'Morrison's Pill,' by which he appears to mean mere law-making without any conversion of the national heart and conscience. He would have things done, without the slow, the only available pacific process of getting them done in England. The ministerial autocracy of the recent crisis might have satisfied Carlyle in some degree. But, with all his cry for justice, he never more than half-perceived the value of positive law, putting as it does the brake upon, if it can never quite stop, some far-off unforeseen injustice. He saw through the rough, prosaic moral psychology of the Benthamites, with their 'calculus' of pleasures, but he did not see how little it tainted their practical achievements. His strength lies elsewhere—in the proclamation that behind all such doings, as a condition of making the right law and administering it well, lies the health of the national soul. 'Not a May-game is this life'; the well-known and noble peroration is in his loftiest manner; and Carlyle brought a breath of upper air, he sounded a sharp bugle-note from the mountains, during the confused fray over the social question; and he soon heard the answering call of Ruskin.

Chartism, published three years earlier (1840), exhibits the same ideas in a rougher shape. Sauerteig's sudden lantern-slide presentments of English history (an evolution 'foreseen, not unexpected, by Supreme Power') are somewhat oblivious of the doctrine of the strong man, or hero who moulds events. It would seem after all that the work has been strangely done, in the course of generations, by persons mostly fools. Ten years later, in the *Latter-Day Pamphlets*, with their hoarse iteration, Carlyle utters his loudest, longest shout against officialdom, professional philanthropy, and complacent democracy. The hero has not appeared who shall rule England and set her right.

The book was partly prompted by the upheaval of 1848, which seemed to Carlyle to portend the reign of anarchy in Europe. He sat down to record 'the ruinous, overwhelmed, and almost dying condition in which the world paints itself to me.' He lost awhile his faith in the event, and forgot that the world, even if it does not visibly go forward, at any rate goes on, recuperates, and never dies. It was no conservative kindness for the old order that made him lift his voice, but rather his contempt for the ideals of liberals and democrats, with their belief in the franchise and in 'model prisons,' and their soft-headed objection to hanging fellows who deserved nothing better. There is plenty of mere din in the *Pamphlets*, like that of a ship's great screw spinning round in the void, with no water to churn, and making no way at all. But we are to remember their sound and prophetic passages. Carlyle's scorn, vented in the chapter on 'Downing Street,' for feeble administration, for the worship of the capitalist, and for the superfetation of American wealth and luxury, is healthy enough. While too amorphous to live, and too unconstructive, the *Latter-Day Pamphlets* did good with their phrases that festered.

The Reform Act of 1867 drew from Carlyle the fierce incoherent pamphlet entitled *Shooting Niagara : and After*.[1] It is strange to see him drifting in his old age into a kind of disconsolate Whiggery. The remnant of his hopes is invested in the chance of the landed aristocracy, with their good bearing and inherited authority, becoming local kings or administrators. To merit this position, no doubt they must change themselves profoundly; but then they are to be replenished from below, by the captains of industry' who, though somewhat 'Orsonish' in manners, are yet rulers of men duly certified by the event. In November 1870 he burst out once again, in *The Times*, applauding the confiscation of Alsace-Lorraine. This act is commended, he says, by divine law and the facts of history. He praises 'noble, patient, deep, pious, and solid Germany,' and sees, in her rise to be 'Queen of the Continent,' 'the hopefullest public fact that has occurred in my time.'

When he had purged his mind of the *Pamphlets* and had not yet settled down to *Friedrich*, Carlyle was happily moved, in 1850-1, to write *The Life of John Sterling*, the most humane and harmonious among his compositions of middle length. Sterling, who had died seven years before, had done nothing—his books being stillborn—but leave behind him amongst his friends a vivid kindling memory, which had been ill satisfied by Archdeacon Hare's clerically-toned memoir. He would quickly have been forgotten but for Carlyle's art, which is never more delicate or better sustained than in this affectionate portrait. Unconsciously, the book is a truer mirror of Carlyle himself than Froude's perverted skilful account. It shows the essential kindness behind his show of acerbity. The picture of the friendly wrangling of the pair, 'not divided *except* in opinion,' and the deeper notes of musing reminiscence, rising to an elegiac gravity which is never blind or hysterical, reveal the real Carlyle. 'There are wonders in true affection.' The water-colour landscapes, and the pictures of individuals smaller and greater (the most noted being Coleridge) are of the same quality, and have the same spontaneity, as Carlyle's talk or letters. Sterling himself, in retrospect, appeals to him not only as a cherished companion and sacred friend, but as a type of his age :

> It is in the history of such vehement, trenchant, far-shining and yet intrinsically light and volatile souls, missioned into this epoch to seek their way there, that we best see what a confused epoch it is.

'Light and volatile' may be a thought too harsh ; but Sterling had run through, in a somewhat passionate and headlong way, the characteristic phases of the young English mind at that time ; had started as a doctrinaire radical ; had been shocked out of that creed by the stress of circumstance ; had come under the spell of Coleridge ; had taken orders for a brief while, and quitted them ; and had ended, if anything, as a Carlylean, who was at last ready to find some salvation in Goethe and to launch into the open. The biographer is full of the wisdom of the heart. He is not sentimental, and extenuates nothing ; and the book, allowing for eruptions and iterations, is a noble and pious memorial.

VIII

History is usually invoked to instruct the present in the wisdom of the past ; but Carlyle likes to invert this process and to read the past in the light of the present. His picture of the French Revolution is visibly affected by his feeling that in the years after the Reform Bill parliaments, nobility, lawyers, and churchmen alike were impotent to mend the lot of the poor or even to perceive the nature of the social problem. Faith was the motive power of Cromwell, the spring of his efficiency ; there was no such faith, no such man, in Carlyle's own day. The new franchise only led to a greater confusion of counsel by a larger number of fools, whom there was no Frederick to drill into sense, or at least into obedience. The chronicle of Abbot Samson shows how these thoughts preoccupied Carlyle. He may have been right ; but they gave to his exhibitions of the past a certain twist which is a more serious drawback than his picturesque bias in the choice of material. One deep misconception of history he encouraged. In the introduction to the *Cromwell* he applies the notion of the 'heroic' to whole periods of time. Study the heroic ages, he says ; the 'unheroic' only merit oblivion. But which, we ask, are these ? No doubt the eighteenth century, apart from Frederick, is judged to be one of them ; indeed Carlyle says as much. His own age he reckons no better. The world, however, will persist in studying the ages of seed-time; when great men are scarce and the sages and poets are silent, but when a Renaissance, or a Reformation, is being prepared. Such a time was the fifteenth century in England. Carlyle's view reflects the distaste of an artist for an uncongenial subject. It also accords with the contempt, which grew upon him, for the 'dim common populations' of mankind. They, he is convinced, have not the ghost of an instinct for the means of their own salvation. *They* have no share in the realisation of the divine idea. Long before, Carlyle had proclaimed that such an idea works itself out, not only vertically through long periods of time, but horizontally, through the brotherhood of man, and through the 'filaments,' that unite classes, and peoples, and races, in the same age. Their wrongs and claims, we are still told, are immense and indubitable; but they are blind. It is a pity that Carlyle forgot the teaching of *Sartor*.

One source of the discomfort felt in reading his histories may be briefly noticed. They are often called epics, or dramas, or picture-galleries, or a series of lightning-flashes, or the like. And they also profess to read events in the light of certain universal principles. But how does Carlyle make a rational connexion between these principles and the scenes represented? When the play is over and the lamps are down, we are at a loss to answer. Secondary causes, enlightening uniformities, proximate explanations, are what we do *not* end by perceiving. The sharp impression of things seen remains, the primary tenets remain; but there is an ugly gap between, which we must go to other historians to see made good. The reason of this omission may be found in Carlyle's scorn and lack of science. Figures, and the growth of law and institutions, are not in his line. Sometimes, as in *Latter-Day Pamphlets*, he embarks on these waters, but in truth he does not think the voyage worth while. He is not like Thucydides, who can both depict and reason.

Carlyle reduces the philosophy of history to a single article: There is one God, and right will at last prevail. So far, this is as simple as the creed of Islam. The methods of providence may, no doubt, be distressing and ambiguous through long periods of time. But any institution, race, or nation which in the end has proved to work, and to be stable, can only have done so by virtue of some divine right inherent in it. Make the test long enough, and only what is justified will survive. This seems the fairest statement of the much debated doctrine of 'might and right.' Carlyle, however, complicates it by his view that the 'hero as king' is always the chosen instrument of providence, and by neglecting both the play of impersonal forces and the intelligence—call it even the 'horse-sense'—of the mass of mankind. But his real thesis is that 'might and right,[1] so fearfully discrepant at first, are ever in the long run one and the same.' Here Carlyle has defined for thousands, from whom other doctrines have fallen away, their residual faith; and it has a great emotional and fortifying power. Whether it will bear looking into is another matter. 'At any moment,' says Sir Leslie Stephen, a keen critic, 'the test of success may be precarious, while that of justice is infallible.' It would have been more natural for the prophet of righteousness to adopt the criterion of justice, and not the criterion of the event. But for two reasons he would not do so. First of all, I judge, he dimly felt the truth that all civilised achievement is based on most ambiguous beginnings and is evolved through an infinite amount of incidental egotism, rapacity, and injustice; and he demanded some robust faith that could survive, and could also seem to explain, such a spectacle. Secondly, he was drawn one way by his passion for righteousness, and another way by his passion for personality; which, in its full energy, is often 'frightfully discrepant' with righteousness. It is not true to say that he approves all wars of successful conquest; many such wars, he tells us in *Friedrich*, are sheer waste. He does not say that victory is always a stately exhibition of providence. He falls back on the doctrine of the 'long run.' But how long a run? The case of a small heroic nation being hopelessly beaten out of existence by pirates is a case that he does not consider. Frederick's performances in Silesia are warranted, we are led to suppose, by the ultimate consolidation of Prussia. But in that case, why drag in providence, and why not say with Treitschke that the State is above right and wrong? However, the problem of the scientific frontier between ethics and politics, or between the canons of private and public behaviour, is not of Carlyle's making, and the only thing to be said against him is that he, like others, has failed to solve it. But he did not leave the question unaltered; he tried earnestly to test his peculiar faith upon the unsoftened facts of history. If we think the test broke in his hands, that may be the fault not of Carlyle's but of the nature of things. It remains to speak of him as a writer, with a prefatory note on his literary judgements.

IX

One of the best and worst of our critics, Carlyle is full of unconscious ingratitude. He despises Rousseau; but no Rousseau, no Carlyle; the modern inventor of the literary confession is the source and fountain, if any one man can be so called, of Romanticism, and in a score of ways Carlyle is a romantic. Voltaire he treats as void of reverence and of the higher insight; but, again, Carlyle, in his own despite, inherits from the Voltairian 'enlightenment,' or how else could he have come to discard what he termed 'old Jewish rags'? It is singular how many great or good writers of all ages he maltreats at one time or another; he speaks in disparagement, being usually in the wrong, of Scott, Coleridge, Wordsworth, Lamb, Hazlitt, Shelley, and Keats; even of Virgil. He thought that the poets were too much concerned with 'vocables,' though he was instinctively studious of vocables in his own prose. He is most unsafe as a critic. Yet safety is not everything in a critic. Time sifts away the naughtinesses of Carlyle, and they now mislead no man, and are never dull. Often they get home. Who can forget his word on Walt Whitman, 'It is as though the town bull had learned to hold a pen'; or on Baudelaire, 'Was ever anything so bright-infernal?' And time keeps fresh his inspirations also. The review of Lockhart's *Life of Burns*, with its praise of the 'little Valclusa-fountain' of the songs; the repeated vindications of Johnson, and in passing of Boswell, which have really fixed the English estimate of both writers, and have, or ought to have, effaced Macaulay's paradoxes; above all, the praises of the greatest, of Goethe, of Dante, and of Shakespeare, which befit the theme—these are the salt of Carlyle's critical writings. He speaks mostly of them as men—as prophets and sages; but what he lets fall concerning art and song has the same accent. He might talk himself hoarse about the Eternities and Immensities, but his eye was fixed on them nevertheless; and there are few of whom this can at any time be said.

People talked from the first, and talk still, against 'Carlylese,' and cried out that it was bad in itself and a bad model. The grammarians picked it to pieces, with its ellipses, gestures, capitals, interjections, iterations, and so following. All that is true from the grammarian's point of view, and it has been an easy game now for about eighty years. But it does not much matter. The truth is that as we look back on the English prose of the nineteenth century, this old man, if anybody, predominates in it. With all his tricks, with certain real and too manifest vices of language, he has not only a millionaire's stock and fund of speech, but a certain fundamental and nail-hitting rightness in the use of it. The vices are those of a man; the bad pages are those of a man raging, at any rate, and not mere musical wind, like so much of Ruskin, or sheer sterility, like so much of Newman. Carlyle has let himself be misjudged, because in the region of ideas his power of expression is so much greater than his range of thought; but then this is not his only region, perhaps not his more native one; and some distinctions may be made, in order to see wherein his strength, if he be taken purely as a writer, lies:

> He rolled forth Latter-Day Pamphlets by the hour together in the very words, with all the nicknames, expletives, and ebullient tropes that were so familiar to us in print, with the full voice, the Dumfries burr, and the kindling eye which all his friends recall. It seemed to me, the first time that I sat at his fireside and listened to him, that it was an illusion. I seemed to be already in the Elysian fields listening to the spirit rather than to the voice of the mighty 'Sartor.' Could printed essay and spoken voice be so absolutely the same?

This evidence, borne by Mr. Frederic Harrison,[1] gives a key to Carlyle as a writer. He talked for half a century, in numberless letters, journals, monologues, and books. He did not talk like books; his books talked like *him*. All 'models of style' and the like count for little; they colour or discolour the native stream for a moment, but they are soon absorbed. With its volume and onset, its long sounding course, its fertilising range, its turbid tumultuous rapids, that stream is after all the largest in our present field of country. The current gathers slowly and the first stretches are unpromising. *The Life of Schiller* was published at thirty; it lacks accent; were it unsigned, some future thesis-monger might have to prove that Carlyle wrote it. To trace the essays chronologically is to mark the accent sharpening, the touch of commonplace and rigmarole dwindling, the incandescence growing steadier, the fated style emerging. Meantime, Carlyle also becomes an easy, manly, companionable writer. But of his true style he is scarcely in regular command before the age of thirty-five, though it is announced by many a sally. It is just before that age that his younger prose, whether lyrical or monitory, culminates. In the elegy on Goethe, in *Characteristics*, and in some of the pages upon Burns, it is noticeably pure and untroubled. There is a specially tender and harmonious strain in his diction at this period. Like Shakespeare when he turned to his greater tragedies, Carlyle begins to torment expression when he embarks on harsher and deeper matter. Expression is wrestled with, 'as in a war-embrace,' and is at last victorious. Carlyle may fairly remind us of Shakespeare in two respects: in the immense resources of his language, and in his power to extort from language its blessing. The comparison need not go further; for one thing, Carlyle, however much he may describe and interpret, has none of the dramatist's self-identifying gift; he is always and invincibly himself. The metaphysical prose of *Sartor* shows one kind of his power: other kinds are seen in his landscapes, his battles and riots and tumults, his flowing sardonic narratives, his pictures of life and manners; all these swell the grand total. Everywhere, of course, there is the unmistakeable Carlylese, on which a little must be said.

It is late in the day to play the friendly schoolmaster to the idiom of *Sartor* and the other 'prophetic books.' There is little to add to the strictures of Sterling, quoted in the *Life* (part II. ch. ii). Barbarous coinages, 'new and erroneous locutions,' 'the constant recurrence of some words in a quaint and queer connexion' ('quite,' 'almost,' 'nay,' 'not without,' and the like); Germanised compounds, frequency of inversion, fatiguing over-emphasis; 'occasional jerking and almost spasmodic excitement'—such are the reproaches, to which others can be added: sentences of telegraphic cast, whimsical archaic use of capitals, italics, and so following. These things besprinkle both the high bravura passages, and also the grotesque-humorous commentary. Here Carlyle loves to repair to some feigned spokesman, Teufelsdröckh or Sauerteig or 'an author we have met with before,' his wilder self to wit, upon whom to father extravagance. Such alarums relieve the march of the discourse. But the idiom is still everywhere, and its origins have been rather unsuccessfully conjectured.

Two features stand out from the rest. One is the *noise* of the style, and the strident emphasis, betokened by the trick of italicising, which Carlyle uses more and more to the last; and the other is the intense self-consciousness of all his writing, good and bad alike; the self-reference, the self-lashing, the self-scrutiny, the self-distrust; a quality which is deep down in the man, and which sometimes mars the form, even as egoism of another and nobler cast does not mar the form of Dante. On the whole, Carlyle's much-debated 'style' is his natural speech, not something affected or excogitated, and he could not and would not change it, any more than the tones of his voice, for a hundred Sterlings or a thousand reviewers.

X

Carlyle meets the tax laid upon his English in one way when he is holding forth by way of monition, exposition, counsel, or tirade, and in another way when he is presenting occurrences or things seen. The distinction is worth developing. He may be said to have a small capital of large ideas; and he has a limitless fund of words, and of the best words too, for their utterance. He therefore repeats himself, in this field, without measure. But then it is his business to do so, as an educator, as a natural orator. He pounds away for half a century; iterating catchwords with a boisterous self-confidence beyond parallel, straining his voice, circling round the same notions; but he is never *flat*; from that risk he is saved by his sheer gift of words. If three-quarters of his sermons were gone, we could judge of his ideas perfectly from the remainder; nothing would be intellectually lost. Yet we would not wish to lose anything he has said; for it is fired by an undying faith and sustained by an unfailing style. And much of it is perfectly said; and yet, again, from the very nature of Carlyle's gift, it is seldom finally said. Plastic skill, economy, and proportion, we do not always get from him; but the life-long continuance of such noble talk, kept at the same height and fearless of repetition, is an earnest of the soul behind and the instrument of its power.

Carlyle meets one test which critics tell us to put when we wish to try the metal of an author quickly. How does he speak, we may ask, of death, of love, and of nature?

The week-day man, who was one of us, has put on the garment of Eternity, and become radiant and triumphant; the Present is all at once the Past; Hope is suddenly cut away, and only the backward vistas of Memory remain, shone on by a light that proceeds not from this earthly sun. (*Death of Goethe*, 1832.)

Two plain precepts there are. Dost thou intend a kindness to thy beloved one? Do it straightway, while the fateful Future is not yet here. Has thy heart's friend carelessly or cruelly stabbed into thy heart? Oh, forgive him! Think how, when thou art dead, he will punish himself. (*Journal*, December 15, 1870.)

But sunwards, lo you! how it towers sheer up, a world of Mountains, the diadem and centre of the mountain region! A hundred and a hundred savage peaks, in the last light of Day; all glowing, of gold and amethyst, like giant spirits of the wilderness; there in their silence, in their solitude, even as on the night when Noah's Deluge first dried! (*Sartor*, 1834.)

There are hundreds of such passages, which begin to explain the remark, usually misquoted, that was made by Goethe to Eckermann (July 25, 1827):

Carlyle is a moral force of great importance. There is in him much for the future, and we cannot foresee what he will produce and effect.

The above quotations are taken from his earlier books. But consider, again, the *Inaugural Address*, delivered at the age of seventy-one. Nothing is new, but the old themes are handled with undiminished force. Two years later, Carlyle was asked to give a valedictory address to the same young Edinburgh hearers. His letter declining the proposal has still the same accent, high and moving; the style keeps its savour to the end:

Bid them, in my name, if they still love me, fight the good fight, and quit themselves like men, in the warfare, to which *they* are as if conscript and consecrated, and which lies ahead. Tell them to consult the eternal oracles (not yet inaudible, nor ever to become so, when worthily inquired of), and to disregard, nearly altogether, in comparison, the temporary noises, menacings, and deliriums.

The same is true of Carlyle's more private utterances. In the language of his heart, as disclosed in the sketch of his wife in the *Reminiscences*, or in the outpourings of his journal, the old elegiac power is turned to new and sad uses. In these fierce self-reproaches that are almost fanatical, revealing as they do a pride and tenderness of heart which torture him with the memory of the smallest unkindness, real or supposed, offered to the dead, the theme is uniform, while the variations are infinite; but the language is responsive, to the last shade. The world took these confessions to the letter, at Carlyle's expense; often they only show his noble excess of scruple. In such pages he never thought of how he was writing; but nothing better shows his sheer power as a writer.

This habit of wheeling over and over the same spot disappears when the work in hand compels Carlyle to get forward; when a tale has to be told or a scene exhibited. In this case the matter is continually changing, and it is given to him, and not spun out of him; and another fount, as printers say, of language is drawn upon. His narratives are not all equally good; he often merely alludes to, or takes oracularly for granted, something which ought to have been related, and which the reader does not know. This defect is often seen in *The French Revolution*: in *Friedrich* and in *The Life of Sterling* there is more clearness and more continuity. Still, Carlyle's management of the level parts of a history or biography can easily be under-estimated ; it ought not to be obscured by the excellence of the great coloured passages which are quoted everywhere. When he chooses, he tells a plain story wonderfully well, though not of course with the classical thrift of Hume, or with the ordered and spaced-out rhetoric of Macaulay. 'There are thin tints of style,' as he says somewhere of Goethe, 'shades of ridicule, or tenderness, or solemnity, resting over large spaces, and so slight as almost to be evanescent.' The account of the boyhood of Friedrich, of the Spanish adventure of John Sterling, of his own Irish or Parisian journeys, are models of narrative, some of them only set down for his own eye. He is a master of prose that is just doing the day's work of prose ; and his indescribable nerve and virility give him an advantage over more reserved and finished writers, like Thackeray or Newman, of his own time. He has, when all is said, a better eye and a better mind than most of them, and he gives a stronger satisfaction. Genius, like generalship, is not all grand strategy ; much of it comes down to a series of small strokes, each of them going an inch further than mere talent can manage.

This is when Carlyle is moving forward ; but when he stops to describe heads, or landscapes, or scenes of blood and disorder, or sarcastic-comic interludes, then, no doubt, we are in presence of his central gift. These passages are not patched in ; they come naturally in their places. His ear was at least as keen as his eye, and his impressions of voices, modes of laughter, and inarticulate sounds and noises, find the right words instantly. Such is the well-known portrait of Thiers, flung on paper for Carlyle's private eye after a meeting in Paris in 1851 ; we hear the 'good-humoured treble *croak*, which bustles itself on in continuous copiousness,' and the 'monotonous low gurgling key, with occasional sharp yelping warbles,' all proceeding from the 'placidly sharp fat face, puckered eyewards.' But here is a less familiar sketch, taken from certain old discarded chapters on the early Stuarts. Gardiner describes the career of Alexander Leighton,[1] author of *Sion's Plea against Prelacy* (1630), and fits it into his story ; and he has also duly read, and summarises, that work, which Carlyle declares 'will never more be read by any mortal,' and which he does not summarise.

Instead, he presents Leighton's headpiece, after long poring upon some old print of it :

A monstrous pyramidal head, evidently full of confused harsh logic, toil, sorrow, and much other confusion, wrinkly brows arched up partly in wonder, partly in private triumph over many things, most extensive cheeks, fat, yet flaccid, puckered, corrugated, flowing down like a flood of corrugation, wherein the mouth is a mere corrugated eddy, frowned over by an amorphous bulwark of nose ; the whole, you would say, *supported* by the neck-dress, by the doublet-collar and front resting on it, surmounted by deluges of tangled tattered hair : such is the alarming physiognomy of Dr. Leighton, medical gentleman, etc.

We may be glad that the study of physiognomy was a kind of Lavaterish superstition with Carlyle. He looked at Southey or Daniel Webster in the flesh ; he is said to have hung up the pictures of Cromwell and other historical persons before him while he wrote. When he can, he likes to begin with the face and voice of the man whom he is describing. He was now and then comically beguiled, as in the case of the innocent-looking practical jester Squire ; and often there is a ragged cutting edge to the description. But the coloured photography of Macaulay and other 'vivid' writers is killed at once by the side of Carlyle's presentments. He is alone of his kind, and his imitators are below notice. It is the same with his incidental landscapes, which are perfect ; such are the visions of London and of the Vale of Glamorgan in *The Life of Sterling*. Each of his major books, *Sartor*, *Past and Present*, and the three histories, has its own different stamp of descriptive genius. As time goes on, Carlyle applies his gift more and more to realistic purposes ; leaves behind the grotesque-sublime-fantastic and big confused scenes of tumult, and draws with a minuter veracity, often highly humorous. This change appears in *Friedrich*, where the battles on the one part, and the domestic passages on the other, mark the extremes of his craft. Leaving out the domain of Ruskin, there is certainly no such gallery in English as the works of Carlyle. His ideal, we know, as an historian or chronicler, was to recover the *life* of things, either long buried or as they fleeted by him ; and, though unhappy in some ways, he was happy in this, that his gift exactly fitted, as it doubtless determined, his ideal. The result, no doubt, is scarcely commensurate with his gift. Such a vision, such a moral passion, such a fountain of language ! Yet they did not, as might be hoped, produce any large harmonious masterpiece of thought or art. Whim, and temper, and the gaps in his philo-

sophy, and want of construction and economy, disabled Carlyle from such achievements. But when all is said, he is a real prophet, if not precisely a 'sage'; it will be long before his prophecies and counsels are so fully realised as to be obsolete. The battle goes on for ever, for which he sounded the call to arms. And to 'recover the life of things,' past or present, as Carlyle does, and with his fidelity and intensity, has been granted to no English writer since he died. The great ship is not wholly weather-tight, its freight is not all precious still; but its displacement, its onset, are hard to match in its own day; and the roar of its guns, the blast of its syren, cannot soon be forgotten.

XI

Carlyle's talk and writing are full of a shearing kind of satire; and at times there is a mellower suffusing humour. He was not exactly a wit; and the deficiency is supplied by Mrs. Carlyle, who has left nothing except her correspondence. He was delighted, at any rate in retrospect, when her wit singed his own beard. Not all were equally grateful when it flicked their way; but it did them no real harm, and posterity is grateful. It is French in ease and lightness, though there is no precise parallel in French. It is Scotch in mental fibre, and in its fundamental hard sense. But wit, in Mrs. Carlyle, ministers to many other gifts; and, above all, to her alarming and riveting genius for feminine description. Her accounts of the prayer meeting, of the mesmerist, of the 'money rows,' of friends and visitors, of Miss Jewsbury, and Mazzini, and Mrs. Mill, are as clear and sharp in their own kind as anything of Carlyle's own. Her strong head had to contend with a large native power of being miserable, which was increased by circumstance, by what has been called Carlyle's 'deficiency in the small change of affection,' and by something of a morbid streak in her nervous system. And the demon drove her to utter everything, or to write it down. The household drama was no worse than thousands that never find words at all. The true, net impression is one of fundamental honesty, courage, and spirit in both parties.

On Sterling, Mill, and the Carlyles, and their talk, a gentle and clear light is cast by Caroline Fox in her *Memories of Old Friends*. Her letters and journals range from 1835 to 1871, and Wordsworth, Hartley Coleridge, Tennyson, Bunsen, Maurice, and many figures more move across her vision, and are told of in her 'musical little voice,' by her 'swift, neat, pen,' commended by Carlyle. Caroline Fox had the curiously trained memory which can carry away the pith of a discourse at the meeting-house, and it helped her to record some of the *Lectures on Heroes*, and many a monologue and conversation. Sterling's humming-bird disquisitions on German thought and poetry are noted, and Mill's on conduct and affairs, touched with his high feminine sentiment and his late-discovered love of the poetic ; it is pleasant to find him drawing out a 'calendar of odours,' every month its flower, for his friend. There is not a little dreary culture, rather solemnly taken, and now extinct—pulpit discourses and scientific holdings-forth are chronicled ; but the nimbleness of Caroline Fox's mind and her dainty intellectual temper rise above even that atmosphere. It was surely an age of unmatched eagerness for talking on 'subjects,' for listening and inflicting ! But we get the sense of an eager, mirror-like intelligence at work, and also of a heart of gold, which the slightly formal style cannot disguise.

CHAPTER III

PHILOSOPHY AND LETTERS

I

THE fifty years that ended with the death of Bentham were not, in Britain, a great age of philosophy[1] or of philosophical writing. There was no Kant, Fichte, Hegel, or Schopenhauer. Late in the day Coleridge, followed by Carlyle, began to acclimatise German thought, and to ask the public to think on fundamentals; but neither of these transmitters and interpreters of genius can be called, from the European point of view, an originative mind, nor were they methodical thinkers. The writers who merit the latter title, like Godwin, Bentham, and James Mill, had started by banishing metaphysics; and their power and service lay in the sphere of applied philosophy, in sociology, in legal reform, in political economy, and in the frontier-ground between positive law and ethics. The elder Mill greatly advanced psychology as a natural science. In political thinking the group is in sharp contrast to Burke and to all for which he stands. They share nothing with him except his dislike of 'first philosophy.' They descend, in the first instance, from the traditional English school, with its emphasis on what is given to the mind by experience, and its inclination to derogate from what may be given either *in* or *by* the mind; and they draw, more immediately, on the ideas of the French Revolution, of which a crude and naïf version is found in Godwin. The principle of the rights of man lives on in the individualism of the 'philosophic radicals,' but it becomes obscured by the principle of utility, or of the 'greatest happiness.' The aim of this school was, first of all, to state in a rational way the conditions of welfare for the individual, especially for the unenfranchised and ignored classes; and next, to proclaim and fight for the changes of privilege required for the attainment of those conditions. The campaign was a great one, and was partially successful, and had its influence on literature. Its intellectual history was well written by Sir Leslie Stephen.

Bentham and James Mill could not foster a great, or even a very good, philosophical style, which seldom flourishes where metaphysics are considered a perilous luxury. But the want was to be made good by their adversaries like Hamilton, Mansel, and Ferrier, and also by their truant son, John Stuart Mill, who broke away from radical orthodoxy. Their own notion of life was decidedly bleached; they remained cheerfully or grimly blank to scenery and poetry and art, to imagination and mystery. They would only reckon with what reason gave, and ignored much that is given to reason to judge, including the sub-reasonable or unconscious element in man. They are anti-romantic. The key to John Stuart Mill, the leading English thinker of the mid-century, is found in his effort to repair these deficiencies, and in fact to *edit* Benthamism; to fit the missing feelings and ideals into philosophy, while trying to crutch them on reason and logic as still understood. In his passionate effort to do this Mill becomes a very good, a very considerable, all but a great writer. An unusually pure, high, and honest mind, with a true strain of magnanimity, he always remains. Before approaching him it is well to note some of the links between philosophy and letters during this period, without affecting to write its intellectual chronicle.

In one way the disappointment continues. To the last no philosopher arises in England who makes an epoch in general thought. There is no book to compare with Hegel's *Æsthetik* (published 1832), or with Schopenhauer's *World as Will and Idea* (1819). Neither of these works was put into English for many years. Comte had not so long to wait. Still it was not all an evil that our philosophy for a time kept its insular stamp. The native genius could thus work more freely and yield all that was in it.

Its character can be seen best in three books, which may be taken as landmarks. The first is Mill's *Logic* (1843), another is Darwin's *Origin of Species* (1859), the third is Herbert Spencer's *First Principles* (1862). In the long series of writings thus inaugurated, the *Liberty* (1859), *The Descent of Man* (1871), and *The Data of Ethics* (1879), are further landmarks. Much of the controversial writing of the age can be referred directly or otherwise to these six volumes. Conspicuous later in the war is Huxley, an athlete of noble temper and a genuine gift of style, who lies somewhat buried under his own trophies. On the liberal side, Mill and Huxley stand above the rest as writers; there is the best quality of the classical age in the style and mind of Sir Leslie Stephen. In the other camp,

Mansel and Ferrier are both masters of a philosophical diction of rare excellence. But we must not, on either side, confound literary with philosophical importance. These, in the case of Herbert Spencer, do not coincide. Darwin, while not a philosopher in the accepted sense, and not exactly of mark as a master of words, leavened universal thought. Indeed, the year 1860 may be taken as a watershed. Thereafter the conception of evolution, with its endless applications and fresh vocabulary, became really current. John Stuart Mill it never fairly penetrated; he lived till 1873, but his mind was formed long before Darwin wrote. He was greatly moulded by his early revulsions, as becomes clear when we glance at the prominent *a priori* thinkers before 1860. The first of these, the most influential teacher in Britain, Mill attacks along the whole line in his *Examination of Sir William Hamilton's Philosophy* (1865), a work in which many of the vital issues between the philosophical Right and Left are arrayed.

II

It was in 1829 that Sir William Hamilton (1788-1856) began to write in the *Edinburgh Review*, where his distinctive theories of perception, of predication, and of the 'unconditioned,' were first presented. His lectures on logic and metaphysic were given from his chair in Edinburgh, beginning in 1836. Their posthumous publication (1858-60) explains why Mill's attack, so late in the day, could still be fresh. Hamilton had, however, published his edition of Reid, with dissertations appended, and some volumes of *Discussions*. His lore was very great, in letters as well as in philosophy, and, though it is more critical, it reminds us of the cascade of erudition in writers like Cudworth. He might be called a humanist with the brain of a schoolman. He was deep in theology, in Greek, and in Latin and neo-Latin poetry. He planned to edit George Buchanan. Like a true Scottish professor he dearly loves a quotation. He comes back with a sigh and a 'But to return' from his roll-call of obscure names and curious parallels. As we turn his pages we see the Northern faces in the classroom, drinking in the difference between the five main theories of immediate perception, or lighting up at the resonant hexameters of Fracastorius on the Platonic Ideas. Hamilton's diction flouts the graces; he can use words like *redargue*, *potence*, *astrict*, or *transeunt*, and can say that Dr. Brown 'evacuates the phenomenon of all that desiderates explanation.' It is a pity that

Lockhart, as 'Peter,' patrolled Edinburgh too soon to put Hamilton in his 'letters to his kinsfolk.' Yet there is a certain grand rhetorical air, a glow and direct appeal, which the Universities of the South are ready to despise, but which is exhilarating all the same ; and this air Hamilton commands. With all his pedantry he rivets the mind. He contrives to unite logical and historical exposition without confusing the young, or the reader, which is no easy feat. Mill regrets that Hamilton did not keep to the history of philosophy. For such a task he was equipped by his learning ; but he is not remarkable for apprehending the point of view of other minds, and if he had remained a mere historian he might have sacrificed much of his power. For his chief desire is to make others think ; and the sight of the teacher reasoning aloud, refuting and constructing, whether well or ill, prevents the dead hand of the past, the purely historical treatment, from chilling initiative. He certainly knows the right way to usher in philosophy. He begins by copious definition and discrimination of the central terms, *subject*, *substance*, *reason*, *realism*, and of their synonyms in languages ancient and modern. He unsealed British ears to the greater German thinkers. It may be true, as Mill says, that much of his precision is only apparent ; but he lays out the ground in a large way, and states the perennial problems sharply, with such reiteration and harking-back as befits the educational scene. In his dissertations and notes to Reid, where his object is not first of all to stimulate, the method is much the same, while the rhetoric is absent.

Hamilton is not judged, even by those of his own lineage, to have left much that is of original or lasting value for thought. But he raised up the study of metaphysic in Britain, opening up anew the larger horizons of the history of philosophy, and he gave a point of departure for two diametrically opposite schools, represented by Mansel and by Herbert Spencer. As a philosopher, he holds that the infinite and the absolute are past our knowing ; but, in the sphere of rational theology, he seems to offer them as objects of belief. Hence the divine and the agnostic use his conclusions in opposite ways. Hamilton quickened the study of psychology ; and he has his ties with the romantic movement, dwelling much on the hidden fund of human feeling and experience, as it emerges in dreams, in the phenomena of dual personality, and in the sense of the mysterious. He also awakens, as none of his opponents do, a lively sense of the populous past of thought—of the human wisdom scattered amongst the philosophers, and of the philosophy that is to be found in the poets.

Hamilton is cumbrous, with all his abundant energy. But his follower, Henry Longueville Mansel[1] (1820-71), professor at Oxford and latterly Dean of St. Paul's, is the master of a pure and precise diction—classical and never too scholastic—of a pithiness and rigour in demonstration, of a grim order of wit, and sometimes of a pure and exalted music. Even if his main thesis be thought an historical curiosity, Mansel is plainly a logician born. His *Prolegomena Logica* (1851) are designed, in the first place, to defend the innate and universal nature, and to state the exact function, of the principles of formal thinking; secondly, to establish the restriction of human knowledge to that which is purely finite and 'conditioned'; and then to apply, more fully than Hamilton had done, these conceptions to the data of theology. Such is the aim of his Bampton Lectures, delivered in 1858, on *The Limits of Religious Thought Examined*. The long preface to the fourth edition (1859) forms part of the argument, which is to the effect that

> the history of mankind in general, as well as the consciousness of each individual, alike testify that *religion is not a function of thought*; and that the attempt to make it so, if consistently carried out, necessarily leads, firstly to Anthropomorphism, and finally to *Atheism* (ch. viii.).

The italics, which are not Mansel's, contain the essence of his view. He argues that reason can only go bankrupt in the endeavour to control the region of faith, wherein the truths of theology lie; yet that this is no disproof of religion; since reason, in her own field, encounters difficulties fully as great as those raised by faith—a new turn given to the argument of Butler; and that, moreover, the orthodox creed is irresistibly commended by the moral consciousness, the voice of the heart, and the teachings of history. Mansel's pleading for his principles and their applications is of signal ability, and it is seen again in his reviews and in his *Philosophy of the Conditioned* (1866), a rejoinder to 'Mill on Hamilton.' He naturally raised a hornet's nest. Some of the orthodox found that he had conceded altogether too much; the Broad Church, in the person of Maurice, entered the fray in the name of the free reason, and there was a painful exchange of amenities; while Mill, taking up Mansel's proposition that human and divine goodness might signify very different things, since our moral notions can only be 'relative,' exclaimed that if Mansel's God could send him to hell for denying such a discrepancy, to hell he would go. A later philosopher, Höffding, echoes the feeling concerning Mansel's general view, that 'this weapon is only too apt to wound those that use it.' But it is admirably forged and chased, and will not soon cease to be regarded for its handiwork. In his directly religious appeals, Mansel is able to rise to a grave but piercing eloquence, of the real, the best, the indefinable Oxford sort. Few there are, however rigorous-minded, in whom the old city leaves no touch of mysticism. His irony and sarcasm are also Oxonian ; and the best example of these qualities, in prose, is the article on *Sensation Novels*, wherein twenty-four such productions, which are mostly trash, but which also include *Lady Audley's Secret* and *No Name*, are faithfully and sourly dealt with. His Aristophanic skit, *Phrontisterion*, was prompted by the report of the University Commission of 1850. The allusions to Lord John Russell and the 'Manchester man' were soon mouldy, but the chorus of Hegelian and Straussian professors, who were to supplant the college tutors, still dances to most excellent anapæsts. Mansel spoke for Oxford conservatism in the most formidable sense of the term. Some, however, of the reforms of 1850 remain, and so do the tutors, and so does his copy of good verses.

A professor of genius must now be mentioned ; Scotch, of course ; an acute-minded and glorious dogmatist, who called his system 'Scottish to the core.' This is James Frederick Ferrier[1] (1808-64), who lectured at St. Andrews for twenty years ; the author of *Institutes of Metaphysic* (1854), of a course on early Greek philosophy, and of a number of shorter articles. All thinkers except possibly Plato and Berkeley had asked the wrong questions, or in the wrong order, or had answered them wrong, or had only a glimmering of the answers. To set matters right, Ferrier would establish an idealism of a new kind and by a new method. The pupil and friend of Hamilton, and with him the champion of metaphysic against the still potent school of 'common sense,' he breaks away and pursues an independent path. He is no mere expounder of Hegel, or of any one else. The path is in three stages ; a theory of knowledge, a theory of ignorance (on which Ferrier lays especial stress), and a theory of being. Everything follows rigorously from the primary and self-evident proposition that 'along with what every intelligence knows, it must, as the ground and condition of its knowledge, have some cognisance of *itself*.' The form of proof is like Spinoza's : a string of geometrically stated theorems, with demonstrations and glosses appended; and everything leads up to a final definition of 'Absolute Existence.' For clearness, Ferrier adds a string of consistent 'counter-propositions,' which form a complete *corpus* of philosophic falsehood. In a letter to De Quincey he tries to put the whole system in a nutshell; but it is best apprehended from his *Introduction to the Philosophy of Consciousness* (1838-9) and his *Berkeley and Idealism* (1842), where he is not fettered by scholastic method.

No British metaphysician writes with more relish and confidence, or more as one to the manner born. The magisterial style carries us along. Mill, who thought that Ferrier begged every one of his propositions as it came, called the *Institutes* 'the romance of logic,' very justly. It is good to read Ferrier every few years, as a tonic; not only for his peculiar rigour in the statement of the most abstract matter, and for the jaunty ease with which he moves in the metaphysical Zion, but also for his rhetoric, which often amounts to eloquence. He beats his way to the Absolute upon a drum. He sets up his foe, the 'materialist,' like a stuffed image, and then hurls him to the abyss, not indeed of falsehood, which is too good for such a being, but of nonsense, of the 'contradictory,' of total and stark and irredeemable inconceivability—of what is inconceivable, be it noted as vital, not only to *us*, but 'in itself' and 'to any *possible* intellect.' This is all most exhilarating; there is no finer canter for the mind. The sallies and perorations, the passages on the apparent unfruitfulness of philosophy, and on Plato (' over deep and over shallow he rolls on, broad, urbane, and unconcerned'), are not inferior. The college lectures on Parmenides, Heraclitus, and their company, are models of the art. Ferrier presents highly rarefied ideas as firmly and vividly as Macaulay presents detail. He is a most brilliant blossom of the *a priori* stock, and he initiates the return, of which note will be made in the next chapter, towards an absolute idealism. His school never died down; but it was eclipsed for some decades in the public eye by that of 'experience,' which enlisted for a time the best or most popular writers, and whose appeal was strengthened tenfold by the prodigious development of science, its natural ally, and of the accompanying concept of evolution, which altered so many 'values.'

III

Is there any one alive who still speaks of '*Mr.* Mill,'[1] as people did for some time after his death in 1873? A certain special dignity hung round his name; and his letters, the mass of which only appeared a few years ago, do not impair the impression. They fill in, but do not essentially alter, the portrait. They are, it is true, largely discourses; they are like the reports of a grave public servant to a trusted colleague; or they are guarded, finished replies to earnest questioners. Mill's intellectual passion, which is everywhere latent, comes nearest to the surface in his early outpourings to Sterling and Carlyle; and also in his subsequent correspondence with Comte, which has been long before the world. He was the most conscientiously receptive of philosophers; anxiously he drew on other minds, and balanced his accounts with them, yet always in an independent spirit; he made a religion of the 'conduct of the understanding.' He hardly saw why others should not return the compliment; and we can watch him impinging vainly and seriously, with the best of arguments, upon the fixed conclusions of Comte, Spencer, or Carlyle. This openness is his strength; but it leads him less to a rigid foursquare system of thought than to a living and changing body of principles. I can only glance at some of the mental traits and vicissitudes which are mirrored by his admirable style, without trying even to summarise his philosophy. His life (1806-73) falls into several chapters which may be separated by the years 1826, 1843, and 1858.

The first may be taken to end with his twentieth year (1826), when the too famous paternal drill which he has described, and on the whole defended, in his *Autobiography*, led to a mental crisis. His gifts were precocious; he was brought up on Benthamism; he painfully shed a good deal of it; and part of his work in life was to amend, to enlarge, and, as I have said, to edit Benthamism; and at last he edited it almost out of knowledge. This task proceeds during the second phase, which ended with the issue of the *System of Logic* in 1843. During those seventeen years Mill, whose profession was that of an official in the India House, was chiefly a journalist and reviewer. He had started in the newly founded *Westminster* (1824), and was soon a leading contributor; from 1835 onwards, for some years, he superintended the *London* (afterwards the *London and Westminster*) *Review*; and he wrote in other journals. Many of his papers reappear in the four volumes of *Disser-*

tations and Discussions (1859-75), and he went on reviewing long after the end of this period, which shows his mind in the making, and produced some of his weightiest work. The *Logic* was his first real book ; but his name and influence were much increased by the *Principles of Political Economy* (1848). These two are Mill's only monumental books. The third chapter lasts for ten years, until 1858, when he retired from the India House, and when he also lost his wife, formerly Mrs. Taylor, whom he had married, after a long friendship, in 1851. This bereavement is the second turning-point in Mill's career. A fourth period produced a series of political and social writings, including the *Liberty* (1859), his most popular book, and his best composed and best written. It was preceded by *Thoughts on Parliamentary Reform*, and followed by *Considerations on Representative Government* (1861). In a fifth and final stage, Mill is seen inclining more to pure philosophy ; and the fruits are seen in *Utilitarianism*, which had been sketched in 1854 ; in the *Examination of Sir William Hamilton's Philosophy* (1865) ; in *Auguste Comte and Positivism* (1865) ; in the notes to his edition (1869) to his father's *Analysis of the Human Mind* ; in *The Subjection of Women* (1869) ; and in the *Three Essays on Religion*, which came out after his death. Mill sat for a few years as independent member for Westminster, and his speeches, which were much respected, may count amongst his many essays and articles on current politics.

IV

Mill's premature surfeit of history, chronology, logic, and the solid sciences has often been deplored ; but it trained him as nothing else could have done for the work of his life, and he paid, like every one, the price for his training. He got a durably wrong notion, as his inspiring inaugural address (1867) at St. Andrews shows, of the amount of diet that the youthful mind can assimilate. But the worst of it was that he was not allowed to grow ; he was told to watch and set down and justify everything that occurred in his brain. His introspective habit thus begins early ; and the instincts and feelings, when they come, come in defiance of the *régime*, and therefore they have to be *cultivated*. Mill goes to landscape, to music, and to the poets, as men travel for a 'cure' ; and he has to be his own physician, making clinical notes of his case. His constant, serious, depressed attention to his own nature was an unhappy thing ; it left him, he says, aware of 'self-consciousness even in the act of confiding' ; and it is wonderful that he remained signally unselfish, after so long a bout of the spiritual dryness, or *accidia*, which easily produces an incurable egoist. But he had healthy impulses ; he had a boy's liking for fiction and fantasy, and also, what is rarer in boys, for scenery. He was sociable, and was delighted when he got away to France. Indeed, he seldom uses the word 'English' without some aversion ; this is a trace of the very considerable dourness of his upbringing. He applied to the poets, and found that Byron was less stimulating than he was advertised to be ; but he got from Wordsworth satisfaction in things that do not depend upon the march of intellect. His pleasures were thus increased, but he never expected too much from them. Poor man, ever arguing that happiness is the chief good, and getting so much less than his share of the commodity! He has the thorn in the spirit. Still, we find him liking his garden, and latterly contriving a humane sort of existence down at Avignon.

In the end there are two 'ruling passions,' which seem to 'swallow up the rest,' and can hardly be distinguished. One is for his wife [1] and for her memory ; the other is for humanity at large, and more especially for its oppressed portions. There is no doubt that the woman of whom Mill wrote in print with such disconcerting extravagance not only furthered his work, but cleared and kept alight his enthusiasm for mankind. She must have been somewhat uncommon, though we have little but Mill's word for it ; and it is easy to see how so pure and pent a nature as his, unused to the easy commerce of youth, might idealise such a person. The reader may be left to guess who it was that pronounced her to be 'far otherwise than a paragon, one might safely say,' the speaker's wife adding that she 'was not the pink of womankind, as her husband conceived, but a peculiarly affected and empty body.' We have nothing that she wrote except one article which Mill edited. It is on the same topic as his *Subjection of Women*, which, as he tells us, bears the stamp of her inspiration, and which contains his most fervent writing. Dr. Georg Brandes,[2] whom Mill visited in Paris in 1870, has said no more than the truth :

> He talked first of his wife, whose grave in Avignon he had just quitted. . . . It may be thought that the man who expressed himself in this style was anything but a great portrait-painter, and the actual correctness of his judgement may be questioned; but he cannot be reproached with considering marriage a mere contract, as sometimes has been done owing to the extremely rational standpoint that he took up on the question of women. Great poets like

Dante and Petrarch have set up an imaginative memorial to the women they had loved in imaginative wise ; but I know not that any poet has given such a warm and sincere testimony to a loving admiration for a feminine being as Mill has left to the merit of his wife and to her enduring significance for him.

But the true liberator of Mill's intellect had been Carlyle,[1] with whom he made acquaintance in 1831, when Benthamism was already dust upon his lips. A correspondence followed, and many of Mill's letters to Carlyle are published. For a moment he even catches the celebrated, the highly catching manner ; sets down his spiritual debt to Carlyle ; and helps to launch *The French Revolution* with intelligent praise. He feels it his business, at this period, to 'translate the mysticism of others into the language of argument' ; that all truth *can* be thus translated he entertains no doubt. He himself is a 'logician-in-ordinary' and no more, and Carlyle sees truths that lie beyond his reach. Mill never completed the work of 'translation,' for the rift between the ethical and social faith of the two men became apparent. For one thing, Mill trusted more and more in the mechanism for representing the popular judgement ; this was to be perfected by the 'proportional' system and similar devices, which for Carlyle could only measure the more precisely the folly of mankind ; not to name womankind, whom Mill includes in his ideal electorate. The real issue was whether the collective sense of the units, if faithfully registered, could be trusted—better, at least, than anything else—to steer aright, and on this point there could be no agreement.

Carlyle, whether right or wrong, was here consistent. But Mill was entangled in the contradiction which wrecked the philosophical radicals in practice. He had himself little faith in Demos ; he was too much of a bureaucrat, and too fastidious in grain, to have it. He always speaks shrewdly of business matters, as a highly capable functionary ; but his calling deepened his distrust of the unskilled vulgar mind. New Demos might become merely old Cæsar writ large. The tyranny of the majority, repressing 'individuality as a means of well-being,' became Mill's dread. His only hope lay in the better education of Demos. This remedy Carlyle preached also, but with next to no hope ; and, since no Cæsar was forthcoming, relapsed into tirade. Moreover, what was yet more fundamental, Carlyle and Mill had different ideas of justice, as their respective action in the case of Governor Eyre demonstrates ; and a real divergence on such a point wrecks any friendship worthy of the name.

V

Mill, meanwhile, turned to many other sources of wisdom in his quest for a larger faith. He read history, of which his own school had long conceived in a narrow way. He was the son of the historian of British India; but he wanted a more sympathetic reading of mankind and the past; a creed that should indicate the progress, however slow and broken, of the human spirit. His papers on Guizot and Michelet, and those on Grote, show his lines of study. But he cared less for the pageant or chronicle of history than for its philosophy. He was drawn to the Saint-Simonians,[1] who revealed to him the 'organic stages' in the growth of society, and who fortified his belief in the claims of labour and of women. But that school dispersed in a sorry fashion, and the letters of John Stuart Mill become almost flippant in describing their rout. But he was thus led on to Comte,[2] who left a deeper imprint. The tale of Mill's connexions with Comtism and its founder is too long to tell here. The correspondence lasts some five years (1841-6), begins in enthusiasm, and ends chilled. Mill's mature view is seen at length in *Auguste Comte and Positivism*, published long afterwards. He there mocks with horror at the *politique positive*, with its philosophic despotism, termed by Huxley 'Catholicism *minus* Christianity'; but from the earlier *philosophie positive* he drew not only more than one fruitful idea, but something like a religion; and a passage from a letter written in 1854 gives his reading of the faith which affected some of the strongest minds in England at that time:

> Je soutiens comme lui [Comte] que l'idée de l'ensemble de l'humanité, representée surtout par les esprits et les caractères d'élite, passés, présents, et à venir, peut devenir, non seulement pour des personnes exceptionelles mais pour tout le monde, l'objet d'un sentiment capable de remplacer avec avantage toutes les religions actuelles, soit pour les besoins du cœur, soit pour ceux de a vie sociale. . . . Restent sa morale et sa politique, et là-dessus je dois avouer mon dissentiment presque total.

And again:

> When we see and feel that human beings can take the deepest interest in what will befall their country or mankind long after they are dead, and in what they can themselves do while they are alive to influence that distant prospect which they are never destined to behold, we cannot doubt that if this and similar feelings were cultivated in the same manner and degree as religion they would become a religion. (*Letters*, ii. 379 (1854).)

Such a creed softens, though it does not exactly belie, Mill's original tenet that the duty of man is to glorify Reason and enjoy her for ever. Apart from its special doctrines, such as that of the 'three stages,' positivism gave Mill's reason fresh material to work upon, urging him to interpret the growth of the world instead of eternally arguing in the dialectical void.

But he could not always be content even with the 'service of man,' founded on an agnostic basis. He had been reared, in a fashion then of the rarest, wholly without positive beliefs, nor did he ever acquire them. For some months in the year 1854 he tried the experiment of putting down one valuable thought each day; and these *pensées*, which were first printed with his letters, contain some of his most striking sayings; here his mind is free, and he is not bound to reconcile his moods. He utters his satisfaction in the belief that

> The belief in a life after death, without any probable surmise as to what it is to be, would be no consolation, but the very king of terrors . . . all appearances and probabilities are in favour of the cessation of our consciousness when our earthly mechanism ceases to work.

And again, thinking of his wife, he cries out that

> if human life is governed by superior beings, how greatly must the power of the evil intelligences surpass that of the good,

—when such a creature must perish; and he adds, in a way that recalls Newman's picture of human life in the *Apologia*,

> If, indeed, it were but a removal, not an annihilation—but where is the proof, and where the ground of hope, when we can only judge of the probability of another state of existence, or of the mode in which it is governed if it exist, by the analogy of the only work of the same powers which we have any knowledge of, namely, this world of unfinished beginnings, unrealised promises, and disappointed endeavours—a world the only rule and object of which seems to be the production of a perpetual succession of fruits, hardly any of them destined to ripen, and, if they do, only lasting a day.

Mill does not draw Newman's theistic inference; but the passage shows the line of thought which is familiar in the *Three Essays*, the work of his later years. In 1860 he wrote:

> It may be that the world is a battle-field between a good and a bad power or powers, and that mankind may be capable, by sufficiently strenuous co-operation with the good power, of deciding or at least accelerating its final victory. (*Letters*, i. 240.)

The consequence, suggested in the essay on *Theism*, comes out in another letter :

> The cultivation of the idea of a perfectly good and wise being, and of the desire to help the purposes of such a being, is morally beneficial in the highest degree, though the belief that this being is omnipotent, and therefore the creator of physical and moral evil, is as demoralising a belief as can be entertained. (*Letters*, ii. 308.)

Mill's Manicheism thus consists in dallying with the pious conjecture of a deity who is limited in strength but of unexceptionable intentions and is doomed to wrestle with a power foreign to himself. Whatever the value of such an idea, nothing better shows the need of Mill to stay his imagination, which had been starved in early days, upon something or other. It is these needs, guesses, and reachings forth, and refusals to close his mind, that make him so attractive and genuine a writer.

VI

His earlier reviews [1] are unexpectedly lively, and we must go to them if we want rhetoric from him. Some of the sallies in the manner of Thomas Paine he cast out in the reprinting ; as in the paper on *Corporation and Church Property* :

> Much property is set apart by the laws of all idolatrous nations, for the special use and service of their gods. Large revenues are annually expended in offerings to those gods. To resume those revenues would manifestly be robbing Baal ; they are his by law ; law cannot give a clearer right of property than he has to them. A lawyer, addressing a court of justice, would have nothing to object to this argument : but a moralist or a legislator might say that the revenues were of no use to Baal, and that he would never miss them.

Quotations in his later work become rare, but here he is ready to cite Figaro or *Hudibras*. Nor is his range a narrow one. The articles on poetry and on Tennyson show connoisseurship, and have the real note of pleasure. Mill is one of the first to see (in 1835) that Tennyson

> has the power of *creating* scenery, in keeping with some state of human feeling, so fitted to it as to be the embodied symbol of it ;

and he adds that Wordsworth 'seems to be poetical because he wills to be so, not because he cannot help it.' He says that 'all poetry is of the nature of soliloquy,' which is true of the kinds he liked. In 1838 he writes with judgement on Alfred de Vigny, then hardly known in England.

There are two classic articles, on Coleridge (1840) and Bentham. Coleridge he tries to understand from within, whilst remaining outside his fold ; but less as a critic or poet than as the voice of that higher conservatism, to which the article is Mill's salute. The portrait of Bentham (1838), one of the 'great intellectual benefactors of humanity,' is in his best style, which comes too seldom ; it is easy to read in it his own contrary experience, if not a touch of envy :

> He had neither internal experience nor external ; the quiet, even tenor of his life, and his healthiness of mind, conspired to exclude him from both. He never knew prosperity and adversity, passion nor satiety ; he never had even the experiences which sickness gives ; he lived from childhood to the age of eighty-five in boyish health. He knew no dejection, no heaviness of heart. He never felt life a sore and a weary burthen. He was a boy to the last. Self-consciousness, that dæmon of the men of genius of our time, from Wordsworth to Byron, from Goethe to Chateaubriand, and to which this age owes so much both of its cheerful and its mournful wisdom, never was awakened in him. How much of human nature slumbered in him he knew not, neither can we know.

The cool and detached survey of Benthamism was a blow to true believers like Grote and Molesworth. Other massive essays, of various date, are those on Guizot and on *Civilization*. The review of *The French Revolution* has been mentioned, and elsewhere Mill says that Carlyle has perfected the second-best way of writing history, which is to recreate the life of the past. The best way, of course, is the philosophical, and of this Mill finds a pattern in Grote's *Greece*. His own picture of a free reasonable life can be seen from his remarks on Athens, and from his references in the *Liberty* to Pericles. Bain says that Mill was, 'quite as much as Grote, a Greece-intoxicated man.' Grote's account of the myths, which is now out of date, and his analysis, which is by no means so, of the myth-making spirit, especially attracted Mill. Bayle had whetted his irony on the gods and heroes, both sacred and profane. He tried to show up fable ; Grote tries to explain the birth of fable and its significance. Mill's sympathy with such an adventure marks him off from the older rationalism. But history was not his field, and his chief writings must now be glanced at.

VII

Mill, we must not forget, was a reformer in grain, and his gaze is fixed on the far-off living consequences latent in the most abstract doctrine. He was not, indeed, bribed by the fear or hope of these consequences, and he makes it his religion to be judicial, succeeding, perhaps, in that intention so far as mortal may. But his real aim is to find a scientific foundation in the laws of human nature for economic, social, and political theory. This explains his earnestness and tension, and the touch of tartness with which he declines to see the 'predicate quantified,' or insists on the three different senses of the term 'inconceivable.' The ordinary man does not understand such emotion; but Mill feels that an error at the outset may in the long run vitiate practice. Much of the *Logic* and of the work on Hamilton is to be read in this light. The most important and contested chapters are those on the theory of causation,[1] which forms the bridge between pure and applied philosophy. Upon it rests the whole inquiry as to the *organon* of reasoned truth, the methods of proof and disproof, and the inquiry how we are to come right, and to know when we are right. The problem of causation, again, leads straight back to ultimate questions concerning the nature of the connexion between mind and things, and the make of the mind itself. Mill is torn between his own bent for metaphysics, where he perceives more and more that the true issue lies, and his positivist desire to have as little of them as possible. He also has to justify the leap from a purely subjective and sensational starting-point to a fixed external order. The *Examination of Hamilton* shows more fully the detail and development of the campaign, and represents a later stage in his mind; but the *Logic* is more of a book, and is his nearest approach to a great book, and has its place in every chronicle of philosophy or of literature. It was the arsenal, for a whole generation, of the empirical school in England, and not least at Oxford. There it also gave provocation; and memory can still hear the far-off, irritated, high accents, sometimes Scottish, of tutors bombarding 'Mr. Mill,' who was fain to sweep away every *a priori* element in the mind, and who showed the very worst that could be done in that direction. The crown of his edifice was to be the establishment of fixed laws, or uniformities, in human proceedings. Mill dreamed of a science of human character, 'ethology.' This came to little; but the merit of the *Logic* is not to be measured by asking how much is now left of it. It offered (drawing something from Whewell's *History of the Inductive Sciences*, 1837) its elaborate far-reaching theory of the inductive process.[2] Somewhere Mill pours scorn on the saying that the chief good of such inquiries lies in the seeking, not in the results. The lay reader, who cares little about the method of concomitant variations, still catches the spirit of the quest, the spirit of the man behind the book. Gladstone called him, inaptly, 'the saint of rationalism.' This he is not; but he is an unresting, rather irritable seeker for the exact truth; the adversary of the 'idols of the cave,'—the vicious mental twist in each one of us; and of the 'idols of the theatre,' or the equally vicious preconceptions of the schools. Mill shows this temper above all when he crosses the border into social and political philosophy.

VIII

In the *Liberty* Mill comes nearest to classic form. Brief, transparent, and studiously proportioned, and nobly animated, the tractate carried far, reaching even the East. It was a stroke in the general war of liberation, and one which helped to clear the battle-ground, not only at home, for the already surging conflict of ideas. The motto is taken from Von Humboldt: 'the absolute and essential importance of human development in its richest diversity.' Mill has in mind the hindrances offered to such an ideal in heavy, tyrannous, custom-ridden Victorian England. Macaulay was surprised at the complaint that in the age of new inventions, phrenology, Comtism (which was 'absurd enough'), spirit-rapping, and 'spasmodic' light literature, any one should complain of a want of the 'individual' or eccentric element. 'He is really crying "Fire!" in Noah's Flood.' But this misses the point of Mill, who is thinking of the social cold shoulder turned to the unorthodox. Also he is thinking first of elect minds like his own, rather than of mankind at large. He wants free play for the thinker, the reformer, and even for the eccentric or unconventional 'character,' whom Mill worships by a convention of his own. It is not too plain at first what the thinker is to do with his freedom, once he has it, except try experiments in living and thresh out the truth by endless debating. He is to 'follow his intellect to whatever conclusions it may lead'; he is to cast out the devil, who tempts him to fix those conclusions in advance; he is not 'to sophisticate with an intellect which he cannot silence'—a stroke which has been supposed to glance at Newman. This done, he is to have a hearing, like his opponents. The utterance of opinion must not be coerced by law or society. Here the question arises: Since there must be some limit to the free action of the individual, if not to his utterance, where may, and where must, law and society step in to impose the limit? Mill's general answer is to place the burden of proof upon law and society for interfering; his own bias was against their doing so. It was a bias into which he had not settled without oscillations. Lord Morley tells us that Mill had been 'inclining towards over-government, social and political,' and that 'the composition of this book and the influence under which it grew kept him right.' He now dreads the meddling of the state, when the state is only the stupid majority organised into officialdom. The actual issues that he raises in regard to the liquor traffic, education, and the like, have quite changed in aspect since his day; and all the time, it must be borne in mind, he is thinking of a state of peace and order. He also, no doubt, moves overmuch in the region of pure ideas; but this is also his strength; for no one saw clearer that the ultimate conflict, in political and social affairs, is between ideas; and that not only before they are, but whilst they are being, organised into action. Mill could not complain of the lack of 'discussion' over his *Liberty*. His hardest-headed critic was Sir James Fitzjames Stephen, who is presently to be noticed, and whose *Liberty, Equality, and Fraternity* (1873-4) is an attack along the whole line.

The spirit of the *Liberty* rules in the work *On the Subjection of Women*, which is written with high-pitched ardour and remains the best English record of the 'feminist' cause in its earlier phase. It shows all Mill's force and weakness. He had a fixed idea that sex can and should be made to count for far less in human life than it has ever done. In one of his private 'thoughts' he lays down

> that what any persons may do freely with respect to sexual relations should be deemed to be an unimportant and purely private matter, which concerns no one but themselves. If children are the result, then indeed, etc.

Meredith's Mrs. Berry could here have told the philosopher something; he clearly did not see all the complexities of the case. We echo Von Sybel's[1] cry, 'Does Stuart Mill really depict the world we live in?' However, if it be said that he did not know much about women, neither do we. Mill's premisses are needlessly wide in view of his conclusions. Women may claim a fair field without our ignoring the irremoveable differences of sex. Once more Mill's bad old psychology of the *tabula rasa*, which attributes all differences to training and opportunity, disserves him. Herein he goes back, behind Bentham, who was a conservative in his views of female development, to doctrinal revolutionaries like Condorcet. Mill is on surer ground when he simply pleads, against *a priori* objections, that women should have all civic opportunities, and also advocates equality in the home and before the law. He does not touch on the question, now seen to lie near the root of the matter, of economic equality. His spirit is best seen in the 'solemn promise,' now printed in his correspondence, which he voluntarily added to his marriage vows. All this pleading is conceived in the interest not only of the removal of unjust restrictions, but of 'human development in its richest diversity,' both male and female. Mill assumes that a world of diverse and original types will be noble and picturesque; or at any rate, for the sake of 'the greater good of human freedom,' he is ready to take the risks of a rich diversity which includes an allowance of Pecksniffs, Sir Pitt Crawleys, and Rastignacs. This, no doubt, is a sound view; and Mill, in his cult of originality or colour, or difference from other men ('du moins je suis autre') is more of a Briton than he might have cared to admit. Yet we are struck with the quaint absence of colour in his colour-worship, and with the abstract fervour of his advice to be concrete and individual.

His views on the franchise and popular rights appear in the article on De Tocqueville and in *Considerations on Representative Government*. It is interesting to see him trying to conciliate his dislike of Whiggism and privilege with his equal dislike of mob-rule, and with his growing sense of the difference between man and man. He believes in the educative power of the vote, but not in the ballot; in stretching the franchise downwards, but also in giving more than a single vote to the better-trained citizen; and in proportional representation. These guards and refinements cut him off, together with a few friends, from the vehement popular movement of his time; and the practical issues have long since changed. In one respect he threw over *laissez-faire*, and those who call Mill 'sentimental' or 'doctrinaire' might remember his letters of the early months of 1871, in which he advocates national military service: the words find an echo to-day, though some of the proper names are different:

It will be an uphill fight to get a really national defensive force, but it may be a question of life and death to this country not only to have it, but to have it soon. I do not know which are most smitten with imbecility, those who are for trusting our safety solely to our navy, on the speculation that no foreign army can land in

England, or those who, after crying at the top of their voices that we are utterly without the means of facing an enemy in the field, turn round next day and demand that we should instantly go to war with Russia for the Black Sea or with Germany for France. (*Letters*, ii. 304.)

The *Principles of Political Economy* (1848) gave Mill a wider authority than the *Logic*; it held the field for a generation; its large plan, its clear and dignified manner, its outlook into political philosophy, and above all the enthusiasm that it reveals for the good of the worker, duly enhanced its fame. Mill's power of quickening a technical discussion by keeping its remoter applications in sight was never better seen. The ultimate problem is again that afterwards stated in the *Liberty*, but worked out in a special field. What are the conditions and limitations of useful state interference with the arrangements of production, distribution, and exchange? Mill starts, avowedly as an hypothesis, with the Ricardian idea of the economic man, as a purely wealth-seeking animal, and illuminates it by the facts of economic life. On his way he encounters all the vital questions: co-operation, peasant ownership, the Malthusian formulæ, and the relationship, actual and possible, of capital and labour; and the great individualist ends, it has been said, 'well on the way to state socialism.' In later editions Mill revised, amongst other things, his defence of private, and especially of landed, property. I cannot trespass on the field of economy; the works of John Elliot Cairnes, William Stanley Jevons, John Ramsay M'Culloch, and others, belong to science; but here may be named in parenthesis, since Mill prompted the book, Edward Gibbon Wakefield's *View of the Art of Colonisation* (1849), a classic of controversy. It is a series of discursive letters urging emigration, and the principle of 'federal-municipal,' as against Whitehall, government. Wakefield's writing is informal and racy, his satire is pointed; his labours are part of the history of Australasia.

Mill's short book on *Utilitarianism* has been much assailed, not to say riddled; one of the most effective criticisms was the modest and acute *Examination* (1870) by John Grote, Professor of Moral Philosophy at Cambridge. Mill's frankness and clear style help to cast light upon any fissures in his thinking. His faith in unselfish service, which every page exhibits, has to rest on the rebuilt masonry of the old empiricism, and the question is whether such a foundation is strong enough to bear the fabric. An inducement, on Benthamite premisses, has to be found for practising the absolute 'altruism' preached by Comte. The natural purity of Mill's own motives may have obscured for him the pinch of the problem. The *Three Essays on Religion* were not printed till after his death, and must be read along with his letters and *Autobiography*. Mill never minded speaking out, but he showed a certain canniness in his dealing with his public, preferring to give it only one shock at a time. The course of his religious opinions had been affected in his youth by reading the hard, literal, and very robust attack on 'natural religion,' by 'Philip Beauchamp,' published in 1822. 'Philip Beauchamp'[1] was in fact Bentham, whose manuscript was edited and fortified by Grote. Nothing better shows how the whole complexion of the debate changed during our period, than a comparison of this book with the *Three Essays*.

IX

Mill's solicitude to be fair all round tames down his ordinary style. There is a good deal of this kind of writing, which accounts for Carlyle's epithet of 'sawdusty':

> But though each side greatly exaggerates its own theory, out of opposition to the other, and no one holds without modification to either, the two doctrines correspond to a deep-seated difference in two modes of thought; and though it is evident that neither of these is entirely in the right, yet it being equally evident that neither is wholly in the wrong, we must endeavour to get down to what is at the root of each, and avail ourselves of the amount of truth that exists in either. (1861.)

For anything like sharp eloquence we must wait until Mill is morally indignant, be it with Whewell[2] or Brougham or Mansel. His sarcasms against the Comtian hierarchy show a contemptuous skill. A more exalted strain is heard in *The Subjection of Women* and the *Liberty*; we have the image of Mrs. Mill prompting the philosopher. But Mill's emotion, his ardour for justice and freedom, is always apt to break out, to flame up, through the measured phrases. He has a keen vehement sensibility to manage; he has none of the calm assurance of the eighteenth century. He is the antipodes of Hume; he has not the same kind of tranquil grandeur, nor does he say his destructive things in the same urbane, talking voice. Mill's inner life may be described as an incessant race between his reason and the feelings that are ever seeking to outrace it. Usually this element is repressed, though it still animates the discourse. The ordinary tone is that of a man trying to convince the intelligent reader, to reform his intellect, in the end to sway his vote, and not to bore him. Mill writes not for the expert, but for everybody. His style is just fitted to the purpose. He does not swamp the page with Spencer's technical polysyllables ; he uses little decoration, but expounds in an equable, punctilious, not exactly genial way, seldom changing his pace. His literary aim is to make the truth self-evident. His pains in laying out and proportioning his material are great. He omits well. He has the best French-academic manner. When he approaches to oratory, we feel that a little more, and the tones would be too piercing ; but this danger is rarely present.

Mill, then, ranks high amongst our speculative writers, though he has none of Ferrier's colour and daring, nor yet the classical form and felicity of Mansel. The soundest way is to compare him with authors of his own ancestry, and here only Hume is his superior. A thinker will not soon arise who cares more truly to be in the right. It is good to read him after the emphatic and capricious authors, Ruskin and Carlyle, whose aim is different. He left no issue where he found it, and his candour enables us to see just where he left it. This quality is best seen in the regions where it is hardest to preserve : in social and moral philosophy, and in politics and in natural theology, where the coals are always hot.

X

The name of Alexander Bain (1819-1903) should be mentioned here. His writing has little more grace than a safe-deposit ; but the safe is stacked with invaluable documents, and Bain is a weighty and honest thinker, never mistaking, or being able to mistake, a sentimental for a scientific transition. He wrote in his industrious formal way on rhetoric and composition, for which he had little ear. He was for twenty years professor at Aberdeen until 1880, and there upheld an unimaginative but rigorous version of the philosophy of experience ; making it his affair to put that creed into a more fully methodised and pedagogic shape than John Stuart Mill (whose *Logic* he helped to revise), and working in sympathy with him, but independently. Bain had won his rank by his treatises on *The Senses and the Intellect* (1855) and *The Emotions and the Will* (1859) ; these were compacted later into a *Manual of Mental and Moral Science*. He signally advanced the study of the mind, isolating it from metaphysics into a separate science, correlating it with physiology, deepening the theory of association, and more than foreshadowing the study of experimental psychology. He also wrote treatises on logic, did good service to education, and in 1876 founded the philosophical quarterly *Mind*, which keeps its high repute. Bain doubtless belongs to science more than to letters; his hard rationalism, which recalls the elder Mill rather than the younger, limits the 'experience' to which he appeals, and he easily, sometimes comically, misses the force of the 'emotions' which he chronicles. But his faithful and precise records of the two Mills (1882) show him in a much more humane light, like his rather melancholy *Autobiography*; and the accurate cutting of his language is welcome after much oratory.

The Stephen family, several members of whom call for mention in our survey, is eminent for its performance not only in law, philosophy, and controversy, but in pure literature: in biography, criticism, and essay-writing. The father, Sir James Stephen (1789-1859), a barrister, a distinguished public servant, and latterly Professor of Modern History at Cambridge, is best known for his *Essays in Ecclesiastical Biography* (1849, reissued from the *Edinburgh Review*), which are full of the family vigour. His second son, Sir James Fitzjames Stephen (1829-94), won high professional note as a judge, Indian legislator, and jurist; his *General View* (1863-1890), and his *History* (1883) of the English criminal law are standard works. Stephen, though a scion of the Utilitarians, travelled far towards the political Right. A champion at intellectual quarterstaff, he enlisted the gifts of a great lawyer and some of the convictions of Carlyle in the labours of critical and conservative journalism. At Cambridge he was an intimate of Maine, another distruster of liberalism, and also a member of the 'Apostles,' a club of candid 'intellectuals' which has numbered many men of note. In 1855 he joined the staff, along with Freeman, Goldwin Smith, and other swordsmen, of the newly-founded *Saturday Review*, of which the ideal was plain speaking, contempt of sciolism and sentiment, and a somewhat arid and ill-humoured but genuine devotion to truth. Some of Stephen's contributions are garnered in his *Essays by a Barrister* (1862), and in three series of *Horæ Sabbaticæ*, of which the first is dated 1892. These papers are pure exposition and criticism, showing in the highest degree the power to eviscerate and judge a complex argument. The treatises of Jeremy Taylor, Chillingworth, and Hobbes, and the mental posture of Laud and Clarendon, are dissected with precision; not a cut is wasted. Stephen's most elaborate work of this kind, *Liberty, Equality, and Fraternity* (1873-4) is another string of rescued articles, and appeared just after Mill's death. It is a clear, telling piece of argument, harsh enough in tone. The general happiness is still the canon; something of the earlier Benthamite temper revives in Stephen; but this temper is oddly united with an authoritarian spirit, which is partly natural and partly encouraged by the teaching of his friend Carlyle, and which comes out strongest in the chapter on the 'subjection of women.' Stephen's writing is rather bleak, and much of it is purely negative in character; but its solid sincerity, strength, and disdain of flourishes are admirable; and it comes like a refreshing east wind after the preciosity and subtlety of some other styles—after a course of Walter Pater, for instance, or, for that matter, of Newman. Sir James Fitzjames Stephen's son, James Kenneth (1859-92), died young, after producing two little volumes of sharp-edged and highly-finished satiric verse; and his younger brother and biographer, Leslie, afterwards Sir Leslie Stephen (1832-1904), will be noticed hereafter as a philosopher (Ch. IV.), and as a critic and climber (Ch. XI.).

CHAPTER IV

PHILOSOPHY, SCIENCE, AND LETTERS

I

THE advances and annexations of science are the boldest feature of all in the intellectual map of the last century. After 1830, and yet more after 1860, the spirit of science increasingly permeates philosophy, and also invades literature, in a manner that may now be sketched. The classic achievements of men like Sir John Herschel in astronomy and physics, of John Dalton in chemistry, and of Michael Faraday in electrical science, are not in question here ; nor is the more popular but valued work of the geologist, Hugh Miller, whose gallant record in his autobiography, *My Schools and Schoolmasters* (1854), is to be remembered. But the impact of geological and biological discovery upon general thought, the influence of Lyell and Darwin, is more relevant. For the old 'catastrophic' view of geological change was silenced by the labours of Sir Charles Lyell (1797-1875) ; the history of the earth was reduced to the operation of natural uniformities, and the whole question of its age revolutionised, by this 'attempt to explain the former changes of its surface by causes now in operation.' Lyell's first great work, *The Principles of Geology*, appeared in 1830-3, received many increments and revisions, and ran through eleven editions in his lifetime. His *Antiquity of Man* (1863) and his *Elements of Geology* (1838) were not less influential. Geology included a study of the changes in the organic world ; Lyell discussed the origin and extinction of species ; and his conversion, which was not immediate, and which entailed some reserves, to the views of Darwin, powerfully affected opinion. The 'anti-transmutationists,' Huxley wrote, 'regarded him ever afterwards as Pallas Athene might have looked at Dian, after the Endymion affair.' But to the last he resisted the argument of *The Descent of Man*. Lyell's style is plain, grave, and weighty ; he told by the mass and strength of his reasoning, and by the extreme cautiousness, noted by Darwin, of his mind ; and his orthodox belief, set forth at the conclusion of the *Principles*, in a designing intelligence, doubtless aided in reconciling prejudice.

Darwin, in his 'historical sketch' introductory to the *Origin of Species*, has a good word for the once popular, and still readable, *Vestiges*[1] *of the Natural History of Creation*, which appeared unsigned in 1844. Twelve editions, involving revisions and corrections, were issued in twenty years. The writer was Robert Chambers, the Scottish publisher, co-founder of *Chambers's Journal*, and compiler of *The Book of Days* (1862-4): a busy and capable person of letters. The authorship of the *Vestiges* was only revealed in 1884, thirteen years after the death of Chambers. Rumour had guessed at Lyell, or Thackeray, or the Prince Consort! The book had raised no little dust in its time, and in Darwin's judgement it had

> done excellent service in calling attention in this country to the subject, in removing prejudice, and in thus preparing the ground for the reception of analogous views.

He also speaks of the want of accuracy and scientific caution shown in the earlier editions; and the book was soon antiquated as a contribution to knowledge: no wonder, when it strides lightly over the ground of astronomy, geology, zoology, and anthropology. But it served its turn in shaking, before the evidence was really presented, the belief in the doctrine of special creation:

> The construction of the globe . . . [is] the result not of any immediate or personal exertion on the part of the Deity, but of natural laws which are expressions of His will. What is to hinder our supposing that the organic creation is also a result of natural laws which are in like manner the expression of His will?

Chambers assumes the theistic premiss, and the omnipresence of design; his particular view of the origin of species has lost interest; but he has his place in the history of the conception of development; he was the earnest amateur who caught the public ear. And he writes well, with a breath of philosophical as well as religious fervour; believing that

> the present system is but a part of a Whole, a stage in the Great Progress, and that the Redress is in reserve.

The place of Charles Robert Darwin[2] (1809-82) in this review may not at first be apparent. He wrote no polemic; pure philosophy he hardly touched; he had no rhetoric, good or bad, in his composition ; he ceased to care for poetry, and lamented the decline of his æsthetic instincts ; he would not have called himself a man of letters. But letters have a share in his glory and cannot sacrifice his name. He is a writer ; his intellectual power and candour find the style that they deserve ; and it reveals to us, in a transparent way, the majestic figure of the man himself, standing back and watching, ever so modestly and with some surprise, the effect of his work—the huge displacement caused by the tidal wave of his great idea, as it flooded the mind of the world, and so penetrated, by many a winding channel, into literature too.

His first book, the *Journal* (1839) of his voyage in the *Beagle*, is full of the sense of enjoyment, and also of the 'æsthetic sense,' and of appreciation of things seen. 'I am sure now,' he said afterwards, 'that I felt most sublime in the forests' of Brazil ; and not, as he had at first thought, on the mountains. The charm of the tale also lies in its humanity, but above all in its fidelity to fact, and in its unity of purpose. Darwin's mind is a pure mirror ; he does not, like Kinglake and many travellers, impose his own prejudice or irony on the scene. In this he recalls his friend, the co-discoverer of the principle of natural selection, the long-lived Alfred Russel Wallace [1] (1823-1913), whose *Travels on the Amazon and Rio Negro* (1853) and *Malay Archipelago* (1869) also have the note of the open-air, gypsy, all-enduring naturalist, and who afterwards produced notable works on the evolutionary theory (*Geographical Distribution of Animals*, 1876), and on many other themes. Some eminent biologists have been most at home in the laboratory, and have gone out of doors to get a holiday from observation ; but Darwin's affair, like Wallace's, was to study live creatures in their habitat. His notes breathe a spirit of happiness, and show a mind as patient as nature herself, matching itself against her, and tracking down her processes. This temper is reflected in his language, and explains some of the popularity of a book like *Formation of Vegetable Mould through the Action of Worms* (1881).

Many years of intense work passed between Darwin's return from his voyage and the publication in 1859 of his chief work : *On the Origin of Species by means of Natural Selection, or the Preservation of Favoured Races in the Struggle for Life.* He has told at length, and many have retold, the history of its slow inception and painful execution. Well known, too, is his honourable and fraternal treatment of Wallace ; the outcry that greeted the *Origin* ; the appearance of Huxley in the lists, and his disposal of Bishop Wilberforce at Oxford in 1860. Huxley's chapter, inserted in the *Life of Darwin*, on the 'reception of the *Origin of Species*,' was published in 1887, and is classical. The famous volume, which reacted on universal thought, is still difficult reading, and that not merely for the laity. Darwin took immense pains over the style, and lamented it as bad; 'no nigger with the lash over him could have worked harder at clearness than I have done.' But his judgement was too severe. If the style is not always clear, that is due partly to the rival claims of concision, partly to the intricacy of the matter, and to the puzzling but necessary interlacement of the methods of induction, deduction, and analogy. The hypothesis of natural selection is set out first, and next the general view of evolution, for which that hypothesis for the first time provided a *vera causa*. The evolutionary idea had long been current; its most recent exponent had been Herbert Spencer; it now received definition; and Darwin's theory, while it avowedly did not admit of direct proof, affected every one's mental picture of the living world as a vast and sensitive web of interrelations. The conception of the 'struggle for life,' suggested to both Wallace and Darwin by a reading of Malthus, implied an ubiquitous process, self-acting from the first, by which the balance of power amongst species and individuals was only kept stable, or altered slowly, by war. Somehow this process had brought man also into being; and could it be supposed to fail throughout the course of his own history, once he had appeared? All these and more implications, or misapplications, of Darwin's idea, told upon general thought and figured in the literature of controversy.

He himself went on with his proper work, *The Descent of Man, and Selection in Relation to Sex* (1871), and *Expression of the Emotions in Man and Animals* (1872) may be mentioned. Like his numerous other books, which are mostly in the fields of botany or geology, they are re-trials, in one or another field, of his main hypothesis, which itself became enriched and extended as he worked. *The Descent of Man* is another many-sided argument, masterly and lucid in conduct. *The Expression of the Emotions* is, owing to its subject, the most humanly interesting of Darwin's writings, along with his letters and his chapter of autobiography; and his account of his grandfather, Erasmus Darwin the poet, is to be remembered too.

He is not so much impressed by the waste and cruelty of nature as are some of those to whom he furnished material;

and the spectacle of a world developed through the workings of internecine strife does not make him melancholy:

> When we reflect on this struggle we may console ourselves with the full belief that the war of nature is not incessant, that no fear is felt, that death is generally prompt, and that the vigorous, the healthy, and the happy survive and multiply.

Darwin has little of the tragic or mystical sense which is evident in another great observer, J.-H. Fabre, whose wasps and spiders seem to be moved by a blind instinct, mechanically indeed, but as if with a purpose not their own. The same happy naturalism is seen in the descriptions of shame or terror in *The Expression of the Emotions*. These are not themselves emotional, nor yet are they impassive; but they are full of the pleasure of demonstration, and are human too. We read without surprise of Darwin that, 'although he was so anxious to observe accurately the expression of a crying child, his sympathy with the grief spoiled the observation.' Quiet lucidity and grace (the former quality being painfully earned) distinguish his style, and are not less apparent when he strays into general speculation. Nothing can be more limpid, or more unconsciously fresh and original, than his utterances on theology, collected by his biographer. Here Darwin contrasts well, even as a writer, with the professional disputants in either camp.

There remain for mention some of the men of science who expanded or applied his conceptions, or who otherwise impinged upon philosophy, and who are also of mark in letters. Spencer, Huxley, Lewes, Tyndall, and Clifford may be selected. They were all aggressive; all of them, except possibly Spencer, were investigators; and they were all, in more or less degree, conduits between the sources of pure thought or knowledge and the lay educated world: some of them irrigated even the 'low fat levels' of public opinion. They gave, that is, publicity to the conclusions and the claims of science. The surprising change they wrought during this period may be measured by a glance at Sir John Herschel's *Preliminary Discourse on the Study of Natural Philosophy* (1830), a well-worded book which inspired Darwin, and which, besides sketching a theory of induction, was a still needful defence, from the orthodox side, of the freedom of physical inquiry, and a popular outline of its results.

II

The works of Herbert Spencer [1] (1820-1903) belong to the history of thought and science, but they also have more connexion with literature than might at first be feared. No criticism can be risked here on Spencer's philosophy, and no description of it; but some landmarks [2] may be noted, and some features of his singular mind and temper and of his writing.

He began to publish about 1842; his period of ferment lasted till 1858. He began as he ended, an out-and-out individualist, as can be seen from his work on *The Proper Sphere of Government* and his *Social Statics* (1850); and the first version of his *Principles of Psychology* appeared in 1855. He also wrote many essays, where most of his fruitful ideas can be seen in a scattered form. He always had a view about everything; 'from principles of ethics,' as he proudly says, 'to a velocimeter, from a metaphysical doctrine to a binding-pin.' He had been trained as an engineer. Pictures of those implements appear in his *Autobiography* (1904). The topics of his essays of various dates range, in fact, from Comtism, the nebular hypothesis, and 'personal beauty' to railway policy and the philosophy of style. But in January 1858 he wrote to his father: 'Within the last ten days my ideas on various matters have suddenly crystallised into a complete whole.' The programme of the great scheme of *Synthetic Philosophy* was published in 1860, with an imposing list of backers, including Charles Kingsley, and 'George Eliot, Esq.,' J. A. Froude, and F. W. Newman.

The plan was closely adhered to, and took thirty-six years to execute; Spencer showed a sublime tenacity and devotion to his work. *First Principles* (1862) was followed, with sundry overlappings, dislocations, and revisions, by the *Principles of Biology* (1864-7), of *Psychology* (1870-2), of *Sociology* (1876-96), and of *Ethics* (1879-93). Spencer also presided over the large syndicate-enterprise, *Descriptive Sociology*, and wrote many lesser articles and tractates on heredity, government, and other things. Outside the *Synthetic Philosophy*, his most popular and pointed works are *Education* (1861) and *The Study of Sociology* (1872).

The huge synthesis, designed to cover almost the whole range of philosophy, has not affected the higher thought like Hegel's or like Comte's; but in vogue it had no rival. It has had its chance in most of the Western languages, and in Russia, India, Japan, and America. It proffered a comprehensive and coherent outfit of truth. It was an effort to apply one large key-conception to matter, to life, to mind, to society, and to conduct. The crown of the fabric was the inquiry into man, considered as a being only partially moralised and rationalised, and therefore imperfectly happy, in an organised community. Spencer wrote both before and after Darwin, whose conclusions he saluted as verifying in a special field the broader idea that he had himself announced. It is due to Spencer almost as much as to Darwin that we now cannot but think in evolutionary terms. But he gave his own colouring to the word. Evolution, as he elaborately defines it, comes to him to mean progress, and progress means hope. It is this transition in his argument that has been most keenly attacked. Spencer's conclusion and outlook were thus broadly optimistic. It was a large and encouraging, if not exactly cheerful, reading of the universe, with the supernatural excluded and, what was more, with the belief in the supernatural explained away. No bigger and braver attempt had been made to put heart into naturalism, or, in the ebb and chaos of beliefs during the later Victorian age, to find a substitute for the old religious emotions. Comtism made a similar attempt, but Spencer had a far wider public than Comte, whose system he attacked at every point.

So vast a target was naturally shot at from all sides. *First Principles* was assailed by Gladstone, Mansel, and Martineau. The Oxford Hegelians, like Thomas Hill Green and William Wallace, dissected Spencer's metaphysic or want of metaphysic. His ethical and other theories were sharply sifted at Cambridge by Henry Sidgwick; and his friend and brother-in-arms, Huxley, saw conflict rather than harmony between the process of the cosmic order and the moral effort of mankind. Spencer's views in every field of science were criticised; his definition of life was mocked at by men of letters; his hatred of state control set him in conflict with the whole movement of socialism. Yet all this meant that he was taken seriously. Each of his major works keeps at least an historic position. We are told on authority [1] that his *Biology*, with all abatements made, remains a classic. Psychology has grown, partly on the experimental side, partly through a larger gleaning of the 'varieties of experience,' partly through a restatement of its metaphysical basis; but some of Spencer's results have been used and absorbed. His collections of material, as well as his speculations, impelled the growing science of anthropology. Probably his most fruitful work was in the field of sociology and ethic.

III

Two paradoxical traits in Spencer may be picked out here. The first is best seen in his *Data of Ethics*. This cold-tempered, comically detached theorist, self-absorbed and rather cheerless, is a preacher of *happiness*. He had not had enough of it himself. 'Life,' he says, 'is not for work, but work is for life.' 'Be a boy as long as you can.' Pleasure, or happiness, he defines in terms of life, or life in terms of pleasure, it is hard to say which. The 'tide of life' is a favourite phrase with him. All conduct, he says, is an adaptation, and moral conduct is an adaptation of life to the ends that intensify life most and that ensure survival. Moral intuitions express in shorthand the experience of the races that have lasted through obedience to them. We must have faith in the far-off completion of the coincidence between personal and 'altruistic' ends. Still, only 'relative happiness,' or the choice of lesser evils, is possible as yet. Virtue brings happiness to the individual only 'in the majority of cases.' It has not brought happiness to Herbert Spencer, who, though moved purely by the 'desire to further human welfare,' has had little pleasure in the long run, nor a 'feeling appreciably above equanimity.' None the less is he sure that

> no contemptuous[1] title of 'pig-philosophy' will alter the eternal fact that Misery is the highway to Death, while Happiness is added Life, and the giver of Life.

To that ancient tenet the conception of evolution gives a new depth. In the age of Carlyle all this needed saying; and Spencer's language, often creaking and cumbrous, rises to dignity when he declares his faith.

Another trait separates him from some of his mental ancestors; it is the sense of mystery. In this impersonal, pedagogic mind there is the fatal seed of romance; and Carlyle's own 'immensities and eternities' reappear in a heavier dialect. In his youth Spencer had read *Prometheus Unbound* with enthusiasm. Science, not less than the historic creeds, is pronounced bankrupt in face of the ultimate riddle. The Absolute, or the Unknowable, must inspire an emotion which can neither be effaced nor defined. Spencer, in the wake of Hamilton and Mansel, limits knowledge to the finite; but he quits them promptly when they, passing into the religious sphere, affirm many things concerning that which has no predicate but existence, save that somehow it is the ground of all existence. But he sees that the questions which can never be answered must always be asked. In his old age he owns to feeling a certain 'sympathy, based on community of need,' with the discarded churches. He has no such answer as theirs, but he wishes that he had one. He would like to find more *sense* in the Universe. 'What if of all that is thus incomprehensible to us, there exists no comprehension anywhere ?' What is meant by the teeming life on the ocean-floor, by the dead 'thirty millions of remote suns,' or by the growth of mind 'out of what seems unconscious matter' and by its prospective relapse thereinto ? In such passages Spencer commands an eloquence of the soul, and even of language. His is a kind of inverted mysticism, without the mystic's revelation. His 'Absolute' or 'Unknowable' was of course another target for critics. To some it seemed a mere zero 'hypostatised'; others urged that he really professed to know a good deal about it after all; others called it a question-begging label for that which as yet is, but may not always be, unknown. But there is grandeur of vision in Herbert Spencer, when he foresees the day when no man shall ask why he need help his neighbour, or when he muses on the Nameless, of which the natural order is both the inevitable consequence and the impenetrable screen. Indifferent to the past, he does not know when he is only making rediscoveries ; but he is all the fresher for that : his 'lack of regard of authority,' he rightly says, 'is a principal cause of what success I have had in philosophical inquiry.' It is true that everything accepted—a machine, a theory, or a custom—had to prove its innocence to Spencer, and usually failed to do so, and that he was ever ready to put it right.

He is certainly a Philistine on a royal scale, with a delightful apathy to the history of culture. His *Education : Intellectual, Moral, and Physical,* which was translated, so we are informed, even into Mohawk, is a plea for making science the staple training for the young. Often he is before his time ; he urges bodily training for girls, humaner discipline for children, and instruction in the business of the citizen for everybody. But languages and letters, like history, go very much to the wall. Spencer could not get through Plato, or trouble with the 'languages of two extinct peoples.' 'Had Greece and Rome never existed, human life and the right conduct of it would have been in their essentials exactly what they are now.' Cromwell having been dead so long, why trouble, with Carlyle, to understand him ? Spencer tells us with sorrow how one of his assistants, a graduate in the humanities, actually thought that mammals were endowed with gizzards. So much for the historic universities. In the same sense he retorted on Matthew Arnold :[1]

The men of letters, in their early days dieted on grammars and lexicons, and in their later days occupied with *belles lettres*, Biography, and a History made up mainly of personalities, are by their education and course of life left almost without scientific ideas of a definite kind.

So much for humanism. Elsewhere Spencer calls the refrain of a ballad ' the inane repetition of an idea.'

For all this, he is no outcast from letters. Like Mill, he began as a journalist, and has some of the instincts of the craft. He implies that in writing *Social Statics* he made a point of being lively : and his use, at this stage, of exclamatory questions and rhetorical instances reminds us of Macaulay. 'Though my style is lucid, it has, as compared with some styles, a monotony that displeases me.' Lucid it is, and it is also consecutive, carrying us along well. The massive argument is unreeled without halt or disorder.

There appears to be in me a dash of the artist, which has all along made the achievement of beauty a stimulus ; not, of course, beauty as commonly conceived, but such beauty as may exist in a philosophical structure.

Spencer said that he was ' never puzzled,' meaning that he did not travail in thought, but let his ideas settle of themselves and emerge into harmony. The effect is felt in his writing, and contrasts with Mill's eager searchings and qualifications. For example, Spencer's description in his *Psychology* of his feelings by the sea-shore is simple and excellent, and his sarcastic recitals in such chapters as that on ' Ceremonial ' in his *Ethics* are piquant enough.

The philosophy of Comte,[2] first actually decocted by Harriet Martineau (*Positive Philosophy*, 1853), was much translated, preached, reviled, and analysed during this period. The religion founded on the negation of ' first philosophy ' enlisted a notable band of ' joined members,' and a few of its temples still stand in England. The *Philosophie positive* (1830-42) was assailed in the Sixties by Huxley and Spencer, and judged by Mill. Few except the professors of the faith had a good word for the *Système de politique positive* (1851-4), with its quasi-Catholic cult, its pedantic hierarchy, and its tyrannous philosopher-rulers. But the ethical fervour of Comtism powerfully coloured the writing of George Eliot, and also that of her companion George Henry Lewes (1817-78); who was a capable dramatic critic, a wretched novelist, and editor awhile of the *Fortnightly Review.* Lewes was the first Englishman to attempt a *Biographical History of Philosophy* (1845-6), afterwards enlarged. But his denial of the value of metaphysic (which impenitently went on flourishing) did not qualify him for the task. Lewes writes with vigour, and with a lively and attractive ease. He was a scientific naturalist; and he advanced psychological study, especially on the biological side. In his *Problems of Life and Mind* (1874-9), moving away from Comtism, he tried to distinguish between the metaphysics which are permissible, and those which are not ('metempirics'). His work on *The Physical Basis of Mind* has been praised by experts. But his best book by far is his *Life of Goethe* [1] (1855), a vivid, open-minded piece of exploration and narrative, on an inexhaustible subject. Lewes was perhaps more at home with Goethe's human than with his intellectual or artistic side; but his book remains the best, on its own scale, in English.

IV

In the case of Thomas Henry Huxley [2] (1825-95) there is no impediment to the happy union of science and letters. He is, indeed, one of the best prose writers of his time, with his pure, rapid, and athletic English, his controversial skill and honesty, his ironic wit, and his note of life and experience, which is most unlike the detachment of Herbert Spencer. Huxley had a long apprenticeship as a voyaging naturalist and investigator, which qualified him for his illustrious work in zoology and biology, before he was known to the general public. Many of his researches are gathered into the volumes of his *Scientific Memoirs*; and his teaching manuals of physiography and other sciences are accepted patterns of their kind. He came into general note after the appearance of the *Origin of Species*, as the most powerful champion of Darwinism and of the whole theory of evolution. His support gained in force from his critical reserves. His book, *Evidence as to Man's Place in Nature*, appeared in 1863, eight years before *The Descent of Man*, and is a good example of a rigorous demonstration that can be comprehended by the layman. He said in 1880, on the occasion of the 'coming of age of the *Origin of Species*':

Having conceived a tender affection for a child of what appeared to me to be of remarkable promise, I acted for some time in the capacity of an under-nurse, and thus came in for my share of the storms which threatened even the very life of the young creature. For some years it was undoubtedly warm work. . . . A theory is a species of thinking, and its right to exist is coextensive with its power of resisting extinction by its rivals.

Huxley wrote thus at the height of his renown, and in the press of his full and laborious life. He had, meanwhile, come to devote himself somewhat less to original inquiry, and more to the business of teaching, lecturing, and disputation. He was a great professor, and had in a high degree the teacher's power of discovering and training independent minds, as well as all the possible gifts of a popular expounder. He plunged deep into affairs, educational and administrative. Much of his best writing was produced just before or during the Seventies, and is found in the bundles of articles and addresses entitled *Lay Sermons* (1870), and *Critiques and Addresses* (1873), and in the little book on *Hume* (1878). Later came *Science and Culture* (1881), and *Essays on some Controverted Questions* (1892). The Romanes Lecture (1893) on *Evolution and Ethics*, with the *Prolegomena* to the edition of 1894, contain his final speculations. He collected his *Essays* in nine volumes in 1893. Despite all the obstacles of his earlier career—slow recognition and a competence long-deferred—and through the endless calls and distractions of later life, Huxley's wit and spirit triumphed to the last. He managed, as he had vowed in youth, to 'leave his mark clear and distinct'; although, as he said to Herbert Spencer, he cared less to leave his mark than to 'give a push.' [1] He certainly left it not only on the mind of his age, but on literature. Some of his letters rank among his best writings, and can be found in the excellent biography by his son.

His conception of his work in life is modestly and distinctly set out in a letter of 1873:

The part I have to play is not to found a new school of thought or to reconcile the antagonisms of the old schools. We are in the midst of a gigantic movement greater than that which preceded and produced the Reformation, and really only the continuation of that movement. But there is nothing new in the ideas which lie at the bottom of the movement, nor is any reconcilement possible between free thought and traditional authority. One or other will have to succumb after a struggle of unknown duration which will have as side issues vast political and social troubles. I have no more doubt that free thought will win in the long run than I have that I sit here writing to you, or that this free thought will organise itself into a coherent system, embracing human life and the world as one harmonious whole. But this organisation will be the work of generations of men, and those who further it most will be those who teach men to rest in no lie, and to rest in no verbal delusions. I may be able to help a little in this direction—perhaps I may have helped already. (*Life*, i. 397.)

Huxley's expositions and polemics, like his discoveries, in the field of exact science, exhibit all his gifts; but they have passed into the general stock and chronicle of knowledge. Here, as oarsmen say, he pulled his weight to the utmost, and with a powerful stroke, and he remains eminent. His contributions to metaphysic and to theological discussion are equally clear-cut; their form is first-rate, and they are not obsolete, even for those who may doubt if they achieved their object. Still fresher are Huxley's words on ethics, on education, and on life at large. Wide as he ranges, his work is bound together not merely by its literary worth, but by a certain noble unity of mental temper, which is not marred either by some inconsistencies, or rather changes, of view, or by the atmosphere of disputation in which he worked.

V

His philosophic tenets are best summarised in the *Hume*, in the 'prologue' to the volume of *Controverted Questions*, and in the Romanes Lecture. The *Hume* is a manifesto in which Huxley, ever with his eye on the adversary, expounds his own solution by the way; 'here and there,' as he confesses, 'more is seen of my thread than of Hume's beads.' Like Mill and all the votaries of 'experience,' he has to rest the validity of the law of causation, which is assumed as obtaining among things, upon something within the mind itself. But Hume, the great simplifier, had reduced the mind, and with it phenomena, to a series of sensations. The question is how we can arrive, on such a basis, at a permanent order independent of ourselves. Huxley, after Berkeley and Hume, inclines to the idealist solution, or statement, of this problem; by which things themselves are reduced to something mental. He thus disclaims any sort of 'materialism' except that which is a kind of 'short-hand idealism.' The situation was not thus to be saved; but Huxley's treatment of the miraculous received more attention. He has not, like Hume, any *a priori* objection to the miraculous; the question for him is only one of evidence; he asks for nothing but sufficient proof, though it is pretty clear that he does not expect to get it. This attitude he maintains throughout all his discussions of the supernatural. 'I have always had a certain horror of presuming to set a limit on the possibilities of things.' In this spirit he coined the term 'agnostic'[1] and its derivatives, which are now fixed in the language. Huxley's tone fluctuates in some degree concerning the highest theorems of theology; but in the end he seems to have held that the question of their truth or falsehood lies outside the limits of what can be proved or disproved; and therefore that he could have none of them. After 1885 he set himself to pulverise the evidence for the biblical-supernatural. The creation, the flood, and the miracle (which he treated as crucial) of the destroyed pigs were amongst the topics. The last of these incidents occasioned a resounding prize-fight in the magazines, waged between Gladstone and Huxley, conducted with immense relish and under the strictest rules of the ring. Huxley's own metaphor, however, for the procedure was the entomological one of 'pinning-out' the adversary. He also contended with the Duke of Argyll, with Mr. Lilly, and with many others, in papers that are still excellent reading and classics of scientific *Boxiana*.

In the 'prologue' of 1894, above referred to, Huxley sets forth the dozen or so propositions which are to form a 'common body of established truth,' and to which 'all future philosophical and theological speculations will have to accommodate themselves.' Together with the Romanes Lecture, they form a sort of *Credo* of scientific naturalism. Huxley finds himself, at last, as far away from the qualified optimism of Spencer as he does from the later croakings of Carlyle. Buoyant and brave in temper, he nevertheless ends with a reasoned but very cautious hopefulness. The race may possibly advance, while it lasts, but it will do so slowly. It will advance, if at all, in the teeth of an indifferent or unscrupulous universe outside it. Huxley writes to Leslie Stephen in 1894:

> You are charitable enough to overlook the general immorality of the cosmos on the score of its having begotten morality in one small part of its domain.

He sees no sign that the 'cosmic order' of non-human, or at least of non-living, nature has developed in the interest, or even as though in the interest, of human happiness and virtue. At any rate it sets a wretched example. Earlier, however, he had spoken of the warning 'slap in the face' with which 'nature' visits our misbehaviour before executing her final sentence, and of the fixed laws under which such punishment is inflicted. The two views are not strictly incongruous, but Huxley never reconciled them in form.

His views on the traditional theology are full of curious interest. He gave it all up; but he thought that it contained more ethical truth than cheap optimism of whatsoever brand. He was led to this position by reading and also by experience. As a boy he had dived into Paley, and retained a taste for theology; he always prized the Bible and advocated its use in schools.[1] In youth he was stirred by Carlyle, to whom he traced his lifelong abhorrence of imposture, and also his strain of sympathy with the poor, which is of a less sentimental cast than that of Mill and other radicals. Carlyle's sterner Calvinistic strain also struck a chord in Huxley, chiming in as it did with his scientific recognition of the reign of law. He had, as we have seen, a severe sense of the penal regulations of life. He is not like Spencer, who always speaks as if Plato had never discoursed of the two steeds, or Paul of the law in our members. A letter written to Charles Kingsley in 1860, 'in a humour of savage grief' on the occasion of a bereavement, shows that he did not win his faith easily. In old age, when repudiating any sympathy with the Comtists, and denying at the same time that his teaching had been purely 'negative,' he describes himself as one who

> has graduated in all the faculties of human relationship; who has taken his share in all the deep joys and deeper anxieties which cling about them; who has felt the burden of young lives entrusted to his care, and has stood alone with his dead before the abyss of the eternal.

It is this 'graduation,' this note of conflict and reality, that distinguishes Huxley from many philosophers.

His opinions on education show a broader spirit than either Matthew Arnold's or Herbert Spencer's. There is, we know, nothing like leather; and Huxley naturally pleads for a regular training in science. He also mocks at our public schools and older universities, with their disdain of the laboratory, their class superstitions, and their Latin elegances. But this he does in the interest of the humanities themselves. In the dark days which many yet remember (and they have not wholly vanished), Huxley advised the genuine teaching of modern history, of foreign tongues, and of the native literature. The adult, also, should receive no narrow culture, but should be conversant with the great expounders, both Israelitish and Greek, of life and conduct; not to name the wisdom of Goethe,[2] whom

Huxley prized highly, and whose aphoristic descant on *Nature* he translated. This strong-headed catholicity of view is felt even in Huxley's addresses on technical and professional training.

In his political and social ideas he went a way of his own. In many respects he was anti-radical. He believed much more than Mill and Mill's followers in State action, or at least in the chance of a bureaucracy not becoming too foolish. He became an unionist; perhaps he would have been more of a liberal if Mr. Gladstone, whom he cordially distrusted, had never been born. But, in the great test case of Governor Eyre [1] (1866) which brought out the sharpest of cleavages amongst English thinkers, Huxley sided with Mill, Spencer, Darwin, and Goldwin Smith, and against Tennyson, Ruskin, and Carlyle. He thought that Eyre, whatever his intentions, had committed legal murder. Yet Huxley had unhopeful views of the negro,[2] and was no democrat. One of his papers is entitled *The Natural Inequality of Men* (1890). On such matters—for instance on the 'emancipation of women,' for whom he claimed a fair field but no favour—his attitude may be described as liberalism controlled by anthropology.

VI

Huxley, as a writer, is a vigorous slip of the fighting, expounding eighteenth-century stock. He has no tricks. Rather vociferous and rhetorical at first, he settles down into an easy, manly, pure elocution, which is mostly argumentative, often sardonic, again and again truly eloquent, but which never loses the tone of reasonableness. It is like a speech made in court by an honest advocate—before the court of science, where any amount of banter or icy politeness, without vulgarity, is allowable. He does not lose himself in refinements; if he has a fault, it is that he sheers all too buoyantly through them. Since his time there has been no such disputant among men of letters in this country. But a fighting style is the most transient of all, and no doubt Huxley has suffered from his very victories, and from the shifting of the issues for which he strove. In the literary struggle for life mere militancy is a clog unless it is vitalised by a great theme, a strong mind, a desire for the truth, and the gift of form. Huxley's work is often thus preserved. There is no English Bossuet. Newman is famous in controversy; but Huxley, like many a reader, could truly say of Newman what no one can reasonably say of Huxley: 'After an hour or two of him I began to lose sight of the distinction between truth and falsehood.'

Still, Huxley's style is not essentially combative in its higher, or in all its ordinary, forms. He is a teacher, knowing the pace at which an audience can take things in. The discourses *On a Piece of Chalk* and *On the Method of Zadig* are exemplary, and would have pleased Buffon. The address on Priestley is the model of a scientific *causerie*. The paper *On the Hypothesis that Animals are Automata* (the paradox of Descartes) is a skilful union of history, argument, and demonstration: the manner is dignified without being slow, and exact while not too technical. The *Prolegomena* (1894) to *Evolution and Ethics* are the work of a past master of reasoned statement; they are simple in diction and brilliantly arranged.

Huxley admired Tennyson's precise and poetical treatment of science; and in his own science there is a strong vein of poetry, which comes out best when he is disowning the opinion that science can explain everything. The passage is familiar, but may be quoted once more, as it is worthy of any philosophical humourist:

> I do not wish to crow unduly over my humble cousin the orang,[1] but in the æsthetic province, as in that of the intellect, I am afraid he is nowhere. I doubt not he would detect a fruit amidst a wilderness of leaves where I could see nothing; but I am tolerably confident that he has never been awestruck, as I have been, by the dim religious gloom, as of a temple devoted to the earth-gods, of the tropical forest which he inhabits. Yet I doubt not that our poor long-armed and short-legged friend, as he sits meditatively munching his durian fruit, has something behind that sad Socratic face of his which is utterly 'beyond the bounds of physical science.' Physical science may know all about his clutching the fruit and munching it and digesting it, and how the physical titillation of his palate is transmitted to some microscopic cells of the grey matter of his brain. But the feelings of sweetness and of satisfaction which, for a moment, hang out their signal lights in his melancholy eyes are as utterly outside the bounds of physics as is the 'fine frenzy' of a human rhapsodist.

Darwin said, 'What splendid fun Huxley is'; and so he is still. Of the geologist Hutton he observes that,

> like most philosophers of his age, he coquetted with those final causes which have been named barren virgins, but which might be more fitly termed the *hetairæ* of philosophy, so constantly have they led men astray.

His pages are full of such things; they are not forced or

thought painfully out, but spring up as if in talk. His letters to his friends and family have the same spontaneity. He can write excellent nonsense about a cat, or about his own Privy Councillorship. His gallant good spirits, resting on and surviving the conviction that the universe is a grim affair, come out to the end, especially when there is fighting to be done. Huxley, certainly, is an artist in his many-sided business of explaining, refuting, and deriding; but amongst our scientific writers he stands out, above all, for humanity and imagination.

William Kingdon Clifford[1] (1845-79), a mathematician of note, and perhaps also the Marcellus of philosophy, left only his book called *The Common Sense of the Exact Sciences* (1885) and a handful of speculative papers. He writes with brilliant simplicity, and sketches his conception of 'mind-stuff,' which implies some incredibly far-back embryo of mind latent even in the inorganic world; the aim being, naturally, to turn the flank of the question,—At what point does life emerge in the eternal process? Clifford also dreams of a creed, secular and scientific in foundation, but idealistic in effect, which shall extend our sympathies beyond humanity itself. He borrows, it is said from Henry Sidgwick, the term 'cosmic emotion'; and, writing in the Seventies, fervently quotes Swinburne, the 'singer before sunrise'; and rejoices in the spirit of *Hertha*.

A kindred enthusiasm is also seen in the physicist, John Tyndall (1820-93), whose *Heat as a Mode of Motion* (1863) and other works proved him to be, along with Huxley, the most expert and eloquent populariser of his time. Tyndall's address at Belfast to the British Association in 1874 was saluted as a sonorous statement of the new materialism; it really points to a kind of mystical dualism, denying that 'logical continuity can be established between molecular processes and the phenomena of consciousness'; and it is a plea, founded on an historical review, for freedom of scientific inquiry. Tyndall was influenced by his friend and master Carlyle, on whom he wrote well; he is full of poetic and pictorial feeling, which finds no very restrained expression in his style, and which is well seen in his essays, his *Fragments of Science* (1871), and his *New Fragments* (1892), and in his works on glaciers and mountaineering. Inferior to Huxley as a thinker and writer, Tyndall is a clean hitter, and his language has a compensating touch of colour which is not yet faded.

VII

Thus many of the apostles of experience and utility, of science and evolution, proffered not only a philosophy, but some kind of natural religion or working faith, denuded of the supernatural. So, in another way, did the Comtists, or those who without being Comtists inhaled their spirit. But the men of science are often hostile to Positivism ; nor have they, in the nature of the case, any formal cult in common ; but each goes his own way, while in accord with the others on many fundamentals. This heroic effort to beat out a lay creed will always signalise the second half of the century in English history. Its manifestations in letters are not easy to fix, but they abound. In the stories of George Eliot, in the verse of Swinburne, in that of James Thomson, there is a conscious rejection of the old doctrines and a resolution to make what can be made of life without them. But a deeply secular tinge, without any strife or crying, also comes over inventive literature at large, and is seen in the novel, in poetry, in fantasy, and in criticism ; *servat odorem.* To come, outside the sphere of controversy, on a writer like Christina Rossetti, of truly conservative faith and principles, who is also an artist, is exceptional. The purely intellectual movement told, not so much by direct attack as by silently loosening the ancient anchorage, at least for the time.

Within philosophy itself, a new phase opens during the seventh and eighth decades. Naturally, the battle-ground becomes more and more that of morals, and of the ethical sanction. For the new creeds were on their mettle to show that the basis and inspiration of conduct were not lost with the old dogmas. They might own their debt freely to the historic faiths, and professed to have cleared them of unscientific accretions. Such a challenge explains the temper of writers like Sir Leslie Stephen, whose *Agnostic's Apology* (1893) is still the most powerful, and indeed poignant, expression of it ; the *Essays on Freethinking and Plain Speaking,* twenty years earlier, are also of mark. Unlike Spencer, Stephen was well qualified on the historical side, and produced in 1876 his deeply-informed *History of English Thought in the Eighteenth Century,* which explores the byways and main roads of speculation. His *Science of Ethics* (1882) is much beholden to Spencer, but is less ambitiously deductive in character ; he starts with the accepted moral code in its better shape, and seeks to interpret that code in the light of evolution, in a manner which was naturally challenged by conservative thinkers.[1] He was, however, first of all a man of letters and critic (see Ch. XI.). A somewhat different lay religion was sketched by the Positivist, James Cotter Morison, whose *Service of Man* (1887) is a typical piece of polemic and of hasty reconstruction, with the note of passion that marks the time. Cotter Morison is much happier in his short volumes upon Gibbon and Macaulay.

Two other scions of the school of experience, Henry Sidgwick [2] (1838-1900) and Shadworth Hollway Hodgson (1832-1912), are more dissident from its tradition, and in pure philosophy are more original, than Stephen. Sidgwick, while deeply attentive to literature, is primarily a close hard thinker, chary of the graces. Much of his work dates from the Nineties, and some was posthumously published; his books on economic and political science are of high value (*Elements of Politics*, 1891); but he is best known by his *Methods of Ethics*, published in 1874 and frequently revised. It is a tribute to this long, toughly-written work, and also to the spreading interest in philosophy, that six editions of it were demanded in twenty-seven years. In a complex argument, Sidgwick turns round on the utilitarian scheme of morals and gives it a disconcerting wrench. He seeks, in the first place, to restore the absolute character of one intuition, which the school of 'experience' had obscured or explained away. It is that of duty, or absolutely rational conduct, regarded as binding in its essence. Sidgwick analyses this idea, and also, in his most Aristotelian chapters, the 'morality of common sense'; and from both of them, and from what is left of the utilitarian creed, works up to his own conclusion. During the process, the deep fissure in that creed comes into light—the fissure between 'egoism,' which starts with the happiness, more or less intelligently conceived, of you or me, and 'universalism' or 'altruism,' which starts with the happiness of others. Sidgwick's point is that no sophistry can ever make these wholly coincide, or can answer the question '*Why* should I seek the happiness of others more than my nature inclines me to do?'—Nothing can do this except 'a hypothesis, unverifiable by experience, reconciling the Individual with the Universal Reason.' Failing which, 'the Cosmos of Duty is thus really reduced to a Chaos,' and the hope of a rational ethic is foredoomed.

It was characteristic of Sidgwick to be haunted by the question and to end with the hypothetical answer. The *Data of Ethics* did not appear till 1879; nor, from the other camp, Green's *Prolegomena to Ethics* till 1883. Sidgwick criticised both these works with much dialectical and judicial power, but did not visibly change his point of view. In a purely naturalistic universe he saw an unfillable hole—no sufficient *motive* for doing what you know you ought to do. He could not be expected to see that the most promising answer to the difficulty was offered by a life and temper like his own, which was markedly disinterested and exalted, and by what Sir Leslie Stephen calls his 'hopefulness not damped by provisional scepticism.' In some ways, like Stuart Mill, he provides a pattern for the 'conduct of the understanding.' His acute, honest, minutely-balancing mind is ever on the alert against believing merely because it would give anything to be able to believe. 'How I sympathise,' he once exclaims, 'with Kant! with his passionate yearning for synthesis, and condemned by his reason to criticism!' In his published letters, with their fervent musings on duty, immortality, and happiness, and their comments on *In Memoriam* and on George Eliot, we seem to touch the very pulse of the Victorian age, in which Sidgwick was formed; with its special questionings, its disquieted, high-strained 'nobleness.' Sidgwick was a powerful and effectual champion of liberal education, for women equally with men, and won great influence, especially at Cambridge where he spent his days. His style grew more flexible and easier, but offers few bribes to those who require them; it is full of doublings-back, qualified qualifications, and densely-crowded sentences; but it holds the mind, and leaves an impression of caution rather than of scepticism. A little more form, or concession to form, and Sidgwick doubtless would have reached the laity more than he did.

Shadworth Hollway Hodgson's difficult and subtle work on *Time and Space* (1865) was succeeded by his *Theory of Practice* in 1870, and in 1878 by *The Philosophy of Reflection*; his elaborate *Metaphysic of Experience*, which gives his maturest thought, did not come out till 1898, so that he is hardly within our limits. He may be said to attempt a restatement of the ethical problem, by sinking a shaft down to the bedrock that is common to the opposing camps. Hodgson's analysis of the passions and virtues, while abstruse, shows great conversance with life: he does not, like many moral philosophers, work at six removes from reality, or simply methodise platitudes. There is a warmth of direct observation in his pictures of veracity, envy, or love; for the barren antipodes to his pages (in *Theory of Practice*) on Eros and Anteros, we may turn to Bain's account of the tender feelings in *The Emotions and the Will*. Hodgson also describes the æsthetic[1] feelings from within; his distinction between fancy and imagination, and his accounts of style, of rhythm, and the species of poetry have been much too little noticed. He inlays bits of Greek and other quotations in his nice and fastidious style, the exactness of which suggests a close reading of Aristotle.

VIII

But to return to the philosophers of the 'right wing' who succeeded Ferrier and Mansel, and who were all this time at work countermining the new naturalism. After 1860 they drew new weapons from Hegel, who had died in 1831, but who for long was most imperfectly known in England; and there came also a notable revival of Kant. The empirical writers had to face the attack in their fortresses of logic, psychology, ethics, and political science; but the citadel was metaphysic. They were to be told that they could not get on without it; that they had a metaphysic already, but a bad one; and that if they went to the Germans they would find salvation or remission. This movement, at once offensive and reconstructive, culminated in the last quarter of the century. It belongs to the history of mind more than to letters, all the more that many of its champions were not good or not easy writers, and spoke to an academic or elect audience, not to the general public. Their veteran, however, James Hutchison Stirling (1820-1909) has an eccentric eloquence, sometimes coloured by reminiscence of Carlyle; who bore witness, though himself now impervious to metaphysics, to the valiant service done by Stirling against the empirics of the age. *The Secret of Hegel* (1865) is an effort to translate, and to expound in plain English, the wickedly technical 'dialectic' of the master. In this task Stirling shows great and rampant ability. He breathes with ease, and can only breathe, in that strange heady atmosphere, which seems to seal the ears of the devotee to the conceivability of any other point of view. Stirling's work as a pioneer and acclimatiser was always recognised by his successors. In 1874 *The Logic of Hegel* was translated and commented by William Wallace, later Professor of Moral Philosophy at Oxford, who was a skilled interpreter of German thinkers (including Schopenhauer), and who wrote with elaborate finish and much power of clarification. The quickening power of Hegel on an unsystematic mind is well seen in the earlier career of Benjamin Jowett. In 1876 came the *Ethical Studies* of Francis Herbert Bradley, who was to be the most original philosopher and philosophical writer in Britain during the next generation; and, in 1879, *The Philosophy of Kant*, by Robert Adamson, another independent thinker, with a consummate knowledge of the history of thought; his *Fichte* (1881) also exemplifies his powers. But these two writers use the Germans rather than depend on them, and inaugurate a new 'moment' in our philosophy. Green and the two Cairds, on the other hand, though no mere importers, devote themselves in great measure to representing and adapting Hegelian or Kantian conceptions.

It was a pity that so strong and serious a spirit as Thomas Hill Green (1836-82) should have stooped so seldom to the common idiom of literature. In 1874-5 he published, along with T. H. Grose, an edition of Hume's *Treatise on Human Nature*, with a long, dense, unreadable and hostile introduction, showing great dialectical skill and pertinacity. It sent many an unregenerate student to Hume for mere relief. Huxley's work on that thinker, which appeared a few years afterwards, and Green's, belong to different worlds, and it is hard to bring them into any sort of contact; but there is no doubt which of the two men is the writer, and which the metaphysician. Green's aim was to cut empiricism at the very root; and Hume's tree, in the *Treatise*, is naked and distinct enough, without any of the foliage of the *Essays*. Of Green it has been well said that

> he appealed [1] to 'Englishmen under five-and-twenty' to close their Mill and Spencer and to open their Kant and Hegel; and this appeal marks an epoch in English thought in the nineteenth century.

Green's major work, *Prolegomena to Ethics* (1883), is far less forbidding in form, though still very close-grained; it is also less purely critical. It is an impressive deliverance of the 'philosophy of spirit'—of a fresh, thorough-going, and lofty idealism. But he writes somewhat as though his system had all the loftiness to itself; and on his showing it is not so easy to explain the ethical afflatus that is strong in the writers whom he judges to be steeped in error, and in the votaries of 'humanity,' who abandon the sacred wells of metaphysic. The same sincerity and no less weight are evident in Green's later and scattered writings on social and political science. He was a power in Oxford, and beyond; but his influence was checked, much more than Henry Sidgwick's, by his anti-popular form.

This defect is less apparent in the writings of the brothers,

John and Edward Caird. John Caird (1820-98) is more of a divine, Edward (1835-1908) more of a philosopher ; but they have much ground in common. In his *Introduction to the Philosophy of Religion* (1880) John Caird eloquently assails, on Hegelian lines, the scientific ' materialism ' of Huxley, and the Spencerian cult of the Unknowable. He tells the religious world not to be afraid lest the conception of development should force them to admit that Christianity is merely ' elaborated out of pre-Christian religions and philosophies, any more than that life can be elaborated out of inorganic matter ' : a sentence which well indicates Caird's position. It does not follow, he says, that Christianity is not ' a religion of divine or supernatural origin.' The whole book is in the nature of an insurance offered by metaphysics to liberal orthodoxy. Edward Caird, the younger brother, was professor at Glasgow from 1866 to 1893, and afterwards Master of Balliol. Much of his work, published in his later life, embodies the teachings of a quarter of a century ; and perhaps only Carlyle had a stronger influence in Scotland. His short books on *Kant* (1877) and on *Hegel* (1893) show great expository skill ; and in other works Caird reviews the progress of religion from the idealistic point of view. He is a smooth dignified writer, with a marked gift for comprehensive and sweeping surveys, and his tone is exalted and sincere. But for those who are not already converts Caird is a most elusive thinker, moving from abstraction to abstraction so that the reader loses foothold. That may be the case with Hegel too ; but in Hegel we come on lumps of monumental granite upon which to stay our steps. Edward Caird's outlook on literature is also a wide one, as his articles on Carlyle and Goethe testify. He naturally cares most for the ideas and creeds that are to be extracted from the poets and visionaries.

The revulsion from the school of experience takes yet another form in James Martineau (1805-1900), long the leader of thought and letters in the Unitarian community. Martineau was much more of a divine than of an original philosopher, though he wrote profusely and keenly on philosophical matters ; and he was greater as a preacher, and as a personal and spiritual force, than as a theologian. His activity was prolonged and wonderful. He began to write in 1836 ; but his most elaborate and massive books were not published until he had reached his vigorous eightieth year ; *Types of Ethical Theory* (1885) and *A Study of Religion* (1888) being, with the *Study of Spinoza* (1882), the most important. The best work of his earlier life he collected in four volumes of *Essays, Reviews, and Addresses* (1890-1). Brought up in a rigid form of empiricism, Martineau broke away early, and his philosophical *vita nuova* began in Berlin, where he studied Kant and Hegel. In the end he elaborated a theistic doctrine profoundly ethical in its complexion, opposing alike the Utilitarians and Mansel, and ranging over almost every current controversy. Martineau's lofty temper, like his keen dialectical power, can be felt in all he writes, and his rhetoric is not empty. It is, however, diffuse and ornate, and his genuine faculty for writing was somewhat dispersed and lost. How well he could describe when he chose can be seen from his account of the person and character of Charles Kingsley. But he figures more in the history of religious thought and feeling than in that of letters. Yet a last representative of idealism may be named, Alexander Campbell Fraser (1818-1914), another of the Scottish Guards, and long a professor of veteran rank at Edinburgh. To write of Berkeley is to be near the rose of literature ; and Fraser's commented edition (1871) of the noblest writer amongst English thinkers, who made philosophy musical and Apolline, was a timely reminder of the powers of our language in the age of Herbert Spencer.

IX

For there was no Berkeley during all this period, nor yet a Hume, nor a Hobbes. Despite the powers of Mansel and Ferrier, of Mill and Huxley, none of them quite rose to the immense intellectual occasion. There was an atmosphere of combat only to be paralleled in Berkeley's own day. The style of philosophy and science is affected by this medium, as well as by the new ideas which clamoured for expression. It is apt to be the language of the streets, or else of the laboratory or the schools. The technicalities of science lumber it ; and the forms of the review article, the rejoinder-pamphlet, the public lecture, the lay sermon, the open letter, and the occasional oration, all make for a journalism which may not be ignoble but is not enduring. These forms multiply greatly, and the salvage for literature is not encouraging. But we have had to note some true practitioners of that 'close, naked, natural way of speaking' which is the voice of science. Darwin wrote as calmly as Aristotle, and as well, while the fighting prose was being whetted and edged all around him. Tribute has already been paid to other writers ; and I shall but cite some stray new words and phrases of learned origin that now stole into the language, or acquired new senses, as a result of the movement of ideas.

Greek, the mother-language of thought, and Latin in a less degree, were once again drawn upon. Endless neologisms appeared in the special sciences, which themselves, like *anthropology*, got new names as they arose. The popular spread of such words and phrases is a very rude index of general culture. How many who speak of the *survival of the fittest* or of the *struggle for existence* understand the true sense of such phrases? We can at least apply them (the first is fathered on Darwin and the second on Wallace) to the fortunes of the vocabulary itself. Words appeared that have dwindled or died, not 'of their own dear loveliness,' but because they were not wanted; or have survived painfully in professional circles. So with *metempirical*, suggested by Lewes; and with *eject*, formed by Clifford on the pattern of *subject* and *object*, to denote our consciousness, which is for ever indirect, of minds other than our own. Other terms, like Hamilton's *cosmothetic*, and John Grote's *felicific* (not a word itself that makes for happiness) are similarly interned. The appearance of *subjective* and *objective* is noticed by Edward FitzGerald in 1840-1, in a spirit of regret. The former, he says, 'has made considerable progress in England . . . so that people begin to fancy they understand what it means'; and in the same strain he mentions *exegetical* and *æsthetics*. All these have held their ground in the semi-learned language. *Psychology*, which was earlier domesticated, has passed into working English; and also, in the sense of character or play of motive, into the slang of the press. We are told to 'understand the ex-Kaiser's psychology,' as though he were a Hume or a Lotze. One of Comte's inventions, *altruism* and its derivatives, came in through his translators and expositors, and is still in use, even outside works on ethics, amongst formal speakers. *Egoism* and *egoist*, already in existence (*egoism* as far back as 1800, in its modern sense), were captured by the schools to express a particular theory of morals. They are used in a hostile, or at best in a neutral, sense; and they escape into fiction and into common parlance. Meredith's tale *The Egoist* was published in the same year (1879) as *Data of Ethics*, where the word figures largely. *Ethology* was coined by the younger Mill to denote the science of human character, and it might have lived had such a science really existed. It occurs in the *Logic*, which also promoted the circulation of the words *connote* and *connotation*. These are well enough in their place; they are heard, in donnish circles, instead of *imply* and *implication*.

The new religions or no-religions did not want for titles. *Hedonism* and *hedonist* are now established words: the latter is said to be the invention of Christopher North. The *New English Dictionary* quotes first De Quincey, in 1856 ('I am a Hedonist; and if you must know why I take opium, that 's the reason why'), and next Pater, in 1876. He said: 'I wish they wouldn't call me a Hedonist; it produces such a bad effect on the mind of people who don't know Greek.' Indeed moralists' Greek, when it migrates into English, can sometimes produce as bad an effect as thieves' Latin. Again, the epithet *cosmic* had its day. A 'cosmic philosophy' was evolved in America in 1874; the 'cosmic emotion,' which so few can feel, was recommended by Clifford; and the 'cosmic process' was, we have seen, censured on high moral grounds (in 1893) by Huxley. The words *agnostic* and *agnosticism* were hatched in the Metaphysical Society, and are now found in census returns, and also (profanely clipped) in undergraduate slang. *Secularism*, *secularist*, are in use, but they still have a raw, dogmatic, outlaw air. Many of the new words, though taken from the noble languages, are dissonant: and the worst is the gnashing and hissing *scientist*, to which the epithet 'Christian' (being considered a contradictory one) was not prefixed until after this period, but which was used by writers of repute as early as 1840. Lastly, the diction of philosophy was enlarged by the need and hampered by the problem of finding English equivalents for German terminology. This task confronted the translators of Kant, Fichte, and Hegel, and even those of Schopenhauer, who writes more like a man of this world than the rest. Expressions like *Vorstellung*, *Begriff*, *Anschauung*, not to name the jargon of Hegelian logic, always gave trouble, for no one English word was exactly conterminous. The word *moment*, in the sense of element or constituent phase, made its way into our technical vocabulary. But the greatest of our insular thinkers—Hobbes, Berkeley, and Hume—have proved that a special dialect, however useful, is not requisite to philosophy, and that the nicest shades can be expressed, unscholastically, in the mother tongue.

X

Nothing can better show the vigour, or the manners, of the philosophical prize-ring, or the nature of the stakes, than a glance at two of the most flourishing of the weightier magazines, and also at the record of the 'Metaphysical Society.' The most notable journal, on the advanced side, was the *Fortnightly Review* [1] (which in fact was issued monthly) under the editorship, from 1867 to 1883, of Mr. John Morley, now Viscount Morley of Blackburn. Its pages were not merely an arena; it found ample room for pure letters; Walter Pater, Dante Rossetti, Swinburne, and George Meredith were among the contributors. But the *Fortnightly* was correctly regarded as the organ of fighting rationalism, philosophical, political, and more especially religious. During the latter half of 1877, we are told, 'nearly every number contained an attack by some powerful writer, either on theology as a whole, or on some generally accepted article of theological belief.' No label, however, was really apt except the elusive one of 'liberalism,' of which the *Review*, at that season, was the great exponent. The tone of the *Nineteenth Century*, though by no means calmer, was more impartial; the aim being to pit against one another the toughest producible combatants from all sides, to fulfil the object glorified in Mill's *Liberty*.

This journal was founded in 1877 by James Knowles, and it may be regarded as the offspring of the Metaphysical Society, which the same *impresario* had suggested, which was started in 1869 and lived on for some twenty years; dying then, it was said, 'of too much love.' The Society contained so many notable men, representing the extremes of 'Rome and Reason,' and also every intermediate shade of opinion, that it is easier to name the absent, who included Mill, Newman, Browning, and Herbert Spencer, than to recount the members, who numbered from first to last more than seventy. Lively descriptions may be found in the biographies of Huxley, W. G. Ward, and Tennyson. The object of the debates was to discover some common ground of conviction; their result was that the width and depth of the chasm between the two principal parties was measured, most amicably indeed, but more hopelessly and precisely than ever before. Providence, miracles, the nature of the soul ('Has a Frog a Soul?'), the possibility of its survival ('What is Death?'), and the stability of ethics, were all discussed in the light of the claims of the new thought and science. These were among the *agenda*. The hard hitting, the brisk dialectic, the good temper, the sense of humour, and the firm refusal of so many *open minds* to be convinced, which appear to have distinguished divines and heretics alike in these wit-combats, are signally British characteristics; and the scene can hardly be imagined in any continental capital.

CHAPTER V

PHILOSOPHY, HISTORY, AND LETTERS

I

THE links between science and history are riveted by the writers who endeavour to read the facts of history in the spirit of science. Certainly all true historians make this effort, unless their bent, as with Carlyle, be for portrayal mixed with prophecy. Freeman, Stubbs, and Gardiner are scientific; for their method is rigorous: they have the conscience of the naturalist, they seek to prove all things, and they look for some general laws amid the welter of events. But they are concerned more with political and constitutional matters than with thought and art, or with manners and religion. With abstract philosophy and her perplexities they have but a bowing acquaintance. But with Lewis, Buckle, Lecky, Maine, and Bagehot speculation is never far in the background; their operations include, but reach far beyond, politics in the stricter sense; and their collective labours mark a new departure for the English mind.

They do not all write equally well, and their ideas are often above, or else below, their powers of expression. One of the earliest in the field is Sir George Cornewall Lewis [1] (1806-63). A dry mind (not without dry banter) and a slow-going writer, but very full and very sound. A methodical, pigeon-holing man, who begins with the alphabet, defines and sub-defines without mercy, multiplies polyglot illustrations, and plods surely towards conclusions of unmistakeable value. Like Hobbes and Bentham, Lewis truly thinks that mankind is much befogged by the ambiguities of words; and he has the bookman's faith that mankind will mend when such darkness is cleared away, and when it clearly knows the meanings of *republic*, *balance of powers*, *state of nature*, and the like. The *Remarks on the Use and Abuse of some Political Terms* (1832) are Benthamite in spirit, and may owe something to *The Book of Fallacies*. This *nominalism* marks the early radicals, and is healthy enough; but Lewis has much more learning than his masters ; and learning is one of the things that kept the school alive, and saved it from the condemnation of Matthew Arnold, when he exclaimed (in his pleasant indifference to connected thinking) that it was 'doomed to sterility.' The thinking of Lewis is British and solid, without a ray of imagination. It is, in fact, his principal task to shatter vain imaginations ; '*Hypotheses non fingo, immo destruo*' might be his watchword.

In his *Enquiry into the Credibility of the Early Roman History* (1855) Lewis treats destructively the guesswork of genius which had marred the speculations of Niebuhr: his acids corroded many a hypothesis. The authority of the great German, which had inspired and oppressed Thomas Arnold, was thus shaken in England. Lewis went to the sceptical extreme ; but Macaulay, for instance, had jumped at Niebuhr's theory that the legends of the Roman historians are drawn from a lost fund of Roman epic or ballad poetry.[1] Lewis asks in vain for the evidence of this connexion, and of *metrical* originals, and with polite irony commends the theory for having begotten, at any rate, the *Lays of Ancient Rome*. The most enduring of his works seems to be the *Essay on the Influence of Authority in Matters of Opinion* (1849). It covers part of the same ground as Mill's *Liberty*, but the temper and mode of analysis are different. Like Mill, but in a quieter way, Lewis is adverse to the control of intellectual conviction by church or state. But while Mill urges with passion that such control *ought* not to exist, Lewis pleads coolly that it *cannot* effectually exist, at least not without grave evils. He also wrote a long work on *The Methods of Observation and Reasoning in Politics* (1852). He certainly has a liking for leaden titles. But this treatise ends with the confession of a sober but firm belief in human progress, in the spheres of politics, ethics, and religion, though not in that of art ; a faith the more striking, because the idea of evolution makes no figure in it.

One of Lewis's liveliest and most rapid compositions is the *Dialogue on the Best Form of Government* (1863). Here the monarchist, the aristocrat, and the democrat make their pleas, and Crito, the impartial judge, who is Lewis, decides that there is no best form of government, and that all forms are relative ; though he seems to least dislike a modified aristocracy. Bagehot says that Sir George Lewis was lighter in talk than with his pen, and we can believe this from the *Dialogue*. He quotes the saying about O'Connell : 'He was a man whom you ought to hang, and to whom you ought to build a monument under his gallows.' Lewis was a typical, in some ways an ideal, publicist and public servant; a fair-minded Whig, some time editor of the *Edinburgh Review*; a good Chancellor of the Exchequer, if an odd figure at the War Office; with real statesmanship, and not much literature, in his composition.

The spirit of Lewis is critical; and first in the field with a large constructive effort was Henry Thomas Buckle[1] (1821-62), with his *History of Civilization in England*, of which the first volume appeared in 1857, and the second four years later. It is a huge torso; or, to use a truer figure, a huge ground-plan, as grandiose as the 'new Delhi,' with two or three outbuildings more or less completed, while the central mansion is hardly begun. For the architect, dying all too soon, never fairly reached the history of civilisation 'in England.' The outbuildings are the chapters, so sharply canvassed, on Spain and Scotland. These countries are presented as the most notorious in all the realm of darkness. The ground-plan is the series of theses concerning those impersonal laws which in Buckle's opinion have determined, and must ever determine, the arrest or progress of mankind. Each thesis would be matter for a long debate, and most of them provoked violent criticism. Buckle's view of the fatality of statistical averages, the fallacy of which is well exposed by Lecky, is not required by his argument, and is only an embarrassment. His statement that the 'aspects of nature,' where, as in India, they are fierce and impressive, cow the reason, and only kindle vain and slavish imaginations, is ludicrous as applied to the home of metaphysic. When he tells us that religion and art and letters are only the 'product,' and not a 'cause,' of 'civilisation,' we reply that these things *are* civilisation. His notion that great men are disturbing by-products, mere creatures and not causes of mighty changes, is simply pseudo-science run mad, and a sufficiently cavalier disposal of Cæsar and Mahomet. It was perhaps prompted by the exaggerations of Carlyle. But in two directions at least Buckle blazed a fresh track for English readers. His very materialism, when he traces down national characters and fates to the influence of climate, food, and soil, is a revelation of facts till then hardly appreciated, and is also a forecast of our larger conception of geography. But he came, or rather departed, too soon to appreciate the idea of evolution. And his intellectualism, which caused him to set down all improvement on this earth to the march of mind, is salutary too. He intensified the general sense of the reign of natural law throughout the whole sphere of human action; though he would not see, what Lecky was to trace so well, that there has also been a certain progress in the moral conceptions, and even in the moral practice, of the West. In support of his views Buckle marshalled a great mass of facts, often ill-verified and half-digested, but in the mass impressive. With all his faults he widened the horizon of English thought. His work was that of a self-trained bookman, but it was fresh. He owed something, as critics have remarked, to the speculations of Comte, and there is a trace of the French habit of mind in his union of sweeping generalisation with minute note-taking.

His style, however, has not the French virtues. He is a hard-hitting, but often a diffuse writer, with little sense of scale. He is visibly honest, with many a spurt of sentiment and passionate, cutting invective. His outbursts against the Inquisition and the tyranny of the Kirk are well inspired. But he holds fiercely to his own remnants of theology, and can rise to eloquence in maintaining them. At the end of his book there is a queer sudden argument to the effect that the theory of a moral government of the world is a 'slur on the Omniscience of God,' seeing that a truly infinite wisdom would never need to be 'meddling here and meddling there.' In a review of Mill's *Liberty* he defends, in a strain that recalls Tennyson, the belief in personal immortality, on the strength of the vehement desire felt by the bereaved for reunion. His most moving passage occurs at the end of his third chapter, when he finds that his task is too heavy, and that he will never reach his history of 'the free, the noble, and the high-minded English people.' So he settles down, savagely enough, to his 'examination of the Scotch intellect during the seventeenth century.'

II

William Edward Hartpole Lecky[1] (1838-1903) writes much better, and inspires more confidence than Buckle ; he is a better scholar, and sure where Buckle is rash ; he does not start with a case to prove. But, as a surveyor of moral and intellectual history, he admires and praises Buckle,[2] though with many reserves, and owes to him not a little of his large outlook ; and he comes in Buckle's wake, for the *History of the Rise and Influence of the Spirit of Rationalism in Europe* appeared in 1865, four years after Buckle's second volume. The *History of European Morals from Augustus to Charlemagne* (1869) was published when Lecky was barely thirty. His reputation was now assured. As he says himself, the two works, which are really one, form an essay in the science[3]; which had been founded by Vico in the seventeenth century, and expanded by Condorcet, Herder, Hegel, and Comte, and latterly by Buckle too: the science that conceives of history as 'not a series of biographies, or accidents, or pictures, but a great organic whole.' It is Lecky's praise that he truly enriched this conception. His lecture (1892) on *The Political Value of History* presents his ideas in their ripest form, and in his most limpid style.

He makes it his business to steer between the extremes of Buckle, whose idea of history, he says, implies 'leaving out the men and women,' and of Carlyle with his 'heroes.' Few historians have steered so well. Lecky seems happiest and most at home when he is moving among impersonal forces, and tracing the growth and decline of ideas as they have coloured human feeling and action. But he is also alive to the influence of persons, and presents them with much skill. And he appreciates an element for which neither Buckle nor Carlyle duly allows —the element of *accident*,[1] meaning thereby the fatal ironical twist that may be given to events by small and apparently irrelevant personages. He appreciates that saying, which gives trouble to the scientific historian, about the length of Cleopatra's nose. A campaign, and all that turns upon it, *may* be determined by 'some obscure captain who perhaps moved his men to the right when he should have moved them to the left.' Once, in a letter, he notes the effect of a woman upon the course of recent Irish politics.

The ruling ideas of the *Rationalism* often tally with those of Mill's *Liberty* (1859). Error, if honest, is innocent; the individual may form and utter his opinions freely; it is fatal for the church or state to endeavour to subdue the mind. But Lecky's treatment is historical, not controversial, and covers a spacious field. He traces the belief in the miraculous (including magic and witchcraft), and the causes of its decline. Then he traces the history of persecution, and of toleration. He finds the roots of superstition and cruelty in the darker forms of theological dogma, and their decline he explains by the decay of belief in that dogma. And his handling is the fresher, that he does not *argue* about the reality of miracles or of witches. His picture shows the human mind, in Matthew Arnold's phrase, in the act of 'turning away' from such beliefs. In the age of W. G. Ward and Mozley, of Huxley and the dispute over the 'possessed pigs,' this picture, though it did not decide the philosophical question, told as much as all the arguments. Lecky shows that mankind does not reason itself out of such tenets, but suddenly finds, without much surprise, that it does not hold them. But he also does full justice, in his chronicle of toleration, to the great reasoners and champions—to Zwingli and Montaigne, to Hooker and Taylor, who in the long run made this conversion swifter.

The book on *European Morals* exhibits the natural history of some of the moral sentiments, the changing weight attached to different virtues in the course of centuries, and the measure in which that change has made mankind happier. The book is a pendant to the *Rationalism*, which had described the decay of certain opinions that retarded morality. Part of the ground is thus gone over again. But in the *Morals* Lecky feels bound to declare from the first his own speculative position. He takes sides in the great schism among the moral philosophers, and opens with a long defence of the intuitional theory of ethic. I do not know that the rest of his book—his account of the Stoics, or of the Roman games, or of the Christian virtues, or of the cult of celibacy, or of the position of women—could have been very different had he found himself in the opposite camp. The utilitarian thinker can accept it all. Still, the line that Lecky took, though never prompted by mere tactics, won the very audience that had to be convinced. Lecky, by his tone and antecedents, was just the man to forestall conservative alarms. He was no radical firebrand, or self-taught, like Mr. Buckle. He was judicial, moderate, reassuring, Dublin-trained. He was of Irish Protestant (and English) stock, and had thought of taking orders. He did not, like Mr. Mill, stand pointedly outside the great ruling caste. Nor was he dull and tame. He was capable of rare sallies of impassioned rhetoric, such as occur in his essay on 'the position of women'; and, with all its touch of the pulpit, it was good and generous rhetoric. And his tone, though it could not be called puritanical, was 'Victorian'; it was that of the refined student who brings himself, with much reluctance and some apologies, to lift the veil from ugly corners of moral history when truth and completeness so require. Yet he was not timid. Lecky's intellectual conscience bore him on at times to daring conclusions, always backed by an array of references and authorities:

> Had the Irish peasants been less chaste, they would have been more prosperous. (*Morals*, ch. iv.)
>
> Herself the supreme type of vice, she is ultimately the most efficient guardian of virtue. (*Morals*, ch. v.)
>
> That vice has often proved an emancipator of the mind, is one of the most humiliating, but, at the same time, one of the most unquestionable, facts in history. (*Rationalism*, ch. iv. pt. ii.)

III

Strokes like this are rarer in Lecky's capital production, *A History of England in the Eighteenth Century,* the labour of some nineteen years. The first two volumes of the original eight appeared in 1878, the last two in 1890. Equity, comprehensiveness, the tone of a judge's charge, are among its virtues ; Irish wit and paradox, though not Irish eloquence, are absent. Lecky seems to have been aware of the risks, for he writes (1882) :

> People begin to talk of me as if I were another 'judicious [1] Hooker,' so moderate, so judicious, etc., so I fear I must be growing very dull. I am afraid that nothing short of some great indiscretion or paradox can save me.

In Froude, the effect of whose *English in Ireland* he desired to counteract, Lecky had found worse than indiscretion and paradox ; but he did not need his own warning. Nature had given him a nice and fine historical conscience ; he knew that truth is complicated ; he wished, and his wish was granted, that those who desired the truth should consult his *History.* He had to present and judge the history of the Whig party, of the American war, and of the French Revolution in its reaction on English affairs ; the chronicle of intellectual and social toleration ; the record of the Kirk, and that of the English in Ireland. He had to portray not only the English statesmen, but Junius and Wilkes and George the Third, and Washington and Franklin. He had also to expound the conceptions of the moralists and social philosophers, in so far as they influenced events ; and his gallery ranges from Paley to Voltaire and Rousseau. In two of his most animated chapters he sketches the life and manners of the people, their tastes and amusements, and also the record of English music and architecture. Certainly this was a gallant effort to conceive of history as 'a great organic whole,' and the result is one of the widest, soundest, and best-ordered surveys produced in the Victorian age.

If the *History* ever drags, it is where the matter is almost impracticable. The confusions that followed on the fall of Walpole, and the debates on the Regency, are no doubt important ; but they are mean and thorny topics, and are treated with a strong sense of duty. Lecky's temper is Whiggish, of the cautious slowly-innovating type ; he has not the party zest that carries Macaulay through this kind of work, and he cannot bring himself to imitate Macaulay's emphasis. Nor are his portraits so compact and distinct. He dissects rather than portrays—dissects with an invaluable rightness and fairness. He does not spare points and anecdotes, but they come in to lighten the dissertation, rather like the tales in the *Gesta Romanorum*.

Nothing can weaken our admiration for his catholicity, width, and sureness. There is plenty of life in his narrative. The American battles, the affair of Benedict Arnold and André, the breach between Burke and Fox, are related in a masterly way, though not in Carlyle's way. Lecky learnt from Macaulay the craft of arraying pointed instances in order to illustrate a custom, an abuse, or a superstition ; and he is most himself when he does this to make us realise some far-spreading principle or tendency. Such had been his habit in the *Rationalism* and the *Morals*. The variety of his gifts and the complexion of his mind are nowhere better seen than in his chapter on Methodism. The recital is alive, the documents are ample, the sketches of character are admirable. The temper is better still. It is not that of the aggressive radical, still less of what is called the religious world. It is easy to hear the undertone of measured disgust with which Lecky, the refined, the liberal, the intellectual, beholds the narrowness of the Methodists and their alienation from the *mind* of England. He is describing it from without ; him it does not touch. Yet he feels in every line that he is dealing with a potent national force, and with a cult which, as he points out with real emotion, has consoled millions of dying persons. It is not his own cult ; but it is the last touch of Lecky's fairness, that there is no reluctance in his admiration for the good things in Methodism. It is easy to see how far he stands from the contempt felt by the 'enlightenment' for 'enthusiasm' ; for that very contempt is part of his theme and takes its place in his pattern.

This great work was originally two books in one : the history of England, and the history of Ireland. In later editions Lecky unpicked the history of Ireland, which had grown out of scale ; wove it together again, and published it singly, with a clear gain in shapeliness and proportion. He had qualified long before as a student of his own country. His youthful work, *Leaders of Public Opinion in Ireland*, with its sketches of Swift, Flood, Grattan, and O'Connell, he afterwards cut down and greatly recast.[1] He had to explain that his respect for an Irish Parliament of propertied and Protestant gentry consisted perfectly with the Unionism of his later years. In the *History of Ireland in the Eighteenth Century* his equity was put to its severest trial. He belonged to the school for whom the difference between history and politics is only one of date; 'history is past politics.' Yet he also believed that the historian exists to describe things as they really and precisely were, without reading back the conceptions of later into earlier times. We may agree or not with Lecky's opinions, but few writers have done more to conciliate these two ideals of the historian's task. The *History of Ireland* closes with the establishment of the Union. In one way it is less of a *book* than the *History of England*, for it contains fewer of Lecky's brilliant 'characters,' or of his reviews of manners and customs. Instead, there are immensely long summaries of speeches, letters, pamphlets, and documents, the result of personal digging and inquiry. It is in this material, coupled with the severe coolness and impartiality of the tone, that the worth of the *History* lies. Nor does the historian hide his own final judgement; his condemnation of Pitt for repudiating the pledge to the Catholics is decided enough. And, as the work proceeds, it is plain that the shadow of 1887 lies over it. The latter pages were written in 1890; and they form a transition to Lecky's writings on democracy, and to his Unionist speeches and pamphlets.

Democracy and Liberty (1894) is a series of separate yet connected studies on English, French, German, and American democracy: on the growth of Socialism down to the Fabian Society inclusive; on the marriage laws, the history of toleration, and almost every great social question. The tone is tinged with doubt and even with gloom; it is that of a man who sees the old reasonable Liberal landmarks slipping away, after the second Home Rule Bill and the increase of mob-power. A noteworthy 'character' of Gladstone precedes the edition of 1896. The praise is fair-minded, though it is bestowed against the grain; the mistrust is cordial. It is one of Lecky's most careful portraits, but it produces a sense of bewilderment and externality rather than of wholeness or clearness. The traits are unharmonised, and the note of repulsion, almost of alarm, contrasts with Bagehot's gay and masterly sketch of many years before. Lecky produced in 1899 a miscellany of reflections and essays called *The Map of Life*: a not very salient work, comprising *media axiomata* on compromise, marriage, success, money, and many other things; and he wrote some refined verse. A posthumous gathering of *Political and Historical Essays* is much more nutritious, with its notices of Carlyle and Newman, and its account of the influences that moulded Lecky's own mind.

IV

The effort of Bentham to find a new foundation for legal science in the principle of the greatest happiness was carried on by the eminent jurist John Austin (1790-1859), author of *The Province of Jurisprudence Determined* (1832), and the teacher of many publicists and thinkers, including Cornewall Lewis and John Stuart Mill. Austin was not, like most of his school, a democrat, and judged that a wide franchise did not make for the greatest happiness. Mill, however, acknowledges a heavy debt to his inspiration: and Austin's skill in analysing and clearing up the fundamental ideas of sovereignty, punishment, and legal right make his work a landmark. His influence seems to have been chiefly indirect, and on the few, and his rigorous style is hardly that of a man of letters.

The study of institutional history in its larger bearings was signally advanced by Sir Henry James Sumner Maine[1] (1822-88), another of Austin's debtors and admirers. A master of clean-cut brilliant exposition, his great achievement, apart from his actual contribution to knowledge, was to drive into the educated mind the truth that the study of law, past and present, so far from being an isolated or stationary thing, opened out new vistas in the study of history, custom, philosophy, and religion. This idea, as well as the scientific method of applying it, Maine made common property. His work won European recognition. A son of Cambridge and a senior classic, he became a noted lecturer on jurisprudence, and founded his reputation by his *Ancient Law* (1861), which threw fresh light on the historical import of such ideas as the 'law of nature' and the social compact, and also on the connexions between theology and jurisprudence. The phenomena of early communities he illustrated from Indian law and usage, his knowledge of which he greatly increased by his seven years' stay in India; where he held the post of legal member of Council and supervised the work, initiated by Macaulay, of codification. Maine's contact with the life of the East added colour and pungency to his subsequent writings, and the experience is reflected in his *Village Communities* (1871), in *The Early History of Institutions* (1875), and in *Early Law and Custom* (1883), a work in which he draws on Indian as well as on English, French, and Slavonic history. His mastery of statement, and of a style at once rigorous and attractive, is nowhere more apparent.

There is no better Cambridge prose than that of Sir Henry

Maine. By Cambridge prose I mean a prose of which logic, reason, and dislike of surplusage form the mental basis, and which is distinguished by the great eighteenth-century virtues of closeness, orderliness, incisive clearness, and freedom from rhetoric. These qualities are found in the writings of the Stephen family, of Henry Sidgwick, and in men of the older generation like Mill. The poetic strain of Oxford (which extends to her prose), her appeal to the heart and imagination, and also her vices of weakness, vagueness, and 'preciousness,' are more rarely found in the sister university. Most of the Cambridge poets have written in verse. Maine has plenty of the best sort of academic pungency ; his experience as a lecturer makes him careful of the pleasure of the lay reader. His manner and temper can be illustrated even from a few sentences, which occur in his last considerable book, *Popular Government* :

> Towards the close of the poem this line occurs—'I heard a voice say, What is Freedom ?' It is impossible that the voice could ask a more pertinent question. If the author of *Towards Democracy* had ever heard the answer of Hobbes, that Freedom is 'political power divided into small fragments,' or the dictum of John Austin and M. Scherer, that 'Democracy is a form of government,' his poetical vein might have been drowned, but his mind would have been invigorated by the healthful douche of cold water.

In the same work Maine quotes with approval the saying of Machiavelli, that 'the world is made up of the vulgar,' and he seems to be always mentally adding that the vulgar can never be trusted. In this attitude he did not stand alone, but represented a formidable weight of learned and philosophical opinion. For the new study of history, politics, and law, though greatly enriched in material, and also refreshed by the principle of natural selection, by no means exclusively favoured an encouraging view of human progress, and still less the reading of such progress in democratic terms. The opposition to Mill—who was indeed no pure-blooded democrat—and to his school was partly provoked by Mill himself, but was now reinforced from the ranks of the learned, and may be regarded as a legacy, transformed and reinvested, from the old reaction against the French Revolution. It is enough here to point to the diverse criticisms of Sir James Stephen, in his *Liberty, Equality, and Fraternity* (1873), of Maine himself in *Popular Government* (1885), and of Lecky in his *Democracy and Liberty* (1896).

V

If we must wait for a generation in order to measure the staying power of a writer, there are good omens for Walter Bagehot[1] (1826-77). In his lifetime he was chiefly known as the editor of the *Economist*, which he conducted for many years; as the writer of *Lombard Street* (1873), a classical picture not only of the principles and forces of banking, but of the actual temper and motives of the market; and also to a wider circle, for his *English Constitution* (1865-7), of which the most obvious feature was Bagehot's power of beginning at the right end, namely with living and working realities as distinct from paper theories, and of exhibiting those realities. After his death were collected various groups of essays, biographical, literary, and economic; Richard Holt Hutton, Bagehot's friend and fellow-collegian, edited these volumes, and wrote two short memoirs; but Bagehot's biography and letters only appeared a few years ago. He emerges, beyond a doubt, as one of the freshest and alertest of the neglected Victorian writers. His beat is entirely his own, his eyesight is his own, and his English, though sometimes careless, is most excellent and overflows with life. It seems almost unfair that an authority on silver and the exchange, consulted by Gladstone and immersed in banking, should not only speculate, in his *Physics and Politics* (1872), on the working of Darwinian principles in early societies, and interest Darwin thereby, but should also be a critic of Shakespeare and Lady Mary Wortley Montagu and Hartley Coleridge, with a queer psychological gift of his own; a gift which he applies, with equal relish, to Brougham and Bolingbroke and Lyndhurst, to Cobden and Adam Smith. On these essays, along with *The English Constitution*, Bagehot's reputation as a writer rests. And he is a good writer, if not exactly a great one; above all, at his best, he is a *satisfactory* writer, a wise converser who keeps you awake; not rhetorical, and free from the professional solemnity and moral strain that tire us in some of his contemporaries; yet never common, or familiar in the wrong way. One or two clues to his peculiar cast of thinking may be suggested.

The liveliest of men, with a glancing brain and restless temper, Bagehot is fond of dwelling on the ubiquity, and also on the value, of dulness, or rather of slow-wittedness, in human affairs, for the conduct of the tough work of the world. He delights to tell us how, above all in Britain, the labour of administration, of enterprise, of trade, of politics, of committees, is done by the mutual friction of opaque, safe, honest intellects, not too sensitive for the job. He likes such statesmen as Lord Althorp (he might have added the late Duke of Devonshire),who share, guide, and understand such a spirit. He understood it himself, humorously; he saw it every day in the City. He felt that 'there is a sickly incompleteness about people too fine for the world, and too nice to work their way in it.' This attitude is one reason why his portraits of men of affairs are so good. He saw them as specimens; in their setting, in their action on the national life, in their place in the great game. He is equally alive to what such persons lack, and to the world of sensibility which they so comfortably and efficiently dispense with. His cameos of Lyndhurst and Brougham exemplify this acuteness of view. He imagines Brougham, the incalculable, the perverse, the lawyer-tribune-reformer, not quite sane, yet a benefactor after all, rushing about Coventry, not 'hanging' or musing 'on the bridge,' but putting everything right, talking of the 'schooling of the porter's eldest boy,' and deficient in the 'stillness,' the power of mental retreat, which is the condition of imaginative work, and therefore in the capacity for the truest oratory. Bagehot's most difficult subject, of this order, was Gladstone; and for analytic power his article still holds the field, telling us more than the biographies. Here he has to reckon with the man's inner life, and with the strangest complex of faculties, as well as with the maker or marrer of history; with 'the soul of a martyr,' as he says, 'and the intellect of an advocate.' At the other extreme, his memoir of James Wilson, his father-in-law, the Indian administrator, an admirable but pure man of affairs, is a pattern of how such things may be done.

Bagehot, from his youth up, was deeply conversant with the later history and the different layers of English public life. His union of information and shrewdness qualified him, like his actual contact with business, to write his *English Constitution*. This work, we remember, was much quoted some years ago when the Lords were deprived of the absolute veto; it had already become an authority, not only with professors, but in practice. The chapters on the Cabinet, on the Upper House, on the place filled by the sovereign in the popular mind, are classical; and they are remote in standpoint from any political party of Bagehot's own time or since. Some of the interest of the book, no doubt, depends on the change of conditions. It makes us wonder how Bagehot would have spoken of the rise of labour, the Liberal 'split,' the last Coalition, and the reaction of the war on the seat of political control. His own point of view may be described as anti-radical rather than actually conservative. He had little of Burke's mystical reverence for the established edifice, but he liked, as I have said, the slow-going British habit of mind as a check on mere plunging experiments ; like Prospero he said, ''tis a good dulness.' This note is anticipated in his early, rather flippant letters from Paris upon the *coup d'état* ; the unballasted French, he then thought, required a master. But he afterwards saw through the pasteboard Cæsar, and prophesied, in 1865, that 'the present happiness of France is happiness on a short life-lease.'

VI

Most of Bagehot's literary studies were written between 1850 and 1865. Matthew Arnold, in 1856, wrote to him in praise of his paper upon Shelley. This and some companion essays, he says,

> seem to me to be of the very first quality, showing not talent only, but a concern for the *simple truth* which is rare in English literature, as it is in English politics and English religion.

Matthew Arnold may have been predisposed towards a critic who was somewhat deficient in popular sympathies and distrustful of golden dreams, and who, like himself, looked askance on Shelley. Bagehot's emphasis on Shelley's eager and hectic side shows a distinct misreading of Shelley ; and this is not one of his best papers. But Matthew Arnold rightly assigns to Bagehot a 'concern for the simple truth,' just as he is right in denying it to Macaulay. Still, on Macaulay, Bagehot is the sounder critic of the two :

> Macaulay is anything but a mere rhetorical writer ; there is a very hard kernel of business in him. . . . This is what Macaulay does for us in history, at least what he does best : he engraves indelibly the main outlines and the rough common sense of the matter. Other more refining, and perhaps in some respects more delicate minds, may add the nicer details, and explain those wavering, flickering, and inconstant facts of human nature which are often either above common sense or below it. . . .

This keeps the balance better than Matthew Arnold's onslaught, some fourteen years earlier, on the 'rhetorician,' or than Mark Pattison's contemptuous words on the 'materialist.' It forecasts the deserved, and perhaps now assured, reaction in Macaulay's favour.

Bagehot has been cried up as a critic for excellences at which he did not aim, and has also been cried down as an amateur. He is an amateur, but it is a pity that there are not more like him. He must be judged from his own point of departure. He does not begin with theory, or philosophy, or learning; nor, again, does he begin with form; in fact, he often never gets to form at all, being beguiled on the way by the study of character. He begins with character, with life and its strangeness. A writer is one of the oddest varieties of the *genus homo*; let us see what he was like, let us find his mental habitat, his climate, his *humour*; it is all to be read in his work. There was nothing new in this idea; it was the age of Sainte-Beuve, who made such a quest his profession. Walter Bagehot is unprofessional; he starts from men and business; he finds in literature a new digging-ground, yet more interesting than business in that it expresses the higher and rarer part of the mind. What interests him in a writer—in Hartley Coleridge, or in Cowper, or in Dickens—is this rarer part, as it interacts with the daily career and habit of the man. He adventures on Shakespeare, and quotes the passage from *Venus and Adonis* on the hare, and adds:

> It is absurd, by the way, to say we know *nothing* about the man who wrote that; we know that he had been after a hare. It is idle to allege that mere imagination would tell him that a hare is apt to run among a flock of sheep, or that its doing so disconcerts the scent of hounds.

Shakespeare's 'amazing sympathy with common people,' his command of their ways of thought and of their wandering diction; his capacity, nevertheless, for solitude, and his strain of melancholy, which is not pessimism; his belief in the fairies, in the 'paganism of the South of England'; all this is well conceived, and as well said. It is worth any amount of gush, and a good many treatises. One of Bagehot's best papers, in another style, is that on Lady Mary Wortley Montagu, an ideal subject for a *causerie*; and another is that, of early date, on *The First Edinburgh Reviewers*, with its analysis of the Whig soul, and its contrast between the competent mundane arbiter Jeffrey and the long-slighted, enduring Wordsworth. The remarks, too, on the 'singular delicacy of expression and idea' to be found in the novels of Dickens (1858) are those of a true but discerning believer.

Bagehot, without any claim to prowess in metaphysics, has a distinctly philosophical background to his mind, which is not seen merely in his political reflections. He had, like all of us, his working supposition as to the meaning of the universe, and he was strongly influenced by Bishop Butler. He gives us a taste of his natural theology in the remarkable paper (1862) on *The Ignorance of Man*. 'In a large universe like this,' he writes in an early letter, 'we must not expect a very exact nicety.' The phrase is characteristic, and in the article referred to he gives his own variant on the old idea that life is a probation for our faith and our ignorance. The world of matter, of gravel, and ugly plants and insects—what can it all *mean* ? Well, it can only be in the nature of a screen ; it looks irrelevant, but really, if all things were clear, morality would no longer be disinterested ; for the consequences of every action would be too obvious and overpowering, and the moral will would have no choice. Our fellow-men, too,—what if they were much less visibly imperfect ? Then, also, there would be no theatre of struggle, no morality ; blessed, once more, are the uses of stupidity ! All this Bagehot sets out in his regular style, on which there is little to say except that it is very natural and very good, and that we do not much notice it, which is what he would have wished. He seems to have no particular pedigree as a writer, though he has been compared with some truth to Hazlitt. There is some jerkiness and restlessness ; but it is a good epistolary style, naturally right and sharp, untrimmed and unconscious. Legibility, he says in one place, is given to those

> who are willing to be themselves, to write their own thoughts in their own words, in the simplest words, in the words wherein they were thought.

CHAPTER VI

MACAULAY AND FROUDE

I

Admired by the world and read in many languages, Macaulay has been challenged by the judges in the name of historical science and equity, of philosophic truth and depth, and of literary delicacy. And he has been damaged, beyond question, upon every count; the *Hastings*, the *Bacon*, the *Byron* are in evidence. Yet there Macaulay stands, not to be criticised away, for the instructed reader as well as for the larger public. There is his fabric, with its great shining surface, its solid skilful grandiose architecture, its bold bright colouring, which must be judged, in fairness, from a little distance off; it has a pillar broken, a façade tarnished here and there; but the thing stands. The *History of England*, and the best of the *Essays*, and most of the *Lives*, and some of the *Speeches*, and Macaulay's verses too, live by weight and truth of substance as well as by their workmanship. His achievement has the unity of a political creed and temper, limited it may be, but never ignoble, and inspiring, though often warping, his treatment of history; and it has also the unity of a style, not of the rarest kind or without blemishes, but a style which faces the wear and tear of an immense task, which speaks to all men, and which, at its best, is brilliant, classical, and pure.

The life of Thomas Babington Macaulay[1] (1800-59) as a man of letters falls into three acts. The first opens in 1825, when the curtain rings up and the house fills in order to applaud the essay on *Milton*. There is a slender prologue to be remembered, for the contributions to *Knight's Quarterly Magazine* (1823-4) include the dialogue of *Cowley and Milton*. But the nine years from the appearance of the *Milton* to Macaulay's departure for India in 1834 established his name. The fruits were some twenty essays in the *Edinburgh Review* and ten parliamentary speeches delivered in the years surrounding the Reform Act. Long ere he was thirty he was taken to the bosom of the Whigs. He was launched and applauded by the old set as the new man destined to carry on their work. There was a true and vociferous mutual esteem. Jeffrey, who, so Macaulay thought, was, 'take him for all in all, more nearly an universal genius than any man of our age,' was to live to see the first volumes of the *History*, and to write, in 1848 :

> I have long had a sort of parental interest in your glory : and it is now mingled with a feeling of deference to your intellectual superiority which can only consort, I take it, with the character of a female parent.

Sydney Smith, and Jeffrey, and Praed, and Lord Holland —we must remember them all to understand Macaulay : eighteenth-century men, sharp rational men, touched with romance less rather than more ; whom he outlived, less touched with it than most of them ; sitting through, we may say, the next imaginative age, and still less touched by that. We can listen to the growls of Carlyle[1] over the whole 'phenomenon' :

> 'an emphatic, hottish, really forcible person, but unhappily without divine idea' (1832) ; 'he has more force and emphasis in him than any other of my British contemporaries (coevals). Wants the root of belief, however. May fail to accomplish much. Let us hope better things' (1833). 'Essentially irremediable, commonplace nature of the man' (1848). 'No man known to me in present or past ages ever had, with a peaceable composure too, so infinite a stock of good conceit of himself' . . . 'the limited nature of his world-admired talent' (1876).

The essays of this early time include some of the most truculent, those against James Mill and Sadler, and the versifier Robert Montgomery. The attack on Croker's edition of Boswell was deserved, although, as Lockhart said, 'it might have been done in the style of a gentleman.' The *Machiavelli* and the *Hallam* furnish clues to the writer's political programme and views of statecraft, and the six speeches on Reform, and that on the government of India, exhibit the same principles on the field of battle, and remain among the best of his writings. For writings they are properly to be called ; many of them had to be recomposed from memory, years afterwards, for the press. From 1831 to 1834 Macaulay's activity is surprising : ten essays, besides the speeches, were produced. The *Burleigh*, the *Hampden*, and the *Mirabeau*, betray in their substance the heat and haste of the process ; but the celebrated style, the oratory of the essayist, rolls on without let or strain. The first essay on Chatham (1834) shows Macaulay triumphing in his true field ;

and the ten years that close with the second essay constitute a new and distinct phase in his career.

This period covers his stay in India (1834-8), where he presided over the drafting of the Penal Code which is his greatest contribution to the practical good of mankind and has earned the highest praise from skilled lawyers. The 'Great Minute'[1] that determined the future course of Indian education in the direction of English rather than Oriental studies is also a telling piece of literature. Macaulay's case is good, but the sciolism with which he sweeps away as worthless all Indian thought and religion is edifying. On his return he wrote two of his best essays, those on Clive and on Sir William Temple; also the *Warren Hastings*, which ought not to add to his fame; he dealt faithfully with Gladstone, he dashed at Ranke, he essayed a sketch of Frederick the Great; and for a while threw himself, more happily, on pure literature, on the scene that he knew and loved best, on the 'Restoration' dramatists, on Addison, and on Madame D'Arblay. Meantime he was again in the Commons, as member for Edinburgh, and as War Minister under Melbourne. The speeches on Ireland and Maynooth, on theological tests in Scotland, and on the Corn Laws form a group in which the old Whiggism is seen widening into Liberalism, though carefully guarding itself against the Radical tar-brush, and remaining, as Macaulay puts it gaily in conversation, 'in favour of war, hanging, and Church Establishments.' The oration on the gates of Somnauth is a display, in a good cause, of the old-fashioned reviewer's invective and derision. All these speeches retain the literary character; yet we hear, on the evidence of Gladstone, that the House of Commons was, listening to the speaker, afraid to 'miss a single word that he said.' He also found time for the *Lays of Ancient Rome* (1842).

Happily for letters, he lost his seat for Edinburgh in 1847; he was re-elected later, but letters had regained him for good. The last phase now begins, and the most prosperous of all. The original plan of the *History of England* is on record in a letter of 1838; the first two volumes appeared in 1848. The essayist, the orator, is now also a great historian. The instant success of the work, the honours heaped upon it, the editions printed of it, and the translations made from it, are a familiar story. It was the climax of Macaulay's immense and well-won good fortune, which the very gods appeared not to envy. The work, alas, could not be finished according to the scheme. The third and fourth volumes were published in 1855, the fifth posthumously in 1861; Macaulay, who had been made a peer in 1857, died, happy man, in the midst of affection, friendship, honours, and fame, two years later. Better still, his powers had never declined; the minor works of his last five years show, if anything, an enhanced skill in proportioning, and in purity of form. The short biographies, written for the *Encyclopædia Britannica*, of Atterbury, Bunyan, Goldsmith, Johnson, and the younger Pitt may fairly be ranked for their peculiar virtues among the masterpieces of the *eighteenth* century. And in the best tradition of that age he also wrote his noblest piece of verse, the *Epitaph on a Jacobite* (1845), which is the crowning grace of the Whig historian.

II

Macaulay's tastes and character are fully and fairly revealed in his *Life and Letters*, by his nephew, Sir George Otto Trevelyan. This classical biography was published in 1876. The letters and journals often have the note of *Io Triumphe!*, of Macaulay's honest pleasure in his success and fame and numberless editions. There is also the note of the Whig optimist; and there is a good deal of what John Mitchel,[1] reading the *Essays* on shipboard while on his way to a convict settlement, called

> altogether a new thing in the history of mankind, this triumphant glorification of a current century upon being the century it is.

All Macaulay's virtues are there too, his frankness, his courage, his integrity, his love of literature. There are no half-lights, everything is explicit and self-evident. But Macaulay's mind, if not mysterious, is less simple than may appear at first sight, and some of its other features are worthy of remark.

We might think of Macaulay as a humanist, or interpreter of classical thought and art, diverted by circumstance into politics. He missed the narrowing mill of the public school, but he learnt the ancient languages in a free yet not inexact fashion, winning Cambridge honours in that field. Pattison, a good judge, said that his 'command of literature was imperial,' and as to classical literature the observation was true. The classics are alive to Macaulay in a measure that is rare amongst those who give their entire lives to the study of them. His 'thoughts,' says his biographer, 'were often for weeks together more in Latium and Attica than in Middlesex'; he was 'as familiar with his Lucian, and his Augustan histories, as other men of letters are with their Voltaire and their Pepys';

and he 'could not read the *De Corona* even for the twentieth time without striking his clenched fist, at least once a minute, on the arm of his easy chair' ; a description in Macaulay's own ringing concrete manner. Everything in the record confirms its truth. His early writings in *Knight's Quarterly* hold out, indeed, some hopes that are not to be fulfilled. The scraps of the *Roman Tale* and the *Athenian Revels* show lively promise of that gift for imaginary dialogue which is realised in the *Conversation between Mr. Abraham Cowley and Mr. John Milton Touching the Great Civil War* (1824). The grace and unrhetorical ease of this composition, qualities soon to be trampled out in the arena, are studied, we may think, from Plato or Lucian ; and Macaulay's marginal notes on his Plato—an old folio with Ficino's Latin beside the Greek—are full of gusto and independence, though critically sometimes blunt or even obvious. To wish that you had been in the shoes of Polus and had shown the right way of standing up to Socrates is an aspiration that many must have cherished ; but how would the duel have ended ? Plato's criticism of the Whig theory of the state, or of the review of Montgomery, would have been worth hearing. But nothing daunted so voracious a humanist as Macaulay. The voyages to and from India were his holiday, the catalogue of the volumes that he perused on board ship is famous ; and he had gone on reading even while he drafted the Penal Code. The fruits of this lifelong fervour are seen throughout his writings. There are the pages in the *Atterbury* on the *Phalaris* dispute, and there are endless casual allusions to the ancient writers. The career of Cicero is surveyed in lengthy notes, the Latin of Milton and Addison is compared, the protests of Erasmus and Politian against purism in diction are cited. The Greek tragedians are enjoyed and discriminated, and Macaulay overcomes a youthful prejudice, common in his time, against Euripides : 'the *Orestes*,' we hear, 'is one of the very finest plays in the Greek language.' His own manner, we may think, owes something to these studies. They gave him models of freedom and largeness, of lucidity and order. He has, at his best, at any rate the *march* of a great antique writer. Delicacy, rarity, the higher sense of beauty, are another matter. His reading of the ancient orators was not without its special influence, though his iterations, rhetorical questions in the form of chain-shot, and other devices which in the long run go back to the classics, are English and recent in their immediate derivation.

More deeply still is Macaulay moulded, as to his political

ideals, by those of Athens and free Rome. This influence lies behind all his Whig principles and helps to animate them. It was no mere flourish that led him, at the age of eighteen, to tell his father :

> My opinions, good or bad, were learnt, not from Hunt and Waithman, but from Cicero, from Tacitus, and from Milton. They are opinions which have produced men who have ornamented the world, and redeemed human nature from the degradation of ages of superstition and slavery.

The juvenile tirades on liberty in the essay on Milton are in the same spirit, which was to be deepened and trained by the study of history, which has nothing in common with a Radical or Jacobin enthusiasm for Brutus, and which was also tempered by Macaulay's robust faith in modernity and progress. Still it is the spirit that lifts the most eloquent parts of his speeches, like the peroration on the government of India, above commonplace optimism into a prophetic strain. His debt to the ancient historians he constantly acknowledges.

The passion for humanity, toleration, and the moderate extension of political privilege was also in Macaulay's blood, and was fostered by his rearing. In his father, Zachary Macaulay, it was concentrated on one cause, the abolition of negro slavery, and was inspired by a single-minded and narrow, though not intolerant, devotion to evangelical Protestantism. The anti-slavery cause was won during Macaulay's youth, and the enthusiasm that had won it widened in his case into other channels. The Protestantism slipped off from him, leaving little mark on his character, which was, as his biographer says, 'high and simple,' but was also naïvely secular. Macaulay's temper towards religion [1] must be understood. It is external rather than exactly hostile ; it is that of the eighteenth century, yet qualified, and in a sense reconciled, not by any personal sympathy, but by the new historic sense, and by a lively and learned curiosity. In the first chapter of the *History* Macaulay repudiates the contempt felt during the preceding century for the cults of the Middle Ages. It is at this point that he parts company with the age of reason. Yet he remains outside cathedral, church, and chapel ; he is not even in the porch ; neither does he throw stones, except for a stray fling against the abstruser dogmas, as to which his temper is agnostic and distrustful. He describes religious experiences and ecclesiastical institutions with much zest and colour, and often powerfully. Three times he portrays the inward struggles of

Bunyan, and he has made the contents of *Grace Abounding* familiar to thousands who will never see the book. He does all this in a pictorial way, and by virtue of his power of vivid memorising; but he has not the gift of entering into the heart of the experience. Once he praises Goethe's *Confessions of a Fair Saint* for a similar achievement; but then Goethe performed it by the force of his deep and flexible dramatic sympathy. Macaulay also, in his essay on Ranke, depicts in the tone of one who will not underrate the enemy, the solidity and the adaptive genius of the Roman Church; and, in one of the most striking pages of the *History*, he analyses the aims and character of the Society of Jesus. His own sympathies as a statesman were, allowing for many a Whiggish reserve, with the Church of England. But neither the churches nor yet the anti-church seem to have touched any fibre in his heart. There is no trace of religious emotion, any more than of the passion of love, in the record of Macaulay's buoyant, fervent, and healthy nature. Such a temper, no doubt, cut him off from many things; but it was a good soil for intellectual and political tolerance, and also for impartiality as an historian. He tolerates all creeds when they cease to persecute. He is a combatant for the rights and franchises of dissenter, Catholic, and Jew. His *History* is in great measure the history of the progress of religious liberty. Yet all the time there is, to quote John Mitchel, the anti-Briton, once more, 'a tone of polite, though distant recognition of Almighty God, as one of the Great Powers. . . . British civilisation gives Him assurances of friendly relations.'

But the campaign has two sides to it. If the churches are to be free, neither must they usurp. Macaulay has his firm, immoveable, Erastian, Whig conception of the sphere of government. The theory is set out, in its bearing on ecclesiastical affairs, in one of his most closely argued and best composed essays, *Gladstone on Church and State*. But he has his own version; he always insists that the business of the state is *secular*, that government is an 'experimental science,' and that it exists

> for the purpose of keeping the peace, for the purpose of compelling us to settle our disputes by arbitration instead of settling them by blows, for the purpose of compelling us to supply our wants by industry instead of supplying them by rapine. This is the only operation for which the machinery of government is peculiarly adapted, the only operation which wise governments ever propose to themselves as their chief object.

At a later date Macaulay admits that there exist some 'secondary' aims of government, such as education; his Indian experience brushed away some of the objections to interference which he had shared alike with his own school and with the philosophic radicals. Yet his bias remained against interference. Nothing is more characteristic, more British, in Macaulay than his readiness to qualify mere doctrine under the hard knocks of common sense and experience. He is magnificently, savingly, almost savagely empirical. The cautious plea for retaining the established church, which occurs at the end of his article on Gladstone, is a case in point; and the churchman will be better pleased with Macaulay's conclusion than with the reasonings that lead up to it.

III

The 'essay,' as written by Macaulay, is something of a new invention, but its origins are clearly visible. It begins as a review of the current, dogmatic, *Edinburgh* kind: a kind of composition of which the plainest feature is the insolence by which its censure, its commendations, and its wit are alike distinguished. Macaulay is blunter than Jeffrey and less good-natured than Sydney Smith; the noisy, hard-fisted vulgarity of some of his remarks on Walpole and Boswell exceeds even their injustice, and some of his pages only retain the interest of an obsolete mode of behaviour. It was all part of the rough horseplay of the time, like the practical jokes of Theodore Hook, and it was all the worse for being prompted by a sense of duty. Still, much of Macaulay's hard hitting is deserved, as in the case of Croker; and it is at least preferable to the vague praise, or the cautious innuendo, which now often does duty for criticism. Moreover, he hit without malice, and though his own skin was thick he sometimes repented of his violence. The worst was that he had little or no eye for new talent among his contemporaries; it is rare to find him encouraging or saluting it. He was incapable of jealousy, but not of indifference. Sometimes he wrote a conscientious and fairly polite review of the book in hand; but more frequently, if it is not scarified, it is speedily dismissed, and the essay is a discourse at length on the topic of the book.

Did Macaulay speak essays, or did he write speeches? In any case, he thought oratorically, mused in antithesis, dreamed in figures. His style has many varieties, but its uniformity of mould in essay, speech, diary, and correspondence and journal shows that it was natural to him : as philosophers say, it was the form of his thought. There is just the same way of stating the case, the same elocution in the essay on Jewish disabilities as in the speech on the same subject. The only difference lies in the presence or absence of the forms of debate. The peroration to the *Hallam*, written in 1828, and forecasting a serious change in the franchise, might have come, though graver in tone, from one of the subsequent discourses on Reform. This oratorical habit determines not only the style of the *Essays*, but their clear structure and efficient masonry.

The proportion of political theory to historical narrative varies greatly in these essays. The three papers directed against Mill and the utilitarians are Macaulay's chief adventure in speculation, and resolve themselves into an attack on Radical theorising in the name of Whig empiricism, or, as Macaulay terms it, of induction. He makes many shrewd hits against the doctrinaire, and is careful to separate the honoured Bentham from his disciples. He treated Bentham as the author of one of the rejoinders, and when the veteran published a contradiction he had to retract somewhat awkwardly, explaining how much more ferocious he would have been if he had not made the mistake. He afterwards withdrew some of his rampant language against James Mill. Macaulay, it should be said, did not himself reprint these three essays ; they only reappeared after both he and Mill were dead. But the true milk of the Whig word can be found in the dissertations on Hallam and Mackintosh. The latter, with its recital of the four or five chief blessings conferred by the Revolution, is a clear exposition of the standpoint afterwards adopted in the *History of England*.

The historical essays are probably better known than the *History*, but many of them are far from water-tight. More than one of them has disseminated error and injustice in a way that no disproof or annotation can ever eradicate. Macaulay is still read by thousands who would never look at a note. How many people will always misconceive and mispraise Bacon, or miscondemn Impey and Hastings, through Macaulay's fault ? How many, on the strength of the *History*, will continue to libel Penn, or to accept the caricature of Frederick William the First ? Even worse, how many of those whose faith has been upset by these miscarriages will then do proper justice to the admirable papers on Clive, and Temple, and Chatham ? The best that can be hoped is that, since Macaulay's essays will always be taught to the young in the English-speaking lands and in India, they may be taught with some critical discrimination.

IV

The worthiest of Macaulay's judgements on men of letters concern the period which in his *History* he never reached, but which he knew best of all, namely, the eighteenth century. The *Milton* he himself condemned, in terms that are even too harsh; the *Dryden*, which he did not reprint, need not be dwelt upon; it is a slapdash, unmeasured composition, which disposes lightly of the 'absurd metaphysics' of Dante and argues that 'the critical and poetical faculties are not only distinct, but almost incompatible.' And in the *History* he is over-hard on Dryden's conversion to Rome. But the study of Leigh Hunt's edition of the Restoration and Revolution comedy is the work of a critic, and an example of Macaulay at his happiest. Lamb's contention that the world revealed by Wycherley and Congreve is a world outside good and evil and can only be judged as a kind of fairyland, is true for Lamb himself, and for the few who are like him; and his paradox tells us more, as usual, than the hard sense of others. But Macaulay, to the letter, is right; he hits the mark when he calls, in his *History*, the school of Wycherley *hard-hearted*; and he has George Meredith on his side. It is unfortunate that he never reached Vanbrugh and Farquhar, and that while speaking, with some exaggeration, of Jeremy Collier, he never mentions Etherege on the credit side of the Restoration drama. But he is just to Congreve, who has always been more admired than read:

> The wit of Congreve far outshines that of every comic writer, except Sheridan, who has arisen within the last two centuries. . . . The dialogue [in *The Old Bachelor*] is resplendent with wit and eloquence, which indeed are so abundant that the fool comes in for an ample share, and yet preserves a certain colloquial air, a certain indescribable ease, of which Wycherley had given no example, and which Sheridan in vain attempted to imitate.

This reminds us of Lamb himself, or of Hazlitt. The *Addison*, on the other hand, is a masterpiece of biography rather than of criticism. Macaulay sees Addison, both as a man and a writer, out of all scale, and is capable of praising him in a strain that should be reserved for Berkeley. We should never guess from Macaulay the commonplace side of

Addison. Juster far, and even more congenial, is the essay on Madame D'Arblay; it is one of those things which need never be done again. Macaulay, like Carlyle, delivered himself upon Johnson twice. Carlyle's vindication of Boswell's brains and skill disposes, it may here be repeated, of Macaulay's crude sarcasms at Boswell's expense. As to Johnson himself, Macaulay loved him, and revelled in his talk, and knew all the material available, but never penetrated him. I cannot share the general admiration for the *Life* (1856), though it is more measured in tone than the review of 1831. It under-estimates Johnson as a writer; it dwells on his externals with a rough and vulgar emphasis; and it leaves us but half-aware of the depth of his nature, and of the wisdom of his heart. Moreover, Macaulay adopts without warrant Johnson's own prejudiced and damning judgement on the lady who 'fell in love with a music-master from Brescia'; which she had a perfect right to do without being taunted with a 'degrading passion.' The indelicacy here is on the side of the two robust critics. The *Walpole* is a speech for the prosecution, and the cure for it is to read Walpole's correspondence. The fresh, keen independence of judgement that lies under, or upon, the surface of Walpole's comments will somewhat amaze the reader who has not travelled beyond Macaulay's essay. In the *Byron*, on the other hand, there is much sound sense, though not much sympathy; the picture of the Byronic hero is hardly overcharged; and the manly and biting sarcasms levelled against the ethical vagaries of the British public are thoroughly in place. What has made Byron appeal to thousands out of Britain, Macaulay was too British to appreciate. Yet of his work, Macaulay justly concludes (though he forbears to specify), 'we have little doubt that, after the closest scrutiny, there will still remain much that can only perish with the English language.'

Macaulay, therefore, merits anything but contempt as a critic of literature. He himself was modest about the matter, and said that to read a page of Lessing, or of Goethe's judgements on Hamlet, filled him with despair. But so good a lover of books, so good a hater, so fully informed a mind, so ardent and devouring a reader, so rare a memory, could not but leave judgements of note and value. The best of them, perhaps, do not occur in his essays, but are scattered through his letters and marginal notes. The fiction of the previous century he may be said to have inhabited rather than to have judged in set form, knowing as he did *Sir Charles Grandison* and Miss Austen pretty well by heart. Their words and personages lived a delightful second life in the familiar talk of his household. Of Miss Austen he was a most faithful worshipper, nor was his cult ever tempered in later years. He once thought of writing a biography of her, and unfortunately never did so. Such a devotion bespeaks a certain fineness of judgement with which Macaulay is seldom credited. He was, it has often been said, a man of her period. He liked reason and he liked irony and satire and finish, and understood them better than he understood the high poetry and inspiration of his favourite Milton and Æschylus. He says arresting, though not always just or favourable, things about Ben Jonson, Defoe, Chesterfield, Pope, and Paul-Louis Courier. His memory, no doubt, was greater than his critical genius; but we must remember that while literature was his first love, his refuge and his consolation, history and politics were his chief concern.

V

The reaction against his fame was bound to come, and has itself now begun to be reckoned with. A good deal of the adverse criticism, it was rightly said by Jebb, is 'that species of censure which consists in blaming a man because he is not somebody else.' Matthew Arnold led the onslaught, with his cry that Macaulay was a brilliant rhetorician and never got to the 'real truth of things.' But of what things? He got to the truth of some things for which Matthew Arnold cared little, for he wrote a chapter in the history of liberty. The same critic, however, did justice to the *Lives*, and finally called Macaulay a great man of letters. A snarl of Mark Pattison's goes deeper:

> He is in accord with the average sentiment of orthodox and stereotyped humanity on the relative values of the objects and motives of human endeavour. And this commonplace materialism is one of the secrets of his popularity, and one of the qualities which guarantee that that popularity will be enduring.

This comment is more serious; but is it true? It is not without foundation. Macaulay, in his pæan on the national improvement, makes much of the increase of comfort, security, and prosperity during the last two centuries. Here he shows his characteristic 'complacency,' which is part of his cheerful faith in 'progress.' He is eminently 'on the side of the moderns' in that department; and in progress, of course,

Britain leads the way. There is a certain streak of 'materialism,' no doubt, in all this, and special pleading in mitigation is needless. But we must remember that Macaulay is thinking of the welfare of the people, of the mass of 'orthodox and stereotyped humanity,' who had *not* all that time enjoyed security, comfort, and other gross advantages.

In the third chapter of the *History* he describes the bad roads of 1660, and adds that 'every improvement of the means of locomotion benefits mankind morally and intellectually as well as materially,' and that it 'tends to remove national and provincial antipathies, and to bind together all the branches of the great human family.' This may be materialism, but it is true and philosophical. And if the statesman who promotes these improvements is to be honoured, the historian who celebrates them is within his rights. It would be truer to say that Macaulay is apt to interpret all intellectual advance in terms of applied science, or of invention 'for the relief of man's estate'; and that, apart from the great region of legal and constitutional reform, he has not much ear for the rarer phenomena of the human spirit. We must go to others for the history of impalpable developments. His odd mixture, already noticed, of keen interest and thorough-going externality in the article of thought and religion marks this obvious limitation. Hence Carlyle, while granting Macaulay to be 'a really emphatic, forcible person,' adds that he is 'unhappily without divine idea.' Certainly the prophetic or mystical note, the note of Burke, is rare in Macaulay; but there is something of it in his speech on India, which may well seem to-day (1920) one of his most prescient utterances, and which shows his eloquence at its best.

The destinies of our Indian empire are covered with thick darkness. It is difficult to form any conjecture as to the fate reserved for a state which resembles no other in history, and which forms by itself a separate class of political phenomena. The laws which regulate its growth and its decay are still unknown to us. It may be that the public mind of India may expand under our system till it has outgrown that system; that by good government we may educate our subjects into a capacity for better government; that, having become instructed in European knowledge, they may, in some future age, demand European institutions. Whether such a day will ever come I know not. But never will I attempt to avert or to retard it. Whenever it comes, it will be the proudest day in English history. To have found a great people sunk in the lowest depths of slavery and superstition, to have so ruled them as

> to have made them desirous and capable of all the privileges of citizens, would indeed be a title to glory all our own. The sceptre may pass away from us. Unforeseen accidents may derange our most profound schemes of policy. Victory may be inconstant to our arms. But there are triumphs which are followed by no reverse. There is an empire exempt from all natural causes of decay. Those triumphs are the pacific triumphs of reason over barbarism; that empire is the imperishable empire of our arts and our morals, our literature and our laws.

'*Our* arts' and '*our* laws'—there, you may say, speaks the irrepressible Whig and Briton; and the Indian faiths are *superstition*; still, to read that passage takes away the taste left in our mouth by the detractors of Macaulay. For a 'materialist,' for a 'Philistine,' and for a 'rhetorician,' it is pretty well.

VI

Macaulay's much quoted remark, in reference to his *History*, that he wished to 'produce something which shall for a few days supersede the last fashionable novel on the tables of young ladies,' can be misread at his expense, but it is explained by a passage in his essay on *History* (1828), in which he says that 'a truly great historian would reclaim those materials which the novelist has appropriated.' Scott, coming in the wake of the historians, had 'constructed out of their gleanings works which, even considered as histories, are scarcely less valuable than theirs.' The ideal course was to unite the living pictorial interest of Scott with the intellectual interest of Hume and Clarendon. Macaulay, then, sketches a history of England from the time of Chaucer to that of *Hudibras* as he would desire it to be planned out. He adds, as though in forecast of his future work, that the loyalist, the Puritan, and the philosophic republican would all 'enter into the representation,' which would not contain merely battles and debates.

However, another sentence redresses the balance. A history is not to be exclusively a stirring pageant or to resemble a novel that should happen to be true: for

> the history of the government, and the history of the people, would be exhibited in that mode in which alone they can be exhibited justly, in inseparable conjunction and intermixture.

Macaulay in his own way really achieved this aim. He did not indeed complete his design of 'tracing the progress of useful and ornamental arts,' or of 'describing the changes of literary taste,' or of noting 'the revolutions which have taken place in dress, furniture, repasts, and public amusements,' though some of these matters are skilfully panelled into the *History*. But he keeps the balance between the constitutional and the living aspects of the story better than his successor, John Richard Green, whose *Short History*, with all its life and rapidity, lacks the single and dominating purpose which holds Macaulay's great fragment together. The original plan is given in a letter of July 20, 1838. The Revolution was to be the starting-point: but

How far I shall bring the narrative down I have not determined. The death of George the Fourth would be the best halting-place. The *History* would then be an entire view of all the transactions which took place, between the Revolution which brought the Crown into harmony with the Parliament, and the Revolution which brought the Parliament into harmony with the nation.

There is the Whig theory of our history in a sentence, and we see how firm a backbone Macaulay's book would have had. Even as it stands, it is plain that his talent was by no means confined, as is sometimes implied, to the representation of the concrete. His mastery of the abstract principles involved, though doubtless legal rather than properly speaking speculative, was great. A page of Hobbes, or of John Stuart Mill, contains indeed more pure thinking than all Macaulay's disquisitions; we feel at once that we are in the free air of political philosophy. Still, on the purely constitutional side he is strong, and on that side he perceives, and impressively exhibits, the unity and continuity of the national life. On the side of thought and art he does not do so. He has indeed much to say of the manners of the Puritan, on the Royal Society, on the influence of French literature, on Dryden, and Burnet, and Baxter. Yet these persons and phenomena, though sketched with a rapid and arresting brilliancy, are mostly viewed from without, and a certain sense of void haunts us through Macaulay's clamorous and coloured pages. This is only to note the boundaries of his genius. Within his noble and ample territory, what motion, what variety, what splendour, what a power of marshalling! The *History*, if we consider it both as a work of art, and for its weight and worth of substance, is the only great production of the kind since Gibbon that has come from the hand of an Englishman. Macaulay himself, who was modest under all his self-confidence, felt that he could not emulate Thucydides, and did not overrate his own performance.

VII

In his art of construction and arrangement he has something in common with the greatest models. Historical writing consists of narrative, description, and analysis ; or, more strictly, of long steady marches and judicious pauses for relief. The march is the narrative ; the analysis calls a halt ; the descriptive matter either moves or stands still, or both, as it may happen. Macaulay is a master, though not equally a master, in each of these departments, as well as in the art of ordering and proportioning. His art has been styled mechanical ; but few historians of any school have approached it. His battles, his pageants, his debates, his discussions of principle, his portraits, and his reviews of life and manners, are disposed with an enviable skill. It is true that his transitions are often abrupt ; and, if any element bulks too large and is of smaller permanent value than the rest, it is his lengthy expositions of the Whig philosophy, and his imaginary speeches and pleas on either side, and summaries of public opinion. These, he tells us, are gathered from a thousand sources, of which he only specifies a few ; but they are composed, on a convention as obvious as that of Thucydides, by an imaginary Macaulay of the year 1689. They usually take the form of a speech full of dilemmas, rhetorical questions, and contemptuous illustrations, exactly in his own style of oratory. They are wonderful advocacy, and their conclusions may be sound ; but they are made up ; and to check them, it would be necessary to know as much as Macaulay. But that difficulty applies to the whole substance of his *History*, and I am now speaking of its art.

Among his narratives and descriptions it is needful to distinguish. In his passion for a clinching detail he often sins, not so much against the 'dignity of history,' for which he professes little respect, as against fitness of scale and colouring. When we hear that at the trial of Hastings 'Mrs. Sheridan was carried out in a fit' ; or, beside the deathbed of Charles the Second, that 'a loathsome volatile salt, extracted from human skulls, was forced into his mouth' ; we feel that Macaulay is not selecting in the spirit of a great historical painter, or even in the spirit of Hogarth. Hogarth crowds every corner with significance, but the whole effect is harmonious ; Macaulay, as though on principle, teases us with detail. This is but one species of the continual, thudding emphasis which ends by weakening the attention it is meant to quicken. Macaulay, in the long run, fatigues us more than many duller writers.

But for all that he is one of the great masters of narrative, and the world with a sound instinct has fixed upon his best things. The scenes of Glencoe, Londonderry, and Sedgemoor, the last hours of William and Mary, the acquittal of the bishops, the Darien bubble, the detention of James at Sheerness, are perfect in their own kind of art, and only lack, what the roughest page of Carlyle possesses, the note of spiritual genius, and the background of the 'immensities and eternities.' Yet Macaulay, at his best, stirs the blood, and he commands not only the heroic strain but a simple and manly pathos, of which his account of the deathbed of Charles the Second is an example.

His elaborate 'characters,' though always brilliant, are less satisfactory. Beside Clarendon (not to speak again of Carlyle) he seems, with all his acuteness, rhetorical and heavy-handed. His Halifax, his William, his Tillotson, his Jeffreys, apart from all questions of equity, are aggregations of qualities rather than living men. He pursues them with epithets of eulogy or abuse; he will not let them simply show themselves in act; they are good or bad in extremes, like the characters of Charles Dickens; and he seems to think that the subtleties of character are exhibited by an array of antitheses and contradictory attributes. The more he explains away Halifax or Danby the less we seem to understand them. He succeeds best with his secondary figures, like Portland or Schomberg, who are cast on plainer lines.

He excels most historians in the felicity of his interludes. His touches of landscape, which are rare, have the same quality as those in the *Lays of Ancient Rome*; they are not, like Carlyle's, full of deep poetic beauty; but they are true and simple, and are often a record of things seen. As Adolphus remarks of Scott, 'the images which he does supply are placed directly under our view, in a full noonday light.' So Macaulay describes the Highlands and Glencoe, Holland or the Boyne, always seeing, however, with his memory as much as with his eyes:

> That bright and tranquil stream, the boundary of Louth and Meath, having flowed many miles by green banks crowned by modern palaces, and by the ruined keeps of old Norman barons of the Pale, is here about to mingle with the sea. . . . On the Meath side of the Boyne, the ground, still all corn, grass, flowers, and foliage, rises with a gentle swell to an eminence surmounted by a conspicuous tuft of ash-trees which overshades the ruined church and desolate graveyard of Donore.

Nothing is more like Macaulay than his equal and impartial

delight in the 'ruined keeps' and in the 'modern palaces.' It is this that separates him from Scott, who cares less about the fruits of civilisation. But Macaulay is at his best when he is not thus distracted. At St. Germains, or in St. Peter's Chapel, he is alone with the past, and he masses and orders his thronging recollections into a noble picture. Another kind of relief is given by the numberless stories that he tells by the way. In his account of William's amnesties he inserts a page on the Earl of Clancarty, who might 'furnish a good subject to a novelist or a dramatist'; and the subject is certainly worthy of Thackeray. The visit of Peter the Great, 'in the same week in which Whitehall perished,' supplies a more important episode. This is the regular method of the *History*, and it can be trusted to carry us through the tale, itself often as dull and confusing as a kaleidoscope, of ministerial shiftings and rascalities. Lord Acton,[1] who judges Macaulay on some counts with great severity, adds that 'all this does not prevent him from being one of the greatest of historians,' and that 'in description, not in narrative, I think he is quite the first of all writers of history.'

VIII

As to the main question whether Macaulay, after all, can be trusted, the historians themselves have so far given no perfectly distinct answer, and it is not for others to be dogmatic. There has been much criticism in three directions. First of all, he is charged with inaccuracies of fact which have led him into gross misjudgements of character, and into circulating, though in good faith, historical libels. His immense authority with the public makes this question more serious. Nor have the professional historians thus far dealt with it as a whole. No one has done for Macaulay what Mr. Bury has done for Gibbon. No one duly versed in the period has gone over the whole ground in order to show, first of all, how far Macaulay dealt thoroughly and faithfully with the material at his command, and then how far he has been corrected by later knowledge. Still less has any one rewritten his story on the same scale, embodying the results of later criticism. But both the *History* and the *Essays* have been severely riddled,[2] here and there. The pictures of Penn, of Marlborough, and also of William admittedly require modification. The account of Scottish affairs is in the same plight. The biographical part of the *Bacon* was dissected in James Spedding's *Evenings with a Reviewer* (1848), and the philosophical part has long been given to the lions. Impey's legal conduct of the trial of Nuncomar, and also his motives, were vindicated by Sir James Fitzjames Stephen in 1885, and the true story of the Rohilla war was told by Sir John Strachey in 1892. All this must shake the confidence of the layman in Macaulay. Much too has been written, though in a less conclusive style, about his general handling of evidence.

The difficulty here is that he does not fully give his evidence. He has many footnotes; he read and dug immensely; his fabulous memory, though it must have saved him some thinking, was mostly precise; but his method, which is a large and lordly one, almost precludes him from supplying the *pièces de conviction*. His ideas on the position of parties in the reign of William have, he says, been

> derived not from any single work, but from thousands of forgotten tracts, sermons, and satires: in fact, from a whole literature which is mouldering in old libraries.

So he builds up the material, not into a scientific demonstration, but into a picture or panorama, by force of intuition, and perhaps by the kind of 'castle-building' that he described to his sister Margaret:

> The past is in my mind soon constructed into a romance. With a person of my turn the minute touches are of as great interest, and perhaps greater, than the most important events. . . . Precision in dates, the day or hour in which a man was born or died, becomes absolutely necessary. A slight fact, a sentence, a word, are of importance in my romance.

It would be most unfair to charge Macaulay with spinning the history of England into a romance. But the same baffling mixture of minute detail and imaginative construction is evident. One critic speaks of Macaulay's 'audacity in outrunning tangible evidence,' another says that his 'extreme precision and his excessive emphasis' carry him often 'much further than can be justified by any authority.' This seems to hit the mark. We have to be careful with Macaulay's habitual *plurals*; we do not know on how many cases they are founded. Perhaps, if challenged, he could have rolled out an overwhelming avalanche of examples to make good; but perhaps not.

> Alarmists predicted that the wealthiest and most enlightened kingdom in Europe would be reduced to the state of those barbarous societies in which a mat is bought with a hatchet, and a pair of moccasins with a piece of venison.

How many persons, and who, made this lively remark in the year 1696? Six years after Macaulay's death appeared Lecky's *Rationalism in Europe*. Macaulay had taught the fashion of marshalling concrete illustrations, and Lecky employs it; but the new method has appeared; there is a voucher for every statement, nor is the vividness of the picture abated.

Macaulay has been assailed, thirdly, on the broad ground of political partiality and unfairness. So far as the charge may be true, he is condemned out of his own mouth; for he denounces 'the error of judging the past by the present,' says that it is 'pernicious in a historian,' and adds that it 'perpetually infects the speculations of writers of the liberal school when they discuss the transactions of an earlier age' (*History*, ch. vii.). But the accusation has been overdone. In one sense it would have been wrong and impossible for Macaulay not to 'judge the past by the present.' He certainly saw 1688 and 1832 in the light of one another. The middle class franchise, as he viewed it, was the long result of time, of the beneficent process that had begun nearly a century and a half before. Such was the Whig view of history, and Macaulay frankly pleads for it. But the Whigs as a body, and Whig individuals, are plentifully castigated; and the writer has no little dramatic and imaginative sympathy with Tory and Jacobite. He is indeed over-violent with James, and over-civil with William. But it has been acutely remarked that while Macaulay may be unfair to Marlborough or Shaftesbury, 'his diatribes against them are quite independent of party spirit.' And his strong language, whether merited or not, is often due to his intense realisation of the scene, in which he lives in fancy; sharing its passions like a man, and not simply watching them like a naturalist. Once he records 'an event which, even at this distance of time, can hardly be related without a feeling of vindictive pleasure.' The event is the arrest of Jeffreys. Such a spirit may sometimes lead to what has been called 'blacking the chimney'; but it adds immensely to the liveliness of the story.

IX

Turn from a plain natural writer of the higher kind like Goldsmith, or from a master of the more intricate music of prose, to the *Warren Hastings* or the chapter on the state of England in 1685, and you may feel that Macaulay's sentences are fed out of a machine: a wonderful machine, because it is the very mind of the man. Explore as you will his letters or journals, or the reports of his unprepared talk, and you will still come on those sentences. Except, that is, when Macaulay is imitating a past style, as he does in the dialogue of Cowley and Milton; a piece that promises fair, as I have observed; but it is a *pastiche*, and the manner is not natural to him. The college essay on William the Third may be consulted in the *Life* to see how soon Macaulay wrote in the style that is now so familiar. And, as a tune which has arrested all who can read our language, it deserves attention. It is sometimes, no doubt, a very ugly one:

> Logan defended the accused governor with great ability in prose. For the lovers of verse, the speeches of the managers were burlesqued in Simpkin's letters. It is, we are afraid, indisputable that Hastings stooped so low as to court the aid of that malignant and filthy baboon John Williams, who called himself Anthony Pasquin. It was necessary to subsidise such allies largely. The private hoards of Mrs. Hastings had disappeared. It was said that the banker to whom they had been entrusted had failed.

There is a good deal of this *atomic* style everywhere in Macaulay. It seems to be his own; and its peculiarity is the premature full-stoppage of every sentence in what ought, considering the energy of the start, to have been merely its mid-career. The aim is to leave the slowest member of a large audience with no excuse for misunderstanding.

Yet this is only the style in its lowest terms. There is, it is true, a certain framework of rhetoric and rhythm, not easy to state technically, and not be defined by any tricks or figures, but unmistakeable, out of which Macaulay seldom escapes. It has the merit of being wholly natural to him; it is not a thing learnt or affected, though it may be thought by the enemy to be all the more fatal for that. But, within that framework, it is one of the most skilful, and also of the most varied, of styles. For one thing, its abruptness of effect is often a mere matter of punctuation. The short snappy-seeming clauses are not really isolated, but unite into an harmonious group that satisfies the ear, as a whole, and only as a whole; they are the minor ups and downs in a long rolling wave:

> The Chancellor fell down with a great ruin. The seal was taken from him: the Commons impeached him: his head was not safe: he fled from the country: an Act was passed which doomed him to perpetual exile: and those who had assailed and undermined him began to struggle for the fragments of his power.

The sentence, though its components are sharply marked off, is a musical unit gradually swelling in cadence. The usual mechanism of Macaulay's sentence is of this kind, consisting of a series of parallel simple sentences ; or else, so far as it is further organised, the subordinate members fall into further pairs and parallels, marked by antithesis of language coupled with repetition of rhythm. This pedantic statement of the case must be pardoned, as it applies to much of Macaulay's prose, which admits, nevertheless, of great internal variety. His most obvious device is that of the echoed word or phrase, which is used to point the antithesis :

> The *war between wit and* Puritanism soon became a *war between wit and* morality. The hostility excited by a grotesque caricature of *virtue* did not spare *virtue* herself. *Whatever* the canting Roundhead had regarded with reverence was insulted. *Whatever* he had proscribed was favoured. Because he had been *scrupulous* about trifles, all *scruples* were treated with derision. . . . To that sanctimonious *jargon* which was his Shibboleth, was opposed another *jargon* not less absurd and much more odious.

Another constant habit is the clinching of the argument by the concrete instance, very often in the form of a name, or, for choice, of a pair of names, which ring out like a gong at the end of the sentence. In a single page of the *History*, too long to quote, we come upon the following couplets : 'Lords of the Bedchamber and Captains of the Guards' ; 'Jane Grey and Lucy Hutchinson' ; '*Clelia* and the *Grand Cyrus*' ; 'the whole Greek literature from Homer to Photius' ; 'Raleigh and Falkland' ; 'Pitt and Fox, Windham and Grenville' ; 'Sophocles or Plato.'

I must not discharge a notebook on the reader, who will easily multiply, if need be, the list of Macaulay's weapons in discourse. But it is well to notice that his aim was not merely lucidity. He was pleased, we know, when the printer's reader could only find one sentence in the *History* that required to be read over twice. But his other aim, in spite of all *staccato* or hammering effects, was, above all, smoothness to the ear, and this aim he attains. His rhythm,[1] like his language, is easy and effortless ; if we are sometimes forced to think of the piston-rod, it is a rod well-oiled that plays powerfully, swiftly, and steadily. Macaulay's style, whatever may be said against it, carries his readers though their long journey.

His actual diction is so pure and sound that it can almost be appealed to as authoritative. Herein he ranks with Addison,

Hume, and Goldsmith. He rarely uses an obsolete or doubtful word except when he quotes it from the period that he is chronicling. 'Dismission' for 'dismissal' is an apparent exception, but it is an eighteenth-century form, and technical. 'The Chancellor instantly fired': 'an active search was making' after Roman Catholic priests: these are stray examples. In his simpler and higher passages, and in the *Lives* that he wrote during his last decade, his language becomes purer still, it is English of no period; and his mere manner, though still quite perceptible, is more subdued and temperate.

His literary models have been much debated. The riveted antitheses of Johnson, the pendulous clauses of Gibbon, count for a little; the aggressive pointed speech of Jeffrey counts for more. I cannot see, as some have done, any trace of the study of Hazlitt. Sydney Smith may have given Macaulay some lessons in epigram. But it is easier to see his general lineage than his particular creditors. Behind him is the long, twofold, eighteenth-century tradition of plain diction and fighting rhetoric. 'In his hands the thing became,' not a trumpet, but sometimes a machine-gun, sometimes heavier ordnance. Yet such figures must always do injustice to his real power and compass. Macaulay, once more, *stands* as a writer; he will always be there; he will not go down until Gibbon and Swift go down; and although he may not be their equal, he is only less than their equal.

X

Macaulay relates that Leigh Hunt, in the course of a begging letter, wrote to him lamenting 'that my verses want the true poetical aroma that breathes from Spenser's *Faerie Queene*'; and other critics have made it a test of discernment to see no poetry in the *Lays of Ancient Rome*. It is, indeed, almost impossible to miss seeing to what order of poetry the *Lays* do not belong. But let them be judged in their own kind: there is nothing at all in them like

> Field of death, where'er thou be,
> Groan thou with our victory! . . .

and there is nothing quite like

> That yellow lustre glimmer'd pale
> On broken plate and bloodied mail,
> Rent crest and shatter'd coronet,
> Of Baron, Earl, and Banneret . . .

Beside the rarer and more piercing note of Wordsworth or of Scott, Macaulay's bugle has the ring not so much of baser as of less tempered metal, just as the rhetoric of his prose is dulled by the side of Demosthenes. But his verse, like his prose, is genuine for all that. Compare it, again, in its own kind, with that of his successors Aytoun or Sir Francis Doyle, both of them spirited, impetuous makers of martial lays, and its excellence is conspicuous. It is not for nothing that he prints himself on the memory; that is one quality, at any rate, indispensable in popular writing. And *popularity*, the virtue that John Leycester Adolphus so well defined in his praise of Scott, is not to be had for the asking. *Horatius* throughout, and the first appearance of the 'princely pair' in the *Battle of Lake Regillus*, and most of the *Prophecy of Capys*, are popular in the highest sense of the word. And they are more than that. They are noble; not so much by virtue of any rare magic, or of the highest felicity of style, but for their manly ardour and their Roman strength of onset, which are felt in the opening of *Horatius*—indeed in all *Horatius*—and in the close of *Lake Regillus*. Nor do they lack more delicate touches, as in the line about 'April's ivory moonlight' and in the last three stanzas of *Horatius*. Macaulay's massiveness and distinctness, his avoidance of surplusage, give to the *Lays* a real unity of effect; and his scenes in verse often leave a sharper image than his scenes in prose, where he is capable of swamping the effect in excessive detail and in figures of oratory.

The *Lays* are really lays, not ballads, and the occasional ballad-tags ('to witness if I lie,' 'Never, I ween,' 'Then out spake') do no particular good. Macaulay cannot completely sink himself in his imaginary minstrel. The value of the *Lays* does not depend on the truth of the theory or conjecture which happily prompted them, and which Sir George Cornewall Lewis, as we have seen, could only value for that reason. The lost poems that might have lain behind the legends of the Latin historians remain *in nubibus*; it is only certain that they would not have been Macaulayesque. For the *Lays of Ancient Rome*—and it is one of their virtues—are a new species, and not a revival or adaptation of an old species. They come in the lineage, no doubt, of Scott; but their fashion of narrative, and their characteristic rhythm—which is not without lapses or snags, but is quite individual—are only found in Macaulay's own imitators.

His other verse, though not voluminous, is not to be neglected. *The Armada* and *Ivry* well anticipate the *Lays*. The early pieces, written in the manner of his fellow-collegian Praed, are not very neat-handed, and the long Byronic *Marriage of Tirzah and Ahirad* (1827) is only curious as coming from the future critic of Byron (1830). But the *Battle of Naseby*, composed at the age of twenty-four, is as good as the Cameronian diatribes in *Old Mortality*, and is, like them, written from the outside, as a *tour de force*. The pretty song 'O stay, Madonna, stay,' is noticeable as Macaulay's only love-poem. The *Epitaph on a Jacobite* has been named already; it shows, among other things, that the couplet of Pope will always have worthy work to do and is not an outworn mode. Macaulay's most serious and mature, though by no means his best, piece of verse, the *Lines Written in August 1847*, is imitative in form and follows Gray's *Elegy*, but is a true record of the writer's own ideals, and of his unexpected streak of pensiveness.

XI

The ever-questionable Froude has not worn so well as Macaulay; and he is far oftener open to the reproach that his tale asks in vain for confirmation and that he is honestly incapable of dealing justice. He is often correct, he is often fair; but we are never sure; and the more eloquent he is, the more we are haunted by the doubt. He has a rarer mind than Macaulay, and a more enigmatical one; he cares for religion and speculation; and he is a more delicate, though not a more potent, artist. He too has the popular quality, and commands a rhetoric, purer and more chastened than Macaulay's, of his own; but he has not, in handling political history, anything like so massive a store of knowledge or so strong a head. The two are grouped together here because, Carlyle apart, they are the greatest men of letters amongst the historians of their time.

James Anthony Froude [1] (1818-94) came out of a Devonshire parsonage of the old, high and dry, unperplexed, pre-Tractarian type. His early experience was harsh; he was unrecognised and poorly treated both at home and at school; and, though he bore no malice, he broke away. So, before him, did his elder brother, Richard Hurrell, the storm-bird of the Oxford movement, who died before learning to fly steadily, or to see the true direction of the ecclesiastical wind. James Anthony went up to Oriel in 1835. He read the classics, not as a strict scholar, but in his passionate appreciative way, as his papers written long afterwards on Lucian and Euripides attest.

And he was under the same roof as Newman; he began to think, and to be troubled by the religious ferment of the place and hour. Froude's very singular mental journey, in its first phase, lasted till about 1849; by that date his convictions were clear and his task was chosen. He has told much of his story in the essay called *The Oxford Counter-Reformation*, which is to be found in the fourth volume (1883) of *Short Studies on Great Subjects*. There he portrays Keble, Isaac Williams, Hurrell, and above all Newman, whom he honoured to the last. He tells how he revolted from his youthful subservience to Hurrell and to the new intolerant doctrine; how a visit to some devout but not fanatical Irish Evangelicals opened his eyes to the other side; how he helped Newman in one of the *Lives of the Saints*, and how his mental gorge rose up against their absurdities; how Newman startled him by saying that Hume's argument against miracles was unassailable by the natural reason; and how he, Froude, though he had already begun to read Carlyle, was in the end left without doctrinal or other moorings; all the more painfully, because he had taken deacon's orders in the year of fate 1845, when Newman seceded to the old faith; and a nominal parson, or half-parson, Froude was to remain until 1872, when the Relief Act was passed.

By now he was a Fellow of Exeter, but Oxford was not to hold him. His early troubles and his inner conflicts are represented, under artless disguise, in two stories, or sketches, the one called *Shadows of the Clouds*, the other *The Nemesis of Faith* (1849). The latter work was pounced upon and hunted down, and a copy was melodramatically burned in Exeter College Hall. If worthless as a story, it is curious as a document. One Sutherland Markham, who is more or less the author, works his way out of the narrow beliefs of his childhood, and tries to live by reason. He fails; he becomes enamoured of a married lady. 'They did not fall as vulgar minds count falling'; but still Markham has 'reasoned himself out of the idea of sin.' In this condition he is captured by a priest, and becomes a Roman Catholic, but only for a time; his end is left uncertain, but is anyhow a luckless one. He remains bewildered between Newman and Carlyle.

Froude himself ceased to be thus bewildered. He was frowned on by orthodox and heretics alike, and withdrew from Oxford; in fact was virtually turned out. He married, went into the country, and threw himself on literature. He began, in the *Westminster* and elsewhere, to print the essays afterwards to be gathered up in his four volumes of *Short Studies on Great Subjects*, which are the fruit of the leisure that he secured from time to time from the work of the *History*. One of the earliest and happiest of these 'studies' is not a study at all, but a fable, a form in which Froude excelled; it is called *The Cat's Pilgrimage*, and represents a mood which perhaps lies deeper than all his theories; it is the mood of irony, the haunting sense of vanity. The cat goes forth among the beasts to learn the meaning of life, and they all tell her to do her duty; but interpret that mandate in sundry owlish, or doggish, or foxy senses, so that no satisfaction is given to the cat. Froude's paper on the poem of *Reynard the Fox* also shows, in graver form, his queer strain of moral questioning. What has Mr. Carlyle, with his doctrine that right prevails in the end, to say to the Hero as Reynard? Reynard, on the whole, succeeds; and the rascal is happy. How are we to get at him? Why do we, rather sneakingly, admire him? How about the moral government of this world, in the light of Reynard? Froude enjoys performing his egg-dance among these uncomfortable questions, and also enjoys not answering them; he never breaks the eggs. All the while, he believes, as firmly as his master, in the tenet that right does ultimately prevail, and that in history we must judge by the event and the achievement, and take liberal views in appraising the means that are employed by the imperfect tools of Providence.

XII

Some of the *Short Studies on Great Subjects*, issued in four series (1867-83), are reprints of essays published before the *History* appeared; some are of much later date; and the whole collection falls into three or four groups:

1. There are many papers on religion and theology. The account of the Oxford Movement has been mentioned. One of the most eloquent, *The Philosophy of Catholicism*, is an effort to put in plain language the appeal of the old faith to the heart and soul of mankind; to enforce its historic service, and vindicate its relative truth. A strange task for the admirer of Calvin and the assailant of Popery; but it does him honour, and he might well have remembered the spirit of this paper in some of his later diatribes. Not that it would be welcome to Roman readers, for Froude's point of view is that he is doing intelligent justice to an obsolete phase of the human spirit. More characteristic is *Calvinism*, the address given to the

students of St. Andrews, where Froude vindicates the greatness of Knox, the tonic power of the Scottish creed in bracing a nation of freemen, and the eternal truth implicit in the predestinarian dogma. Of the fabric of Calvinistic theory he himself retains but one stone, which he thinks the cornerstone: a belief, namely, that there is a justice at the heart of things, which declares itself through the moral law. He really has no other doctrine; and he once observes that 'God gave the Gospel; the father of lies invented theology.' To cherish this ethical residuum of faith Froude was led, no doubt, by Carlyle; but he was better informed on the speculative side than Carlyle, and much more capable of consecutive statement. Still his looseness of assertion is seen everywhere. On one page he calls Milton a Calvinist; on another, he says that 'only a fourth of mankind are born Christians; the remainder never hear the name of Christ except as a reproach.' Froude forgets the honours paid by the creed of Islam to the prophet Jesus; though he presently eulogises that creed for its likeness to Calvinism. His most striking theological paper is that upon the Book of Job; here can be studied Froude's peculiar cast of scepticism, and also the limitations which he sets to it. The review of Newman's *Grammar of Assent* is of interest from the same point of view; and, in his handling of abstract ideas, Froude often reminds us of Newman; the simple, apparently lucid style hides the incoherence of the argument. In all this kind of work, Froude's skill in popularising 'great subjects' is apparent; it amounts to a fine art; it is impossible not to read him; he is as transparent as Mill, and much more elegant, though his transparency is often delusive and his transitions are lax. He is the ideal author for those who wish simply to be borne along, and to look into nothing. His craft in exposition is more favourably seen in his book, written late in life (1880), on Bunyan, where he expounds with sympathetic insight the state of mind of the unlettered Protestant, and once more proclaims the forgotten verities of Calvinism.

2. The *Reynard* paper has been named already, and also *The Cat's Pilgrimage*. It is a pity Froude did not make more fables and apologues. *The Lion and the Oxen*, *The Farmer and the Fox*, *The Bread-Fruit Tree*, though written in prose, are worthy of La Fontaine or Krylov. The bread-fruit tree is the old faith; an amazing, fertile growth, which nourished men for many ages, and of which no one believed that it could ever decay, but decay it did. *A Siding at a Railway Station* is still better known. A train full of all ranks and classes is suddenly

stopped; their baggage is overhauled, with results disconcerting to the rich and notable, but better for the third-class passenger, Piers the Ploughman. The Last Judgement is here signified; the *karma*, the net result of each man's action, is appraised once and for all. Such is Froude's gospel, and Carlyle's; but their doomsday is purely an ideal one, and is postponed *sine die*.

3. Among the pleasantest of Froude's writings are his notes and diaries of travel, with their sketches of scenery and manners. Here he compares well with Thackeray; there is the same ease and frankness, and the same melodious rendering of immediate impressions. *A Fortnight in Kerry* also displays a good temper, which is remarkable in the author of *The English in Ireland*. The *Leaves from a South African Journal* record a visit paid to the Cape in 1874, and belongs to Froude's later books of travel. *Sea Studies* turns out to be a sympathetic criticism of Euripides,[1] in a happy setting. Froude was an open-air man, a sportsman, a yachtsman, devoted to the sea. The unquiet spark in his composition disappears when he is alone with nature; his scepticism takes a serener cast; and in the region where he then moves there is nothing to call forth his intellectual faults.

4. He is for ever telling us unmistakeably how, and how alone, history should be written. It is not a science. He reviews Buckle with admiring disbelief. The phenomena of history, he urges, never repeat themselves; the event can never be foretold, however well the causes may be known; for who, however well informed, could ever have foretold the growth of Islam or of Christianity? Yet no study which cannot foretell things is a science. Here Froude speaks in the spirit of Carlyle. Yet we feel that, since science is only truth accurately observed and methodised, and politics are only present history, and all reforms presuppose a constancy of operation in human motive, Froude's scepticism goes beyond reason. It is, in fact, of no philosophical interest; but it suggests to him the mode of composition which suits his own genius. This also he plainly defines. A history must be a drama, in which 'the actors shall reveal themselves and their characters in their own words'; 'let us hear the man himself'; the historian need not impose his own colouring or opinions, as even Thucydides and Tacitus do; the true model is rather Shakespeare, in his history plays; or Homer, since a history is more of an epic than a drama. It is obvious to retort that were this the only way, a work like Gardiner's would be futile;

and also that Froude not only composed but perverted his own *History* under the sway of one or two dominant ideas, and that he by no means lets its tale tell itself. But the passage shows that he came to his task with the intentions of the artist rather than of the theorist or of the mere chronicler. The same point of view is seen in the paper entitled *The Scientific Method Applied to History*. And one of the *Short Studies*, first printed in 1852, gives an earnest of Froude's method and spirit. This is *England's Forgotten Worthies*, which furnished Tennyson with the story of *The Revenge*, and which introduces Hawkins and Drake, the heroes of Froude's own county of Devon. He was again to celebrate them, long afterwards, in his Oxford lectures in 1893 on the *English Seamen in the Sixteenth Century*. These noble buccaneers he styles, in his early article, 'the same indomitable god-fearing men whose life was one great liturgy.' The phrase gives a clue to Froude's whole-hearted partisanship, and to the paradoxical relish with which this sworn believer in justice and righteousness strove to make the best of his robust heroes. Indeed, the 'hero as mariner' is added to the gallery of Carlyle. Hawkins and Drake took the blame and the praise, took all the risk and a share of the loot. They did not mind being disowned by their mistress if they failed, or if they succeeded too well. They were the unauthorised founders of the navy which was to save Protestant England and spiritual freedom. In these narratives, early and late, the style excels itself in skill and clearness, and irony and finish. The irony is at the expense of the modern liberal who throws up his hands against piracy; and Froude evidently sighs that those good days should have gone for ever.

XIII

The scope and object of the *History of England* now come in sight. The first two of the twelve volumes appeared in 1856, and the last instalment in 1870. The preface which finally preceded the whole work is dated in the latter year, and clearly explains the author's intention. He had meant at first to narrate the whole reign of Elizabeth; but was led, on the one hand, to go back to that of Henry VIII.; and, on the other, to bring his tale to a natural and dramatic ending with the Armada, with a consequent alteration of the original title. These changes of plan he justifies by his ruling purpose, which was to vindicate the English Reformation, both politically and spiritually, to the discomfiture alike of the High Churchman and of the secular Liberal. For the Reformation meant, in the sphere of affairs, the establishment of the royal instead of the papal authority over the whole realm, including the Church; while in the sphere of religion it meant the removal of all human intermediaries between man's soul and God's word. The first four volumes are chiefly devoted to the vindication of Henry from this point of view. The other eight, covering thirty years of the reign of Elizabeth, continue the story, with the difference that the queen, instead of being 'white-washed' or too much glorified, is portrayed with all the shadows, and with the further difference that Froude now relies more on the mass of manuscript authorities, hitherto unexplored, on which he spent immense though by no means sufficiently skilled labour. Throughout he held to his epical or dramatic conception of a history, and to his master-theory, that Protestantism saved England and freedom of thought, and that the two Tudor monarchs saved Protestantism; and that this they did by the aid, above all, of the navy, which had been made possible only by the seamen-adventurers.

Four-fifths of Macaulay's *History* had appeared by 1856; and Froude's early volumes were also very popular; in spite of coming in the wake of so powerful a craft, their course was hardly disturbed by its wash. Froude sailed, for that matter, with more ease and lightness than Macaulay; in another way, he was even smoother reading; he was the master of a style commoner amongst essayists or novelists, than historians, and it spoke to all. The scholars, reviewers, and High Church divines, however, were soon up in arms; and the teapot storm which had greeted *The Nemesis of Faith* swelled into a gale (to continue the figure). It blew in Froude's teeth, though without appreciably altering his course or arresting his speed, for the rest of his days. The criticisms upon his errors of fact, transcription, and inference blew hardest at a somewhat later date. At first he was chiefly attacked for his Henry-worship, for his general partisanship, for his condonation of atrocities when they happened to be committed by his own side, and for misreading the character, so imperfectly representative, of Henry's parliaments. Some of these charges are pressed hard, from the Whig standpoint, in the *Edinburgh Review* for July 1858. Many of them have been generally accepted by later historians; and it is equally clear that, as one of them has said, Froude's 'work will have to be done again,' and that no one has done it, as a whole, since his time, even as no one had done it before. It is agreed that though history is an interpretative art as well as a scientific record, still founded in science it must be ; and that Froude, despite his immense labour in researching and transcribing, did this work in an untrained and careless way, which falsified his record at many points, and shakes our confidence generally. It is also clear that though he freely admits that there were bad men on the side he favours, and good ones on the other side, still his whole temper is unjudicial ; and, further, that he deals intolerably and also needlessly in moral paradox. His larger thesis did not require all that whitewashing and special pleading. By his own favoured theory, heaven uses extraordinary instruments, who serve its ends unawares and from doubtful motives. Why, then, strive to make them out cleaner than they were ? Certain Catholics were detrimental to the state, and had to be made harmless : but why seem to extenuate the practice of killing them ? Froude's lectures on the seamen are full of reasonings of this kind : when he comes to some piece of sharp practice or cruelty, he cries, 'Let us have done with cant,' and urges either that the enemy was just as bad, or that the offenders were fighting in a great cause ; it was life or death for the country, and we must not scrutinise too closely. The effect would be better if he did not show a kind of glee in these apologies ; and moreover, he provokes a feeling of revulsion against his heroes, which no plain recital of their doings would have produced.

We must, then, read the *History* with a constantly suspended judgement, as to its reading of character and policy. As to errors of detail, Froude's name has not suffered so greatly as his principal assailant, Freeman,[1] desired. Freeman, in his long series of *Saturday Review* articles, is pronounced to have much exaggerated his case, and to have been sometimes wrong himself. It is unluckily, however, no plea in the courts of truth that Froude made his mistakes like a gentleman, while his adversary brawled. Froude's honesty and industry are not now disputed ; he was the first to dig, at Simancas and elsewhere, at all deeply into the original documents. But his inaccuracy and fallibility in doing so are admitted. He pursues Mary Stuart unrelentingly ; and one who had really investigated the story, Andrew Lang, observes :

> He is quite untrustworthy ; he has taken fragments from three letters of three different dates, and printed them, with marks of quotation, as if they occurred in a single letter. He accuses Mary Stuart of a certain action, on the authority of an English

ambassador, and when we read his letter we find him saying that rumour charges Mary with the fact, but that he does not believe it.

I remember long ago hearing one eminent student of 'psychical research' say about another: 'He thinks he is making a scientific transition, when he is only making a literary transition.' This seems to apply well to Froude. It was by a sound instinct that he scouted 'science'; it did not suit him. He is a patriot, a Protestant, a force-worshipper, a tale-teller, a portrait-painter, an artist. And what sort of an artist?

XIV

His epical choice of theme was a just and a distinct one. 'The English Reformation I sing, and the temporal defeat of the Catholic supremacy.' He stopped at the right point for his purpose in the year 1588. The laying-out of his story is less excellent. With all its clearness of style, it becomes swamped in detail, especially in the later volumes, which are the fullest of extracts from the documents. The chapters on economic and social life are not well fused with the rest. And Froude's two or three ruling ideas, being inadequate to the complexity of the phenomena, fail to ensure the due impression of unity in the whole. He is undoubtedly best in episode, and in those episodes which suit his pictorial gift. Here, indeed, he is hard to match. The murders of Rizzio, of Darnley, and of Murray, and the last scene at Fotheringay, are told in a way worthy of a great novelist. They leave a sharper impression, be they accurate or not, than the poetic treatment of Swinburne. Froude also loves pageants like the coronation of Anne Boleyn or the reception of Philip by Mary; and herein is himself a true Elizabethan. He revels in the martyrdoms of Hooper and Latimer; he makes a perfect short story out of the Nun of Kent; and he rises to his highest in describing the last hours of his hero, Henry. The rhetoric is restrained; the colouring, though never faint, is clear and pure; the English is limpid and right, and is never made turbid by the manifest passion of the writer.

But the *History* also lives, as a piece of literature, by its more abstract passages of argument and reflection. Froude is sparing of formal and balanced periods; his sentences are cast less in Gibbon's mould than in Hume's. But he rises without strain from the plainer march of the narrative into a more musical and elaborate cadence, when he comes to his patriotic outbursts, or to his celebrated praise of the English liturgy, or to discuss the ethics of persecution. Here again the form is excellent, but these passages, like his descriptive ones, gain by extraction. He has a habit of leaving them in the air, and of promising something important which never comes. The anthologies quote the page in his opening chapter beginning, 'For, indeed, a change was coming upon the world,' and its peculiar music is hardly to be paralleled outside of Newman. But he never says clearly what the change was ; unless, indeed, as a similar passage (ch. xlvii.), and an equally disappointing one, may indicate, it is the change produced in the general mind by the Copernican astronomy. Froude's chapters often begin with this kind of overture, and drop suddenly, without due transition, to the day's work. At other times there is a real connexion, and an impressive one. One short passage may be quoted as characteristic alike in spirit, diction, and rhythm ; it shows Froude, as a writer, at his best :

> Súddenly,|| and from a quárter|leást|expécted,|| a líttle cloúd|róse|over the hálcyon|próspects|of the queén|of Scots,|| wrápped|the heávens|in bláckness,|| and búrst|òver her heád|in a tornádo. On the political stage Mary Stuart was but a great actress ; the 'woman' had a drama of her own going on behind the scenes ; the theatre caught fire ; the mock heroics of the Catholic crusade burnt into ashes ;||and a treméndous|doméstic|trágedy|was revéaled|before the astónished|éyes|of Eúrope|.

Whatever the faults of the *History*, Froude's *English in Ireland* (1872-4) is an altogether less worthy production, and its chief merit is to have provoked Lecky to supply the corrective in his classical volumes.

> The right of a people to self-government consists and can consist in nothing but their power to defend themselves. No other definition is possible (i. 3). . . . The right to resist depends on the power of resistance (i. 5). . . . The worst means of governing the Irish is to give them their own way. In concession they only see fear, and those that fear them they hate and despise. Coercion succeeds better : they respect a master hand, though it be a hard and cruel one. But let authority be just as well as strong, give the Irishman a just master, and he will follow him to the world's end. Cromwell alone. . . . (ii. 138).

In such a temper, with conclusions fixed in advance, and simply making out a case, Froude reviews three centuries of our history—its thorniest chapter. Such a method any man can judge without regard to his own political sympathies ; the book that superseded Froude's was written by a convinced Unionist. It is, however, strange he did not see that the argument resting solely on force and the event is double-edged, and that any successful rebellion, on his own showing, would justify itself as the will of providence. His book suffers throughout in tone and style from its fundamental prejudice.

Oceana, or England and her Colonies (1886), partly a political pamphlet and partly a diary of Froude's trip to the Cape and Australasia, is one of his most agreeable books. The chapters on South Africa, which got him into warm water as usual, have their interest for historians. The meditations, which are sceptical and pessimistic but serene in tone, drift with the motion of the ship. The descriptions of men, manners, and places have the old lightness and ease. The book is held together by the spirit of imperial patriotism, which glows and expands more than ever under the Southern Cross. Froude was all for a closer bond—a bond not of forms but of reciprocal sympathy—between the mother and daughter countries ; his moral here is a true and sound one, and the contribution of the colonies and dependencies during the world-strife of yesterday has more than borne out his hopes and aspirations.

Froude wrote a great deal besides : books, of no great substance, on Cæsar and on Luther ; a novel, *The Two Chiefs of Dunboy* ; a sketch of Lord Beaconsfield ; and minor studies in his earlier field, like *The Divorce of Catherine of Arragon* (1891). In 1892 he followed Freeman in the Oxford chair, and showed himself once more an artist, not only in words, but in the craft of half-popular, half-academic lecturing. Among his courses were that on *The English Seamen*, already touched upon ; and there were others, less durable in print, on Erasmus and on the Council of Trent. Froude's uncritical habit was now an old story ; but it did not much trouble the hearers whom he had in mind. His dealings with the memory of the Carlyles have been described in a former chapter, and belong to the early eighties. In literary skill, unluckily, they are excelled by none of his writings ; the English is of the purest and simplest. Froude has the art of making everything he says appear self-evident, until it is examined ; and when he is right, it is the truth which becomes self-evident, clothed in impeccable form.

The character of Froude's style is by now evident. It has an ineffaceable Oxford stamp. His English is not curious and inlaid like Pater's, nor is it conscious like Matthew Arnold's ; it does not crutch itself on formulæ and reiterated phrase. It is not Ruskinian. It is natural to think of Newman, with his plainness, ease, and melody, as Froude's model ; and such, in some degree, Newman must have been. But it is probably truer to regard both writers as carrying to perfection a variety, which was cherished and encouraged at Oxford, and of which the animating principle, besides the love of purity and elegance, and a corresponding dislike of rhetorical tricks, may be found simply in the wish to remove all obstacles between the writer and the reader : the old aim, in fact, of Addison, Law, and Hume. Other and diverse examples are found in the contemporary styles of Pattison and of Jowett. The plain tradition, academically touched, and imaginatively too, such is Froude's inspiration. There are few good writers from whom the meaning of a whole page can be gathered in a quicker flash. This, it may be said, is but the gift of the superlative journalist ; and Froude is often no more than that. He has the defects of the type. We glide on through his pages hardly noticing our progress, and are suddenly jarred, when our judgement asserts itself, and some laxity of thought is perceived, or some inaccuracy of fact detected ; and our confidence, after a time, is impaired or ruined. But Froude's assurance never deserts him, for he is honestly deceived by prejudice, and also by his own art and skill. Yet a certain fineness and delicacy of speech seldom quit him. His rhythm and music too are his own, and of no little variety. He passes the difficult test, that it is impossible to imitate or parody him, any more than Goldsmith or Thackeray. He is thus at the opposite extreme to Carlyle ; and in absorbing his master's ideas, Froude may well have made up his mind wholly to avoid his master's manner.

CHAPTER VII

OTHER HISTORIANS

I

In our present chronicle there is no Gibbon, no Ranke, and no Mommsen; but there are the three writers of great mark already reviewed; there are the historians of definitely philosophic bent, described in the fourth chapter; and many other names remain, which it is hard to select and classify. The choice becomes no easier as the century advances. The general proficiency of historical authors increases, to an almost fatal degree; and a kind of adequate, colourless, impersonal style, a style-of-all-work, becomes common property. This body of work shades off at one end into mere compilation, or into matter of purely scientific value; but at the upper end it runs, without any fixed frontiers, into work of individual note and power, which is still alive and calls for record. Every degree and combination are found of scientific capacity and literary gift. In a survey of letters it is well to keep on the safe side, and rather to omit some worthy than to include much inferior writing. But the chapter is a fruitful and honourable one in literature as well as in historiography. The chief historians of Greece and Rome, along with Milman, may be referred to first; next, the later, more avowedly scientific school, who are mainly though not wholly concerned with British history; and lastly, two men of letters, Napier and Kinglake, who shared in, or were close to, the great affairs which they describe.

II

To Connop Thirlwall[1] (1797-1875), Bishop of St. David's, and one of the leaders of the historical revival in England, Mill pays a high tribute in his *Autobiography*; and Thirlwall's force of brain and speech impressed all his contemporaries. The best-known fruit of his humaner studies is his early paper, published in the *Philological Museum*, on *The Irony of Sophocles*. Thirlwall extends the sense of the term irony to the detached temper of a judge who hears contending parties. So too, in the *Antigone*, the spokesman of each of the eternal principles, law on one side and piety on the other, states a case. The point of view recalls that of Hegel in his *Æsthetik*, which was published about the same time. But the more familiar sense of 'irony' is naturally exemplified from the *Œdipus Rex*, where the words of the tragic sufferer have another meaning for the audience. The grave and rigorous style of Thirlwall is already seen in this justly famous essay. His liberal ideas in the matter of university tests drove him from his post in Trinity College, Cambridge; he went into a country living, and became bishop in 1840. Thirlwall was a linguist, and could preach to his flock in their native Welsh. He was a pioneer in England of German lore and letters; and translated, along with Julius Hare, two volumes of Niebuhr's *History of Rome*. His own *History of Greece*, preceding Grote's (1845-56), appeared in eight volumes (1835-44); a new and enlarged edition was complete by 1852. Thirlwall did not write much else except sermons, episcopal charges (a form of composition in which he excelled), a small sheaf of essays, and a number of excellent letters.

The *History of Greece* is severely planned and proportioned, from the opening geographical survey down to the Roman conquest. The backbone of Thirlwall's chronicle, as of Grote's, is political; but the politics are those of long ago, with no special application for to-day, and they are judged without passion, bias, or visible preferences. The writer is equitable and remote, a judge who has never been an advocate. He concentrates on his story, and has few digressions on speculation, art, or letters. His sketch of Athenian tragedy has some warmth of colouring, but is all too brief. His descriptions of the great figures, Pericles and Alcibiades, have a classical concision, but they are descriptions rather than portraits. The general effect is therefore somewhat grey, though not tame; but, in requital, Thirlwall is positively unable to care for anything but the truth, and he is the master of a pure and pointed, if restrained, style. Only too modest, he hailed Grote's performance as entirely above his own. He had, however, done much more than till the ground, and had embodied his German reading attentively: and his book abides, though the study of Greek antiquity has been transformed since his day.

Thirlwall's mind and temper are much more freely disclosed in his correspondence, which includes the posthumously printed *Letters to a Friend*. To this lucky young Welsh lady, Miss Johns, the Bishop discourses, in his keen finished manner, upon many things: the infallibility of the Pope, the arguments for immortality, the breakfasts of Monckton Milnes, the possible end of the world, the ethics of suicide, and his interview with Queen Victoria. His mind, though devout, is not specially ecclesiastical in tone; it is sure and balanced, and also marked by a sharp independence of view. He sometimes lets loose an irony, not of the Sophoclean kind, but highly pertinent. It is pleasant to come on his dislikes and prejudices, when he drops the crozier for the small-sword. Amongst the great Germans there was one whom he failed to admire:

> I have so much faith in the force of truth as to believe that sooner or later Hegel's name will only be redeemed from universal contempt by the recollection of the immense mischief he has done.

It is to be wished that Thirlwall had written an imaginary conversation between Cardinal Newman and Socrates, whom he exalts above all other Greeks: we can guess from the following sentences how it might have run:

> His mind was essentially sceptical and sophistical, endowed with various talents in an eminent degree, but not with the power of taking firm hold on either speculative or historical truth. Yet his craving for truth was strong in proportion to the purity of his life and convictions. He felt that he was entirely unable to satisfy this craving by any mental operations of his own. . . . Therefore he was irresistibly impelled [to seek an infallible guide, etc.]. No doubt this was an act of pure self-will. He bowed to an image which he had first himself set up. There was at once his strength and his weakness. He could deceive himself and could not help letting himself be deceived. . . . [As to Newman's belief in angels] Surely it is one thing to believe that all is regulated by a Supreme Will, and another thing to believe that this Will employs a machinery like that of *The Rape of the Lock*.

Thirlwall's less formidable side is seen in his delight in *The Earthly Paradise*; the latter poem is 'even more delicious' than the *Jason*, and

> a godsend when I can take it out on the grass and read it, while the haymakers are at work, and the dear horse is pacing up and down quite unconscious of the help he is giving. The 'season' is not complete without such a reading in harmony with it.

The philosophic Radicals aimed at a rational recast of law; they tried to explore the natural history of the individual mind, and to base a programme of social reform on sound principles of economy. The achievement of George Grote [1] (1794-1871) was to apply their scientific method, and their democratic canons to the study of ancient history. William Mitford, the chief English pioneer in this field, whose *History of Greece* (1784-1810), and especially of Athens, reflects the Tory reaction of his time, was the provoker of Grote ; who in 1826 fired a shot into his bows in the *Westminster*, and whose own *History* was partly written as a corrective to Mitford's. It is, he wrote long afterwards,

so much the custom, in dealing with the Grecian history, to presume the Athenian people to be a set of children or madmen, whose feelings it is not worth while to try and account for . . .

whereas in truth Athenian politics are present history, and the world's great object-lesson in democratic experiment. It was well that Grote waited twenty years over his task ; the first two volumes of his twelve did not appear till 1845, and the book was not completed till 1856. He had meantime plunged into affairs. He had visited the Paris liberals, and had sat for nine years in the Commons, only retiring when he found that the cause of the philosophic party was outworn. He had written long before (1821, 1831) on parliamentary reform. There could be no better schooling ; nor was Grote's life as a banker alien to the student of Greek finance. He knew what is meant by the swirl of parties and the fight of a minority, and how law is battered into shape by open discussion. Hence the air of great events circulates through his book ; and his writing, though heavy and buckram in style, is often lighted up by modern instances. He compares the license of the sedition-stricken 'Korkyra' with that of revolutionary France, and finds modern French parallel to the mutilation of the Hermæ.

Grote's limitations, which are now well understood, have by no means left his work obsolete. As Freeman said of Gibbon, 'whoever else is read, he must be read too.' Authentic history begins, for him, late in the eighth century ; the discovery of Ægean culture now places the beginnings, in some sense, two thousand years earlier. Modern archæology has been born, Aristotle's book on the constitution of Athens has been found, comparative mythology has transformed the study of beliefs ; and Grote, in the light of it all, has had to be re-edited. But his work, or great and solid blocks of it, must remain. His injustice to some of the autocratic states, and many details in his book, have been corrected. That culture, art, and letters figure little except as illustrations of his political text is, after all, it has justly been said, only a criticism of his title. What endures is his story of the great men, military events, and constitutional struggles of the fifth century. Even his account of the myths, though superseded, is full of shrewdness ; his analysis of the state of mind expressed in the phrase *fingunt simul creduntque* strikes deep, and marks a distinct advance on the older view that the priests, or 'godsmiths,' invented the gods ; I have already noted how John Mill welcomed Grote's exposition of this subject.

The *History of Greece*, in one sense, is literature only by courtesy. It is not elegantly written, though it is plain and massive in construction. Grote suffers because his business is to put two great writers, his two chief authorities, into his own decidedly creaking English. Herodotus becomes heavy in hand, and 'the condensed and burning phrases of Thucydides,' as Grote calls them, lose their virtue. We have to face expressions like 'the reciprocal indulgence of individual diversity.' Yet somehow we read Grote, and that not merely for his matter. He swings along in an ugly, powerful stride. The greatness of the subject does get into his language. His chapters on the plague, on the spirit and work of Pericles, and on the Sicilian tragedy, are worthily written. He had never been to Greece, he does not describe scenery ; like all his school, he rather thinks than sees ; yet he communicates the passion of the scene. His philosophical interests and gifts, hardly represented in his *History* save in his well-known plea for the Sophists, appear in his later studies of Plato and Aristotle. His *Minor Works*, edited by Bain in 1873, throw light on his mind in other ways ; but the best record is *The Personal Life of George Grote* (1873), written by his notable and formidable wife. The history of their love affair, and of the doings of the villain of the piece ; the historical emotion betrayed by Grote at Pæstum, Rome, and Terracina ; the learned intercourse in talk, or in dignified correspondence, with Lewis, Hallam, and Molesworth ; Mrs. Grote's claim, seemingly incorrect, that she inspired the writing of the *History* ; and Grote's later falling away from the true faith in the matter of republicanism and the ballot ; are all described with a vigour, pedantry, and *naïveté* which make the memoir one of the most amusing of the period.

A true link between the age of romance and the spirit of historical science is to be found in the labours of George Finlay[1] (1799-1876). A strong-headed young Scot with some legal training, and already filled with a lifelong passion for Greece and its past, Finlay drifted in 1823 to Cephalonia, volunteered as a Philhellene, and fell in with Byron.

During the two months I remained at Mesolonghi, I spent almost every evening with Lord Byron, who, Mr. Parry says in his book, wasted too much of his time in conversation with Mr. Finlay and such light and frivolous persons. I left Mesolonghi nine days before Lord Byron's death.

After some adventures Finlay was invalided home, but was in Greece again a few years later under the rule of Capodistrias. Wishing to 'help in the material improvement of the country,' he bought land in Attica, and lost 'his money and his labour' under the reign of Otho. Then he 'planned writing a true history of the Greek Revolution in such a way as to exhibit the condition of the people.' This portion of his work, where Finlay speaks with the liveliness and honesty, if sometimes with the prejudice, of an eye-witness,[1] was the latest (1862) to appear during his lifetime, which was mostly spent in Greece itself. Thinking backwards, he conceived and gradually executed his great scheme of describing the age-long preparation for this event, namely the 'history of Greece under foreign domination' for two thousand years. The story begins about 140 B.C., or rather, in outline, from the death of Alexander the Great, and finally goes down to A.D. 1864. Finlay's work appeared in instalments, the arrangement of which causes some perplexity, from 1844 to 1877; after he reaches 1453 the form of chronological essay gives way to that of narrative.

By his account, above all, of the Byzantine empire, Finlay established his fame as a true pioneer with a sound method, and he is always saluted by those who have built on his labours. He is throughout distinguished by his grasp of economics, statistics, numismatics, and institutional history. No book is a better purging medicine for the cheap idealist. 'Good roads and commodious passage-boats have a more direct connexion with the development of human culture, as we see it reflected in the works of Phidias and Sophocles, than is generally believed.' He broke up soil over which Gibbon had passed more swiftly and with another aim; and he often seems to be quietly correcting Gibbon, to whom he is opposed in political and religious temper. He is always thinking of the 'condition of the people'; and he has the democratic faith—chastened and yet confirmed by his long, sombre, and, as he calls it, 'uninviting' survey of centuries of slavery—in the popular and municipal institutions that have kept the Greek nation alive all that while. He is also a believer ; and, while fair to the Moslem and cool to the hierarchy, he drives home the historic service of Christian ethics in preserving the seed of national unity.[1] Just laws and government are the only political antiseptic ; this truth, while reviewing age after age, Finlay enforces with a certain smouldering eloquence. He was also the first writer clearly to point out the continuity of race, institutions, language, and territory, in the case of 'the only existing representatives of the ancient world.'

Finlay has some of the aims, qualities, and drawbacks of Thucydides. He mostly eschews rhythm and the graces,[2] and cares only to pack his story with meaning. He rewrote much for the sake of greater compression ; he taxes the attention, but he keeps it. Yet he is beguiled by vivid incident ; his stories of the Empress Eudocia, and of the anarchy which he had himself beheld at Athens, are well told ; and his survey of the first Byzantine sovereigns [3] rings with sonorous and well-placed names, like a page of Macaulay. Byron or Landor would hardly have treated in a livelier way, or with more of the spirit of romance, the fortunes of Andronicus the First. But Finlay's strength lies in the interweaving of good narrative with political reflections that grow naturally out of the particulars and rise above them. A clue to his sustaining creed and a brief example of his manner may be found in his passage on the ill doings of the timariots :

> The permanent laws of man's social existence operate unceasingly, and destroy every distinctive privilege which separates one class of man as a caste from the rest of the community, in violation of the immutable principles of equity. Heaven tolerates temporary injustice, committed by individual tyrants, to the wildest excesses of iniquity ; but history proves that Divine Providence has endowed society with an irresistible power of expansion, which gradually effaces every permanent infraction of the principles of justice by human legislation. The laws of Lycurgus expired before the Spartan state, and the corps of janissaries possessed more vitality than the tribute of Christian children.[4]

The Greek revolution, ending after many days in constitutional government, seems to Finlay a long-delayed design of Providence, of whom the peasantry and people, not the officials or diplomatists, have been the chosen instruments. 'The best despot cannot in the end prevent so much evil as a moderately good representative system.' His creed was thus not a mere doctrine, but, unlike that of the older radicals, a conclusion from historic data ; and his disenchanted view of the Greeks, and the stern melancholy with which he describes their vices and their long durance vile, really plant his confidence in their destiny upon a firmer basis. Could he have brought his narrative up to 1920, Finlay would have recorded yet more disappointments, but his faith would yet again be brighter. His chronicle is the plain prose of Byron's cry that 'the peoples will conquer in the end.'

III

Hare and Thirlwall's translation (1828-32) of Niebuhr's *History of Rome*, helped to transform for English scholars the whole conception of historical inquiry. Niebuhr had himself owed much to his acquaintance with British institutions, and the debt was now to be repaid. He taught not only by the example of his imaginative and constructive power; he made an epoch in the critical study of historical material. He has even been described as 'the scholar who raised history from a subordinate place to the dignity of an independent science.' His greatest disciple in this country was Thomas Arnold[1] (1795-1842), who from 1828 onwards was headmaster of Rugby, and in 1841 became Regius Professor of History at Oxford. Devoted from the first to history and the classics, Arnold figured, in his earlier years at Oriel, chiefly as a divine: the ally of Whately, Hampden, and the broad churchmen (see Ch. VIII.), he was the foe of the Tractarians, whom he held in a deep and continuous abhorrence. His article in the *Edinburgh Review* on *The Oxford Malignants* might have served his son Matthew for a text on the virtue of urbanity. A priesthood, says Thomas Arnold, in his muscular way, is 'the first and worst error of Antichrist.' His gestures in debate are those of the irate headmaster, brandishing his professional weapon. Arnold's own ecclesiastical dream recalls, and possibly derives from, that of Coleridge. Church and state are to be one, the church being the soul of the state, and Christian ethics the right mainspring of politics;[2] in this way both sacerdotalism and Erastianism are to lose their sting. Subscription is to be on generous terms, but is to exclude Romans, Unitarians, and Jews. All citizens must promise obedience, though they must not be forced to avow belief. The jarring creeds must bury smaller differences and concentrate on fundamentals. The guiding class is to be a spiritual aristocracy, both lay and learned, like the 'clerisy' imagined by Coleridge. This ideal is sketched in Arnold's letters, articles, and lectures, and in his *Fragment on the Church*. Something like it is to be found long afterwards in Seeley's *Natural Religion*.

Arnold's management of Rugby, and the lofty, masculine spirit which he inspired, along with much true culture, into his boys, has powerfully affected the character of the English ruling classes. Sometimes, no doubt, as in the case of the sensitive Clough, that spirit could be charged with encouraging overstrain, or in some characters with puffing up moral self-importance. But Arnold really taught the coming generation 'manners, freedom, virtue, power.' His sermons are raised into eloquence by the temper which his son delineates in the verse of *Rugby Chapel*. He also found time to make himself, what he hardly was by nature, a man of letters. His claim to the title rests, above all, on his unfinished *History of Rome* (1838-43). He had already produced a valuable edition of Thucydides, with a commentary which is full of life. In 1845, after his death, appeared the *History of the Later Roman Commonwealth*; but his masterpiece is admitted to be the third volume of the original *History*, containing the story of the second Punic War.

Here, it has been said, 'his powers of thought and expression were mature, and he was no longer impeded by his loyalty to Niebuhr.' In the earlier volumes, especially in the first, he had made it his mission to put the conclusions of Niebuhr into popular shape, though in an independent spirit. But the story at last rises to an epical force and life, as the contrast deepens between the Marlowesque figure of the pursuing Hannibal, and the collective courage and policy of the senate. Arnold almost thinks of Rome as a person—'thy dæmon, that 's thy spirit that keeps thee'; but he can find no individual Roman worthy to compare with Hannibal until he comes to Scipio. The historian died before he reached the date of Zama, but the torso of his work is little impaired. He had meant at first to prolong the story down to Charlemagne.

In Arnold's conception of history there is a marked admixture of theology. The fall of Hannibal is the work of Providence, operating chiefly through the integrity and firmness of the Roman spirit. But the Cæsars, both Julius and Augustus, who are unscrupulous as to means and methods, are hostile to the divine purposes. This view is urged, to the point of fanaticism, in some ruder pages of earlier composition, which describe the latter days of the Republic. Arnold thus stands at the opposite pole to Mommsen, who judges by results and *Realpolitik*. The clerical or didactic reading of history is too rigid when applied to a complex many-sided civilisation; but when it is enlisted in the praise of senatorial and republican virtue it is less out of place. And in his chosen field Arnold shows much impartiality. With all his modern instincts, he is full of admiration for the Roman aristocracy which held the city, and he thinks that an aristocracy, if only it can be good and generous, may be the best rulers of all; like his own virtuous school prefects, brave, incorruptible, severe, conscientious, well-educated, and not too clever.

'There floats before me an image of power and beauty in history,' wrote Arnold in 1840, 'which I cannot in any way realise,' and in the next year he begins to regard his task 'with something of an artist's feeling, as to the composition and arrangement of it.' These two passages tell us something of his literary gifts. His style is not wanting in variety. The more mythical tales, like that of the Sabines, he deliberately tells in what he calls a 'more antiquated' diction than the rest. It is an excellent diction for the purpose, and unaffected; it is meant to mark the popular, invented quality of the stories. The regular style of the *History* is, in its own kind, hard to excel. It is not great and strange, like Carlyle's, nor pleasing and insidious like Froude's, nor pyrotechnical like Kinglake's; nor is it heavy, or tame, or cold, or stiff; vices of which the examples are too many to specify. It is well fitted for describing hard facts, like the topography and geography for which Arnold had an exceptionally keen eye, and also for military operations. It is good for character-drawing, and for dramatic incident; its terseness suits the high, sententious passages. In the great episodes, like the battle of the Trasimene and the siege of Syracuse, it catches the grandeur of the subject. There is evidence that Arnold paid more heed to finish as he proceeded with his work. The Homeric quality of his narrative is perhaps best seen in the chapter on the battle of the Metaurus; the writer's grasp of character, in his portrait of Scipio; and his historic vision, and the compass of his period, in such a passage as the following:

> He who grieves over the battle of Zama should carry on his thoughts to a period thirty years later, when Hannibal must, in the course of nature, have been dead, and consider how that isolated Phœnician city of Carthage was fitted to receive and consolidate the civilisation of Greece, or by its laws and institutions to bind together barbarians of every race and language into an organised empire, and prepare them for becoming, when that empire was dissolved, the free members of the commonwealth of Christian Europe. (Ch. xlii.)

The labours of Arnold were taken up and continued, though in another style and spirit, by Charles Merivale (1808-93), Dean of Ely, the writer of a *History of the Romans under the Empire* (1850-64). One quarter of the work, in spite of the title, is given to the prelude of thirty years; and this portion Merivale recast for the general reader in the attractive *Fall of the Roman Republic* (1853); which opens, some eighty years earlier still, like a story by a follower of Scott, with 'Tiberius Gracchus, a young plebeian, of the noble family of the Sempronii, traversing Etruria in the year of the city 617.' The story of a hundred years marches well and is ably condensed; it closes with the arrival of Augustus, and with admiring excuses for Julius Cæsar, which contrast almost absurdly with Arnold's censures. These opinions are developed more formally in the larger work, which is written in the same gently ornate fashion, and which carries the story down to the Antonines. Merivale is praised for his sound knowledge of all the literary sources; he wrote other historical works, and was an accomplished classical scholar; he turned the *Iliad* into rhyme, and Keats's *Hyperion* into Latin verse. 'He was pre-Mommsen,' it has been said, 'in his unavoidable neglect of epigraphic material,' and so belongs to a past school. But, at the date of his writing, none had covered the same ground with any sufficiency. His work is not only a careful narrative, but a reasoned eulogy, or at least vindication, of the early empire, of the *pax Romana*, and of monarchical institutions generally. As a writer, he has less nerve and style than many of the other historians mentioned in these sections; but he does not want for dignity.

IV

The plays of Henry Hart Milman (1791-1868) were written before 1830, and have been named in an earlier *Survey*. They are ardent, ambitious, Elizabethan, and their afterglow touches his prose again and again into a tempered richness. In 1829 Milman commenced historian; but his *History of the Jews*, like his *History of Christianity* (1840), which ends with the abolition of paganism in the empire, provoked some alarm, and is said to have delayed his preferment. Like Thirlwall, Milman was an early student of German criticism; his tone is judicial, scientific, and up to a point naturalistic. His liberal orthodoxy accepts the miraculous element quite honestly, but in a thrifty spirit. He begins to treat the Jews like any other nation or tribe, and their records like any other literature. He protests against Strauss and Renan, but on critical grounds, and not in the tones of the pulpit. He is very devout, and quite free from unction of the wrong sort. His work is also free from the evasions, if it lacks the vision and suggestive power, of the later *Ecce Homo* (1865). It suffers, no doubt, because much of it is a dilution of the scriptural text into a level modern paraphrase. Milman manages to take most of the colour out of the life of Christ, and is more at his ease when he reaches the post-apostolic age, and has less to fear from comparison with his documents. But all this was the prelude to a larger achievement. *The History of Latin Christianity*, 'including that of the Popes to the pontificate of Nicholas v.,' appeared in 1854-5, when Milman had for some years held the deanery of St. Paul's.

Already, in 1838, he had edited Gibbon, and his edition was long to hold its ground. In his *History* he now retold part of Gibbon's story, not controversially, but by way of a silent readjustment. To Gibbon the historic disputes of the faith were an aimless series of absurdities which delayed the march of reason; but they had made, and marred, secular history, and accordingly they demanded a lucid and ironical exposition. Milman, too, often seems to utter under his breath a quiet *tantum religio!* but he does so in the name of religion itself; and, moreover, he sees the great controversies as stages in the very march of reason, and as conceived in the only terms which reason, at each successive period, could command. And he sees, throughout, the spirit of Christianity surviving persecution and bloodshed. He does justice to the most doubtful instruments of Providence with anxious candour. Indeed his history is a sort of *Decline and Fall*; the decline, if not the fall, of Latin Christianity is its real theme. The ten centuries of his chronicle are the prelude to the rise of 'Teutonic Christianity,' or Protestantism; and of this, he says in one passage, Latin Christianity was the 'Avatar.' The ultimate overthrow of the Latin sacerdotal monopoly, after it had done its divinely appointed work for civilisation and the human spirit, is kept in view throughout.

Milman is a considerable historian, a writer of many-sided competence. He can tell an intricate story, or a simple one, very well. His pictures of the First Crusade, or of the Sicilian Vespers, or of the fortunes of Becket, approve his skill. His biographies of St. Francis and of Abelard show that the poet is not dead in him; and his accounts of the Northmen and of the code of chivalry are full of catholic sympathy. He is at home, too, in abstract matter; and while expounding the great heresies he is careful to keep in mind not only their arguments but their sources; as he puts it, 'divergencies of religion, where men are really religious . . . arise from the undue domination of some principle or element in human nature.' Above all, he excels in panoramic views. In his first chapter he divides the long drama into a dozen or more acts, or phases, and he keeps to his plan; and then, in his ninth volume, when he has finished, he turns and surveys the mind of Christendom in the fourteenth century, very summarily, and often avowedly using second-hand sources, but with an impressive sweep and clearness. For the great schoolmen his chief authorities are in French and German; for 'in England,' he laments, 'we have no guide,' now that Dr. Hampden, who promised so well in his article on Aquinas, 'has sunk into a quiet Bishop.' Milman had great learning, but he often felt at a loss for tools. The huge accumulation of knowledge since his time it would be absurd to regret; but something has been lost, if the day has departed when a single mind could venture to stride through the record of a thousand years.

As a writer, Milman modestly disclaims all competition with Gibbon, and seems to guard himself against any imitation of Gibbon's style. The note of irony is rare. There is no very marked manner or rhythm. But Milman is never flat, and he has no tricks, if his language is slightly old-fashioned and decanal. His sentences are often long and accumulative, but are seldom worked up into formal periods. He has not exactly Gibbon's power of carrying us through the tiresome parts of the story. But he is much more satisfying than the pictorial Stanley, and more convincing, if less exciting, than his friend Macaulay. His work is readable as well as honourable and valuable, if it lacks the absolute stamp of decision and distinction.

V

The commanding position of William Stubbs [1] (1825-1901) amongst the English historical scholars of his time is founded not only on his immense and precise erudition, his mastery of textual criticism, and his judicial weight and grasp, but also on a literary gift which, though to some extent swamped by his material or buried away for the laity in his massive volumes, is undeniable and arresting. He first became eminent as a church historian; then, some years before becoming Professor of Modern History at Oxford, a post which he held from 1866 to 1884, he began his long list of contributions to the Rolls series (*Chronicles and Memorials*, etc.), which contain some of his most learned, vivid, and pointed writing; and the same is true of his introduction to the edition of *Select Charters*, which appeared in 1870. His most continuous, best-known, and greatest work, *The Constitutional History of England*, came out in three volumes (1873-8), and covers the whole span down to 1485. It handles not only the growth and structure of institutions, but almost every activity, except war, of the body politic. The book confirmed Stubbs's position as the master, in Britain, of the scientific band of historians, and won him European note. The style is naturally close and severe, and Stubbs's shorter writings give him freer play. Amongst them may be named his mass of statutory lectures, such as those *On Mediæval and Modern History*, and those *On European History*, as well as his summary book on *The Early Plantagenets* (1876). At Oxford he lectured in the wilderness, sometimes 'to two or three listless men,' but exerted great influence nevertheless, and benevolently watched the progress of historical studies, which was due largely to his own teaching and example. He afterwards became Bishop of Chester, and then of Oxford, continued his work notwithstanding, and ended full of honours. Part of Stubbs's work was corrected by Maitland and others, but much of his edifice is acknowledged to stand fast.

In his private convictions Stubbs was not only orthodox but vehemently anti-liberal; as an historian, he is the shining example of a judge in equity. He saw that no period is so remote, but that our judgements of it may be coloured by a prepossession imported from a later day, either for or against a person, a party, and nation, or a creed; and such a prepossession in his eyes is the sin against the light. Or, more dangerous still, it might be the result of speculation *a priori*; and accordingly Stubbs has, he says,

> no belief in what is called the philosophy of history[1] . . . in nine cases out of ten a generalisation is founded rather on ignorance of the points in which the particulars differ than in any strong grasp of one in which they agree.

In this spirit he works ever upwards, in Aristotelian fashion, from the particulars, washing out the truth from their infinite multitude, like a master-digger; and reaching, in the most wary way, generalisations of his own. In judging character he is the embodiment of caution. He by no means belongs to the school which, on the plea of being scientific, is averse to moral judgements; he is for ever passing moral judgements, often in very strong language; but they are the fruit of intricate analysis, with every item weighed. These habits of mind are seen in his historical portraits,[1] which are packed with thought and drawn with many incisive distinctions; often each detail is borne out by the authorities in a footnote. Such are his pages on Charles the Fifth, on Henry the Fourth of France, on Richard the First, and on John: on the last of whom is bestowed an epitaph hard to match for its severity. These 'characters,' often embedded in a stiff learned dissertation, are artistically among the best of Stubbs's writings; but he can also, when he will, tell a story excellently: his account of the last days of Henry the Second at Chinon is an instance; and both in portraiture and narrative his close, vivid, stripped style reminds us of the best of the saga-men.

Edward Augustus Freeman [2] (1823-92) carried on the torch of Grote and Arnold, by virtue not only of his devotion to scientific method, but of his firm faith in the study of history —especially of classical history—as a school of affairs and a source of political wisdom. 'The history of ancient freedom' is 'one of the most living pursuits for the ruler and the citizen.' He was, moreover, a liberal of the Gladstonian type; the oppression of the Eastern Christian by the Turk, the struggle of the modern Greeks for constitutional government, were to Freeman but another phase of the eternal strife, and were to be judged by the same canons as the fight against the 'tyrants' of the fifth century B.C. History, he holds, is continuous, not only because the divisions of 'ancient,' 'mediæval,' and 'modern' are artificial in themselves, but because the truth of great political principles is independent of time and place; those principles, in the most civilised communities, being to Freeman's mind democratic. And they are also, at root, ethical. With the extra-moral, or non-moral, view of history, he is in sharp conflict; and he censures Mommsen for judging the deeds of Cæsar merely by the event, and without reference to right and wrong. At the same time, like Stubbs, he keeps in view the changing moral standard, and sees the unfairness of simply judging the actions of one age by the canons only consciously realised in a later one. Like Maine, he familiarised the English scholar with the 'comparative' method in the study of institutions—the method which detects the same principles and phenomena in diverse ages and countries.

Freeman, though little under the spell of Oxford, was and remained a convinced high Anglican. But his bent and interests were from the first sharply defined, as though with a knife. He cared little for theology, or for any but political philosophy, or for any art except architecture; or for literature, except as an amusement. But he had a passion and a genius for the analysis of political structure. One of his college essays is said to show the germinal idea of the *Norman Conquest.* He dreamed of, and in the end was to execute in part, a *History of Federal Government*, ancient and modern. The completed portion upon Greece, despite its mass of learning, attracts the lay reader by its clear argument and vigour of style. The long history of Greece he saw as a whole; and his admiring reviews of Finlay's great work explain at once his enthusiasm for the experiment of the Achæan League and his ardent desire to see the last of the Turk in Europe. Freeman's many-sided interest in classical history is best seen in the essays scattered up and down his four series of *Historical Essays*, which are mostly reprinted articles, and in the *History of Sicily*, which he did not finish. It is not the interest of a humanist; we hear little of the religion, or thought, or art, or literature of Greece and Rome, or of the life of their peoples; and this remarkable limitation must be remembered; but, in recompense, Freeman concentrated upon their polity, and on their struggles for constitutional freedom, and for national or imperial unity. 'To read,' he says, 'the political part of Mr. Grote's *History* is an epoch in a man's life.' 'We profess a religion of Hebrew birth; but the oracles of that religion speak the tongue of Greece, and they reach us only through the agency of Rome.' Rome, indeed, was the spot to and from which almost all roads led in Freeman's eyes. His mind and style are seen at their best in his large surveys, which sweep easily down the ages, and radiate from some great focus of civilisation and war, be it Rome or Athens, Sicily or Constantinople. His article on Sicily in the *Britannica* is a good instance of his powers; he gains greatly by enforced compression.

His industry was intense, and his work voluminous beyond belief. He wrote over seven hundred articles for the *Saturday Review*, and countless more in quarterlies and monthlies. In 1865 he set to work on his *History of the Norman Conquest*, which appeared (1867-79) in six volumes. Apart from the learned labours, which he duly acknowledges, of Kemble and Sir Francis Palgrave, he had a clear field. The work is one of vast erudition, and is of the first importance to historians; and the story is told with all Freeman's energy; but the diffuseness and minuteness of treatment, and a certain hammering monotony in the style, leave much of it outside the bounds of literature. The subject is politics and war; Freeman was wise in neglecting aspects of history for which he did not care. He followed with two volumes on *The Reign of William Rufus*.

In 1884, when already sixty, Freeman became Regius Professor at Oxford, a place which he found a Sahara of examinations, not a living fountain of historical studies. His force, however, did not abate; he poured forth lectures, articles, and books, of which the most important are *The Methods of Historical Study* and the *History of Sicily*. His earlier Rede lecture (1873) on the unity of history, is a classical exposition of his favourite doctrine (originally inspired by listening to Dr. Arnold), on which he discoursed to the last.

Freeman's style has been rather too much abused. It certainly resembles some hewing or pounding instrument rather than an artist's pencil. He has the reiterating and recapitulating habit of the lecturer, and deliberately thrusts the same truth many times down the hearer's throat, to make sure of him. Such a habit, in print, defeats itself. It is possible to be lucid beyond endurance, especially if we have a persistent craze for 'Teutonic' English, as for everything else Teutonic, and if we are aggrieved to find how many Romance words we are really using, and how insidiously like 'Saxon' words they often manage to look, so that we must console ourselves by the timely recollection that 'we may make sentence after sentence out of Teutonic words only, we cannot make a single full sentence out of Romance words only.' This fancy for a 'native' vocabulary was not prompted by mediæval or artistic feeling, as it was with Morris, but by theory, and the result is disagreeable.

Another proclivity of Freeman's, also making for tedium, but much more respectable, is what may be called his nominalism. After the manner of Hobbes, and still more of Sir George Cornewall Lewis, he is for ever dissecting and defining abstract terms—*federal*, *democracy*, *monarchy*—in order to see what lies at the bottom of them, and to show up latent fallacies and ambiguities. This he does in his usual copious and iterative manner. The effect is pedantic, but the practice is a healthy one, and makes for precision. Freeman's inveterate harping on verbal, which express real, distinctions in the end serves his large and, as he likes to call it (using a term which is *not* 'native'), his 'œcumenical' view of history.

All this, as well as his exhaustless facility and fertility of production, weighs down Freeman as a writer and makes it the harder to read him for pleasure. Yet he is a relief after the decorative and high-flying historians ; and when we are in the mood to detest, as he did himself, oratory and the graces, he is refreshing. And he is not only always informing, but he always (except in some of his churlish invectives against Froude and others) writes in a manly way. His sheer intellectual grasp, his big vision, get into his language ; in describing signal events and characters, Godwin or Edward the First, or in summing up the service of Athens to the world, he rises to a plain strong eloquence and to grandeur of outlook.

Macaulay had shown how scenery, colour, and portraiture could quicken political and constitutional history, with the life of the people as a background. Every one had to read the *History of England.* But then he had not written the whole history of England ; he had not covered a century of it. Nor had any one worth naming, since Hume, written or even sketched it in a vivid and competent way. The new science did not favour such adventures ; and Freeman, Gardiner, and the rest devoted themselves to single portions or aspects of the story. There was room, therefore, for a swift and living survey of the whole, on a moderate scale, conceived somewhat in the spirit of Macaulay; a survey that should do justice to the great scenes and personages, and should also, without becoming too abstract, keep alive the sense of continuity in the national record. Such was the aim of John Richard Green (1837-83), whose *Short History of the English People* appeared in 1874, and was thirstily received and read. The book was the greatest popular triumph since Macaulay's, and it also holds its place amongst serious histories.

Green writes under the influence of a certain revulsion against the predominance attached to military, diplomatic, and courtly affairs.

> I have devoted more space to Chaucer than to Cressy, to Caxton than the petty strife of Yorkist and Lancastrian, to the Poor Law of Elizabeth than to her victory at Cadiz, to the Methodist Revival than to the escape of the Young Pretender.

In this sense he called his work a history of the English people ; but the word should be 'nation.' He sets out to delineate the 'constitutional, intellectual, and social advance in which we read the history of the nation itself.' He gets far above the 'people.' He dwells on the conceptions of Bacon and Hobbes, on the school of Spenser, on *Comus* and *Paradise Lost.* His literary judgements are often excellent. In the *History of the*

English People (1877-80), an enlargement with corrections of the shorter work, he says of Dryden :

> Dryden remained a poet. . . . But he was a poet with a prosaic end ; his aim was not simply to express beautiful things in the most beautiful way, but *to invest rational things with such an amount of poetic expression as may make them at once rational and poetic*, to use poetry as an exquisite form for argument, rhetoric, persuasion, to charm indeed, but primarily to convince.

Not a complete account of Dryden, but his genius has seldom been better described. The pages on Chaucer and Bunyan, which bring us nearer to the common folk, are just as good. It is in his handling of thought and letters, and in the kind of emphasis that he gives to them, that Green differs from Macaulay. They now become part of the story in their own right ; they are not merely telling illustrations of 'history,' brought in from some region outside it ; they *are* history. Thought, of course, like literature, has also an internal history of its own, but that is not Green's business. He applies the same principle to Wyclif, to Laud, and to Puritanism. He does not reach the Tractarians, for his book ends with Waterloo, a mere 'epilogue' being appended. *The Making of England* and *The Conquest of England* expand particular chapters of the story, and show similar gifts.

The value of this generous conception of the subject does not wholly rest on Green's actual performance, which is unequal enough, but in the difficulty of ever going back on it once it has been so strikingly executed. He was charged with an imaginative use of authorities, and with errors of detail ; but the severe historians gave him their blessing, especially the accurate Stubbs, who spoke of Green's 'deep research and sustained industry' :

> There was no department of our national records that he had not studied, and I think I may say mastered. . . . Like other people, he made mistakes sometimes ; but scarcely ever does the correction of his mistakes affect either the essence of the picture or the force of the argument.

Green, indeed, is more open to attack as a writer than as an investigator. His page is often crowded, even dull, when he is dealing with wars and factions, about which he cares little. Some of his portraits, like those of Elizabeth or Burke, are indistinct and laboured. With all its rich variety, there is a certain scrambling effect about the *Short History* that prevents it from being a classic. The style is simpler and more even in the *History* than in the *Short History*, but some of the colour has gone. Green's *Stray Studies from England and Italy* (1876), and his second series of *Stray Studies*, many of them reprinted from the *Saturday Review*, are among his happiest writings ; it is surprising how much work and style he put into these casual and 'middle' articles, which are usually ephemeral things. Many of them return to the historic life of the city and municipality—London, or Yarmouth, or Como—a subject which always inspired the writer. Others are reminiscent of his life as an East-end parson ; others are old reviews, still with vigour in them. Some, again, are purely human and not learned at all, but the work of a holiday mood which flings learning off ; such are *Carnival on the Cornice, Buttercups* (a delightful study of the young heart-free schoolgirl), and *Children on the Sands*. The *Oxford Studies* are of a more professional cast ; but they have Green's animating quality, like all he writes.

VI

'It is not too much to say that Gardiner [1] found the story of the first Stewarts and Cromwell legend, and has left it history,' wrote York Powell, speaking of 'this English Polybios.' 'The result of his labours was to make the period he treated better known and better understood than any other portion of English history' (C. H. Firth). Another scholar declares that 'he has left us the most exact and impartial account of any period in the history of our race' (G. P. Gooch). Samuel Rawson Gardiner (1829-1902), unlike Freeman, Froude, and Lecky, was never drawn into the stream of contemporary politics, but kept to his proper work like a Benedictine ; and he has noted in a philosophic spirit the relationship between the historian and the statesman. The former can only help the latter indirectly ; the point of contact between the two is found 'in the effort to reach a full comprehension of existing facts' ; but the historian 'uses his imagination' to trace out the causes of those facts, the statesman in order to 'predict the result of changes to be produced' in them.

He, therefore, who studies the society of the past will be of the greater service to the society of the present in proportion as he leaves it out of account. If the exceptional statesman can get on without much help from the historian, the historian can contribute much to the arousing of a statesmanlike temper in the happily increasing mass of educated persons without whose support the statesman is powerless.

Gardiner, then, up to a point follows the banner of Ranke, and another sentence shows by whose example he had taken warning :

Certainly the politics of the seventeenth century, when studied for the mere sake of understanding them, assume a very different appearance from that which they had in the eyes of men who, like Macaulay and Forster, regarded them through the medium of their own political struggles. Eliot and Strafford were neither Whigs nor Tories, Liberals nor Conservatives.

And he adds that 'the constant or unavowed comparison of' the past with the present is 'altogether destructive of real historical knowledge.'

Gardiner's forty years of devotion to his master-work left him time for valuable labours as a lecturer, populariser of history, and editor ; his somewhat sequestered life in no way weakened his discernment of human or political motives in his *dramatis personæ*. He hardly paints, and has no flashes of genius, but he analyses down to the last fibre, without cynicism and without false sentiment. The comparison may be strange, but Gardiner is a kind of Browning in prose, so sharply does he realise opposing points of view, and the tragic deadlock that results. Like Browning, he also has an ideal strain that reveals to him the ultimate harmony, which was in part to be historically realised (though the struggle still persists) between the one-sided principles of the two great parties at strife. It is this strain that carries him beyond his immediate theme, and makes his story one of instruction to the statesman and the citizen, as well as to the student who wishes to 'see the thing as it really occurred.'

Gardiner's first ten volumes came out in instalments and under various titles, between 1863 and 1882: together they form the *History of England (1603-1642)*. Three more (1886-91) describe *The Great Civil War*, and another three *The History of the Commonwealth and Protectorate* (1895-1901). He reached the year 1656, leaving a chapter of the sequel for print ; the work was completed under the title of *The Last Years of the Protectorate*, by Professor Firth. *Cromwell's Place in History*, a course of lectures given at Oxford in 1896, is an excellent example of Gardiner's style when he is freed from narrative, and of his quality as a philosophic historian. It is the ripe fruit of a lifetime given to inquiry and to thinking, and it contains, not a picture, but a subtle and many-sided presentment of the Protector

> as he really was, with all his physical and moral audacity, with all his tenderness and spiritual yearnings, in the world of action what Shakespeare was in the world of thought, the greatest because the most typical Englishman of all time.

Gardiner's English is not energetic and clumsy like Grote's; but it has been justly charged with some flatness or bareness. He cares little for colour, and nothing for mounting rhetoric or cunning elegance. But his style improves on acquaintance, and as his work progresses. It is a faithful reflection of his mind and a transparent medium for his story. He describes adventures like the voyage of Raleigh or of the *Mayflower*, or scenes like the death of Charles, with effect. He can also handle unclean matter, such as the divorce of Essex, with clean hands, and describes a court scandal without moving a muscle. Indeed, the comedy of history is almost absent from his pages. His manner is fitted for weighing nice probabilities, for the clear and convincing exposition of obscure motive, and for the statement of condoning or aggravating features in a complicated case. He has the acuteness of survey, and the decision united with simplicity of character, which are sometimes found in judges.

For Gardiner is not only by common consent a great scientific historian, a master-investigator in the fields of foreign policy, constitutional history, and in the wide borderland lying between theology and politics. This achievement he crowns by his power to realise and convey the ethical atmosphere of another age. We go to him, as we do to Lecky, not only for truth of fact but for truth of estimate. The severity, even *naïveté*, of his own moral standard, which in cast is markedly Puritan, or at least Protestant, so far from hindering, actually seems to quicken this gift of trained appreciation. He does not write under the influence of any theory that the historian should cultivate what is called an objective or detached state of mind; on the contrary, he is full of enthusiasm, because he regards the warfare of the time as unconsciously working towards a far-off goal of toleration [1] and freedom.

> At last, after a terrible struggle, teeming alike with heroic examples and deeds of violence, a new harmony would be evolved out of the ruins of the old.

But he is always warning the reader against intellectual anachronisms, and pointing how much and how little enlightenment can be expected at a given moment :

> Where then was the remedy ? It is easy for us to say that it was to be found in liberty, in the permission to each new thought to develop itself as best it might ; but the very notion of religious liberty was as yet unheard of [1629], and even if it had been as familiar as it is now, its bare proclamation would have been of little avail. . . . The time would come when it would be understood that liberty of speech and action is all that either a majority or a minority can fairly claim. But that time had not yet arrived (vii. 39, 43).
>
> Even the intellectual perception of the value of toleration had not yet dawned upon the world. The obstacle was, however, not purely intellectual. The real difficulty was to know who was to begin. The problem as it presented itself to men of that generation was not whether they were to tolerate others, but whether they were to give to others the opportunity of being intolerant to themselves. Was Laud to allow Leighton to gather strength to sweep away the whole Church system of England ? Was Winthrop to allow the dissidents to gather strength to sweep away the whole Church system of New England ? It is only when a sentiment of mutual forbearance has sprung up which renders it improbable that the spread of any given opinion will be used to spread other opinions by force, that the principle of toleration can possibly commend itself to a wise people (vii. 158-9).

Gardiner's account of the code of bribery, and of its refinements, in the age of Bacon, is one good example of this passion for accurate perspective ; another is his review of Laud's position (' a lawyer in a rochet, and that not a lawyer of the highest sort ') ; or, better still, his tracing of the changes of attitude towards the prerogative. His patient analysis of Charles is a thousand times more telling than Macaulay's invective, and in the end, as has been remarked, he has no word of condemnation for the regicide. Gardiner's glory, then, apart from his exhaustless industry, his accuracy and equity, rests on his possession of the historic sense that enables him to recover, not the faces indeed, but the actual minds, of ' our vanished fathers,' and to make clear, while not unduly simplifying, the determining motives of men, of parties, and of national movements.

VII

Sir John Robert Seeley [1] (1834-95), being also a divine and a critical essayist, stands somewhat apart amongst the historians. He was a brilliant Cambridge classic; he held the chair of Latin at University College, London, when he published, anonymously, his *Ecce Homo*,[2] *A Survey of the Life and Work of Jesus* (1866). The authorship was not acknowledged for many years. The aim of the book is to treat Jesus, without prejudice, like any other great religious reformer: to pick out from the gospel texts the character of his moral teaching, and also of his supposed theocratic programme; and so to justify, in the light of each other, historic Christianity as an institution, and the thought of the founder. Other questions Seeley does not profess to ask or answer: whether anything like the doctrine of the churches was in the mind of Jesus, or whether Jesus held a true view of his own origin. But the supernatural, though much in the background, is by no means denied or ruled out. Jesus, we are told, did work miracles; were it not so, the fabric of the Christian cult would be shaken; but he displayed much 'temperance in the use of supernatural power': a sentence which, like the whole essay, failed to satisfy thoroughgoing minds of either extreme.

Long afterwards, in 1882, Seeley produced another speculative work, *Natural Religion*, this time under his name. The book was less popular and made less stir than *Ecce Homo*, but contains intenser thinking. It is one more endeavour to construct a working faith, mainly on naturalistic lines. But here again Seeley is seen abiding in a half-way house. In his closing pages he tells us that the supernatural element is after all to be retained, but as a kind of second string. Without it we might fall into pessimism; yet we must not have too much of it; it must not 'come in to upset the natural and turn life upside down'; still, there it is. The main purpose of the book, however, is to stretch the meaning of the term 'religion' and identify it with all the higher activities of the human spirit —civic, ethical, philosophical, artistic, and scientific. Even paganism, even pantheism, must be laid under judicious contribution. On this catholic foundation may be built an universal church, the soul of the state. There must be give and take on all hands, but doctrinal theology must give a good deal more than she takes. The term God may, or must, be retained for the sake of its associations. Seeley, in framing this ideal, was much influenced by Goethe, on whom he wrote a luminous essay, *Goethe Reviewed after Sixty Years*; and also by Wordsworth, whose nature-worship is impressed into the argument. For an historian, Seeley shows little sense of the depth of the cleavages in human opinion which must be mended before his dream can be realised. It has some affinities with that of Matthew Arnold, and some with that of the Comtists. The ruling conception is that artists, thinkers, and saints and simple souls are alike banded against their common enemy, who in the gospels is called 'the world.' Seeley's temper is always lofty, but his religious books lack the edge and clear outline that mark his historical thinking. As a critic of letters he is calm, plain, and pointed, in the best French academic manner: his style is still abstract, without much colour; and his two papers on Milton are a good example of his methods.

In 1869 he became Professor of Modern History at Cambridge. A keen, thought-propagating teacher, he now found his true calling. His first historical work on a large scale, *The Life and Times of Stein* (1878), relates the political and mental rebuilding of Germany. Stein is the chief actor, but Fichte, Humboldt, and Niebuhr, each of whom had powerfully influenced English thought, are also shown in clear outline and proportion. The English public now had a trustworthy account of one of the great national recoveries of modern times, and of the fateful growth of Prussia. Seeley was the first to digest the literature—since his day hugely augmented—of the subject, and the worth of his work was recognised in Germany. Yet the task gave little scope for his peculiar gifts. It is a minute narrative, and its wheels drive heavily. Seeley, however, excels in rejection of detail, in quick and lucid review, in reducing a complex story to its purest elements, and in tracing the large impelling forces of political history. His work stands to Carlyle's somewhat as anatomy, or at least as physiology, stands to portraiture. Both kinds are indispensable, though Seeley pours unjust scorn on the theory that the main affair of the historian is to present a picture of the past and the shades of contemporary opinion; for that opinion, he says, in judging of great events and issues, is commonly wrong. He is concerned with tracing causation; the persistent impersonal forces which may indeed work through, but which eclipse and outlast, the energies of great individuals. To Carlyle, who is concerned with scenes, and passages, and 'heroes,' history illustrates no law at all except the moral or providential; Seeley carries his opinion to an extreme in his short book on Napoleon, whom he regards, not very consistently, as at once the Ahriman of modern history, and the creature of external forces. But when he comes to his proper task his impersonal standpoint is better justified.

The Expansion of England in the Eighteenth Century (1883) and *The Growth of British Policy* (1895) are part of the same enterprise, and are filled with the same spirit. Seeley thinks of history as given for our political instruction, and of present politics as history for the guidance of the future statesman. The truth of the tenet is self-evident; and it not only does not clash with, but depends for its force upon, the doctrine that the historian must rid himself of party prepossessions, avoid judging past in the light of present standards, and see 'the thing as it really took place'; else the lessons taught by history to politics will be tainted at their source. Seeley himself needed no such warning; he had no party bias; he disliked equally the 'bombastic school,' which exults in the superior morality and governing capacity of the empire-founding Briton, and the pessimist, or 'little Englander,' who wishes us well out of our dangerous responsibilities. Imperialism, as he conceives it, is not, as with Froude, a passionate sentiment, but the acceptance of a long inevitable process pregnant with endless consequence. The 'expansion of England,' he says, has come almost unawares; historians have tended to treat our acquisitions (which are not 'conquests') in the East, the Pacific, and the New World as mere incidents; whereas they, and not the wrangle of party politics and the fall of cabinets, are the essence of the story. Seeley traces the expansion of Britain first in America and then in India. The process was utterly different, even opposite, in the two cases; but his conclusion in both is dead against disruption. He believes in drawing tighter the bond with the colonies and dependencies; and he thinks that, at least for a long while yet, the abandonment of India would be 'the most inexcusable of all conceivable crimes.' *The Expansion of England* is a book that illustrates its own precept; it affected opinion powerfully, and through opinion affairs; it is a piece of history written for the statesman.

The Growth of British Policy is more formal in cast, and carries the review much further back. The foreign policy of the sixteenth and seventeenth centuries is shown as the main formative influence in our history. This work, which was posthumously published, is also in the lecture form. The needs of the lecture, which is Seeley's natural unit, force him to leave out everything inessential; he does not exhaust the topic, and still less the pupil, but makes him think, and launches him on inquiries of his own. The story is made vivid without any of the usual aids; there is no painting, hardly an anecdote, little analysis of character, and not much humour, though plenty of sharp pertinence. Seeley's elegant and concise language is never obscure or oracular, though it runs to epigram. To generalise, to state a problem, to unravel the main threads of an intricate web, it is admirably fitted. There is something Gallic in Seeley's deft manipulation and presentation of general ideas. A good deal, no doubt, is sacrificed which more imaginative writers provide; but as an expounder of English history and policy from the oceanic point of view he did memorable work.

Here may be named, though he is not properly an historian, that accomplished publicist, journalist, university reformer, and life-long disputant, Goldwin Smith (1823-1910). His brilliant and restless mind had many facets. He began as a prize classic, and worked awhile at Virgil with Conington. He did far-reaching service on the Oxford University Commission of 1850. For eight years he was Regius Professor of History at Oxford; and though he had not been drilled in investigation, and added little to historical knowledge, he brought the breath of contemporary life and thought into his discourses. His *Lectures* of the years 1859-61 are a singular medley. In one he pleads for the basing of historical on humanistic studies; in others he attacks scientific determinism, jeers at the new conception of progress, defends the providential view of history, and denounces the supposed sceptical consequences of Mansel's Bampton lectures. The Positivist 'calendar of great men' and the speculations of Francis Newman are also castigated. Goldwin Smith certainly could manage, and loved to manage, the whip. He was also capable of condensed, effective, and impassioned rhetoric. His tone is rather different in his discourse on the foundation of the American colonies, and comes nearer to that of the historian. Meantime he was also deep in politics; in his volume of collected letters to the press, entitled *The Empire* (1863), he appears as an old liberal of the purest stamp and undoubtedly a 'bonny fighter,' thirsty for the dust that he raises. His collection of opinions has a curious interest to-day. He is all for the cession of the Ionian Islands, and also of Gibraltar. The colonies and dependencies he would see independent realms. To India we are at present committed—it must remain British in a sense; yet, in the long run, it should be no longer ruled from home, but by an absolute Governor-General—'by a line of able and honourable despots.'

Goldwin Smith's language and tone here and elsewhere seem to show a close study of Burke; there is the same attempt at condensations and richness, and the same appeal to general principles. The result, of course, has not the same permanence. Goldwin Smith wrote profusely, always pointedly, often eloquently, but mostly on the sand.

After ceaseless penwork against slavery, against the South, against Governor Eyre, and against university conservatism, Goldwin Smith, while in mid-career, broke with Oxford and England, resigned his chair, and migrated to Cornell University. Here he flung himself into the work of organisation and teaching; he also found himself standing up for the old country during the *Alabama* quarrel. In the last phase, after 1871, he lived in Canada, published journals, *de omnibus rebus*, sometimes wholly written by his own hand, argued for the annexation of Canada to the United States, and fired off pamphlets, books, and letters upon almost every public question. Two of his later works were upon the political history of the United States. He was anti-imperialist, anti-clerical, and anti-home-ruler. The course of political events seldom went as he would, but every one read the sallies in the English press by the tireless old Ishmaelite in Toronto. Goldwin Smith had his own refuge from controversy. His style softens into a different sort of felicity when he turns to pure literature, and his short volumes on Cowper (1880) and on Jane Austen (1892) are unexpectedly sympathetic, as well as skilfully laid out and written. But his great natural faculty of words was chiefly spent in warfare.

VIII

I have only professed to touch, and that in their relation to literature, on certain leading writers; the professional chroniclers of historical scholarship during the period have many names [1] to add to the list. And it is needful to break off at an arbitrary date. The year 1880 has, in this chapter, no special significance, for the story is continuous down to the present day. The army of inquirers, soundly trained in modern method, and with their conscience well steeled against mere literature, has grown steadily, like their body of production; and the events of the Great War alone will find work for their own and the next generation. I will but mention three historians of mark who prolonged the great tradition during the last quarter of the century. Some of them had passed their noviceship long before. Mandell Creighton (1843-1901), latterly

Bishop of London, had issued several shorter volumes before his great *History of the Papacy* began to appear in 1882; a work of acknowledged authority and equity, and also of signal detachment of view. The noble labours of Frederic William Maitland (1850-1906), a master of the institutional and social history of the Middle Ages, and also a born writer, are more recent still. The unique career of Lord Acton (1834-1902) opens much sooner. In the early sixties he is seen, a young man of immense information and courage, striving, in journals like the *Rambler* and *Home and Foreign Review*, to establish a liberal form of Roman Catholicism, founded on the scientific and faithful study of history. Acton figures much in the correspondence of Newman, and still more largely in the *Life of Gladstone*. His magazines were silenced by the Ultramontane party, but he was again in the fray in 1870, fighting against the decree of papal infallibility, which seemed to strike at his dream of conciliating the spirit of science and liberty with the old faith; to which, nevertheless, he remained firm. In the idea of freedom, its progressive conception and realisation, Acton came to find the key to the purpose of history, and the safeguard of the hopes of man. The work of his life was to be a history of freedom on a great scale. He gathered vast materials, but only produced massive fragments in the form of lectures and articles. Acton was said to know more than any Englishman of his time, and he knew too much to accomplish his task. He had written much polemic, and also many historical studies, during twenty years; but his weightiest body of work was produced after 1880. As the founder of the *English Historical Review*, as the successor to Seeley in the chair of Modern History at Cambridge (1895), and as the planner and inspirer of the *Cambridge Modern History*, Acton exerted a profound and shaping influence upon the work of others. His manner in speech and writing was finished and burnished to the point of artifice, and often allusive and obscure in its conciseness. It is the English of a man who thinks in several languages. But it well reflects not only his learning and his grasp, but also the grandeur of his vision, and the austerity of his moral and intellectual habit. He carries to an extreme the high ethical view of history, and almost refuses to the historian the right of allowing for the moral standards of another age; a refusal which, however it may influence Acton's judgement of values, could not for a moment alter his resolve to win the truth at whatever cost.

IX

This chapter may conclude with a note on two writers who saw history in the making. 'Napier,' observed the Duke of Wellington, 'may be somewhat Radical, but, by God, his history is the only one which tells the truth as to the events of the Peninsular War.' The remark was handsome, for Napier speaks freely of some of the Duke's miscalculations. But the Duke's verdict is borne out in substance by the modern historians. Napier's hate of the Spaniards, his enthusiasm for Napoleon, and his views on home politics may call to be discounted ; but his real topic is the campaign itself. The great work of Sir William Francis Patrick Napier [1] (1785-1860) began to appear in 1828 ; the last volume came in 1840 ; the full title is *History of the War in the Peninsula and in the South of France, from the Year 1807 to the Year 1814*. 'The author,' he says, 'was either an eye-witness of what he relates, or acquired his knowledge from those who were.' Napier played an illustrious part ; he was at Coruña, Talavera, Badajoz, the Nivelle, and many other scenes that he describes. 'You knew what you were about,' said a friend, 'and were not afraid of anything.' Napier seems to have gone through 'anything' without the thought of making anything into literature. After coming home, he slowly formed the plan of writing a commentary on the war ; but this grew into a history. His primary motive was to vindicate his hero and leader, Sir John Moore. He first took the story down to Coruña, but was moved by its reception to go on. He was also provoked by Southey's *History*, which he describes as 'smooth and clear in style, but nerveless as the author's mind' ; also it was prejudiced on the wrong side, on the Tory side ; and Napier, unlike many soldiers, had strong popular sympathies. He would now be called a moderate Radical ; he was a delighted reader of Cobbett. He was also encouraged by the unexpected afflux of material. The Duke allowed him to see many official documents, and to the Duke the work is dedicated. He received important information from Soult, of whose talent he makes the fullest acknowledgement. The *History* was greeted with abundant criticism, to which Napier replied, cudgelling back with a will ; but its success was fairly gained : it became a classic, and it was translated into many languages.

Napier took to letters late, and was at first backward with his pen. He was in a sense self-taught. As a boy he had rejoiced in the same romances as Don Quixote, and their breath is in his pages. but for his task he had gone to the right school, the school of the classics, studying Cæsar and Thucydides: and some of their qualities he really had, or acquired. The effects of the Renaissance are eternal; Napier, the tried warrior, writes like Montaigne or Machiavelli, with a classic example ever on his lips, and finding in the ancient world some lesson of chivalry or parallel of policy. These graces and decorations are naïf, not artificial, and they grow naturally out of the heroic theme:

> Epaminondas, mortally wounded at Mantinea, was anxious for the recovery of his shield. Moore, mortally wounded at Coruña, sustained additional torture rather than part with his sword! The Theban hero's fall dismayed and paralysed his victorious troops. It was not so with the British at Coruña.

In the same way, his more reflective style, the excellence of which is sometimes overlooked in the colour and energy of his descriptions, is often packed with analysis; the scene might be Melos or Corcyra:

> Former failures there were to avenge on one side, and on both leaders who furnished no excuse for weakness in the hour of trial; the possession of Badajoz was become a point of personal honour with the soldiers of each nation; but the desire for glory on the British part was dashed with a hatred of the citizens from an old grudge, and recent toil and hardship, with much spilling of blood, had made many incredibly savage: for these things, which render the noble-minded averse from cruelty, harden the vulgar spirit.

Napier, by acclamation, is held to possess the cardinal gifts of the military historian: science, grasp of strategy and of intricate operations, insight into motive, and lucidity in exposition. All these gifts might be coldly exhibited, and the result speak only to the brain. But Napier's language burns with the flame of his personal memories and of his patriot soul. He keeps his head, yet he writes in a manly passionate style, not without sallies and exclamations, but without the consciousness and studied epigram of Kinglake, another great describer. He has also a saving streak of Plutarch in his composition. The brilliant, endlessly quoted and quotable pages on the fight of Salamanca, the siege of Tarifa, and the retreat from Burgos, show his mastery both of subject and of form; and that kind of work forms the staple of his narrative: but he is also strong in heroic episode. His *History*, as he remarked, 'is no whining affair.' No one could have told better the story of the scouting officer, Captain Colquhoun

Grant, who was caught, complimented, and betrayed by Marmont; who then, escaping to Paris, 'frequented the coffee-houses, and visited the theatres boldly,' and who finally got off, armed with the certificate of a discharged American sailor, to the British fleet.

Napier worked hard for twenty years after finishing his *History*. He gave much of his time to narrating and defending the actions of his brother, Sir Charles Napier, who won Scinde in the old imperial fashion. The histories of *The Conquest of Scinde* (1845) and of the *Administration of Scinde* (1851) are vehement, generous, and partisan writing. *The Life and Opinions of General Sir C. J. Napier* (1857) was another *apologia* in the same spirit.

It is natural to associate with Napier the name of another military historian, also of a high and virile temper, namely Alexander William Kinglake [1] (1809-91), the chronicler of the Crimean War. Kinglake was not a soldier, but first made his name as a traveller and observer. His ever-young *Eöthen* (1844), with its engaging arrogance, its heady unabashed rhetoric, and its light wit, records his wanderings in Servia, Turkey, Palestine, and Egypt. Fidelity to the fleeting mood, a refusal to admire in ways expected, and the 'notion of dwelling precisely upon those matters which happened to interest me, and upon none other'; that is Kinglake's pose, or rather it is a good resolution, which he carries through without mercy to others or to himself. His tempers and passing lusts of the eye, his slight shame and greater relish in hustling Orientals, his amusing inflated raptures in presence of the Sphinx ('Mark this, ye breakers of images,' etc.), and his humorous impressions of Lady Hester Stanhope, as well as his highly edited talks with Pashas and officials, are a mixture of light comedy and pleasant rant. Whether he writes well or ill, he is always himself, and little debt to Beckford, Hope, or other forerunners can be detected. It does *Eöthen* wrong to take it heavily, but it still retains its savour.

Kinglake's early unsigned reviews in the *Quarterly* [2] have something of the same liveliness; there is a flippant one on the 'rights of women' (1844), a cause with which the voice from the East ('Eöthen') does not sympathise; and another, on Eliot Warburton's work, *The Crescent and the Cross*, is a mere excuse for a tirade on 'the French lake,' namely the Mediterranean, and for anti-Gallic ebullitions.

Kinglake retained his vein of mingled prejudice and chivalry, his whimsicality and irony, and his eye for colour and adventure.

These graces and foibles were again to come into play, and his epical skill and historical judgement were to be tried, in a sterner field. He saw some warfare in Algiers. In 1854 he found himself in the Crimea, still an unofficial traveller, but the guest of Lord Raglan, whose widow afterwards entrusted to Kinglake her husband's official papers. Kinglake saw the Alma and much else, and stayed on till the beginning of the siege of Sebastopol. He went home, and started on the task which occupied him, first and last, for a whole generation. He developed a genius for digesting a vast mass of evidence, printed, manuscript, and oral, into a clear and living narrative. The first two of his eight volumes appeared in 1863, the last two in 1887. The full title is *The Invasion of the Crimea, its Origin, and an Account of its Progress down to the Death of Lord Raglan*. The successive volumes roused fierce criticism ; and Kinglake's political opinions, his accounts of military operations, his unfairness towards persons and even whole nations, as well as his scale, and proportioning, and style, were all viciously assailed. The opinions of experts still clash over his book ; there appears to be no complete and authoritative criticism upon it ; and, though so heavily shelled and battered, it has not yielded its position. Some of its obvious faults would have sunk a writer of less mark and energy.

Kinglake's accounts of policy and statecraft are warped by preconceived ideas. Not only partisan reviewers but historical students have condemned his obsession against Napoleon the Third. Much of his work in this department is little more than bitter and brilliant, but not first-rate, pamphleteering. Gladstone remarked that the book was too bad to live and too good to die. Kinglake's pictures of his heroes, like Lord Stratford de Redcliffe and Lord Raglan, do the heroes no good, being often in a strain of absurd eulogy. His tribute to Todleben and other heroic Russians is generous, and is more reasonably uttered. Todleben himself, though admiring Kinglake, called his work, so we are told, a romance rather than a history. Kinglake is certainly safer as a painter of incident than as a judge of character. Apart, however, from certain obvious excesses of admiration or dislike, he is even painfully anxious to measure out military glory and censure justly. He worked very hard to get the narrative clear, and the threads distinct, and the details accurate. It was objected that eight volumes were excessive for recording the events of two years ; but it is a sufficient answer that we read to the end. It was not Napier's method ; but Kinglake wished to show, as though on a cinematograph, all the scenes and stages of a confused, bloody, and momentous affair. And he leaves a wonderfully clear impression; the march of the drama is not obscured by the pauses which he makes to relate individual feats of heroism. Nor is a whole long volume, upon such a plan, too long for such a battle as Inkerman, though it may take longer to read through than the battle took to happen.

Kinglake's style was much copied and admired, and even more widely abused. At least it could not make us angry, if it did not keep us awake; a quality for which we must have a kindness, seeing how soporifically many histories are written. Matthew Arnold called it Corinthian, and other hard names; and though his own tricks are not much better than Kinglake's, it is hard to deny his charges. The *Quarterly Review* hit the worst blot when it said that 'events of the most unequal importance are related in the same stilted and magniloquent periods.' And it is certainly an unsafe style, full of false hot colours, and too often overcharged. Rhetorical devices, such as the use of an elaborate icy politeness towards uncongenial persons, are much overdone. And perhaps the writing is too visibly filed to the last point of acuity; it is possible to be too highly finished and polished. Yet somehow these vices are not fatal. Kinglake can describe with the clearest precision, whether he is treating of events or of motives; and in commemorating heroic behaviour he can even be simple. The life always runs high in his pages, and sometimes we catch the emotion of the eye-witness, as in his account of the stricken men whom he saw after the battle of the Alma:

> For the most part, the wounded men lay silent. Now and then a man would gently ask for water, or would seek to know when it was likely that he would be moved and cared for; but, in general, the wounded were so little inclined to be craving after help or sympathy, that for dignity and composure they were almost the equals of the dead.

CHAPTER VIII

CHURCH AND LETTERS

I

THE Oxford,[1] or Tractarian, or Puseyite, or Anglo-Catholic, or High Church movement, and the Anglo-Roman movement that ensued upon it, may now be outlined in their relation to letters; which is the smallest aspect, no doubt, of the phenomenon. A fierce, if insular, battle raged, and is not yet extinguished; the frontiers between faith and reason, the canon of doctrine, the connexion of church and crown, the seat of clerical discipline, and the modes of ritual and observance, were all in debate. The 'dead ground' lying between philosophy and theology was strewn with relics of the fray. One of the results was a body of writing which has not all perished, and without which our view of the Romantic revival is incomplete. The Oxford authors took their share in that return to the past, and notably to the Middle Ages, which had already been quickened in art and poetry and fiction. But they went further than the poets and critics; for in the Middle Ages they found not only a treasury of stories and pictures, and food for the fancy, but a school of dogma, and a link in the chain of revelation and authority descending from the Apostles. And they went back further still, in the same quest; they went to the early Church. And in so doing they disregarded much of the mediæval mind, even in the field of religion. Not for them, by supposition, are Wyclif and Langland, or the 'prelude to the Reformation'; the mass of pious-amorous poetry is foreign to their severe temper, and so are the founders of humanism, Petrarch and Boccaccio. They take from the Middle Ages just what they want. Traces, however, of Dante, may perhaps be found in *The Dream of Gerontius*; and one of the best introductions to the poet, the essay by Dean Church (1878), is a tardy fruit of the Anglican revival.

The Tractarians owe a little to the poetry of the preceding age. The author of *The Christian Year*, and the still gentler poets, Frederick Faber and Isaac Williams, have Wordsworth behind them, partly as a watcher of nature, and still more as a devotee of the English establishment. Newman studied the pure plain prose of Southey. Coleridge had tried, in his own way, to reanimate the pattern of a national church, with its exalted 'clerisy,' and its old doctrine reinterpreted; and, despite his tendency to attenuate doctrine into symbol, Coleridge attracted Newman. Scott, above all, had awakened the historical imagination, and with it a general, genial prejudice in favour of the past. His influence is seen in the efforts of Newman and Wiseman, and of Kingsley in another camp, to apply his method to the moving or heroic incidents of early Christian times. *Callista* appeared in 1856, *Fabiola* in 1854, *Hypatia* in 1853. As it chances, of the three, the 'broad churchman' shows the greatest sympathy and power.

A second literary influence was that of our seventeenth-century divines. The Anglicans, in the course of their argument, soon came on these monumental writers, beginning with Hooker, and took off some of the rust that had gathered upon them during the 'age of reason.' Their learning, their blocks of solid reasoning were willingly appropriated; and Pusey, in point of erudition, could be claimed as one of the true breed. But after all the age of reason, with its conception of modern prose, has come between. The quaintness and cumbrousness of the old writers are shunned, in favour of a plainer, more transparent style. Yet the new Anglicans are narrower than the old. They have, on the whole, less lay culture; they are less weighty minds; they are not exactly, like Taylor or Chillingworth, to be honoured as preachers of toleration; and they have left less good literature behind them. Where, amongst them, are the counterparts of the liberal Hales, and of the large-minded, Aristotelian Barrow? The best writer of the school is a man of problematical, *abnormal* mind, of the strangest texture; that, precisely, is the interest of Newman; and he is great, when great he is, just because he is not representative. Newman reminds us, at his best, more of William Law than of any seventeenth-century author; he has the same severe earnestness, and the same turn for irony, and for the moral dissection of the backslider or self-deceiver; some of his 'characters' might have come out of the *Serious Call*. Nor must we forget that he also schooled himself amongst heretics. His notion of the 'sceptic' is formed largely on his memories of Hume and Gibbon; the full-blooded unbeliever of his own day he seldom pictures, save in general and dreadful terms. The style of Gibbon he knows only to avoid, save now and then in his historical sketches; his own periodic, flowing sentence, when it comes, has a different drapery altogether; he prefers, especially before his conversion, to be short and simple. He read Addison, and their affinities are manifest. The fatal simplicity of Hume may have helped to temper his dialectical weapon. We know that he liked Johnson, but as writers they are nothing akin.

All this, however, comes to little, and the literary origins of the Tractarians and the converts remain somewhat elusive. As for their salvage, it is hard to refer at length here to more than one of them. Yet it will be right to attend awhile to William Ward, to James Bowling Mozley, and to Dean Church, if only to see Newman in truer perspective; he comes out, under the process, as more of a writer than they, but less of a thinker. A history of doctrine or of ecclesiastical learning would apportion the emphasis very differently.

The 'movements' produced, first and last, a surprising bulk of ecclesiastical journalism. The bibliography would fill many of these pages. Few even of the old irritant manifestoes—book or memoir or sermon—now retain their sting. A chapter could be given to the political, anti-Erastian side of the campaign alone. One of the provocative forces, if not the deeper ground, of the Oxford revival was the protest against the temper which treated the Church as a mere branch of the civil establishment. The Crown appointed the sacred officials, and the findings of a lay council might determine what was sound belief. The contrary view, in Gladstone's language, was that the Church, an *imperium in imperio,* had in the bishops 'the ordained hereditary witnesses of the truth, conveying it to us through an unbroken series from our Lord Jesus Christ and his Apostles.' This note of political independence is heard again and again in *Tracts for the Times* (1833-41); it had been sounded in Keble's sermon on *National Apostasy*, preached on the 'birthday of the movement,' July 14, 1833. It is repeated in the *Remains* (1838-9) of Richard Hurrell Froude,[1] the Rupert of the war, who died young in 1836. Froude's amusing and fanatical flings at the heroes of the Reformation enraged the 'Protestants,' and disconcerted the 'high and dry' upholders of the Establishment. His high and fierce courage, his incapacity for compromise, and his natural affinity with the older Church goaded the more hesitant mind of Newman, who always kept his sharpest arrows for the Erastian. This trait, we know, has persisted in the High Churchmen. Gladstone, in his volume (1838) on *The State in its Relations with the Church*, diverged from the rest in a fashion that is not unjustly described in Macaulay's essay ; but the book only lives as the occasion of that typically Whig retort.

Another mass of writing was produced by the Anglo-Roman controversies of the period. But the *Ideal Church* of William George Ward, the appeals of Wiseman, and the harangues of Manning are now covered with dust. Much capable writing lies buried in the religious periodicals, which rose greatly in credit during the half century. A competent map, or survey, is much to be wished for of the material to be found in the *British Critic*, led by Newman in his Anglican days ; in the Ultramontane *Dublin Review*, as conducted by Ward ; and in the *Home and Foreign Review* (the successor of the *Rambler*), the capable organ (1862) of the liberalising Catholics, led by Sir John Acton. Here again the issues are political as much as doctrinal ; and, from the nature of the case, historical inquiry on the one part and philosophical analysis on the other were notably advanced. But these enterprises can only be named in passing. For literature, the central figure is John Henry Newman,[1] who was born in London in 1801, became Fellow of Oriel in 1822, joined the Church of Rome in 1845, was made Cardinal in 1879, and lived till 1890.

II

Apart from his preaching, Newman's talent for words flowered little before he was thirty. In 1832-3 he visited the Mediterranean, found out that he was a poet, and wrote about a hundred brief pieces, including *The Pillar of the Cloud* ('Lead, kindly Light'). They show the hidden, the ecstatic, the aspiring side of his nature ; he was lonely always, and cherished his loneliness jealously. Somewhat ruggedly he sings, or rather speaks in rhyme, of human vanity and unrighteousness, and of his craving for rare and lofty consolations. This mood may have been fed from the first by his Evangelical upbringing ; and certain traces of an original bleakness long appear in his musings. Already, however, he had enlarged his mind through his intercourse at Oriel with the clerical 'intellectuals,' headed by Whately. He was soon to break with them, but the experience fostered his dream of a large ecclesiastical communion.

The 'movement of 1833,' as he liked to call it, brought out Newman's turn for dispute and exposition. The next twelve years, ending with his conversion, really inaugurate his prose. He became the living voice, the fighting chieftain, of the

Tractarian rebels. His works, during this phase, divide into treatises, tracts, and sermons. The tracts went on till 1841, the sermons went on all the time. Of the treatises the chief (besides the stiffly-written work on the *Arians of the Fourth Century*, and the *Lectures on Justification*) is the *Prophetical Office of the Church* (1837), which was long afterwards, in his Roman days, reissued with destructive notes as *The Via Media of the Anglican Church*. It brings to a point the main contentions of the once-famous, the once-perturbing *Tracts for the Times*, which must now be strange reading, if read they ever are, for many of the Anglican fold.

Newman wrote about one-third of the ninety tracts ; and their literary interest comes in, and goes out, it must be said, with Newman. Not that he is always easy to recognise, for his imagination is kept down ; he is sharp, precise, and pugnacious, and he courts simplicity and astringency. He draws the mouth up like an unripe sloe. His fierceness is genuine enough, but it is also politic. The opening numbers are 'written as a man might give notice of a fire or inundation, to startle all who heard him.' '*Choose your side*,' he cries in No. 1 to the stagnant clergy who are slow to proclaim 'our apostolical descent.' He had the instincts of a superlative pressman ; the same faculty is felt long afterwards in the papers called *The Tamworth Reading-Room*, and in his *riposte* to Kingsley. Sometimes the cold fierceness is dropped ; in No. 47 there is an exhibition, astonishing enough, of pulpit self-righteousness : 'When we say that God has done more for us than for the Presbyterians. . . .' Not all these numbers can be certainly fathered upon Newman, but he has been credited with them. In No. 73 the writer flies out at 'rationalism,' on which he was not very well informed ; in No. 85, on *Scripture and the Catholic Creed*, the basis of the *via media* is laid with elaborate skill. In No. 90, which raised the storm and was condemned, and which Newman wrote, the position of the English, as a 'branch' of the Catholic Church, is defended by a special reading of the Articles, which seems now strained enough to the lay reader. The plea, in effect, is that the Articles only condemn certain vulgar perversions of Catholic doctrine, the acceptance of the doctrine itself being implied in the condemnation. The aim of No. 90 was honestly tactical ; it was to keep within the Church the extreme spirits that were ready to fly Romewards. Newman's honesty in all this need not be doubted, any more than his generalship.

The *Tracts* had altered their complexion in the course of

their issue, with the formal accession of Pusey to the cause. They became learned and solid; some of them are books. Pusey discoursed on fasting or on baptism, exhibiting an immense procession of Caroline and other theologians. With Newman and Keble, he also edited the *Library of the Fathers*, in many volumes of translation; the series went on, and outlived the schism, and was a true contribution to scholarship. A number of saints' lives, extracts from divines, and the like, were also annexed to the *Tracts*. There were other contributors, including Keble, Hurrell Froude, and also Isaac Williams, whose articles on 'reserve' caused superfluous alarm. Many of the numbers are miserably feeble; there are imaginary dialogues of clergymen with prize boys who are grounded in the right arguments against the Erastian. It would be hard to find anywhere a more bigoted and sawdusty page than the unidentified No. 36, *An Account of the Religious Sects as at present Existing in England*. It is a relief to go back to Newman, in his true capacity as a preacher, a dreamer, and a shepherd.

We have to read in the long-subsequent *Apologia* his own story of the inner struggle that came to a crisis before 1845. The vulgar enemy, the alarmed friend, and Rome herself, saw the goal to which Newman, at first unawares, was making. But none of them saw the path he took; nor did he see it himself till late in the day; and he spent his time—with a sincerity of feeling that is more seldom questioned now, whatever may be thought of his mental processes—in fortifying and defending his high Anglican halting-place, and in warning others off the country that lay beyond; warnings which he had later, penitentially, to retract. The chief material for judging Newman's history during these years is to be found in the *Prophetical Office*, in his last lecture on the 'difficulties of Anglicans,' and above all in his letters; in these the story is given from point to point, with all the vacillations, and not as it is rounded off afterwards in memory, or used for controversy.

III

Many of Newman's sermons are doctrinal arguments, like his treatises. The Anglican series 'on the theory of religious belief' anticipates his essay on the *Development of Doctrine*. They contain a scornful picture of a 'theophilanthropist,' who wants happiness and makes much of God's kindness, but little of sin and God's justice. Many other sermons turn on the dividing-line between faith and reason, a subject which restlessly exercised Newman's mind. Nor can his doctrine be severed from his moral and imaginative preaching. Emotion and fancy must rest upon a hard rock of dogma; and so dogma in its turn becomes charged with passion. But his higher style and vision are less often found in his controversial pages. When he speaks as a seer and artist, it is unmeaning to argue or contradict him, and it is then that he is a great writer.

'Come, long sought for, tardily found, the desire of the eyes, the joy of the heart. . . .'—'At length the white throne of God, at length the beatific vision!'—'The year is worn out; spring, summer, autumn, each in turn, have brought their gifts and done their utmost; but they are over, and the end is come. All is past and gone, all has failed, all has sated. We are tired of the past; we would not have the seasons longer; and the austere weather which succeeds, though ungrateful to the body, is in tone with our feelings and acceptable.'—'Life passes, riches fly away, popularity is fickle, senses decay, the world changes, friends die. One alone is constant; One alone is true to us; One alone can be true; One alone can be all things to us; One alone can supply our needs. . . .'

These were the plangent tones, this was the musical voice, that sank into Newman's hearers. The reader can recover in some degree the effect that he produced, of which there are many descriptions. The unearthly note of lyrical prose recurs at all times in his life, but is never purer than in these Oxford sermons. The style is mostly so simple that the speaker's idiosyncrasy cannot be seized through any analysis of the form. But we can begin to piece together, by reference to his letters and other works, some of his ruling and haunting ideas. He is disheartened by the changes and decay of visible things, and appalled by the aspect of the natural man, and of what the natural man has made of the world and of history. This it is that drags Newman out of the solitude, which he shares with his Maker, and in which he is 'luminously' conscious only of those two presences. The world is a veil, 'beautiful,' he says in a letter, but 'still a veil.' But one thing at least in the world is real, namely evil. '*If* there be a God,' he says later, '*since* there is a God, the human race is implicated in some terrible aboriginal calamity.' History is a bad dream, hope falls to pieces, without that *if* and that *since*. The children of Adam, left to themselves, simply work out their own curse. This is an orthodox view enough, but Newman holds it in a literal way and with a living intensity. For a precisely opposite one, we can turn to the representation, in the prose dreams of William Morris, of the 'children of Adam' as *he* sees them; the kindly, beautiful lovers, craftsmen, and warriors of the future, not exempt from anger and failings, but living in brotherhood, and unperturbed by fears, as they are unmoved by hopes, of the hereafter. It is this innate mood which determines the note of Newman as a preacher of conduct. His religion is often one of gloom, denunciation, fear, and distrust of human nature. In the rigours of his school, in the diaries of Hurrell Froude and the youthful Pattison, there is the same note. Some of Newman's sentences are nightmares ; the restraint of the form conceals their sinister character. It is the same temper that sharpens his bent for moral analysis—for 'realising,' as he says, 'our more recondite feelings happily and convincingly.' He does not speak much against crime or vice, they are too remote from him ; but he is a skilled surgeon, a ruthless confessor, when he touches on the struggles of the waverer or the Protean temptations of the 'world.' He deals in sarcasms and threats of judgement. And his expression is often classical, however little his ideas and temper may attract us.

IV

An Essay on the Development[1] *of Christian Doctrine* (1845) was written while Newman was 'on his deathbed as regards the Anglican Church,' and was finished, with a lyrical warning to the reader 'not to determine that to be the truth which you wish to be so,' when the struggle was over. In order to be more telling, it was printed without revision by Rome. The date is significant. Hegel, twenty years before, had expounded the philosophy of history. The world, in his view, was a theatre on which the human spirit and the divine idea slowly unfolded themselves through an incessant clash of contradictions. Hegel was little known in England, and to Newman was apparently not known at all. It was also the hour of the earlier Comtist zealots, the importers of the *Philosophie positive*, for whom theology was only a primitive stage, doomed to obsolescence, in the march of truth ; not therefore to be accounted the queen of sciences on any terms. Newman does not appear ever to allude to this reprobate theory, and his general apathy to lay thought except in certain restricted forms is noticeable. But he was all the more original, or rather independent, in pleading that truth, by a divine inevitable process, is purged and *developed* in the course of history. Development was not yet a current biological notion in 1845. Religious truth, says Newman, is beaten out by the agelong clash of heresy with authority; in the original revelation, its dogmas are only implicit, but they are drawn out more and more fully, and never quite finally, in successful official pronouncements, which are themselves made under supernatural guidance. He propounds certain tests of truth; the chief of which are the continuous identity, the adaptiveness, the assimilative capacity, and the power to survive, of a really vital doctrine, as distinguished from a mere 'corruption' however long-lived. These requirements prove to be satisfied only by the creed of Rome. The argument is really an appeal to the event. But apart from this application, Newman has a true and distinct vision of the life and fortunes of an idea: how it exists at first only as a germ, grows under the stress of combat with other ideas, meets new conditions as they come, and is tried in numberless arenas; how it satisfies fresh needs of mankind as they rise up to challenge it; until at last it is crystallised into a general formula, or explicit truth, which lay within it from the beginning. Such a test certainly admits of being applied to the scientific concept of evolution, or to the idea of liberty, of which Lord Acton hoped to write the history. Newman applied it to dogma; and he has been of course criticised by all who deny the supernatural inspiration of his tribunal, or who cannot swallow the view that the full-blown doctrines of the churches are 'implicit' in the untechnical language of the gospels. The study of comparative religion, which grew up after his day, has widened the whole issue; but his book is notable as an early essay in that science. He wrote it not simply as an historian or philosopher, but also as a record of his own mental history, and as an appeal to others. With all its acumen, its manner is stiff and embarrassed. This may be due to Newman's want of conversance with philosophical, as distinct from theological, literature. The same want is evident later, in the *Grammar of Assent*, but there the style has become flexible and easy. In the *Essay*, as in the *Grammar*, we feel that he is coining his terminology as he goes along. The *Essay*, moreover, reflects his transitional stage, as he painfully struggles with his own mind and affections, in retreat at Littlemore.

V

The crisis over, Newman undergoes a great relief and unbending of the spirit. For five years he does little but preach; and also he writes a novel, a 'story of a convert,' *Loss and Gain*, a string of dreary conversations touched with gleams of humour.

Then, in 1850, he lets himself go, in his lectures on *The Difficulties of Anglicans*: a piercing call to his old friends, some of whom were hopefully, others doubtfully, moving in his own tracks, while others were always to stay behind. These discourses are affectionate to the point of tears, ironical to the point of mischief, and relentless to the point of cruelty. They show Newman's gift, which is one of the sources of his power, of getting into the skin, and speaking with the voice, of a real or supposed objector, who in this instance is his own, his not long since discarded, self. He tries to shut off every loophole from the wavering Tractarian, who can neither change the English Church, nor yet form an inner church, or a 'branch church,' or a sect. Rome is the only logical goal of the 'movement of 1833.' Newman thought so; and the rationalist may think so too, and the Protestant. Still, such has not been the historical outcome; the High Church, within the English pale, has grown and persisted, with results that must soon be glanced at, in the field of letters, learning, and theological thought; it is not only an affair of ritual and of clerical politics. Newman lived to see, if not to recognise all this; at the time, he turns and rends his old *alma mater*, and weeps over her, and makes fun of her, and lashes himself and her. The effect is not agreeable even to a detached reader; the inclination, for so it must be called, to *scratch*, is too strong. But Newman always had a streak of womanish temper, which, to apply a phrase of his own, 'much resembles a nun's anger, being a sweet acid.'

The *Lectures on the Present Position of Catholics in England* are a retort to the No-Popery clamour of the hour, following on the proclamation of the English Catholic sees. The addresses were spoken in 1851, to the lay brothers of the Birmingham Oratory, who were to go forth and stem the popular illusions concerning the Roman Church. The immediate audience was thus a domestic one; and the tone is often that of savage, witty parody, running even into farce. We can imagine the strange angry laughter of the hearers. The picture of John Bull seeing red and running amok is hardly overdrawn, though it is slightly tainted with the vulgarity of its subject; and it is marked by an almost hysterical tone of contempt. There is wit in the sketch of the young Protestant Scripture Reader, who strays in to Benedictions, and 'finds four priests, a young priest with a wand, and a whole congregation, worshipping a gold star glittering like diamonds, with a lamp in it.' Newman, in spite of his appeals, has few illusions: he sees that however tolerance may increase among the educated, and conversions grow, John Bull will not be changed, and England will hardly be saved. The passion of the time is reflected in Newman's fierce humour. In these lectures he attacked Achilli, the disreputable unfrocked priest, who won an action against him for libel. In later editions the pages on Achilli are left out; they show how Newman might have been a power at the bar; and in their place stands the legend, a perfectly fair and just one, *de illis quæ sequebantur posterorum judicium sit*. The book is one of the most remarkable that Newman wrote; it amounts to the portraiture of a *character*—that of the bloodshot Protestant, whose blindness is an act of his will, and who, multiplied by millions, stands for an undying enemy. This person, indeed, is Newman's bogey; and there is room for some writer of equal power, who has not yet arisen, to describe Newman's notion of the communions of Chalmers and Wesley. However, it is the Evangelical Churchman that chiefly moves his ire. Alien to either side is the historical view that the various religious societies and their articles arise in response to the needs of various natures, types, and races.

The *Discourses to Mixed Congregations*, a gathering of Newman's earlier sermons as a convert, faithfully reflect the change in his chameleon temper. The delicate balance of tone has gone, the reticent though impassioned sobriety has broken down. The polemical parts are less restrained than before, and Newman is harsher to the Church he has left than he ever was to the Church whither he has travelled. The note of revulsionary scorn is loud. The devotional parts are also of another stamp; there is both loss and gain to notice. The unction is of a new kind, the rhetoric is more Southern, more Latin, and the preacher dwells with an almost florid opulence on the poetry of dogma and symbol; the series of sermons on the Virgin is an example. Newman feels that he has reached his true home, and the note, which we miss in the Anglican discourses, of delighting to believe without restraint, is continually heard. But the magical, the Platonic touch, with its exquisite propriety and nicety, has departed, or become rarer. In fact, Newman tries, much more than of old, to *excite* by his oratory; to do what he had reproved before, in his sermons on the *Danger of Accomplishments*, where he is a thorough Platonist in his distrust of fiction, poetry, oratory, and singing, as likely to 'excite emotions without ensuring correspondent practice, and so destroy the connection between feeling and acting.'

VI

Newman never shows more courage, or is more himself, than when he has to find his own chart for a nice and dangerous course. The lectures and articles that are gathered up under the title *The Idea of a University* [1] were composed, the first set in 1852, the others in the years 1854-8, when he was Rector of the Catholic University of Ireland, which was planned for the higher education of the flock, and as a counterpoise to Trinity and the godless colleges. The scheme failed after a trial; Newman's hands were tied by the hierarchy, and his conceptions were too large for his public; he resigned, and went back sorrowful to the genial St. Philip Neri. But the discourses retain a living value; he left behind him an 'idea,' rigidly limited no doubt on this side and that, yet embodying some of the finer genius and remembered essence of his Oxford life as tutor, college reformer, and humourist. He now uses the word *liberal* as one of praise; it no longer means, as it had formerly done, anti-theological. He seeks to adjust it to the ground-plan of a university in which Catholic theology shall of course be present, nay paramount, but where she shall rule with a wise reserve, and 'steady' the work of intellectual education. The omission of theology, he cries, had marred the programme of Sir Robert Peel's undenominational colleges. She must receive due homage; but she must leave room for science, medicine, and letters to work themselves out freely. Newman proceeds to define this ideal more exactly.

The primary aim is to teach the

> diffusion and extension of knowledge rather than the advancement. If its object were scientific and philosophical discovery, I do not see why a University should have students.

The increase of learning he naïvely relegates to mere academies; he seems to have no notion that a university can train an investigator. It soon appears that the aim is to fit the student, in point of information, intelligence, and manners, for the world, not for the study or laboratory. Of course it is the *Catholic* student, who in Ireland had so long been starved and handicapped. Still, the dream is otherwise the old Oxford one of the man of 'general education,' and it is a dream which has found some warrant in the spheres of English public life and business. The programme is generous accordingly. The world is mixed, and to face it we must know it; and to know it, the young Catholic—Newman speaks, of course, only of men

—must candidly study in his pupilage the facts of science, and still more the literature of the natural man. It is fatal to shut him off from 'Homer, Ariosto, Cervantes, Shakespeare, because the old Adam smelt rank in them.' So far he had been turned out, as we should say, unvaccinated into the germ-laden world. The university must not be a mere seminary. Nay, he must not shirk meeting even the enemies of the faith. English literature is not, and is never likely to be, distinctively Catholic. Newman is never more liberal himself than when he urges this programme; he does so with the aim of preserving the souls of the faithful.

> We may feel great repugnance to Milton or Gibbon as men; we may most seriously protest against the spirit which ever lives, and the tendency which ever operates, in every page of their writings; but there they are, an integral portion of English Literature; we cannot extinguish them; we cannot deny their power; we cannot write a new Milton or a new Gibbon; we cannot expurgate what needs to be exorcised. They are great English authors, each breathing hatred to the Catholic Church in his own way, each a proud and rebellious creature of God, each gifted with incomparable gifts.

It is a most characteristic passage; Newman is never shaken in his seat, but he always feels the force and the tug of the adversary. Measure him, he seems to say, for you cannot get rid of him, he will always be there; you should even admire Milton, very much as you do Milton's Satan. We can hardly expect Newman to concede more than this; and his curriculum, from his own standpoint, cannot be called a timid one. Elsewhere he delineates the secular side of his Catholic Athenian. The language may seem rather general and didactic, but so was that of Pericles; and there is something in it which is wholly lacking in the school of Brougham, with its cry for the 'diffusion of knowledge,' so keenly derided by Peacock as well as by Newman.

> A University training is the great ordinary means to a great but ordinary end; it aims at raising the intellectual tone of society, at cultivating the public mind, at purifying the national taste, at supplying true principles to popular enthusiasm and fixed aims to popular aspiration, at giving enlargement and sobriety to the ideas of the age, at facilitating the exercise of political power, and refining the intercourse of private life.

The well-known character of the 'gentleman,' which matches Ruskin's, is all in keeping with this picture. It comes in the eighth discourse of 1852. Newman, though he had never been at one of the great Protestant schools, perceives that with all their faults they do form character. He believes in a large measure of 'self-education.' Crabbe's village boy, he says, who learns his own poetry and philosophy from the shepherd and the sea-gulls, is healthier than a mere thing of examinations. Still, the college training must be thorough so far as it is carried; and Newman has judged in advance another modern vanity, when he declares that

> the stimulating system may easily be overdone, and does not answer on the long run. A blaze among the stubble, and then all is dark.

There are many things that these discourses do not contain. Newman's liberalism, no doubt, is relative. There is no real sense of the scientific method and temper. The scholarship commended is of the delicate but narrow 'English' description. There is no provision for revealing what Pattison calls 'the grand development of human reason, from Aristotle down to Hegel.' Yet Pattison [1] himself, the escaped Tractarian, who proclaimed as one in the wilderness the ideal of university research, testifies to the 'breadth and boldness' of Newman's exposition; and such a witness is not to be despised. I have not mentioned the haunting and musical passages on the everlasting moral laws, 'these awful, supernatural, bright, majestic, delicate apparitions'; or on the early Irish Church; we may remember that Newman provided for the 'special encouragement of Celtic literature,' engaged Eugene O'Curry to teach and publish, and 'went to the expense of having a fount of Irish type cast for the use of the university.'

VII

But his hopes in Dublin failed, and for many years he suffered from despondency and frustration, and lay, as he says, 'under a cloud' of popular suspicion. He wished to edit, with *prolegomena*, a translation of the Bible, but was baffled. He tried, impossibly, to mediate between the Ultramontane and the Liberal Catholic. His life in his new Church was a record of failure; and was to remain so until in his old age he received the belated tribute of the cardinalate. The result, meantime, was isolation; and when, in 1860, being now fifty-eight, he reads a new poem called *Tithonus* in the *Cornhill*, he feels that he too is fading out from the world, and having nothing to do with its interests or its affairs. I have fallen off in flesh and shrunk up during the past year, and am like a grey grasshopper or the evaporating mist of the morning. And, as I get older, so do trouble and anxieties seem to multiply.

Apart from sermons and a few verses, most of his writing thus far had been exposition or polemic, done for an occasion, and not always for a great occasion. It had little unity to show, and the inner clue to it was unknown. It might, as literature, have receded into a very dim region. But he was now to give a clue, and to write a real book. Late in 1863 began his war with Kingsley,[1] who foolishly misquoted him and taxed both Newman and Rome with confessed indifference to veracity. After an exchange of letters and pamphlets, Newman next year produced his *Apologia*[2] *pro Vita Sua,* which left him cleared, honoured, and triumphant.

The *Apologia* came out in serial parts, like a story, and must be read in its original form, with the controversial portions adroitly marshalled, the more general ones coming at the outset, and the particular 'blots' in Kingsley's argument at the end. This framework was shorn away in the next edition (1865), and the sub-title, *History of My Religious Opinions,* became the title ; the text was also revised. The work, in its fulness, is a confession, a document, a piece of English history, and a work of art. The retorts on Kingsley are in the classic dialectical manner, the manner of the *grand siècle* ; wonderful in wording, in cadence, and in attitude. The anger and sarcasm are in part forensic ; Newman felt, he says, that he must say something 'sharp' ; but they are genuine too. The actual charges hardly required a master of fence to dispose of them. Kingsley had quoted without book, and his apology made matters worse. Newman was able to make his own personal credit the issue, and not the historic doctrines of the casuists, Roman or Anglican, about mental reservations ; a point which was never fairly discussed at all. It is odd that Kingsley did not see his own weakness. Any British committee, in such a case, insists that the offender shall appear in a perfectly white sheet. Had he gone further in making amends, Newman might well have lost his opportunity, and could never have written his formidable, inimitable letter[3] (February 13, 1875) after Kingsley's death, in which he observes :

As to Mr. Kingsley, much less could I feel any resentment against him when he was accidentally the instrument, in the good Providence of God, by whom I had an opportunity given me, which otherwise

I should not have had, of vindicating my character and conduct in my *Apologia*. I heard, too, a few years back from a friend that she chanced to go into Chester Cathedral and found Mr. K. preaching about me, kindly, though, of course, with criticisms on me. And it has rejoiced me to observe lately that he was defending the Athanasian Creed, and, as it seemed to me, in his views generally nearing the Catholic view of things. I have always hoped that by good luck I might meet him, feeling sure that there would be no embarrassment on my part, and I said Mass for his soul as soon as I heard of his death.

Well he might: on the other hand, a confused good faith is equally manifest in Kingsley, who blundered into the man-trap through what one of his critics called his 'animal scent'—his scent for something really wrong in Newman, that was immaterial to the case before the court. What this is, Newman's whole career sufficiently indicates.

He was not like his friend Ward, who walked straight over the worst abysses on a tight-rope of syllogisms. He never professed to move by processes purely intellectual. The intellect, he says, 'cannot without intrusion exercise itself as an independent authority in the field of morals and religion.' Arguments he has in plenty, and he shows the gifts of a considerable schoolman in presenting them. But avowedly they only count *amongst* his mental impulses. Everything shows the subordinate part played by reason in the moulding of his convictions, as distinct from their self-justification afterwards. As he moves Romewards, we watch the slow, painful interrupted drift of the man's whole nature. Signs and omens, a sudden intuition, a phrase like *securus judicat orbis terrarum* (which haunted him after he had read Wiseman's article on the Donatists in 1839), all play their part. It is a frank and moving history, although, to minds otherwise built, it is sometimes puerile; but he does not care for that; it is a true history. 'Du moins je suis autre'; he seems, like Rousseau, always to be saying that. As we listen, in his letters, to his cries of sadness and irritation and pique, to his words of dependence and affection, and to his strange feminine jests, we may feel that we do not love him, or much like him, or trust his thinking, but that we credit him; and this is what he wants. The *Apologia* has been attacked for inaccuracies, but few records of a long-past crisis could stand literal scrutiny. The finding, in general, is confirmed by his correspondence. Not that all his story is plain, for Newman is as hard to fathom as Fénelon; but then no Sainte-Beuve has yet appeared to chronicle the inner life of the Oxonian and the Roman movements in England. Newman's challenge, *Secretum meum mihi*, cannot soon be met. One point, however, is plain ; his real indignation is against a more difficult and treacherous adversary than Kingsley. This is British public opinion. No wonder he had been misread and mistrusted. John Bull frowned angrily and suspiciously on a mental pilgrimage so alien to his own. Newman had estranged his former public, and soon became unhappy—not so much doctrinally as politically—in his new Church. He had never had a chance of speaking out. When he did so, John Bull still neglected the refinements, but granted that Newman must be, in his unintelligible way, an honest man.

VIII

The *Apologia* contains some of Newman's great, moving, poetic passages, which arise so easily from the argument ; and it really left his mind in the 'region higher and more serene' of which he speaks. This is apparent from his poem, *The Dream of Gerontius*, written in 1865. He could now live awhile in his true life, the life of vision and imagination, though he was doomed to mix again, and that immediately, in ecclesiastical broils. We find him, in the same year, anxiously reviewing and disparaging Pusey's *Eirenicon* on the one side, and Seeley's *Ecce Homo* on the other. But during the long remainder of his days he published little : only one work, indeed, of note, *An Essay in Aid of a Grammar of Assent* (1870). He was also painfully exercised over the papal definition of Infallibility, in the same year ; not as to the doctrine, but as to the timeliness and fitness of defining it. He accepted, of course, the definition once it was decreed ; and in 1875 wrote his *Letter to the Duke of Norfolk* in reply to Gladstone's pounding pamphlet on *Vaticanism*. He occasionally took up his pen again ; at eighty-four he is found explaining, in reply to the searching attacks of Dr. Fairbairn, his peculiar attitude to Reason, and disclaiming the time-worn charge that he had fled to Rome for fear of his own scepticism.

Veteran pastors at Oxford, thirty years ago, were still shaking their heads over that 'scepticism,' and quoting Huxley's saying that a 'primer of infidelity' could be made up from the writings of the Cardinal. But the point is easy to misstate, and cannot be duly drawn out here. There is abundance of scepticism in Newman, but it is all *contingent* scepticism, which never comes to anything, since the contingency that would make it real cannot, for him, ever arise. How could it, when his first principle, his theistic premise, stands on the footing of an intuition, as certain as his own existence ? Without that everything would crumble ; but then his assurance is unshakeable. So that he feels safe in displaying the worst consequences of its negation. Thus his famed picture of the world, as it seems to the natural reason, moving 'as though from unreasoning elements, not towards final causes,' is a contingent one ; he does not think, he is not tempted for a moment really to think, that the world is like that at all. He dwells, with surprising vividness, on his vision of what the world, without religion, seems to be and would be ; but in doing so he thinks more of others, of the waverer and stray sheep, than of himself ; he remains inveterately a shepherd and winner of souls. He sees quite sharply, too, how and why others may misconstrue him, and he writes of an old friend :

> My surmise[1] is, that he thinks me a profoundly sceptical thinker, who, determined on not building on an abyss, have [has], by mere strength of will, bridged it over, and built upon [it] my bridge—but that my bridge, like Mahomet's coffin, is self-suspended, by the action of the will—but I may be putting it too strong.

This misreading was no doubt encouraged by the *Grammar of Assent*, which cost him several years of hard work and is his chief formal contribution to philosophy. The book shows Newman's power of tortuous analysis and dialectic, but its chief interest is autobiographical. He had always been sure that he was sure ; but he had always been vexed, more for others than for himself, by the question of method. How could he convince others of their right to such assurance ? The *Apologia* had been a memoir, not a demonstration. To make the omission good, Newman wrote his essay on the psychology and logic of belief. He asks what is the ground of certitude and the warrant for a reasonable assent. He makes his well-known distinction, which is psychologically a good one, between 'notional assent,' a mere intellectual affair, and 'real assent,' where the conclusion is also embraced by the will and feelings. He nicely graduates all shades of acceptance from the faintest to the most complete. Then, adapting Butler, he applies his theory of 'probability' to show that real assent not only may, but must, accept many a conclusion in advance of the logical evidence. Nay, in religious inquiry we are not 'justified' in waiting for full demonstration ; for it may never come, and meantime we must live and choose. Accordingly, Newman discovers a special 'illative faculty,' which allows and forces us to make the leap in question. The application, of course, is to matters of faith ; and the faith in question is Newman's own. The book has been hammered at both by theologians and by lay heretics ; and we are certainly left wondering whether the illative sense remains the warrant for its own conclusions being objectively true, and whether Newman does not offer us a psychology under the guise of logic. His fluctuating, personal, and subjective attitude is ever in contrast with the hard fabric of the orthodox Roman philosophy. But he does his work with address ; he is trying to speak both to the trained minds which can follow his subtleties, and to the unlettered, who are to feel that they may safely believe without any such capacity.

The theme gives many chances to an ironist and a musician in words. The poet and the Virgilian speak in the contrast of the 'notional' assent given by the schoolboy with the real assent given by the mature man to the Greek or Latin lines which are 'the birth of some chance morning or evening at an Ionian festival, or among the Sabine hills.' The romantic rebel against the march of intellect speaks in the satire against Brougham, Peel, popular cheap instruction, and what Thomas Love Peacock had called 'the learned friend' ('the Lord deliver us from the learned friend!'). Elsewhere Newman is more melodious ; he gets poetry out of the Athanasian Creed ; and when he takes the clauses on the Trinity, and 'illustrates the action of the separate articles of that dogma upon the imagination,' as they are enhanced by chant and ritual, he rises to his full height, and it becomes easier to see why so many followed his voice.

IX

In reasoning, his style is by no means so good, with all its show of rigour ; at the best it is a great philosophical style—*manqué*. How loose it is appears at once if it be confronted with a page of Bishop Butler, or of Bossuet's book on the Protestant churches, or even of the Anglican divine, Mozley. The clearness and candour of John Stuart Mill help us to see any gaps in his argument ; but these gaps, with Newman, are covered up by scholastic over-niceties, or by poetry and fancy. He was a sophist,[1] and an honest one, and all the more formidable for that. There was no Socrates to expose him to himself, nor could Socrates easily have done so. His own gift, in one respect, is Socratic. It is to spur to their natural destinations, whether to right or left, the minds that are content with halfway houses. He was naturally attacked, on all sides, by those who objected thus to be dislodged. He tries, at different times, to threaten the Protestant with liberalism, and the liberal with scepticism; to quicken the dry Anglican, to draw the quickened Anglican to Rome, and to warn the convert against intellectual reserves. It is true that he himself, once he has 'gone over,' shows a relative liberalism, and resists the extremist; but much of his writing, from first to last, is determined, as to its tone and theme, by the propulsive instinct. His crook is pointed like a goad, and he uses it at either end, as may serve his turn. And he propels not by argument alone, but, wherever that fails, and whether it fails or not, by every possible assault that he can think of on the conscience, the imagination, and the mystical feeling: thus repeating for others his own experience, and holding out the 'light' that had led him 'o'er moor and fen.' In this effort a singular, though very fitful, gift of writing is displayed.

We have to watch and wait for Newman as an artist. For an artist he can be; but what long and sterile tracts, what belts of unwatered thin vegetation, separate the solitary peaks and the happy valleys! In his histories, his disputes, his apologies, and his fiction, how much, even on a liberal showing, is ephemeral! For the historians of theology and of English opinion his works are a necessary document; but as a writer he is best in selections. He has left three books of original stamp; but the *Essay on Development*, the *Grammar of Assent*, and even the *Apologia* are all cumbered with mortal matter. He holds out best through a short composition, a lecture, a sermon, a chapter, or a harangue. Even here, we remember single pages and short solos rather than the whole. Perhaps he is surest in his letters, and in his easier, familiar speech; there, he is as natural as Ruskin is in *Præterita*, and his variety is surprising. His impatience, his affections and sudden hardnesses, his melancholy and his rarer moods of buoyancy, are expressed without hindrance; the style calls no attention to itself. He is full of more or less gentle mischief. There is something childlike, or womanish, in his slang, when he talks of 'tease' and 'fidget' and 'jobation' ('I had a most horrible jobation from Coleridge'—in the Achilli trial). Sometimes, as in the *Letter to Pusey*, there is the true pat of the ecclesiastic's claw, gently drawing blood from an old friend who has been 'rude.' There is another vein in the letter which begins: 'St. Philip of Birmingham presents his compliments to Our Lady of the Immaculate Conception.' Newman has the power in a high degree, as his biographer says, of 'adapting his mind to that of his correspondent.' How to write at need to a Cardinal-Archbishop, very sourly, but 'kissing the hem of the sacred purple'; or to a pious feminine doubter of moderate intelligence; or to an intimate like Ambrose St. John (*carissime!*); or, in the crushing manner, to an insolent Monsignore, who invites us to Rome to speak to 'an audience of Protestants more educated than could ever be the case in England'; or for our own eye, in our private notes;—Newman's letters would be a manual of such instruction, if only it could be followed.

But though subtle he is not supple; he is absurdly unlike the stock notion of the Italianate cleric. He has only too little of the wisdom of the serpent; he is not like Manning. There is something in him of the plain indignant Briton, only asking for fair play and the rigour of the game. This physiognomy is not merely a mask, or *persona*; though he makes the most of it in his retorts to Kingsley, or in his protest against the popular caricature of the Roman Catholic. The voice often corresponds; Newman's English can be the pure, central English of Goldsmith, or even of Swift. He cannot be imitated; he is the least mannered writer of his time. All the others, except perhaps Thackeray and Froude, can be and have been well mimicked, by disciple or parodist.

There is variety in his technique. His clauses are generally short, but except for a purpose they are never curt, and they are linked into a natural harmony. They recall Shairp's account of his Oxford preaching:

> Each separate sentence, or at least each short paragraph, was spoken rapidly, but with great clearness of intonation; and then at its close there was a pause, lasting for nearly half a minute; then another rapidly but clearly spoken sentence, followed by another pause. It took some time to get over this, but, that once done, the wonderful charm began to dawn on you. . . . Subtlest truths, which it would have taken philosophers pages of circumlocution and big words to state, were dropped out by the way in a sentence or two of the most transparent Saxon.

Such is the staple; but as time goes on Newman elaborates more and more, chaining his sentences tighter, and building them up, not into a complex Ciceronian paragraph, but into a series of parallel members similarly framed, which come out right at last into a clinching phrase or climax. The page in the *Apologia*, on the aspect of a world without a God, is a well-known example; and here is another, which may be given without any comment on its amazing contents:

> She [the Church] holds that, unless she can, in her own way, do good to souls, it is no use her doing anything; she holds that it were better for sun and moon to drop from heaven, for the earth to fail, and for all the many millions who are upon it to die of starvation in extremest agony, so far as temporal affliction goes, than that one soul, I will not say should be lost, but should commit one single venial sin, should tell one wilful untruth, though it harmed no one, or steal one poor farthing without excuse. She considers the action of this world and the action of the soul simply incommensurate, viewed in their respective spheres; she would rather save the soul of one single wild bandit of Calabria, or whining beggar of Palermo, than draw a hundred miles of railroad through the length and breadth of Italy, or carry out a sanitary reform, in its fullest details, in every city of Sicily, except so far as these great national works tended to some spiritual good beyond them.

In the form, everything here is well; the diction, the movement, the simple artful rise and fall, the valuing of the vowels. Such effects are commoner in Newman's Roman period; yet they do not represent his usual cadence. Principal Shairp's description could be illustrated freely. When Newman is speaking, as though to himself aloud, on the nature of music, or the consciousness of the animals, or the presence of the angels on the earth, or on the fragility of life and hope, or the fall of the year, or on Virgil; then indeed the new capacities that he discovered for English prose are undeniable: but one example out of many must serve here:

> We have had enough of weariness, and dreariness, and listlessness, and sorrow, and remorse. We have had enough of this troublesome world. We have had enough of its noise and din. Noise is its best music. But now there is stillness; and it is a stillness that speaks. We know how strange the feeling is of perfect silence after continued sound. Such is our blessedness now. Calm and serene days have begun; and Christ is heard in them, and His still small voice, because the world speaks not.

The distinction of such passages, and the purity of their utterance, rests at last upon the solitariness of temper which is Newman's deepest characteristic. They express a certain ecstasy; the soul is far withdrawn into an internal fastness What if he is an unwilling solitary, never *more* alone than when alone, and always craving for the human intercourse which never fully satisfies him when it actually comes? That makes him all the more appealing, perhaps all the stranger; but it saves him from the touch of coldness with which the great solitaries pay for their prize. His inmost communings, no doubt, are most fully expressed in his small sheaf of verses, which remain to be noticed. Here can best be felt, what Burne-Jones remarked in him, Newman's 'glorious scorn of everything that was not his dream.'

X

They are written with an effort which is foreign to his prose. They are often rough; their form bears marks of the inner conflict that inspires them. The moods of self-abasement, or of painful self-examination, are strained to the breaking-point; the ascetic note of the early days of the movement, of Hurrell Froude's diary, is audible, in spite of joyous revulsions and ecstatic interludes. These remarks apply to the brief lyrics, already alluded to above, which Newman made while on his Mediterranean voyage, sometimes two or more in a single day. There is little decoration. One of these pieces, 'Lead, kindly Light,' owes part of its charm to an unexplained element; questioned long afterwards, Newman could not quite interpret its meaning. His supernatural touch is felt more than once, as in the lines 'When Heaven sends sorrow'; but he seems to be most himself in his choric Agonistes-like fragments; or they remind us of *Empedocles on Etna*:

> Thus God has will'd
> That man, when fully skill'd,
>   Still gropes in twilight dim;
> Encompass'd all his hours
> By fearfullest powers
>   Inflexible to him.

The translations, made some years later than this, from the Roman Breviary, are more assured in their form; but *The Dream of Gerontius*, Newman's only long poem—written, we have seen, amid and just after the stress of disputation—carries us at once into the land of lonely vision where his true life is lived. The soul dialogues with itself first, as it expects to leave, and then as it leaves, the body, when the priestly voice has said the word *Subvenite*. Then it falls 'over the dizzy brink Of some sheer infinite descent,' and time is now compressed or abolished. Angels, somewhat scholastically, instruct the soul in mysteries, and it approaches the cleansing pains of purgatory. This part of the *Dream* marks Newman's highest reach in verse. The rest—the ritual of prayer, the songs of the angels—if less remarkable, is well in keeping. None of Newman's contemporaries ventured on the same theme, none of them had at once the skill and the faith to make such a picture convincing. He owes little enough to others ; but his form, the dramatic monologue, is close to that favoured by Tennyson and Browning. It is not clear that any particular model has served for the blank verse, in which the best of the *Dream* is written. It is hard to suppose that Newman cared for Marlowe, of whom we are sometimes reminded: Gerontius, speeding from his guardian angel to his judge, is a contrast to Faustus, but speaks in similar tones :

> The eager spirit has darted from my hold,
> And, with intemperate energy of love,
> Flies to the dear feet of Emmanuel.

And there is the same ring elsewhere :

> Now let the golden prison open its gates.

XI

The quickening of sacred verse and hymnody by the High Church movement may here be sketched. Behind lay the peaceful *Christian Year* (1827), described in a previous volume ; and Keble continued the same strain in his *Lyra Innocentium* (1846) and other works. During the first heat of the fray, in 1836, appeared the *Lyra Apostolica*, with Newman for chief contributor. The poems were collected from the *British Magazine*, and amongst other authors were Keble, Hurrell Froude, and Isaac Williams. The verses by Newman reflect the stern interior life and lonely consolations of the captain in the intervals of warfare. Christina Rossetti, that sure artist in sacred verse, wrote later, and will be considered in another context. The temper of her feelings and meditations is High Anglican, but she kept aloof from the disputes. Some lesser poets must be named. In Isaac Williams (1802-65), who remained in the Anglican fold, there is undeniable poetic instinct, though his work is much diluted. *The Cathedral* (1838) is an effort to versify in their symbolic senses and associations the inside and outside of a cathedral building, point by point ; *The Altar* (1849), in a sonnet form which is used easily and has some of the Wordsworthian virtues, represents the incidents of the Passion. The devout and modest, yet independent temper of Williams is happily reflected in his autobiography. A more prominent figure was Frederick William Faber [1] (1814-63), who followed Newman to Rome, became head of the Brompton Oratory, edited Lives of the Saints, wrote profusely, and found much acceptance as a preacher. Much of his sacred verse has the preacher's unction and facility, rather than any distinct style. But he wrote *Pilgrims of the Night*, and other pieces too that have deservedly taken root in the hymnals. He too descends, in a measure, from Wordsworth; and he is most truly a poet in his secular hours. When he sings of the Cherwell and of Oxford—'City of wildest sunsets'—and of the 'main glories of that winter wood'—Bagley Wood—he stands for a moment beside the author of *Thyrsis* as a master of windy landscape in water-colour.

The High Churchmen did well for letters when they disclosed the treasures of the Latin hymnody. This work was begun, for the public, by the philologist, Richard Chenevix Trench,[1] afterwards Archbishop of Dublin, in his volume, *Sacred Latin Poetry, chiefly Lyrical* (1849), which is a small garland of first-rate examples, introduced with much historic sense and sympathy. Trench handles well the vital question of the Latin metres and their changes; his apologies for certain 'tares' and 'doctrinal blemishes,' which he excises or avoids, seem timid now, and are needless; but his aim is to rescue from the monopoly of Rome the great chants, the *Dies Iræ*, or the *In Exequiis Defunctorum* of Prudentius, as 'immortal heritages of the Universal Church.' The work of actual translation was taken in hand by John Mason Neale (1818-66),[2] a very learned ecclesiastical scholar, and a metrist of unwonted skill and resources, who was also versed in music. He faced the greatest of the mediæval poets, Bernard of Morlaix, Adam of St.-Victor, and many more, keeping in most cases near the original measures, and getting over with no little skill the constant risk of turning the Latin double endings into a heavier equivalent. His style, if most unequal, and not of the rarer sort, has at least the indispensable rush and ardour. Try to put into similar English rhythm *Nunc mæsta quiesce querela*, or *Vexilla prodeunt*, without slipping into a false gallop, and you can measure the courage, now and then well rewarded, of Mason Neale. In one of his happiest experiments the measure is his own. The tripartite dactylic hexameters of the *Rhythm* of Bernard of Morlaix are hardly to be reproduced in English without the special inspiration which carried Bernard, as he so gratefully claims, through the task. But the three familiar hymns, 'Brief life is here our portion,' 'For thee, O dear dear Country,' and 'Jerusalem the golden,' are centos picked out of Neale's renderings from the *Rhythm*. He also was the first to dress in English verse the cadenced prose of the Greek sacred odes; he adapted many mediæval carols, and 'Good King Wenceslas' is of his own making; but his hymns and carols are of less interest than his translations. Best, as hymn and poem, is 'The strain upraise'—the great *Cantemus cuncti*, or 'Alleluiatic sequence,' which is not sung in churches, so Neale laments, to the original music.

XII

No one will refuse a parting salutation to the shade of the Cardinal, even if it be only in the poet's words, 'Go honoured hence, go home.' The winding and embarrassed course that he was driven to steer, and the cries that his perplexities drew out of him, produce a mixture of distrust and regard. It is something of a relief to turn to the disciple who outran Newman, and vexed him, and loved him: this is William George Ward [1] (1812-82), the most consecutive and extreme reasoner of the Anglo-Roman movement. Newman's charm, poetry, delicacy, are gone; and in recompense there is a purely intellectual but very clear perception of the exact issue. Ward was a pure-blooded disputant, careless of history and literature, and happiest in the hot corners where divinity joins in the *mêlée* with philosophy. He had heard Newman in St. Mary's, had taken orders, had taught vigorously at Balliol, and had lashed in the *British Critic* the apathy of the Church and the tenets of the Reformation. In an overgrown volume, *The Ideal of a Christian Church* (1844), which caused much stir, he 'characterised' Lutheranism, 'that hateful and fearful type of Antichrist, in terms not wholly inadequate to its prodigious demerits.' Convocation, in consequence, boiled over and censured Ward. Why had he signed the Articles? He replied, so we are informed by Jowett, that in subscribing they were not 'all dishonest, but all honest together.' Ward, anyhow, was honest, and was soon received by Rome, and became one of her picked swordsmen, fighting Protestant, Anglican, liberal Catholic, and infidel with equal relish. He struck with one hand at Sir John Acton, the freer-minded English Catholics, and the *Home and Foreign Review* (1862), and with the other at John Stuart Mill; with whom, in a sporting spirit, he exchanged private letters on speculative subjects; and his bouts with Huxley in the Metaphysical Society are historical. Ward believed in proving all things, and in keeping the truth bright continually by the 'tierce and quart of mind with mind.'

The phrase is Tennyson's, concerning the 'most generous of all Ultramontanes.'

Ward had humour, and was full of whim: his active, buoyant style has been too much disparaged. His quality is seen in the *Essays on the Philosophy of Theism* (1867-82), especially in that on 'Science, Prayer, Freewill, and Miracles.' He discusses every burning question of theology, but does not enter much into the main stream of thought or into the minds of other men. The empirical philosophers were put on their mettle by Ward's dialectic. As he is now little read, one expressive passage may be quoted:

> We begin, then, with imagining two mice, endowed, however, with quasi-human or semi-human intelligence, enclosed within a grand pianoforte, but prevented in some way or other from interfering with the free play of its machinery. From time to time they are delighted with the strains of choice music. One of the two considers these to result from some agency external to the instrument; but the other, having a more philosophical mind, rises to the conception of fixed laws and phenomenal uniformity. 'Science as yet,' he says, 'is but in its infancy, but I have already made one or two important discoveries. . . .'

This empirical mouse, a John Mill in mouse's clothing, finds out some of the sequences, or laws of the vibrations, and he divines yet other laws: 'to their exploration I will devote my life.' Next let the piano become an imaginary instrument, a 'polychordon,' with two hundred intermediate 'laws' between the player and the sound:

> Well, successive generations of philosophical mice have actually traced 150 of the 200 phenomenal sequences, through whose fixed and invariable laws the sound is produced. The colony of mice, shut up within, are in the highest spirits at the success which has crowned the scientific labours of their leading thinkers; and the most eminent of them addresses an assembly: . . . 'Let us redouble our efforts. I fully expect that our grandchildren will be able to predict as accurately for an indefinitely preceding [*sic*] period the succession of melodies with which we are to be delighted, as we now predict the hours of sunrise and sunset. One thing, at all events, is now absolutely incontrovertible. As to the notion of there being some agency external to the polychordon—intervening with arbitrary and capricious will to produce the sounds we experience—this is a long-exploded superstition, a mere dream and dotage of the past. . . .

XIII

Few other writers of mark followed Newman to Rome. But the Oxford movement continued to be a power in letters. The work of Stubbs and Freeman shows its influence, in diverse ways, on historical study; and it deeply coloured the stories of Miss Yonge. In the field of divinity only a few representative names can be added. Keble will be mentioned again as a literary critic (Ch. x.). After the departure of Newman, the most potent personage in the Anglican camp was Edward Bouverie Pusey (1800-82); he was also its most learned divine. Pusey gave a strong impulse to the study of the early ages of the Church, and to that of German theology; he spent much of his life in resisting liberalism, university reform, and the modern spirit generally. Pusey has something of the massive manner of our older theologians, but his admirers seldom claim a place in literature for his many volumes. The most acute and weighty thinker that remained in the fold was James Bowling Mozley [1] (1813-78), a pattern of the cautious, able English Churchman, who remains firmly on the defensive, yet is quite ready to make a counter-attack. In his Bampton lectures on miracles, Mozley grapples hard with Mill; elsewhere he assails the cult of Comte, tries to bring Maurice to the point, derides the eclectic church of Dr. Arnold, and is strong on the insufficiencies of Luther. He distrusts Carlyle's hero-worship, especially in the case of Cromwell. We see the spell of Newman persisting, when Mozley hails the *Grammar of Assent*, as 'a powerful defence of a common Christianity.' Mozley's ink is rather thick; he is a slow and hampered writer, but full of matter, with a streak in him of Bishop Butler; and sermons like those on the Pharisees and on gratitude recall Bourdaloue in their turn for moral analysis. His style satisfies the brain much better than Newman's, for his transitions and connexions are logical rather than emotional.

The truest man of letters among the orthodox divines who remained was the historian of the Oxford movement, Richard William Church [2] (1815-90), Dean of St. Paul's. Church embodies the comparative stability and peace of mind that ensued after the foreign elements had been expelled from the Anglican system. His clear and fair outlook is welcome after so many partisan readings of history; and his style, though it entirely lacks the sting, the restlessness, and the subtle strangeness of Newman's, is an excellent one, and well befits his task, which is threefold. Church is preacher, historian, and critic. His sermons and addresses, such as those on the *Gifts of Civilisation*, or on *Early Sacred Poetry* (in which he introduces the Vedas to the religious public through Max Müller's translation) have a markedly historical cast. Indeed, he is at his best, and most at his ease, in a big rapid review. Church is thoroughly well informed, the very opposite of a sciolist, though he left no large monument of his powers. He usually plays the part of a safe and masterly populariser who has escaped the snares of that industry. He writes first of all for the cultivated layman, for whom he makes matters easy without stooping to concessions or becoming 'unscientific.' His sense of proportion and perspective, not always present in the professional digger, is constant, and is well seen in his small book on *The Beginning of the Middle Ages* (1877), a sketch of some eight centuries and lucid in its plan—a good map not cumbered by a crowd of names. The article (1854) on *The Early Ottomans*, like that on *Cassiodorus*, shows the same qualities, though the Oriental lore is avowedly second-hand. *St. Anselm* (1870) is a monograph which is based on research, and has held its place, and it forms a transition to Church's critical or appreciative papers.

Here again he is first of all an introducer and interpreter. The Dante scholar, weighted by his load, or hump, of learning, too often repels the mere lover of letters. Church's essay on *Dante* (1850) makes us wish to read that poet. He was abreast of contemporary scholarship; and though much has been added since to Dante lore, the value of the essay, with its exalted enthusiasms, its sympathy with the austerity and still more with the tenderness of the poet, and its lightness of movement, is little affected. One of Church's best and most characteristic passages is his praise of the *Purgatorio*, to be found in his preface to Vernon's *Readings* in that poem (1889). The same relish for good poetry is found in his paper on Wordsworth, and, with some qualifications, in his book on *Spenser* (1879). Church was perhaps too rigid, or mentally timid, to do justice to the Renaissance; he shrank, though some surprised and reluctant admiration is mixed with his censure, from its full tide of life. The age of Machiavelli, he once declares, could not be redeemed even by Leonardo and Raphael. This temper is seen in his otherwise excellent book on *Bacon* (1884), and in his essay on *Montaigne* (1857). He feels bound to preach not a little; yet he enters, calling resolutely on his constitutional fairness, with unexpected vigour into the windings of the sceptical spirit, so alien to his own. We can turn for relief, if we like, to Pater's *Gaston de Latour*, with its free and intimate treatment of Montaigne.

Church's chronicle of *The Oxford Movement, 1833-1845*, is both history and portraiture, and appeared in 1891. He had been and remained a friend of Newman, he had known the other *dramatis personæ*, both those who had stayed behind and those who had crossed over; and he had played his own part in the story, which he tells with an almost impossible equity and avoidance of emphasis, on the historical, the political, and the personal side alike. He wrote the book a quarter of a century after the dust had settled. His own standpoint is made clear in various tracts and pamphlets, and especially in his *Lancelot Andrewes* (1877), where he defends the English Reformation and church settlement; its very compromises and inconsistencies appeal to him as part of its historic task. Church's writing, everywhere, is of a good academic stamp. It cannot be called masculine, or very genial, but it is pure and equable, not always without colour, and never common. Reserve, or a certain didactic turn, or some other obstacle, keeps it from being easy to remember. With the dignified figure of Church our list of the divines who sprang from the Oxford Movement must end, at the cost of excluding the eloquent preacher and apologist, Henry Parry Liddon, and others. Some of its offspring will appear amongst the novelists; others, who broke away leftwards, like James Anthony Froude, are discussed in other connexions.

XIV

The liberal divines within the Church have left less salvage for letters than might be expected from the share they took in the formation of English opinion. At first, in the common rooms of the Thirties, they were styled 'noetics,' [1] or, as we might say, 'intellectuals'; but after the middle of the century they came to be known, somewhat unwillingly, as 'Broad Churchmen.' [2] After 1860, the year of *Essays and Reviews*, their foes gave them other names like 'latitudinarian,' an old term revived. Their effort is scattered; they touch on doctrine, exegesis, history, and the humanities, and philosophy and education, at points mutually distant. From the nature of the case they disagree among themselves, and have no common body of articles, even in the negative sense. But they have a common spirit and tradition. It is the modern spirit cautiously imbibed; it is the tradition of the rights of reason, temperately claimed. It was thus that Hampden, Hare, and Thomas

Arnold in one generation, Maurice and Stanley and Jowett in the next, tried to reanimate their church. Not, of course, as the Anglo-Catholics did, through mediævalism. The broad churchmen are of the Left Centre, and face leftward. Yet, rather to the general surprise, they stoutly keep their seats, conscience-clear, and refuse to be chased or pelted in that direction by missiles from the Right. They have counted for much, and for good, in our public life ; in schools, and colleges, and pulpits, and in philanthropic and liberal enterprise. They also did much, amongst them, for learning, and much too for the diffusion and propagation, if not strictly for the original advancement, of thought. Their love for mental compromise acquires the force of a principle. They fill their place in the intellectual series lying between such extremes as William George Ward and Herbert Spencer. Their influence and merits are not to be rated by their thoroughness or consistency in speculation.

Their fighting archbishop, Richard Whately, quitted Oriel for Dublin in 1831, and lived and wrote till 1863. He had already produced his Bampton lectures, his *Historic Doubts*, his *Logic* and his *Rhetoric*. He edited and amplified the work of Paley, and carried it on in his robust way. Religion has still to be 'proved by evidences,' in open court ; and abundant emphasis, though not much heart or imagination, is put into the task. Religion, so conceived, does not include the special tenets, nor does it allow for the emotions, either of the Oxford High Churchman or of the Evangelical Protestant. Whately thinks he can refute feeling by many discourses. He belongs, like Bentley and Whewell, to the *bear*-family of writers ; his claws and hug leave their marks. The notes to Bacon's *Essays*, and the 'apothegms' in the *Commonplace Book* (1818-61) display Whately's acuteness and hardheadedness. His largest conception, namely the broadening of the basis of the Church, sank into the mind of Newman, who had sat under him at Oriel, and who was to give to it, in Whately's opinion, a truly pestilent turn.

A typical writer of another stamp was Renn Dickson Hampden, who was appointed Regius Professor of Divinity, in spite of his Bampton lectures of 1832, to the fury of the High Church party. His book is singular and by no means dull reading. Hampden was learned, not only in Aristotle, but in the historical changes of theological terms, and foreshadows the critical treatment of the subject. Theology, he declares, cannot be an exact science ; the language of scripture is not technical, and fathers and councils have no right to go beyond it. There has been a 'mystery attached to the subject which is not a mystery of God.' Still Hampden professes and duly recites the fundamental dogmas. His consistency in so doing was assailed by Newman and others; but he continued, in a second edition, to protest that he was innocent of heresy.

The implements of German exegesis, of physical science, and of literary criticism had thus long been at work on the accepted theology; and in 1860 there came, within the pale, the inevitable shock. The volume of *Essays and Reviews* [1] is now mild reading, and only one of its seven essays endures. This, apparently the least heterodox of all, is Mark Pattison's on the *Tendencies of Religious Thought in England, 1688-1750*, a luminous and learned inquiry. Here, as always, Pattison's pen is like a graving-tool, and his standpoint is scientific. Jowett's paper *On the Interpretation of Scripture* contains large views and sharp sayings, but is somewhat diplomatic, and lacks the freshness of his Pauline discourses. Temple's paper *On the Education of the World* is a harmless account of the services which Greece, Rome, and Judæa have done for mankind. The essays that really drew blood from the orthodox were, first of all, Rowland Williams's review (of Bunsen's inquiries) which refined away, to say the least, the evidence for inspiration, prophecy, and miracle; secondly, the historical survey by H. B. Wilson, the planner of the volume, with its glance at other Eastern races than the Jewish; and further, the study of evidences by a veteran disputant and mathematician, Baden Powell. The book was condemned as to some points by the church courts, but their decision was reversed by the Privy Council, and the number of opinions on matters of faith, legally tenable by Anglican shepherds, was distinctly multiplied. According to an epigram of the hour, 'hell was dismissed with costs.' All of which so far bears upon our record that the Church, with her mental boundaries now more elastic, comes to contribute more to pure literature. The next notable discussion of the kind was to be in 1889. Then came another joint production, *Lux Mundi*, wherein negotiations with secular thought were opened by the truant grandsons of Puseyism.

XV

The brilliant season of the 'Broad Church' was the third quarter of the century, and, for our purpose, Maurice, Jowett, and Stanley may be taken as its representatives. A shadowy figure now in literature, though a most copious writer, John

Frederick Denison Maurice (1805-72) exercised a deep influence on the course of religious sentiment in England. The historians of doctrine are hard put to it to define his tenets. No markedly original idea is linked with his name ; he is justly taxed with much elusiveness and obscurity in thought and style ; he seems hardly to have had any mental centre. His personal character was lofty, self-sacrificing, courageous, and full of charm. He has a gallant record as a fighter for social and educational reform. But this by itself would not account for his note as a divine. Maurice took one or two large and generous conceptions, already in the air, applied them in many fields, and, without ever strictly working them out, gave them a living currency. He impelled to the historical study of the religious spirit by his effort to find the points of common aspiration in Christian and non-Christian creeds. He also dreamed of an *eirenikon* between the Christian churches, which no one exactly accepted, and was of course attacked by those whom he strove to reconcile. He disagreed with High and Low Church, and Nonconformist alike, as to the dogmas which could be safely and rightly sacrificed ; and having considerable dialectical skill, coupled with a good deal of asperity in debate, and also being very hard to pin down to a positive profession, Maurice caused wrath and perplexity. A mystical element in his mind separates him from the secular and rationalising camp of Broad Churchmen. But he was a *solvent* ; and his power is not to be measured by philosophical or artistic tests. His *Moral and Metaphysical Philosophy,* and his *Religions of the World,* are ambitious and pre-critical works. His rejoinder to Mansel's celebrated Bampton lectures is elaborate and wordy. His most popular work, *The Kingdom of Christ,* which is still reprinted and which sets forth his plea for the unity of religion, is by no means clear-cut in its thinking. His volume of essays, *The Friendship of Books,* has little substance. Maurice's letters, too, which enhance our impression of his wide, exalted, and inspiring mind, show his want of defining or shaping power.

In point of courage, address, and width of experience, Benjamin Jowett [1] (1817-93) may figure as the Odysseus among the liberal divines. He did not, indeed, travel in the body ; he stayed at Balliol, first as tutor, then as master ; was, as he said, 'married' to his college ; made it finally the premier college, and himself the chief potentate, in Oxford. He fought steadily, cunningly, and successfully for many academic improvements, and did more than all the rest to make the university a power in the nation. He never welcomed, or perhaps understood, the true and ancient, the continental idea of a university as mainly a nursery of learning, and he lacked the stern devotion to knowledge which distinguishes Mark Pattison, as well as Pattison's note of intellectual pertinacity and consistency. Jowett was a man of intellect, of course, but of much more character than intellect. His literary judgements [1] were apt to be narrow and blind. He left his mark on many men who have made history, and whom Plato had taught him to train for the good of the state ; it is true that he lectured them all their lives, but they did not seem to mind that ; he had also taught them how to get on, and told them what to do, making it plain that he did not readily forgive failure. He had an extraordinary gift for shepherding kindness, backed by hard severity, and had also a gift for friendship. But Jowett, with all his world-worship and adroitness, had further a deep strain of idealism ; and he influenced ideas considerably, although his mind was not originative, through the spoken and the written word. He had, indeed, his own mental Odyssey, which is curious and representative of the time, though it resulted in no particular contribution to thought.

He began as a theologian, with the Germans ; studied Baur, and also Kant ; and was awhile, despite his unconstructive mind, much inspired and enlarged by Hegel. In 1855 he produced an edition of the Epistles to the Thessalonians, Galatians, and Romans, which was much besprinkled with heretical and subtle remarks. The essays on ' natural religion ' and on ' The imputation of the sin of Adam ' show the finer edge of Jowett's style, and are among the freshest of his writings. His singular mixture of piety and scepticism is already apparent. In the end he came to distrust philosophical and theological system, and his religious doctrines were, latterly at least, vague and attenuated. In a remarkable memorandum [2] of 1886, he forecasts apparently without antipathy, the victory of something very like the pure agnostic position (' doctrines may become unmeaning words ') :

> Yet the essence of religion may still be self-sacrifice, self-denial, a death unto life, having for its rule and absolute morality, a law of God and nature—a doctrine common to Plato and the Gospel.

This was written in Jowett's old age, but his earlier writings can be read in the light of it. His paper in *Essays and Reviews* has been mentioned already. Such utterances, as well as his zeal for reform, exposed him for a time to a bigoted persecution, which deservedly strengthened his influence.

His lasting performance is a translation of all the dialogues of Plato, accompanied by introductions. It first appeared in 1871, and was afterwards much revised. The Greek scholarship in this great work would not, it appears, always have satisfied Browning's Grammarian; sometimes the exact meaning was altered in the process of refining away every trace of effort from the style, but the same process adds to the delicacy and naturalness of the English, which rises or falls, becomes exalted or playful or homely, just like the original. Jowett when translating paid great attention to his rhythm, rewriting again and again, and was well rewarded for the toil. He also published a similar version of Thucydides; it is smooth, and therefore unlike Thucydides; but the combing-out of tangled sentences was part of the plan. Some of the essays in the *Plato* carry the art of exposition to a very nice point, and contain much of the editor's philosophy of life as well as Plato's.

Jowett's own prose has a somewhat ambiguous quality, which is felt in reading his lectures and college sermons, and which could also be felt by the listener. Who could forget that strange figure, with the pink and silver colouring, the bitter-sweet voice, the studied silences, the reverend bearing, the secular epigrams, the cool oracular evasion of merciless ultimate questions? Manner and prestige told for much in the effect. There were commonplaces without number, shrilled out in the shape of mild paradox, and there were flashes too of noble good sense and observation. The English was pure and clear, indeed fastidiously graceful as to diction, and thoroughly well expressing the utmost that Jowett had to say; the sentences were *staccato* in delivery, but are less so in the reading. Other rhetorical effects, of the kind so well managed by eminent pulpit voices of that hour (*compressa quiescunt*) like Liddon's or Magee's, were wholly absent. This was Jowett in his latter plenitude of local authority; perhaps he is to be thought of most cordially as he seems to have been in earlier days—fighting, often alone, against obscurantism, dreaming of 'Plato and the Gospels,' and loosening the mental crust of the ancient city.

Jowett's friend Arthur Penrhyn Stanley[1] (1815-81), Dean of Westminster, the chief dignitary and popular apostle of the Broad Church movement, and a valiant champion of toleration, both ecclesiastical and academic, was also a copious and successful writer. He has much more style than Maurice, and much less than Jowett; his rather flowery English is not cheap or common; but little of his work seems to have the mark of permanence. His first noticeable book, the *Life of Thomas Arnold* (1844), skilfully and piously executed, is still widely read; its chief interest, however, lies in Arnold's letters. *Sinai and Palestine* (1856) is an attractive geographical and historical record interspersed with notes of travel. Stanley's liberalism was rooted in the historical and concrete bent of his mind. By history he understood the picturesque realisation of the past, and the sympathetic tracing of the fortunes of institutions and ideas. Himself in the thick of affairs, he bids the student of the Creeds imagine the actual process by which they were hammered out into a compromise, after the manner of committees:

> a new turn given to one sentiment, a charitable colour thrown over another; the edge of a sharp exclusion blunted by one party, the sting of a bitter sarcasm drawn by another. Regard confessions of faith in their only true historical light.

The doctrinal point of view is again submerged by the historical in Stanley's *Lectures on History of the Eastern Church* (1861) and on the *History of the Jewish Church* (1863-76). He drew much inspiration from Ewald; but his own work in these regions is that of a populariser. His views on doctrine and polity, as set forth in his *Christian Institutions* (1881) show the distinctive uncertainty, or *Halbheit*, which marks his school, and which consists with the purest sincerity. He was more on his native ground in his *Historical Memorials of Canterbury* (1855) and of *Westminster Abbey* (1865). Stanley gave new life, not only to the historical spirit, but also to the old seventeenth-century text, with all its practical corollaries, that 'vitals in religion are few.' He drove home to the popular mind—in terms however vague—the conception that the category of growth applies to the future as well as to the past of theological beliefs and institutions. In his ardour for a larger comprehensiveness and charity he often recalls Chillingworth, or Hales, or the author of *The Liberty of Prophesying*, though all these are stronger writers than Stanley.

XVI

Amongst the scholar-clerics the strongest and most original spirit, the most learned man, and the best writer was Mark Pattison [1] (1813-84), Rector of Lincoln College. He published little ; but his *stylus* is pen and dagger in one. Pattison narrates his own mental history up to the year 1860 in his *Memoirs*, which were posthumously published, and the sequel to which was withheld ; for he spared his contemporaries, living or dead, no more than himself. He came from an Evangelical home ; was at first swept along by Newman, writing two Lives of the Saints and doing some translations ; but after a time, and many struggles, he revolted and escaped. He quitted first the Anglican and then the 'Catholic' standpoint ; became and found his real bent as a humanist ; and gave his life to study. What Pattison says of Macaulay is true of himself: 'his command of literature was imperial.' In Oxford he stood for and fulfilled the old ideals of scholarship, which he truly judged were being smothered by a parasitic system of examinations, tutors, and committees. The *Memoirs* and the *Suggestions for Academical Organisation* (1868) embody his academic views. Pattison was also, less nobly, embittered by an intrigue which robbed him for many years of his college headship. He became a recluse and somewhat formidable figure, admired by a small public.

He was perhaps most at home in the literature, both lighter and graver, of the sixteenth, seventeenth, and eighteenth centuries. His most substantial volume is his *Isaac Casaubon* (1875) ; here, as usual, he does work which need not be done again, and converts his great learning into literature. The outlines of a still more notable work on Joseph Scaliger are to be seen in a magazine article and in a fragment which has been saved. He wrote on Erasmus, More, and Grotius (and also on Macaulay) in the *Encyclopædia Britannica*. The Renaissance he approached less as a flourishing-time of art and poetry than as a new birth in 'the grand development of human reason': and this process, again, he studied less on the purely philosophic side than as laying the foundations of critical knowledge. His own ultimate creed, he tells us, was slowly won ; he passed

> to that highest development when all religions appear in their historical light, as efforts of the human spirit to come to an understanding with that Unseen Power whose pressure it feels, but whose motives are a riddle.

But the reference to pure thought and pure letters always invigorates Pattison's writing, and is well seen in his treatment of the poets and theologians.

His paper, already named, in *Essays and Reviews*, upon the *Tendencies of Religious Thought in England, 1688 to 1750*, has worn well, and is a worthy companion to Sir Leslie Stephen's *History of English Thought in the Eighteenth Century.* His *Milton* (1879) is still the best short book on the subject in existence. Here, and in his edition of Milton's sonnets, Pattison responds to the grace as well as to the grandeur of the poet. Again, in his editions of Pope's *Essay on Man* and *Satires and Epistles,* his conversance with the mind of the time and the byways of literature is most remarkable. His fairly numerous periodical articles and reviews have the same stamp; the *Academy,* in the Seventies and Eighties, contains many of his notices that are worth unburying, including one on George Meredith's *Poems and Lyrics of the Joy of Earth* (1883). His style is hardly popular, though its lighter side is seen in his pages on *University Novels* ; but it is never hard or pedantic. Its mark is compressed strength, united with elegance and exactness ; and he likes to pack his mind into a Tacitean epigram, as when he calls the Oxford training 'the exaltation of smattering into a method.' His manner may be considered too scornful, and his life and temper were superficially inhuman; but he often rises to the higher strain :

> I shared the vulgar fallacy that a literary life meant a life devoted to the making of books, and that not to be always coming before the public was to be idle. It cost me years more of extrication of thought before I rose to the conception that the highest life is the art to live, and that both men, women, and books are equally essential ingredients in such a life.

A sentence that well illustrates Pattison's manner, and may avert some misconceptions as to his character.

The list of theologians, orthodox or vagrant, must not be extended further ; few of the remainder belong to literature proper. Yet it would be amiss not to name Francis William Newman (1805-97), the younger brother and polar opposite of the Cardinal ; though he has left little for our purpose except his religious autobiography, *Phases of Faith* (1850). The pilgrimage of Francis Newman was from the rigid Evangelical to the Unitarian point of view, and he relates it without the moving grace of his brother, yet with a simple sincerity and fervour. He has, it may be hazarded, a freer and more open mind than the Cardinal. Another of his books, entitled *The Soul, its Sorrows and Aspirations* (1849), shows a kindred strain of interest in what he calls 'the pathology of the spirit,' and is an impassioned effort to find room, in a system purely theistic, for the characteristic religious emotions and experiences—the feeling for the infinite and the sense of sin and of forgiveness. Francis Newman wrote besides on most things under the sun —mathematics, Oriental languages, history, divinity—with undoubted learning; he translated Homer amid the mockery of Matthew Arnold; and there seems to have been some twist of ineffectual queerness in many of his activities.

Many other religious writers are perforce omitted from these notes. Names like those of Lightfoot, Hort, and Westcott, and of the many-sided William Robertson Smith, are within the competence of the historians of biblical exegesis. That of the long-lived Thomas Erskine of Linlathen (1788-1870), whose published work falls very early in the period, and partly before it, belongs to pure theology and devotional writing, on which his influence was marked. So, too, the sermons of Frederick William Robertson (1816-53) of Brighton, posthumously published from notes and reports, won fame in the religious world for their fire and independence. But the record of 'applied literature,' with the problems of choice and treatment which it raises, must now draw to an end, although it will reappear at times in the pages on the travellers and essayists, and on the social writings of Ruskin and Matthew Arnold. There remains the literature which is to be judged purely as art: the poetry, the fiction, the imaginative or descriptive prose; and there remains also literary criticism, or the judgement of such art.

CHAPTER IX

JOHN RUSKIN

I

THE unity of John Ruskin's [1] life (1819-1900) and of his purpose, at first sight so distracted, comes into clearer light with time. A generation has passed since his labours ended. His writings every scrap, and his letters and memoranda, have been edited with pious care and precision. They fill thirty-nine volumes; and a glance at the last of these, containing the big index, will throw some light on that many-faceted, rash, and passionate spirit, which flung itself on every theme, with unvarying self-confidence, not always with knowledge, but with arresting intensity, and with transparent honesty of aim. The face of nature; the art of painting, sculpture, architecture, and literature; war and trade, economics and education, the differences and relations of the sexes: over them all Ruskin ranges, trying to cover a field for which the mind of Goethe might possibly be adequate, and yet more often profound than ridiculous, more often penetrating than indiscriminate. In expression, once his style has been matured, it is not easy for him to go wrong; and when we say that Ruskin writes ill, we are mostly thinking of what he says, and not of how he has said it; for his most painful pages give his meaning as faithfully as the wisest and sanest. His position as a master of words is impregnable; his position as a critic and thinker, though a high one, is much more equivocal. But to estimate this with any fulness a long patient discussion would be needed, as well as the special gifts of the artist and the economist. I shall only try to take certain bearings in the wide map of his works, a map that is crowded with names, and confused as to its frontiers; for within it art and ethics, ethics and theology, theology and science, science and art once more are seen interwinding with endless curious enclaves.

One clue at least has been plain for a long time. Ruskin did not, in the midway of his life, about the year 1860, abruptly abandon art and commence reformer. He was always a reformer, and an artist he always remained. There was only a remarkable change of emphasis. His campaign in behalf of Turner and Tintoret, of Gothic and the study of natural forms, is united by many a thread to his campaign against the mercantile economy, *laissez-faire*, and social apathy or injustice. This connexion is best expressed by saying that Ruskin was always a preacher; he is, indeed, the last great preacher whom the English-speaking nations have found. He would be great in a different way—he would persuade, or revolt, the judgement in a different way; he would not be Ruskin, if he were not concerned, first and foremost, with pointing out the ways of salvation. And he is a preacher with a measure of religious doctrine—sometimes more, sometimes very little, but always some—in his mind, and therefore on his lips. It is his ethical passion, if anything, which binds all his activities together; to this in the end they are all subordinate. It is the spring of his best and rarest utterance; and also of his principal weakness, which may be defined as a propensity, borne along by spiritual fervour, and on the wings of his own eloquence, to take premature and illegitimate short cuts to some conclusion which could only be reached and assured, if at all, by a long circuit of reasoning. But first to sketch his career as a man of letters.

The first volume (1843) of *Modern Painters* revealed a new vein of wealth. I shall speak presently of Ruskin as an artist in words; but it was clear that the tradition of high philosophic prose was suddenly refreshed, that new pathways were opened for the imagination, that the criticism of art was now renewed, almost created, in England, and that a new language had been found, not less exact than beautiful, and unknown even to the poets, for the notation of natural phenomena, both in themselves and as they are represented in fine art. 'Word-painting' Ruskin always repudiated, and it is a phrase that means little; but he had the gift of translating the impressions of the eye into speech, with an accuracy which it was easy, in the glow of his images and the melody of his numbers, to overlook. To this gift he added the gift of spiritual passion; but description, passion, and theory all served for the present one ruling purpose. This was to vindicate and interpret Turner, who had long been noted and prosperous, but who had not been intelligently valued, and whose later work had been attacked by journalists of the hour. Ruskin also praised other landscape painters of the British school, such as Copley Fielding. As a foil, he held up to scorn the admired masters of the 'classical group,' especially Claude [1] and Salvator Rosa. In later volumes these censures, showing a peculiar power of mingling analysis with invective, were more fully reasoned out, and in some instances qualified. And the book was all the stranger because it was steeped, as the author was afterwards to deplore, in a brewage of fanatical, evangelical sentiment: 'to this day,' we are told, absurdly, 'the clear and tasteless poison of the art of Raphael infects with sleep of infidelity the hearts of millions of Christians.'

Ruskin was afterwards to leave a balanced judgement on Raphael, and to revise his first volume. But nothing could quite eradicate the Protestant bias. The extreme zeal of it, and his whole temper of mind, often led him, so his first readers might excusably think, to explain or explain away nearly all artistic excellence in terms of religion and the virtues. Yet, after all, one of the prime virtues, in his eyes, was simply truthfulness; by which he meant fidelity, in observation and in representation, to natural fact, though by no means always the literal and complete portrayal of it. Here, then, Ruskin was back on strictly artistic ground. Such truthfulness, moreover, was a supreme characteristic of Turner, whom he praised for it abundantly. And who, then, in the year 1843, was the anonymous Ruskin?

II

Only his own pen could have fitly contrasted the 'two boyhoods'—his own, and that of Carlyle, who was afterwards to be his acknowledged fountain of wisdom. We know the story of the struggles of Teufelsdröckh. Ruskin wrote in his old age a crystal narrative of his youth, *Præterita*, in which he relates his surprising early good fortune; and indeed he needed all the happiness that his *Fors* might give him, for prelude to a life that was to have more than its share of discord and tragedy. He was precocious; and his home, like Milton's, though in some ways strictly puritanical, did not by any means starve his imagination. His parents believed in him, and they were very well to do; the father, the 'entirely honest merchant,' in the wine-trade, and a sagacious guide in affairs, perceived his son's genius; and the son was left, like Milton, to follow his star. He was somewhat unhappily sheltered from healthy mental rough and tumble with his peers. But he lived near the London galleries, he was taken abroad to France, Switzerland, and Italy, and he knew Turner well personally. His own drawings were most faithful and delicate, and he soon wrote remarkable prose; as well as verse in plenty, which counts for little. He went to Christ Church, but got little from the regular studies of the place, unless we are to credit them with inspiring the enthusiasm for Plato which colours much of his thinking. He wrote on Alpine geology in *Loudon's Magazine of Natural History*; and his papers (1837-8) in the *Architectural Magazine* upon 'The Poetry of Architecture' visibly forecast the subject and temper of the *Stones of Venice*. He had also made, though he did not print, a defence of Turner against the tirades of *Blackwood's*. Thus, though a very new graduate, being only twenty-four, when the noted first volume came out, Ruskin was by no means unpractised.

The book was at once recognised; English art criticism being then in a very poor and parochial condition, and having fallen as far behind artistic production as the Elizabethan critics, in 1600, fell behind the poetry that was sounding in their ears. Hazlitt, the most eloquent lover of pictures in the last age, had died in 1830. Ruskin has little to say to Hazlitt, drawing chiefly upon Burke, Reynolds, and Dugald Stewart; of whom Reynolds had by far the most to teach him. But Reynolds he was to attack, ten years later, respectfully but strongly, for his heresy (already well denounced by Blake), that the grand style in painting consists in an abstract and general treatment of the object, and not in fidelity to particulars. This criticism was to be developed in the third volume (1856) of *Modern Painters*. Meantime Ruskin's own verbal notes of nature were themselves concrete and true. He gave eyes,[1] to all who could use them, for cloud and sunlight and the shapes of shadows, for flower and leafage, for ice and flame, for stone and crystal, for serpent and bird—in fact for *opera omnia*; and he was ever ready with his fervent *Benedicite*. And, he says in effect, although truth of presentation is the artist's first law, it must be truth working under the further law of the imagination; no Dutch literalism, or delineation hair by hair, being sufficient or useful for art. I am anticipating much that comes out plainer in the subsequent volumes of *Modern Painters* but is traceable from the first, when I add that on this great body of observations, drawn partly from nature and partly from painting, Ruskin builds up his immense, and often fragile, superstructure of values, ethical, spiritual, and theological; a procedure which he follows, indeed, in all his works. But the stride which had been made in the actual analysis of art is better realised in the second volume, published in 1846. Here Ruskin expounds a complex conception of beauty, draws upon the poets as well as the painters, goes wider afield for his examples, and reveals the true magnificence of his descriptive power, as well as the fuller harmonies of his prose.

For he had meanwhile travelled through the galleries of France and the Swiss valleys, had reached Venice, and had found Tintoret, whom in this second volume he glorifies. The manner, which he afterwards regretted that he had modelled upon Hooker's, leaves some impression of artifice, but it is a dignified, spacious medium for an elaborate theory [1] of the beautiful. This theory, which he was never to carry much further, has a place of honour in the history of English æsthetic; and it was produced, like Burke's book on the *Sublime and Beautiful*, at the age of twenty-seven. The arrangement is over-scholastic, especially in the chapters on the 'theoretic,' which Ruskin, in his Platonic way, steadily refused to call the 'æsthetic,' faculty; the types of sundry divine qualities, such as 'unity,' 'purity,' and 'infinity,' have no true logical principle of division; and the insistence on the religious symbolism which is to be extracted from natural objects amounts to a fixed idea. But the essay on the different types of imagination, 'associative,' 'penetrative,' and 'contemplative,' is one of the most satisfactory in the language. In passing, Ruskin illuminates the poets; he quotes from Dante, Spenser (a fellow-Platonist), Shakespeare, Milton, Scott, Wordsworth, and Shelley. The comments upon Dante's flames, upon Wordsworth's fraternal yew-trees, and upon Shakespeare's 'imagination penetrative' ('How did Shakespeare *know* that Virgilia could not speak?'), show that Ruskin himself has the kind of imagination he describes; and no one can be the same after having once read them. And the other passages, the great coloured ones that get into the anthologies, like those on the Soldanella flower, on Turner's dragon, on Tintoret's Last Judgement, and on Perugino's Michael, are not mere patches, but arise out of the argument, and are examples, themselves, of veracity working under the law of the imagination, with that faculty at full stretch.

III

The writings of Ruskin down to 1860 can be regarded, despite their variety of matter and their connexion with those that follow, as forming a single group. The bibliography [2] hides the real assortment of the topics. For *Modern Painters* appeared in five volumes, covering seventeen years; in 1843, 1846, 1856 (vols. iii. and iv.), and 1860. It embraces six or seven distinct compositions, each of them being scattered through various volumes ; and Ruskin's subsequent endeavours to sift out and reorder the material were incomplete, while the first two volumes he largely revised. Moreover, *Modern Painters* was interrupted by two other books which grew out of it, namely *The Seven Lamps of Architecture* (1849), and *The Stones of Venice* ; of which the first volume appeared in 1851, the second and third in 1853. And there is an array of lesser works, mostly produced after 1850, to add : reviews, letters to the press on art and politics ; the so-called *Notes on the Construction of Sheepfolds*, of which more hereafter, and which disappointed both farmers and clergymen ; many catalogues and observations dealing with Turner ; and a series of *Notes on the Royal Academy*, eloquent or biting, an ensample of what is called art journalism. More substantial is the pamphlet called *Pre-Raphaelitism*, which in 1851 brought timely succour to Millais and his friends ; who, after Turner and Tintoret, were Ruskin's third great discovery, and whom he upheld and chastened to the last. He also produced a very popular manual on *The Elements of Drawing* (1857) and a harder one on *The Elements of Perspective*. Of wider scope are the Edinburgh *Lectures on Architecture and Painting* (1854), a lucid summary of his earlier gospel ; and *The Two Paths* (1859), also lectures consummate in arrangement and expression and setting forth one of his chief articles of faith, namely that all high design in sculpture and painting depends on the observance of the forms of organic nature.

Towards 1860 there are many signs of the change of emphasis, to which I have referred, in Ruskin's interests. It intrudes into the last volume of *Modern Painters* ; and still more prophetic are the Manchester discourses of 1857 on *The Political Economy of Art*, in which the faiths and frays of the following decade are seen to be taking shape, and which was afterwards augmented and named, significantly enough, '*A Joy for Ever*' (*and its Price in the Market*) (1880). Out of all this output it is not easy to wash the gold. A note on some of the major works, and on some features of Ruskin's mind and creed, must here suffice. Of his many practical doings, in connexion with the Oxford Museum, the Working Men's College, and the Turner collection, his biographer gives an admirable account. The parable of the sower might have been written of Ruskin. The Turner Gallery, which he did not live to enter, is perhaps, amongst things that can be seen, the principal fruit of his labours.

IV

The Seven Lamps, which grew out of notes made for *Modern Painters*, may be regarded either as a side-chapel to that great irregular edifice, or as a portal to a much more symmetrical and finished one, *The Stones of Venice*. It is Ruskin's first essay in vindication of Gothic. The names of the lamps, which he managed with some trouble to limit to the mystic seven, express the sacred principles which he considered to preside over this, the noblest sort of architecture. And the lamps really do give light; for in this, beyond all the other arts, it is least unfair to trace a direct relationship between the artistic result and the moral qualities, not only of the designer and workman, but also of the society that produces and employs them. The lamp of Sacrifice prompts men to spend freely, beyond what is needed for mere use, and for the sake of noble effect, upon costly materials and ample spaces. The lamp of Truth forbids all kinds of deception like the marbling of wood or the use of machine-made ornament. The lamp of Memory enjoins the preservation of good or great ancient buildings, and forbids the 'restoration' of them. The lamp of Beauty shows us that in ornamentation and design all the 'most lovely forms and thoughts are directly taken from natural objects.' The significance of the lamps of Power and Life is less distinct; and the lamp of Obedience, more questionably, warns us, as Ruskin did all his days, against the 'pursuit of that treacherous phantom which men call Liberty.' The book has been a living influence, and has affected actual architecture, as well as triumphantly interpreting the Gothic ideal. It is based on laborious study; Ruskin's own drawings complete its value, and we may wonder whether they will not outlive many of his sermons. There remains a touch of immature didacticism in the style of *The Seven Lamps*, but it is one of Ruskin's clearest and most orderly books. Some of its pages foreshadow the transference of his interest from the work of art to the condition, in mind, body, and estate, of the individual workman: 'Was the carver happy while he was about it?'

Much of *The Stones of Venice* comes near to the ordinary forms of scholarly exposition for which, when he chose, Ruskin displayed a real genius. Many chapters are filled with close technical analysis, which was the fruit of immense toil conducted on the spot, often hidden or suppressed, like that of the workmen in the churches which he describes. But there is also a far-reaching statement of principle. The famed chapter on the nature of Gothic is in organic connexion with the rest of the book, and with Ruskin's lifelong creed. It was joyously declaimed, as a confession of faith, by some of the 'Pre-Raphaelites.' It was reprinted separately for working men. It was, essentially, a reasoned vindication of the great mediæval revival, which for a whole century had been inspiring creative work in poetry, in prose, in painting, and in building, but which had never given a very articulate account of itself, although the word Gothic had long ceased to be derogatory. But now all future champions of Gothic must start, if only they can, where Ruskin left off. He gives much less space to its external or material forms than to the nature of its 'mental expression,' which is analysed under many headings. Not all of these are equally apt, but all are suggestive. Under 'changefulness' is demonstrated the principle of infinite life and variety that quickens Gothic arch and tracery. In the section on the grotesque, a subject expanded afterwards in *Modern Painters*, Ruskin works his way into the problem, which for such an idealist as himself is the most searching of all; namely what feelings of pathos, or oddity, or strangeness may rightfully, though with an apparent effect of discord, modify the expression of beauty. Many things that are good he shrinks from admiring; but no one has yet probed further into the question. Perhaps the most enlightening section is that on 'naturalism,' a term which Ruskin uses not in its later sense, but as a middle one between the 'purism,' like the art of Perugino or Stothard, which represents only what is perfectly good or pure, and 'sensualism which perceives and imitates evil only.' The naturalists, he says, the 'second or greatest class,'

> render all that they see in nature unhesitatingly, yet with a kind of divine grasp or government of the whole; sympathising with all the good, and yet confessing, permitting, and bringing good out of the evil also. Their subject is as infinite as nature, their colour equally balanced between splendour and sadness, reaching occasionally the highest degrees of both, and their chiaroscuro equally balanced between light and shade.

This subject is resumed in the third volume of *Modern Painters*, and 'naturalism' seems to imply a perfect balance between the idealising spirit and the recording gift.

V

The main text of *The Stones of Venice* is not simply the supremacy of Gothic art, but the wider one that art, and architecture in particular, is the most sensitive index of the moral goodness and greatness of a people. 'The rise and fall of Venetian Gothic art depends on the moral or immoral temper of the state.' It is usually admitted that Ruskin established the connexion, or at least the coincidence, of the moral and artistic phenomena, in the case of Venice. In this light he traces the development of the Gothic from the Byzantine style, and its decline into that of the Renaissance, with wonderful clearness, for the lay as well as the learned reader. More questionably, he extends his principle to the history of art at large.

This, however, is one of the instances in which Ruskin's way, already noted, of taking an intellectual short cut spoils his case and conceals the element of truth which it contains. He tries to make out that art is a 'function,' in the scientific sense, of national morality, varying in excellence along with it. He often had to meet, and never seems to have met, the retort that much good and even noble art has arisen among nations, and during periods, which cannot be credited with special elevation or purity of morals. The Athens of Phidias, the Italy of Leonardo, and the England of Wren have little right, on his showing, to produce what in fact they did produce. The retort, however, does not dispose of Ruskin's principle, but only shows that his calculus is much too simple. An 'age' is not all of a piece ; and it is clear that the *Pilgrim's Progress*, for example, appearing in the time of Wycherley, is a work of art, which speaks for the deeper and unspoilt elements in the society of the Restoration. Ruskin liked to read a little Plato every day ; and if we think of the servile basis, and of the sexual code, of the community from which the Dialogues emerged, apparently like flowers from a dunghill, the proposition that art is a function of national morality will be seen to be neither wholly true nor wholly idle. An art like that of Balzac, which portrays the whole of a society in its heights and depths, presents yet other riddles, for which Ruskin's canon is inadequate. In such cases there is nothing for it but an intricate, and above all a disinterested, analysis ; the question cannot be solved by a rush.

Ruskin's strength and weakness are fully displayed in *The Stones of Venice*. The rigmarole in the third volume against the 'poison-tree' of the Renaissance, especially in its later developments, such as the 'pride of science,' the 'pride of system,' 'infidelity,' and the rest, is all the more melancholy reading, because Ruskin pounces on some genuine defects, but sees them in lurid disproportion. And his attack widens far beyond its original reference to the history of architecture; and much of his abuse of modern civilisation seems to be rooted in the primary absurdity of thinking that the Renaissance came on the whole to be a bad thing, and to mark a step backwards for the human spirit. It is needless to dwell upon the blindness to the whole later course of mental and moral history that this prejudice, partly sectarian or pietistic in its origin, involves. It is the price that Ruskin pays for his great achievement, which is also his inalienable glory; namely to have revealed in a new light the greatness of the ages of faith, which culminate in the *Divine Comedy* and in the best Gothic. About the earlier Renaissance he says much that is true and illuminating; he guards himself against the charge of ever slighting for a moment the work of Leonardo and his companions; and he shows a deep sympathy with Spenser, or at least with the Platonic and mediæval sides of that poet's imagination. Any true artist whose genius is of the symbolic or allegorical cast is pretty sure of Ruskin's homage. Nothing is better than his distinction between personification and symbolism, or his comparison of Spenser's emblematic method with that of the painters and sculptors, or his passing touches of moral analysis. Much of this matter is to be found in the chapter on the 'Ducal Palace,' which Ruskin justly calls 'one of the most important pieces of work done in my life.' There are many other things of price in the book, like the prose hymn to colour, which preceded Meredith's poem (1888) by a generation.

VI

The third volume of *Modern Painters*, well entitled 'Of many Things,' recurs to some of the old problems in the light of ten years' further experience. The 'ideals' of 'naturalism' and of the 'grotesque' are re-described. The nature of the 'grand style' is expounded at length; the conditions of its appearance being nobility of subject, love of beauty, and sincerity of treatment; though what, after all, the grand style may *be* is less apparent. It is not bound down to minute particulars, and yet it does not reject them; how far it shall enlist them must depend on the occasion. The true test is to ask how far the imagination is actively at work upon the particulars. One of Ruskin's best chapters is that upon 'Finish,' true and false; and true finish is defined, most pertinently, as 'the completeness of the expression of the idea,' and, simpler still, as 'telling more truth.' The same principle is applied to the problem which had always vexed Ruskin (and indeed it is a fundamental one), namely how far the artist's imagination is to be bound by things seen, as they are seen; in fact, what is the law guiding his selecting, rejecting, and combining power. Ruskin had praised Turner and Tintoret for free creative genius, and the 'Pre-Raphaelites' and Dürer for rigorous observance of fact, and he sought some elastic formula that should cover all such cases. Again and again he seems on the verge of stating what would now be called the purely 'artistic' canon, which first and foremost judges the excellence of the handiwork as an expression of the artist's idea or subject. In his third chapter he reviews the relationship of technique to theme and expression. But he is soon off again in search of one or other of his spiritual 'lamps'; and, with all his disclaimers, he is ever prone to judge the work of art rather by the high feeling which its topic, or its conception, may arouse than by the actual performance.

A long section of this volume (chaps. xi.-xvii.) contains one of Ruskin's most delightful, coherent, and trustworthy studies; all the more trustworthy, that he is here safe on his own territory of rock, and valley, and lowland. He sketches, at its salient points, the sentiment of landscape in poetry and art—but at first more fully in poetry—from Homer down to Turner. He draws chiefly on Homer for antiquity, and on Dante for the Middle Ages, and on Scott and Wordsworth amongst recent poets. Of course there are outcries against the Renaissance and modern life; and one chapter, that on the 'moral of landscape,' opens with the question whether we 'may wisely boast' of the pleasure which landscape gives, and may 'unhesitatingly indulge it.' But this extraordinary qualm is allayed; and then we are told, with a delicacy only equalled in the *Prelude*, of Ruskin's own nascent feeling for scenery during his childhood. The penetrating discussion of the 'pathetic fallacy' is equally well known; though it is often forgotten that, in Ruskin's view, the 'fallacy' does *not* consist simply in imputing human feelings to natural objects. To the last chapter, on 'the teachers of Turner,' is appended—such a dance does Ruskin take his readers—an epilogue on the Crimean war, with a great prose dirge on the soldier-boys who had perished in it; and there is also a word of praise for a certain 'great emperor,' Louis Napoleon namely.

The fourth and fifth volumes of *Modern Painters* (1856, 1860) form together a splendid if exasperating medley which defies any brief description. There is always the purpose of explaining Turner, and of enforcing the 'moral of landscape.' To this the more systematic chapters are devoted; and the analysis of the aspect of mountain, tree, and cloud, begun in the first volume, is resumed, naturally with an immense enrichment of material. This part of the book has been acclaimed both by mountaineers and by artists; nor is there much of Ruskin's writing that bids fair to stand firmer, or to last longer. And, after finishing the pages on 'Turnerian mystery,' 'Turnerian topography,' and 'Turnerian light,' he might well have said, like Chapman on completing his *Homer*,

> The work that I was born to do is done.

Turner was now to be safe on his pillar in the House of Fame. But Ruskin's work, as we shall see, was not done; in one sense, he had hardly begun it. Prompted by his father, he forced himself to bring *Modern Painters* to a stop; and it is evident from many signs that he was preoccupied with a great new campaign, this time in the field of economics. But these volumes, the fourth and fifth, show his thoughts raying out, in the strangest brilliant fashion, to all quarters of the compass.

Sometimes there is an historical thread, as in the unsympathetic account of the Dutch painters. 'The Mountain Gloom' and the 'Mountain Glory' describe the influence of scenery upon national, and especially upon rustic, character, with the sharpest possible portrayal of the unhappy scenes and faces which lived in Ruskin's memory. In the chapters with poetic headings, 'The Nereid's Guard,' or 'The Lance of Pallas,' the treatment is free to the point of incoherence, and the wandering capricious style of a later phase, that of *Fors Clavigera*, is foreshadowed. As we near the end, we never know whether we shall light on a profound reading of a great picture, or on a gallop into etymology or mythology, often fantastic, or upon musical *suspiria* lamenting the condition of lost and blackened England, or on a whirl of Bible texts, or on a passage of sober and consecutive analysis, like the chapter on 'Vulgarity,' which is worthy of Plato. Instead of attempting a vain summary, it may be convenient to halt at this central point of Ruskin's life, and to review quickly, looking both before and after, three different but connected aspects of his mind and gift. The first of these is his temper towards religion; the second, his ethical view of art; and the third, his position amidst his fellow-masters of the English language.

VII

Ruskin was brought up in an acrid sort of Evangelical Protestantism, which he afterwards reacted against violently, trying to weed the signs of it out of the reprints of his earlier books ; or, where he could not do that, to recant in footnotes. It took, however, the form less of insisting on the special dogmas of the school than of a bitter anti-Romish sentiment which discoloured his view of history and interrupted his criticism of art. In the *Notes on the Construction of Sheepfolds* (1851), his only quite unreadable volume, he dreams, like Leibniz long before him, of a union of the Protestant Churches ; and his dislike of the Anglo-Catholic and Anglo-Roman movements is intensified by their weakness for bastard Gothic. But in time he came to ask himself the question put by Matthew Arnold : 'O Evangelical Protestant, is thine own religion, then, so true ?' or, in his own words, he perceived that he had not seen the absurdity of thinking the divisions of Protestantism wrong, but 'the schism between Protestant and Catholic virtuous and sublime.' And so, at any rate after 1860, Ruskin comes to shed much of his Protestantism, though still upholding 'the authority of scripture' ; and yet to reduce, during a long and perplexed interval, his actual tenets to a very few, to which he clings as to a raft ; doing, withal, a kind of despairing justice to the agnostic or secular school, whom he sees beginning to prevail around him, and appealing to it (as in *The Crown of Wild Olive*) in the noblest terms—and almost with a momentary sympathy ?—to make the most of the one life that it was sure of, and to back him in his crusades. Then again, latterly, under the old spell of the ages of faith and their art, Ruskin, without any stiffening of dogma, was ready to call himself, in the largest sense of the term, a 'Catholic' ; standing, generally and as of old, for 'faith' against 'unfaith,' which he found to be the taint of the modern world at large. This is but a rough chart of the journey which led through many a winding, and in the course of which Ruskin submitted to many influences. The greatest of these, beyond doubt, was that of Carlyle. In both these thinkers we are at first perplexed by the mixture of intense conservatism of temper with extreme paucity of dogma. Such eulogists of the times of faith *ought*, we feel, to have had more of that commodity themselves ; *ought* not, along with so many sons of the new world which they revile, to have thrown over most of the venerable consolations. But the solution may be found in the compensating intensity with which they held to their primary tenets: to the faith that is in a divine order of the world, and (in Carlyle's case at least) in the ultimate might of goodness. Often their creed comes to no more than this, but it seldom comes to less.

Still it is hard to give a simple account of the religion, or religions, of Ruskin. He was never a mere Protestant; for all he might say, he was, like Milton, very much a child of the Renaissance. He would have been very different if the manuscripts of Plato had never been discovered. And his artistic theory and his religious creed interpenetrate. Often, in his earlier works, he talks much like a Christian Platonist, who sees in the Divine at once the source and the identifying principle, of goodness and beauty. This view comes out plainest in the second volume of *Modern Painters*. And there is an odd seasoning, as of Paley, in Ruskin's blending of Plato and Spenser with the Bible; there is an emphasis on the presence of design in nature, but a transfer of that emphasis from utility to beauty. For beautiful natural forms, in their perfection, are *made* for us to love, admire, and live by; so that the main or ultimate function of art, in representing them, comes at once into sight. Ruskin never swerved from this point of view, though he elaborates it in many ways. Whatever we think of it, the point for remark is that he never suffers it, for any edifying purpose, to warp his actual record of natural facts; working steadily, in that sense, by the light of his own 'lamp of truth.'

Ruskin's tendency to take an ethical view of art is the best-known and most obvious feature of his writings; and also, some would say, the most obsolete one. The identity of the great triad, truth, beauty, and goodness, is not a thing that he tries to prove; he assumes, applies, and illustrates it. This immense jump of his, from beauty to morals, over chasms by Ruskin unperceived, can escape no reader. It never gives him the least trouble, and he bridges it over, or covers it up very considerably, in Platonic fashion, by his use of the word *noble*, good and fair, *καλός*; *noble* is perhaps the commonest epithet in his writings, as well as the truest and most comprehensive one that can be applied to them. There is little doubt that his constant straining of this term, which led him to find 'ethics' in the 'dust,' and 'temperance and intemperance in curvature,' and sermons, not only in the stones of Venice, but in those of the field, had its share in provoking the revulsion, which becomes so marked towards the end of the century, against the notion of building, between art and ethics, any particular bridge at all. And certainly, if we followed Ruskin, we should cut ourselves off from the appreciation of many good artists and writers, simply because of his driving of an undeniable truth too far, and because his conception of 'nobility,' after all, is not a perfectly catholic one ; leading him, as it does, to avert his eyes from what may be called great mixed art, or art that profoundly expresses mixed humanity ; or, to put it in a word, from art as *expression*.

It is clear, however, that this question of the relation of art and ethics is bound up with another one of a more purely æsthetic sort, namely the relation of the artist's subject, or motive, to his technique and execution ; and Ruskin's position here is often misread. He is careful to repeat that virtue alone cannot make any man an artist or any nation artistic. A mass of his writing, both critical and pedagogic (like *The Elements of Drawing*), is concerned purely with execution. He has left a great body of judgements on particular painters, which are entirely concerned with the way in which they did their work, apart from the question of their ulterior motives. He analyses Turner's actual quality of vision, in terms of line and colour, at length, on its own merits. And even when Ruskin deserts this ground, and flies off to his application and his moral, that procedure, think of it what we may, does not falsify what he has to say on the technical or executive side. I repeat this point, because we are thus able to trust Ruskin so much more than might have been expected ; owing, once more, to his fidelity to the 'lamp of truth.'

But it is time to speak of him, and of his own technique and performance, as a writer ; considering it apart, so far as may be, from his ideas, and from what is called his 'message.'

VIII

For the year 1860 quickened a change, which had long been coming, in his style.[1] 'The art of language,' as he remarks, 'is certainly one of the fine arts' ; and what kind of an artist, in language, is Ruskin ? He had another art, that of the pencil, of which I am not competent to speak ; but it is impossible to think of his books apart from the hundreds of examples of his nice and often exquisite handiwork. He also, in early days, wrote much verse which is full of feeling and is technically right, but which leaves very little impression. In prose he is, accurately speaking, the central figure of his time : central, because the prose of Carlyle, though greater in itself, and of stronger fibre, is well away from the centre, from the type and long tradition, from the English prose of the past, the present, and the future; while Ruskin's in its pure and classical quality, and in the distinctive character of its beauty, is in the full stream of that tradition. The first instalments of *Modern Painters* opened, as I have said, new pathways in imaginative, descriptive, and expository prose. Landor and De Quincey had still work before them, but they really belonged to the previous age. John Stuart Mill was a very good, but not exactly an inspired, writer. The novelists, Dickens and Thackeray, did not attempt the prose of ideas. Thackeray, indeed, is one of Ruskin's two contemporary rivals in the command of pure, flowing, and incorrupt English; but grandeur and splendour and prophecy, not to speak of intellectual analysis, lie so far from his powers or purpose that the comparison cannot go further. The other rival was Newman, who had already written much and had preached his best in St. Mary's. Newman, in 1843, was the most delicate living master of the prose instrument; and was also a master, in his own way, of spiritual appeal, though chiefly to those of his own fold. But Ruskin from the first had sympathies far wider, and a far deeper sense of human needs, than Newman, and therefore a rarer moral intuition; as well as a style, at first less Attic in stamp than Newman's, but of incomparably more sweep, and variety, and greatness: a more *generous* style, and altogether the voice of a more generous brain. But I am now to speak of his English; [1] and Ruskin has one of the surest styles in our language.

Like Newman's, it is secured, at the very foundations, by an intimacy with the Authorised Version,[2] of which no secular writer has made fuller use. The mere quotations and references fill endless double columns in the great Index. Ruskin tells in *Præterita* how the whole Bible was dinned into him every year by his mother in his childhood, 'hard names and all.' Unlike many children, he was grateful, and read it daily afterwards. From the Bible comes much of the best of his language and cadence: it is never far off in his magic melodies; no other literary influence can be compared with it. Nor any mental influence; for it affected his whole temper towards nature, art, and humanity. It kept the vernacular part of his vocabulary fine as well as pure. The vocabulary of a writer like Cobbett is pure, but not fine; but Ruskin appropriates both the plain idiom and the poetical and imaginative part of the scriptural diction. Hence, as his biographer observes, it 'is ingrained in the texture of almost every piece from his pen.' Not that this influence is wholly for good. When he is angry, a text easily becomes a 'war substitute' for an argument. There is often an unpleasant pulpit twang. The peroration is apt to become a confused shower [1] of quotations, and we wait until it is over. The end of the lecture on 'Work,' in *The Crown of Wild Olive*, is a painful instance: in contrast with the pertinent and moving close of *Unto This Last*, one of the summits of Ruskin's writing, where his vision of a better society on earth instinctively falls into high biblical speech.

Naturally, that kind of speech does not much colour his working or weekday prose; for which should be consulted, not the heightened or formal passages, but Ruskin's ordinary letters, diaries, private notes of travel and things seen—which are now accessible in plenty—as well as the level, connective parts of his books. Take him when he is talking to himself or to a friend, or to the reader, without his trappings and also without his weapons. His books are written, he tells us,

> in honest English, of good Johnsonian lineage, touched here and there with colour of a little finer or Elizabethan quality.

'Elizabethan'? hardly; unless the term is to include a writer like Jeremy Taylor, of whom Ruskin at times reminds us by his richness of bright or tender imagery, and also by his early excesses and over-richness. 'Johnsonian,' undeniably, but only when the subject so demands, which often it does not. The following is an average piece, chosen because it is unexciting; it is just sound, eighteenth-century, traveller's English, with a little added colour:

> Five minutes more, and we are in the upper room of the little inn at Mestre, glad of a moment's rest in shade. . . . The view from its balcony is not cheerful: a narrow street, with a solitary brick church and barren campanile on the other side of it; and some conventual buildings, with a few crimson remnants of fresco about their windows; and, between them and the street, a ditch with some slow current in it, and one or two small houses beside it, one with an arbour of roses at its door, as in an English tea-garden; the air, however, about us having in it nothing of roses, but a close smell of garlic and crabs, warmed by the smoke of various stands of hot chestnut. There is much vociferation also going on beneath the window respecting certain wheelbarrows which are in rivalry for our baggage; we appease their rivalry with our best patience, and follow them down the narrow street.

But turn from this to an expression of critical judgement, in which the sentences are not long, but where the clauses are poised into antithetic pairs, after Johnson's manner, though less ponderously, and with a less formal tune ; and remember that Ruskin took *The Idler* with him on some of his early travels :

> Salvator possessed real genius, but was crushed by misery in his youth, and by fashionable society in his age. He had vigorous animal life, and considerable invention, but no depth either of thought or perception. He took some hints directly from nature, and expressed some conditions of the grotesque of terror with original power ; but his baseness of thought, and bluntness of sight, were unconquerable ; and his works possess no value whatsoever for any person versed in the walks of noble art.

This habit of doubling and balancing remains to the last, though it is more marked during Ruskin's earlier, oratorical period. It is of great value to his longer, more magnificent sentences of description ; the antithesis gives something for mind and ear to rest upon, amid the rush of imagery, and then it starts the rhythm again, with a strong-winged beat, upon its journey towards a distant close. These complex harmonies recall De Quincey rather than Johnson ; but the secret of them is Ruskin's own. This statement may sound somewhat abstract, but an illustration should bring it home to the reader :

> Let us watch him with reverence as he sets side by side the burning gems, and smooths with soft sculpture the jasper pillars, that are to reflect a ceaseless sunshine, *and rise into a cloudless sky* ; but not with less reverence let us stand by him, *when, with rough strength* and *hurried stroke, he smites* an uncouth animation out of the rocks which he has torn from among the moss of the moorland, and *heaves into the darkened air the pile* of iron buttress and rugged wall, instinct with the work of an imagination *as wild and wayward as the northern sea* ; creations of *ungainly shape and rigid limb, but full of wolfish life* ; fierce as *the winds that beat, and changeful as the clouds that shade them.*

IX

But Ruskin becomes more sparing of this device of mechanism; nor is that sentence an example of the manner into which he came to settle, when employing the long-breathed sentence. The temporary and avowed imitation of Hooker, in the second volume of *Modern Painters*, mostly disappears, and the whole effect becomes less Latinised. His 'period' more commonly is not a period at all in the sense of the grammarian ; not, that is, a complex sentence which is technically incomplete in syntax till its last word is written. Ruskin adopts a freer style. To speak in school terms, the main clause prolongs itself, not by a chain of dependent clauses, but by a series of absolute, or otherwise supplementary ones, loosely though quite correctly hung; thought giving birth to thought, and image to fiery image, with much the same air of inevitable afterthought as in Shakespeare's poetry, for just so long as the matter may demand:

Far up the glen, as we pause beside the cross, the sky is seen through the openings in the pines, thin with excess of light; and, in its clear, consuming flame of white space, the summits of the rocky mountains *are gathered into solemn crowns and circlets*, all *flushed in that strange, faint silence of possession* by the sunshine which has in it so deep a melancholy; full of power, yet as frail as shadows; lifeless, like the walls of a sepulchre, *yet beautiful in tender fall of crimson folds,* like the veil of some sea spirit, that lives and dies as the foam flashes, fixed on a perpetual throne, stern against all strength, *and yet effaced and melted utterly* into the air *by that last sunbeam that has crossed to them* from between the two golden clouds.

It is a dangerous way of writing. Some of Ruskin's sentences sprawl gigantically, in a seventeenth-century fashion. But he usually stops in time, and then there are no harmonies like his. To scan his prose brings out its beauty, but the subject is too technical to elaborate here. Some have blamed him, and others more justly have defended him, for admitting so many lines of blank verse, so much iambic movement, into his sentences. The defence is that this feature is not so easy to notice, and that it does not sensibly impair the character of the prose rhythm. Still, I think that in his earlier books Ruskin sometimes overdoes the iambic, which forces itself upon the ear: a peril that may be judged from those portions of the last two quotations which I have italicised. His cadence, in its full perfection, eschews this tune. A passage from *Fors* will show that he could not only recover but even better his earlier music; and the fall of the last ten words is incomparable, quite effacing the faint impression of metre which is twice left by the preceding clauses—I will leave the reader to discover where:

Between the shafts of the pillars, the morning sky is seen pure and pale, relieving the grey dome of the Church of the Salute; but beside that vault, and like it, vast thunderclouds heap themselves above the horizon, catching the light of dawn upon them where they rise, far westward, over the dark roofs of the ruined

Badia ;—but all so massive, that, half an hour ago, in the dawn, I scarcely knew the Salute dome and towers from theirs : while the seagulls, rising and falling hither and thither in clusters above the green water beyond the balcony, tell me that the south wind is wild on Adria.[1]

Similar gifts, but other harmonies, are to be found in Ruskin's philosophical and critical prose. Here too he is a master of form, but he uses—sometimes with his Plato in his ears, and sometimes with Dr. Johnson—the more regular build of classical complex sentence, longer or shorter. Thus he has a Greek manner, a Latin manner, a Tayloresque manner, a scriptural manner, and finally his own manner ; which comes out much plainer after 1860, but which often emerges before that date, and about which he has a good deal to tell us. He wrote with toil, and revised incessantly, and played the schoolmaster to his own books, when he reissued them, with a severity that leaves little to be added. He liked to blow away all surplus dust of words, and at the same time to avoid 'affected conciseness.' The changes in his text are of much interest, and are usually inspired by one or other of these purposes, or else by the instinct which he describes most happily :

The constant habit to which I owe my (often foolishly-praised) 'command of language'—of never allowing a sentence to pass proof, in which I have not considered whether, for the vital word of it, a better could be found in the dictionary—makes me somewhat morbidly intolerant of careless diction.

In one passage, he first wrote the words *the golden honour of the sunset*. This was unprecise ; and he next wrote *the bright investiture and golden honour of the sunset*. Then he got rid of the original phrase, keeping the new one, and added to that another, so rendering an exact sensation, and finding the 'vital word' of the whole ; which at last ran, *the bright investiture and sweet warmth of the sunset*. The more Ruskin's 'eloquent' descriptions are examined, the more they are seen to have this stamp of fidelity : a merit that is often hidden, in his earlier work, by a certain excess of rhetorical device and over-conscious skill. At the same time the effect is spontaneous ; there is not that laborious inlaying of words, which is practised by writers like Pater, beautifully enough, yet with the result of delaying the ease and march of the sentence. The pace is naturally slower in later works like *The Cestus of Aglaia*, with their surprising fretwork of allusion and wild abruptness of transition. But it is time to notice some of the changes produced in Ruskin's use of English by the new warfare which he took up, and by the stresses and troubles of his second half of life.

X

He is always complaining that people praise his language and admit that he can write, while they do not care for what he says or believe his report. He came to condemn, with gentle irony, his 'customary burst of terminal eloquence,' and he was minded to get rid of any such obstacles between himself and his reader. And so, in 1868, he wrote : 'Whatever I am now able to say at all, I find myself forced to say with great plainness.' To pink the fallacies of the popular political economy effectively, he needed great precision of fence, and an unencumbered fighting style. 'Plain,' however, is hardly the epithet for *Unto This Last,* where the language, though free from obscurity, is by no means devoid of ornament. There is little of the old formal pomp, of the brocading that stiffened the fall of the drapery and sometimes distracted the reader's attention. The long sentence, the balanced epigram, the tone of passionate appeal, are all present. But the thrusts have become sharp, brief, and rapid ; Ruskin had often hit hard before, but his sheer English had never been so dangerous. In *Munera Pulveris*, a little later, the primary aim is an Euclidian statement of definitions ; the tone is sober, even formal, and the neatness and fineness of outline may remind us, not too fancifully, of Ruskin's own drawings. Many of his other books are addresses or professorial lectures ; and here he shows all the arts of the teacher, 'feeling the mouth' of the audience, laying out the matter ingeniously, and holding the attention by jest and interlude, and by various and amusing stagecraft ; the language itself being studiously lucid, and the eloquent digressions as studiously prepared. So it is in the discourses on birds or flowers, or on wood and metal engraving, or in the manuals made for the tourist in Italy. Few but those who have tried to teach can appreciate the rightness of Ruskin's diction in all this kind of work ; and no one can be so consecutive when he will.

But often, in his later writings, he does not so choose ; and we are there faced, not only by an apparent chaos of outcries, doctrines, and fantasies concerning many things under the sun, but by an answering variety of speech, for which little has prepared us, and which no description can exhaust. Wonder, sadness, admiration, intellectual disgust, Ruskin stirs them all ;

but that, for the present purpose, is neither here nor there, for language, at least, seldom fails to answer to his call. Sometimes, not often, he uses a kind of allusive short-hand; or, as in *Præterita*, is calm and limpid; or, in *Fors* above all, he is swept over by moods that pass into one another one knows not how, like a stream pencilled by changing flaws of air. But he always has the words. Once in *Fors* (No. 67) he explains the principle of this erratic writing, in words that apply to many of his other works after 1865:

> The violence, or grotesque aspect, of a statement may seem as if I were mocking; but this comes mainly of my endeavour to bring the absolute truth out into pure crystalline structure, unmodified by disguise of custom, or obscurity of language.

Could the whole aim of the art of prose be more surely described than in this stray sentence—*to bring the absolute truth out into pure crystalline structure?* Think of much celebrated writing, and ask what would become of it if everything foreign to this aim were blotted out. Substitute *exact meaning* for *absolute truth*, and you have said what Ruskin, more nearly than most writers, accomplishes. What, then, was it that he exactly *did* mean, in these later years? Here, again, I shall but attempt to take a few bearings.

XI

From the first, with his instinct for referring all things to their 'root in human passion and human hope,' he had refused to confine himself to art strictly so-called, or to the world of nature lying outside man. He had traced the influence of architecture upon the workman, and of the 'mountain gloom' upon the countryman, and had discovered in the fine art of a people the index to its morals, and in the defacement of town and country the tokens of national decline. The closing pages of *The Stones of Venice*, the lectures on *The Political Economy of Art*, and many a vehement outburst, had shown his growing preoccupation with the 'condition-of-England-question' and with the causes of social welfare [1] and misery. As we have seen, he took for his master Carlyle, who impelled him along the path on which he had already started. 'I find Carlyle's stronger thinking colouring mine continually,' he writes in 1856, and he acknowledges that Carlyle's idiom and rhythm can often be traced in his own. Carlyle's letters of encouragement and delight, as he receives book after book from his disciple, from *The Stones of Venice* to *Fors Clavigera*, show his conviction that there was one man at least, amidst a population mostly fools, who was capable of living speech, a St. George who might really rip up the belly of the dragon. The book that affected Ruskin most deeply was *Past and Present*, perhaps the most remarkable fruit in English literature of the mediæval revival. Carlyle's deep sympathy—at first deeper than his contempt—for the blind multitude, who were miserable for lack of a heaven-born feudal ruler, found an echo in Ruskin ; so did his derision of all the remedies of all the liberal freethinkers ; while the mysticism of the two men, with all its differences, was akin. And Ruskin's war on the economists was also Carlyle's war, only conducted with far greater precision of attack. Nor was it only a war, for Ruskin perceived and said, much more definitely than his master, what ought to be done next.

Thackeray, the friendly editor of the *Cornhill*, was compelled by the proprietor, to put a stop to the four papers entitled *Unto This Last*; which Ruskin always considered, as most of his readers do to-day, to contain in its purest expression the essence of his teaching concerning the true 'wealth of nations.' As we look through the old volume, No. II., July to December 1860, and see these articles interleaving *Framley Parsonage*, *Roundabout Papers*, *The Four Georges*, and verse by Matthew Arnold and Elizabeth Browning, we are tempted to coin some Ruskinian title for them like 'The Rejected Stone'! Thackeray had to prefer contributions on adulteration, or 'the electric telegraph.' The public dismay and booing were most emphatic. The 'man of genius' had 'gone outside his province,' with deplorable results. The man of genius continued to do so ; in 1862-3 he produced *Essays in Political Economy*, this time in *Fraser*, under the auspices of Froude. That work, the basis of the *Munera Pulveris* of 1872, was also generally reviled ; and the publisher, finding that the supply exceeded the demand, would have no more of the goods : a practical illustration, from Ruskin's point of view, of the 'value of a commodity.' In the miscellany of letters called *Time and Tide, by Weare and Tyne*, addressed to a working man, he returned, intermittently but hotly, to the charge ; and also in many a letter to the press and passing utterance, and in *Fors Clavigera* afterwards.

Political strife, in the ordinary sense, Ruskin did not touch. He was of no definable party, and though he called himself a Tory of the old school, and was full of feudal notions of paternal kingship and heaven-born aristocracy, he was also much too full of explosive material to be a Tory really ; indeed, he attacked the assumptions of Tory, Whig, and Radical alike, at their roots, and by constant implication. All of them were more or less devoted to the policy of *laissez-faire*, which to Ruskin simply means the neglect by the State both of its obvious duty and of the instinct of self-preservation. This neglect he condemned at every point. But it was on the old 'mercantile economy,' now sometimes called 'plutonomy,' that he opened fire ; choosing the younger Mill and Fawcett for his targets, but actually criticising the more abstract school of Ricardo and Mill the elder, with its central conception of the 'economic man' and his impulses. Ruskin denied that a separate and valid science, inductive and deductive, could be framed on the basis of disregarding every human motive, in commercial affairs, except that of profit. Or, if and so far as such a science could be framed, he denied that it deserved to be called 'political economy.' The social feelings and the play of disinterested motive were not casual factors that could be neglected, as Euclid neglects the breadth of a line, but vital and inherent ones. The orthodox economy was only concerned with 'certain accidental phenomena of modern commercial operations,' and not with the total forces which really move, or ought to move, the whole body politic. 'Wealth,' hitherto defined in terms of the market, must be re-defined in terms of 'life' : and the science of political economy is meant for the furtherance of human life, understood in terms of virtue and happiness. On this showing, many alleged eternal necessities go by the board : the 'laws' of supply and demand, the competitive system, the policy of non-interference. They are not eternal at all, said Ruskin, and moreover they are inherently poisonous, and ought to vanish. Wages, in particular, must be fixed, not by the law of the market, but by the law of justice. For Justice, to put the case no higher, pays, and a fixed minimum wage is good national economy. Such is the drift, in *Unto This Last*, of Ruskin's eloquence, which has a sharper and more flashing edge than ever before. The book is full of impassioned appeal and text-flinging, of fantastic touches and of satire ; but its power lies in the fierce precision of its analysis.

Yet Ruskin was stung to utterance not so much by the printed fallacy as by the sight of the industrial and social system itself, by the evidence of actual suffering and injustice, and by the exclusion, under existing terms, of whole multitudes of men from any reasonable and hopeful way of living. Like the dreamer in *Hyperion*, he was one of those to whom the miseries of the world 'are misery, and will not let them rest.' Carlyle had long since assailed the 'dismal science'; the novelists and poets, Dickens and Hood, Mrs. Browning and Tennyson, had denounced bumbledom, or sweating, or adulteration, or legal cruelty to children. The tide of sympathy and indignation had overflowed into literature; the Christian Socialists of the Maurice group were full of it. Ruskin went along with this tide, and his work swelled its volume; but in two respects he was peculiar. In the first place, he had approached the whole question, originally, from the artistic side, asking himself in what soil of character, and in what sunshine of welfare, the living art of a nation must be nourished, and thence proceeding to the economical social problem. And secondly, while the rest were angrily, or generously, or musically, sorry ('there is such lovely, lovely, misery in this *Paradise*,' he wrote, ironically, of Morris's poem), he, in his irregular but pertinent style, reasoned. He reasoned, not only critically or aggressively, but with no little constructive and practical instinct. He was much derided, but produced an effect which he did not live to appreciate. He helped, by his rays of insight and foresight, to quicken the arrival of legislative and social changes which many other forces were conspiring to produce. His admirers, with good right, enumerate the reforms which he proposed in 1862, in the preface to the collected papers of *Unto This Last*, and which have since been, or have begun to be, realised: national education, elementary and technical, state-controlled; the fair and fixed wage; the old age pension; and the handling of unemployment by the State. The 'Oxford graduate' had travelled far, and his Odyssey was still only half through; reckoned by years, even less than half.

XII

The contents of *Munera Pulveris* [1] are too intricate to be specified here, and can only be understood in the light of Ruskin's many stray expansions and applications of them. The general aim is to lay a basement for the edifice of a new and true 'political economy.' Ruskin begins by closely defining the essential terms, 'wealth,' 'money,' and 'riches,' and develops the definitions under the headings of 'storekeeping, coin-keeping, commerce, government, and mastership.' He manages to touch on almost every branch of economy: urges, truly, the evil of expenditure on luxury, also the illegitimacy of interest—a favourite craze, afterwards much insisted on in

Fors. He ranges from the different species of law to a classification of the forms of government, and from the nature of currency to the ethical training of a nation. The edifice was never built; the plan of it has to be partially pieced together by students: a turret here, a traceried archway there, and miscellaneous half-hewn material everywhere. The work of interpretation is well worth doing, and has been well done; and the result establishes, despite all Ruskin's fantasies and excursions, his power of divining, through seeming paradox, the commonplaces of the morrow. *Munera Pulveris,* which begins in good order, goes off into ironies, and parables, and interpretations of Dante, which are often delightful to read but do not make for clearness. *Time and Tide* is yet more discursive and indescribable, but contains much scattered good sense and wit. A more definite impression can be gained from three other works of this period, *Sesame and Lilies* (1865), *The Ethics of the Dust* (1866), and *The Crown of Wild Olive* (1866). Here Ruskin's thought and style are perhaps at the fulness of their power. *Sesame and Lilies*, one of Ruskin's very popular works, consisted at first of two discourses. The first, *Of Kings' Treasuries*, is a noble and sagacious plea for the right use and valuation of books. The second, *Of Queens' Gardens*, set out a high and gracious, yet altogether too limited and domestic, ideal of female character; *The Angel in the House* is the favourite poem. There is a certain, doubtless unconscious, note of condescension and pedagogy in Ruskin's references to women, amid all his reverence for them: a mixture of avuncular scolding and garland-offering, which I confess to finding faintly offensive. This is very well in the dialogues with little girls, entitled *The Ethics of the Dust*, which are managed with brilliant skill, and which are nominally, and in part really, lessons on the construction and beauties of crystals. But Ruskin's highest qualities are shown in the lecture on *The Mystery of Life and its Arts*, which was afterwards appended to *Sesame.* It ranges far, and contains much of the essence of his creed, in respect of art and of life. But, above all, it reveals his inner temper at its sanest, and also on its more mystical side. This Dublin lecture of 1868 is also noteworthy, like the preface to *The Crown of Wild Olive*, for Ruskin's strong and pathetic appeal to the agnostic school. We ought to mark this stray point of fiery contact between Ruskin's thought and the secular movement of his time. In *The Crown of Wild Olive*, with its three lectures on work, on traffic, and on war, there is something of the same quality; but on war the prophet confesses, like most other men, that he has two minds, and he is equally emphatic in either of them.

XIII

Some of Ruskin's other writings are shaped by the requirements of the lecturer. He held the Chair of Fine Art at Oxford twice, from 1869 to 1878, and from 1883 to 1885, a serious illness occurring in the interval; and he gave many addresses elsewhere. Many of his books are almost too disorderly to classify, though he often shows his power of perfect and shapely disquisition. But the habit of letting his mind and his subject drift grew upon him; and though it delighted his pupils, who never knew what was coming, it is apt to tax the reader. Yet his power of recovery is wonderful. Ruskin's simplest, quietest, and most continuous production, *Præterita,* was begun (1885) in the intervals of a fierce brain-disturbance, which only occasionally ruffles its even stream. Most of his remaining works may be grouped somewhat as follows:

(1) Studies of natural things. These are often designed to give a simple sort of instruction, and are studies in the 'science of aspects,' with not a little of science, in the ordinary sense, interposed, and also with plenty of digression upon things in general. Thus *Proserpina* is concerned with flowers, and *Love's Meinie* (1873) with birds and their feathers; while a whole volume of the standard edition is filled with work on geology and mineralogy, Ruskin's earliest loves; *Deucalion* being the chief single item. The controversy with Tyndall and others over the origin of glaciers falls into this department. *The Ethics of the Dust* may be mentioned once more, with its account of crystals. A transition to the next heading is formed by *The Eagle's Nest*, which discusses 'the relation of natural science to art.' Ruskin often—not always—reviled science, and did so ignorantly; and had no conception of the philosophic bearings of scientific discovery, and abused Darwin and Huxley in a wild helpless fashion; having less excuse for this procedure than Carlyle (from whom he may in part have borrowed it), seeing that he was himself, in his own field, scientific. When he is not enforcing an imaginary rivalry between science and art, he is mostly beating at an open door. His plea amounts to saying that they are different things, and that science must not pretend to give what art alone can give. He says, for instance, that 'sight is a spiritual power,' and not simply the subject of optics. When he gets back to art and to

things imaginatively seen, he becomes luminous again; the pages on the eye of the snake and of the eagle are in his best style. There is a touch of Blake in his marvelling temper, and the motto of *The Eagle's Nest* is taken from the *Book of Thel*.

(2) While his powers lasted, Ruskin showed immense industry as a critic and teacher of fine art. His biography must be studied to see how seriously he took his work, and into what endless practical activities it led him. He retained his former power, though he wrote no great comprehensive book. *The Laws of Fesole* treats of perspective, *Aratra Pentelici* of Greek building and sculpture, *Ariadne Florentina* of engraving, *Val d'Arno* of early Tuscan painting. Padua, Verona, Venice, Florence are his chief hunting-grounds; his guides, to their paintings and buildings, his descriptions and judgements fill several volumes. Handbooks like *Mornings in Florence* and *St. Mark's Rest* have been used by generations of devoted visitors. In this kind of labour Ruskin is distinguished by precision and business-like method; but his inspiration and his strange wild vitality of touch never disappear. Of quite another stamp are the Oxford lectures that he gave, towards the close of his second tenure of his chair, on *The Art of England*.

These are kindly and genial, with the inevitable sallies and back-lashings; they deal, for example, with Ruskin's old admirations, Rossetti and Burne-Jones; with Leech and Tenniel, Allingham and Kate Greenaway; and with Watts, a fellow-idealist. I heard these addresses: the voice comes back to the mind's ear, with its singular wailing [1] quality, which seemed to the young imagination like that of a wandering and saddened angel, full of a quite woeful, open-eyed, inexpugnable *surprise* that the incorrigible world of men should be what it is, and yet never be ashamed of itself. This was the last course but one; the last was that on *The Pleasures of England*, delivered not long before Ruskin's last retirement and the breakdown of the 'physical basis of mind'—a calamity, though, which did not come on all at once; and the happy intervals permitted the composition of *Præterita*.

(3) *The Queen of the Air* (1869), which partly reproduces *The Cestus of Aglaia*, stands in a class somewhat apart; though its object, namely the curious, and often arbitrary, interpretation of myth and symbol, was most congenial to the author. It is connected with his fancy for chasing, as though with a butterfly-net, the etymological roots of words, and also with his love for finding secondary, or spiritual, meanings in all things however

innocent, one of the pleasantly mediæval traits of his intellect.

(4) As of old, Ruskin wrote much on literature, and a small volume might with profit be put together containing his criticisms of books. He read as a poet reads, not academically; but he read a great deal. His dislikes are not always interesting, or safe, but where he is at home with his author his critical judgements are among the best to be found anywhere. They are not, as a rule, concerned with form or expression, though in the papers called *Fiction Fair and Foul* he returns to the subject of the 'grand style,' which he had discussed long before, in reference to fine art, in *Modern Painters*. His Shakespearian examples are as apt as Matthew Arnold's, and are taken from *Henry the Fifth* and *Coriolanus*. But the grand style is only the perfect expression of a noble spirit; and the quest of Ruskin, here as ever, is mostly for 'nobleness,' as distinct from simple beauty, and still more as distinct from expressiveness: the cult of which, involving as it does the exhibition of life in its meaner discords and intractable matter, is alien to him; so that we must not expect him to care for the kind of poetry or fiction that dwells upon it. Ruskin's drag-net, therefore, for 'foul fiction,' *fiction mécroyante*, is altogether too sweeping, for it would include almost every exhibition of the horrible-grotesque in literature; and of fair fiction his exemplar is Scott, to whom in *Fors* he returns continually, and of whom he is a sworn and sound admirer, and a lifelong praiser. The unsentimental side of Ruskin should never be forgotten; and what Johnson says of Shakespeare's plays Ruskin, perhaps in echo, as justly observes of the Waverley Novels:

> Marriage is by no means, in his conception of man and woman, the most important business of their existence; nor love the only reward of their virtue or exertion . . . we shall often find that love in them [the Waverleys] is merely a light by which the sterner features of character are to be irradiated.

Of Dickens he writes with more reserves, yet with great affection. But his fullest allegiance is paid to the poets, and above all to Dante. He quotes from all parts of the *Divine Comedy*. Dante, by the force of his 'imagination penetrative,' and of consummate style, effects a fusion of faithfully observed imagery with spiritual meaning, in a degree, and with a constancy, that has never been equalled. Hence of all writers he spoke most intimately to Ruskin, who is for ever dissatisfied with the mere face of things, seeking for some ulterior significance in simple beauty, and for moral type and symbol in life everywhere. But Ruskin's explorations of literature would take long to indicate. In *Fors* there are 'readings' in Plato, Shakespeare, Chaucer, Marmontel, Froissart, and other authors. His admiration for Wordsworth, Keats, and Tennyson, and also for Coventry Patmore, is to be expected; his good word for Byron, less so; his prejudice against Shelley is an aberration. The series called *Bibliotheca Pastorum* comprises a translation of the *Economist* of Xenophon; a selection (called *A Knight's Faith*), with comment, from the biography of Sir Herbert Edwardes, that devout soldier, administrator, and one of the saviours of India in 1857; a reproduction (*Rock Honeycomb*), again with comment, of some of Sir Philip Sidney's versified psalms; and, growing out of this last, a confused little manual, done with immense relish, on *The Elements of Prosody*. All these enterprises fit aptly enough into Ruskin's characteristic enthusiasms, social, ethical, and religious; and so does his sponsoring of Miss Alexander's *Story of Ida* and her *Roadside Songs of Tuscany*.

XIV

Fors Clavigera [1] is a series of ninety-six open letters addressed 'to the workmen and labourers of Great Britain,' and issued nominally every month, between 1871 and 1884. The title, with the triple sense attached to each word in it, is untranslatable; and the medley of the work itself is hardly to be sorted out. Written in the intervals of Ruskin's other industries, *Fors* is a descant on almost anything that could anger, or grieve, or inspire, or amuse, or otherwise interest him; on the evils of England and Europe, economic and spiritual, and on the remedies for them; and on books, pictures, and travels. *Fors* relates all his dreams, actual or feigned, nightmarish or happy, his whims and humours, Ariel fancies or Puckish mischiefs; his memories and disappointments; and all grave things and all trifles that crossed his brain, just in the state of order, or disorder, in which they crossed it. A friend complained to him of the disorder:

> But he might as well plead with a birch-tree growing out of a crag, to arrange its boughs beforehand. The winds and floods will arrange them according to their wild liking; all that the tree has to do, or can do, is to grow gaily, if it may be; sadly, if gaiety is impossible; and let the black jags and scars rend the rose-white of its trunk where Fors shall choose. (*Letter* 50.)

Fors itself is more like a jungle than a tree; and, so far as we can clear the jungle, so far does it lose its character of mingled charm and provocativeness. It contains few ideas that are fresh to the reader of Ruskin, who returns to his crusade and reiterates his gospel; but the old thoughts are presented from new angles, in marvellous re-wordings; not in form and order at all, but in personal monologue, and as part of the author's confession to himself and to the world, in a private mental journal now made public. We might judge *Fors Clavigera* either as a contribution to thought, or as a piece of writing, or as completing our knowledge of Ruskin as a man.

In the first of these aspects, *Fors* must be considered as part of his entire campaign, militant and prophetic; and brings up at once the large question what Ruskin has really done, in that capacity, for the English mind. And this at least is the beginning of an answer: that he must at any rate be honoured for his far-reaching prophecies, and for his unfailing valour, in the cases where history has actually borne out the one, and truth has profited by the other. The old 'economy' *has* been transformed, Ruskin helping, and its subject-matter absorbed in that of sociology, or the science of social welfare. The duty of the community to labour, to children, to the aged poor, and to education, art, and craft, *has* begun, Ruskin helping, to be acted upon. He did not create, but he divined, in his irregular way he quickened, the mental forces at work. In the *Daily Telegraph* of September 19, 1918, there is a report of the aims of the American Federation of Labour (a formidable body), presented to the Inter-Allied Labour Congress, which contains a sentence with a remarkably Ruskinian ring:

> That in law and in practice the principle should be recognised that the labour of a human being is not a commodity or article of commerce.

Much of the guerrilla warfare of *Fors* is directed to enforcing this truth. No doubt, all manner of world-forces, and many schools of thought, have worked in the same direction. Of Marxite or other thinkers Ruskin seems to have known nothing; but his prescience is not less remarkable because he laboured alone. And, no doubt, we are loth to complain if a man who did so much, labouring alone, overshot the mark. But Ruskin's general attack on the modern world, or the English world of the Seventies and Eighties, becomes an impossible one. Apart from his special and vouchsafed revelation, he knew little to the purpose of its thought and literature, or of the larger political forces at work. His fanatical view of science is now only a curiosity. Much of *Fors* might have been written in a dream ; but it contains starry pages, piercing sallies, gentle humour, as well as much dreary invective and positive silliness. The style is perfectly expressive everywhere. But it is difficult not to find *Fors*, as a whole, repellent and painful. It is the memorial of an unique genius and temper ; but the temper is jarred, and the genius is too often in disintegration. To treat it, as some do, as Ruskin's masterpiece is to do him much wrong. We must remember that after *Fors* came *Præterita*, with its appendix *Dilecta* ; and these, as I said, were written when that noble and much-vexed spirit was passing through a season of calm weather, in spite of the thickening storms.

CHAPTER X

EARLIER CRITICS: AND MATTHEW ARNOLD

I

FOR a time after 1830, English criticism [1] was at something of an ebb; and this while Sainte-Beuve was writing his earlier *Portraits*, and Gustave Planche his articles, in the *Revue des Deux Mondes*. Our romantic discoverers, Lamb and his company, had departed—all but De Quincey. Carlyle and Macaulay had begun to speak, but they are not critics of art first and foremost; and both of them are infected by the arrogant official tone of the journals in which they write. The heavy papers of the *Quarterly* type, which made or marred the fortunes of books before 1850, are mostly dead reading now; even a man of talent like Lockhart is weighed down. Good things, it is true, have been saved from the files. Such are the scholarly and pointed articles of Whitwell Elwin, the editor and prosecutor of Pope; and there is lively good sense as well as information in the *Essays from the Quarterly*, by James Hannay. Also there is the figure of the assiduous reviewer, journalist, politician, and talker, Abraham Hayward (1801-84); but his letters and his prose translation (1833) of *Faust* are of more interest than his opinions on literature. The truth is, Matthew Arnold so completely changed the character of criticism that we too easily forget the other writers who kept it alive about the middle of the century. One of these undoubtedly was Walter Bagehot, who has been described; and, among the rest, Keble, Brimley, and Dallas are decidedly the most original.

Keble's [1] *Prælectiones Academicæ*, delivered from the Oxford Chair of Poetry from 1832 to 1841, were published in 1844. They were unluckily in Latin, and have seldom been read except by students, but can now be seen in an English version. They are discourses of mark in themselves, and also historically significant. The general topic is *De Poeticæ Vi Medica*—on the curative, or 'cathartic,' power of poetry; the motto comes from Plato's *Ion*, where the souls of poets and lovers of poetry are described as links in the magnetic chain hanging from the original loadstone, itself divine; and the dedication is to Wordsworth, who is a provider not only of sweet poetry but of sacred truth. Keble's point of view is thus sufficiently defined. The Greeks, supported by Wordsworth, give him his canon and principle, half-artistic and half didactic; and Greek poetry is his main subject. Homer and Æschylus, Sophocles and Pindar are expounded at length; Euripides is well defended against his detractors; his strength, says Keble, lies in painting 'domestic affairs and affections.' Theocritus, Lucretius, and Virgil follow; and Keble, like Fénelon (of whom he often reminds us), excels in discovering the more elusive beauties of landscape in the poets. Lucretius he duly exalts; but we are near a point of danger when that poet's irreligion is extenuated on the score of his mental affliction.

But Keble's theory of poetry is by no means illiberal or sectarian. Poetic utterance, he says, is at bottom a relief or vent for powerful emotions or oppressive thoughts; the act of shaping these into musical words steadies and balances the soul; to linger over diction and cadence occupies and diverts the spirit. The result, to both poet and hearer, is a certain mood of composure, or 'tranquillity'—a view which is an obvious reminiscence of Wordsworth's. Yet poetry has its origin in passion; that is indispensable; in fact poets are to be divided, in respect of their rank and value, by no other criterion. So far Keble is a disciple of Wordsworth and Coleridge, and says nothing very new; but his distinction between 'primary and 'secondary' poets is the most original part of his treatise. Joseph Warton and others had long before, while trying to put Pope in his place, drawn the distinction between the poets of 'nature,' which is 'eternal,' and the poets of 'wit and satire,' which are transitory. Keble goes deeper: primary poets, he says, are those who write under the impulse of their own original passion; such is Homer, such are Æschylus and Dante. Horace is not one of them, with all his gifts. Horace has no 'serious regard' for any one of all the subjects which he versifies so admirably. Nor is Dryden a primary poet; he does not care enough about anything; he is not consistently noble and sincere. Keble really means that Horace and Dryden are not, in the high sense of the term, *religious*; for primary poetry and religion are to his mind not only harmonious, but almost conterminous. We hardly expect any other attitude from the author of *The Christian Year*; but he ranges far for his illustrations; he quotes not only Scripture, but the lay of Ragnar

Lodbrog, and the songs of Lapps and Polynesians; and his sympathies are often wider than his theories. His manner is somewhat that of the intelligent pointer-out of 'beauties'; but he does not lack for subtlety or nicety. Had his 'prelections' been in English, Keble would at once have taken his just rank amongst the critics. His English writing, gathered up in his *Occasional Papers and Reviews* (1877), hardly contain enough critical matter to give his measure; but the article (1838) on Sir Walter Scott contains, in brief, a theory of poetry and a classification of poets almost identical with that in the prelections.

George Brimley[1] (1819-57) was librarian of Trinity College, Cambridge, and a small sheaf of his periodical essays, chiefly written before 1850, was reprinted after his death. Brimley, in his own field, is a delicate, neat-handed man of letters. He is usually on the defensive; he tells the public, very modestly, why it really ought to like Tennyson and Wordsworth, and *Esmond* and *Westward Ho!* and *The Angel in the House*, and Shelley too; and he tells them in a fashion which is not yet antiquated. On Shelley he is much nearer to the truth than Matthew Arnold. Not every one could write in 1851, or in 1920 either, so much to the purpose as this:

> After the passions and the theories which supplied Shelley with the subject-matter of his poems have died away and become mere matters of history, there will still remain a song such as mortal man never sung before, of inarticulate rapture and of freezing pain—of a blinding light of truth and a dazzling weight of glory, translated into English speech, as coloured as a painted window, as suggestive, as penetrating, as intense as music.

Brimley is expository; his essays would serve excellently to introduce the poets to strangers; but this professor-work is in its nature not original. He is also extremely moral—an idealist of the kind that people call 'mid-Victorian,' although in fact the type is eternal. He shakes his head, with a half-unwilling admiration, over *The Lady of Shalott*; its 'serene beauty,' we are told, and 'clear landscape features,'

> only make one more angry that so much skill in presenting objects should be employed upon a subject that can only amuse the imagination.

Yet Brimley, throughout, loves more things in poetry than he can well approve of. More than once he breaks his chain; and he must have been one of the first writers to do full justice to

Maud; refusing, as he sturdily does, to be frightened by those current epithets of 'morbid' and 'hysterical,' which really indicate the dramatic virtue of the work. In his paper called *Poetry and Criticism* he comes near to adopting a free disinterested standard:

> All, then, we have to ask ourselves in reference to the form of any particular poem is, whether it does so express the emotion of the writer, and what quality and degree of emotion it expresses—that of a great soul raised to the height of its subject, or of a little soul vainly striving to warm its thin blood, but puny, starved, and shivering, even in presence of the central fires of the universe.

This is not dead writing, and I hope it may lead some reader to reopen Brimley's pages. But he produced little, and his range is not considerable, and his subjects are nearly all English. Even while Brimley was discoursing Matthew Arnold had begun to preach the Greek harmony of structure, and the grand style of Homer and his peers.

The author of a singular book, *The Gay Science* (1866), now too little remembered, Eneas Sweetland Dallas (1828-79), is much more of a philosopher, if less of a critic, than Brimley. The 'gay science' is the science of criticism, the term being transferred from its original, Provençal sense of the craft of poetry. Dallas, with Matthew Arnold's proclamation in his ears that the movement of the time is 'critical,' seeks to found the science on first principles; and, after many a circuit, he concludes that since the end of art is pleasure, as Aristotle said, and not edification, or mere imitation, the science of criticism must first of all be the science of pleasure. So he plunges back into psychology and æsthetic, showing much reading and shrewdness by the way, but often going off at tangents; and ends in a most acute disquisition on the 'mixed' pleasure involving pain, which is inherent in drama (comedy as well as tragedy), on the 'pure' and painless pleasure given by many kinds of art (such as *L'Allegro*), and finally on the 'hidden pleasure,' which issues from the 'hidden soul,' and speaks to, or from, the depths of unconscious experience. Mystical verse like Wordsworth's Tintern lines gives this kind of pleasure. The sequel, which includes a defence of fine art against the charge of mendacity, is less interesting, and is indeed slaying the slain; but it would be hard to name any one who has attacked the problem of artistic enjoyment at precisely the same angle as Dallas. He is a very lively, in fact a discursive and jerky writer; he hardly ever gets to literature itself; he does not exactly get to anything; but he throws by the way a sharp light on the plot of ground that is common to æsthetic, to psychology, and to ethics. Herein his work is still fresh. In his emphasis on the 'unconscious' he is an avowed disciple of Sir William Hamilton; and we trace in Dallas everywhere the infection of Matthew Arnold's pronouncement that poetry and letters are, or should be, or may become, the most important things in the world.

II

Our review of the poets must here be partially anticipated. It would do wrong to Matthew Arnold (1822-88) [1] to sever his prose, which is so often that of a poet, from his verse, into which the thoughts and the temper of his prose—and sometimes, alas! its movement—continually find their way. We must here study both together, in order to see what he has to say and to discover some of the influences that went to his making. Speaking of Byron, Matthew Arnold says that he himself was old enough 'to have felt the expiring wave of that mighty influence.' Yet only the spray of the wave reached him. He speaks of Byron with more admiration than sympathy; he stood well outside Byronism. Matthew Arnold had his own quarrel with the world as he found it; but Byronism revolted against the conditions of life itself. He obeyed the precept of Carlyle: 'Close thy Byron, open thy Goethe'; Goethe, the wise man who 'bade us hope,' and who was full of counsels upon life and conduct. This was the Goethe whom Matthew Arnold 'opened' as Carlyle had done before him; but he opened another Goethe too, about whom Carlyle cared much less; and this was the poet of *Iphigenie*, the man who had turned to the Greeks, and had attained something of the *symmetria prisca*, and was the apostle of form, and sculpturing, and artistic self-restraint. Matthew Arnold, however, was more affected by the Greeks themselves than he was by Goethe; and by the Greeks he meant, we find, chiefly Homer and Sophocles, and in some degree Theocritus. This influence was profound in its way, but the strongest one of all was nearer home; it was that of Wordsworth. Matthew Arnold ranked Wordsworth extravagantly high amongst European poets; bore witness to his 'healing power'; and repeatedly, as we find, in his sonnets and in *Mycerinus*, follows Wordsworth's poetic style. But he was most of all affected by the Bible; and the forces which made him, if they can be named in the order of their importance, I take to be, first of all, the Bible and Wordsworth; and, next to these, the Greeks and Goethe. Many other things told upon him powerfully; amongst them the poetry of Milton, and certain masters of French prose, notably Sainte-Beuve; but these, after all, were secondary in importance. And all the time, receptive as he is, by nature and also on principle, Matthew Arnold is still himself, with a mind and a tune of his own—*ein eigenste Gesang*.

He began, both as poet and critic, by rejecting the former generation. He was afterwards to speak nobly of Keats and handsomely of Byron; but against the romantic movement in England, though himself one of its children, he rebelled. He found a deficiency of substance, and of satisfactory 'subject-matter,' in its productions; nor was he always content with 'Wordsworth even, profound as he is, yet so wanting in completeness and variety.' He disliked no less the romantic looseness of structure and excess of imagery; and he found the romantic dissatisfaction with life a sterile mood. And in his poetry Matthew Arnold tries to make all these defects good, while in his prose he tries to prescribe for the mental maladies that produce them. The poet must find something great and sound and real to write about; he must have plastic power, or a command of structure; and he must possess a great, or an adequate, poetic style. The critic, on the other hand, and the man of culture, must find their food and medicine in the contemplation of the great style itself; in the study of many literatures, and of the 'best that has been thought and said'; and further, in the discipline of impartial thinking, or of striving 'to see the object as it really is.' Matthew Arnold's own labours were dispersed, but this is the underlying purpose that gives them unity.

He paid, no doubt, for his purpose; he paid for it as a poet, when it makes him flag and become dull, as it does in *Merope*; and he paid for it also as a critic. We often want to call him a bad, great critic; he is a great critic—when he is a good one. It was his purpose, his moral and spiritual purpose, that made him unjust to Carlyle,[1] Shelley, Victor Hugo, Charlotte Brontë, and Tennyson. He found it hard to like writers who seemed to ignore the ideal which he had set before himself, or who disconcerted the missionary twist in his composition. But then the very same purpose gives to his judgements, when they are true and sound—his judgements of Homer, on Dante, and on Milton—much of their value and inspiriting power. It is a relief to find that when he is wrong, as he is about Shelley, he is wrong beyond recovery, and without qualification. In the same way, as a poet he is seldom mediocre ; he is either musical or unmusical, seldom nearly musical ; and either Apollo visits him and carries him off, or else Apollo deserts him, finding that one 'haunt' in particular of Matthew Arnold's, namely the pulpit, is by no means 'meet' for Apollo.

Humourist as he was, with a streak of Horace in his nature, Matthew Arnold would have made excellent fun of the picture of himself as a person drearily prosing away in verse as well as in prose, in the hopes of saving a stray soul in a sleepy congregation. He knew quite well that a writer must please ; he is always talking about charm, and urbanity, and delicacy, and good temper, and he had these qualities himself, along with a certain cheerful insolence too. Still, he regarded them at bottom as a means of winning men to moral and intellectual virtue, and Matthew Arnold's glory is to have commended this purpose so well ; but there is something he misses, something which can best be indicated by attending to the accent in which he speaks about *beauty*. He is constantly referring to the 'laws of beauty,' and to the 'Greek instinct for beauty.' And he deeply felt, and he could sometimes create and commánd, both the grander and austerer sort of beauty, and the more gracious, simple, and holiday sort. It is the beauty of Pallas and Hera, or else that of the guardian gods of woods and streams, of 'Flora and the country green,' of Cumnor and Isis. Aphrodite is not there, nor the song of Pan ; nor yet any mixed and strange divinities of doubtful loveliness. So that the word *beauty* sounds quite differently on his lips, and on those of Rossetti, or of Walter Pater, or even of Keats, who can abandon himself to sight and sound in a way which Matthew Arnold is hardly capable of doing. No doubt, by meaner men, such words as *beauty* and *beautiful* came to be made repulsive or ridiculous, and were fair game for Messrs. Gilbert and Sullivan, and for *Punch*. We may not ourselves care to repeat them too often ; but they are the sacred words of a true religion nevertheless. Matthew Arnold's sacred words, however, are different ; they are *conduct* and *righteousness* in the first place ; and, in the second, expressions of his own coinage like 'culture' or 'sweetness and light.' I am not judging between these two creeds, or points of view, but merely marking a difference. Matthew Arnold repeated his holy words continually, and made them pass current ; which, in the approving words of Disraeli, was 'a great achievement.' He repeated them, and set people by the ears over them, much to his satisfaction ; and then they began to be worn out of shape, and to become tiresome, so that it takes some courage to-day to revive them, and to urge how much truth and value is really to be found in them. But they too represent a genuine religion, a religion in which the severity of the ruling idea, that of conduct and righteousness, is softened and reinforced by the ideas of charm, of balance, and of trained intellectual integrity. Who can say that these conceptions are done with, or that we can all take them for granted?

III

Matthew Arnold was a critic almost as soon as he was a poet; and, in spite of his later verse like *Westminster Abbey* and *Geist's Grave*, it is fair to say that he remained a critic longer than he remained a poet. Some chronology must now be pardoned: for it will show how through many years he was writing his best 'with both hands.' Apart from collegiate prize pieces, his first volume was *The Strayed Reveller, and Other Poems, by A.* (1849). It was soon withdrawn, though it contained the sonnet to Shakespeare and *The Forsaken Merman*; and so, too, was *Empedocles on Etna, and Other Poems, by A.* (1852), although in this volume were *Tristram and Iseult*, and the *Lines written in Kensington Gardens*. The *Poems* of 1853 bear the author's name, and include a selection from the earlier books (though not *Empedocles*), as well as new pieces like *Sohrab and Rustum*, the beautiful *Church of Brou*, and *The Scholar-Gipsy*. And there is the noteworthy Preface, the first of Matthew Arnold's statements of poetic theory, and one of the clearest and the best. More *Poems* followed in 1855, including *Balder Dead* and *Resignation*; and, in 1858, the tragedy of *Merope*, with another closely reasoned preface. He was now Professor of Poetry at Oxford, and held the chair until 1867, for ten years.

During the Sixties Matthew Arnold's powers were at their fullest. He gave, and in 1861 published, his *Lectures on Translating Homer*, followed a year later by his *Last Words* on that topic. In 1867 appeared the *Lectures on the Study of Celtic Literature*; the first series of *Essays in Criticism*, originally magazine articles, having preceded them in 1865. The precious *New Poems* (1867) contained the rescued *Empedocles*, besides *Thyrsis*, *Dover Beach*, *Rugby Chapel*, *Heine's Grave*, and other delightful things; indeed all in that little book is good. Some of the threads which unite Matthew Arnold's poetry with his criticism will appear presently. But first the poems may be classified, following the author's own division, into narrative, dramatic, elegiac, lyrical, and sonnets; and out of these groups may be separated one other, conveniently called *associative*, which tells us most of all about the writer himself.

Two of the stories, *Sohrab and Rustum* and *Balder Dead*, have the character of heroic episodes; and in both of them Matthew Arnold follows the antique model as devoutly as any poet of the Renaissance. Both are designed to be Homeric, in subject, temper, plan, and diction; but Virgil, and scenery, and pathos are always breaking in. They have a similar scheme, the same sort of blank verse, and the same virtues. *Balder Dead*, for which Arnold had his special liking, is dignified; but *Sohrab and Rustum* is the more concise and the more alive of the two. It is perhaps not quite alive, as we may feel by applying the author's own test. 'Everything depends upon the subject'; and, as King Edward the Seventh is reputed to have said to a student of Shakespeare, 'You could not have chosen a better subject.' But then who reads *Sohrab* for the subject, or for the story? The poetry, where it tells the story, hardly rises to its full level;—only once, it may be, and that is when Sohrab's soul departs,

> Regretting the warm mansion which it left,
> And youth, and bloom, and this delightful world.

No, it is read for 'beauties' and descriptions; for the Miltonic use of melodious names, *Aralian, Afrasiab, Kai Khosroo*; for the simile of the diver, and the picture of the Oxus, which is none the less perfect for being unlike the Greek manner. *Tristram and Iseult*, though noble in spirit, fails in essential passion; nor are the style and subject so nearly harmonised as in *The Sick King in Bokhara*: where the style is natural and fluent, not epically draped at all, and prepares us for that of *The Earthly Paradise*:

> 'Now I at nightfall had gone forth
> Alone, and in a darksome place
> Under some mulberry-trees I found
> A little pool; and in short space
> With all the water that was there
> I fill'd my pitcher, and stole home
> Unseen; and having drink to spare,
> I hid the can behind the door,
> And went up on the roof to sleep.'

As for *The Forsaken Merman*, which is not a story, but a chant involving a story, its grace and half-human pathos make it a very rare thing; and further (what does not always happen with Matthew Arnold) the tune and the words, both of them almost perfect, are born together.

The Preface of 1853 explains why he had suppressed *Empedocles on Etna*, which was saved at the instance of Robert Browning. The subject was wrong—almost, we might be led to fear, morally wrong. Wrong, because the reflections of Empedocles, instead of leading to anything, except to the plunge in the crater, eddy round and round inconclusively; 'the suffering finds no vent in action'; or, as Matthew Arnold put it in a letter, 'everything is to be endured, nothing to be done'; whereas a poem, especially one that calls itself dramatic, ought not so to behave. Dramatic *Empedocles* is not; but the future writer of *Rabbi Ben Ezra* might well perceive its special excellence. The philosophic lyric that forms the centrepiece is as rugged and jagged, and as full of matter, as anything of his own. Some of it strays into unduly metrical prose. But the ruggedness befits the matter; you could not have a suave Empedocles. This lyric embodies many of the thoughts which beset Matthew Arnold himself, and which recur in his verses. Age brings the decay not only of pleasures—to these, indeed, we had never any right—but of intellectual hope and of faith in the gods. The conclusion is that we should measure our aims by realities, conform inwardly to the stern law of life, and not abate our effort. Empedocles finds the strife on such terms impossible, and perishes; but not so Matthew Arnold himself, who was to work out a faith of his own of a different complexion. The setting is valley and mountain, the accompaniment is the songs of Callicles. The blank verse, describing here the Sicilian slopes, and there the days of youth in the Italian cities—which surely are Trinity, and Balliol, and Oriel, and Corpus—is of Matthew Arnold's best, and is free from the touch of consciousness which attends that measure in his epical experiments. Many traits and thoughts of the historical Empedocles [1] are inlaid in the poem; the wandering mind of man which only mirrors the world in fragments, the purgatorial transmigration of the human spirit through the elements, the evil lot of our life. But Matthew Arnold builds on all this a creed of resignation which recalls his favourite Marcus Aurelius more than it does the ejected democrat of Agrigentum.

IV

In *Thyrsis*, Matthew Arnold's only elegy in the traditional form, he is safe, musically and plaintively piping down in the water-meadows. There is no knottiness, inherent in the very thought, to be got over; the difficult stave, which is that of the earlier *Scholar-Gipsy*, is nobly invented; and the Oxford country, which already had been happily limned by Faber, finds its destined artist. Some thought that there was too little about Clough, and this idea occurred to Arnold himself; but Clough's ghost is there all the while, though his bones are in Florence. Together they watch the Tree on Foxcombe Hill, together they mark the traces of '*our* Scholar.' We think of Clough's own verse, of his eye for a different sort of landscape, in *The Bothie of Tober-na-Vuolich*; 'he had,' wrote Matthew Arnold, 'this idyllic side too.' *The Scholar-Gipsy*, Joseph Glanvill's gipsy, haunts both poems; but the earlier one is the more symbolic, though the symbolism is not obtrusive, and it is the more widely imaginative of the two. In style and execution the poems match, as they are meant to do; and, for single strokes of magnificence, it is easy to confront

> Still clutching the inviolable shade

with

> The morningless and unawakening sleep
> Under the flowery oleanders pale.

Thyrsis is a true elegy; and so, on another scale, are the beautiful Heinesque *Requiescat*, and the lines of piety on the author's brother, *A Southern Night*. But elegy and lyric fade off into the form, itself of no little range and variety, which I have called *associative* poetry, where the ethical and reflective element easily overpowers the elegiac, and which circles round a place, or a person, or both; such as the Grande Chartreuse, or Haworth and the Brontës, or Montmartre and Heine, or Rugby and Thomas Arnold. Some of these subjects might seem more tractable in prose; and might have gone better, with only a touch or two changed into one of Matthew Arnold's skilful, *numerous* periods, instead of into verse which is sometimes uncertain, and, to speak frankly, jaw-breaking:

> But something prompts me: Not thus
> Take leave of Heine, not thus
> Speak the last word at his grave!
> Not in pity and not
> With half censure—with awe
> Hail, as it passes from earth
> Scattering lightnings, that soul!

This painful effect occurs above all in the metre, of triple beat and unrhymed, which Matthew Arnold seems to have invented, and which he likes to use for intimate utterance. Its danger is ungainliness ; but 'the strong passion,' it has been well said,[1] 'fuses it' into 'something grave and noble in *Rugby Chapel*.' There the metre turns to a slow marching or climbing chant, comparable to that of *A Grammarian's Funeral*, as the thinned mountaineers, after the journey of life, come at last 'to the lonely inn 'mid the rocks.' To grandeur of spirit Matthew Arnold often approaches, to grandeur of form less often ; but here the form responds. And it responds again, in another way, in the *Fragment of a Chorus of a 'Dejaneira,'* which is in a style that would serve well for a translation of Sophocles ; and in *Dover Beach*, with the *Lycidas*-like rhymes on 'the sea of faith' with 'its melancholy, long, withdrawing roar.'

Others of these poems are in stanzas that lend themselves to the panel-pictures—something like Tennyson's, but simpler and more straightforward—in which Matthew Arnold excels :

> And the domed Velan with his snows
> Behind the upcrowding hills
> Doth all the heavenly opening close
> Which the Rhone's murmur fills.

These Alpine passages in *Obermann once More*, and those too in *Stanzas from the Grande Chartreuse*, are true poetry, while the verses on the Roman noble, and on Byron and Shelley, which show the same kind of skill, are but splendid poetic eloquence. Both pieces reveal the solitary-mindedness of the writer, and his disenchanted romanticism. Romance has gone, faith has gone, a new faith has not come, and there is no spiritual resting-place, not even—nay, not at all—in monastic peace. And the lines portraying the work achieved by Christ in the world anticipate the tone of Matthew Arnold's theological prose ; and the tolerance, which there also we find, towards the old faith has its root in poetic rather than intellectual sympathy. There is plenty of mountain air, too, in *Obermann* and the *Stanzas*, but never so much lyrical energy as in the earlier series called *Switzerland* ; which, be it a record of experience or no, is full of young, direct, and genuine emotion, and which contains at least one outburst—'Yes ! in the sea of life enisled,' which is passionate and resonant beyond Matthew Arnold's habit.

As to his lyrical faculty, which seldom reaches the point of *singing*, and is always being arrested by thinking, and too rarely sweeps the thought along with it—this faculty, it may be, works most freely at unexpected points, for instance when it is turned to the utterance of indignation :

> Charge once more, then, and be dumb!
> Let the victors, when they come,
> When the forts of folly fall,
> Find thy body by the wall!

This is a ringing cry, as of a 'soldier in the Liberation War of humanity'; and the religion of culture would be none the worse for a little more of it. Though smothered up in his praises of sweetness and urbanity, it is a strain ever-latent in Matthew Arnold. It breaks out again in *A Wish*, where he prays that in his last hour he may keep away from the doctor and also from 'his brother doctor of the soul.' The wish was granted in a sense, for he died suddenly, near the Mersey and the 'wide aerial landscape spread.' There is another kind of sharpness in the lines entitled *Old*, published when he was but forty-five; they forecast a palsy and apathy of spirit of which he was never to be in danger. The more usual note of lyric is struck happily, as we have seen, in the songs of Callicles and *The Forsaken Merman* and in *Requiescat*. Matthew Arnold had sometimes to contend with a certain imperfection of ear; he is capable of such a hissing line as 'My melancholy, sciolists say.' But then this defect has been much exaggerated; his idea often demands a discord of sound; and his real defect is not that he is unmusical, but that the turn and movement of his verse are apt to be those of high prose rather than of poetry, so that the presence of verse strikes us as accidental. Unawares, he speaks rather than chants. But his best things are not thus disabled at all; and on his own upland of contemplative, intellectually impassioned poetry, and in purity of tone and colour, he has few companions.

Not all the best of his sonnets are inspired by Wordsworth. The greatest of them, though not verbally perfect, is still that on Shakespeare. It contains none of the critical reserves which always weaken poetry; and there is no cult in it—nothing about the value of poetry for the higher life, or the equivalence of poetry and religion. The spirit of it is 'free,' and therefore the less 'abides our question.' The third sonnet, on *Rachel* ('Sprung from the blood of Israel's scatter'd race'), has some of the same quality; but *Austerity of Poetry* and *East London* are the most harmoniously built of those in the orthodox form.

V

So far as we can judge, there was a singular and happy absence of dark corners in Matthew Arnold's nature and imagination. Indignation is there, and satire, and melancholy; yet there is nothing of the strain which we find in every other poet of the same time or rank—in such work as *Guido Franceschini*, or *The Bride's Prelude*, or *Faustine*. He felt 'the sick hurry, the divided aim,' and how the time was out of joint; but there are many kinds of fever of which he must have had little apprehension, as may be guessed if we compare his *Empedocles* with Tennyson's *Lucretius*. Nor does he show any liking for this element in the work of others. This deficiency is one of Matthew Arnold's great charms. When we have had enough of tragedy or pathology, it is a relief to turn and listen to his pure, sound strain:

> Thin, thin the pleasant human noises grow,
> And faint the city gleams;
> Rare the lone pastoral huts—marvel not thou!
> The solemn peaks but to the stars are known,
> But to the stars, and the cold lunar beams;
> Alone the sun arises, and alone
> Spring the great streams.

The passage is from an early piece; the distinctive mood and style are soon perceptible; and so, too, is another of Matthew Arnold's traits, his special intimacy with nature, and his power of making nature poetical. This is found in his prose also. In the essay on George Sand there is a page on the river-country of Berry, with its 'shelving gravel and yellow wagtails,' which has the charm of *Thyrsis*. The East he had not visited, but those who knew it praised the veracity of the descriptions, taken from books, in *Sohrab and Rustum*. Still, in spite of the 'beds of sand and matted rushy isles' of the Oxus, the landscape is of necessity more general than it is in the Swiss or English poems. And of these the foreign pictures are the more rapidly done, and have the movement of travel in them; but the Thames valley, long known and haunted, is Matthew Arnold's chosen plot, and he has given eyes to those who knew it already. It is here natural to think of Tennyson; and, while both poets are at their best in this kind of work, Tennyson, with his concentrated vision, gives us, at the end of it, the pleasure of 'many a golden phrase,' always a little curious; but Matthew Arnold is the more transparent in his language, and so makes us think less about the words and more of the object. His simplicity seems no trouble to him, and there is no lack of air and colour :

> Men who through those wide fields of breezy grass
> Where black-wing'd swallows haunt the glittering Thames,
> To bathe in the abandon'd lasher pass.

But with all their differences the two poets, considered as painters, have this in common, that they are more English than anybody, as English as Constable. In English scenery, said Alfred de Vigny, we feel everywhere the hand of man ; *tant mieux ; partout ailleurs la nature stupide nous insulte assez.* The same gift, however, is found in *The Church of Brou*,[1] which the poet, as he afterwards said, 'found he had described wrongly' ; for the pines and valleys of the poem are not at Brou at all, but in Edgar Quinet's prose, whence Arnold took the description only. Yet it is one of his noblest things, and and he never wrote better rhymed verse :

> So sleep, for ever sleep, O marble Pair !
> Or, if ye wake, let it be then, when fair
> On the carved western front a flood of light
> Streams from the setting sun, and colours bright
> Prophets, transfigured saints, and martyrs brave,
> In the vast western window of the nave.

VI

The examples of Homer and Sophocles lie behind much of Matthew Arnold's criticism, as they do behind some of his poetry ; and so, we should add, do the examples of Dante and Milton. These are the masters who bring him to insist first of all on the necessity of design, proportion, and wholeness in a poem, and then on the continued presence of the grand, or at least of the high style, or else of one that has charm and magic. They also bring him to insist on poetry being a 'criticism of life.' These are the three great articles of his creed ; he draws many lines of connexion between them, and it is easy to misunderstand them apart.

It was no new thing to preach structure and unity. The Renaissance, with its eye on the great old models, had done so ; and though Matthew Arnold did not study the Renaissance much—indeed, was shy of it—still he is obeying one of its ruling passions, and is therein a true man of the Renaissance. But ages had come between. The neo-classical centuries had worshipped structure, building on Aristotle with an almost theological licence, and disguising his teaching almost out of knowledge. But the result became petrified and pedantic; the rules of tragedy, the rules of the epic, had reduced themselves to absurdities, and the world grew sick of them. Lessing did something to explode them. The strongest heads of the 'age of prose,' such as Johnson, in the end gave them up. The romantic age followed; and Coleridge renewed the conception of unity and design in a larger sense, finding those qualities not as imposed by rule, but as developed through a living inherent law, in Shakespeare. But the romantic poets themselves, in their longer and more imposing works, forgot these virtues again, as may be seen in *The Prelude*, *Prometheus Unbound*, and *Don Juan*; in the last of these, indeed, the absence of design is part of the programme. It is in well-made works of the middle scale, like *The Ancient Mariner* or *Michael*, that these virtues do appear and shine; and, still more, in shorter works like the odes of Keats or the lyrics of Shelley. The *Lines Written among the Euganean Hills* have a true pattern and unity of their own.

Well, Matthew Arnold, nursed on the Greeks and Dante, and reacting, as we have seen, against many things in the romantic poetry, fastened on its want of large design and structure. In his preface of 1853 he puts his case with a plainness and point that he never afterwards surpassed; and he also put it, more formally, in his preface to *Merope*. It was a true service to pull men's admiration back from beauty of detail to the artistic whole, and to the eternal qualities of the ancient writings from the neo-classic travesty of them. Arnold does not apply his criticism to the more ambitious poems of his own age; but it condemns them. Think of *Idylls of the King*, or *The Ring and the Book*, or even of *Sigurd the Volsung*, from the point of view of harmonious proportion, unity, and design, and not one of them will hold water for a moment. *The Life and Death of Jason* is a partial exception. But it is mostly, once more, the works of middle or lesser scale that are really well put together, like *Sohrab and Rustum* itself. Nor has this ceased to be true of our poetry since Matthew Arnold's time.

The exposition of the 'grand style' is to be found in the lectures *On Translating Homer*, and in their sequel, *Last Words*; and the same idea is expanded and carefully qualified in *The Study of Poetry*:

> The grand style arises in poetry *when a noble nature, poetically gifted, treats with simplicity or with severity a serious subject.*

This is the conclusion, and the lectures on Homer lead up to it. They form one of the most satisfactory efforts in the language since Coleridge's chapters on Wordsworth, and along with Pater's paper on *Style*, to work out a critical problem. True, Matthew Arnold has not, like Coleridge, a large metaphysical background of ideas—he has not that sort of wheelwork in his head at all; but then for his purpose he does not much need it, and he is in no danger of slipping into philosophic jargon, as Coleridge easily does. Also he is talking of something that has to be *done*; not simply of what has been the wrong way, but what is to be the right way, of getting Homer into English with as little loss as possible. What are the right diction, movement, and metre for that enterprise?

> Homer is rapid in his movement, Homer is plain in his words and style, Homer is simple in his ideas, Homer is noble in his manner.

The exposition and illustration of these qualities, the weighing and contrasting of Chapman, Pope, Cowper, and other translators according as they attain to or miss them, and, not least, the discussion of the metrical problem, must always form a point of departure for any treatment of this question. There are but two unsatisfactory points in the *Lectures*. One is the carping at Francis Newman, whose version, after all, no one took very seriously—it would have died of itself; there is a certain strain of bullying and inurbanity, such as Matthew Arnold was justly hard upon in other people, and which is not cancelled by his half-apologies. The other unsatisfactory point, as he saw, is his own hexameter translations, which have neither a good Greek nor a good English rhythm. They are, in fact, far less musical and effective than the Spenserian stanzas of Philip James Worsley,[1] whose version of the *Odyssey* appeared in 1861, just after the *Lectures*. Arnold had dismissed this complex stanza, as a vehicle for Homeric translation, on grounds of which Worsley well disposes in his preface. His formal criticism is as good as Matthew Arnold's own, and as well expressed, when he pleads that

> whatever objections may be urged against a rhymed translation of Homer diminish in weight precisely as the correspondences become more and more involved; though it is doubtful whether such involutions could safely be carried beyond the limits laid down by Spenser. It is one great merit of the Spenserian stanza, that the number of styles possible under the laws which it introduces is practically unlimited.

It is also true that the real proof is in the result; Worsley's rendering of the tale of Nausicaa, or of the picture of the garden of Calypso, is rich, sweet, and above all natural; and the associations of the stanza well suit the temper of these parts of the *Odyssey*, though they suit the *Iliad* less well.

Yet I believe that the true measure for Homeric translation is still Chapman's,—Chapman's, purged of the roughness and fantastic sallies, the gnarls and interruptions, which Chapman has associated with it. These faults of his blind us to the excellence of his fourteen-syllabled line, usually broken at the eighth syllable, which is a near equivalent to the hexameter in the amount of matter it contains, which admits of much continuity as well of salient single lines, and which gets the onset and directness of the hexameter; although, it is true, it misses the rushing ripple of the dactyl. But the dactyl, we know, is very expensive to reproduce in English at all. No, before we prefer any other measure, let us have a whole book of Homer done by a sufficient scholar-poet into a style like this:

> The Princess with her women train without the fort he found,
> Beside a limpid running stream, upon the primrose ground;
> In two ranks seated opposite, with soft alternate stroke
> Of bare, white, counter-thrusting feet, fulling a splendid cloak
> Fresh from the loom; incessant rolled athwart the fluted board
> The thick web fretted, while two maids, with arms uplifted, poured
> Pure water on it diligently, and to their moving feet
> In answering verse they sang a chaunt of cadence pure and sweet.

These lines are from Sir Samuel Ferguson's *Congal* (1872). He hardly keeps up this excellent style, though his aim (see Ch. XIX., *post*) was to be Homeric; yet in such a passage there is little to wish away, in verse or language, before we are reminded of Homer. Another medium might be the *Sigurd* measure used by Morris for translating the *Odyssey* (1887). Matthew Arnold had not this alternative before him. The *Sigurd* measure has, we shall see (Ch. XVI., *post*), many advantages and felicities; but the diffuseness of Morris, and his special diction, do not suit Homer; and it is difficult to think them away and to judge how the measure, without them, would serve for Homer in English.

Arnold's *Lectures* gave the impulse to all discussion of this kind; and they are so excellent not only because they contribute to the subject, but because they stick to the subject. There is nothing in them about culture and conduct, or about poetry being the ultimate religion, and there is no polite scarifying of John Bull. Nor has the writer's way of balancing and comparing yet become too artificial, as it does later in the articles upon Byron and Wordsworth. And it is here that he leads up to his amended description of the 'grand style,' which, like all Matthew Arnold's formulæ, can be neither ignored nor accepted, and over which one critic more must now needs vex himself.

It is easy to pick holes in it, and to say that he describes, not the grand style at all, but the conditions of its appearance, namely the 'noble and poetically gifted nature,' and the adequate and serious subject; and that he then gives two of its attributes, alternatively, namely 'simplicity and severity'; so that we never get to the grand style itself at all. But then he says, what is true, that you can only feel it, not define it, and that you can only feel it through examples. These, then, he provides; these he reiterates; and he works through them steadily, saying that

> if we have any tact, we shall find them, when we have lodged them well in our minds, an infallible touchstone for detecting the presence or absence of high poetic quality, and also the degree of this quality, in all other poetry which we may place beside them. Short passages, even single lines, will serve our turn quite sufficiently.

It was not Matthew Arnold's fault if he did not 'lodge them in our minds'; and his examples roused ample debate, as he desired. He finds other examples when he quits the region of grandeur for that of charm, felicity, and 'natural magic.' And he chooses his lines well; but the whole procedure, especially in his later essays, like those on Byron, Wordsworth, Goethe, and Milton, where he plays off against one another the test-passages not only from these poets, but from their critics—becomes a little too talismanic and dexterous, and also too arbitrary. For one thing, the examples are too short, and 'single lines' cannot 'serve our purpose quite sufficiently.' If we are to have a talisman, a whole speech of Satan or Macbeth is a better one; if only because grandeur or charm of style cannot be severed from grandeur or charm of rhythm, and in a line or two rhythm cannot have proper scope.

VII

The account of poetry as a 'criticism of life' has been much battered, and people have exhausted themselves in saying that the novel also is a criticism of life, and that so are the Ten Commandments, and that poetry is art and not criticism.

All this is true ; but it seems more to the purpose to add that there was nothing else for Matthew Arnold to say, once he was pressed to explain what it was in poetry that he really valued. By a criticism of life he meant something that would illumine and inspire us in the highest degree for the business of living. This includes, then, not poetry only, but all high literature ; an extension familiar to us in the tribe of minds which is represented by Sidney and Shelley, with their ancestor Plato. And high literature really gave Matthew Arnold his working religion. The best comment on his phrase we find by glancing at his interesting notebooks, where he put down a *pensée* from Pascal, or Johnson, or the Vulgate, or Goethe, to carry him through each of his hard professional days. And a very good religion it is. But it can only, we are told, be good for a small handful of mankind. 'Ah ! yes, but then,' replies Matthew Arnold in effect, 'I say not only that poetry is a religion, but that religion, that is, the real, essential, though often unconscious part of religion, is just poetry ; and that is what the multitude really live by, though they do not know it. So let us purge their religion of its false doctrine, and they will get nearer to the real essence of it ; and then poetry and religion will meet at last, like long-sundered lovers.' This application of course does not come out clear till he begins to write on theology ; but it is implicit from the first. We must keep, however, for the moment to his literary judgements ; the lectures *On the Study of Celtic Literature* came after the *Essays in Criticism*, but may be mentioned first.

Here he frisks wildly about his theme, and how far he knew any of the originals in Welsh and Irish remains obscure. He expands into humorous and shaky race-theorising—one of his most serious intellectual faults. He canters round and round in a wonderful circle. Take a few examples from Celtic poetry, and find a certain quality, say 'natural magic,' in them. Lay down that this can only be 'Celtic' ; and then, when you find anything like it in a 'Saxon' such as Shakespeare or Keats, say that such a 'Saxon,' of himself, *cannot* possess that quality and can only have 'got' it from the Celtic strain in him. The Celtic scholars have always smiled at much of Matthew Arnold's commentary, but still they have been grateful to him ; and well they may be. The praise of 'Ossian,' the true sympathy with the Welsh spirit and genius, the delightful quotations, the opening up of a fresh, endless field of letters, hardly known thus far except to the scholars themselves—what could better earn their gratitude ?

In the first series of *Essays in Criticism*, which really brought Arnold into reputation as a prose writer, and which are still wonderfully fresh and alive, we see, full-blown, his conception of criticism and its business. It is a temper of mind, he says,

> which regards Europe as being, for intellectual and spiritual purposes, one great confederation, bound to a joint action and working to a common result ;

it is the temper of 'seeing the thing as it really is' ; of keeping the mind a clean mirror, untarnished by personal, national, provincial, or doctrinal prejudice. Others, like Mill or Huxley, might cultivate this temper in philosophy or science ; their material lay in the facts of nature, or in the forces of history. Arnold's material lies in 'the best that is known and thought in the world'—in literature, that is, in the large sense in which we have seen him taking the term. And the method of getting at this 'best' is, once more, that of comparison. The actual ideal of a federation of minds was in the air at the time ; but the method approaches the method of Sainte-Beuve, and the *Essays in Criticism* are a modification of the *causerie*.

Sainte-Beuve, who lived in 1869, and went on writing to the last, knew and appreciated Arnold, who wrote after his death an admirable sketch of him, and termed him 'the master of us all in criticism.' But Sainte-Beuve has no mission, and treats his readers as urbane and rational already. Matthew Arnold tries to scold and banter them into becoming so ; and he has his mission, which is to enforce his ideas of culture, literature, and the intellectual life. Hence his *Essays* of 1865, and many of their successors, are not the *causerie* pure and simple at all. They are a salad, mostly deftly and harmoniously mixed, of jests, eloquence, topical allusion, disquisition on the national failings, genuine literary judgements, and the lofty idealism just indicated, which finds salvation in criticism, letters, and culture. Some of the subjects had the charm of discoveries. No one in England seemed to have heard of Joubert, with his beautiful intelligence and nature. French readers were shocked at seeing Joubert named in the same breath with Pascal ; but he was a discovery all the same, like the De Guérins, brother and sister. Matthew Arnold wrote on them with happy sympathy. But, while he praised them, he could slight Victor Hugo and even Racine. He managed to combine a true feeling for French prose with a singular deafness to both the form and the spirit of French verse, though he had heard Rachel and Madame Bernhardt.

The essay on *The Influence of Academies* is an attempt, Addisonian in spirit and not without practical effect, to reform the blatant and metallic reviewing that still survived, and to put the merely rhetorical gift, as Arnold judged it, of writers like Kinglake and Macaulay, in its place. Macaulay, however, stands much firmer than Matthew Arnold thought. The opening essay, on *The Function of Criticism at the Present Time*, sets forth with real power Arnold's characteristic ideal—the federal ideal of thought and literature, drawn from the study of 'Germany, France, Christ, Moses, Athens, Rome,' and of Persia and Britain too. He thus enlarged the whole material for critical judgement, and brought new territories into its field of vision. This ideal has now (1920) been thrown back for the time, by the public convulsion. As Matthew Arnold states it, it sounds rather too much for our short life ; but it is his real contribution to the English thought of his age, and it was probably suggested to him more by Goethe than by any one else. The way to realise it is by the practice of comparison. We are to draw on all these great writers and religious founders, in order to attain not a body of formal truth, but a temper and a critical *organon*, which will keep us from harbouring wrong admirations in life and literature, and set us in the right way. Spinoza and Marcus Aurelius join the company of torchbearers.

VIII

Arnold's religious and social writings, which begin with *St. Paul and Protestantism* (1869-70), and with *Culture and Anarchy* (1869), expanded these ideas, and diverted their current, leaving him the freer for pure criticism whenever to that he returned, as he did in his studies of Wordsworth, Byron, Keats, and Gray, and in *The Study of Poetry*. These and some others are collected in the second series of *Essays in Criticism* (1881) ; and behind them, of various dates, stand further studies, of Tolstoy, Amiel, Emerson, George Sand, and of the critics of Goethe and Milton. The method varies a good deal. In the *Gray* and the *Keats* it is concise, and all the better for that ; moving still from quotation to quotation, from formula to formula, swinging between praises and reserves in a way that became widely but not well imitated, and ending on a generous note. *The Study of Poetry* is a chapter of *poetic*, a confession of faith, concerning the uses and destinies of poetry and the tests of absolute excellence in it. This essay did more than anything else to spread Matthew Arnold's ideas broadcast.

In the *Emerson*, which heads the *Discourses in America*, delivered in 1883-4, there is more of personal retrospect; and the chief interest lies in the pages on Carlyle, for whom Matthew Arnold had never greatly cared, but whom he now salutes with more cordiality, and perhaps with a sense of not having done so duly before; and in those on Newman, for whom he had always much of the old Oxford leniency, and even felt reverence. In *George Sand* he tells of his visit to Nohant; in another article [1] he honours her at the expense of Balzac, whom he cries down, as we might, alas! expect; and he predicts, most dangerously, that George Sand will outlive Balzac. In the papers on *Amiel* and on *Count Leo Tolstoi* he is once more an introducer. Matthew Arnold tells a story well, and his sketch of *Anna Karénina* is a model of that sort of writing.

He also reviewed excellently, though not often. He justly praised Stopford Brooke's little *Primer of English Literature* (1876); in the last years of his life, he did not praise Dowden's *Life of Shelley*. The biographer, who otherwise did his work well, had sentimentalised; in producing his painful new material, he had seemed to salve, or evade, what was indefensible in Shelley's behaviour to his first wife; and he is duly beaten for doing so. But Matthew Arnold could never value Shelley properly; and, since it would take too long to examine all his antipathies and blindnesses—which are as interesting as Johnson's, and never merely freakish—let us take Shelley for an example.

> Those who extol him as the poet of clouds, the poet of sunsets, are only saying that he did not, in fact, lay hold upon the poet's right subject-matter; and, in honest truth, with all his charm of soul and spirit, and with all his gift of musical diction and movement, he never, or hardly ever, did. Except, as I have said, in a few short things and single passages, his poetry is less satisfactory than his translations; for in these the subject-matter was found for him.

And then we hear that Shelley's letters may well outlive his poetry. This, in effect, is the reasoned defence of the famous sentence about the 'beautiful and ineffectual angel.' I shall not argue for Shelley; Mr. Swinburne has answered the case once for all; and besides, *securus judicat orbis*. It is, however, strange that such a hoper for mankind as Matthew Arnold saw nothing in Shelley's evangel. Why was it? One is tempted at first to say it was sheer Whiggery, the impatience of the English gentleman with Shelley's 'set' and 'world' and the free Italian life; or again, that it was lack of ear. But it is something more than that, and the clue is found in a striking letter of 1865, where Arnold speaks of the need

to keep pushing on one's posts into the darkness, and to establish no post that is not perfectly in light and firm. One gains nothing on the darkness, by being, like Shelley, as incoherent as the darkness itself.

That is it. You cannot formulate Shelley, or put him into a *pensée* to get through the day with. He is drink, not meat. He is 'incoherent as the darkness itself.'—But then so is the sunrise 'incoherent,' and so is the 'prophet of Israel's restoration.' Nothing can better show the concrete, ethical turn of Matthew Arnold's mind, at least as it tended to become, than these deliverances. In his 'notebooks' there are bits from *Rasselas*; and there was a good solid eighteenth-century strain in him, poet as he was; and, much as he talked of the 'age of prose and reason,' it was the strain that gave discipline, and force, and pungency to his own prose. In his preface to the *Six Lives* from Johnson he pays his tribute to that age.

Yet this, of course, is but one side of Matthew Arnold, and it is not the one we finally think of when we watch him at work as a critic. He is truly of the tribe of Sainte-Beuve, to whom one always comes back. And with far less psychology, flexibility, and science than Sainte-Beuve, he has, at his best, a loftier view, and, in the phrase of his favourite Goethe, a more 'panoramic' one. We see this in his notable words on Sainte-Beuve [1] himself, which are an admirable example of his style. It is here free from the repetitions of phrase which became his trick, and which, like a number of reflecting mirrors, distract us from the clear sculptured outline of his thought:

As a guide to bring us to a knowledge of the French genius and literature he is unrivalled—perfect, so far as a poor mortal critic can be perfect, in knowledge of his subject, in judgement, in tact, and tone. Certain spirits are of an excellence almost ideal in certain lines; the human race might willingly adopt them as its spokesman, recognising that on these lines their style and utterance may stand as those, not of bounded individuals, but of the human race. So Homer speaks for the human race, and with an excellence which is ideal, in epic narration; Plato in the treatment at once beautiful and profound of philosophical questions; Shakespeare in the presentation of human character; Voltaire in light verse and ironical discussion. A list of perfect ones, indeed, each in his own line! and we may almost venture to add to their number, in his own line of literary criticism, Sainte-Beuve.

IX

Arnold's excursions into theology, social preaching, and politics fill many of his volumes, and are sometimes called a mere sojourn in the wilderness ; but this is an erroneous view. They contain some of his best exposition and satire ; he put his heart into them, and they made their mark on opinion. It is true that they are journalism—though often good and superlative journalism, for they are addressed to a stage of living thought—and that they are therefore in part written in the dust. The moving impulse is to be found in Matthew Arnold's faith in the saving power of literature and poetry. Read the Bible, he says, in that light ; it gives us 'morality touched with emotion,' and poetry, both in the grand style. Find, he says, the secret of Israel in his sublime expression of the need of mankind for righteousness. Study the books of both Isaiahs in this sense, taking them in their historical setting, and using modern criticism, and correcting the Authorised Version sparely and with literary tact. The two little volumes, *The Great Prophecy of Israel's Restoration* (1872) and *Isaiah of Jerusalem* (1883) were an effort to apply such ideas to practical teaching. Find, Arnold proceeds, the secret of the Gospels in the 'sweet reasonableness' and other qualities of Jesus, using similar methods and safeguards in interpretation ; and that of Paul in his deep, mystical, and unmethodised apprehension of the appeal of 'rich single words,' like *faith*, *grace*, *love*, or *the will of God*, in which he develops the 'secret of Jesus.' Do all this, keeping your head and literary sense, knowing that Israel and Jesus do not 'Hellenise,' or make refined and connected systems, and seeing clearly when Paul Hellenises and when he 'Hebraises,' and then you will be on the track, at any rate, of true religion, of the only religion which can survive the accretions that have gathered round the popular cult. Such is the broad sense of *St. Paul and Protestantism* (1869-70) ; of *Literature and Dogma* (1873), with its sequel *God and the Bible* (1874-5), a reply to critics ; and of *Last Essays on Church and Religion* (1876-7).

In all this Matthew Arnold cut clean across the recognised divisions of English opinion. Far is his temper from that of the philosophic liberals, the men of science, and the positivists, though he has certain affinities, after all, with these last. He called Comte a 'grotesque old French pedant' in his cheerful way, and he was assailed by devotees for want of seriousness. Behold, they said, society groaning and travailing, 'and me'—so Arnold expressed their charge—'me, in the midst of the general tribulation, handing out my pouncet-box.' Still, his large and catholic conception of literature, and his effort to preserve and clear the ancient sources of religious emotion, bring him much nearer to these critics than to the scientific liberals. He has also certain ties with the Broad Churchmen; but he was outside the fold, he was free, and he threw over the whole cargo of orthodox doctrine with a cheerful completeness which staggered the compromisers. He is, in fact, an agnostic (though he would have positively reared at the description) as regards the ordinary propositions of theism. Miracles must go; they 'do not happen,' and we know how men come to believe in them. The official creeds must go; they are the creations of 'pseudo-science.' What we can be sure of is the working of an 'eternal law, not ourselves,' impersonal it appears, though naturally and inevitably personified, and 'making for righteousness.' If religion, as a motive power, is to be saved, it must be transformed in this sense.

All this is set forth with point and eloquence, largely by the use of a relentless iteration and flogging of the key-phrases, and its tenor is not obscure. However, Matthew Arnold perplexed his position, and also his readers, by his practical conservatism. He is all, it would seem, for keeping up the ordinary religious language, and certainly for keeping up, in some improved form, the Church of England; which has not been very grateful for his consideration. He was consistent in his way, since he thought that, for England, the Church of England was the best and safest depositary of culture; and he wanted to save culture, which the Nonconformists, with their bleak antipathy to it, would never do. Salvation, so we make out, involving the rescue of religion from the radicals, the pedants, and the men of science on the one side, and from the Nonconformists on the other, is to come from a renewed Church of England, which shall be cleared of legendary theology, and which shall thus work freely on the national mind through its reformed apprehension of what Israel, Jesus, and Paul really meant; being aided thereto, above all, by a study of the 'best that has been said and thought in the world.' This was the way in which the English soul should and could be reanimated. And the man who propounded all this thought Shelley a dreamer!

In *Culture and Anarchy* (1869) he rings the changes again on Hebraism and Hellenism with little mercy, and on yet another set of phrases too: the materialised upper class, the vulgarised middle class, the brutalised lower class, Barbarians, Philistines,

Populace. It is a rather dull book, with lively passages. The satire on the middle class is brisker in that odd, almost faded *jeu d'esprit*, which still contains some good reading, called *Friendship's Garland* (1866-70), with its imaginary professor and his comments on British society and education. On education Matthew Arnold wrote much. He was for forty years an inspector of elementary schools, and some of his reports have been published. He went to France and Germany, there to investigate education officially, and his book on *Higher Schools and Universities* in those countries is the fruit ; he wrote articles, too, like *A French Eton* and *Porro Unum est Necessarium*. All this may be taken as part of his effort to bring home to his countrymen the best that had been thought, and said, and done, for their example.

The result is valuable, if not always exactly literature. He saw some of the problems clearly. He saw how the public schools and old universities were a preserve for certain classes, not for the nation ; and how, even there, humanism itself was deadened by some of the ancestral recipes for producing it. He saw the absence, in the universities especially, of the teaching of the realities of antiquity, and the weariness and futility, for the mass, of much 'composition.' The son of Thomas Arnold could never forget how his father had quickened the teaching of history, and of religion too, not only for Rugby, but for England ; and so to his mother he writes :

> My one feeling on closing the book [J. T. Coleridge's *Memoir of Keble*] is papa's immense superiority to all the set, mainly because, owing to his historic sense, he was a sower, wonderfully, for his nation, time, and profession, European ; and so got himself out of the narrow medium in which, after all, his English friends lived.

The two little editions of Isaiah show the same impulse of the educator, which was perhaps the deepest thing in Matthew Arnold when he was not, and sometimes also when he was, a poet.

His value as an educational reformer was lessened in several ways. He had an imperfect notion of the spirit and value of science, and though he made his bow to it, he was inclined to set it in a false and needless opposition to the humanities. He also had a strong anti-English bias, and fell in love with the foreign bureaucratic organisation, without really studying it long or seeing that England would never digest it. He sometimes had the State on the brain. He saw how well the State might unify and direct, but not how horribly it might meddle. Still, he did more than anybody to interest the reading public in education, and much to temper the dreariness of the topic for human perusal. This was no slight service. Working as Arnold did under the yoke of a system he disapproved, and before free education and its consequences had prevailed, he wrote much that is now only of historic note. But his professional reports are full of light and humanity; he is always for the living word and the quickening spirit, never for mere mechanism and the dead 'result'; and this is the epitaph which, as an educator, he would have preferred.

Matthew Arnold's politics need only be glanced at. He wrote more than once on Ireland, with less sympathy than he supposed. He wanted a new temper towards Ireland to arise in England, and saw that there was the difficulty; but when it came to the point he shook his head over the charming Celt, and took, like many others, a strong Whig line. In this department the genius of Matthew Arnold is not seen at work. He admired Burke, but his political utterance has nothing of the stamp that we find in Burke's most casual pamphlets.

X

On the morrow of his death Matthew Arnold was saluted in the press as 'a guide, a representative, a glory' of his country. He had become an institution, all the more that, like a true Briton and his father's son, he had turned aside from pure letters into the public fray. Hardly any other critic was widely read before the arrival of Pater; except Macaulay, who was read by the multitude. English society felt that Arnold was a poet who had a right to talk about poetry, a thinker who derided philosophy, a scholar without being a pagan, an eminent public servant with a good conservative streak in him; and that no one had, no one deserved, more friends. There was, indeed, his odd religion; some thought he had too much religion, some that he had too little. But, to the earnest reader, he seemed mysteriously to be on the right side after all. When attacked, he 'only took snuff,' smiled, and reiterated generally. The 'great middle class,' when it did read him, rather liked his jibes and 'far-singing arrows,' and went on as before, every one thinking that the hits at other people were very good. All this made Matthew Arnold a considerable, a very attractive, figure. But we like best to think of him as what George Sand called him, a *jeune Milton voyageant*, in his youthful and melancholy ferment of thought, before he had discovered the creed of culture; seeing himself on the frontier between two faiths, the one extinct, the other hardly born; feeling 'the expiring wave of the mighty influence' of Byron; going night after night to see Rachel act, and reading the 'too bold dying song' of Emily Brontë, which, he tells us, 'stirr'd, like a clarion-blast, my soul'; and solitary-minded, with something of Alfred de Vigny in him, and something of Keats. And all the time, all his days, there hovered before him the true artist's ideal of what he himself calls 'the law of pure and flawless workmanship'; and that is Matthew Arnold's real praise.

CHAPTER XI

WALTER PATER: AND OTHER CRITICS

I

Many of our critics have walked in the high road of life, and written for all men in the language of the world. Such was Dryden; and such, when he dropped long words, was Johnson. In their pages, and in Matthew Arnold's too, there is abundance of fresh air; and the want of fresh air is the great deficiency in Walter Pater, and a source of the discomfort which he causes to most readers, unless they are like himself. Yet he is our greatest critic since Coleridge. He left behind him a little creative writing, and a sheaf of what he called 'appreciations.' Time has little dulled or worn that fabric; it is dyed too fast. What Pater may have lost by his esoteric and not wholly healthy habit of mind, and his indifference to the broad energies of mankind, he more than recovers by his delicacy of sense and his unimpeded concentration. Much of Matthew Arnold's writing is, to use his own agreeable phrase, 'touched with caducity': he was very English, and he could not keep off politics. Pater was rewarded for knowing so well what he could do. His influence stole out from a narrow circle; it has never reached the larger public, but it has never retreated.

He wrote one really continuous book, *Marius the Epicurean* (1885): the fragment called *Gaston de Latour* would have been another. His integer was the article, the *étude*, or the lecture, of magazine length. This limitation may have suited his talent, though it also encouraged his love for condensed and over-studied sentences. The first essay that he printed was on Coleridge, in 1866; the next was on Winckelmann. After the appearance of his *Studies in the History of the Renaissance* (1873) his reputation was secure. *Marius* took some five years to finish; *Gaston*, and the four short *Imaginary Portraits* (1887), are experiments of the same order. Here, as in *Emerald Uthwart* and *The Child in the House*, his imagination works freely, instead of on some historical personage. Meantime appeared *Appreciations* (1889), which contain his theory of style and composition, and his judgements on English literature. Latterly he turned more to Greece; the fruits are *Plato and Platonism* (1893), a course of college lectures, and *Greek Studies*. Some reviews, originally published in the *Guardian*, should not be forgotten.

Walter Horatio Pater [1] (1839-94) was at the King's School in Canterbury; the art and atmosphere of the cathedral left their trace on his mind, and the Anglican spirit and ritual always appealed to him strongly. In the Oxford training for 'humaner letters,' with its direct introduction to the Greece of Pericles, he found another of his primary interests. His headquarters after 1864 were at Brasenose, where he resided long as tutor; and he lived for an interval in Kensington. He travelled to France and Italy, their scenery, art, and literature sinking into him; Ruskin he had read in boyhood. His reading was deep, and what may be called intensive. In each of these great fields—antiquity, the Renaissance, modern thought and religion, modern letters—Pater chose a definite plot of ground and wrought on it, caring for it from first to last, and returning to it faithfully. To perceive, to know, to enjoy, to find the words for his pleasures, seems to have been his existence. His pages mirror one side of the Oxford spirit: its leisured humanism, its backward gaze, its charm, its eclecticism—something most unlike the refreshing east winds of contemporary Cambridge; which, however, were not further from Pater than the academic 'causes' and wrangles of his own university.

II

He has given a clear account of the discipline of mind and sensibility that is required for the 'æsthetic critic'—that is, for himself. An early paper called *Diaphaneitè* shadows forth an ideal of character and 'culture,' which is severed from the world by its simplicity, mental integrity, and lofty remoteness. Pater speaks of 'culture,' now and afterwards, in the accent that others keep for words like 'grace' or 'holiness.' In writing of Coleridge, he celebrates the 'relative spirit,' which shuns fixed principles in metaphysic or criticism and tries to see life and art in their real complexities, taking each belief or mental product, each poem or school of painting, as it comes; not judging it by canon, but considering how it may have grown, what human need or emotion it may serve, and how far it attains full or appropriate expression. All this the critic exists to feel, and then he has to find words for his feeling;

thus acquiring, like Goethe it may be hoped, a sense by which 'no touch of the world of form, colour, and passion is disregarded'; and, further, 'an intellectual *finesse* of which the ethical result is a delicate and tender justice in the criticism of human life': a phrase to be recalled by those who may fancy that Pater was at any time a true Cyrenaic.

This view is developed in *Winckelmann* (1867), in the light of the supposed teaching of Goethe. Extract, by hard study, the secret of every form of culture, and enjoy it 'with a kind of passionate coldness,' so reaching 'the supreme, artistic, view of life'; the Greeks will lead you that way if they are well understood. In the *Renaissance* the cult is defined in terms suggested by Aristotle. The virtue of 'all works of art, and the fairer forms of nature and human life,' lies in the 'special, unique impression of pleasure' that they give. Pater did himself some wrong in the sentences, afterwards cancelled, in which he seemed to reduce the quest of life itself to a series of disconnected 'moments' of pleasure. Apart from any false psychology involved, his own creed implies a strict perception of the difference of spiritual or artistic quality between pleasures. This is clear enough in his study (1874) of Wordsworth. He still, no doubt, uses the vintner's terms; we are to find the poet's 'peculiar savour'; or the playgoer's—we value art and poetry 'as they afford the spectacle' of 'the concentrated presentment of passion,' and this we are to 'witness with appropriate emotions.' But, when he comes to the analysis, it is after all the solemn and spiritual parts of Wordsworth that are defined, and his purer gift; and the pleasure of the 'spectacle' becomes nothing less than the sharing of that life of 'impassioned contemplation,' which is judged by Wordsworth himself to be the highest. Of his country folk we hear, for example:

> Breaking from time to time into the pensive spectacle of their daily toil, their occupations near to nature, come those great elementary feelings, lifting and solemnising their language and giving it a natural music. The great, distinguishing passion came to Michael by the sheepfold, to Ruth by the wayside, adding these humble children of the furrow to the true aristocracy of passionate souls. . . . A sort of Biblical depth and solemnity hangs over this strange, new, passionate pastoral world, of which he first raised the image, and the reflection of which some of our best modern fiction has caught from him.

So with Shakespeare. We are told that he, too, 'sits as a spectator, and knows how the threads in the design before him hold together under the surface,' as he watches (in the way that the critic should imitate) the course of events in his *Measure for Measure* (1874). There seem to be two fallacies in this. First of all, you cannot simply sit aloof, and also have the 'appropriate emotions,' combining enjoyment with detachment. 'Plunge in, man,' we exclaim, 'and take your share (be sure that Shakespeare did so before he earned his right, if he ever claimed it, to sit on the bank and look on); plunge in, trouble about *things*, and you will get unexpected emotions enough that way, whether "appropriate" or not! Else you will exclude life itself from the fine art of living.' Secondly, contemplation is not the same thing as detachment. None the less, Pater's account of Angelo or of Isabella, and of the 'finer justice' involved in the issue, and of the varying levels of workmanship in the play, continues, or revives, the great tradition of Shakespearian criticism.

For he is always proclaiming his cult, and always rising well above it, so that it does not do him much harm; in its cruder shape it was by no means good for everybody. By sheer sensibility and wits, or perhaps through some human experience of his own, Pater winds deep into the spirit of Wordsworth, or Raphael, or Sir Thomas Browne. His actual *organon* of criticism is only half indicated in his theory. Moreover, the theory is quite half true; for all the romantic critics, and many others, had said that pleasure is the end of art, as knowledge is the end of science. Aristotle had spoken of the 'special pleasure' of one or another art; and the principle is duly extended to this or that writer or production. It was the slightly perverse formulation of this truth, and the mannered, hushed style of Pater's language, and his Epicurean pose, that bred suspicion and may divert the reader from his real gift. Also he talked about *art* and *beauty* in a way which is not easy to avoid while expounding him, but which make us feel that the words require a rest. Some of the 'Pre-Raphaelite' group do the like; and his essay, afterwards withdrawn and certainly rather turgid, on *Æsthetic Poetry* (written as early as 1868), may be his tribute to that connexion; along with one on Dante Gabriel Rossetti, written in 1883, which is much maturer.

III

The appreciative temper, in itself, might not seem to favour the quest for first principles; it fears to hamper itself by discovering 'rules.' But this anxiety is vain; for mankind must needs seek for universals, and if you or I find ourselves brought up short in that direction, it only means that we have not the requisite philosophical intelligence. Pater is not thus checked; he has an æsthetic and a 'poetic' of his own. He does not, like Aristotle and Hegel, exalt the drama, but he sees in music the perfect type of all art, precisely because in music it is impossible to 'distinguish the form from the substance, or matter.' Not fulness, then, of matter, but independence of matter, is the criterion of rank in an art. Thus poetry is 'all literary production which attains the power of giving pleasure by its form, as distinct from its matter'; all invention, be it in verse or prose, being thus included. Later criticism has shown up the equivocations lurking in this distinction. How can you enjoy the form of *Michael* apart from its matter? You cannot enjoy even the metre by itself. You can enjoy Lucretius apart from his scientific purpose; but that is only a part of his 'matter.' 'Substance' is not the same as purpose. Afterwards, Pater insisted more fully on the natural frontiers between poetry and prose. In his essay on *Style*, which is a classic in spite of some over-condensation and obscurity, he vindicates prose as a fine art, and as one specially distinctive, in its surprising developments, of the nineteenth century. It is his own art, and the ideal that he sets forth reveals his own way of working. This is the well-known cult of the 'unique word'—the word which alone is 'absolutely proper to the single mental presentation or vision within.' Search, as Flaubert did, for this word, or idiom, or figure, or cadence—or rather wait for it; it is itself waiting somewhere—where, in whose mind, or in what Platonic overworld, is too curious a question. This theory has come to be associated, not quite fairly, with a slow and painful attitude in composing; the pace, however, is not the real question, and Pater himself well sees that 'Scott's facility, Flaubert's deeply pondered evocation of "the phrase," are equally good art.' In one way, namely in his respect for structure, Pater is a good Aristotelian, like Matthew Arnold. 'How wholesome! how delightful!' he says, is the intellectual satisfaction given, for instance, by the evolution and spacing of *Lycidas*. In Pater's own writings there is the concern for structure everywhere. It is easy to connect it with his attention to 'composition' in painting and sculpture.

His readings of the writers and painters mark a renewal in English criticism; or rather, a recovery of that direct sympathy and understanding which we associate with Lamb and his companions, and which Matthew Arnold, with his caprices and *ex cathedra* sentences, had a little interrupted. Pater was more widely read, and more steadily trained, than the romantic writers, and thus retrieves some of his inferiority to them in spirit and passion. He had also, more than most of them, the philosophic bent. Not, indeed, in the way or the measure of Coleridge, whom he portrays as only defeated and distracted by his long pilgrimage towards metaphysical truth. Pater studies, while he abjures, metaphysics ; but he studies them, not for the solutions they may offer, but as an ineradicable mode of expression for certain needs of the soul. This point of view is not enough for the philosopher, who indeed usually neglects it ; but the critic it may carry far. For if he does not affirm, neither does he refute ; he only seeks to understand. Pater's study of Pascal (1894) is a good example of his attitude. The Jesuit doctrine of sufficient grace, the Jansenist doctrine of foreordinance, do but formulate two deeply-rooted, eternally recurrent aspects or types of character ; and one of them finds its born exponent in a great writer, Pascal. It was this kind of contrast, quite as much as art and ritual, that drew Pater to theology. Jowett was wrong when he said, 'Mr. Pater, you seem to think that religion is all idolatry.' The interpretations of Bruno (in *Gaston de Latour*) and of Spinozism (in *Sebastian van Storck*) owe their value to this, the truly 'relative,' method. Still, Pater is more at ease with Montaigne and with the poets and fantasts. They have no systems, the question of whose validity he might be taxed with eluding ; and yet they are charged with thought, which is moulded in turn by emotion and coloured by temperament, and which is therefore to be judged, in the long run, by its expression ; and here the æsthetic critic is unshackled.

IV

In approaching the Renaissance, Pater does not claim to do the work of the excavator, or the professional 'expert' ; some errors of detail in connoisseurship have been found in his book. Nor does he try, like the orderly historian, to show the whole story in perspective. He leaves a great deal out. For instance, while making it plain that the 'pre-Renaissance,' as we may call it, in the twelfth and thirteenth centuries reached far beyond France, he does not touch on the many premonitions of it which can be traced in England at that time. He makes 'studies' ; he takes half a dozen typical great figures, Leonardo, Pico, Michelangelo, and paints each of them on a rather small canvas, every inch of it crowded. He makes Botticelli's Venus, or Leonardo's heads, the subject of a *poème*, or lyrical page, of his own. These are the burnished passages which made the book famous; justly enough, but somewhat to the obscuring of its intellectual force and grasp.

For it is a study, though not a systematic study, of mind. There is, above all, a steady outlook on the various clashes, intermixtures, and attempted reconciliations of thought that mark the fifteenth and sixteenth centuries. The mythology of the artists, compounded of sacred and profane; the play of Platonism on Christianity, of science upon art, of Rome upon the Pleïade, are handled with a sure instinct. *Winckelmann* is a study of the Greek Renaissance in Germany two centuries later. The Renaissance, properly so-called, is again presented in the address on Raphael: the delicate, not strong, but carrying voice of the lecturer is still in the ears of those who heard it delivered at Oxford in 1892. Ronsard, who figures in the essay on Du Bellay, reappears in *Gaston*; where the physiognomies of Montaigne and Bruno also come in, bringing the survey down late in the sixteenth century.

Of the three Shakespearian studies, that on *Measure for Measure* has the sharpest edge, and is a truly noble piece of criticism, bringing out not only the atmosphere and poetry, and the disconcerting inequalities of the play, but also, with unexpected force, Shakespeare's 'power of moral interpretation', never more fully tasked than here. Among Pater's 'appreciations,' it stands high as revealing the qualities for which we otherwise turn to *Marius* or *The Child in the House*—the sense of pathos and the humanity; for which his 'Epicurean' theories, even at their best, are too flimsy a vessel. *Shakespeare's English Kings* comes next; and Sir Frank Benson's subtle performance of Richard the Second is the best comment on Pater's picture of the royal 'æsthete,' enjoying the pangs of the lovely poetry which he makes out of his own weakness. As to *Love's Labour's Lost*, the light world of that play and its sportful sentiment receive justice, perhaps for the first time. As to the studies of *Charles Lamb* and *Sir Thomas Browne*, it is enough to guess how Lamb himself would have admired their handiwork; it resembles his own, in so far as both writers are *trackers*, with an Indian's eye and ear for trifles—a breath, a fallen twig, a half-effaced trail—that will carry them to the retreat of the quarry:

The leading motive of Browne's letter [*Letter to a Friend*] is the deep impression he has received during those visits, of a sort of physical beauty in the coming of death, with which he still surprises and moves his reader. There had been, in this case, a tardiness and reluctancy in the circumstances of dissolution, which had permitted him, in the character of a physician, as it were to assist at the spiritualising of the bodily frame by natural process; a wonderful new type of a kind of mortified grace being evolved by the way. The spiritual body had anticipated the formal moment of death; the alert soul, in that tardy decay, changing its vesture gradually, and as if piece by piece. The infinite future had invaded this life perceptibly to the senses, like the ocean felt far inland up a tidal river.

There is much in this of Lamb's perceptiveness, and also of his instinctive, never servile echo of the style of the writer who happens to be before him. Pater, of course, has a learning, and has an intellectual and historical point of view, which are denied to, but are not required by, the 'belated Elizabethan.'

In his criticisms, Pater is never tempted artificially to separate the soul from the body of literature, the idea from the expression; because he is alive to both of them equally, and also to their contexture. Herein is his strength; for if the mere study of ideas ignores art, the mere study of expression ignores the roots of expression itself, and therefore mutilates art. On the other hand it is true that in some kinds of art, such as the lyrical, the element of ideas may be at a minimum, and the result is still poetry—very much poetry; while the study of ideas in themselves is the affair of philosophy or history, whose conclusions need not be stated in terms of art, or in literary form at all. For the critic, therefore, it is the worse extreme to neglect the form. But Pater is not faced with such a choice of evils. His power of seeing both sides is well discovered in the *Postscript* to *Appreciations*, originally published in 1876 as *Romanticism*: it is a well-known attempt to define that term, and his phrase the 'union of strangeness and beauty' has become current since. More properly, it is 'the addition of strangeness to beauty,' over and beyond the classical quality of 'order in beauty,' that 'constitutes the romantic character in art': the root-instinct at work being that of 'curiosity.' This, no doubt, is one of the historic 'notes,' as Cardinal Newman might have said, of that new or revived ingredient in our modern literature, which we trace from the time of the poet Collins onwards. But then it is only one of the 'notes'; and those who have worked out over the ground may well become shy of using the term 'romantic' at all, since it covers so many phenomena, and moreover has to be defined in opposition to the term 'classical,' which itself has half a dozen senses —themselves well-discerned in Pater's essay. Still 'strange beauty' is clearly the quality that Pater himself felt most keenly, and liked most, in this body of literature.

V

Marius the Epicurean is as far from the propagandist stories written by Newman or Wiseman about early Christian converts, as it is from the laborious resuscitations of the antique world once familiar in *Charicles* or *Gallus*. It is a new offshoot of the historical novel. It exhibits the outer and inner life of Rome in the day of Marcus Aurelius. Banquets, processions, ceremonies, the lecture hall, the Christian catacombs, the Italian landscape—these are the setting, which is exquisitely done; and the learning, which is profound and alert, never troubles the reader. In the midst are the figures of Apuleius, Fronto, the emperor, and Lucian, whose words are often given through actual translation. These speakers, again, illuminate the real subject, which is the spirit of the age, in its interior changes and disturbances, as they are seen reflected, facet after facet, in the rather shadowy Marius. Each of the dying philosophies says its utmost for itself in turn. The nobler pretensions of the Cyrenaic, which passes into the Epicurean, scheme, are sympathetically arrayed, with a definite side-glance at Pater's own day and mental experience. But for Marius they are not enough; nor yet is Stoicism enough, with its tendency to shelve evil and to condone, as Marcus Aurelius did, the cruelties of the games. All that goes against the old Roman piety, and the strain of kindness, in Marius. He seeks for some more ideal satisfaction. Where shall he find the impulse to a cheerful courage, less careless than that of the Greek; and some compelling motive to self-sacrifice? In the end he dies of the plague, which he has risked for the sake of a Christian companion, Cornelius. Marius has visited a Christian house, and felt its charm, and he conceives a new ideal of brotherhood, of chastity, and of piety towards the dead; though, indeed, he is not actually received into the new faith. This somewhat hackneyed topic Pater manages to refresh; but his pictures of the unregenerate *viveurs* and heathen thinkers are still more vivid and natural.

The story of *Marius the Epicurean* is carefully laid out and built up. The translations bulk large, but we do not wish them away. *Cupid and Psyche* is a story within a story, like

Fielding's *Man of the Hill*, and is more in keeping with its context. There is often a tint of the irony which is said to have marked Pater's talk; it is polite, a little feline, like that of Renan. The inlaying and artifice are less apparent than elsewhere, and the thought is less overloaded. Most of the varieties of Pater's style are to be seen in this book, including the really noble one which he always commands when describing the nascent stir of thought in his boyish heroes, and which is seen again in the unfinished *Gaston de Latour*. Here the same gift is applied on a smaller scale. The time is now that of Charles the Ninth, which one of Pater's favourite authors, Mérimée, had depicted in his novel. In Gaston the fighting and politics leave little impression. The conflict is again intellectual. Catholicism, humanism, scepticism, contend, with results that are hardly apparent, for the spirit of the young Gaston, who is attractive of course, but otherwise somewhat questionable. He is meant for the Church; already, indeed, in due order, 'the fair surplice ripples down over him.' But he is drawn by 'the beauty of the world and its sorrow, solaced a little by religious faith, itself so beautiful a thing.' (All the 'preciosity' of the author, and of the Eighties in Oxford, seems to echo in the phrase.) Gaston first visits Ronsard; then he lives a long while with Montaigne; at last he comes to sit under Giordano Bruno. The portrait of Montaigne is one of Pater's best. The scenery, the hospitality, the talk of the château, are perfectly drawn, and the creed of the host, with his canon of 'suspended judgement,' seems their natural product. Along with *Gaston* must be named the 'imaginary portraits' of 'Denys l'Auxerrois' and others, where Pater shows a curious taste for wild cruel legend and the dark corners of human nature—for Pan when he is showing his teeth. So Denys, the young organ-builder, degenerates, falls mad, seems possessed, and is at last torn up by the mob who accidentally catch sight of his blood. All this, perhaps, is the *underside* of the cult of beauty.

VI

The *Greek Studies*, beginning in 1876 with one on Dionysus, spread over nearly twenty years; some are upon myth and folklore, as revealed in art, poetry, or custom; some on sculpture. *The Bacchanals of Euripides* is a sequel to *Dionysus*. *Hippolytus Veiled* is an imaginative, composite retelling of the tale from all the records. *Demeter and Persephone* traces a mythical idea from its primitive state, through poetry and marble, up or down, to its full symbolic development. *The Marbles of Aegina* and its companions form part of an unfinished work. In all of these Pater's large learning lies easily at the service of his interpreting gift. The historical imagination is nourished at every point by knowledge. The conceptions, still fresh in Pater's day, of animism, of evolution and of anthropomorphic fancy, he applies continually. Perhaps he reads a good deal of his own into the early history of myth ; but his peculiar eloquence is seen to great advantage : he speaks thus of the original Dionysus :

> He is the soul of the individual vine, first ; the young vine at the house-door of the newly married, for instance, as the vine-grower stoops over it, coaxing and nursing it, like a pet animal or a little child ; afterwards, the soul of the whole species, the spirit of fire and dew, alive and leaping in a thousand vines, as the higher intelligence, brooding more deeply over things, pursues, in thought, the generation of sweetness and strength in the veins of the tree, the transformation of water into wine, little by little ; noting all the influences upon it of the heaven above and the earth beneath ; and shadowing forth, in each pause of the process, an intervening person—what is to us but the secret chemistry of nature being to them the mediation of living spirits.

These mythical figures, as well as the nobler gods, however they be imagined or embodied by art, come in each case to represent to Pater what he calls the 'spiritual form' of certain conceptions, and such conceptions contain the true bequest of Greece to the European world. Thus Apollo becomes at last

> the 'spiritual form' of inward or intellectual light, in all its manifestations. He represents all those specially European ideas, of a reasonable, personal freedom, as understood in Greece ; of a reasonable polity ; of the sanity of soul and body, through the cure of disease and the sense of sin ; of the perfecting of both by reasonable exercise or *ascesis* ; his religion is a sort of embodied equity, its aim the realisation of fair reason and just consideration of the truth of things everywhere.

—'Represents'—but to whom ? To what Greek did Apollo mean all that ? The critic dreams before the marble, and reads modern significance into it, just as we are tempted to see much in Hamlet of which Shakespeare never thought.

Plato and Platonism is a course of lectures circling round the *Republic*, which is a staple book in the Oxford 'school of humaner letters.' A sketch of the Pre-Socratics and of the Platonic Socrates and his thoughts, the book comes nearer than the rest of Pater's to the common forms of exposition. The leading idea is that Plato, and Plato's language, and the Parthenon, and the Greek mythology all form part of a harmonious whole, which it is necessary for the modern world, and for the author's happiness, to understand. The Greek spirit is not only a matter for the scholar, but is to be distilled into 'the uses of our lives.' Pater's own language, here as elsewhere, has what he calls 'a certain crafty reserve in its exercise, after the manner of the true expert.'

VII

His general way of writing is faithfully enough indicated by his essay on *Style*. He belongs to the cell-building tribe of authors, whom we know better amongst the poets ; Gray and Tennyson belong to it. That is, he seeks for exact and perfect rightness, beginning with the single word, and working outwards. Of Dante he says, in his introduction to Mr. Shadwell's delicate translation of the *Purgatory* :

> He is one of those artists whose general effect largely depends on vocabulary, on the minute particles of which his work is wrought, on the colour and outline of single words and phrases.

This holds good of Pater himself. A 'minute and sensitive fidelity,' as in the same essay he calls it, to the single word, to the perfection of the cell, is ever with him. Another of his phrases, applied to Lamb, is 'the value of reserve in literature,' and this he practises even to the point of sacrifice. Bold, emphatic words are kept out, or only used for special effects ; in one page, on Mérimée, come *naked*, *fierce*, *slavish*, *duped*, *horror*, *blood*, spaced over it artfully ; but this is exceptional. Everywhere, as may suit the matter, be it description, or philosophy, or criticism, the exact tint or wash of vocabulary is observed. Pater may be said to invent new resources of prose for each of these species, superimposing all kinds of suggestion and overtones on the bare meaning, and not being well satisfied, until he has done so, that the meaning is really won. And the sentences are built with great variety, with much characteristic parenthesis and interjection, sometimes into excessive complexity, with a direct avoidance of rhetorical movement, and falling away down to a gentler level, like the end of an Italian sonnet. They are often simple ; but even then, it is not too much to say, hardly one of them could have been written by any one else, unless it were an imitator of Pater himself.

He had fled to the south from the first forbidding days of a hard winter which came at last. Or again: *Angels might be met by the way, under English elm or beech-tree*; the rhythm alone would make these individual. Some of Pater's pictures, like that of London, remind one of Girtin's noblest water-colours:

the great city with its weighty atmosphere, and portent of storm in the rapid light on dome and bleached stone steeples.

The ultimate test, it may be thought, of such a method is whether the result sounds natural—natural not only to the author, for authors acquire a terrible second nature—but to the reader who has goodwill. Pater, when he elaborates, cannot always be said duly to meet this test, or to earn the praise that he gives to Pascal's prose, when he calls it 'a pattern of absolutely *unencumbered* expressiveness.' We could find passages confused in their 'minuteness,' obscure in their conveyance of thought, where the labour is painfully felt and is not therefore repaid. Pater cannot be read aloud quickly—his movement is too clogged, and his music too ritualistically solemn for that. It is not, however, a fault, but a characteristic. Neither is elaboration a fault, when it is the right and only way of saying something subtle. This, on Pascal, could scarcely be simplified without loss, though it is not simple, or like Pascal's own style, in the least:—

Observe, he is not a sceptic converted, a returned infidel, but is seen there as if at the very centre of a perpetually maintained tragic crisis holding the faith steadfastly, but amid the well-poised points of essential doubt all around him and it. It is no mere calm supersession of a state of doubt by a state of faith; the doubts never die, they are only just kept down in a perpetual *agonia*. Everywhere in the 'Letters' he had seemed so great a master—a master of himself—never at a loss, taking the conflict so lightly, with so light a heart: in the great Atlantean travail of the 'Thoughts' his feet sometimes 'are almost gone.' In his soul's agony, theological abstractions seem to become personal powers. It was as if just below the surface of the green undulations, the stately woods, of his own strange country of Auvergne, the volcanic fires had suddenly discovered themselves anew.

Nevertheless, the great things in literature are usually simple in expression; and Pater's powers of thought and style are best displayed when he comes nearer to the traditional manner, reminding us of Thackeray at his best, and hinting how he might possibly have distinguished himself in that effort to 'treat contemporary life nobly,' which he ascribes to Tennyson. It is in his brief imaginative sketches, like *The Child in the*

House, or *Apollo in Picardy*, that he thus succeeds. The aspirations of youth, and the hidden memories of boyhood, appeal to him especially, and link these little pieces for a moment with such famous productions of the romantic movement as *Dream-Children*. Emerald Uthwart, the boy who has been condemned to military disgrace for bravery in defiance of instructions, comes home to die:

> In his worn military dress he seems a part of the ruin under which he creeps for a night's rest as darkness comes on. He actually came round again to the scene of his disgrace, of the execution; looked in vain for the precise spot where he had knelt; then, almost envying him who lay there, for the unmarked grave; passed over it perhaps unrecognised for some change in that terrible place, or rather in himself; wept then as never before in his life; dragged himself on once more, till suddenly the whole country seems to move under the rumour, the very thunder, of the 'crowning victory,' as he is made to understand.

It is not easy to fix on any definite or guiding models for Pater's English. It is unlike that of some of the writers whom he most admired; one of them was Newman. Nor is it like that of any of his favourite Greeks or Frenchmen—Plato or Victor Hugo. He is removed from all of these, if only by his inveterate tessellating habit. The tones of Ruskin are traceable now and then in his earlier pages, but Ruskin is not his master; that full tide of eloquence, sweeping precious things and rubbish along with it, is not for him. Lamb and the fantasts count for something more. But Pater's origins are composite, and eclectic, and obscured. Historically, he represents a sharp reaction from the dissipation and rhetoric of so much Victorian prose. For he wishes not to do much, but to do what he does perfectly; to determine on a clear, noble, not necessarily a large, design, and to pack it close with beauty and meaning, economically. The lesson was wanted; who shall say it has been learned? No one taught it better; yet we come back with some relief to the freer, more careless masters of prose, as they stride over the open down, whistling.

VIII

This Renaissance cult of beauty, as applied to art and letters and fortified by the historical spirit, is also conspicuous in John Addington Symonds (1840-93), whose passion for the Greeks was redoubled by his special conversance with the revival of learning. His writing has suffered from the fatal contrast of its looser texture with the closer thinking and surer handiwork of Pater, who follows the same cult, though not wholly in the same spirit, and many of whose interests are the same. Symonds is said to have disliked this comparison, and also the peculiar savour of Pater's style; and in spite of his dispersion of effort, he has advantages of his own. He was a genuine historian, and wrote a long connected history; he is a very good translator of poetry, and a poet in his own right; and he does not, like Pater, jealously keep his own secret, but confides it, in arresting fashion, to the world. In a volume, printed in the year 1893, on Walt Whitman, Symonds tells how he was brought up, at Harrow and Balliol, in the traditions of the great English caste, and how the reading of Whitman set him free from the incubus, in a way that his favourite Greeks and Italians had failed to do. Travel, made imperative by recurrent lung trouble, carried him to Italy, where he came to live more and more, and where he died. There, in the hills, too seldom able to descend to the city libraries, he worked with unfailing courage, living the open life of the country, mixing with *contadini*, sharing their talk in little taverns with some large old book open on his knees, and indomitably getting through his principal task, the *History of the Renaissance in Italy* (1875-86).

He had begun, however, in 1873 with *Studies of the Greek Poets*. The aim, which is successfully attained, of this series of reprinted articles was 'to bring Greek literature home to the general reader, and to apply to the Greek poets the same sort of criticism as that which modern classics receive.' The style is too prolix and too splendid; there is a sort of pseudo-Ruskinian, inflamed fine writing, which only a Greek of the decadence could have applauded. There is also the subtler fault of implicitly imputing to the Greeks the author's own code, at once formal and feverish, of beauty-worship. For all this, the substance of his praises is continually true, his delight in his subject is infectious, and his versions from the poets are admirably done.

The long work on the Renaissance, in many volumes, is flanked by separate studies of Michelangelo and Boccaccio; nor should Symonds's sketch of Italian history in the *Encyclopædia Britannica* be overlooked. Though he worked under such serious difficulties, he managed to amass or reach many of the necessary books and documents. The political history, though well sketched, does not interest him so much as the course of learning, art and letters. Italy, during the last thirty years, has poured forth an immense mass of writing on her Renaissance, and Symonds, in point of lore, is sometimes antiquated. He lacks, too, the grouping and condensing power of Burckhardt. But his first-hand appreciations are still fresh. His clear study of Bruno, the last notable mind of the Italian Renaissance, compares well with Pater's difficult pages on the same subject, and his study of Tasso is not inferior. As a full and rapid survey of its theme, the work has not yet been superseded in English.

Symonds also wrote much, sometimes laxly but never tamely, on the English poets. His short volumes on Sidney, Ben Jonson, and Shelley, and his longer one on *The Predecessors of Shakespeare* have much the same defects of facility and fluency, and the same quality of fervour and intrinsic soundness. Of more lasting value are his sonnets in the collection called *Animi Figura* (1882), which are subtle, analytic, and confidential, and complete the ample confessions of his prose. With all his pluck and surface cheerfulness, Symonds was often a sick man, in mind as well as in body, and that is why he is personally interesting. He has more than his share of the malady of his time ;—and whence comes that malady ? From the long stagnant peace, which furnished no rallying-point in action for the national soul ? or from the exhaustion following on a sanguine inventive epoch ? or from over-exoticism of sympathy ? or from the habit of introspection, which at such a period gains ground ; or from what ? Each of these elements seems to be in operation at one time or another. Rossetti's sonnets, Thomson's pessimism, Pater's 'Cyrenaicism,' Patmore's religious-erotic exaltations, Symonds's over-excitement,—all these precede and influence the tone of certain later poets, critics, novelists, and penitents, whose career lies beyond our chronological limits. But the phenomenon comes clear into view in the Seventies, and still more so in the Eighties ; nor can it be disguised by the survival into the Nineties of a band of veterans. Oxford men of that date well know, if they cannot put into words, the symptoms and the atmosphere ; for Oxford, certainly, was one home of that singular sleeping sickness, with its dreams, the worst of them now all blown away by the great war ; or so we hope.

IX

We can, at least, now turn to Cambridge for contrast—to a critic less troubled by dreams, a man of severer if less imaginative cast, whose philosophical books have been already named.

This is Sir Leslie Stephen[1] (1832-1904), whose essays, one may safely predict, are bound to wear well, and to outwear much fine writing, what with their acumen and sound judgement, and what with their excellent Queen Anne English, so finished and quietly ironical. Stephen's true line was not soon apparent. His *Sketches from Cambridge, by a Don* (1865), reprinted from the *Pall Mall Gazette*, and his mountaineering book, *The Playground of Europe* (1871), show his quality, and are most agreeable reading. The easy, trained stride of the pedestrian, covering the miles imperceptibly, may serve as an image of his general style. He was also a born editor and literary pilot. In 1871 he began to conduct the *Cornhill*, writing some of the best articles himself. Mr. Thomas Hardy and Henry James, soon to be eminent, were among the contributors. The flower of Stephen's critical studies is contained in the three series of his *Hours in a Library* (1874, 1876, 1879). In 1875 he was able to discard the clerical orders which he had assumed in youth; but in spirit he had broken loose before. His riper mind in speculative matters is seen in his *Essays on Freethinking and Plain Speaking* (1873), in his most massive work, the *History of English Thought in the Eighteenth Century* (1876, see *ante*, Ch. IV.). The final fruit, on the philosophical side, was *The Science of Ethics* (1882), while Stephen put much of his mind and heart into the briefer *Agnostic's Apology* (1893).

For many years Stephen conducted that great and triumphant venture, the *Dictionary of National Biography*, which was projected in 1881 and began to appear in 1886, and which ate up much of his time and energy. We are told that he contributed no less than '378 articles,' covering over 'a thousand pages.' He excelled in the craft of biography, especially on a miniature scale. In the *Dictionary* he delivers endless judgements in a brief Tacitean manner without a touch of arrogance. He found more room in his little books, in the *English Men of Letters* series, on Hobbes, Pope, Swift, Johnson, and George Eliot, all justly prized; and more room yet in his full biographies of Fawcett, and of his brother, Sir James Fitzjames Stephen, which is conceived in a candid spirit, and which sketches the history of the gifted family. Later, when released from dictionary work, Stephen came back to philosophy, and continued his earlier studies in *The English Utilitarians* (1900), which is the best existing presentation of Bentham, the two Mills, and other economists. The *Studies of a Biographer* belong to his latter years, and show an even greater economy of stroke and a yet more gently searching humour.

Stephen was intellectually a child of the 'age of prose and reason.' His natural taste is for tough arguers like Bishop Butler; he also relishes paradox-mongers like Mandeville; and he can digest the obscurest forgotten deist without any visible trouble. His dictionary notices of Bolingbroke, Hume, and Gibbon reflect this aspect of Stephen's mind. In a subdued way, he inherits their spirit of mischief and their objection to insipidity. He well understands Pope and Johnson, the apostles of wit and sense. His sharp sense of their limitations comes as part of his birthright as a man of the nineteenth century.

He has to make his account with ideas to which those who enjoyed the 'peace of the Augustans' were strangers:—with the enthusiasm for science, with the religion of humanity and its secular idealism. The difference between the old scepticism and the new may be seen by comparing Hume's *Essays* with *An Agnostic's Apology*. Many of the negative conclusions are similar; but the old complacency is gone. There is no peace now, but the stress of battle instead. The need has arisen of constructing some positive faith that shall consist with those negations. Stephen and Huxley are the strongest among the writers who strove not only to clear the mind of dogma, but to build upon the ground which is thus left empty. 'Bear,' such writers seem to say, 'the chill of life as the climber bears the risk of frostbite, and always keep your head. If you lose your companion in the avalanche, mourn him with the courage, though not with the apathy, of the Stoic, and then go on. Get up another hill, and get down again, and at evening you can sup, perhaps cheerfully, or at least humorously, in the wayside inn. Afterwards there is always sleep, which is always good. You have got through your day; and perhaps you have added a new peak, or valley, to the map; and anyhow you were up in time to see the sun rise. And you have not got through upon drugs.' All this is Meredithian too, and Stephen was Meredith's intimate friend.

As a critic, Stephen is rather of the judicial than of the imaginative order. His papers on Shelley and Balzac show too jealous a sense of their deficiencies in the eye of reason. He does not much like an artist to be extravagant: he is shy of being dragged after the chariot of a romantic rebel; and, even with the greatest poets, he does not overmuch let himself go. He is a Wordsworthian; he makes the obvious reserves, but his praise of the poet has an unusual note of intensity. He is deeply, though not pedantically, ethical: he has the 'nobleness' that distinguishes the best minds of the time, though he is wholly unaware of the fact and would have mocked at the description. His particular combination of critical balance, humanity, and philosophic grasp is best seen in his judgement of George Eliot. He had lived through her fame and its decline, and, as we shall see, he came forward as a guarded but sincere champion of her slighted merits. His sympathy with his subject is guaranteed, for he had passed through somewhat the same course of spiritual history. The problem was simpler in the case of Crabbe or of Miss Austen; with such writers he is perfectly at home, taking them frankly as they are and untroubled by the sense of what they do not understand, though he well knows what that is.

X

Some critics of more professorial stamp claim final attention. The abundant production of Edward Dowden[1] (1843-1913) belongs mainly to the following period; but his wide sound scholarship and many-sided sensibility are already to be seen in *Shakespeare, His Mind and Art* (1875), and in *A Shakespeare Primer*. Dowden mastered the Shakespearian lore of the Germans, but used it without pedantry and with an Irish sense of humour; he was long professor at Trinity College, Dublin. He was the first of our critics to expound in a clear attractive way the general phases of Shakespeare's 'mind and art,' working on the scientific basis for the canon and order of the plays which had been established by the spadework of a generation. Widely and deeply read, a skilled editor of Shakespeare's texts, and an eminent professor, Dowden also had a keen sense of all intellectual and artistic currents, and traces them with much insight. He suffers from some want of salience; he writes with a soft, not with a sharp pen; he is capable of sentimentality, and sometimes rather diffuse. But his taste and skill are remarkable; and he has left a little intimate poetry, delicate in execution. His monographs on Shelley, Wordsworth, Southey, and Browning appeared mostly in the Eighties and Nineties; his *French Revolution and English Literature* (1897) is a good example of his method. A paper on *The Interpretation of Literature*, in *Transcripts and Studies*, gives Dowden's conception of criticism, and links it, as will be seen, with the more strictly æsthetic canon, which had already been stated by others:

In the first stage of approach, however, the critic, while all the time full of athletic force, must cunningly assume a passive aspect, and to do so he must put restraint upon his own vivacity and play of mind. His aim is now to obtain a faithful impression of the object. His second movement of mind will be one of recoil and resilience, whereby having received a pure impression of the object, he tries to surprise and lay hold of the power which produced that impression. And these are the two chief processes of the critical spirit in literature.

Dowden, though keenly alive to form, applied these principles more readily to the appraisement of an author's thought and feeling, often with high success. Not a commanding writer, he was endowed with an unusually gentle, catholic, and harmonious spirit.

Some of these remarks apply to another Irish scholar and critic, Stopford Augustus Brooke (1832-1916). He was not a professor, but a divine; originally an Anglican, he joined the Unitarian community. He is, therefore, more of a preacher than Dowden. He is also less of a scholar, though in his ample discourses on Shakespeare, Tennyson, and Browning, he covers much of the same ground. His interest in the ideas of the poets and in their 'messages,' however, tends to disguise his critical faculty, which is, or might have been, no less distinct than Dowden's. In fact his definitions and descriptions are often clearer cut. Much as Brooke wrote, his quality is still most apparent in his little *Primer of English Literature* (1876), which was honourably reviewed by Matthew Arnold, and is hardly to be bettered as a piece of miniature-work. Brooke's *History of Early English Literature* (1892) is also still fresh and inspiring in spite of imperfect formal scholarship and much propensity to guesswork.

A word of honour is also due to two Scottish professors of literature, who balance the Irishmen. These are David Masson of Edinburgh (1822-1907) and William Minto of Aberdeen (1846-93). Masson, a picturesque figure, was much more of a *savant*, biographer, and historian than a critic, as can be seen from his monographs on Chatterton and Drummond of Hawthornden, both issued in 1873, and above all from his labours in honour of Milton, with whose name his own must ever be associated. His *Life of Milton in Connexion with the History of his Own Time* (1858-80), in six great volumes, is a vast and unshapely book; Masson wrote eagerly and awkwardly, and James Russell Lowell, a critic much overrated in his day, twanged off sundry cheap jokes at its expense. But the *Life of Milton* remains and the jokes are forgotten. Its title expresses its aim, and the aim is achieved. It is a masterly work of reference, in which all possible information can be easily found and safely trusted. The same is true of Masson's various editions of the poet, and of his editorial work on De Quincey. His little book on Carlyle should be remembered too. The other professor, Minto, left no such monument. A journalist in earlier life, and latterly also a novelist, he was a teacher of philosophy as well as of letters. But despite these diversions he left some sound, unambitious, and hard-headed criticism in his *Manual of English Prose Literature* (1872); and still more, in his *Characteristics of English Poets from Chaucer to Shirley* (1874), where he follows, in a more collegiate and orderly way, the free method of Hazlitt. Minto's plain efficient style is not a dull one, and in his short book on Defoe (1879) he drives a clear track through a thorny and almost impassable jungle.

This is not a history of scholarship; yet one representative name may be selected from the army of skilled masons who laid a surer foundation for the study of English literature. Indeed, the incessant labours of the long-lived, the immeasurably lively and dauntless Frederick James Furnivall [1] (1825-1910) were not merely those of the mason. As a founder and ruling spirit of the Early English Text Society, and of societies for the study of Chaucer, Shakespeare, Browning and Shelley, Furnivall gave an impulse which is hard to calculate. He made the interpretation of many poets possible. Often he interpreted them himself, eagerly, pugnaciously, rashly, teasingly, but never idly or tamely. His best single composition is perhaps the introduction to the so-called 'Leopold Shakespeare,' published in 1877, in which he gives a most humane reading of the poet. Furnivall is not clogged by the mass of accessory learning which he cites; his whimsical taste for archaic diction and spelling does no harm, for it finds no followers.

To this chapter may be added the name of Richard Holt Hutton [2] (1826-97), best known as the co-editor and arch-critic of the *Spectator* from 1861 onwards, and as the opponent, from a very broad theological standpoint, of the scientific and agnostic creeds, which he strove judicially to understand. Hutton's natural turn was for philosophy; in literature, he cared first of all for the ideas, and for the 'application of the ideas to life,' and this bent is seen in his patient and serious, though not very exhilarating, judgements on the poets. His pages on Shelley, Tennyson, and Browning have the tone of the courteous Mentor-journalist, instructing the public in undiscovered beauties. One of his more elaborate papers, a review of Lewes's *Life of Goethe*, makes the utmost of the familiar case against the great poet's egoism, self-absorption, and so forth, and shows no little subtlety of attack; it is a most characteristic sample of the moral gravity and idealistic temper which people now call 'Victorian.' But Hutton was very far from being a mere preacher, though he was sometimes, as his verdict on George Eliot (see Ch. XXIII.) shows, disproportionate in praise. He was catholic in his likings, and also in his dealings as editor. No narrow puritan would have printed, in a weekly addressed to the stable and 'thoughtful' classes, Swinburne's *Faustine* or his review of *Les Fleurs du Mal.*

CHAPTER XII

MISCELLANEOUS PROSE

I

There remain for notice some of the essayists, makers of memoirs, and travellers, as well as certain writers like George Borrow and Samuel Butler who would have scorned to be classified. Selection here becomes the harder for the increasing mass of printed matter which is heaped on the debateable ground lying between literature and mere books. The periodical press grew enormously; the appetite of the public for any record of a 'life' or a 'journey,' or for a lay sermon, became insatiable; circulating libraries multiplied, and books were cheapened. The demand for commodities that fed this desire and were forgotten enhanced the supply. The heap still grows, and it is a curious question whether within fifty years any man will dare to sift and describe the literature of our own day. In the present case the attempt, though not made at random, can only be provisional; and I would wish, whatever may be left out, only to include what can still produce some interest or pleasure.

Among the essayists, it may be proper to mention first the authors of that once esteemed but disappointing work, *Guesses at Truth*, of which the first instalment appeared in 1827: a string of maxims, often swelling out into essays, on matters literary, philosophical, or theological. Descriptive poetry, Wordsworth's *Laodamia*, the minutiæ of prose style, Hegel's idea of history, the 'French paste' of Voltaire's epigrams, are typical subjects of discourse; and the inspiration, for good and otherwise, of Coleridge, can often be traced. But the *pensée*, or single aphorism, has not flourished well in English, in spite of Halifax, and Swift, and the author of *Hudibras*, and Hazlitt. The book was at first anonymous, 'by two brothers'; and these were Augustus William Hare and Julius Charles Hare [1] (1795-1855); and they have a way of starting, ingeniously or solemnly, in a promising manner, and raising hopes—*et puis rien!* Yet there are gleams of delicate observation; and Julius Hare was a man of some mark, who did much to introduce German thought and letters to the English public; translating parts of Fouqué, and also, in partnership with Thirlwall, of Niebuhr's *History of Rome*. Hare collected at his Hurstmonceaux rectory one of the best German libraries in England. He became Archdeacon of Lewes, wrote much controversially, and was recognised as a veteran founder of the liberal movement in English theology. He is a somewhat heavy and eccentric writer, having views of his own, afterwards adopted by Furnivall and others, about the reformation of spelling; *forein*, *firy*, *soverin*, *pluckt*, are examples of his practice. His memoir of his friend John Sterling was a provocation to Carlyle to write a masterpiece of biography.

The movement of English thought in this period, said Matthew Arnold truly, 'is *lay*'; and while this great, lay, central movement of thought pressed on to its extremes, in Spencer, Huxley, or Clifford (extremes often lying far asunder), it could not but also touch many sincere and admirable spirits, reared in this fold or that; who are seen pressing on beyond the bounds and fences of any 'free church,' yet still holding hard to one or two primary tenets, and trying to reconcile the blessings of faith with those of emancipation. Clough is such a figure, in poetry: in prose there is no one so gifted as Clough; but there are some essayists, middlemen and transmitters of thought, who, though not strictly initiative minds, are of more than historic interest, and who can still be read. One of these, James Hinton (1822-75), a surgeon and aurist of note in his time, and born in the Baptist community, is best known for the work, published anonymously in 1866 and called *The Mystery of Pain*: a singular corrective in advance to the sheer happiness-worship which Spencer, thirteen years later, was to proclaim in *The Data of Ethics*. The painful doubts and moral searchings of the hour are reflected in Hinton's argument, no less than in *Middlemarch* or *Dipsychus*; and his style, if not that of a rigid reasoner, is both plain and fine; it suggests the hand of the surgeon touching an open nerve. Pain, always an evil in itself, and often an evil undeserved and unredeemed, becomes, he says, less mysterious when viewed as an element of self-sacrifice; which itself, though sometimes useless, is the true path to the higher satisfaction. Hinton works out this familiar idea on its own merits and with little reliance on any doctrinal stay: and it is here that he is, or was, original.

William Rathbone Greg (1809-81), millowner, philanthropist, essayist, and reviewer, is a writer of less delicacy than the retiring Hinton, and is easier to discover ; but he has a wider range and sharper edge. Greg was a liberal, who took alarm early in the day at the onset of democracy and fulminated accordingly, in a Whig-Conservative tone, in defence of property and the rule of the wise. His fair-minded and balanced eulogy of Peel is a good specimen of his political writing, and contains shrewd touches worthy of Bagehot. He is better known for his speculative works such as *The Creed of Christendom* (1851) and *Enigmas of Life* (1872).[1] He was an 'advanced' thinker, who still held fast to theism and a faith in survival, but in an odd provisional fashion. He preferred to keep them ; but he thought they could neither be proved nor disproved ; and he did not ask anyone else to keep them. On such a base he builds his uncertain faith in the future of mankind He is full of the scientific optimism of the period, and of the improvements wrought, or to be wrought, in 'lighting, locomotion, and communication,' and in housing and hygiene. But he is also a pessimist, who finds that life is a tragedy in its essence, and one by no means lightened by the prospect of mob-rule. Sanguine hours alternate with jeremiads, and the result does not always illuminate. Still Greg can both write and think. His pages on the 'value of false religions' (which are vitiated, yet also inspired, by the claim laid by each of them to absolute truth), and his picture of a heaven which does not efface the earthborn personality, have an independent stamp. His want of coherence is partly retrieved by a catholic and lofty temper, and he is one of the more interesting halfway minds of his time. His form is often good, his English, though not improved by a strain of pulpit rhetoric, is better than easy, being efficient and well-trained.

II

Ruskin, in one of his whimsical and surprising passages, couples Sir Arthur Helps (1813-75) with Plato and Carlyle as a writer who has done him much good ; and speaks, less immoderately, of his 'quiet and beautiful English.' Helps could in fact write in a rather too quiet, but still in a polished and very graceful fashion, and is an attractive essayist. Old Victorian private libraries, kept together in public institutions, can almost be dated by the prominence of such writers on their shelves ; and Helps is a minor landmark of this kind. He wrote a great deal, including a history of *The Spanish Conquest of America* (1855-61), and also dramas, biographies, and books of aphorism. But he is at his best in his imaginary dialogues, called *Friends in Council* (1847-59), wherein the grave Milverton and the lively Ellesmere, with their lady friends mostly silent around them, exchange thoughtful remarks on war, government, slavery, style, and human nature. Helps was an eminent civil servant, and there is some official flatness and propriety about his thinking, but he appealed to his cultivated, sedate, reflective public. His *Companions of my Solitude* (1851) contains a discussion, frank and open for its time, on the problem raised by 'the great sin of great cities.'

Much of this mid-Victorian discoursing wears but a cold greyish hue to-day; estimable and well-balanced, it shows little free play of mind, and its moderate, edifying tone still provokes some protest from the old Adam within us. One of its best practitioners, who says what he has to say with pointed neatness and no pretence, is Philip Gilbert Hamerton (1834-94), a person of repute and expert judgement as a critic of painting and etching, and the conductor of sundry art journals. Of his general essays, the best-known bundles are *The Intellectual Life* (1873), and *Human Intercourse* (1884), the latter being dedicated to Emerson. Both works are well informed, well worded, neither commonplace nor yet distinguished; *Human Intercourse* is the fresher of the two. The headings of the chapters tell us a good deal: 'of passionate love,' which is discussed dispassionately and earnestly; on 'companionship in marriage,' illustrated by the leading cases of Goethe, Shelley, Byron, John Stuart Mill, and George Eliot; and on 'a remarkable English peculiarity,' namely that of observing a 'freezing silence' during foreign travel. On such ground Hamerton is at his best; he lived much abroad, and his *French and English, a Comparison* (1889) is not only an alert observant record of manners, but a real and penetrating study of national differences. Some of the chapters, like those on 'thrift,' 'patriotism,' or 'purity,' have an almost Baconian conciseness and impartiality, if they also show the Baconian habit of using a note-book, packed with 'antitheta,' or the pros and cons of the topic in hand. Hamerton's criticism is often excellent. Matthew Arnold, who must have known French novels better than he knew French life, and who sometimes talked like any ignorant British gentleman, charged the French nation with the worship of 'the great goddess Lubricity,' a myth disposed of by Hamerton's quiet recital of the social facts. Yet such is the unfairness of literature, that the phrase has stuck and the correction is forgotten. Hamerton writes for truth, not for effect, with a mild Gallic elegance, and manages to be entertaining. But now for a writer with more blood in him than all of these.

Brevity is the soul of pathos, as well as of wit; that is one reason why real pathos, which keeps its power through all changes of taste and time, is rare. Dickens commands it, but it has to be painfully sifted out from his mass of false pathos. Thackeray commands it, though he deadens the effect by bearing too hard and going on too long; he sometimes leaves us dead sick of pathos. The great poets concentrate their expression of it into some phrase that has all the force and weight of the drama behind it; as in the epitaphs on Cordelia and Desdemona ('What wife? I have no wife'). In a lyric or short tale there is no such weight behind; but there should also be no time for any risk of overstrain and self-defeat. These remarks will not, I hope, be thought beyond the occasion; for Dr. John Brown's *Rab and his Friends* is a flawless example of pathos in a brief compass. The hospital scene has no equal in its kind; the strength of the subject forbids any sentimentalism; the warmth and depth of the Scottish heart, here uttered without reserve, could not find surer words; while the overture of the dog-fight, and the constant feeling for the dog's point of view, 'balance,' as painters used to say, 'the composition.' *Our Dogs*, though not tragic, is again excellent portraiture. *Marjorie Fleming* equally full of humorous and tender good sense, consists chiefly of the letters of the wonderful child; and it has also inspired the poet's vision of

> Some happier island in the Elysian sea
> Where Rab may lick the hand of Marjorie.

The writings of Dr. John Brown [1] of Edinburgh (1810-82) are nearly all covered in the three volumes or series of *Horæ Subsecivæ* ('odd hours,' 1858-61). One group, nominally given up to professional subjects, is headed, from its opening article, *Locke and Sydenham*; but Brown manages to introduce a eulogy of Henry Vaughan, who was a medical man as well as a poet; and, further, a wonderful Elia-like page descriptive of the Irish *pwcca*-goblin, whom Crofton Croker, in his *Fairy Legends*, had delineated. The memorial notice of Brown's father (*Letter to John Cairns, D.D.*), and the paper upon Thomas Chalmers, take us again deep into Scottish life. Who can forget the picture of the brutal drover weeping, and the flock drawn from their seats and 'converging' on the great preacher? Brown's *perfervidum ingenium* does not mar his grace and economy in the use of language. There are also his elegiac pages on Arthur Hallam and Thackeray. The most cheerful of the *Horæ*, entitled *Mystifications*, relates the performance of Miss Graham Stirling, a born impersonator, who dressed herself out as a witty eccentric lady of the old school, and deceived, after fair warning given, the Lord Advocate, Francis Jeffrey. John Brown also wrote with taste and relish on Leech, Raeburn, and other artists. In his letters there are many flashes of his peculiar felicity; he speaks of a 'brilliant and *procacious* lecture' of Matthew Arnold's; remarks that George Eliot has 'fully as much talent as genius'—a left-handed stroke; and says of his friend Ruskin,

> I am sure he has wings under his flannel jacket; he is not a man, but a stray angel, who had singed his wings a little and tumbled into our sphere. He has all the arrogance, insight, unreasonableness, and spiritual 'sheen' of a celestial.

A note may here be made on Richard Jefferies (1848-87), though the greater part of his work was not published till after 1880. He had already shown his quality in stray articles; but the first book in which it is fairly discovered is *The Gamekeeper at Home* (1878). The son of a farmer, Jefferies was born on the Wiltshire side of Swindon, and grew up among the copsed downs, the fat valleys, and the rolling woodland of that noble countryside. He was a born watcher, a man of trained and intensified senses and of patiently accurate habit; he had besides a strong poetic sense, and a vein of mystical rumination which is never suffered to falsify his report. His faculty of minute description is seen in such works as *Wild Life in a Southern County* (1879) and *The Life of the Fields* (1884). His more usual style is plodding and slightly literal, at any rate circumstantial; but such a manner has its own charm. Not only beasts and birds, fish and insects and spiders, but rustic mankind as well, are part of his scene. In *Hodge and his Master* (1880) and elsewhere he describes the country labourer, and the men of his own class, perhaps more truly, because more from within, than any novelist. In other papers the treatment is freer; Jefferies has an eye for the human comedy, and especially for the beauties and graces of the human body; this is seen in contributions like *The Bathing Season*, or *Sunny Brighton*, or *Beauty in the Country*; all of which are collected in the volume entitled *The Open Air*. His most remarkable book is his autobiography, *The Story of My Heart* (1883), which is a record, touched with a real but not miserable melancholy, of dream and aspiration rather than of external fact.

III

Samuel Butler,[1] born in 1835, died in 1902; but one of his fancies was not to believe in death, or in survival either, in their ordinary senses. A man's identity and personality go on, or go out, according as he is remembered or forgotten, or rather according as his mental impulses continue in others or fade away. This sort of continuance, however, Butler does not phrase in moral terms, like the authoress of the lines about the 'choir invisible,' but in intellectual terms; and he mused a good deal about his posthumous reputation, wishing however that it might be in the hands not of the 'cultured critics,' whom he would have hated, but of 'nice people.' From his own point of view, he was not much alive in his lifetime, save in a dubious fashion; but certainly, after his disappearance, he is having his share of life. In the same strain he remarks of Shakespeare:

> Whilst he was alive, very few people understood his greatness; whereas now after some 300 years he is deemed the greatest poet that the world has ever seen.—Can he be said to have been truly born till many a long year after he had been reputed to be truly dead? Whilst he was in the flesh, was he more than a mere embryo, growing towards birth in that life of the world to come in which he now shines so gloriously?

Butler, born in a parsonage, went to Shrewsbury and Cambridge; was meant for the Church, but conceived doubts and escaped that calling; kept sheep with success in New Zealand, and there began to write; came to London, commenced painter, made some way in the art, and resumed writing, producing in 1872 *Erewhon, or Over the Range*; and also, about the same time, two works, ironically couched, in disproof of the Resurrection. The puzzling *Erewhon* was read rather than comprehended. Indeed Butler seems hardly to know himself whether his Utopian society is a satiric parody, like Brobdingnag, of our own, or an ideal polity, like that of the Houyhnhnms, held up for our shame and instruction. The book was the piecework of many years, and he revised it more than once; each of its main ideas is fairly distinct, but they do not dovetail well together. His most striking point, reflecting the new speculations as to the influence of environment, is well known. The reception given by society to vice or crime, and that given to illness or misfortune, are interchanged. A youth is accused and found guilty of pulmonary consumption, and severely sentenced. But the murderer, embezzler, or bad-tempered person, is openly pitied, but not shamed; he is painfully set right by a mind-doctor, or 'straightener.' The real virtues are health, beauty, and efficiency; the Erewhonians are something like what we dream the best Greeks to have been or wished to be. But they are not perfect. They still pay homage to an effete, inoperative religion. And they pay yet more homage to the goddess Ydgrun, Grundy, or convention; who, none the less, has a good deal to say for herself. There are many other things in *Erewhon* (Nowhere); but the excellence of its descriptions of scenery and mountaineering is not so often noticed. The supposed explorer is one of Defoe's or Swift's plain men, who takes no thought of style, and whose own mind is furnished barely and inexpensively.

From 1877 onwards Butler struck into scientific controversy, and, as an amateur of genius, challenged some of the ruling ideas of Darwin and Wallace. He produced *Life and Habit* (1877), *Unconscious Memory* (1880), *Luck? or Cunning?* (1886), and other works. 'Cunning,' he says, is the element of purposive effort, which must needs reside in the plants and animals that survive in the struggle for existence. The doctrine of merely accidental happy variations cannot account for the facts. The modern biologist [1] acknowledges that Butler's reasonings and intuitions were really to the purpose during a stage, now past and gone, of the great controversy. They are also bound up with other ideas which affected his whole view of life. Sometimes he was tempted to see purpose, or the rudiment of mind, even in the inorganic world, and to merge mind and matter in one. He always asserted a true continuance of personal identity as between the successive generations of living things. Thus bodily death becomes insignificant, and all the 'values' of life itself are changed. Such thoughts are to be found, presented in facet after facet, in Butler's essays, notes, and journals of travel.

In 1881 he published the most agreeable of his books and the freest in treatment, *Alps and Sanctuaries of Piedmont and the Canton Ticino*. It is charged with Butler's intense feeling for art and for natural beauty, and is adorned by his own sketches. It also contains the text of the ballad of *Wednesbury Cocking*, which he recited with much success, in order to console the youth whom he found 'in a flood of tears over the death of his grandmother,' aged ninety-three: an incident that we may imagine happening to Borrow. A sequel was *Ex Voto*, an account of the artistic remains at Varallo, in the same district. In London Butler settled down to literature and music. He adored Handel and thought of him every day of his life; and composed music of his own. He wrote ingenious cranky works, one to prove that a woman wrote the *Odyssey*, another to prove that Shakespeare addressed his *Sonnets* to a plebeian. In 1901 came *Erewhon Revisited*, a well-arranged and brilliant satire, describing the birth of an official religion out of a purely imaginary Resurrection. But the book has not the fresh spontaneity of *Erewhon*; and there is nothing in it like the chapter, which reminds us more of Plato than of Swift, on 'the world of the unborn.' Here there are foolish and restless souls who forgo their birthright immortality and pine for our world of life and death. Despite all warning, they drink a Lethe potion, and they are then 'allotted by chance, and without appeal, to two people whom it is their business to find and pester until they adopt them.' The idea accords with that merciless presentment of the parental relation which rules in Butler's posthumously published novel, *The Way of All Flesh*, which was begun about the same date as the appearance of *Erewhon*.

Butler starts from a revolt against every sort of stuffy convention (as he judges it to be) in science, religion, and conduct. His method is paradox; but he ends, after all, in a creed of hard common sense, illumined by a few scientific ideas. He does not end in romantic rebellion, or in the anarchical temper. He believes in health of mind and body, in honest money and in the satisfaction it brings, and in an unexacting standard of virtue; he will tolerate many faults in the flesh and temper, so the mind remain uncorrupted. He keeps a kind of respect for institutions. Ernest Pontifex, in his novel, breaks away from his dreadful parent, Theobald, the embodiment of complacent and cruel convention; breaks with the Church, and with the social caste and code; does time for an assault; marries a drunken maidservant, who luckily proves to have a husband already; turns tailor and earns his bread; and comes into a fortune by a windfall. The book has been described as 'imperishably graven out of the flint of life,' and certainly every line has the print of experience. Still, it is a pamphlet in novel shape, *ex parte*; it gives Butler's own case against his early environment with absolute sincerity and expressiveness.

Butler, in fact, from the first writes with a chisel. His unit, or ideal of style, is the maxim, or *pensée*, consisting of a few syllables. He is sometimes roguish, sometimes just whimsical, sometimes defiant, always mordant, always short:

'To live is like to love—all reason is against it, and all healthy instinct for it.'—'Behold and see if there be any happiness like unto the happiness of the devils when they found themselves cast out of Mary Magdalene.'—'The fight between them [theist and atheist] is whether God shall be called God or shall have some other name.'—'What a pity it is that Christian never met Mr. Common-Sense with his daughter, Good-Humour, and her affianced husband, Mr. Hate-Cant.'

Butler joins his *mots* together carefully, and his style is continuous and good; but it is bare and blunt, and its atomic origin remains visible. He is, and tries to be, at the opposite pole to the flowing and decorative writers. Some one, before now, must have inquired into his likenesses to his namesake of *Hudibras* fame, another aphorist, another critic of things accepted, and another strange honest man, another *philosophe* judging philosophers, another evangelist of common sense.

IV

Some more formal 'Lives' may now be named, exhibiting very different types of humanity. The remarkable memoirs of the painter, Benjamin Robert Haydon (1786-1846), were published in 1853 by Tom Taylor, and consist of an autobiography, which goes down to the year 1820, and of diaries and correspondence which Taylor arranged and condensed. The earlier part of the story belongs to the age of romance. Haydon was the friend of Wordsworth, Keats, Lamb, and Hazlitt; and in aspiration, if not in accomplishment, he was one of them; he has a breath of their spirit, and his admiration for them is clear-sighted. His very failings remind us of Hazlitt's: though his headlong antipathies and suspicions, his quarrel with the world at large and the Royal Academy in especial, his streak of *paranoia*, or belief in a general conspiracy against him, are unhappily not balanced by the masculine hardness of head which carried Hazlitt through so many vagaries. Haydon has also something in him of Keats; he has the same fundamental ardour for truth and beauty, though not the same power of expression. His long, tragical-grotesque struggle with the public, with debt, and with himself ended in suicide. He seems to have known that he was not quite sane, and his egoism deprived him of a clear view of himself. But Haydon's passion for his art was fierce, his labour and self-criticism were unremitting. His many observations on men and manners show his keen eye for comedy :

In our meetings Hazlitt's croakings, Leigh Hunt's wit, and Lamb's quaint incomprehensibilities made up rare scenes. Lamb stuttered his quaintness in snatches, like the Fool in *Lear*, and with equal beauty; and Wilkie would chime in with his 'Dear, dear' [1813].

Haydon, unlike most painters, often finds the only right words for his visual impressions :

The Chancellor [Brougham] sat to-day. His eye is as fine as any eye I ever saw. It is like a lion's watching for prey. It is a clear grey, the light vibrating at the bottom of the iris, and the cornea shining, silvery, and tense [1833]. . . . [O'Connell] has an eye like a weasel. Light seemed hanging at the bottom, and he looked out with a searching ken, like Brougham, something, but not with his depth of insight [1834].

The latter years of the memoir, though full of painful sallies of disappointment, self-reproach and invective, are not less interesting. The Duke of Wellington is much in evidence ; his sittings to Haydon, his stories, and his replies to the painter's importunate letters, are all memorable. The wizened figure of Wilkie also flits in and out. Haydon, in 1845, met the old Mrs. Gwatkin, with 'great remains of regular beauty,' who had known Reynolds, Johnson, and Burke : she told how

Garrick sat on Goldsmith's knee ; a table-cloth was pinned under Garrick's chin, and brought behind Goldsmith, hiding both their figures. Garrick then spoke, in his finest style, Hamlet's speech to his father's ghost. Goldsmith put out his hands on each side of the cloth, and made burlesque action, tapping his heart, and putting his hand to Garrick's head and nose, all at the wrong time.

Haydon's notes are a storehouse of such things, an unsortable medley of anecdote, art, technicality, devotion, despair, vanity, and shrewdness.

The best prose writer of Young Ireland, John Mitchel (1815-75), has left one of the most vivid of diaries in his *Jail Journal, or Five Years in British Prisons.* A solicitor with a scholarly training, Mitchel was drawn into the cause by Thomas Davis, wrote for the *Nation*, and in 1848 began to serve his sentence of fourteen years' transportation for treason-felony. He was taken to the Bermudas, and thence to Van Diemen's Land, whence he got off to America. Much of the *Journal* is a pungent tirade, burning with hatred of England ('the Carthaginians ') and above all of Whiggery ; but Mitchel has not the political sense and thinking of writers like Gavan Duffy. Very different are his descriptions and conversations, and the story of his sufferings and escape. They have something of the precision and colour of Carlyle, as well as of his actual manner ; we are always coming, in our survey, upon Carlyle ! and the discipleship is all the stranger in this passionate and extreme man of genius, who said, truly enough, that 'Carlyle cannot write rationally about Ireland.' The waterless Bermuda brings to Mitchel's lips a piece of Milton, and also the ditty, with its burden of *Ullagone dhu, oh !* on the 'misty vales' and the 'fair hills of holy Ireland.' He *listens* to the floggings of the drunken obscene convicts who looked black on him for receiving treatment superior to theirs. He talks with the railway swindler who had looted a fortune to spend at Pernambuco ; he paints the Tasmanian scenery, and tells of the breathless and almost baffled plot for his release. Proudly playing the game, Mitchel informs the dull magistrate that he resigns his parole ; then challenges arrest, and rides off openly amid official stupefaction and the hue and cry. Mitchel also wrote *The Last Conquest of Ireland* (*Perhaps*) (1860), which relates, with equal wrath but fewer flourishes, the events of 1848-9. The eulogy of Davis, and the denunciation of O'Connell in his later phase, the account of the *Nation* and of *United Ireland*, bring the story up to and beyond the beginning of the *Jail Journal.* The pamphlet called *The Crusade of the Period* is Mitchel's well founded, though not well managed, attack on Froude for his *English in Ireland*, the libel on which Lecky was to deliver the verdict.

The multifarious Harriet Martineau (1802-76), sister of James Martineau, wrote for the most part ephemerally ; her histories, novels, books of travel, and speculative writings are no more, despite their facility, lucidity, and energy ; and Miss Martineau, to save the critics trouble, made her own epitaph as a woman of letters, in words that are duly brought up against her :

> With small imaginative and suggestive powers, and therefore nothing approaching to genius, she could see clearly what she did see, and give a clear expression to what she had to say. In short, she could popularise while she could neither discover nor invent.

This self-judgement is in one respect too modest. Miss Martineau did popularise, but in a very skilful and pleasing way. Her *Illustrations of Political Economy* (1832), of *Taxation* (1834), and of the *Poor Laws* are designed either to expound the Ricardian views,[1] then in the height of their vogue, concerning capital, wealth, and distribution, or to attack slavery and other abuses; all by means of little tales, which are elementary and even infantine in cast but neatly told. Miss Martineau lived to abandon the orthodox economic faith in favour of a more generous one. Her *Feats on the Fiord* and similar books have the deftness, without the dose of argument, and are well designed for her audience of children. Her *History of the Thirty Years' Peace, 1816-1846*, is journalism, but it is very lively journalism, and introduces allusions to minor events and persons (including criminals), which would be welcome in many a more learned and ponderous chronicle. Her philosophical works, which show her passage from the Unitarian fold to a purely agnostic or atheistic position (announced most intrepidly and firmly held) are not original, though they throw light on her character; but her digest (1853) of the *Philosophie Positive* left its mark on English opinion, and held its ground awhile as an exposition of Comte. Her novel, *Deerbrook* (1839), once popular, but now not very digestible, is an early attempt to describe bourgeois life with unromantic fidelity. But Miss Martineau left at least one work, her *Autobiography* (1877), which is still full of interest, instruction, and oddity. It relates her precise and vivid memories of a repressed childhood; her launch, about 1830, on literature for a livelihood, and the history of her writings; her illnesses and retirements from society, during which her religious views matured; the final hardening of these opinions, and her stoical acceptance of death as the end of all; and, in particular, her acquaintance with, and her judgements concerning, an immense number of contemporary persons. She knew her London well in the Thirties, and has left her comments on Carlyle and Coleridge, on Jeffrey and Sydney Smith, and Bulwer and Monckton Milnes, and on scores of others. She always read widely, and has her views of Margaret Fuller, of Charlotte Brontë, and of Macaulay. Literal, rigorous, and honest, she often has a keen eye for character; and though little given to mere admiration, she is not small or ungenerous. Room may well be found for her observations on Carlyle:

> His excess of sympathy has been, I believe, the master-pain of his life. He does not know what to do with it and with its bitterness, seeing that human life is full of pain to those that look out for it; and the savageness which has come to be the main characteristic of this singular man is, in my opinion, a mere expression of his intolerable sympathy with the suffering.

Miss Martineau herself, being much more of a woman than she would have us believe, has abundant 'sympathy with the suffering'; but her special mark, no doubt, is a high hard intellectual courage which in her day was rarely possible to women. 'My business in life,' she says, 'has been to think and learn, and to speak out with absolute freedom what I have thought and learned.'

Many of the biographers of this period have been touched upon already: Carlyle and Froude, Sir Leslie Stephen, and Lewes, and Bain and Masson; and out of the rest one name may be chosen. Official and competent records like Sir Theodore Martin's *Life of the Prince Consort* (1875-80) are chiefly a quarry for the historian; the legal biographies like Lord Campbell's *Lives of the Lord Chancellors* and Lord Cockburn's *Memorials of his Time* are chiefly, despite their professional wit or acrimony, for professional readers; but the labours of John Forster (1812-76) are more to our purpose. Forster was a most capable and independent journalist, editor, and writer; not elegant, not inspired, but energetic, careful, and outspoken. His *Life and Adventures* (enlarged as *The Life and Times*) *of Oliver Goldsmith* (1848, 1854) is a humane and sympathetic biography, and became a classic in its own kind; the *Life of Landor*, though valuable, is heavier; but the *Life of Dickens* (1872-4) cannot be superseded. There may be rather too much in it about Forster; but the broader lines of a character which it would be easy to exaggerate or distort are faithfully drawn, and are in harmony with the story told by Dickens's letters. Forster, though a blunt man, was full of discerning affection; he was charged with being too candid; but Dickens belongs to the world, and moreover comes out well under the test. No one can ever know so much about him as Forster knew. The same style and spirit are found in Forster's biography of Swift, and in his monographs on Sir John Eliot and other seventeenth-century subjects; though these are less definitive, considered as authorities.

The period is rich in political memoirs which are the quarry of the investigator; but few of them can be classed as literature (not the *Croker Papers*, still less the *Creevey Papers*) for the purpose of this review. The journals of Charles Cavendish Fulke Greville (1794-1865), who in boyhood was a page to George the Third, and who was Clerk of the Council from 1821 onwards, for more than a whole generation, are of another class. His diary opens with the reign of George the Fourth, and continues till 1860; and it appeared, under the auspices of his friend,

Henry Reeve, in three instalments (1874-87). Greville's birth and official position gave him a front seat for the political drama, or rather a post of vantage for the play behind the scenes; and he is its faithful, acute, and sardonic recorder. He thinks very little of himself, and says that his intellect is to Macaulay's as a hurdy-gurdy is to a great organ; but his portraiture of Macaulay is sober and free from antithesis, and has a quality of *finesse* which Macaulay himself lacks. Greville is, in fact, one of the last writers of the old-fashioned 'character,' or true epitaph; he only cares to be right, and does not practise emphasis; he describes wits and statesmen, the Duke of Wellington, Talleyrand, D'Orsay, Rogers, at first-hand, never borrowing his opinions. The judgements of his later years are milder, though not less decisive, than of old. The 'characters' are the halting-points in a level narrative; and of this the staple is political; its theme is the actual and inner story of public events. Greville is a gentleman; he is no dealer in seamy chronicles, but he avoids dulness without any effort; and his material is used, and much trusted, by the professional historians.

V

Some few classics, greater or smaller, of the immense literature of travel may now be named in passing. Darwin's and Huxley's *Voyages*, Kinglake's *Eöthen*, Froude's *Oceana*, and other such incidental works by men of science or letters, have been referred to before. The professional travellers and explorers fall into two chief classes, according as their scene of action is Asia or Africa. The most salient figure among them all is that of Sir Richard Burton[1] (1821-90), who wandered over both those continents and recorded endless adventures and escapes. A great linguist, anthropologist, and observer, he left on many volumes the imprint of his fierce and flawed and splendid personality. His Indian days are recorded in *Scinde, or the Unhappy Valley* (1851) and other books; his penetration of Somaliland in *First Footsteps in East Africa* (1856). The pictures of his reception at Harar by the Amir, and of his fight at Berbera, by the side of Speke, against tremendous odds, are in Burton's most stirring and grimmest style. Between came his best-known adventure, told in his *Pilgrimage to El-Medinah and Meccah* (1856). Like Palgrave after him, Burton passed as a Musalman; he got not only into the dress, but into the mental skin of the Oriental; he was the first Englishman to reach Mecca; and his chronicle, as usual, is a contribution to knowledge, as well as an outpouring of biting description and vivid prejudice. It is rather overloaded with lore, and is written in Burton's hasty, abrupt and hammering, but always virile style. He was also a pioneer in Africa, and his books on the great waters and lakes brought him into one of his hot disputes with his partner Speke. His journeys in Brazil, West Africa, and Paraguay produced yet more volumes. Later came his translation of *The Arabian Nights* (1885-8), which led to a storm. Burton's Arabic scholarship and his debt to other Orientalists have been much canvassed; and he had included many notes and disquisitions of a naked kind on the sexual custom and pathology of the East; these are part of a vast mass of material, both anthropological and literary, which he brought together for the first time.

Burton could not discuss any topic with scientific coldness, or with anything but gusto. He is given to long intemperate digressions; his English, though charged with vigour, is often clumsy and untrained, and in his translations is needlessly packed with archaism and affectation. His book certainly brings out the sickly monotony and unreadable dulness of many of the celebrated *Nights*, but it is a great and valuable work. He also made a remarkable translation of the *Lusiads* of Camoens, which has been highly praised in spite of its deliberate coinages and artifices of diction; but the effect is not poetical. Many of Burton's labours belong less to literature than to learning, and to the history of action, and to the records of national achievement.

There is far more charm and craftsmanship in another tale of adventure, the *Narrative of a Year's Journey through Central and Eastern Arabia* (1865). The author, William Gifford Palgrave, was the son of Sir Francis Palgrave, the learned historian, and the brother of Francis Turner Palgrave, the anthologist and poet. First a Jesuit missionary and afterwards in the diplomatic service, Palgrave made his way, in the guise of a Syrian merchant and physician, through the country of the fanatical Wahabees. His original aim was to survey the ground for religious propaganda, but his actual work was to study and describe geography, Arabian politics, and men and manners. Palgrave's easy, rather digressive style, and his pervading sense of colour, comedy, and character make his *Narrative* something of a work of art. He further wrote a very attractive story, *Hermann Agha* (1872), which continues the tradition of Hope's *Anastasius*, though in a more romantic fashion. The hero is a young German kidnapped by the

Turks; his passages with his beloved Zahra, and his blood-brother Moharib are delicately told, and the book should be rescued. And there is also vivid matter interspersed in the grave monumental books of Sir Austen Henry Layard on Nineveh (*Popular Account of Discoveries*, 1851; *Discoveries in the Ruins of Nineveh and Babylon*, 1853); Rossetti's *Burden of Nineveh* was inspired by them; but they are mostly archæological, and were eagerly greeted as revelations of a new old world.

Apart from Burton, the great African discoverers hardly claim to be men of letters; they are more like Hakluyt's voyagers in their simple directness, though the interest of their story is imperishable. The nice observing faculty, as well as the charity and piety, of the dauntless David Livingstone shine unconsciously through the pages of his *Missionary Travels in South Africa* (1857). John Hanning Speke, in his *Journal of the Discovery* (1863), and his *What Led to the Discovery of the Source of the Nile* (1864), impresses us with his minute watchfulness, scientific temper, and irresistible patience; he is one of Carlyle's 'wearied unweariable men' triumphing over infinite small rebuffs and miseries, and over endless black human obstacles. For such men Africa loses every touch of glamour, yet her call is not to be resisted. The discoveries of Sir Henry Morton Stanley (*How I Found Livingstone*, 1872; *Through the Dark Continent*, 1878; *In Darkest Africa*, 1890) were of lasting scientific and political importance, and his books were numerous; their matter keeps them from being merely ephemeral, and their manner, strongly tinged by that of American journalism, has the virtues appropriate to such a schooling. The *African Sketch-Book* of William Winwood Reade, a narrative of his experiences in Equatorial and West Africa, is full of a downright bluntness, a keen descriptive power, and a rough rhetoric, that remind us at times of his uncle, Charles Reade. The tornado, the gorilla-hunt, the disappointing flirtation with the coloured beauty Ananga, and the story of the Swiss murderer are all excellently, if sometimes too vulgarly, related. Winwood Reade wrote other records of travel, and also a singular, crude, speculative book, which had a long popularity, called *The Martyrdom of Man* (1872).

The Crescent and the Cross (1844), by Eliot Warburton, already named in connexion with Kinglake, is a much ampler, more methodical, and more responsible record of travel in the near East; with something in it of the guidebook, in a day when the ground was far less trodden. The fullest chapters are those on Egypt, the most vivacious perhaps those on Constantinople and the Ionian Islands. Warburton's rhetoric is heavier than Kinglake's, and he does not deal in wit; but the extreme zest of his narrative and its multitude of small vivid strokes keep it alive. Far superior in style, without the fireworks of Kinglake or the prolixity of Warburton, is the *Visits to Monasteries in the Levant* (1849) of the Hon. Robert Curzon, afterwards Lord Zouche. The visits were paid more than ten years earlier; Curzon, who afterwards figured in the diplomatic service, was not simply a well-to-do youth of rank travelling for curiosity, but an expert collector of ancient Oriental books and manuscripts. His spoils, honestly paid for and brought from the monasteries of Egypt and Mount Athos, were of great value. Curzon's style is light and rapid, marked by a cheerful but not offensive impertinence and *sang froid*, and his dialogue is full of point. The accounts of the Orthodox Patriarch who could not understand how a mere Archbishop, though of Canterbury, could be the head of a Christian community; of the other dignitary who softened, under the influence of the drink called 'rosoglio,' to bargain for treasures; the writer's ascent up the vertical ladder, in places broken, to the monastery of Barlaam, and his visit to that of Meteora, well so named; his overawing of a group of bandits, and his defeat by a battalion of fleas,—are all clear-cut stories, amusing, well-bred, and well written.

In fashion akin to *Eöthen*, but with less of real savour, are Lord Dufferin's *Letters from High Latitudes* (1857), relating the author's stay in Iceland and his voyage in a schooner yacht through the perils of the Polar bergs. His modesty cannot hide his nerve and coolness; he has an eye for the strangeness of those heavens, and for the 'pale lilac' of the peaks, and for the hues of the ice, of which he feels the obsession; he writes, too, with the mounting spirits of his Sheridan blood; and he has a genuine enthusiasm for the old Northern stories. An amateur in knowledge, he retails them, like everything else, romantically, and, alas, 'brilliantly' at times, and not at all in the thrifty and impeccable saga-style. The book is still capital popular writing, if deficient in fineness. The spirited young lord jokes easily and generously about the remote, hospitable islanders, whom he has hardly time to understand. The 'letters,' it is likely, are only such in name; they seem to have been made up at home afterwards, from documents and memories, and rounded off.

Last may be mentioned, somewhat in a rank apart, the *Greater Britain* (1868) of Sir Charles Dilke (1843-1911), which chronicles his tour through Canada, America, Polynesia, Tasmania, New Zealand, Australia, and India, and which, besides being an easy and humorous narrative, is bound together by its wide and statesmanlike point of view, and pervaded by a steady vision of the future and unity of the English-speaking countries. His *Problems of Greater Britain* (1890) is a maturer expansion of the same thesis. Dilke returns more especially to the questions raised by the position of the subject and coloured races, black, yellow, and red, and of special communities like the Mormon; and by the Russian threat to India. Much of his thinking is by no means antiquated. His bent of opinion is of course liberal, but is the very reverse of insular, and he judges no question on party lines. He also had, it may be added, a vein of pleasing and unexpected wit. In his little satire, or squib, *The Fall of Prince Florestan of Monaco*, printed anonymously in 1874, a young German princeling succeeds to the throne of Monaco, has some trouble with his microscopic army and still more with the Jesuits, who are the real potentates, and soon resigns his job with much relief and returns to Cambridge. In spite of many topical allusions, now lost, this elegant light romance remains a model of its sort.

VI

There is no expressive name for the kind of book which George Henry Borrow [1] (1803-81) was the inventor, and which died with him. His work has plain affinities with the vagrant, or tramping, novel of Lesage and Defoe; but then it is not fiction, for it is mostly a record, in the spirit if not in the letter, of fact. Nor is it, in the usual sense, autobiography; for no one can measure the precise degree of fancy, conscious or involuntary, with which Borrow invests the truth. He had, no doubt, an exceptionally strong memory, not only for the vocabularies of foreign tongues, but for the incidents and conversations of years long past. But on either side of all such memories, however precise, there is always a sharp knife-edge of darkness; and this darkness the artist fancy, perhaps masquerading as memory, ever seeks to invade, as though with a silent, silk-spinning motion of the hands: and soon fancy comes to know what might, what must, what *shall* have been the antecedents, the fillings-out, and the sequel, of this well-remembered dialogue, or of that occurrence. This, I think, is not to put too fine a point upon Borrow's procedure, if we add that he often well knows what he was doing, and practises plenty of conscious arrangement and invention too; while at other times he gives, as it were, a phonographic record. His art is essentially roguish in its gravity; and his delight in posturing as a mystery-man, polyglot traveller, and scholar gives us the pleasure which he means it to give. Where precisely Borrow's loomwork [1] begins and ends has been much disputed. Detail apart, it is probably most active, first of all in his long inserted stories, like the postillion's in *The Romany Rye*, and secondly, in parts of the dialogue. Some of these things would defy the longest memory; and we cannot be too grateful to Borrow for working as he did. The creative process is more freely at play in some of Borrow's books than in others. His original works are five in number, which really group themselves into three; and to them may be added his correspondence.

The first two are the fruit of the work that Borrow did in the Peninsula from 1835 to 1840, as the agent of the British and Foreign Bible Society for the circulation of the Scriptures. *The Zincali, or An Account of the Gypsies in Spain* (1841), is a monograph, somewhat disjointed, but one of the first of its kind in the language, upon a subject till then hardly explored.[2] The ethnological and philological matter in the book is of much less value than its lively direct faculty of observation. The gypsies also take their turn in the pageant of *The Bible in Spain* (1842), the publication that first brought Borrow into note, not only with the eager pious public but with the lay world. Long stretches of *The Bible in Spain* are transcripts, more or less trimmed up, but sometimes almost verbal, of the letters [3] that he wrote to the Society and afterwards recovered. Such letters, as they stand, are good literature; they needed little trimming. But for the material of at least half the book no original letters are extant; and it is clear that in the dialogues (of which in the letters there are few) the artist is at his ease. Not all the coincidences are too strange to be true, and most of the facts and personages are drawn from life. Borrow, however, is consciously picturesque and naturally 'romantic'; *The Bible in Spain* has the familiar note of newness, like Gray's letters and *Waverley*. 'No one has seen this landscape before,' Borrow seems to say: '*my* brigands, gypsies, and thieves, are *new* brigands. I am the first to make you feel the fierce, un-English sunshine, coming sheer down on the barren rock. The Lord has left it to me to depict these primitive, knifing passions, which by no means work themselves out into honest British fisticuffs.' One bye-product of *The Bible in Spain* is Borrow's strain of religious unction, which recurs in his later writings. He seems to have learnt this idiom, half sincerely, half diplomatically, during his earlier service under the Bible Society in Russia, when he worked as editor, transcriber, and printer of a Manchu Testament. Of that sojourn, apart from certain translations, Borrow's letters are unluckily his only memorial. *The Bible in Spain* is full of the anti-Romish rhetoric and virulence which the author during his stay in the country had discreetly repressed. It also contains not only abundance of rich and coloured writing, but many examples of the plainer and yet subtler manner into which he was afterwards to settle down. Both these varieties of Borrow's English can be traced in the well-known passage which describes his journey through the 'Black Pass,' on the way from Santander to Madrid. He appreciated Richard Ford's description of the book as a '*Gil Blas* in water colours.'

> The sun had set about a quarter of an hour. Suddenly a man, with his face covered with blood, rushed out of the pass. 'Turn back, sir,' he said, 'in the name of God; there are murderers in that pass; they have just robbed me of my mule and all I possess, and I have hardly escaped with life from their hands.' I scarcely know why, but I made him no answer and proceeded; indeed I was so weary and unwell that I cared not what became of me. We entered: the rocks rose perpendicularly, right and left, entirely intercepting the scanty twilight, so that the darkness of the grave, or rather the blackness of the valley of the shadow of death, reigned around us, and we knew not where we went, but trusted to the instinct of the horses, who moved on with heads close to the ground. The only sound which we heard was the plash of a stream, which tumbled down the pass. I expected every moment to feel a knife at my throat, but 'it was not so written.' We threaded the pass without meeting a human being. (Ch. xxxv.)

There is more history and more scenery in *The Bible in Spain* than in Borrow's other books, apart from *Wild Wales*. The bright sharp atmosphere of the country is conveyed, as it is in R. A. M. Stevenson's study of Velasquez. The pace and zest of the narrative, the ever-changing pageant of motley talk and adventure, are surprising. The vogue of *The Bible in Spain* was deserved, and there is nothing quite like it. But one volume has earned a place beside it, namely the learned, accurate, and vivid *Handbook to Spain*, first published in 1845, and written by Borrow's friend Richard Ford,[1] the traveller, connoisseur of art, *bon vivant*, and wit. Ford's lightness and gaiety serve to correct Borrow's more sombre tone. *The Bible in Spain* is imposing; but in workmanship it is not so strange or so fine as its two successors, the poor reception of which is a classical instance of the follies of criticism.

VII

Borrow, who had married an English lady whilst in Spain, returned, settled down, living mostly at Oulton in Suffolk; and during ten years brooded over his *Lavengro: The Scholar—The Gypsy—The Priest*, which appeared in 1851. Its sequel, *The Romany Rye*, waited till 1857; but the two form one continuous work. In the opening lines of *The Romany Rye*, the author 'awoke at the first break of day'; the postillion's story, finished on the very night before, forms the conclusion of *Lavengro*. And *The Romany Rye* itself ends suddenly, with the author walking away from Horncastle Fair in the year 1825, and 'thinking he will go' to India; which he does not do. The two works together, therefore, form a fairly continuous autobiography, from the writer's earliest recollections down to his twenty-third year. The next seven years, 1825-32, are the so-called 'veiled period,' of which he has left no record, and of which the history is but raggedly pieced together from external data. The Russian episode occupied the two years that followed. Then, late in 1835, he started for the Peninsula. He seems to have been about thirty-eight when he formed the plan of chronicling his early life, and fifty-four when he completed it. The result could hardly be more particular and vivid had he kept a diary. But he says:

> I have endeavoured to describe a dream, partly of study, partly of adventure, in which will be found copious notices of books, and many descriptions of life and manners, some in a very unusual form.

Thus opens the preface to *Lavengro*; and half the illusion of the dream is caused by the habit of prosaic—not tedious—diffuseness and iteration. The linguistic disquisitions, which really are tedious, but can be run over lightly, help the illusion too. Doubtless Borrow showed off before his unlettered hearers, and half-bored, half-impressed them, in just that way. His tirades against the Pope have the same effect; Borrow for some reason addresses that potentate by the Russian term *batuschka* [*batyuschka*], which is *not* translateable as 'little father,' or 'daddy,' as he intends it to be.

There is little in *Lavengro* and *The Romany Rye* that does not wear well. All but the best fiction of the time has lost hold on us in comparison with Borrow's notable passages—his poisoning by Mrs. Herne, his battle with the Tinman, and the noble, clean, and wonderful idyll of Isopel Berners, which marks the summit of Borrow's writing and the effect of which is enhanced by his want of heart, and even of shame. The ordinary narrative is hardly inferior. From the Jew who called the infant Borrow 'a prophet's child,' down to the final chat with the recruiting-sergeant, all is sustained, little is superfluous. The speech of the gypsies, like that of jockeys and postillions, is sometimes artificially raised and made bookish; but Borrow gives the gypsy soul and essence, so we are assured by those who know them best, more truthfully than anyone before or since his day. He sees them in daylight as they are, without false romanticism. He does not hate them for their vices, though the only commandment which they keep is the seventh; and his sympathy with their passion for liberty is profound. He knows that he can leave them at any time; but he has no greater pleasure than to talk awhile with people who are not respectable; or who have character, whether they be within or without the pale.

It is Borrow's art, perhaps, rather than Borrow himself that is mysterious. He is indeed full of contradictions; but there is truth in his remark to Mr. Petulengro:

'There you are mistaken, Jasper. I am not cunning. If people think I am, it is because, being made up of art themselves, simplicity of character is a puzzle to them.'

The chief puzzle in Borrow seems to arise from his callousness and self-centredness. He probably sees how well we should like to break his head when he torments Isopel with Armenian verbs or questions Ursula under the hedge; but he does not care, or prefers that we should be angry. His ruthless egoism, which is quite consistent with some good nature and an admiration for good things, is necessary to the production of his effects, and is at least on no mean scale. He was in part of Cornish, in part of Huguenot origin; but he was born in Norfolk, and adopted that shire, and acquired, if only by protective mimicry, some of the true East Anglian hardness; nor would anything less have carried him through all his rebuffs and tight corners. We do not ask Odysseus to be sentimental, or to conform to the ideals of *Middlemarch* or of the author of the *Egoist*.

Yet Borrow's thirst for questioning, understanding, and worrying his fellow-creatures is rooted in a true sympathy, which is half curiosity, yet is by no means inhuman. He really drew people out, all sorts and conditions of people, digging into their histories during the first five minutes, and making them talk. The response that he nearly always found is a proof of this gift of sympathy. He was a great listener and cross-examiner, a true historian of things seen and heard, with something universal in his temper, which is not indeed the temper of the great poetic interpreters, but for which no mere theory of human brotherhood, or humanitarian exaltation, can ever be a substitute. Yet all this would have been lost without his queer selective skill and wordcraft; and to do justice to that we must consult the last of his original works, *Wild Wales*, which appeared in 1862.

Wild Wales, its Peoples, Language, and Scenery was worked up from four notebooks or diaries, written during a trip which Borrow made along with his wife and step-daughter, in 1854. Much of it records the trampings of the tall, white-haired, black-clad, wideawaked figure, equipped with the celebrated green umbrella to which he devotes one lyric page; wherein the musical word *umbrella* recurs like some *motif* in De Quincey's *Dream-Fugue*. Thus *Wild Wales*, like *The Bible in Spain*, but unlike the intervening volumes, bears the stamp of a literal transcript from written material. But it is a transcript expanded at great length with the minuteness at once of a guidebook and of a professional interviewer: Borrow's long memory, with who knows how much of his Defoe-like piecing-out faculty, is still as vigorous as ever. The rough material for just such another survey can be found in the notes of his walking tour in Galloway,[1] made in 1866—jotted scraps which the artist took home but unhappily never wrought up. He has a signal power of catching at once, chameleon-wise, the physical and mental atmosphere of any land in which he finds himself. As he goes in the train across England, he is in turn 'enthusiastically Saxon'; then, as he sees a Danish name on a station, Danish; then in Birmingham a 'modern Englishman,' still 'enthusiastically'; then, refusing to harbour any 'Norman enthusiasm' at all, he glows 'with all the Welsh enthusiasm with which I glowed when I first started in the direction of Wales.' All this is very genuine, though playful, and it is also a cunning overture. Welsh he had learned to read and translate in his youth; and a Welsh groom had taught him to speak the tongue sufficiently to serve as a passport. The result is one of Borrow's most delightful and satisfactory, though not his greatest, books. It would take long to describe the merits of *Wild Wales.* The publisher, Murray, at first feared that, owing to its 'want of stirring incident, it would not succeed'; but he added truly that it is 'beautifully written and in a style of English undefiled, which few writers can surpass.' And in the historical portions, as in the pages on the Welsh poets, there is a sober eloquence, unlike the *bravura* manner of *The Bible in Spain.* There is little declamation: Borrow had vented his ire and prejudice, it would seem, in the splenetic but most entertaining appendix to *The Romany Rye*, which had been too much for his public. But the essence of *Wild Wales* lies in its delicate notes of scenery, in its portraits and conversations, and in the instinctive skill with which, one after another, Borrow's wayside companions reveal their natures under his leading. The book forms a gallery of national types—the Welsh American, the magistrate's clerk, the hog-driver, the waggoner, the country clergyman, and a score of others. Borrow's sympathy did not extend to the English rustic, and he often resents the loutish manners of the Anglo-Saxon; a twist in his temper which at once put him in sympathy with the Welsh dislike and mistrust of the Saxon. There are a few scenes of the old salience, such as the sudden meeting with Captain Bosvile, and the page in which Borrow, under threat of a beating, falls in with the mistake of the Irish reapers, and, in the character of Father Toban, gives them a Latin blessing. But the narrative is mostly even and quiet; inn after inn, valley after valley, talk after talk, succeed with a sameness that is not monotony. Borrow, like Hazlitt, is one of those who can make literature out of a breakfast-table. He has the same passion for the roads, and for the 'noble art,' and for literature; and though his range of intellect is smaller, and he is not so strong in the article of general ideas, he is less fierce than Hazlitt, and more sociable, and readier to get inside the skin of others, if only for the moment.

VIII

There is no sign of his owing any debt to Hazlitt; nor is it easy to see where he learned the indefinable open secret of his English. Some clues there are; Borrow more than once pays his tribute to Defoe; both writers depict humble life and the outlaw world, and create their illusion by the method of 'minute particulars,' and by the use of a subdued key. But in all else they differ; and part of the likeness is maybe simply due to a common taste for the literature of 'low life,' and for its artistic virtues. Borrow in his youth compiled *Celebrated Trials,* in six volumes, for the sweating bookseller Sir Richard Phillips; and in a well-known passage, which will bear re-quoting, he gives his notion of the *non imitabile* in style:

What struck me most with respect to these lives was the art which the writers, whoever they were, possessed of telling a plain story. It is no easy matter to tell a story plainly and distinctly by mouth; but to tell one on paper is difficult indeed, so many snares lie in the way. People are afraid to put down what is common on paper, they seek to embellish their narratives, as they think, by philosophic speculations and reflections; they are anxious to shine, and people who are anxious to shine can never tell a plain story. 'So I went with them to a music booth, where they made me almost drunk with gin, and began to talk their flash language, which I did not understand,' says, or is made to say, Henry Simms, executed at Tyburn some seventy years before the time of which I am speaking. I have always looked upon this sentence as a masterpiece of the narrative style, it is so concise and yet so very clear. (*Lavengro,* ch. xxxvi.)

This 'racy, genuine language,' as he calls it, Borrow seeks to attain, and constantly does attain, especially in plain description and in dialogue. One thing which he may have learnt from the Newgate model is when to stop:

'Brother, I have been with you near three hours beneath this hedge. I will go to my husband.'

'Does he know that you are here?'

'He does, brother.'

'And is he satisfied?'

'Satisfied! Of course. Lor', you gorgios! Brother, I go to my husband and my house.' And, thereupon, Ursula rose and departed.

After waiting a little time I also arose; it was now dark, and I thought I could do no better than betake myself to the dingle; at the entrance of it I found Mr. Petulengro. (*Romany Rye,* ch. xi.)

Borrow 'muses deeply' afterwards on his talk with Ursula, but he keeps his meditations separate; the dialogue itself is sharply finished: there is no fumbling with the conclusion. Every conversation in *Wild Wales,* if examined, will be seen to have this trait. In other passages there is a different kind of craft, suggested by a more sophisticated writer, namely Sterne. But this is confined to a few pages. The conversations ascribed by Borrow to his parents recall those of the parents of Tristram Shandy. But the temper of Sterne is not that of Borrow. Sterne relishes and masters the niceties of language; but his relish is like the ecstasy of an ape—an ape of genius—over the flavour of a rare nut. Borrow has not that sort of connoisseurship, and he writes like a man. To describe his style [1] at its best we might use metaphors drawn from the 'noble art' he admired; it is muscular, middle-weight English, in the best training and without an ounce of needless flesh. He has his own devices for making his dialogue seem actual. One of them is that repetition, or repercussion, of words, the effect of which is to make the talk go slowly, just at the pace of real time, and also rather laboriously, as talk actually does. This effect is cumulative, and could only be shown by long quotation. But a few lines, in which the freedom is taken of italicising the echoed words, will give some conception of it. The fine old English gentleman with the two terriers, the magistrate to whom Lavengro has brought a thousand pounds, administers Madeira to his young guest:

'It is very good,' said I.
'Did you *ever taste* better *Madeira*?'
'I *never* before *tasted Madeira*.'
'Then you *ask for* a wine without *knowing what it is*?'
'I *ask for* it, sir, that I may *know what it is*.'
'Well, there is logic in that, as *Parr* would say; you have heard of *Parr*?'
'*Old Parr?*'
'Yes, *old Parr*, but not that *Parr*; you mean the English, I the Greek *Parr*, as people call him.'
'I don't know him. . . . Suppose we drink his *health*?'
'Thank you, boy, here 's *Parr's health, and Whiter's*.'
'Who is *Whiter*?'
'Don't you *know Whiter*? I thought everybody *knew* Reverend *Whiter*, the philologist. . . .' (*Lavengro*, ch. xxiv.)

For wit and entertainment this cannot compare with a page of *Copperfield*; but it is not dull, and it is much more like the way in which people really chat. Borrow keeps it up, without being dull, for a long time. He, in these dialogues, is always himself, and his interlocutors, who are all different, are always themselves. But the poet Gordon Hake [2] said shrewdly:

Every individuality with which he was brought into contact . . . had to be tinged with colours of his own before he could see it at all.

Borrow has a singular habit of affecting to reproduce a long mental soliloquy of his own, dated many years back. He invents past words which were, avowedly, never even uttered.

Such reports, like the speeches in Thucydides, are nevertheless true in substance; for it is just these ruminations, especially when they were painful, that a man remembers best. No one can forget Borrow's fits of 'the horrors,' or his misery on the eve of his battle with the Tinman, or how he took comfort from his little horse in the dingle. Though there is no theology in the matter, the tone recalls that of Bunyan's *Grace Abounding*:

> Was it possible? Yes, all too certain; the evil one was upon me; the inscrutable horror which I had felt in my boyhood had once more taken possession of me. I thought that it had forsaken me; that it would never visit me again; that I had outgrown it; that I might almost bid defiance to it; and I had even begun to think of it without horror, as we are in the habit of doing of horrors of which we conceive we run no danger; and lo! when least thought of, it had seized me again. . . . (*Lavengro*, ch. lxxxiv.)

Borrow's other writings, earlier and later, are in the nature of curiosities.[1] He had a large unpublished library of translations, or plans for translations, and actually published versions from the Danish: *Romantic Ballads*, 1826, from the *Kjœmpeviser*; also from Ewald's *Death of Balder*, posthumously printed. He produced in 1835 his *Targum, or Metrical Translations from Thirty Languages and Dialects*; in 1860, *The Sleeping Bard*, from the Welsh of Elis Wyn; *The Turkish Jester*, translated from the Turkish; and his *Romano Lavo-Lil* (1874), a wordbook of Romany, which the learned forthwith pronounced to be out of date, but which contains some refreshment in the way of description. Few will profess to check Borrow's knowledge of the 'thirty languages and dialects'; but, to judge by examples, some of his versions are wildly loose, while others, like that from Filicaja, are stiffly literal, with some genuine poetic feeling piercing through. Not many have the air of poetry, though the vigorous *Sir John*, from the 'Old Danish,' is an exception; and the artificially-phrased translation of Pushkin's *Talisman* catches the sweep of the original rhythm. The prose works are variegated with words and quotations from many tongues. It is delightful to find Borrow assuring his wife, in respect of Turkish, that 'there was a time when I wrote it better than any other language'; and informing Lieutenant-Colonel Napier, at Seville, that he had learned Romany 'some years ago, in Moultan.' These things reward the close reader of Borrow. But his linguistic gifts, while useless for scholarship or philology, were wide and genuine; and they were the keys that enabled him to talk to almost everybody, and to unlock human nature in Russia, in Spain, in Wales, and among the English gypsies.

Borrow's art is all his own, and his temper is unique, and he carries the piqued and slightly alienated but constant reader through everything. He resembles some notable, rather disagreeable acquaintance in real life, whom few quite like, but of whom everyone talks the moment that he has left the room, and who, when all is said, is inveterately *there*. And Borrow is there, amid the teeming literature of his time, with its acres of fiction, essays, chronicles of travel, often, alas, undeniably meritorious, but rapidly yellowing and fading. Borrow's colours do not fade; his work stands, not by its queerness, not by virtue of anything except his vision, his essential veracity as a craftsman, and his mother-English.

CHAPTER XIII

TENNYSON

I

THE public coronation of Alfred, Lord Tennyson[1] (1809-92), may be dated in 1850, the year of *In Memoriam* and of the Laureateship. His title had really been established by his volume of 1842; and to ourselves, as to a few observers at the time, it is clearly prophesied in the volumes of 1830 and 1832. It was natural that Arthur Hallam should write that 'the true heir is found'—the heir to Keats; and Wordsworth, who was hard to please, saluted Tennyson as 'decidedly the first of our living poets.' The greeting of Coleridge,[2] who died in 1834, and had not *Ulysses* before him, was more dubious, although the young Tennyson was really a poet in his own tradition. But the interregnum had not actually been long, since the death of Byron in 1824; and the competitors were few. Beddoes and Darley had the true gift, but their flights were brief, and they were too much entangled with the Elizabethans. Wade, Sir Henry Taylor, and some other writers of the transition will be noted hereafter (Ch. XVIII.). The field was clear for Tennyson, and also for Browning, whose fame was to be much longer delayed.

We think too much of Tennyson as suspiciously respectable, as the voice of Victorian England, and as somehow breaking with the freer traditions of romance. His more popular work lends some truth to this view; but we must look at his best work, whether popular or not; at his classical poems, his lyrics, his dramatic monologues, his monodrama, and his early passionate fantasies, if we are to see how close was his bond with the age of poetry in which he grew up. He inherits most of these forms, and carries them further; he does *not* break with romance. And he carries on the succession also in his allegorical and speculative verse; where, indeed, the technique is often much more original than the contents.

Up to 1842 his development is not wholly unlike that of Keats. Both poets begin with a passionate absorption in natural beauty—in colours, sounds, and odours ; both command the rich, sometimes confused melodies that attend on such a temper. From such 'fine excess' both of them move away towards the expression of the plain, the grand, and the heroic ; away from Spenser (the sleepy Spenser, not the Platonist) towards Homer and Dante. And both of them get to the grand style ; they get to it, *fortunati ambo !* in their youth, not too late to preserve intact the full rich capital of their sensibility to things seen and heard ; they retain their hold of the words that seem to *be* such things rather than merely to represent them. This capital Tennyson never squandered, though he lived more than thrice as long as Keats. But to compare further would be misleading ; Tennyson is a craftsman of very singular temper, and it is not enough to say that his progress is from the luxurious to the heroic.

Perhaps his strongest impulse as an artist is to pack his material. He was elaborate and condensed to begin with, and without effort. His diction was naturally curious and his rhythm somewhat slow. Then he followed two different paths. He perfected the elaborate style, the many-faceted verse and image, applying it to ever-new purposes—to reflective writing, to impassioned writing, and above all to natural description, in which he is one of the masters. But from this style, which is his regular and instinctive one, he also tries to get away ; he seeks to be bare and simple, above all in the utterance of lyrical or heroic emotion. And this end also he attains ; but then Tennyson has more than one kind of simplicity, as Matthew Arnold, in somewhat unfair terms, has indicated. But I pass over the risks of false simplicity, or *simplesse*, which we come across often enough in Tennyson. For he attains two kinds which are not false. The first, the commoner kind, is a noble and genuine one, but it has the air of being striven for, the result of a simplifying process. We come on it even at the end of the prize poem on *Timbuctoo* (1829) :

> and I
> Was left alone on Calpe, and the Moon
> Had fallen from the night, and all was dark !

There is much of this in Tennyson, and it gives great and just pleasure. But the other kind of simplicity seems not to have been sought for at all, but to have taken him by the throat ; it is natural and passionate speech that is born in a tune. *Tout le reste est littérature !* we exclaim ; often splendid literature too, no doubt. You can have the great style, perfect music, even undeniable song, without having what Burns and

Heine give us continually, or what Tennyson himself gives us in *O that 'twere possible!* . . . the lines that were the seed of *Maud*, or in *Break, break, break!* or in the first verse of *Come not, when I am dead*, or in

> The voice of the dead was a living voice to me.

When Tennyson writes like this, we may think of the result either as something rather alien to his natural gift, and bestowed on him by the powers from time to time ; or, more truly and handsomely, as his real genius and flame breaking out and overcoming the bent of his talent, which, eminent and delightful as it is, tends to take him away from such utterance and to cover it up. For his character is at times in conflict with his art. He has plenty of primitive instinct ; yet much of his writing is out of keeping with it, and with his natural, recorded talk, and with his leonine side ; the side which is perceptible in his biography, although there the lion may be somewhat over-groomed, with his mane parted in the middle.

II

The *Poems by Two Brothers* (1827) tell us little about Alfred Tennyson except his poetical reading. The two brothers were in fact three, and I shall return to Frederick Tennyson (1807-98) and to Charles Tennyson, afterwards Tennyson Turner (1808-79), both of whom had poetic faculty. In the prize poem *Timbuctoo* the omens are plainer, though as a whole it is turbid. But in the *Poems* of 1830 there are *Mariana, The Dying Swan*, and *The Ballad of Oriana*. Here the lyrical magic and the power of imaginative landscape-painting are already assured. In *Adeline, Lilian*, and their companions the effect is often mawkish ; they are rather like the female heads, long ago beloved by undergraduates, of the late Frank Miles. But the lines in the *Ode to Memory* on Tennyson's home at Somersby are another thing : they were 'written very early in life,' and they are the real Tennyson : they portray

> the brook that loves
> To purl o'er matted cress and ribbed sand,
> Or dimple in the dark of rushy coves,
> Drawing into his narrow earthen urn,
> At every elbow and turn,
> The filter'd tribute of the rough woodland.

In the *Poems* of 1832 (dated 1833) the signs of power are abundant. In *The Poet*, Tennyson's statelier style had already come in sight ; in *A Dream of Fair Women* it has arrived ; and it has also arrived (despite the blind alley of a moral) in *The Palace of Art*. The Greek poems now begin with *Œnone* and *The Lotos-Eaters* ; and *Tithonus*, though not printed until 1860, belongs to the same period. And the first of the mediæval poems, Malorian only in its names, is there also ; Holman Hunt was to draw the *ventus textilis*,[1] as Edgar Allan Poe called it, of *The Lady of Shalott*. In *Fatima* the thirst of Oriental passion is not weakened by any hunt after far-sought phrase. The painful *May Queen* and *The Miller's Daughter* contain, at the worst, admirable description.

Many of these pieces are less known to the public in their earlier shape. Some, like *The Lady of Shalott* and *Œnone*, were largely rewritten. Tennyson corrected all his life with almost invariable tact, and a study of his textual changes is the best clue to his genius. In the *Poems* of 1842 these revisions begin. A number of the old poems are weeded out, some to reappear long after as *Juvenilia*. It is well to have them all, not least *The Kraken* and the *Supposed Confessions*, an early experiment in the difficult form of the imaginary soliloquy. But the new pieces of 1842, by common consent, contain many of Tennyson's chief titles to honour. The intricate style has now gone far ; some of its varieties may be seen in *St. Simeon Stylites*, *Love and Duty*, and *The Two Voices*. There is many an essay in simplicity, not always successful, as *Lady Clare* and even *Dora* may be thought to show. But in *Morte d'Arthur* and *Ulysses* the simplicity of grandeur, if not without signs of effort, is really attained, and Tennyson shows that he can render a large poetical idea, as distinct from a simple mood or emotion, adequately. *Sir Galahad*, *St. Agnes*, and *Sir Launcelot and Queen Guinevere* counted for much to the 'Pre-Raphaelite' artists, and link them closely with Tennyson. The mobility of his gift is plain if we set all these poems beside *Locksley Hall*, or again beside *Will Waterproof's Lyrical Monologue*. He was now the master of many measures, including one that seemed to mark him out for some poetic adventure, on a large scale, that should be worthy of it. But what would he attempt, what would he execute, in his new and peculiar species of blank verse ? Where, asked his friends, was his subject ?

He at once used his metre, not for a great subject, but for a 'medley' ; this was *The Princess* (1847). And he had his great subject, in the loss of his friend ; although, quite rightly, he did not use blank verse for it. *In Memoriam* (1850), the fruit of seventeen years of intermittent labour, was too dispersedly written for complete unity, though it expressed Tennyson's inmost mind and experience. The same year brought him happiness in his long-deferred marriage, as well as the Laureateship. Now, like Pope, he could 'live and thrive' by poetry; and his life had not so far been easy at all; but the long remainder of it was hardly to be troubled except by the paper darts of criticism. Apart from the *Ode on the Death of the Duke of Wellington*, in 1852, he produced little more for five years.

Then came *Maud, a Monodrama*, in 1855, an unpopular triumph; not at all what was expected of Tennyson; but none of his longer poems is fuller of his genius. And he had for years been nursing his Arthuriad, which was to more than appease the public, and which had begun so well, though it had begun at the end, with *Morte d'Arthur*. Four of the *Idylls of the King* appeared in 1859, three new ones in the volume of 1869, one two years later, and one in 1885. Tennyson meant the *Idylls* to be his most serious contribution to poetry—the long-tarrying work on a large scale and a great theme. The rest of his writing, apart from his plays, consists of sheaf after sheaf of poems, many of them brief and few of more than middle length. He went on inventing; he was always finding out new species and new measures, and the old veins were still rich. In the volume (1864) which is named after *Enoch Arden*, that magnified 'English idyll' with a tropical interlude, came *The Northern Farmer*, *The Voyage*, *In the Valley of Cauteretz*; and, in unmerited small print, the *Experiments* in classic metre and translation. In *Lucretius* (1868) Tennyson's dramatic monologues and also his classical poems culminate. In 1875 his dramatic adventures begin with *Queen Mary*; and he continues to revive the 'chronicle play' in *Harold* (1876) and *Becket* (1884); and he writes romantic dramas like *The Falcon*, *The Cup*, or *The Foresters*. Most of these pieces were acted, with all possible advantages, and in each of them there is poetry; but it is seldom the right poetry for a play, and hereafter they are more likely to be read than seen.

Tennyson's lyric energy was still fresh and young. In *Ballads and other Poems*, published in his seventy-first year, are to be seen *The Voyage of Maeldune*, and *The Revenge*, and *Rizpah*. In *Tiresias, and other Poems* (1885) come the twenty lines *To Virgil*, Tennyson's poetical forefather; nor will anything that he wrote live longer. Here too is *The Ancient Sage*, which intimates rather than defines the settled faith of his later life. There are many sequels, or experiments in familiar kinds, which, like *Locksley Hall Sixty Years After* (1886), are not always fortunate ; the skill is there, but the verse does not stick in the mind as of old. We feel this, but we have to be careful, in reading *Demeter, and other Poems* (1889) or *The Death of Œnone, Akbar's Dream, and other Poems* (1892) ; for at the last he writes *Crossing the Bar* ; and already, at the age of eighty, he has celebrated *The Progress of Spring*, exclaiming that

> The groundflame of the crocus breaks the mould.

The truth about Tennyson's contemporary reputation[1] and its fortunes, and about his relations to the critics, has only lately been cleared up. He had to struggle for his fame, not only in the Thirties but in the Forties, longer and harder than had been supposed. The best judges saw that it was due, but they were seldom the professional critics. The public, however, knew better than the reviewers, and bought the books. After 1850 and till his death Tennyson had the suffrages of all, except of one or two of those very judges, Carlyle and Fitzgerald, who repined at his lack of a 'subject,' and of Taine, whose chapter on Tennyson in his *Histoire de la Littérature anglaise*, though acute and salutary, is deformed by a preconception of the poet's character. Respecting Tennyson's attitude to his critics, it is most unsafe to say, as was long said, that he altered his text at their instance ; but it is true that he took their censures bitterly, and was stung, so it is reported, when 'Apollodorus says that I am not a great poet.' Apollodorus, at times, even seems to have silenced the poet, as well as discouraging him. But in the long run Tennyson went his own way, and got out, we may think, all that was in him. Before trying to see, as a whole, what he really achieved, it is well, without strictly heeding dates, to review his work under its natural species, and to begin with his best.

III

The antique, after its long partial eclipse during the age of prose, had come more and more—and this largely through the influence of Milton transmitting it—to inspire the age of romance. And the antique, more and more, had come to mean the best Greek poetry—Homer, and Æschylus, and the anthology, and the idylls, and the odes. *Hyperion*, *Hellas*, the writings of Landor, show this inspiration at work. In Tennyson it takes new life ; it produces *The Lotos-Eaters*, and *Ulysses* nine years later ; and then, more than forty years after that, it produces *Tiresias*, so fresh is the old age of the poet. The spirit of Greek verse and the lesson of its art must have sunk far into a man, must have been one of the deep things in his life, to bear such fruit ! And Tennyson's Hellenics—if we may use the term coined by Landor, whose own volume thus entitled appeared in 1846, and if, by a natural extension, we may apply it also to poems founded on Lucretius, Catullus, and Virgil, who were themselves inspired by Greece—Tennyson's Hellenics, then, along with some of his lyrics, include some of his most perfect and permanent work, and they remain, with *Samson Agonistes* and *Prometheus Unbound*, among the chief tributes in our language to the power of the antique.

This is a good deal to say ; and some distinctions must be made. *Ulysses* and *Tiresias* are in the form on which Tennyson finally settled, not only for his classical, but for other highly characteristic pieces : it is the dramatic monologue, of moderate length, and written in a blank verse of which the marks are generally grandeur and composure—the composure not of detachment or indifference but of experience. No one doubts that he was right, master of blank verse as he was, to use it here, for nothing else could equally convey those qualities ; or, again, that he did well in settling on the monologue form, with all its difficulties. But he did not come to it at once ; and whilst on the way to it he wrote things of great and acknowledged beauty, where that form is not yet fully disengaged. *The Lotos-Eaters* opens with the Spenserian stanzas founded on Homer's picture of the lotos ; but most of it is choric ode, in irregular measures : a monologue certainly, but a lyrical one, chanted by the sailors in unison, and therefore expressive of a mood, and not like *Ulysses* of a character. The poem in its earliest form wanted the long ringing close on the life of the Lucretian gods, which enforces the note of grandeur ; but from the first that note is heard—*Why should we toil alone ?*—and it springs up from and begins to overpower the original strain of languor and fatal delightful ease. Still *The Lotos-Eaters* is a lyric ; and *Œnone* is an idyll, keeping the refrain which the Sicilians, and Milton in his *Epitaphium Damonis*, had used so well. And though blank verse is the medium, and though it is mostly narrative and descriptive, *Œnone* is not yet the true dramatic monologue, where the story and situation are not related but are made clear by the way ; and where nothing external happens, or at least need happen, for the movement is purely one of thought and emotion. This kind of poem may be thought of as a single, central speech taken out of an epic or a Greek play—which however does not exist. This is true of Tennyson's usage, not of Browning's; for *My Last Duchess* and *The Bishop Orders his Tomb* have the air of coming out of an Elizabethan or modern drama, not of a Greek one; the pattern of all such compositions being found in the soliloquies of Hamlet. Tennyson, too, approaches that manner in works like *St. Simeon Stylites*, but not in his classical pieces.

In *Tithonus*, another product of the Thirties, the form is fully attained. It is a speech, addressed to Eos, a *muta persona*, who nevertheless is made visible in her tender gestures, like some figure in the Street of Tombs. The blank verse is there, not yet in all its nerve, but in all its grace; the poem is a triumph of grace and pathos. The peculiar *desiderium*, bred of the 'cruel immortality' under which Tithonus suffers, is enforced by the recurrence of certain words which give the dominant mood: *mist*, and *silver*, and *glimmering*, and *tears*, and *beauty*, and *shadow*. Here can still be traced the struggle, or rather now the fusion, between Tennyson's instinct for complexity and his instinct for simplicity; perhaps the former rules. But in *Ulysses* the latter rules; the heroic style has come, in its plainness and strength. It has come, in part, from Dante, who supplies the story, not to be found in Homer, of the last adventure of Ulysses, and whose treatment may be called, in the largest and truest sense, classical. Tennyson catches his strain in a line like

> And see the great Achilles, whom we knew.

But there is also Tennyson's own, his spontaneous intricacy of musical metaphor:

> Yet all experience is an arch wherethro'
> Gleams that untravell'd world, whose margin fades
> For ever and for ever when I move;

and there his own delight in full, cunning vowelling:

> There gloom the dark broad seas.

In *Ulysses* the poetical conception has a more universal application than that of *Tithonus*; the symbolism is latent, but we can find it without violence. The conception of following knowledge, at any cost, beyond the traditional pillars into dangerous waters, appealed as much to the age of Tennyson and Darwin as it had done to that of Bruno and Bacon. The poem was written, said the author, 'soon after Arthur Hallam's death, and gave my feeling about the need of going forward and braving the struggle of life perhaps more simply than anything in *In Memoriam.*' In *Tiresias*, again, the conception is large and adequate, and strikes beyond the story itself; it is the doom of the seer, who lives to see his disregarded forebodings come true. Here, on the whole, elaboration rules once more. *Tiresias* is a good late example of Tennyson's complex and symphonious verse, which recalls Milton not in its actual cast, but in its comparable mastery of the steeds of Rhythm and Language—in its *charioteering* power. The 'diffuse and opulent end,' which the poet supposes his friend FitzGerald to criticise, is not diffuse at all, though it is opulent; and here it is, though I shall not often venture to quote Tennyson at length, as if he were unfamiliar: and let it be said that these qualities do not vanish in *Demeter and Persephone* or in *The Death of Œnone*, the works of his age:

> But for me,
> I would that I were gather'd to my rest,
> And mingled with the famous kings of old,
> On whom about their ocean-islets flash
> The faces of the Gods—the wise man's word,
> Here trampled by the populace underfoot,
> There crown'd with worship—and these eyes will find
> The men I knew, and watch the chariot whirl
> About the goal again, and hunters race
> The shadowy lion, and the warrior-kings,
> In height and prowess more than human, strive
> Again for glory, while the golden lyre
> Is ever sounding in heroic ears
> Heroic hymns, and every way the vales
> Wind, clouded with the grateful incense-fume
> Of those who mix all odour to the Gods
> On one far height in one far-shining fire.

Except for *Lucretius*, the other classical pieces are lyrics, of the sort in which poets with a brooding, tenacious type of memory excel. Gray is a brother in this craft; and its father, Virgil, Tennyson honours in his anniversary lines 'written at the request of the Mantuans.' He weaves names, and images, and echoes, many of them from the Sixth Æneid, into a majestic harmony: the 'golden branch amid the shadows,' the 'Universal Mind,' the destiny of Rome, now at last (in 1870) the 'Rome of freemen.' Had Tennyson translated Virgil, as so often has been wished, he might have used the long trochaic metre of this poem, which has no little of the 'ocean-roll of rhythm' required. The English hexameter he derided. The lines *To Virgil*, no doubt, are the flower of Tennyson's commemorative lyric, perhaps of all his lyric. His nine monorhymes on Catullus, *Frater Ave atque Vale*, are akin to them; and, what is not easy, he manages to unite tenderness with resonance. The timbrel-tune of the *Attis* echoes in the galliambics of *Boadicea*,[1] as it was soon to do, also worthily, in the *Phaéthôn* of George Meredith. The alcaics on Milton are moulded on the Greek, not on the Latin type, and aim at its 'freer and lighter movement.' They too are distilled, and there is much of Milton in them; but why does the poet prefer the prettiness of a formal Eden to the 'roar of an angel onset'? Of the two translations from Homer into blank verse, the earlier, 'So Hector spake,' is the more magnificent, but *Achilles over the Trench* is nearer to Homer in its cast of language; and its style would have held out better for a prolonged experiment. On Tennyson's general knowledge and appropriation of the classics much has been written; enough to say here that, like Milton, he does not simply insert but incorporates his endless borrowings. In the last year of his life he 'enlarged for some time upon the greatness of Homer, quoting many lines from both the *Iliad* and the *Odyssey*.'

IV

The 'English idyll,' already written by Southey and Wordsworth, was an attempt to extend the lower limits of poetry; to see how near, without ceasing to be poetry, verse could approach in tone to the prose tale of humble life. Southey's *Hannah* is discouraging; but Wordsworth in his *Michael* justifies the experiment, as well as the use of blank verse in such a cause. Blank verse, certainly, is the metre in which prose can most cheaply pretend to be something not itself. The result is easy to detect when the subject is plainly poor or sterile, and the blank verse sinks accordingly; but is not so easy when the verse keeps its dignity, and reacts on the language, and raises the language above any pitch of feeling that can be warranted by the subject. The point of danger is approached in *The Brothers* by Wordsworth, but is just escaped; in a tale like the *Honor Neale* (1838) of Archbishop Trench, the line is passed and the effect is bathos and *pastiche*. What, then, of *Dora*, *Edwin Morris*, and *Walking to the Mill*? Wordsworth praised *Dora*, and Matthew Arnold charged it with false simplicity. The story, taken from Miss Mitford's *Tale of Dora Cresswell* in *Our Village*, is not unfitted for poetry. Tennyson, in telling it, puts a constraint on his natural style and seeks to be Wordsworthian and biblical. The simplicity is not spurious; the force of the story prevents that risk. What is wrong with *Dora* is that part of it is simply iambic prose. The use of verse is not fully justified. Such an effect may serve very well when the tone is light, as it is in the description of the pie in *Audley Court* or of the pack of cards in the *Prelude*; but then *Dora* is wholly serious. Verse on the lowest ledge of diction is agreeable enough, when it slips into satire like that on

> Slight Sir Robert with his watery smile
> And educated whisker,

or when it is interspersed with Tennysonian painting—

> While the prime swallow dips his wing, or then
> While the gold-lily blows, and overhead
> The light cloud smoulders on the summer crag.

The *minimum* style, as we may call it, is like this, when the tone is meant to be serious:

> So left the place, left Edwin, nor have seen
> Him since, nor heard of her, nor cared to hear.

These are three ways of writing; and if we add a fourth, in which Tennyson wrote reams, but in which he is never safe, the declamatory-passionate, like this—

> I choked. Again they shriek'd the burthen—'Him!'
> Again with hands of wild rejection 'Go!
> Girl, get you in!'—

—if we put all these together, with a touch of the speculative, or arguing style, thrown in, we are in sight of the 'medley' of *The Princess*, and of some of the elements out of which *Enoch Arden*, *Aylmer's Field*, and the rest are compounded. Here, as ever, the technique must not be judged absolutely or in the air, but in its relation to the subject; and in general, throughout Tennyson, we find that in his declamatory or spasmodic writing the technique is apt to get above the subject; for when the subject is inadequate the poet instinctively brandishes his rhetorical flail to sweep us off our feet. This drawback is felt most keenly in his blank verse. But then he saves himself when the tirades are truly dramatic in character; as they are in *Maud*, and as they are in *Locksley Hall*: a poem which is not only glorious in its cadence and its dreary landscape, but is also very frank and youthful, and engaging even in its absurdities; unlike that ineffective diatribe, *Locksley Hall Sixty Years After*, where little but the cadence is left.

Some of these observations apply to *Enoch Arden*, but there it is the treatment and the sentiment that inspire misgiving.

The tale as it is told is too good to be true. The old woman who called it 'that other beautiful tract' hit the mark. Every one is noble, no one is angry. There is not much real pulse in the poem, except, be it freely said, in the culminating passage, 'Now when the dead man came to life. . . .' But the little old water-colour village at the outset, and the tropical calenture in the middle, are painted faultlessly. The 'costly funeral' of Enoch has been censured as tasteless; rather, it is out of keeping, which it would not have been had Crabbe told the story, as we may wish that he had done. The *Enoch Arden* volume at first bore the title *Idylls of the Hearth*, which expresses its purpose well enough.

The shot silk fabric of *The Princess* is a delightful thing to hold up and turn over in various lights, in spite of the very considerable hole in the middle of it; by which I mean the confusion in the main idea. Well if Tennyson had kept the tale on the plane of high serious comedy, a kind of inverse of *Love's Labour's Lost*; if he had simply shown the women trying to rule out men from the scheme of things and defeated by nature, and the infant (whom Sydney Smith had said there was no fear of a woman 'deserting for a quadratic equation') playing its part in the story and the lyrics. The jest would then have lain in nature using so unimpressive an instrument as the Prince. As it is, the irony is on the wrong edge, for there must needs be a thesis, and that with the Prince for its expounder. The well-known speech, 'For woman is not undevelopt man,' contains some of the heaviest lines Tennyson ever published; but it is amiss rather in what it omits, yet seems to imply, than in what it says. The type of feminine excellence that it exalts does not leave much room for Emilia Belloni, or for Volumnia, or for George Sand. Tennyson judges more by preconception and theory than by life and the event of what women may do and hope to do if they are given free play. That remains to be seen. Nor did we need to be told what it is they can do which we cannot do at all, or that they always will and ought to do it.

This said, we can enjoy *The Princess* more freely. It was much revised and improved in successive editions.[1] The insertion of the rhymed lyrics in the third (1850) drew the poem together; that of the 'weird seizures,' or trances, of the Prince, in the fourth (1851) has been objected to as detracting from his consequence; but then he had little enough consequence already, and in an avowed medley one curious extra strand can do no harm. Topical allusions to the 'year of revolutions' are also put in. But the old admirable things all remained; the country house, the women's 'Academe,' the pictures, the lectures, the proctors, the daughters of the plough, the masquerade, the war. The style is precisely described by the supposed narrator, as lying in 'a strange diagonal' between what the men wanted, the 'mock-heroic gigantesque,' and the 'true-sublime,' desired by the women. For much of the time Tennyson is amusing himself over his own technique, whilst in the act of extending it, by frolics and experiments with his metre, but still more by playfully exaggerating one of his own faults, which is to deal in images rather beyond the occasion; as in the description of the lady 'Head,'

> Fixt like a beacon-tower above the waves
> Of tempest, when the crimson-rolling eye
> Glares ruin, and the wild birds on the light
> Dash themselves dead.

Altogether *The Princess* is distinguished, in Jeremy Taylor's words, by 'variety and load, and cost, and curiosity.'

V

From *The Two Voices* to *The Ancient Sage*, Tennyson is never long unoccupied with speculative verse—with what has been called 'the poetry of ideas,' argumentative, or rhetorical, or eloquent, or imaginative. He gave it new resources, he found a new style for it, he put, as we say, his weight into it. He inherits it, no doubt, from Wordsworth and Shelley, but his methods are not theirs. The varieties of this kind of poetry are well seen in *In Memoriam*; but Tennyson's first thesis in verse is found in *The Two Voices*. It is direct arguing, by plea and counterplea—a form he did not often use. The skill is signal; but the verse drones, and the end becomes an anticlimax, when the too quick despairer is dissuaded from suicide, strangely enough, by the sight of the citizen family (infant and all) going to church. I said above that *The Palace of Art* has 'a blind alley of a moral.' For the temper of artistic detachment and self-sufficiency there described is a purely fictitious one; it represents no known artist or theory of art; it is more like some of the once prevalent caricatures of Goethe. A mind, moreover, that could admire 'Plato the wise' and 'world-worn Dante' is not likely to 'lose sight of its relation to man and God,' as Spedding expressed it, altogether. The picture-gallery is in Tennyson's best manner, and happily its value does not depend on that of the thesis.

In *The Vision of Sin* the ruling idea, namely that satiety brings in its train not only impotence but malice, is by no means commonplace. The Mænad dance is magnificent, and we could wish that Tennyson had let himself go in this direction oftener. The old rake's lyric that follows suffers from the hammering, ranting vein into which the poet was so easily to fall. In the finale, the bronze-like ringing couplets are worthy of a more satisfactory conception. For the drift is left obscure at the last, and Tennyson's plea that 'the power of explaining such concentrated expressions of the imagination is very different from that of writing them' would not have commended itself, we may think, to Dante, whose underlying thought, however difficult, is always solid and presentable.

None the less, all these pieces disclose a new mastery, almost a new instrument; they do not leave the poetry of ideas where they found it; or at least they take it back to the great age, the age of the *Four Hymns* and of *Nosce Teipsum*:

> Much more, if first I floated free,
> As naked essence, must I be
> Incompetent of memory:
>
> For memory dealing but with time,
> And he with matter, could she climb
> Beyond her own material prime?

That is pure arguing, most deftly done; and the same gift is seen in the epigram of moral analysis, for nothing could be much conciser than this:

> Then some one spake: 'Behold! it was a crime
> Of sense avenged by sense that wore with time.'
> Another said: 'The crime of sense became
> The crime of malice, and is equal blame.'

But the real, distinctive note of Tennyson's philosophic verse is heard when he utters some prophetic vision, as in 'Love thou thy land' and the companion pieces that read like splinters of *In Memoriam*:

> Ev'n now we hear with inward strife
> A motion toiling in the gloom—
> The Spirit of the years to come
> Yearning to mix himself with Life.

This peculiar finish and concision, applied to subtle ideas, is not easily to be found in our poetry before Tennyson; and of these qualities *In Memoriam* is full. The lines on James Spedding's brother (*To J. S.*) have not quite this cast; and they are more simple and direct than most of the great elegy itself, and are not in its measure.

> Verlaine told me that he had tried to translate *In Memoriam*, but could not, because Tennyson was 'too noble, too *anglais*, and when he should have been broken-hearted had many reminiscences.'

So records a living poet;[1] and Charlotte Brontë had made a similar complaint against this 'rhymed, and printed, and measured monument of grief.' There is really nothing in it; it is a complaint that *In Memoriam* is neither a brief lyric nor yet a tragical, Shakespearian soliloquy. Tennyson *was* broken-hearted; in our 'reminiscence,' even if not otherwise, the dead live; and, whatever the speculative value of the poem, it records a great friendship. *In Memoriam* is more impressive than anything Tennyson wrote on the love of women. There is some direct arguing in it; and if we judge this to be, properly speaking, superfluous, since the final consolation and conviction rest not on reasoning at all, but on a mystical intuition which is good for those who have it and meaningless for others, still the reasoning is dramatically in place, for it shows the working of the poet's mind before the intuition came. *In Memoriam* contains some of his best, and some of his most dubious, writing.

Composed at intervals over long years, it was originally no preconceived whole, nor can it be called an artistic whole. The poet tries to make it such by arranging the numbers in an order which is not that of composition, and therefore not that of the moods and experiences related. Quite possibly the same is true of Shakespeare's *Sonnets*, as we have them. In both cases the result falls into certain internal groups, each bound together by its own idea, such as the consolations of friendship or the vanity of fame. But the different members of each group may belong to different times and occasions; and again, the ordering of the groups themselves may be part of the afterthought. All through both poems, meditations on man and the world, on beauty and conduct, and on the power of thought by its own energy to overcome distance or death, radiate out from the main theme, the friend's affection. The comparison need go no further. But the separate numbers, long or short, of *In Memoriam*, have the same kind of unity as the sonnets in an Elizabethan series; that is, they are mostly detachable and complete poems, yet are linked more or less closely with their neighbours, so that the whole has at any rate the semblance of unity; and this is enhanced by the unity of the metre—by the almost irresistible impression, or illusion, of a single atmosphere which a notable and powerful metre will produce in spite of great diversity or even disharmony in the contents. The argument and evolution of *In Memoriam* are intricate, and a brief summary will be unjust to it.

At first the poet is drowned in grief, and plays with it, and makes love to it, as if wearily, sinking into it deliberately, and pausing to cheat himself with sombre fancies. He follows the voyage of the ship that brought his dead friend back, and rethreads the course of the friendship. After many ebbs and flows of feeling he finds that grief is a true possession ; and he begins to found a kind of faith upon it. He finds in the mystery of life itself, and in that of love, some assurance of survival ; failing this, life itself would be a chaos. Then he has a gleam of hope that the dead may care for us ; he muses on the possible nature of the disembodied soul, and on how far it may remember its earthly affections. He revolts against the idea that the soul, after death, is at once absorbed in the Whole ; he judges, as a matter of blind faith, that evil may in the end somehow generate good, in spite of the indifference of Nature to man her chief product. Then follow reflections upon the value and quality of posthumous fame, which Tennyson, unlike the Elizabethans, but like Emily Brontë, holds lightly. At last, in the dark garden, he has the trance-like experience in which he believes that he communes with his friend. After this his love grows afresh, and widens out to include mankind, whose hopes and future occupy him to the calming of his grief. Love, now universalised, is seen to be the principle of human progress. Man's freewill, and the outlook of the race, form a foundation for hope. The epilogue, on the marriage of the poet's sister, is in accord with these aspirations ; the whole work being, as he says, 'a kind of *Divina Commedia*, ending in happiness.'

Thus *In Memoriam* is no simple elegy, but, like *Adonais*, is charged with the poetry of ideas. Its power lies, however, less in playing over ideas than in playing with the logic of feeling—in the analysis of grief and hope, of memory, and vision ; neither Milton nor Arnold have just this habit of mind. Tennyson knows that he does not *know* what he feels till he has shaped it into finished and lucid expression. And though some of *In Memoriam* is condensed to the point of darkness, it is, on the whole, a lucid expression of obscure feelings, not an obscure expression of confused thoughts. Nor, of course, is it all in this difficult style. The simple parts, the picture of the college friendship and of Hallam's character, are only touched with monotony by the metre ; and the sections describing the 'joyless day,' or the coming of spring, are, as to sound and colour, among Tennyson's triumphs.

The metre, the old 'closed' short-line quatrain, used by Ben Jonson and Lord Herbert of Cherbury, Tennyson did not borrow, at least consciously, from those authors. It has, however, an inherent ring of its own, as we see by comparing them all, and we may add Rossetti afterwards—a ring which persists, whosoever may use it. Tennyson, no doubt, gives it most of the variety of which it is capable : uses it for a kind of epigram, or for a long concerted paragraph taken in one breath, or for dream-narrative ; keeps it usually level and lineal, but on occasion breaks the lines or runs on the verses ; now going sweetly, now mustering all the shattering sounds that he can find. Some of these modulations are seen in No. CVII. :

> The time admits not flowers or leaves
>   To deck the banquet. Fiercely flies
>   The blast of North and East, and ice
> Makes daggers at the sharpen'd eaves,
>
> And bristles all the brakes and thorns
>   To yon hard crescent, as she hangs
>   Above the wood which grides and clangs
> Its leafless ribs and iron horns
>
> Together, in the drifts that pass
>   To darken on the rolling brine
>   That breaks the coast. But fetch the wine,
> Arrange the board and brim the glass; . . .

It is easy to find the sweet and fluent, or the grave and sententious, numbers in contrast to this. They are, indeed, everywhere.

VI

In Memoriam, the chief document for Tennyson's religious faith, is also typical of a certain phase of contemporary opinion. It shows, on one side, a great loosening of doctrinal bonds ; it is relatively liberal ; it is leagues away from, it makes dead against, that hardening of dogma which was the aim of the first High Churchmen. It attempts to embody poetically some of the conclusions, as yet but half-divined, of the science of the day. At the same time Tennyson forebodes the results of what has since been called 'naturalism' and was soon (1869) to be called 'agnosticism.' The poem, then, resolves itself into a plea against a negative, or neutral, view on the question of personal immortality, a plea founded in part on the deliverance of the writer's own heart, or of his mystical vision, and partly on the conviction that all the hopes of mankind are staked upon the issue. Without thus much faith, freed though it be from theological terms, he sees all other faith in the future of the world disappearing. How this train of thought appealed to some of the keener minds may be seen from the letter of Henry Sidgwick printed in the *Memoir* of Tennyson, and from the conclusion of his *Methods of Ethics* (1874, see Chap. IV. *ante*). The recorded conversations of Tyndall and others with the poet throw light on these debates.

Tennyson, then, and those who went with him, by no means represent the 'extreme right' among believers, but rather a kind of 'right centre,' which accepts a good many of the new ideas, but remains vehemently conservative nevertheless. Our record (Chs. III. and IV.) of those who sat more to the 'left,' such as Mill, Huxley, and Leslie Stephen, has already disclosed another point of view, which will appear again in George Eliot. It is needless to describe it again; but Tennyson did not study, or did not grasp, at least certainly never states, the full counterplea as put forward by his own contemporaries. But he has his place, and a prominent one, in the protest against the drift of naturalism; with Browning, he stands for the protest of poetry against it. One poet, however, 'Master Swinburne,' as Tennyson was heard to call him, was to express in a single piece, *The Pilgrims* (1871), an ideal of progress, achieved through union in self-sacrifice: an ideal which seemed still to remain all the clearer for mankind after it had lost, or had escaped from, the ancient faiths.

Tennyson rang the changes on the ideas of *In Memoriam* from time to time afterwards. His obscurest lines, *The Higher Pantheism*, seem to identify the outer world with deity, and to say that the spirit of man is only kept by its own blindness from seeing that identity, but that even this blindness may be got over in certain hours of vision. The reference may be to the personal experience [1] which is related by the poet both in prose and in the verse of *The Ancient Sage*, and which he could invite by

> revolving in myself
> The word that is the symbol of myself—

that is, his own name; and then

> The mortal limit of the Self was loosed,
> And past into the Nameless, as a cloud
> Melts into Heaven.

The 'Nameless,' the source of power and life, and the quest of vision, is not spoken of by the sage as having personality or consciousness ; it has no predicates, or it has all, according as we state the matter ; and so far it resembles Herbert Spencer's ultimate reality, the 'Unknowable,' with the salient difference that Tennyson thinks that it can, at moments, be really known. Whether this conception has a purely psychological interest, or has also a speculative value, is a further question. Tennyson manages to connect it with the moral counsel of the sage to the young pessimist who writes desperate (though excellent) lyrics, and also with his own faith in some kind of posthumous survival. The counsels themselves are obvious ones, put into sonorous language ; the young man is bidden not to dress finely, not to

> fold
> Thy presence in the silk of sumptuous looms,

as though to do so were heinous. The poem has been much admired, and is highly wrought, but has not much substance in it save for the description of the trance. In fact, we can say once more that Tennyson is sounder and more truly poetical the more he slips back from metaphysics into psychology or pathology ; and we can pass to the dramatic monologues which best show his power in that region.

VII

These are linked with his classical and also with his speculative poetry by *Lucretius*, the work in which he comes nearest the sublime, though it is the vehement sublime of *Macbeth* or *Othello* and not the controlled sublime of Milton. Many a strand of the *De Rerum Natura* is woven into it, in Tennyson's way, including certain passages betraying suppressed strain and fever, which do not indeed give the tone to the whole work but which justify the modern poet's treatment ; nor does scholarship altogether dismiss the legend as to the cause of Lucretius's death. Thus the disorder of images in the poem is all in keeping, and most of them are suggested by something in the original. The jostling of atoms and gods, of the Oread and the Hetairai, in the mind of the sick man is part of his malady ; and the nobly changeful blank verse reflects and harmonises the fluctuations between beauty and discord. *St. Simeon Stylites*, an earlier work more in Browning's fashion, is also an intense and sustained realisation of the subject ; but so fierce, and here so unvaried, is the tension, that the poem at last begins to deaden itself. And over the admired *Rizpah*, founded though it be upon a fact,[1] and great as is its energy a similar doubt arises ; for it runs off into the clattering passionate rhetoric that was Tennyson's weakness, and it does not suggest the natural speech of self-portrayal.

But in *Maud*, where the pathological soliloquy is tested hardest and longest, the rhetoric, when it comes, is really in keeping and essential to the speaker's character. The public, no doubt, forgot that the speaker was not the poet ; but there was something in its shrewd suspicion that the poet was often the speaker's accomplice. Certainly Tennyson could write, on his own account, very much like the hero of *Maud*, especially in his later works like *Vastness*. But a work of art must be judged as it stands, and all this does not really tell against *Maud*, of which Tennyson exactly describes the construction when he says that 'different phases of passion in one person take the place of different characters.' The story unfolds itself in a string of lyrics, each of them being a more or less independent poem, and each introducing a new moment in the situation, with its special mood, which is embodied in the metre. The return of the metre reannounces the mood. Slow sane iambs, hectic anapæsts, joyous trochees, and many birdlike or dirgelike short measures, form, in their succession and interwoven recurrence, a complete musical fabric ; one extreme being seen in 'Go not, happy day' and in the famous song of the rooks calling, the other in the long-breathed appeal, climbing and falling through a sentence of fourteen plangent lines, to the 'Cold and clear-cut face.' A full study of the prosody of *Maud*, considered as an index of emotion, might be the quickest way to the heart of the poem. The actual facts related, which are sometimes confusing, are cleared up by the notes, by no means superfluous, which the poet added.

The speaker is a *decadent*, a kind of Hamlet without the brains, and Tennyson never dramatised any personage so clearly. The language is that of an abnormal but actual man, and not the wonderfully patterned gauze of words that screens the Lancelots and Arthurs off from us. The novelists had essayed the speech of madness or distraction, sometimes with success, as in Hogg's *Confessions of a Fanatic* or in Maturin's *Melmoth the Wanderer*. Was Tennyson on his mettle to rival or surpass in verse the prose writers of the 'school of terror'? The insane musings of the slayer upon his deed are sometimes worthy of the best Elizabethan tradition—but a little more, and the vein might be that of Sheridan's Tilburina. In the end the narrator is cured, cured by the patriot passion of war, and is made 'one with his kind.' This, no doubt, was the hardest corner for the poet, and also for his critics, to turn. As a matter of psychology the change is natural enough, or at least is made to seem so. But it was here that the poet seemed to be speaking with his own voice. He does not, however, say, though he was rated for saying, that war is good in itself and will cure everybody. He does say that it may cure not only a hysterical youth but a stagnant nation. This idea was unpalatable to minds like that of Mr. Gladstone, who had no enthusiasm for the passion of war. And the war was the Crimean war, which was going on. Even those who approved of it hardly thought that it was a remedy for the evils declaimed at in the poem, of adulterated bread and slum violence. But this inconsequence perhaps might go to the account of the speaker, not of the poet. Altogether, *Maud* was puzzling, and was long and considerably disliked; its artistic qualities were obscured by the dust that it raised. It is really Tennyson's greatest and most genuine production of any length.

VIII

Like Milton and Dryden, Tennyson dreamed in youth of a great poem, epical or dramatic, with Arthur for the chief personage, and his knights around him. But they were all to be moral symbols. 'K. A. Religious Faith...the Round Table ...liberal institutions'—so runs an early note. This was before he had found the natural medium for such a task, his blank verse. He found it, we know, in the volume of 1842; but there, besides *Morte d'Arthur*, come the lyrics *Sir Launcelot and Queen Guinevere*, which is purely romantic and sympathetic, and *Sir Galahad*, which is ballad-like and direct, and, for all the appearance of the Grail, unmystical. *Morte d'Arthur* is set in a scrap of country-house idyll, which was to be shorn away, and another prelude made, when the poem became *The Passing of Arthur*. The style is the decorative-heroic; there is the conscious delight of a still young poet in full-vowelled sequences and consonantal clusters, harsh or sweet as may best serve. These ornaments overlay the simple words of Malory, which are closely followed as to the story; and another thing, the symbolism, begins to overlay them too. Ornament and symbolism often measure the distance of Tennyson from Malory's book or from the *Mabinogion*, the sources of *Idylls of the King*. The ornament is intricate, while the expression of the allegory is often plain enough, however it may be with its meaning.

The poetic idea in *Morte d'Arthur*, while an exalted one, is not so single-minded and effective as it is in *Ulysses*; for the Round Table is but an '*image* of the mighty world,' whereas Ulysses is a person, not an image, though he is also the incarnation and voice of a certain heroic instinct.

In 1856, with *Maud* behind him, Tennyson returned to his Arthurian venture. He began by applying to it a craft, namely the portraiture of women, in which his friend Millais was skilled. He printed privately *Enid and Nimuë*,[1] *or The True and the False*—an Edgeworthian contrast afterwards dropped from the title. In the volume of 1859, *Idylls of the King*, Nimuë is called Vivien, and *Elaine* and *Guinevere* are added. The style is revised and heightened, and the more colloquial touches are weeded out; the Theocritean 'idyl' becomes the heroic 'idyll.' The manner, a not always stable compound of dignity and felicity, is now established. This volume has a symmetry and foursquareness which are absent in the ultimate twelve poems as a whole. The allegory is still faint; there are four tales, four types, four different but not inharmonious frames of mind. The portraits are not all equally good. Vivien cajoles and spits and rails, but remains a description rather than a woman. Arthur, in *Guinevere*, is scarcely a copybook man (as is usually said), but rather the wrong sort of man; all too real, as a pompous lecturer is real. William Morris, in the year before, had published *The Defence of Guenevere*, the book which includes *King Arthur's Tomb* and *The Chapel in Lyones*, poems that owe something to Tennyson's early lyrics. But we have only to compare, to see what Tennyson is not going to give us:

> Must I now prove
> Stone-cold for ever? Pray you, does the Lord
> Will that all folks should be quite happy and good?

Put that beside this:

> Ah, great and gentle lord . . .
> To whom my false voluptuous pride, that took
> Full easily all impressions from below,
> Would not look up . . .

What Tennyson, for our happiness, will give us, what no one else can give us so well, is this:

> She saw,
> Wet with the mists and smitten by the lights,
> The Dragon of the great Pendragonship
> Blaze, making all the night a steam of fire.

Or this—

> But, ever after, the small violence done
> Rankled in him and ruffled all his heart,
> As the sharp wind that ruffles all day long
> A little bitter wind about a stone
> On the bare coast.

Felicity, colour, singularity, magnificence, these we get in delightful abundance. They are all to be found in *Enid*, which was cut later into *The Marriage of Geraint* and *Geraint and Enid*, and in *Elaine*, afterwards called *Lancelot and Elaine* ; but there is something more too. The tale of Enid, drawn from Lady Charlotte Guest's *Mabinogion*, is not only a lovely one, but mediæval in the best possible sense ; it has, says a critic, 'none of the ineradicable falsity of the story of Griselda' ; and the poet, however much he may decorate, keeps to it in spirit and incident. Its sustained note of devotion and pathos may rank it even above *Elaine*, where such qualities are somewhat obscured by the lengthy jealous rhetoric of the Queen ; nor does anything in the story of Astolat come so nearly home as the ending of *The Lady of Shalott* :

> But Lancelot mused a little space ;
> He said, 'She has a lovely face ;
> God in his mercy send her grace,
> The Lady of Shalott.

The Holy Grail and other Poems (1869, dated 1870) included *The Coming of Arthur*, *Pelleas and Ettarre*, and the reset *Passing of Arthur* ; in 1871 followed *The Last Tournament*. The cycle was now announced as complete, but in 1885, in the *Tiresias* volume, came the afterthought, *Balin and Balan*. In the last recension (1888), the order and text of the *Idylls* were finally given as we now have them, after a long succession of changes. This order, then, is very different from the order of composition, the first idyll written being now the last. Tennyson has been criticised as though no result thus attained could be artistic. But if it be not artistic, the to-and-fro nature of composition need not be at fault, but rather the character of the enterprise. We can see how the additional idylls made this more difficult.

They are made at different times, and are various in key, and are the harder to fit into a harmonious whole. *The Coming of Arthur* is a rather desperate attempt to bind together in advance the already existing idylls. One problem is to make the magical environment of Arthur accord with his abstract and idealised character. This difficulty is felt most at the conclusion ; for how, we ask, should such a half-modern, half-symbolic person as Arthur has now become *deserve* to disappear to Avilion? And the curse that hangs over his origin is equally lost upon such a personage. The best poetry in *The Coming of Arthur* is found in the lyric, and in the dream of Leodogran; and of course there is much splendour in the detail.

In *The Holy Grail*, which Tennyson truly called 'one of the most imaginative of my poems,' the great passages of Malory—the girding of Galahad, the passing of the Grail through the hall of knights, and the visit of Lancelot to the chamber whose breath was like a furnace—are transported without loss of keeping, for all the infusion of colour and of exalted meaning. Tennyson is true to mediæval sentiment; no one can say that here he confounds purity with respectability. On the contrary, the flying, holy, crimson lights that shoot through the poem are but the outward sign of the active passion, transcendental and supreme, for purity itself, as the virtue was mediævally understood. The opening picture of homely monkish life and talk is not less genuine. From Malory also came the hint for the idea that the quest for the Grail betokens the break-up of the goodly fellowship; few of the knights prove worthy of that quest; and these shadows become darker in *Pelleas and Ettarre*, with its notes of scorn and faithlessness and the final execration of Pelleas as he flings away into the dark. *The Last Tournament*, which gives the bitter ending of the tale of Tristram without any of the preceding rapture, is in a like strain. In *Balin and Balan*, which in the final arrangement comes as a prelude to *Merlin and Vivien*, there is little of the uplifted spirit and lofty pathos which attends the progress of the brothers, 'in life and death good knights,' through Swinburne's *Tale of Balen*. It is a pity that Tennyson had to discolour these two great stories in order to suit them to his picture of social degeneracy. But the prose argument [1] that he dictated of *Balin and Balan* makes no small amends. *The Passing of Arthur* concludes the whole; and we can now look back on the representative, or allegorical, aspect of the *Idylls of the King*. The allegory, which was in the poet's mind from the first, comes out more as he proceeds, and it is in at the death of Arthur.

Tennyson preferred never to press it, or to make it quite clear; he leaves it suggestive rather than formal. It exhibits 'sense at war with soul'; the code of the Round Table ordains a certain pattern of conduct, chivalrous and pious, in which self-sacrifice, bravery, and purity predominate, and which is proclaimed and vowed. The actors are the knights who obey or disobey this rule, and the women who inspire or discourage them. In time, the cardinal Christian virtue is betrayed by the noblest knight and noblest lady, though not without a remorse which intensifies to the point of repentance. Modred, Ettarre, Vivien are foremost in the scene. Arthur, who as in Spenser binds together all the virtues, is left and dies. It is a tragedy; but, as in Shakespeare, the world is to begin again after it, with the prophecy of a new hope and order. Further than this Tennyson's intention need not be driven; but we have his own words for his faith, the faith which alone, as he believed, can survive any spectacle of the kind:

I have expressed there [in *The Holy Grail*] my strong belief as to the Reality of the Unseen. The end, when the king speaks of his work and of his visions, is intended to be the summing up of all in the highest note by the highest of human men. These three lines in Arthur's speech are the (spiritually) central lines of the *Idylls*:

> In moments when he feels he cannot die
> And knows himself no vision to himself,
> Nor the High God a vision.

Here Arthur is real because he is Tennyson, and not the Prince Consort or another; and the passage that follows in the *Memoir* (ch. xxvii.) shows how this was Tennyson's indefeasible conviction: 'You never, never can convince me that the *I* is not an eternal Reality, and that the spiritual is not the only true and real part of me.'

This is modern-philosophical, not mediæval; and the first proposition is also just the opposite of what a Buddhist would affirm with equal certitude; but whatever we may think of it philosophically, Tennyson has here travelled furthest from his material, and we have to ask how, after all, the symbolism in the *Idylls* will consent to join itself to the story. It does not join; the attempt is a failure, in spite of all the points of genuine contact with mediæval feeling; but the failure is more interesting than most successes; the allegory does not do much harm, and there is always the handiwork to fall back on. The *Idylls* remain idylls, separate poems, interlaced by a hundred threads, with their incongruous elements half-hidden by the execution. Their poetic virtues are those of Tennyson's work at large. But they add profusely to his account, more than any other of his long poems. Their faults delighted their public. Their chief and central weakness is their treatment of passionate love, which is immensely talked about, and also considerably scolded, without ever being allowed to show itself frankly and simply.

But the pictures, the 'interiors' and pageants, the epic similes, which contain some of Tennyson's best observation, the songs, the fresh and subtle prosodic effects, are hard to exhaust. And there is grandeur, not once or twice only, though there is also sometimes the mere imitation of it. And if, not content with imitations, or approximations, or beautiful dexterities, we insist, in taking leave of the *Idylls*, on Tennyson doing his utmost for us in the way of grandeur, this is the kind of poetry we shall think of :

> Then in a moment when they blazed again
> Opening, I saw the least of little stars
> Down on the waste, and straight beyond the star
> I saw the spiritual city and all her spires
> And gateways in a glory like one pearl—
> No larger, tho' the goal of all the saints—
> Strike from the sea ; and from the star there shot
> A rose-red sparkle to the city, and there
> Dwelt, and I knew it was the Holy Grail,
> Which never eyes on earth again shall see.

IX

Tennyson's lyrical gift spans the sixty years of his production. It is not equally active all the time, but comes and goes like a frequent rainbow. It is heard in description, satire, and many other kinds of verse that are not lyrical in themselves. It gets into narrative, not only of the ballad-type, but such as we find in *The Voyage of Maeldune*. It also sometimes gets into the blank verse. The rhymeless lyrics in *The Princess* fall into stanzas, and some of those in the *Idylls* go into triads, with an echo or refrain that recalls the bell-ringer's craft. The same overflow of the lyric faculty occurs everywhere in Swinburne, because he cannot help it ; in Tennyson it is a deliberate use of surplus power.

His lyrics properly so-called, including his songs, share in the general characters of his poetry—its close texture, its consciousness, its studious management of sound, and its usual, though by no means universal, leisureliness of progress. He does not always go slow, as *The Brook*, *The Voyage*, *The Revenge*, and *The Defence of Lucknow* prove in various ways. In the last two of these weight is added to pace ; the waves come high as well as fast, and the troughs are deep between. All four are triumphs of execution ; and what Tennyson does in them is to make English more like Italian, and to circumvent as much as may be the inherent abruptness and knottiness of our language. He is justly famed for the riches and cunning of his vowel-sequences, in which he seeks variety as well as resonance, and for his avoidance of hiatus and conflicting sibilants, and of harsh sounds generally except for a purpose. No one could have written so well, for an English *De Volgari Eloquentia*, the chapter where Dante distinguishes the words that are severally 'glossy,' and 'combed-out,' and 'rumpled.' This kind of skill is best seen and is most wanted in lyric, where sound and substance have to be most nearly blended, because it is here that the substance is least able to excuse or carry off any failure in sound.

He does not, in this province, owe much to any other poet, though we can point to things that other poets might have admired as congenial to themselves. 'The splendour falls on castle walls' might have been envied by Scott as a great thing somewhat in his own style; and the embodiment of hardly wordable feeling in 'Tears, idle tears' would have come home to Shelley; 'the passion of the past,' Tennyson called it, saying he had often felt the like in his childhood. Of the classical lyrics, ode-like or commemorative, something has been said already. Tennyson is possibly more at home in these carefully concerted pieces, be they short, or long with full rolling lines, than in the briefer spontaneous kind; and I have also remarked on the rather exceptional occasions when he attains to, or rather is visited and possessed by, the note of perfectly natural song. The list could be enlarged, of course; we could add the overture to the *Wellington* ode, the first verse of 'Come not, when I am dead,' and other things. Tennyson seems to have felt, however, that these visitations were rare, to judge by his language about Burns and the Caroline singers: 'I would give all my poetry to have made one song like that!' And we can, if we like, measure the rest of his lyric by its distance from this kind of effect. Many of the numbers of *In Memoriam* move lyrically, but their elaborated harmonies, like the alcaics on Milton, are at the opposite pole to song. The patriot narrative chants, of a type that Tennyson more or less invented, are naturally much more direct, yet rather in the way of high oratory, which is not satisfied with any instrument but the most sonorous. *The Revenge* and *The Defence of Lucknow*, both in uniform measure, are examples. In the latter of these the lines are shorter and choppier, and the tension is sharper accordingly, as befits the more terrible nature of the doom, which here threatens women and children and not men only. Still, amongst Mutiny poems, there is perhaps a still sharper suspense in Christina Rossetti's little piece, *In the Round Tower at Jhansi*; and Sir Alfred Lyall's Indian poem, to be noted hereafter, hits hardest of all. *The Voyage of Maeldune*, which is again most highly wrought, leaves behind it a glorious confusion of imagery, as it is meant to do, and it is a great feat, being a lyrical story which is charged with description and yet is not thereby retarded. *The Charge of the Heavy Brigade* is also one of Tennyson's most expert lyrics, though it is rather too cunning in modulation to gain all the suffrages for which it was written.

X

Three of Tennyson's dramas fall, as to subject and spirit, into their place beside his patriotic poems: these are *Queen Mary*, *Harold*, and *Becket*; he wished to produce a series of 'history plays' on reigns which the Elizabethans had left untouched. The Shakespearian inspiration is plainest in *Queen Mary*, the earliest of the seven. But the best parts of it are still Tennysonian and pictorial, like the scene where the younger Wyatt muses over his father's sonnets, or the description of Lady Jane Grey at the block. It is difficult to fill the stage with the character of Mary; her fanaticism, her bewailing of her barrenness, and her passion for Philip are traits that encourage Tennyson's old style of vehement and rather tiresome rhetoric. This, in fact, is his danger all through his plays; and it is not the kind of style that holds the theatre, though it is the supposed needs of the theatre that prompt him to fall back upon it. Thus in *Queen Mary* we feel that Tennyson's strong brain is struggling with an inappropriate form of writing which comes easy to him. But in *Harold*, which was not acted, there is much poetic flame, and the tragic clash of characters, moving towards a predestined end, is conveyed with power; and moreover Tennyson is content with his own style, and makes the utmost of it, not drawing here particularly upon the older drama. The chiming snatch of Edith, 'Love is come with a song and a smile,' is like one of the interludes in *The Princess*. *Becket*, the last of these chronicle plays, was the most successful on the boards, though Tennyson almost despaired of such success; the pageantry, the acting of Sir Henry Irving, and the swiftness of the action, which is little troubled by curious writing, all helped it. Tennyson's long struggle for a dramatic style is better rewarded in *Becket* than elsewhere; but he hardly got free of the habit of tirade, which is essentially of the *Aylmer's Field* order, though it is now transferred to a greater scene.

The romantic plays are rich in poetry ; except *The Promise of May*, with its invented seducer-epicurean-unbeliever ; of this work, least said soonest mended. In *The Cup*, on the other hand, not only is the execution beautiful, but the story is sound. It is called a tragedy, but there is no tragic struggle of motive in it ; it is a short story of righteous vengeance in which both avenger and victim fall ; as simple as a ballad, but decorated with all Tennyson's lifelong skill. The streaks of good nature in the deeply-dyed murderer Synorix are indeed not made credible ; but the light falls full on the radiant figure of Camma who feigns to accept marriage with him, the slayer of her husband, in order to punish him and die with him at the altar. The play is a new kind of 'Hellenic,' a species of poem in which Tennyson had first proved his power more than forty years before. The little scene called *The Falcon*, versified from Boccaccio's tale, is a worthy pendant to *The Cup*, in point of handiwork, though the falcon itself is the only sacrifice ; and *The Foresters* is pleasant.

XI

Books have been written on Tennyson's distillations of the poets, on his management of description, on his political and social ideas, and on his 'teaching' at large. One should be written on his use of words, by some poet of the same stamp. Every one sees his general mastery of them, and also his tricks and obvious gestures of style—such as his use and abuse of the *kenning*, or pictorial description of something that is not called by its own name. 'The word that is the symbol of myself' ; 'the chalice of the grapes of God' ; 'the knightly growth that fringed his lips' : these differ from the old Germanic habit of language, in Anglo-Saxon or Icelandic, because they are longer, roundabout phrases and not mere compounds like the 'surge-floater' or the 'ring-dealer.' But they are due to the same desire to secure dignity, richness, and variety. And there is the further aim of expressing a peculiar sort of beauty, or iridescency of phrase. This occurs especially in connexion with colour :

> But on the damsel's forehead shame, pride, wrath
> Slew the May-white.

Or thus :

> and glowing round her dewy eyes
> The circled Iris of a night of tears.

Such examples are endless; but they blend into the poet's general mode of figured speech, which in his heroic and mock-heroic blank verse spreads out into formal simile of the traditional sort, but more often simply turns to packed vivid metaphor. And if we do analyse the result, we never come on generality or vacancy, but always on something which is first substantially seen or definitely heard, and is then patiently brooded on until the image of it is realised in the predestined words. Tennyson, no doubt, misses the effects that are won by a happy gambling with words, which are flung down for the stake of all or nothing. Such is Browning's way, and his luck in such things is immense:

> Ah, see! the sun breaks o'er Calvano;
> He strikes the great gloom
> And flutters it o'er the mount's summit
> In airy gold fume!

This is not smooth, but it gives an instantaneous vision of the scene. The other method of showing a sunrise, the method of 'the faultless painter,' who waits until all is quite right, is seen in such lines as

> Far furrowing into light the mounded rack
> Beyond the fair green field and eastern sea.

Tennyson's own letters and remarks supply the best notion of this admirable way of working; and when he seemed forced or surprising he always knew the facts behind better than his critics. He remembered when and where he had seen the 'slow-dropping veils of thinnest lawn,' or had heard the wind

> shake the songs, the whispers, and the shrieks
> Of the wild wood together.

In this kind of work Tennyson, so far from being open to criticism, supplies a standard of rightness behind which no one need try to go. The new thing, however, is his peculiar notation, which seems the more his own the more we compare him with any previous poet, be it Keats or another. Its characteristic is a condensation which is only limited by the law of beauty, and the effect of which is always to make the pace of the poetry slower, encrusting the line as it does with gemwork that we have to stop and study, and lending itself, in respect of sound, to a rich crowding of stresses and musical consonants. Thus the imagery does something to determine the cast of the actual versification; and so does Tennyson's habitual compression of his thought, and his careful exploration, in his speeches, of all the resources of rhetoric. To all this the simplest clue is found in a study of his metres [1]; on which excellent chapters have been written, though the subject might fill a small volume. Something has been said of it here in connexion with his lyrics ; and on his main achievement, his blank verse, one remark must serve.

It is, for good and ill, the most conscious blank verse in the language, of any written by a master ; more conscious even than Milton's ; for Milton, intensely as he studies his form, forgets himself more often than Tennyson does in the passion or exaltation of his subject. If this seems too fine a point, let the reader compare *Ulysses* or *Tiresias* with one of the greater speeches of Satan. And we, in these matters, are led by the poet ; *we* too think, in the measure that he does, more of the manipulation and less of the thing said. This is why Tennyson seldom leaves us wholly free to think simply of what he is saying ; and though the remark applies in a measure to all his verse, it applies less to his lyric than to his meditative verse, and most of all to his blank verse. Yet, if this drawback be once reckoned with, and if we also accept, as a general habit, the comparative slowness of his movement in verse, we can then follow the changes and modulations of his blank line, and of his concerted paragraphs, with the pleasure that he designs for us. Much technical statement, which would be out of place here, would be necessary for a full description. The illustrations already given from the English idylls show one or two varieties of his heroic line in its lighter uses ; and of these the great repertory is *The Princess*. The more impassioned dramatic monologues disclose, naturally, a wider range of effect ; and, for a single example, *Lucretius* may be taken as Tennyson's most surprising feat as an executant. In his dramas he seeks to push yet further beyond the ordinary limits of the metre ; there are, by the way, some unusual experiments, including a four-syllabled foot, with a hypermetrical close, and only three full stresses in the line :

> That you may feéd | your fán | cy on | the glór | y of it.

But it is impossible to begin so long a story : let the student think how much there would be to say on the verse-craft of the following four separate lines, to go no further :

> 'The sword rose, the hind fell, the herd was driven.'
> 'Melody on branch, and melody in mid-air.'
> 'Camelot, a city of shadowy palaces.'
> 'Immingled with heaven's azure waveringly.'

Or let him go through the prolonged complex sound-pattern of *Love and Duty*, with its passionate vibrations, from the technical point of view.

Tennyson commanded a style and a music adequate, we may think, for the great poems which he never wrote. They would have been a noble raiment for ideas which never reached him, and are sometimes too good a raiment for the ideas which he expressed; and it is doubtful if this is a fault on the right side. But he had many noble ideas too, not necessarily philosophical, but poetical, ideas; and he arrayed them perfectly. Perhaps the conceptions embodied in his classical poems, such as *Ulysses* and *Tiresias*, wear the best of all. And he invents a new style, an admirable one, for the expression of many strange but real feelings; of these *Maud* is the chief monument. And, as we have seen, he can sing; now and then simply, more often not so simply but still with a wonderful trained voice of much compass. Tennyson is the chief poet, during the nineteenth century, of the tribe to which belong Milton and Gray—and, let us add, his own master, Virgil.

XII

The sonnets of Charles Tennyson [1] (1808-79), who assumed the surname of Turner, number three hundred and forty-two, and are formally distinguished by the great freedom and suppleness of their rhyming schemes, always within the limit of the fourteen lines; and by the natural and imperceptible character of such metrical heresies, which do but follow the movement of the feeling. Great suavity, ease, and simplicity, and a constant and reticent sense of beauty, mark the verse of Tennyson Turner. He is best when he sings, in what he calls the 'quick-spent' sonnet, of small and shy matters; he has a Cowper-like preference and affection for them, though like Cowper he strays now and then into uncongenial declamation. For much of his life he was a parson in a lonely village on the wolds, in what is still one of the unspoilt and unadvertised parts of England. Alfred Tennyson gives the solitude and solemnity of these regions, and their roomy horizons with 'the rounding grey.' Charles Tennyson Turner gives their gentler, homelier aspects and 'old ruralities,' and sings of the April day, the harvest-home, the 'thaw-wind,' the light on the gossamer, the steam threshing-machine, even the 'scarecrow, or malkin.' He is none the worse when he shortens his quiet and pious morals and keeps to description :

> Upon the golden aconites I look'd,
> And on the leafless willows as they waved—
> And on the broad leaved, half-thaw'd ivy-tod,
> That glitter'd, dripping down upon the sod.

Tennyson Turner's range, however, is not a small one ; his sonnets are a diary of his sympathies, travels, and reading. There are children's little themes, the rocking-horse and the dead pet bird ; Wordsworthian notes, like that on the *Moselle Boatman and his Daughter* ; bolder things, well ventured, like *The Lion's Skeleton* ; Greek and Roman memories, with the praise of him

> who set his stately seal
> Of Roman words on all the forms he saw
> Of old-world husbandry ;

and with the beautiful imaginative meditation on *The Lachrymatory* ; and that on *The White Horse of Westbury*, which comes to life and relapses into chalk. There is much else ; Tennyson Turner well merited his brother's praise, and that of their friend Spedding and of Coleridge ; his verse is a relief after the heavily charged and intricately wrought sonnets of another school ; and his extreme modesty and aversion to emphasis cannot prejudice his position.

The verse of the eldest of the brothers, Frederick Tennyson (1807-98), has less definite character than that of Charles, in spite of the manifest force and accomplishment which impressed FitzGerald and other contemporaries. His classical poems, and the blank verse in which most of them are written, are in no sense an echo of the Laureate. But there is a want of concentration in his work. Sometimes, in his earliest independent volume, *Days and Hours* (1854), the inspiration is rather that of Shelley :

> When the poet's heart is dead,
> That with fragrance, light, and sound
> Like a Summerday was fed,
> Where, Oh ! where shall it be found,
> In Sea, or Air, or underground ?
>
> It should be a sunny place ;
> An urn of odors ; a still well,
> Upon whose undisturbed face
> The light of Heaven shall love to dwell,
> And its far depths make visible.

In *The Isles of Greece* (1890) Frederick Tennyson builds up, on the basis of Greek lyrical fragments and traditions, a series of Hellenics centring in the figures of Sappho and Alcæus, under such titles as *Apollo*, *Phaon*, *Myrsilus*, and the like. There is no want of dignity, or of accurate scenery and costume, but the total effect is rather cold. More classical tales followed in *Daphne* (1891); but Frederick Tennyson, publishing as he did so late, just when criticism was beginning to turn even upon his overshadowing brother, won little note; and even apart from such disadvantage, never seems to have attained to finally memorable form.

CHAPTER XIV

THE BROWNINGS

I

IRRITABLE men of letters like Landor and Carlyle found to their relief that Browning[1] was unlike themselves, being in common intercourse hearty, and normal, and unperturbed; a man who might have done well in law or diplomacy or any strong-headed profession. There was even a fancy, latterly, that he had somewhere a private genius, or dæmon, who did his verses for him. In the Eighties, when many intellectual persons were adoring and explaining[2] him, society remarked on his easy suit of chain-armour, which kept the earnest souls at a courteous distance. This mundane behaviour was no mere defence in Browning, but well in keeping with his peculiar talent.

For it suits his thirst for hard and real situations, for history and Newgate annals, for the story of forgotten people 'of importance in their day'; in whose company, as in all companies, he moved so readily; they might be painters, thinkers, musicians, dreamers, politicians, fighters, lovers—especially lovers. However intricate and spiry a fabric he may raise, he likes to feel the firm rock beneath him, and to quarry out of it. Andrea del Sarto, and Pompilia, and Ned Bratts, and Miranda in *Red Cotton Night-Cap Country* had really existed in some such shape as he presents them. When he draws upon fiction and legend, for Ivàn Ivànovitch or Caliban, his aim is similar; it is to preserve keeping; he refuses to be untrue to the story and its associations. And when he invents, it is in the same spirit again; he wants to produce the illusion of fact and not the illusion of dreams—to be *right* about situation and motive, just as if he had history behind him. All this means a wide acquaintance with the big world, past and present, real and imaginary. Browning is a man of the world in this considerable sense of the term. He has been compared with some reason to a novelist; but he is more like a critic who tries to recover the features of past or alien minds and to recreate them faithfully. This too is the way of Walter Pater, otherwise so unlike Browning. The aim is to portray the spirit of Fra Lippo or Leonardo, of Marius or Karshish, in all its windings, in its setting of circumstance : the man in his habit as he lived. Browning makes the man speak for himself, always in some testing and critical situation (as Pater, indeed, points out) ; in his poems there is none of the stillness of the *Imaginary Portraits* ; and the procedure, though perhaps not more difficult than the exquisite analysis of *Emerald Uthwart* or *Gaston*, brings us noticeably nearer to life. Once more, it has to be asked what Browning made of this gift, and into what moulds his invention fell.

The career of Robert Browning (1812-89) falls into some half a dozen acts or phases, which may be thus abbreviated :

(1) 1833-40.—First appeared *Pauline*, *Paracelsus*, and *Sordello*, the early long poems, full of confused wealth, but cast into shapeless and prolix forms which are plainly inadequate to the poet's talent. There is also the first of Browning's plays, *Strafford* (1837). (2) 1841-46.—Next appear the eight numbers of *Bells and Pomegranates*, six of which contains dramas : namely *Pippa Passes*, *King Victor and King Charles*, *The Return of the Druses*, *A Blot in the 'Scutcheon*, *Colombe's Birthday*, *A Soul's Tragedy*, and *Luria*. Browning is now in the full tide of theatrical and other society, and has formed many friendships ; but no contemporary writer, except his wife and possibly Carlyle, was ever to influence his genius. The plays are not exactly plays, but they show his genius clearing up magnificently ; and in other two numbers of *Bells and Pomegranates* (No. iii., 1842, and No. vii., 1845) his true territory, the shorter poem, is disclosed. (3) 1850-64.—Browning's married life (1846-61) is the golden age of his talent and his happiness. During this period the spell of Italy is at its strongest, and it continues afterwards. His correspondence, followed by his acquaintance, with Miss Barrett begins early in 1845. He writes another long work, *Christmas-Eve and Easter-Day* (1850). In 1855 come the two volumes of *Men and Women*, the 'fifty poems finished,' with their *One Word More*. The contents, as will appear, were later distributed under other titles. Both happiness and sorrow now seem to check Browning's productiveness ; but the *Dramatis Personæ* of 1864, the first volume produced after his bereavement, heightens his honours. (4) 1868-9.—On *The Ring and the Book* Browning stands or falls as a master of the long poem ; it extends to over twenty-one thousand lines. (5) 1871-78.—The scale is still generous though not so vast.

The works that follow are said to mark a decline in art, but this is only half-correct. The brains doubtless begin to overpower the poetry; but there is a blessed new store of poetry, as well as of analytic and narrative gift. This period may be thus subdivided: (*a*) Three volumes, *Balaustion's Adventure* (1871), *Aristophanes' Apology*, and *The Agamemnon of Æschylus* are Greek in theme; the first two each contain, and the third consists of, a translated play. (*b*) Two disquisitions in metre, *Prince Hohenstiel-Schwangau* (1871) and *Fifine at the Fair* (1872), precede two criminal stories in blank verse, *Red Cotton Night-Cap Country* (1873) and *The Inn Album* (1875); and in 1878 comes *La Saisiaz*, a return to theology, with the narrative *Two Poets of Croisic*. In *Pacchiarotto* (1876) Browning is already reverting to the shorter poem, and to this form he now remains faithful. But (6) in the two series, 1879 and 1880, of *Dramatic Idyls* he refreshes in a striking way the old pattern of the 'dramatic romance.' Four volumes remain, each with its own unity and colouring. These are *Jocoseria* (1883), *Ferishtah's Fancies*, *Parleyings with Certain People of Importance in their Day*, and the posthumous *Asolando* (1890). Here the good and great things may be sparser, but there is the old range and much of the old savour; Browning's lyric force is never quenched; and, however much he may break the customs and even the laws of poetry, he is never safe against his own genius; some clues to which may now be indicated.

II

Shelley,[1] the 'Sun-Treader,' had only been ten years dead when Browning, a youth not yet of age, produced his *Pauline*, in which the vague flush of imagery and the fervent faintness of outline betray the ruling influence. Long afterwards, in 1852, Browning described the poet who had thus quickened his fancy. Shelley, he says, ranks high amongst those prophetic spirits, of the 'subjective' kind, who do not merely delineate life and their own minds in terms that appeal to mankind at large, but who see all things transcendentally. Such a spirit

is impelled to embody the thing he perceives, not so much with reference to the many below, as to the One above him, the supreme Intelligence which apprehends all things in their absolute truth,—an ultimate view ever aspired to, if but partially attained, by the poet's own soul. Not what man sees, but what God sees—the *Ideas* of Plato, seeds of creation lying burningly on the Divine Hand—it is towards these that he struggles.

So, Shelley's 'noblest and predominating characteristic' is

> his simultaneous perception of Power and Love in the absolute, and of Beauty and Good in the concrete, while he throws, from the poet's station between both, swifter, subtler, and more numerous films for the connexion of each with each, than have been thrown by any modern artificer of whom I have knowledge.

This indeed is 'seeing Shelley plain'; and we may guess that some such ambition came to be Browning's own—namely to interpret this earthly show of 'men and women,' with their mental histories, in the light of that loftier reference; so that he remained, at bottom, a theologian, though a theologian *sui generis*, to the end. In the same essay he recognises that the 'subjective' and 'objective' elements may be variously mixed in one man; and in himself they were thus mixed. His religion, or theodicy, colours his whole reading of life, and interpenetrates (to use a word of Shelley's own) his dramatic and lyrical studies. We may, then, safely expect to watch this union of elements as we pace once more the long gallery of Browning's works.

In *Paracelsus* the drawing is firmer, and the execution often splendid to the point of extravagance. But the whole is ill-shapen and diffuse, and afterwards Browning could have packed it all into a few hundred lines. For one thing, the outer chronicle of the real Paracelsus, a true herald of medicine and chemistry despite his philosophic fantasies, is swamped by the fatally allusive style of narrative; nor is it clearly connected with the mental drama which is the true subject. Paracelsus aspires to know nature and God, and to help mankind. But mankind rejects him, and he is baffled, and dies after long struggle and delirium. Browning's ideal strain is already loud and clear, and there is remarkable richness in the lyrics; yet all is unrelieved and superabundant. Knowing the event, in *Paracelsus* we can now foresee the writer of *A Death in the Desert* or *Easter-Day*, but not the writer of *Pompilia* or of *Caliban upon Setebos*.

Few genuine poets have insulted art more strenuously than Browning does in *Sordello*. With an effort, the story [1] can be made out; for the thing has been done. But no commentary and no undeniable oases can redeem *Sordello*. Dante, who had set the figure of the poet-patriot in the clear immortal light of his *Purgatory*, inspired Browning, but failed to instruct him. Browning buried himself in the obscure history of the time, interwove it with the spiritual drama, treated it with all license, and so hid away Sordello himself in a dense thicket of allusion. Sordello is another baffled aspirant, with his hungry mind fixed on all life and knowledge for its prey. At last he perishes in a conflict between love and ambition. The conception deserves a better fate ; but in spite of the flashes of beauty that flit over the scene whenever Palma, Sordello's love, appears, the poem suffocates itself.

III

Like Tennyson, Browning was a persistent ' maker of plays,' but was never to conquer the theatre. *Strafford* was staged by Macready, *A Blot in the 'Scutcheon* by Phelps, and *Colombe's Birthday* by Helen Faucit ; these pieces and more have been revived by enthusiasts. But the question to-day is how the eight dramas read, and not how they act. In each one of them can be found dramatic material and dramatic moments ; none of them lack life, or poetry, or Browning's natural nobility of accent. Yet hardly one, unless it be *Colombe's Birthday*, is a satisfactory poem. They all show Browning working his way through drama towards monodrama, which is his real field ; and in which he was meanwhile triumphing by the way. Play-writing disciplined his talent and taught him his method.

Strafford is full of energy ; and though it begins barely and drily, the poetry and pathos assert themselves in the final scenes, where Strafford listens to the singing of his children before he finally loses faith in his worthless master. The historians repudiate Browning's Pym, who distracts the interest and whose speeches little justify the awestruck allusions of the other characters to his voice and presence. Still we can see why Macready hailed the work, in the lean years of the drama. Next came *Pippa Passes*, whose lyrical charm, whose tragical force, it may seem insensate to resist. Browning, no doubt, must have all the honours of his conception, which is unique. The little holidaying mill-girl, as we know, lets herself dream that she is each in turn of ' Asolo's Four Happiest Ones ' ; passes the window of each, singing, at some critical instant in the fates of those within ; awakens, being thus overheard, the remorse or resolve of each overhearer, so changing all the issues of their lives ; and, on the last occasion, likewise saves herself, unawares, from an infamy contrived against her, and goes to sleep singing. It must be said that four distinct conversions give us some pause ; as for one or two, let them pass, and Pippa with them. But we are to think that the child's song would perturb a remarkably tough and horny Monsignore while he is engaged with his blackguard agent in a game of mutual blackmail. No doubt we are outside the world of fact all the time; but here there is something too hard a clash between the worlds of criminal fiction and of didactic idyll. It is true that in the most tragic scene of all, the 'bright-infernal' dialogue of Ottima and Sebald (which reminds us of Thomas Middleton's dramas), the poetic reason is convinced; for we are already well prepared for the violent revulsion of Sebald from his paramour, 'magnificent in sin'; and Pippa's singing, quite credibly, turns the scale.

In the plays that followed Browning practised many styles; now, in *King Victor and King Charles*, tracing tortuous intrigue and policy, in language very curt and stripped and also far too allusive; now, in *The Return of the Druses* (a much plainer story) bursting into impassioned Eastern figure, and striking out lines that flash like the sword of Anael or the tiara of the Hakeem; now, in *A Blot in the 'Scutcheon*, improvising a poor violent plot which repels the judgement, and for which the verse, often sweet and moving, is far too good. The young Tennysonian English girl, Lady Mildred, has been betrayed by the young Earl Mertoun; who, loving her nevertheless truly and wishing to make amends, next courts her openly, with the approval of her family; but still, incredibly, visits her window in the night. He is seen by her heroic brother Tresham, who kills him in duel; Mildred dies, Tresham poisons himself. Browning disdained to invent any such story afterwards. Very different is *Colombe's Birthday*; he has left no drama better poised or plotted, none in which the threads of romantic and chivalrous interest are more nicely interwoven. It might be called a political idyll. The verse is unusually simple and beautiful, and the various styles of poetic eloquence well match the speakers—Colombe, Duchess of Cleves and Verviers, threatened with expulsion under the Salic law; Berthold, the claimant, ambitious and unscrupulous, capable of magnanimity but not of love; and Valens, the advocate of Cleves, the winner at last of the Duchess in reward for his loyalty and self-denial.

Next came two plays of historical cast but not founded upon history. In *A Soul's Tragedy* there is excellent prose, spoken by the legate Ogniben, who is a sort of pocket Machiavelli; and there is also one of Browning's favourite studies in slippery character. But there is not enough in Chiappino to bear up the interest. He is man enough to be ready to die for his friend Luitolfo by shouldering the guilt of Luitolfo's tyrannicide, but not man enough to forgo the profit when the crime proves to be glorious and popular. In *Luria*, despite the number of long-winded speeches, there is far more substance and imagination. Luria is one of Browning's more heroic figures, and as well matched with his adversary Tiburzio, as Shakespeare's Coriolanus is with Aufidius. He has the passionate loyalty of the East ; his magnanimity is coldly used and betrayed by the city of Florence, which he has saved. Her treachery breaks his heart and he takes poison. He is in truth done to death by the snake Braccio and the tigress Domizia, who is bent on revenging her dead brothers upon an innocent man. There is a certain deliberate splendour about the language of this play, and in more than one passage can be heard the larger Elizabethan style ; with a difference indeed, but hardly mistakeable :

> Oh world, where all things change and nought abides,
> Oh life, the long mutation—is it so ?
> Is it with life as with the body's change ?
> —Where, e'en tho' better follow, good must pass,
> Nor manhood's strength can mate with boyhood's grace,
> Nor age's wisdom, in its turn, find strength,
> But silently the first gift dies away,
> And though the new stays, never both at once.

IV

From the first it must have been clear to the wise, though not to most of the official critics, that in all these dramas and lengthy works there was much ore, and that only crushing and refining—only that, but an infinite deal of that—was required ; and also that Browning, in his shorter poems, had achieved the process already. Quite early he had begun to find the right shape for his compositions. Shape mattered even more than style, because it usually carried style along with it. In 1836 had been printed the two poems called *Madhouse Cells* ; the first of them being *Porphyria's Lover* and the second *Johannes Agricola in Meditation*. The former would have pleased Baudelaire ; and Browning was always to like a clinical subject. From his vantage-ground of healthy sense he reached out a hand of lively sympathy—dramatic sympathy—towards villainy, crime and craziness of all kinds, the more curious and piquant the better. Herein, by the way, lies the strength of his much-deplored ' optimism ' ; for the faith that could survive the task of creating the alchemist in *The Laboratory*, or Guido Franceschini, or the ' elder man ' in *The Inn Album*, is proof against anything ; and such a writer cannot be accused, like the sentimentalists, of not facing the worst. However, in his early days Browning is less often pathological than he is lyrical and romantic.

It is clear now, though it was less clear at the time, how safely English poetry had been re-established by Tennyson and Browning by the year 1845. The third and seventh bunches of *Bells and Pomegranates* [1] comprise but thirty odd lyrical or narrative poems, none of them lengthy. Many of Browning's future powers and interests are here nobly represented. The lyrics are not all stories, but the stories are all 'lyrical ballads,' mostly of a novel kind. Novel, because of the poet's inveterate way of giving an extra turn to the ethical screw. He must have a problem in casuistry ; must dissect the behaviour of a man in some crisis that is just too strong, or just not too strong, for his moral resources. This habit of mind is seen in *The Glove* ; where we are told that 'Peter Ronsard *loquitur*' ; but that poet would hardly have picked the story thus to pieces, or have urged that a true lover would never have thought twice about the wanton offence of his lady in sending him into the lion-pit after her glove ; nor would he afterwards have married the knight unhappily to a king's leman, and the lady happily to a page. This kind of question Browning was to canvass more sternly in his *Dramatic Idyls*.

Two other characteristics are prophesied in the thirty poems. First of all, Browning gives a fresh turn to the old romantic and rebel mood of impatience. Anything to be free ! *The Flight of the Duchess* is an expression of the longing for escape which is heard in *Youth and Art*, or in the tale of Jules and Phene. Go off to the gypsies, like the Duchess, or to a garret and live on love, or to 'some unsuspected isle in the far seas !' Go with your mate, your lover, and damn the consequences, for 'God 's in his Heaven !' There is something of Blake in this ; and there was plenty of wild sap in the youthful Browning, who himself ran off with his wife, most successfully. The refinements of a deep and serious union, the 'silent silver lights and darks undreamed-of,' are subsequent ; Browning is their poet also. Secondly, these early pieces deal much in the grotesque. *The Boy and the Angel*, with its pure kind of Tennysonian beauty, is exceptional. And the grotesque, whether it minister to the sublime, or to the picturesque, or simply to irony, is naturally signalled by the metre. Browning's acrobatic skill in queer rhyming, without which he would have missed some of his worst failures and his greatest successes, must have encouraged his turn for the grotesque. It is purely impish and childlike in *The Pied Piper of Hamelin*, the story of which he found in his father's library, in Wanley's *Wonders of the Little World*. The scene has often been painted, but the rhymes cannot be painted. The *Soliloquy of the Spanish Cloister* exhibits, like the *Memoir* of Mark Pattison, the uncouth and fearful joy of monastic or academic hatreds. *Sibrandus Schafnaburgensis* is pure fun, while *The Englishman in Italy*, though not exactly grotesque, is homely and joyous, with a joy like that of treading the wine-vat, and the rhymes lift it easily into the higher strain. *The Flight of the Duchess*, with its somersaulting verses and its tumbles into rank imagery, is Browning's greatest feat in the grotesque, prior to *Caliban upon Setebos*; and the grotesque, be it noted, implies not absence of form but precision of humorous strangeness in form; and it need not exclude, though it is content to do without, the beautiful.

Some of the pieces in *Bells and Pomegranates* cannot be classified. *Waring* is all pictures and no story, a lyrical fantasy prompted by the writer's memories of his friend, Alfred Domett, himself a poet worth reading. Domett's [1] *Ranolf and Amohia, A South-Sea Daydream* (1872) contains some subtropical scenery and idyllic passages of a simple beauty. But Waring also embodies, once more, the desire for escape with no certain bourne in view. The other items of the two volumes might be set in a kind of scale, according as they approach more or less closely to pure song. The resurgence of English lyric is assured in *The Lost Mistress*, in *Meeting at Night*, and in 'Nay, but you who do not love her.' The *Cavalier Tunes*, *Through the Metidja to Abd-el-Kadr*, and *How they Brought the Good News* are without subtleties; they are all drums and horse-hoofs, and are all magnificent. In *Rudel to the Lady of Tripoli* the verse advances soft and smooth like the ship that bore the dying troubadour to his lady. Heine had already touched the story, and Carducci [2] was to tell it again (1888); but our reluctant language, which could yield the cadence of

> The far, sad waters, Angel, to this nook!

is not overmatched even by the vowelled Italian:

> —Contessa, che è mai la vita?
> È l'ombra d'un sogno fuggente.
> La favola breve è finita,
> Il vero immortale è l'amor.
>   Aprite le braccia al dolente.
> Vi aspetto al novissimo bando.
> Ed or, Melisenda, accomando
> A un bacio lo spirto che muor.

V

After four years of silence Browning in 1850 produced *Christmas-Eve and Easter-Day*, his fullest though not his final confession of faith. It was the year, too, of *In Memoriam*; and a few years earlier Marian Evans had translated Strauss's *Leben Jesu*, and Newman had published his *Development of Christian Doctrine*. For once the backwash of contemporary thought reached Browning. Though packed with curious lore, he seems to have had no special training in the philosophy of his own or other times. Philosophy? To him philosophy and religion were all but the same, and in this, if in little else, he was mediævally-minded. His imagination was now touched by these extremes of religion which he knew best, the Protestant in its densest vulgarity, and the Roman at the summit of its ritual. To neither of these is he bound, and his reason reacts against them both; but he asks what is their common measure and saving element, and finds it in the principle of love. But love is absent, or only a phantom, in the cult of the German professor, the high mild enthusiast, who worships the critical destroying reason and leaves the divinity and almost the reality of Christ a myth. Browning writes as if there could be no religion of love or 'humanity' outside the Christian pale. *Christmas-Eve* is a poem of curious mark and workmanship. The three scenes of the chapel, the basilica, and the lecture-hall, in which the grotesque and the sublime are variously blended, are bound together, partly by the reasonings, and partly by the vision of Christ, who guides the speaker, either in the body or the spirit, through the journey, and upon whose figure his final faith and love converge. In the end he gets back to the chapel, and is left joining humbly in the hymn. The pictures of the moon-rainbow and of the mass are among Browning's greatest. That of the meeting-house is in the most vivid of doggerel, and this element is allowed to infect the whole work. Much of *Christmas-Eve* is religion in Hudibrastics—with many a touch, it is true, of *Christabel* thrown in. *Easter-Day* is in level short couplets, with hardly a touch of oddity, and with one burst of splendour—the vision of judgement that gives the key to the poem. In the main dialogue two nameless speakers argue and instruct each other; it is not too clear whether they express the poet's own conviction or a more or less dramatic mood. The tone is not catholic and comprehensive as in *Christmas-Eve*, but exclusive and austere. Even the soundest joys of earth and the highest thoughts of man are subordinate to the single-minded service of God. Yet these solicitations of humanity, it is conceded, are steeped from the first in the principle of love; for they too are 'service.' For the later forms of Browning's theology we turn to *Rabbi Ben Ezra, A Death in the Desert, Abt Vogler*, and *La Saisiaz*; and there, though essentially the same, his faith and 'optimism' are less rigidly exacting. The bareness, or blankness, of style which marks many of them is prefigured in *Easter-Day*.

VI

In that Monte Cristo cave-treasure, the volumes of 1855 entitled *Men and Women*, all Browning's former gifts and themes reappear, now greatly enriched and varied. Every poem in them would deserve, but shall not here receive, a review. Classification, too, is difficult; nor can Browning's own be pressed. The *Men and Women* of 1855 consist of the 'fifty poems finished' together with the dedication *One Word More*. But these, in 1863, were combined with the non-dramatic pieces taken from *Bells and Pomegranates*, and the collection thus formed was sifted out under the three classes of 'dramatic lyrics,' of 'dramatic romances,' and lastly of 'men and women' in the narrower sense. Only twelve poems (afterwards increased by one) now bore that title, most of them being dramatic monologues which are neither primarily lyrical nor narrative. But the distribution could not be strict; nor does Browning's poetry ever fit well into departments. *My Last Duchess* figures among 'romances,' but it belongs to 'men and women' every whit as much as the *Epistle* of Karshish. *Mesmerism* and *The Last Ride Together* are also called romances, but if a romance must be a story, they have not much story. The lyric *Rudel* is placed, on the other hand, amongst the twelve 'men and women.' I shall not keep to Browning's classes, but only seek to trace one or two of the patterns that run through the whole shining fabric of his verse up to this date.

His deliberate queerness, to begin with, is as rampant as ever, and it has to find fresh excuses for existing. In *Holy-Cross Day* it is a foil to the solemnity of the concluding march. In *The Heretic's Tragedy* it is there chiefly to enjoy itself—an excellent reason. In *A Grammarian's Funeral* the grotesque is used in the service of grandeur. The rhyming feats (*cock-crow, rock row*; *fabric, dab brick*) echo the broken step of the climbers, and also their recital, half-defiant, half-affectionate, of the dead scholar's purposes, in the world's eye so puerile. The poem presages the gaunter style of *Dramatis Personæ*, and the Grammarian ennobles the gospel of minute 'research' as surely as George Eliot's caricature of it in her Mr. Casaubon leaves that faith piteous and futile. The doggerel in *Old Pictures in Florence* denotes, I suppose, a snap of the fingers at the world's forgetfulness of the good obscure painters who have thought only of the work and not of the praise. And in *A Pretty Woman* half the bitterness against the soulless beauty of the lady would be missed, without the touch of oddness and the slippery dexterous dactyls :

> Shall we burn up, tread that face at once
> Into tinder
> And so hinder
> Sparks from kindling all the place at once ?
>
> Or else kiss away one's soul on her ?
> Your love-fancies !
> —A sick man sees
> Truer, when his hot eyes roll on her !

These effects are not rare in Browning's love-poetry, which is endless in variety, and in which he breaks away from all tradition. No abandoned romanticist, he well knows, like Johnson and Shakespeare, that 'love is but one of many passions'; his grammarian, his rabbi, his saints, stand outside love in the ordinary sense. Still, his own hopes for mankind, and much of his religious faith, are heavily staked upon his gospel of love. Were that to prove illusory, what would be left of the 'optimist'? Once, late in life, in *Ferishtah's Fancies*, he shivers at such a possibility :

> Only, at heart's utmost joy and triumph, terror
> Sudden turns the blood to ice : a chill wind disencharms
> All the late enchantment ! What if all be error—
> If the halo irised round my head were, Love, thine arms ?

This is only a mood ; Browning seldom betrays a doubt about the revelation of love, a subject on which he muses with all possible sympathy and curiosity, concerning himself with strange cases and conjectures, and like Meredith returning to the notion that love is not only man's chief happiness but his chief ordeal. Some of these poems are rapidly flashed pictures, like *Meeting at Night* and *My Star*. Some of the most deeply considered give the feminine point of view ; in *A Woman's Last Word* and *Any Wife to Any Husband* there is the tone of piercing sadness and resignation. Some turn on a favourite idea, the capture or loss of the mystical moment, the one chance, by which the union of spirits may be sealed. In *Cristina* (1842) the chance is caught but lost again, as it is in *Two in the Campagna*. In *A Lovers' Quarrel* it is triumphantly recaptured. In *The Statue and the Bust* it slips away through cowardice; in *Respectability* the world is defied and happiness gained, through courage. *By the Fireside* reveals the secret won: 'the forests had done it'; and this poem may reflect, as *One Word More* avowedly does, a personal experience. Browning did not love only in verse, or by dramatic sympathy; much of his best writing of this kind dates from his married life. In *Love Among the Ruins*, one of his securest masterpieces, the sight of the old relics, and the vision of the dead fighters and charioteers, do not (as in some poem of Mr. Thomas Hardy's they might, just as convincingly, do) lay a cold hand on the lover; but they make his happiness seem the compensation ('Earth's returns') for those departed splendid vanities.

These love-poems, now more than half a century old, last perfectly well. They have no model, they are all quite different, and their handicraft is usually consummate. They are 'concise and perfect work.' There are rough edges to them, but there is no untidy dust or surplusage; and they sound, despite the poet's peculiar idiom, like natural speech; verse propagating verse, as it does in Shakespeare, and the poem never seeming to be thought out beforehand. Browning likes to invent measures, especially curt abrupt ones, which have this air of unstudied impassioned speech shaking itself without effort into rhyme:

> When I sewed or drew,
>   I recall
> How he looked as if I sung,
>   —Sweetly too.
> If I spoke a word,
>   First of all
> Up his cheek the colour sprung,
>   Then he heard.

More intricate are the fervent and lovely chimes of *Women and Roses*. But at whichever end we begin, whether with the impassioned thought or with the technique, we reach the same point of fusion between them. How often we are launched on the music of Swinburne and reach no thought at all, and how often, by the later Browning, we are launched on the thought and find no right expression for it! But that is no matter, when he has left us the 'fifty poems finished.'

Most of the thirteen pieces finally styled *Men and Women* are in blank verse, which is of no uniform pattern. Joyous and free in *Fra Lippo Lippi*, it is faint and dreamy and loth to finish in *Andrea del Sarto*, while in *The Bishop Orders his Tomb* it is broken and tessellated. Blank verse is a kind of standard medium for the dramatic monologue, a form in which Tennyson and Rossetti and others excelled, but of which Browning is the master. It is an exacting form, because it has the air of a speech taken out of a play ; but then there is no play, and the speech itself has to tell the whole story, and also to reveal the character of other persons beside the speaker ; and it has, finally, to sound natural. In *Andrea del Sarto, called 'The Faultless Painter,'* which is all silver-grey and pathos, this feat is accomplished. Andrea is resigned at once to the doom of a too perfect finish in his art, and to the faithlessness of the wife-model whose love, had it existed, might have made of him a Raphael. *Cleon*, a new kind of 'Hellenic,' in which the verse is remarkably stately and finished, has its pathos too, and its problem : Can the pagan artist, in his old age, live merely on his fame, and also on his sharpened sympathy with the youthful life which he cannot, in the flesh, enjoy ? Cleon dreams of 'some future state revealed to us by Zeus,' and has heard of the insane doctrine on the subject preached by one Christus and one Paulus, who are perhaps the same person. A similar idea is developed in *The Strange Experience of Karshish*. Here the Eastern scenery and detail are given with extraordinary gusto, and the 'transformation of all values' in the mind of the risen Lazarus is described in Browning's subtlest style. One of the most finished of these monologues is *How it Strikes a Contemporary* ; it is intensely coloured, and every stroke tells ; and above all it is short, like *My Last Duchess*. The 'contemporary' is the man in the street at Valladolid ; what 'strikes' him is the figure of a poet, a kind of Browning, who sees everything and says nothing, and who becomes the legend and (unlike Browning) the terror of the place. The full savour of the verse is felt in lines like these :

> We merely kept a governor for form,
> While this man walked about and took account
> Of all thought, said and acted, then went home,
> And wrote it fully to our Lord the King
> Who has an itch to know things, he knows why,
> And reads them in his bed-room of a night.

Bishop Blougram's Apology is mostly written in a style which does not encourage, though it does not quite exclude, poetry. Blougram is the half-believing cleric who builds an argumentative house of cards in order to warrant his retention of his stall and his 'sphere of usefulness.' The figure is partially modelled on that of Wiseman,[1] who reviewed Browning in the *Rambler* and dealt him a *coup de patte* which rather misses its mark: 'If Mr. Browning is a man of will and action, and not a mere dreamer and talker, we should never feel surprise at his conversion.' The poem is too long, and anticipates the pedestrian blank verse of the poet's later years, and also his fondness for presenting the sophistical case on the lips of an ambiguous or shady personage. All these, he says, are 'utterances of so many imaginary persons, and not mine'; all, that is, except the *One Word More* addressed to his wife, a poem written in London, but Italian in scenery, and moulded, for once, upon the pure line and colouring of Italian verse.

VII

In *Dramatis Personæ*, which came out in 1864, three years after Browning's bereavement, there is a sharper irony, a harder realism, and a higher grandeur than before. The language is stiffer and more elliptical; there are more monosyllabic lines, harsh knots of consonants, and jingling internal rhymes. These devices, which became the prey of the parodist, are used mostly in the interest of bitterness, just as Shakespeare's 'puns,' on the lips of Queen Margaret or Lady Macbeth, give the effect of a mock grin or *rictus*. The more cheerful variety of this style is seen in *Dîs aliter Visum*, thus:

> A match 'twixt me, bent, wigged and lamed,
>   Famous, however, for verse and worse,
> Sure of the Fortieth spare Arm-chair
>   When gout and glory seat me there,
> So, one whose love-freaks pass unblamed.

This maturer form of Browning's grotesqueness recurs in *A Likeness*, in *Youth and Art*, and in the Morgue-poem *Apparent Failure*. Another variety of it pervades *Mr. Sludge, the Medium*, in which the poet relieves his mind of his cherished disgust at the practices which had impressed Mrs. Browning. The poem would bear separately reprinting to-day (1920), when there is a recrudescence of Sludge. In *Caliban upon Setebos*, a religious satire, eccentricity of form is used in yet another spirit, and the effect is so good as to make us forget that Shakespeare's 'monster' is not eccentric at all, but acts and thinks quite naturally, according to monster-law. Browning's grotesquerie, however, is usually well employed ; it is like some odd-shaped cactus, full of bristles, and more expressive than beautiful, but sometimes breaking, for the benefit of the connoisseur, into a morbid, red, and startling blossom. The most highly wrought poem of this class is *James Lee's Wife*, a series of nine monologues, addressed to the fickle husband, all *staccato* in diction, but all charged with beauty and pathos. None of these poems is theological, except *Caliban*. *The Worst of It* and *Too Late* are purely human and dramatic. Others partly depend for their value on the argument.

And in one of these the argument is monstrous. *Gold Hair: A Story of Pornic* tells of the Breton girl with the wonderful tresses, massed by her own hand so strangely on her deathbed and by her request interred with her untouched. A piece, it might seem, of touching vanity ; but no, one of the Seven Sins was behind it ! The coffin, opened long afterwards, was found to be full of gold coins which had been hoarded in the hair. 'Why I deliver this horrible verse ?' inquires the poet of himself. Why, because the Christian faith, which had been recently attacked in print, was the first or the only faith that 'taught Original Sin, The Corruption of Man's Heart.' Monstrous, I repeat. Such a conclusion requires at least the sin of a Judas or a Guido Franceschini to plead for it. Browning, well as he tells his tale, tells it like any naïf old priest—not, indeed, like the priest in the poem who built an altar out the proceeds of the coffin-gold. The spectre of nineteenth-century criticism also haunts, rather unfairly, the last hours of St. John, in *A Death in the Desert* ; but that poem is a noble statement of Browning's conception of human progress, as at once limited and advanced by the conditions of this life. The turn of the language often recalls Tennyson, as we feel in such lines as

> Stung by the splendour of a sudden thought

or

> Like the lone desert-bird that wears the ruff,

and in the stateliness of the whole movement of the verse.

With Swinburne's *Hertha*, Browning's *Rabbi Ben Ezra* is perhaps the greatest metaphysical poem of his generation. Its power lies in the expression of a lofty austere ideal by means of a series of dazzling and glowing images. The wisdom of age recovers the poetry though not the pulse of youth. The loss of youth and of its joy is repaid by an increase of vision, and of the power to use the memories of youth for the ends of the soul. Life has lasted long enough for the Divine Potter to finish the cup that he is moulding ; and therefore, 'let death complete the same':

> Look not thou down but up !
> To uses of a cup,
> The festal board, lamp's flash and trumpet's peal,
> The new wine's foaming flow,
> The Master's lips aglow !
> Thou, heaven's consummate cup, what need'st thou with earth's wheel ?

Music is yet another avenue to the apprehension of goodness and beauty ; this idea is set forth in *Abt Vogler*, with its heavily undulating harmonies, in which Browning's powers of lyrical execution are seen at their utmost pitch. The whole volume, *Dramatis Personæ*, marks the summit of his speculative verse, just as the volume of *Men and Women* shows to the full his mobility and humanity. But his power to compose a big poem, dramatic in quality though not in form, is tested for the first and last time in *The Ring and the Book*.[1]

Browning had already produced many wonderful short pieces and some unsatisfactory long ones. He had written of love and religion, of painting and music, and of Italy. He had enlarged the scope of the poetical-grotesque. He had played at his ease upon the instrument of blank verse for the purposes of narrative, description, and reasoning. Where, then, should he display all these powers and interests at once, and uncramped, and on the greater scale ? Where find what Tennyson had failed to find in Arthur, and what Morris was almost to find in Sigurd, a subject that was not only great in itself, but great for *him* ? Was he only to be remembered for those wonderful short things ?

VIII

Browning, at any rate, was sure that he had found his subject in the little 'yellow book' describing the old Roman murder case of the year 1697. The book is a sheaf of documents partly in print and part in manuscript. They are in Latin and Italian, official and unofficial, pro and con ; a chance-collection of papers, precious but incomplete, made by somebody, and in no other sense a book. One other pamphlet, outside this sheaf, Browning found and used also. The broken-down Count Guido Franceschini of Arezzo, after committing many other villainies, murdered his wife Pompilia, aged seventeen, and her parents the old Comparini couple. In defence he urged her adultery (the appearance of which he had himself contrived) with the priest, Giuseppe Caponsacchi, who in fact had helped her at an earlier date to fly from the house of torture; an affair dealt with indecisively in a previous lawsuit. The 'book' contains the pleas and counterpleas of counsel; summaries of evidence on either side, including oral depositions by Pompilia, Caponsacchi, and others; the official sentence on Guido, who was duly convicted, and, upon the rejection of his appeal by Pope Innocent the Twelfth, executed; and further, some irresponsible unsigned tracts written on behalf of either side. This was Browning's lump of ore; and in one of his liveliest pages he tells how he found it on a Roman bookstall, mused on it, moulded it, refined it, and after four years of labour spurted on it the final acid, so driving out the alloy,

> Till, justifiably golden, rounds my ring:

—the Ring, which receives its 'posy' of dedication to his 'lyric love,' now for seven years lost to him on earth.

The old book gives the story from sundry points of view; which the poet increases to eleven or twelve, weaving in hundreds of scattered details from the record. But he finds that neither in book nor poem can such a story, or any story, ever be truly told. Not the passionless Pope, not the author, can ever say the last word. The eleven versions offered are all colourable, but they are incompatible. So we see that truth is elusive—that is, man's truth; only by walking round it, by watching facet after facet of it, can we see, and then in outline, God's truth, concerning that far-off Newgate episode. This eternal truth is, indeed, roughly recognised by human justice, and countersigned by the official deputy of God upon earth. But again; such justice, though it may do its work at the time, cannot restore Pompilia, nor can it keep alive her memory, which is buried away in the old yellow papers. So it is for the poet to requicken the story; and had art, he thinks, ever a rarer enterprise—art, which does not simply republish, but which also illuminates? Such appears to be the train of thought that led Browning to invent his peculiar method. Henry James [1] sketched the story of *The Ring and the Book* as a possible novel, with Caponsacchi for the central figure; it remains for some one to conceive it as a play. It would be, I think, a play in which prose and verse were mingled.

For six out of the eleven narratives are prosaic in their very intention; they are on the strictly mundane level, giving the gossip of Rome, or else the bare lawyer-facts of the case as discoloured by lawyer-rhetoric. The sections entitled 'Half-Rome,' 'The Other Half-Rome,' '*Tertium Quid*,' and 'The Book and the Ring' are built up from the scattered documents; while the speeches of the two counsel are taken, often verbally and consecutively, Latin tags and all, from their originals. The employment of verse for this kind of work raises curious questions. No doubt it is the verse that carries us through, where prose might have wearied us—*quod lucro ponatur*, as Dominus Hyacinthus might have said; but then the result is neither poetry nor prose, but something between, with rights of its own certainly, but yielding a mixed kind of pleasure. One of the depositions, that of the serving-maid who describes the horrors of Guido's household, is put into the level kind of verse afterwards used in *The Inn Album*. Perhaps the true justification of this method is the picture which is built up before us, touch by touch, of the hard old cruel Roman world, with its jokes and flying scandal and its taste in oratory, and which also serves for background for the redeeming figures of the girl and the priest and the Pope.

There remain the speeches of these three, and also the two speeches of Guido. The yellow book, which is mostly bare enough in its diction, shows unusual feeling when it comes to chronicle the witness borne by those who saw Pompilia's last hours. These persons were greatly moved by her patience and goodness; and here, perhaps, is the germ of the poet's exalted reading of her character. Pompilia's own deposition in the 'book' is a plain tale told with dignity; she just lives long enough to tell it, and dies leaving her infant of two months behind her. She had heard, she depones, that Caponsacchi was a 'resolute' man, and had gone to him as a last hope. Browning said that he had found all of his Pompilia 'in the book.' In fact, he embodies everything in the book—her childish shifts and rages, her drugging of Guido and drawing of the sword upon him; but he also softens and glorifies it all; with some loss, it may be, of the convincing effect of the real Pompilia's story. More safely, he widens her vision and intelligence out of all recognition, making her love for the unborn or just born Gaetano the mainspring of her action.

He also invents the purged and spiritual love between Pompilia and Caponsacchi, by which an average light ecclesiastic is turned into a St. George or a Perseus. The description of this new birth of Caponsacchi, when he first sees Pompilia with her 'great, grave, griefful air,' standing at her window, is one of Browning's achievements. The unlettered Roman girl becomes the voice of his ideal conception of marriage, which is so often expounded by him, but never in simpler or higher terms. As for Guido, he does not speak at all in the yellow documents, except through the lips of partisans and lawyers. Here, then, Browning was unfettered. Still, the sophistry of Guido's first oration in the poem is quite in keeping with the facts. Nor is there in the yellow book any word uttered by the Pope; there is only his signature. In the poem he reviews the case, confirms the sentence, makes his own last account with heaven, and becomes the spokesman of something like Browning's own theology. He also becomes by the way a considerable satirist and poet. He shows plenty of irony and scorn before he reaches, not too soon, his superb coronation of Pompilia and of the 'warrior-priest.' He becomes, in truth, Dantesque:

> Such denizens o' the cave now cluster round
> And heat the furnace sevenfold; time indeed
> A bolt from heaven should cleave roof and clear place,
> Transfix and show the world, suspiring flame,
> The main offender, scar and brand the rest,
> Hurrying, each miscreant to his hole: then flood
> And purify the scene with outside day—
> Which yet, in the absolutest drench of dark,
> Ne'er wants a witness, some stray beauty-beam
> To the despair of hell.

The whole poem culminates in the Pope's last words; he sees no chance for Guido save in some unlikely miracle that may bring him to 'see, one instant, and be saved.' But Browning's next great stroke is to risk an anti-climax and also escape it, by following at once with the second speech, the great eruption, of Guido, now condemned, a lost but shameless soul. The old document assigns a much more edifying end to Guido, but the poet will have none of that. Then, with another deliberate drop, he adds a satiric epilogue; but at the end he recovers, and delivers his mind on the vital mission of the artist, the ring-maker, the truth-refiner, such as he has tried to prove himself. Once we grasp this bold and successful arrangement of the sections in *The Ring and the Book*, we can imagine no other.

When all is said, it is one of the best, and not merely one of the strangest, poems of the last century. It is not in the Latin taste; the architecture is too eccentric, the ornament is too profuse and whimsical for that. Our ancestors would have called it a Gothic production. But we must leave Browning his own plan. His true subject is the contrast between Heaven and Hell, with the world's voices clamouring all around them and confounding their borders. And his performance, at its best, is very high; the language soars up, or rages down below, without ceasing to be the voice of humanity, or of poetry.

IX

Browning, now enamoured of the long verse *apologia*, practised it steadily for some years more. He became for a while a kind of metrical Balzac. He much admired the creator of Vautrin and of Louis Lambert. He has the same interest in crime, and in ambiguous characters, and in genius that is very nearly mad. He has just as strong, though not so gross, a digestion; he worships goodness when it comes, but he likes to let a scoundrel put his case and make his points. His optimism and idealism are always ready to break in, and though the result is not always poetry, still poetry is always breaking in too. In Balzac its place is taken by a thousand *pensées* concerning male and female nature and social phenomena. The large-scale *apologia* is only an expansion of Browning's favourite form. Poisoners and dukes and murderers and bishops had already had a hearing, the fullest having been granted, so far, to Guido. But the 'modern Don Juan' and the 'saviour of society' talk through whole volumes, and the 'elder man' in the *Inn Album* cannot complain of the hour-glass. The result is not always tedious.

The earliest and most sawdusty poem of this group is *Prince Hohenstiel-Schwangau, Saviour of Society*. It had been drafted twelve years before Napoleon the Third lay sick at Chislehurst; and thus, though published in 1871, it does not allude to his downfall. Browning did not share his wife's admiration for the opportunist visionary, and shared still less the fierce attitude of Victor Hugo. His half-imaginary prince spins a spider's web of self-excuse for the great gulf between his theories and his behaviour. The streak of idealism is true to history, but otherwise the 'prince' is little akin to the real emperor. And the construction of the poem is wantonly confusing. The overture, which at first seems to be describing facts, turns out to have been only a dream. Then the shuttle flies in bewildering fashion between what the speaker did, and what he might have done, and what others think, or might have thought, about his doings. The result is not so much a poem as a long intricate sophism cut into the blankest of iambics.

In *Fifine at the Fair* Browning reverts to rhyme, and lightens the rather lumbering trot of Drayton's old Alexandrine couplet;

and indeed he gets out of it a few long smooth gallops over the sward. His Don Juan is neither sombre nor delightedly cruel, but simply a man who inveterately hunts for experience. Don Juan walks through the fair with Elvire, and proclaims her the perfect type of wife; and he is in earnest for the time. He sets her high above the gypsy Fifine, the newest of all the endless fair women—Helen, Cleopatra, and the rest—who have allured his imagination. He argues and refines on the matter interminably—and at last he goes off to Fifine, with an obvious lie to Elvire upon his lips. Much of Juan's harangue is a weariness; but the book is remarkable for the beauty of its similes, in which much of the poetry takes refuge, and which are drawn out almost to the length of parables. Also there are the lovely Breton landscapes of cliff and foreshore, and the plash of the waters gets into the verse. In the lyrical prologue and epilogue, the one gay and gracious, the other curt and elliptical, the double strain of the poem is repeated.

The facts of *Red Cotton Night-Cap Country* were taken from a recent *cause célèbre.*[1] The opposition is between the idyllic sleepy setting (the *white* cotton) and the tale of blood and avarice (the *red* cotton) there enacted. A further symbolism is implied in the second title, *Turf and Towers*, which contrast the life that drifts at ease with the 'sharpened life' which, Meredith tells us, 'commands its course.' The hero is another sophist, one Miranda, a Catholic who tries to serve both masters, ease and religion, turf and towers. This converted waster, after a surprising chain of events and reflections, gives a show of sincerity to his madness by flinging himself from the top of the 'tower.' The symbolism weighs the story down. When Browning keeps to sheer sardonic comedy he is excellent, and Molière or Henri Becque might have praised the scene in which Clara, the widow of Miranda, defies all his harpy 'Cousinry' and sits firm in her strong financial position. Despite the squalor of the story, the poet remains genial and almost hopeful at the end of it.

So much cannot be said of *The Inn Album,*[2] where he hardly speaks in person at all. The rascal of the piece, the 'elder man,' predominates; and his hypocrisy goes to the length of talking absolutely like Browning. He exclaims to the woman whom he has betrayed and whom he is soon to try and blackmail,

> Let this parenthetic doubt
> Of love, in me, have been the trial-test
> Appointed to all flesh at some one stage
> Of soul's achievement,

which is Satan quoting scripture. By such strokes the villains of Thackeray are outdone; but the *Inn Album* often recalls his novels. There is the same knowledge of the card-room, the club-world, and the half-world. The story is freely adapted from an actual scandal of the last generation, and is too intricate to epitomise easily; but the incidents are closely riveted, and the actual ending is the only possible one. All the characters are unnamed. The 'lady' is no lamblike or saintlike Pompilia, but magnificent in wrath and denunciation. She was ruined, she fled to a dreary marriage; the 'younger man,' one of Browning's best delineations of manly and primitive youth, has loved and missed her, not knowing that her injurer is the 'elder man,' the very man who has taken him up, initiated him, fleeced him, and won his adoration. At the crisis he slays the elder man, and the woman commits suicide. At last, with the two bodies lying before him, he opens the door to a fourth person, the young girl whom he was about to marry and who had sought the counsel of the dead woman. Save for this lightly pencilled figure there is hardly a touch of charm in *The Inn Album*, except one description of an elm-tree:

> O you exceeding beauty, bosomful
> Of lights and shades, murmurs and silences,
> Sun-warmth, dew-coolness,—squirrel, bee, and bird,
> High, higher, highest, till the blue proclaims
> '*Leave earth, there 's nothing better till next step*
> *Heavenward!*'—so, off flies what has wings to help.

The Inn Album is the last remarkable long poem that Browning wrote. It has discomfited some of his admirers, but had it not been in verse it would have taken its sure place in fiction. It recalls the old 'domestic' tragedies like *Arden of Feversham*, where the passions are left naked and their speech is little transfigured out of the ferocity of fact. Still, Browning throws a fine spume of his own over the most literal language; and the dignity of the injured lady lifts *The Inn Album* out of bare realism.

X

Meanwhile Browning began, for refreshment, to produce his 'transcripts' of Greek stories. So might a man, whilst working in mine or sewer, make holiday in the open-air theatre of Athens or Epidaurus. He could not for ever resist the call of beauty. He began with *Balaustion's Adventure*, where cordiality and song predominate, and hope and goodness flower. The setting was partly suggested by Plutarch, but the girl Balaustion, the 'wild pomegranate-flower,' who chants the *Alcestis* of Euripides to the Syracusans for the redemption of the Grecian captives, is the poet's own invention. She is one of his living and delightful figures. 'Herakles,'[1] whom Euripides had presented in a perplexing light (some scholars believing the intention to be merely derisive), is glorified into a type of the rescuer. His 'great voice,' breaking in upon the keeners in the house of mourning, rather suggests the caricature, now well known, of the solid and ruddy Browning surrounded by a shadowy chorus of dreary persons. The play is 'transcribed,' sometimes roughly and literally, but into close and expressive verse, and is commented on from point to point by Balaustion-Browning. All is clear and straightforward; the refining over the vacillations of Admetus is part of the problem raised by the original play. Browning wished to defend his wife's favourite Greek poet, and did something to shake the estimate which had been encouraged by the unintelligent abuse of Schlegel in his *Lectures on Dramatic Literature* of 1808. It is clear what Browning owed to Euripides and to Greece. For the moment they cleared his voice, they brought him back to pure beauty. Already in 1842 he had produced *Artemis Prologizes*, which was meant to introduce a sequel of his own to the *Hippolytus*.

But beauty does not detain him long: in *Aristophanes's Apology* he is off again into the jungle. The actual version of the *Hercules Furens* has the same virtues as that of the *Alcestis*; and it is even closer, because there are lyrical measures corresponding in position to those of the original. Balaustion is again the speaker. While sailing to Rhodes with her husband after the downfall of Athens, she dictates to him the story of her conflict with Aristophanes, who had burst into her house upon the news of the death of Euripides. He makes his 'apology' for his attacks on that poet; it is conceived on conservative lines at the expense of the sophist and eccentric. Balaustion had refuted him by reciting the play. The apology bursts into splendour here and there, but is choked with crabbed learned allusions and jibes, and no Greek would have uttered it or listened to it. Aristophanes makes amends when he chants, in sweet and flowing *terza rima*, the song of Thamyris. Soon afterwards Browning produced his translation of the *Agamemnon* of Æschylus, which few have praised. The measure is not happy and the style is doggedly literal and strained. The mistake, similar to that which Morris made over *Beowulf*, seems to lie in supposing that an idiom which, though difficult, is natural in one language produces the same effect when it is slavishly followed in another language where it is not natural and therefore still more difficult. We are far here from the lovely and stately Hellenic of his youth, *Artemis Prologizes*.

Johnson somewhere shakes his head over the task of 'the most vigorous mind when it is employed at once upon argument and poetry,' and in *La Saisiaz* (1878), whatever the fate of the argument, the poetry must be held to suffer. But the overture is a noble utterance of collected grief. The poet, who had lost his friend and fellow-climber, treads, now alone, the familiar uphill joyous road; and the verse, with its *Locksley Hall* rhymes, echoes his paces. The rest is a plea, lofty in tenor and bleak in language, for the belief in personal survival, without which all human hopes are represented as idle. The Stoical view of the agnostic does not figure among the arguments controverted. Many passages recall Bishop Butler, and Browning gives a new turn to his own favourite idea of life as a probation; the soul requires a troubled progress towards perfection, and this progress can only be consummated in another life. In the same volume, in *The Two Poets of Croisic*, he turns to a lighter mood. This is one of his pleasantest works, with its pensive moral. The poets are historical persons. There is René Gentilhomme, who prophesied truly the birth of a Dauphin, and who was much honoured and then forgotten; and there is Maillard, or Desforges, who disguised himself as his own sister, letting her publish his verses in her name, and who thus cheated Voltaire into saluting him gallantly. Here Browning uses the roguish *Don Juan* metre, though he may not make the utmost of its powers.

XI

He now went back, with a difference, to the lyrical ballad, or story of action. Most of the *Dramatic Idyls* of 1879 and 1880 are of this kind, and are also poems of casuistry. He does not deal in the obvious moral, but likes to exhibit the trial of courage or piety under extraordinary conditions, when a sudden choice must be made carrying with it either self-acquittal or permanent remorse. But he does not show interest in the mere temptation

> To buy the merry madness of one hour
> With the long irksomeness of following time.

We must have strange cases; and in one of them, that of *Ivàn Ivànovitch*, a tale which he had heard in Russia in his youth, the poet surely turns the winch too far. It is the tale of Ivàn's wife, who let the wolves tear her children from her, and resisted furiously, but did not fling herself to die with them ; for which lapse Ivàn beheads her in public, and the village pope hails him therefore as 'God's servant,' and discourses on the duties of mothers. The event may have happened ; but is the sentiment simply dramatic, or does the poet too applaud the atrocity of Ivàn ? If so, his sympathy is better warranted in the case of *Martin Relph*, where the conscience-stricken speaker is a constructive murderer. *Ned Bratts* is versified from the story of 'Old Tod' in Bunyan's *Mr. Badman* : Bratts and his wife are slayers and thieves, but are converted, and plunge into court, and confess, and face their sentence. The speech of Bratts is a grimy, fiery, and splendid explosion. In *Halbert and Hob* there is the just and tragic though not the fatal explanation of a fault ; the father suffers his son to outrage him, just so far as he had outraged his own father long ago, but no further. All these poems are in long rolling rhymes of various pattern, and in all there is the genuine ring. The situation is sharpest and, morally speaking, most intricate in *Clive*, where three separate mental crises are presented. Two are actual ; there is the breakdown of the card-sharper, whose pistol Clive, his exposer, calmly faces ; and there is the test of Clive's courage as he does so. But these only lead up to the third crisis, which is imaginary, and which consists in the humiliation which Clive *would* have felt if his enemy, instead of collapsing, had spared him in assumed contempt. The whole setting and performance of this poem, with the figure of the old officer silently listening to Clive's reminiscence, is worthy of Browning's prime.

In others of the 'idyls' there is also a recovery of charm. Such are the Arab tale of the horse *Muléykeh*, and the Greek tales of *Echetlos* and *Pheidippides* ; and there is all Browning's youthful feeling for beauty in the moon-scenery of *Pan and Luna*, where the silvery images make us forget the occasional jars of sound :

> And thus it proved when—diving into space,
> Stript of all vapour, from each web of mist
> Utterly film-free—entered on her race
> The naked Moon, full-orbed antagonist
> Of night and dark, night's dowry ; peak to base,
> Upstarted mountains, and each valley, kissed
> To sudden life, lay silver-bright ; in air
> Flew she revealed, Maid-Moon with limbs all bare.

Ixion, which comes in the next volume (*Jocoseria*, 1883), is not properly a 'Hellenic' ; for the myth is turned, in a modern spirit, into a scornful condemnation of the unjust Zeus by the tortured Ixion; who appeals to the unknown 'Potency' behind the tyrant, in the name of the ideal rights of man. Shelley in his 'Demogorgon' in *Prometheus Unbound*, had less successfully personified this final court of appeal. *Jocoseria*, besides the famous and musical lyric, 'Never the time and the place,' contains one dramatic monologue, *Cristina and Monaldeschi*, which is a fierce and magnificent exhalation of vengeance planned and satisfied. The scene, with its streak of diabolic humour, shows all Browning's pristine power. The craven and treacherous lover whom the queen draws by her falsehoods to the fatal ambush is solely but sufficiently depicted through the gestures which are described in her narrative. Browning feels an almost savage interest in any kind of coward.

In *Ferishtah's Fancies* (1884), under the guise of an Eastern fabulist, Browning once again reasons out his faith. Again we learn the significance of earthly pain and penance and the value of obstacles to the aspiring soul. The keynote is the worth of love, as compared with knowledge, in supporting us through the struggle; and it is struck in the inserted lyrics, some of which are very fresh and beautiful. The book, for the rest, though seldom obscure, is crabbedly and barely written, with more than the usual play of quirk and eccentricity. I once saw a treasured note from Browning to a young poet who had sent him verses; wherein, speaking as a veteran 'practitioner,' and perhaps echoing his own Abt Vogler, he noted how some chance gathering of common words may suddenly break into a 'star.' The stars of phrase flash out more rarely in these latest volumes, though the force of mind is unabated. *Parleyings with Certain People of Importance in their Day* (1887) is full of curious interest and untired play of intellect. The parleyings are with Christopher Smart, Bubb Dodington, the painter Gerard de Lairesse, and other forgotten persons. Some of the similes and descriptions are rich in colour and energy. The body of Smart's poetry is compared to a decent and dreary mansion in which one gorgeous chapel, the *Song to David*, is concealed. In *Gerard de Lairesse* the figure of Artemis is beheld on the sun-steeped mountain after the clearing of the storm, and the clear tints of *Artemis Prologizes* reappear, with a swifter measure and a freer style:

> What hope along the hillside, what far bliss
> Lets the crisp hair-plaits fall so low they kiss
> Those lucid shoulders? Must a morn so blithe
> Needs have its sorrow when the twang and hiss
> Tell that from out thy sheaf one shaft makes writhe
> Its victim, thou unerring Artemis?

The thought, no doubt, often usurps on the poetic faculty; but the handiwork is still that of a great old age. In the posthumous *Asolando* the poet writes his own epitaph, 'One who never turned his back . . .'; a poem which is in the strain of *Prospice*, and which, if less sublime, is not less courageous. Any signs of age appear rather in the knotting and gnarling of the language than in loss of power. *Asolando*, as a volume, shows also a recovered lightness and freshness of mood, and some of the verse really dances. The double refrain ('Clara, Clara') in *Rosny* recalls the 'Edward, Edward' of the old ballad. *Speculative* is a good dramatic monologue of the early kind. The noble piece called *Reverie* celebrates the trinity of Power, Love, and Faith. 'All these and more come flocking' to prove Browning's unconquerable resilience, one of his greatest qualities.

XII

Tennyson, it was said above, tried to give to English the virtues of Italian; Browning seemed to rejoice in the inherent defects of our language; he liked it to be English to a fault. Not that he was prejudiced, like Morris, against the 'learned' element in it, or against the legacy of Milton; or had any leaning, like Swinburne, to the use and abuse of biblical diction. But he has a passion for the monosyllable, however much it may creak and grind, and the monosyllable is usually of 'native' origin. Nine times out of ten, when his verse is rough or deterrent, that is the reason. Some of his clusters of consonants—*ndgr*, *lpsfl*, *lpss*—recall the names in *Gulliver's Travels*:

> Let us not always say,
> 'Spite of this flesh to-day
> I strove, made head, gai*ned gr*ound upon the whole!'
> As the bird wings and sings,
> Let us cry 'All good things
> Are ours, nor soul he*lps fl*esh more now than flesh he*lps s*oul.'

Such a style, which comes to its acme in *Dramatis Personæ*, is well and duly parodied in the *Heptalogia*; but then it is often the right and necessary style, for the discords are wanted—wanted in the service of an intense or an exalted mood which is fully conscious of the past or present struggle involved in its attainment; and no easier style would serve. And the technique of the verse is of course affected by this congestion of consonants and monosyllables; the result being many 'spondees,' and a slow hindered march, which has its own music, often of a subtle kind:

> Táke the clóak from his fáce, and at first
> Lèt the córpse dò its wórst.
>
> Hòw he líes in his ríghts as a mán!
> Deáth has dóne àll deàth cán . . .

But not infrequently, and above all in the 'anapæstic' measures of which he is otherwise a master, he falsifies the natural accent.[1] Yet he goes on joyously over all snags and boulders; and whether as rough-rider, or when guiding his smooth-pacing Arab, his *Muléykeh,* he is still a master-horseman. His invention and his control of metre are surprising, and to the last he is ever finding new tunes. The slow suave undulations of *Rudel*; the piercing simple cadences of *White Witchcraft*; galloping measures, choppy measures, stately measures, all are there. But to enlarge on this would be to repeat what has been well said by others. The extremes of Browning's power and weakness, of his roughness and smoothness, are to be found in his blank verse.

Something, however, may be added on his grammar[2] and idiom, which have certain constant features. They are, as with Shakespeare, the expression of life and impulse; and, even with the precedent of the Grammarian, it may seem mere pedantry to think of 'properly basing' them. It is not pedantry; but the subject would need a tractate. Some peculiarities lie on the surface. We need not fear the curses launched in *Pacchiarotto* against the 'impudence, ignorance, envy, and malice' of verbal critics; for the result of analysis only tells in Browning's honour.

> Was it 'grammar' wherein you would 'coach' me—
> You,—pacing in even that paddock
> Of language allotted you *ad hoc,*
> With a clog at your fetlocks,—you—scorners
> Of me free of all its four corners?

And Browning's grammar is not so much false as free. It represents an effort to show that, for all the work of the 'classical' and succeeding ages, English syntax is still, in the right hands, ductile. Carlyle made a similar effort, and, for all his incidental contortions, prevailed. Browning is one of the few English poets since Milton who may be said to have a grammar of his own. He is strong enough to have one. It is, no doubt, hit or miss with him. But the grammar is much the same throughout ; it is a deliberately practised idiom that soon becomes second nature. Some features of it may be noticed in a single passage in his 'parleying' with Christopher Smart :

> [a]Such success
> Befell Smart only out of[b] throngs between
> Milton and Keats that donned the singing-dress—
> Smart, solely of such songmen, pierced the screen
> 'Twixt thing and word, lit[b] language straight from[b] soul,—[d]
> Left no[g] fine film[g]-flake on the naked coal
> Live from the censer—[e]shapely or uncouth,
> Fire-suffused through and through, one blaze of truth
> Undeadened by a lie[e],—(you have my mind)—[f]
> For, think! this[g] blaze outleapt with[g] black behind
> And[g] blank before, when Hayley and the rest . . .
> But let the dead successors worst and best
> Bury their dead : with life be my concern—
> Yours with the[g] fire[g]-flame : what I fain would learn
> Is just[f]—(suppose me haply ignorant
> Down to the common knowledge,[c] doctors vaunt)[f]
> Just this—why only once the fire-flame was[a] . . .

a. Nothing can be unliker the traditional poetic paragraph, or 'period,' either grammatically or musically : it is natural, broken speech plunging forward, rather fettered by its rhymes, and straining to be blank verse. *b*. There is some of that deliberate omission of articles which is most marked in passages that require discords and thudding spondees. A similar effect is heard in *Shop* :

> Then off made[b] buyer with a prize,
> Then[e] seller to his *Times* returned,
> And so did day wear, wear, till[b] eyes
> Brightened apace, for rest was earned :
> He locked[b] door long ere[b] candle burned.

c. Omission of relative pronoun—again for *staccato* effect. *d*. Use of the breathless dash, appositive or transitional, eight times. *e*. Use of the absolute clause, and *f*. of parenthesis—both of them causing a stoppage. *g*. Heaped alliteration, for the enhancement, or at the cost, of melody. So we might, it is plain, proceed ; the total impression being one of an interrupted stumbling gallop, of a concision that causes delay, and of a strange rough harmony emerging at the last. This is the briefest of demonstrations ; the special idioms of Caliban, of Bishop Blougram, and of Dominus Hyacinthus, are superimposed on these rude elements. The parody by Calverley in *The Cock and the Bull* is full of such scholarship. For Browning, on the whole, makes good his grammar and syntax, as George Meredith, on the whole, does not. We can 'learn his great language,' and honourably salute it, though with occasional amusement.

XIII

He wrote reams of verse which are not poetry, though poetry is always struggling through. He seems to have been little aware of its absence, and in this he is like Chapman and many a good Elizabethan. He had a similar contempt for the public and the critics, though like Tennyson he was always angrily thinking about them. But all this is only to say that Browning's mental force and alertness outrange, as so often happens with Englishmen of genius, his artistic power. He tried to put into poetry much that should never have gone into verse. It is not true, though Swinburne said it, that Browning is rapid rather than obscure. He can be so obscure as to annul the value of the thought which he less than half conveys. He breaks his fingers on what is stronger than the strongest man, namely the genius of the language. He often commits himself to impossible forms and moulds, as in *Sordello* and *Hohenstiel-Schwangau*; some of these long poems are altogether mis-creations. Yet all this was but the excess and the diversion of strength. It is clear that Browning's noble body of living and consummate work is none the worse for failures that lie outside it.

He has reasoned and philosophised [1] in verse more than any English poet of equal gift. Much has been written on his theology and its 'optimism.' His fervent instinctive theism encouraged the myth that he was of Hebrew blood. It is united with an intense if undoctrinal belief in personal immortality, and with an equally undogmatic and mystical reverence for Christ, whose lineaments he draws after the Fourth Gospel. He so far attends to current controversies as to dismiss certain lurid tenets. This he does in the satire of *Caliban upon Setebos*, and in the *Inn Album*, and *Ixion*, where the doctrine of reprobation is itself cast forth unto reprobation. The very faith in an after-life, proclaimed in *La Saisiaz*, repudiates the conception of reward and punishment, as sapping the moral impulse of man on this earth, who is no longer disinterested if he is to be bribed or threatened. Indeed, the force of Browning's appeal is always moral and imaginative rather than speculative. In the region of ideal aspiration we must seek for his power, in *Abt Vogler* and in *Rabbi Ben Ezra*, and in the musings of Pope Innocent, and in *Prospice*, and in the *Epilogue* to *Asolando*. Luckily it is here too that he is most of a poet ; and when he is once fairly on his way few have equalled him in sureness and nobility of style. His execution, at its best, does not fall behind—it is worthy of—his energetic spirit of faith and courage. Whatever we may think of their validity, we feel that the utmost has been done for their expression. The optimist, at the worst, has had a great innings, and his knowledge of human nature, of traps and pitfalls and stumblings and of the enemy generally, has saved him from too cheap assertion. And he is always best when he *chants* his sermon. Start with Browning where we will, we are apt to come back at last to his lyrical gift.

The web of circumstance and situation in his imaginary world, I began by saying, is very tough and definite, and he gives the taste of life, with its oddity, colour, and splendour, as sharply as any poet, whenever he likes. The pictures of Caliban, and the Bishop of St. Praxed's, and Bratts, and a score of others, cannot be outdone in their intense expression of temperament. Down into the pit of realism, below the sphere of poetry, yet making a kind of poetry out of what he finds, Browning often goes, with a dramatic sympathy that seems to be rather intensified by his moral repulsion (indulgence or complicity being far from him). But short of this, he moves joyously above-ground, with a certain good-natured impatient contempt for the average nature, and also a clear vision of it ; the contempt distinguishing him from Shakespeare, as it does from Chaucer, to whom Landor compared him. His world, nevertheless, is amply peopled. Yet with whom, or with what ? He has more dramatic sense than any poet of his time ; but which of his characters have forced their way into the general memory ? Possibly Pippa, or Pompilia ; more probably Mr. Sludge. No one else, despite all those brains and pains ! There is no Hamlet, no Satan ; certainly not even a 'new Don Juan' ! It may be said that the test is too hard, and that Browning speaks to the lettered public. But his 'Karshish, Cleon, Norbert, and the fifty,' for all their liveliness and eloquence, are hardly persons. Some, indeed, are types not to be forgotten, and Guido and Fra Lippo are more than that. And it is a great thing to create types, as Chaucer created them. But Browning's men are often spokesmen—voices of his own ideas on love and art and faith ; and they are little more for all the colour and detail that surrounds them. They are, from this point of view, wonderful inventions. His women are more real and satisfactory, especially when they speak for themselves. They theorise less; and sometimes, like the lady in *The Inn Album*, they have a poetic reality. Sometimes they too are types, and profoundly representative ones, like the speaker in *Any Wife to Any Husband*. But here we approach Browning's safest and least hindered mode of speech, which is, once more, the lyrical. Now and then, as in the case of Pompilia, the impression is lyrical, while the form is not so. Browning presents situations, but his aim is through them to present passion—anybody's passion; and to present thought too, with a shadowy thinker behind it. From 1842 to 1890, from *Through the Metidja* to *Dubiety*, a poem in the *Asolando* volume, he retains this power, which constitutes his surest title-deeds; he keeps the tones of a perennial youth, which is not like that of Tithonus:

> Perhaps but a memory, after all!
> Of what came once when a woman leant
> To feel for my brow where her kiss might fall.
> Truth ever, truth only the excellent!

There is much, then, in Browning which is not exactly poetry, but which is all the same well worth having. It may be good and entertaining, of the *Ingoldsby* kind, like the beginning of *Holy Cross Day* ('Fee, faw, fum! bubble and squeak,' etc.). More often it is in blank verse, and in the nature of rapid, allusive, and sarcastic narrative or *apologia*. Much of *The Ring and the Book*, and most of *The Inn Album*, is of this order. It cannot be said that the use of metre is unwarrantable; but it is just the metre that carries us through. The level is that of very animated prose, but the style is a new invention—cynical, broken, conversational, crutching itself quite effectively upon the metre:

> And did I spoil sport, pull face grim,—nay, grave?
> Your pupil does you better credit! No!
> I parleyed with my passbook,—rubbed my pair
> At the big balance in my banker's hands,
> Folded a cheque cigar-case-shape,—just wants
> Filling and signing,—and took train, resolved
> To execute myself with decency
> And let you win,—if not Ten thousand quite,
> Something by way of wind-up-farewell burst
> Of fire-work nosegay!

When he likes, Browning can always spurt up from such a level into real poetry; or again, he can slip into a more agreeable, easy kind of verse-talk. In *The Inn Album* this variety abounds, and is delightful. There is one allusion to 'poor hectic Cowper,' and the history of the 'Night-Cap' suggests, perhaps intentionally, the manner of *The Task* :

> And so, encroaching more and more
> It lingers long past the abstemious meal
> Of morning, and, as prompt to serve, precedes
> The supper-summons, gruel grown a feast.

All this brings us back to our starting-point : Browning's normality, sanity, humanity ; he is a man of the world, in the best and strongest sense of the term ; his genius has its sound, stubborn roots in real life. And as to his whole body of performance, we may look on it as on some metal-worker's or lapidary's store, stocked with rubies and chrysolites of the best, and with rings and armlets 'justifiably golden,' and also with the same things half-wrought and ill set, and again with 'cradles' of the unwashed, gold-containing rubble ; one and all being paraded, as if they were the regalia, with a queer unconsciousness of difference. This large absence of self-criticism is one thing that makes Browning so big, so attractive, so Elizabethan. He talked endlessly about art, but hardly knew when he was an artist and when he was not, leaving us to state that matter as best we may.

XIV

The early reputation of Elizabeth Barrett [1] (1806-61) was made by two volumes published before her marriage, *The Seraphim and Other Poems* of 1838, and the *Poems* of 1844. The first of these contained not only highly-pitched romantic lyric like *Margret*, and romantic narrative like *Isobel's Child*, but some less ambitious verse of finer workmanship, mostly reminiscent, such as *The Island*, *The Deserted Garden*, *The Sea-Mew*, and *My Doves* ; while the most popular as well as the most impassioned piece, though not the surest in note, was *Cowper's Grave*. In the *Poems* of 1844 the scope is wider, the hand less uncertain, and the intensity greater ; it contains *The Cry of the Children*, and *Catarina to Camoens*, and *Wine of Cyprus* ; but the form, while often beautiful and melodious, is still inadequate to the occasion.

There are more romances, like the overcharged *Lady Geraldine's Courtship*, and pleasant simple things like the lines *To Flush, My Dog* ; who, she observes in a letter, 'understands Greek excellently well.' But work like *A Rhapsody of Life's Progress* again shows the authoress on a false track ; within a few years she was to find a truer one. Meanwhile in 1844, she contributed a fervent essay on Carlyle,[1] and a good deal of other matter, to *A New Spirit of the Age*, by the poet Horne, the writer of *Orion*.

Miss Barrett's marriage to Robert Browning in 1846 did not merely bring her renewed health and personal happiness after an invalided and hermit life ; it was also a release from a kind of prison. Her father's notion of the *patria potestas*, in the article of marriage, amounted to a monomania, and the wedding took place without his knowledge. It enabled Mrs. Browning to escape from London to Italy, and from a sofa surrounded with books to the great world, Browning's 'world of men,' of great affairs, and of vital ideas : and she herself was afterwards to write :

> I lived with visions for my company
> Instead of men and women, years ago.

The letters exchanged between Browning and Miss Barrett were published after both were dead ; they do nothing but honour to both writers, of course ; yet the reader is shy of overhearing love-letters ; and another record of this fortunate union was given to the world by the poetess in her book of sonnets, first privately printed in 1847, and in 1850 published as *Sonnets from the Portuguese*. They come not from the Portuguese, but from the soul of the writer, and often attain a purity of form that is worthy of their splendid inspiration. Like the nightingale, Mrs. Browning was 'a creature of a fiery heart.'

The Brownings lived and wrote in Italy, their second country, making occasional flights to England. Their headquarters were in Florence, and Mrs. Browning's next book, *Casa Guidi Windows* (1851) is the record of a sanguine, absorbed onlooker, vehement in sympathy with the Italian cause and nourishing an admiration, afterwards to be chilled, for Louis Napoleon. It is most unequal in execution, but is alive with observation and enthusiasm. In 1857, adventuring on blank verse, Mrs. Browning produced the long story, *Aurora Leigh*, which succeeded, but which is now somewhat stranded. Most of the *Poems before Congress* (1860) are political rather than poetical. But the posthumous volume of 1862 contains some of Mrs. Browning's best writing, including *Bianca among the Nightingales* and that triumph in dramatic monologue, *Lord Walter's Wife*. The influence of her husband's *Dramatic Lyrics*, for good and ill, can here be traced ; the style is stronger, and the grasp of situation too ; but Browning's ruggedness does not sit well upon her looser habit of speech.

There have been few good poetesses at any time or in any country. Amongst those who have written in English, it is equally certain that Mrs. Browning is not the surest artist and that she 'has the largest and most comprehensive soul.' She deserves her husband's praises so well, that it is an ungrateful business to criticise her strictly. *One Word More*, and the 'posy' in *The Ring and the Book*, and *By the Fireside*, considered as a description of Mrs. Browning's spirit and nature, do not lead to disappointment when we turn to her own poetry. As to her performance, it is well to approach it with some critical precautions. It would be a mistake, within a week of doing so, to read either Robert Browning or Christina Rossetti, and it is best, perhaps, to begin with a prejudice of the right kind, in order to find how often it is disarmed. Prepare from the first to come, almost anywhere, on a sudden lapse of language into almost every fault except vulgarity, or on a vicious rhyme or a defect of rhythm, or on queer vague matter, diffuse and high-flown, or on hectic writing. Expect all this,—and again and again you will not find it ; but instead will come on passages of melody unbroken and imagery unimpaired ; on gorgeous things, and also on simple things, which are successful, and which leave you free to admire the generous poetic vision which inspires them. If Mrs. Browning had written more things like the *Sonnets from the Portuguese* she might have ranked with a poet like Rossetti, and not, as she does rank, with a poet like Sir Philip Sidney, who was also a sonneteer. The parallel may seem an odd one, but it is true up to the point where I wish to leave it. In both writers there is the same intermittence, the same occasional triumph ; and both of them frequently leave us with the sense of a rightness that has only just gone wrong. Both, too, have the power of recovery, and are always liable to be excellent.

XV

Mrs. Browning from her youth up had a passion for nature, and also a passion for the Greek poets. The copses and orchards, the rich fat rolling scenery, breaking into steepness, of the countryside lying below the Malverns, on their Herefordshire flank, are heard of in her early writings ; nor did Italy ever make her forget them. These Ledbury verses include

The Lost Bower, *The Deserted Garden*, and others already named; also the pretty *Hector in the Garden*:

> Underneath the chestnuts dripping,
> Through the grasses wet and fair,
> Straight I sought my garden-ground
> With the laurel on the mound,
> And the pear-tree oversweeping
> A side-shadow of green air.
>
> In the garden lay supinely
> A huge giant wrought of spade! . . .

The giant is the figure of Hector wrought in flowers, and the child dreams that perhaps the soul of the real Hector may enter into the giant. For more work like this, who would not give away all Mrs. Browning's Byronic or spasmodic compositions like *The Seraphim* and *A Drama of Exile?* And some of her romances too; but we must not ignore *Margret*, with its complaining music and deftly varied refrain. Of the refrain Mrs. Browning was fond; but it is a dangerous device, for while a good refrain may save, a bad one will damn, almost any poem in the world. The nightingales, singing at the end of each verse in *Bianca*, sing aright; but the repetition of the words *Toll slowly* in the *Lay of the Brown Rosary* only tempts us to say with Othello, *Silence that dreadful bell!* Yet, again, the burden of *The Dead Pan* is a true close, and aptly fitted to every stanza: *Pan, Pan is dead*. This piece is a noble fruit of Mrs. Browning's Greek studies, which claim a separate mention.

She read the poets honestly in the originals, from Homer to Gregory Nazianzen, and in *Wine of Cyprus* recites their praises with much colour, gaiety, and ardour. It is her happiest piece of familiar verse, and alludes to her readings with her blind instructor, Hugh Stuart Boyd; the memory of the same scholar is honoured afterwards in three sonnets, of which the last, entitled *Legacies*, is of great beauty. The Greeks did not teach Mrs. Browning their own virtues of form; but she has her place, beside the transcriber of the *Alcestis*, among the poetic humanists of the period. Her dealings with 'our Æschylus, the thunderous' were, indeed, not much more fortunate than her husband's. She produced, and deplored, a youthful version of the *Prometheus*, and afterwards made another one. Her essay (1842) on *The Greek Christian Poets* contains many translations, and is a rapid, not to say scampering, review of an enthusiastic, though not uncritical cast, and is another fruit of the lessons described in *Wine of Cyprus*. Her *Book of the Poets* (1842) is in a similar style, and full of eager enjoyment; the poets are the English poets, and the list closes with Wordsworth, whose reputation was now established, and whose influence is occasionally traceable in Mrs. Browning: and that to advantage, as in the charming piece called *An Island*. *A Vision of Poets* is the counterpart in verse to the *Book of the Poets*. Though not wholly successful, it contains a happy characterisation of Chaucer, and also of Ossian, 'once counted greater than the rest'; and, further, some true Tennysonian scenery:

> A wild brown moorland underneath,
> And four pools breaking up the heath
> With white low gleamings, blank as death.

There is nothing to be said for Mrs. Browning's deliberate way of rhyming falsely [1] whenever she is minded to do so. She says that it is the 'result not of carelessness, but of conviction, and indeed of much patient study of the great masters of English.' Nothing has hurt her reputation more; but the precise nature and extent of her error must be remembered. It occurs chiefly in her early works, little in the *Sonnets from the Portuguese* or in *Casa Guidi Windows*; and chiefly, also, where she is courting the difficulties of double rhyme. English has its traditional freedoms, which are somewhat boldly extended, as the next chapter will show, by Dante Rossetti. In *The Blessed Damozel* are to be found: *untrod*, *God*, *cloud*, and *mild*, *fill'd*, *smil'd*. This is 'consonance': the vowel is deserted, the following consonant-sounds are retained. Mrs. Browning goes further, and passes bounds with her *mortal*, *turtle*; *altars*, *welters*; *enters*, *centaurs*; *moonshine*, *sunshine*. Assonance (which is the retention of the vowel, while the following consonant-sounds are altered) she also uses, but not so freely, though she is commonly reproached with 'assonances.' Such are: *benches*, *Influences*, *Nazianzen*, *glancing*; *trident*, *silent*. But sometimes she combines both processes, and two examples will probably suffice the reader: *angels*, *candles*; *panther*, *saunter*. I do not know whether there be any language in which resemblances like these would be accepted. These practices are the more to be deplored because they often introduce the effect of 'a brazen canstick turned or a dry wheel grating,' in the midst of an otherwise excellent melody. The effect is such that no writer of any credit, since Mrs. Browning, has tried to imitate it.

XVI

The forty-four *Sonnets from the Portuguese* form a sequence, or continuous poem, written in a state of happiness, but mostly ringing the changes on a single theme, namely the writer's sense of humility; with a standing contrast between her present condition and her former one of loneliness and seclusion. The tone is now and then lighter, as befits her joyful estate, and then it runs into playful images and conceits; 'The soul's Rialto hath its merchandise'; and there is a strange flight of this kind in the thirty-seventh sonnet: here, in the sestet, she exclaims that she can set up only an unworthy counterfeit of her love, even as a 'shipwrecked Pagan safe in port' might set up, instead of 'his guardian sea-god,' a 'sculptured porpoise.' This, however, is cheerfulness breaking through. The prevailing note of these poems is so high, the spirit so ardent, and the matter so intimate, that they might seem to claim immunity from the process of inspection. Still, the sonnet-form is the most exacting of all, and besides Mrs. Browning published the book. Everywhere there is the same spiritual fire; none of the sonnets are without beauty; and four or five of them approach the standard of finish which is set by the great, unforgettable examples in the language. They are all in the Italian form, which is observed with due care as regards the rhyme-arrangement, and with some regularity as regards the exact distribution of the thought among the metrical sections. One of the best-wrought, in these respects, is the fifth, where the single image of the ashes of the heart, poured from the sepulchral urn, and smouldering at the feet of the beloved, but flaming up in his face under the passionate gust of wind, is perfectly carried through. The sonnet itself flames up in the last words, 'Stand farther off then! go.' Of the other three that are perhaps the best, the fourteenth ('If thou must love me') has, designedly, the high Elizabethan ring, in spite of its orthodox versification; the most lofty and magnificent, the twenty-second, 'When our two souls,' is as definitely modern in cast, and the most Rossetti-like (like Dante, not like Christina Rossetti); while the forty-third, 'How do I love thee?' a much more even, quiet, and regular piece, may be thought to have the honours in point both of depth and simplicity. A commentary on the *Sonnets from the Portuguese* may be found in the small group of companion-lyrics—in which the style of Robert Browning may be detected—called *Insufficiency*, *Inclusions*, *Proof and Disproof*. Whatever their flaws, the *Sonnets from the Portuguese* stand, by right of subject, occasion, and temper, and frequently by right of workmanship, apart from all other English sonnet series and above most of them.

The first and longer part of *Casa Guidi Windows* records the spectacle of Florence in 1848, when the Grand Duke Leopold made his promise, which came to nothing, of a liberal constitution. The second part, written three years later, is a generous but turbid tirade, telling of the flight of Leopold, of his return under the protection of Austrian bayonets, and of the departure of Pius the Ninth to Gaeta ; the spirit is one of bitter disenchantment. There is much more poetry in the first part ; and though the digressions and disquisitions on art are a kind of caricature in point of style of *Andrea del Sarto* and *Old Pictures in Florence*, the actual diary of things seen—the procession in the streets, the banners, the impassioned crowd—is admirably written. This was a new venture for Mrs. Browning ; as her letters show, she had an eye for a pageant, in its colour and detail, and for popular traits and gestures ; and it is a pity that she did not write thus oftener. The poem is in a breathless measure ; the stanzas of six run on unbrokenly, and the melody is only occasional ; and the general effect is confused.

Aurora Leigh,[1] though a curious document of the time, is, it must be confessed, something of a 'chokepear' for the reader of to-day. It is a long story, interlaced with long discourses, and occupying four hundred pages of blank verse. Like *The Cry of the Children*, it is a proof of Mrs. Browning's deep humanitarian feeling and of her large heart. *Aurora Leigh* could not be omitted from any account of the sentiment which in sundry forms animates Carlyle and Dickens, Ruskin and Kingsley : the overflow into literature of the quickened sympathy for the poor and the dispossessed, and of a noble indignation against the more cruel and irrational kind of social taboo. The real heroine, Marian Erle, a sacrificed, innocent daughter of the people, gives up her betrothed, the exalted philanthropist, Romney Leigh, sooner than drag him down to her level, and then vanishes. Aurora Leigh, his cousin, the woman of letters, who has watched the story and befriended Marian, in the end accepts Romney. None of these persons are particularly real, and we have the painful sense that much honourable emotion has been spent upon a crowd of shadows. And the endless preaching, arguing, and moral philosophising is almost as trying as anything in the verse of George Eliot. The verse is prosaic and high-pitched in turn, as in work of this kind it is bound or doomed to be : as it is, again, in Lytton's *Lucile*. Yet here again, as in *Casa Guidi Windows*, we are aware that in Mrs. Browning there are more than the makings of a poetic observer. The domestic scenes and the scraps of natural talk are the best parts of *Aurora Leigh* ; the speeches of Marian Erle herself, being the simplest, are the best of all. But in form, and temper, and purpose the poem dates itself in the most singular way ; and it is needless to echo that stray fling of FitzGerald, which drove Browning to such a burst of fury ; seeing that, whether we thank the powers for it or not, there *will* ' be no more *Aurora Leighs*.'

Altogether, we leave Mrs. Browning with a mixture of admiration and discomfort. Her faults of form and phrase are never the faults of smallness ; it would have been an honour to have known her. Often we feel we would rather have known her than read her ; this is when the faults become too disastrous. But on her life, as well as on the golden, the exceptional, passages of her verse, it is good to dwell.

NOTES

p. v. **Goethe.** The passage is given by G. Herzfeld, *Aus H. C. R.'s Nachlass* [*i.e.* the MS. in Dr. Williams's Library, Gordon Square], in *Archiv für das Studium der neueren Sprachen*, vol. cxx. (new series, vol. xx.), p. 31 (1804). It is not in T. Sadler's *Diary*, etc., *of Crabb Robinson*, which is only a selection from the mass. Goethe spoke in reference to his antipathy to Egyptians. Crabb Robinson, of course, reports in his own English.

p. 6. **rhythm.** See G. Saintsbury, *Hist. of Eng. Prose Rhythm*, 1912; chs. x. and xi. cover this period. My obligations to them throughout this work are large, and may be cordially acknowledged in advance.

p. 8. **Carlyle.** *Bibliography*, R. H. Shepherd [1881]; and by J. P. Anderson in R. Garnett, *Life of T. C.*, 1887. Many edd. of *Works*, the fullest being H. D. Traill's, 31 vols., 1897-1901. Chief biographical sources: *Reminiscences*, ed. C. E. Norton, 2 vols., 1887 (not Froude's incorrect ed. of 1881); *Early Letters of C.* [to 1826], ed. Norton, 2 vols., 1886; *Letters* [1826-36], ed. Norton, 2 vols., 1888. The last two works reprint, amidst many more, some of the letters already used, often inaccurately, by J. A. Froude in his *T. C.; a Hist. of the first 40 Years of his Life* (*1795-1835*), 2 vols., 1882, and in his *T. C.; a Hist. of his Life in London* (*1834-1881*), 2 vols., 1884. There is also a popular ed. of these four vols. They remain the official biography, which must be corrected as to facts and impressions from the rest of the first-hand evidence, *e.g.*: *Letters of T. C. to his Younger Sister*, intr. C. T. Copeland, 1899; *New Letters of T. C.*, ed. Alexander Carlyle, 2 vols., 1904; *Corr. of C. and R. W. Emerson*, 1834-72, 2 vols., ed. Norton, 1883. There is, besides, the correspondence of Mrs. Carlyle: her *Letters and Memorials*, ed. Froude, 3 vols., 1883; these again must be read in the light of her *Early Letters*, etc., ed. D. G. Ritchie, 1889; of *The Love Letters of T. C. and Jane Welsh*, ed. Alex. Carlyle, 2 vols., 1909; and of *New Letters and Memorials of Jane Welsh Carlyle*, 2 vols., 1903, ed. Alex. Carlyle, introd. by Sir J. Crichton-Browne. For the alleged pathological side of the business, those who have a mind to do so may turn to the reff. at end of the art. 'Carlyle' in *Ency. Brit.*, eleventh ed.; but I feel as if I had read that literature in defiance of the astounded shade of Carlyle and also, still more, of Mrs. Carlyle's (cf. 'I knew the lady; and, if there can be such a thing as indignation in the unseen world over aught that passes here below, O what a face I see, what a voice I hear, as *she* looks down on this transaction!' So Masson, *C. Personally*, p. 17, as to Froude; but the words apply still more now). Shorter accounts, appraisals, etc., are too many to recite; but see J. Nichol's vol. in *Eng. Men of Letters*, 1892 ; Mazzini's articles (1843) in vol. iv. of *Life and Writings*, 1864-70 ; and Taine, *Hist. de la Littérature anglaise*, vol. iv.

p. 9. **witnesses.** *E.g.*, *Memories of Old Friends . . . of Caroline Fox*, ed. H. N. Pym, 1881 ; F. Espinasse, *Lit. Recolls. and Sketches*, 1893, pp. 55-272 ; F. Harrison, *Memories and Thoughts*, 1906 ; *W. Allingham, a Diary*, 1907, *passim* ; Sir C. G. Duffy, *Conversations with C.*, 1892. See too Lecky, *Hist. and Pol. Essays*, pp. 104 foll., 'Carlyle as a Moral Force,' and many notes of interest in the *Memoir* (1909) of Lecky by Mrs. Lecky. The reference from Varnhagen von Ense in text, p. 9, is given in *Last Words of T. C.*, 1892, p. 287 ; there also, p. 289, is the tale of Carlyle, when Goethe was being criticised for ungodliness, asking the company, 'in seiner schwerfälligen langsamen Weise und in seinem ungeschickten Deutsch mit lauter Stimme, 'did they know the old tale of the man who blamed the sun because he could not light his cigar at it ?' 'Die Anwesenden schwiegen erschrocken,' etc.

p. 11. **Goethe.** *Corr. between G. and Carlyle*, ed. Norton, 1887, Eng. tr. ; Eckermann's *Conversations with G.*, July 1827 and 11 Oct. 1828. See too my *Survey* (1912), ii. 406.

p. 12. **the German school.** Not Carlyle's own words, but the substance as given by Dowden, *Transcripts and Studies* (1887 and 1896), ed. 1896, pp. 38-9, of the twelfth lecture 'On the Periods of European Culture,' from a report unspecified. For a first-hand statement see Espinasse, *Lit. Recolls.*, pp. 58-60, letter dated 28 Aug. 1841 : 'It is many years since I ceased reading German or any other metaphysics, and gradually came to discern that I had happily got done with that matter altogether . . . metaphysics is but a kind of disease, and the inquiry itself a kind of disease. We shall never know "what we are" ; on the other hand, we can always partly know, what beautiful or noble things we are fit to do, and that is the grand inquiry for us.'

p. 13. **Plato.** *New Letters* (1904), No. 277, 27 Aug. 1856, to Dr. Carlyle ; ii. 180-1. Cp. the cool sayings on Socrates quoted by Dowden, *Transcripts*, p. 12, from the lectures named in last note : 'his writings seem to be made up of a number of very wiredrawn notions about virtue ; there is no conclusion in him ; there is no word of life in Socrates. He was, however, personally a coherent and firm man.'

p. 15, note 1. **Sartor.** Careful searching ed. by A. MacMechan, 1896, Boston, U.S.A. (Athenæum Press series) ; others, also useful, by J. A. S. Barrett, 1910, and P. C. Parr, 1913. Editors show how portions, little changed, of the odd, highly Teutonic, and mostly mawkish romance by Carlyle, *Wotton Reinfred*, were transferred to the biographic part of *Sartor*. The work is printed in *Last Words of T. C.*, 1892.

p. 15, note 2. **early letters.** See especially those of 1814-21 in Norton's ed. ; that of Dec. 15, 1819 (i. 259) shows the young Carlyle strongly stirred by the troubles of the poor (in the 'Glasgow rising'), and already detaching himself from ordinary radicalism. So *Early Letters*, May 5, 1820 (i. 303).

p. 18. **French Revolution.** Re-ed., with introd. and notes, by J. Holland Rose, 3 vols., 1902, and also (intr. and notes) by C. R. L. Fletcher, 3 vols., 1902. See also the preface to H. Morse Stephen's *Hist. of the Fr. Revol.*, 3 vols., 1897, on the authorities used by Carlyle ; and remarks by Lord Acton, *Lectures on the Fr. Revol.*, 1910, p. 358 : 'The usual modest resources of a private library satisfied his requirements ; but the vivid gleams, the mixture of the sublime with the grotesque, make other opponents forget the impatient verdicts and the poverty of solid fact in the volumes that delivered our forefathers from thraldom to Burke.'

p. 20. **Cromwell.** The *Letters and Speeches* have been fully overhauled and re-edited, with addenda, by Mrs. S. C. Lomas, 3 vols., 1904. Valuable introduction by C. H. Firth, *e.g.* p. xxx: 'he could never surrender himself to his subject, because he was continually summoned from the past by the importunate problems of the present; because he was a prophet and a poet by nature, and a historian only by accident.' On the material gathered up in *Historical Sketches*, etc., ed. Alex. Carlyle, 1902, see *post*, p. 408 (note to i. 37), concerning Alexander Leighton.

p. 21. **Cromwell and assemblies.** See Firth, *op. cit.*; and Gardiner, *Cromwell's Place in History*, 1897, p. 46, etc.

p. 24. **Carlyle and Fichte.** See above all C. Vaughan, 'Carlyle and his German Masters,' in *Essays and Studies by Members of the English Association*, 1910, pp. 186-96—a paper that for the first time defines the debt plainly: also R. Adamson, *Fichte*, 1881, pp. 79-80. These and some other reff. are embodied in the following:—In Aug. 1827 (*Letters*, ed. Norton, i. 72, and cp. Froude, *Early Life*, ed. 1890, i. 385) Carlyle is 'reading somewhat of Fichte, Schelling, etc.'; and his essay, *State of German Lit.* (*Misc.*, vol. i.), appeared in the *Edinburgh* in Oct. He there acknowledges *Das Wesen des Gelehrten* (delivered in Erlangen, 1805); his translations and allusions seem all to refer to the first discourse. The whole can be read in *F.'s Popular Works*, Eng. tr. by Wm. Smith, ed. 4, 1889, 2 vols., esp. i. 209-32. For F. on mysticism (impatient bankrupt anti-rationalism), see *ib.*, ii. 324 ff., in *The Doctrine of Religion*; Carlyle, *loc. cit.*, absolves Fichte from the charge of being the wrong sort of mystic. He was still thinking of Fichte (as a 'resolute Liberal') in 1840, on 8 Oct. (*New Letters*, i. 216-17); and in *Hero as Man of Letters*, *ad. init.*, uttered 19 May 1840, had repeated the same old passage from the *Wesen des Gelehrten*. Nothing *proves* that Carlyle read anything else of Fichte's; but the division of the Heroes into King, Prophet, etc., seems to start from that of the functions of the *Gelehrte*; the exaltation in *Sartor*, etc., of 'blessedness' (*Seligkeit*) over 'happiness' as a worthy end is thoroughly Fichtean: and, as Prof. Vaughan shows, the doctrine of the strong ruler is even more so, and is vehemently asserted in the *Staatslehre* (Vaughan, p. 194). This is at least a striking coincidence, and there are traces of the same spirit already in the *Wesen des Gel.* (*Pop. Works*, i. 213: 'with labourers and hodmen it is otherwise, their virtue consists in punctual obedience,' etc.). My knowledge of Fichte is insufficient for carrying the matter further; but a likeness may be noted between Fichte's manhandling of Rousseau (Lect. v. of the different and earlier discourses on the *Vocation (Bestimmung) of the Scholar*, given in 1794 in Jena), and Carlyle's in *The Hero as Man of Letters*; and lastly, Carlyle's whole quarrel with the age of logic, mechanism, and utilitarian morals compares with Fichte's capital sentence on the *Aufklärung*, or 'third age,' in *Characteristics of the Present Age*, 1804 (*Pop. Works*, vol. ii., lects. v.-viii.); see Carlyle's *Characteristics*, 1831 (*Misc.*, vol. iv.), a paper which is full of Fichtean doctrine in solution.

p. 25. **Icelandic.** See the tribute to Carlyle in Vigfússon and Powell's *Corpus Poeticum Boreale*, Oxford, 1883, vol. i. p. ci.

p. 26. **Jocelin.** The *Chronicle* has been translated by Sir Ernest Clarke, 1907, with all elucidations.

p. 28. **Shooting Niagara.** Some of these later tirades ('The Repeal of the Union,' and other Irish papers, and 'Trees of Liberty') are reprinted in *Rescued Essays by T. C.*, ed. Percy Newberry, n.d.

p. 31. **might and right.** See *Past and Present*, ch. ii. : 'Await the issue. In all battles, if you await the issue, each fighter has prospered according to his right. His right and his might, at the close of the account, were one and the same. He has fought with all his might, and in exact proportion to all his right he has prevailed. His very death is no victory over him. He dies indeed, but his work lives, very truly lives.' Nobly meant and phrased ; but could confusion go further ? Who, in this case, are the *mighty* ? The test of success is abandoned, and no standard of *might* remains except the righteousness of the cause. For a close logical criticism of this point, see (Sir) Leslie Stephen, *Hours in a Library*, ed. 1889, series iii., 'Carlyle's Ethics' ; and, for an historical analysis of Carlyle's political creed in relation to the thought of the time, see the luminous pages in L. Cazamian, *Le Roman social en Angleterre* (1830-50), 1904, pp. 150-164 ; I shall again cite this authority.

p. 33. **Mr. Frederic Harrison.** In his *Memories and Thoughts*, 1906, pp. 99-100.

p. 37. **Leighton.** From *Historical Sketches . . . in the Reigns of James the First and Charles the First*, 1898, p. 242 (ed. Alexander Carlyle) : of this material, what was not used up for the *Cromwell* was buried away, unearthed long afterwards, and sifted, by leave of the author, who would have no more to do with it, by John Chorley. These fragments are often in no way behind Carlyle's best writing. For Leighton, see Gardiner, *Hist. of England, 1603-1642*, vii. 143 ff.

p. 41. **philosophy.** For the ideas and historical importance of the thinkers named in this chapter and the next, see above all H. Höffding, *Hist. of Mod. Philosophy*, Eng. tr., 1900, 2 vols., ii. 293-488. Also J. Seth, *Eng. Philosophers and Schools of Philosophy*, 1912, pp. 240-end ; and W. R. Sorley, in *Camb. Hist. Eng. Lit.*, vol. xiv. ch. i. A. W. Benn's *Hist. of Eng. Rationalism in the Nineteenth Century*, 2 vols., 1906, is a chronicle of great value, which I have also used freely. For some links with the philosophers of the previous age, see my *Survey* (1912), chaps. viii. and ix.

p. 45. **Mansel.** Misc. writings, including *Phrontisterion*, collected in *Letters, Lectures, and Reviews*, ed. H. W. Chandler, 1873. They cover the years 1850-71. The paper 'On the Philosophy of Kant' contains Mansel's tribute to his master Hamilton (pp. 183-4) ; in that on 'Modern Spiritualism' (pp. 255-90) he operates well on 'Mr. Sludge, the Medium.' Saintsbury, *Hist. of Eng. Prose Rhythm*, pp. 416-20, 469, renders deserved and much-needed justice to Mansel's numbers. See Benn, *Rationalism*, ii. 103-112, for an effective, and I think merited, attack on Mansel's metaphysics ; but his power as a writer and preacher is ignored.

p. 46. **Ferrier.** *Lectures on Greek Philosophy, and other Philosophical Remains*, 2 vols., 1875, ed. Sir A. Grant and E. L. Lushington (memoir by the latter) ; uniform with this, last ed. of the *Institutes*, with appendix and rejoinders to criticisms. In *Berkeley and Idealism* is clearly seen the germ of the system, with its essential distinction between nonentity or non-reality on the one side, and the contradictory, nonsensical, or 'surd,' on the other; into this, and *not* into zero, 'matter' relapses without a perceiving subject human or divine. See Elizabeth S. Haldane, *J. F. Ferrier* [1899], which gives, besides biographical detail, an excellent account of Ferrier in his setting among the Scottish philosophers, his attack on the 'common sense' school, etc.

p. 48. **John Stuart Mill.** Sources for Mill's life, besides the *Autobiography*, are: *Letters of J. S. M.*, ed., with introduction, by Hugh S. R. Elliot (with a note on Mill's private life by Mary Taylor), 2 vols., 1910; *J. S. M., a Criticism, with Personal Recollections*, by A. Bain, 1882 (see material in the opening chapters for early life); the Carlyle literature; Caroline Fox, *Memories of Old Friends*, ed. H. N. Pym, revised ed., 1883; John [Lord] Morley, *Critical Miscellanies*, second series, 1877 (three articles); also his *Recollections*, 1917, i. 52-67. Other letters of Mill occur in the biographies of Kingsley, Grote, and Spencer. Among other accounts of Mill see above all that of Sir Leslie Stephen, *The English Utilitarians*, vol. iii., 1900; also Taine's two studies, *Le Positivisme anglais*, 1864, and the chapter in *Hist. de la Littérature anglaise* 1863-(4), tom. iv.; some excellent pages in Höffding, *Hist. of Mod. Philosophy*, Eng. tr., 1900, ii. 394-433; W. L. Courtney, *Life of J. S. M.*, n.d. [?1889], in 'Great Writers' series; C. Douglas, *J. S. M., a Study*, etc., 1895; and J. MacCunn, *Six Radical Thinkers*, 1910.

p. 50, note 1. **Mrs. Mill.** See *Autobiography*, and the letters written after her death by Mill; dedication to *Liberty*; and the views of friends in Bain, *op. cit.*, and in the letters of the Carlyles; also the note in journal, given in *Letters*, ii. 361.

p. 50, note 2. **Brandes.** I translate from the *Samlede Skrifter*, popular ed., 1901, Heft 68, pp. 531-46.

p. 51. **correspondence with Carlyle.** In *Letters*, i. 32-99; the last is dated 28 April 1834, but the association went on much longer. In 1869 (ii. 220-1) Mill writes: 'It is only at a particular stage in one's mental development that one benefits much by him (to me he was of great use at that stage), but one continues to read his best things with little, if any, diminution of pleasure after one has ceased to learn anything from him.' In 1854 (note of Jan. 21, *Letters*, ii. 361), Mill says, 'Carlyle has written himself out, and become a mere commentator on himself.' See too Gavan Duffy, *Conversations with C.*, pp. 166-70.

p. 52, note 1. **Saint-Simonians.** See especially *Corr. inédite avec G. d'Eichthal*, 1898, pp. 13, 29 ff. (1829).

p. 52, note 2. **Mill and Comte.** See *Letters*; *Autobiog.*; and *Lettres inédites de J. S. M. à A. Comte*, 1899, ed. L. Lévy-Bruhl. Mill writes in French; Comte's replies are given. The personal dealings and disputes of Comte with his English benefactors are equitably summed up by Bain, *op. cit.*, pp. 70-6. See too Benn, *Rationalism*, i. 408-50, on 'Comte, Carlyle, and Mill.'

p. 54. **Mill's earlier reviews.** I have found no full bibliographical list. See *Early Essays of J. S. M.*, selected by J. W. M. Gibbs, 1897. These are from the original periodicals, and include a number not reprinted in *Dissert. and Disc.*

p. 56, note 1. **causation.** For attacks on Mill's view by theologians see the Roman Catholic W. G. Ward's *Essays on Philos. of Theism*, vol. i.; and the Anglican J. B. Mozley's *Eight* [Bampton] *Lectures on Miracles*, 1865, especially note 2, p. 279, and note 4, p. 295.

p. 56, note 2. **inductive process.** See W. R. Sorley, *Camb. Eng. Lit.*, xiv. 17, and his whole account of Mill.

p. 58. **von Sybel.** In *Vorträge und Aufsätze*, 1874, p. 61, in the article 'Ueber die Emanzipation von Frauen,' a reply to the *Subjection.* Von Sybel makes this remark on Mill's picture of the despotic husband ; otherwise he has little fresh to say ; he repeats Stephen's plea that one housemate must decide in doubtful cases, and that this *must* be the man. He takes the Prussian view of the *Hausfrau*, with streaks of sentimentalism, and shows on first principles that women can never do many things, which they have visibly and actually done.

p. 61, note 1. **'Philip Beauchamp.'** This symptomatic work should have been named in my *Survey* (1912). It is called *Analysis of the Influence of Natural Religion on the Temporal Happiness of Mankind* ; first ed. 1822, afterwards privately reprinted by Grote, 1866. A full account is given by Sir Leslie Stephen, *Eng. Utilitarians*, ii. 339-59 (the vol. on James Mill) ; and he, having seen Bentham's MS. in the B. M., thinks 'that Grote's share in the work was a good deal more than mere editing.' The book is, as he says, most forcibly written, and is by implication an assault on all, and not only on 'natural,' theology. It dwells on the futility of supernatural sanctions to affect motive, save in so far as they pervert it ; and so reduces actual religion to superstition and to the work of priests—'a particular class of persons incurably opposed to the interests of humanity.' It is an early and curious application to religion of the canon of 'experience' ; all the inferences of 'natural religion' are described as 'extra-experimental.' The publisher was Richard Carlile.

p. 61, note 2. **Whewell.** See the paper of 1851, reprinted in *Diss. and Disc.*, vol. ii., with its lively attack on the old universities ; which, in Mill's eyes, are devoted to buttressing conservative principles by the process of 'adapting' the German philosophers. Whewell figures as a ringleader in this attempt. I have barely named him (William Whewell, 1794-1866, Master of Trinity ; *History of the Inductive Sciences*, 1837, *Philosophy of the Inductive Sciences*, 1840, and much else) in my text ; he hardly figures in letters, and is seldom cited as a thinker, though his *History* is accounted of value. A pleasing epigram on Whewell's *Plurality of Worlds*, by Sir Francis Hastings Doyle, will bear re-quotation :

> Should man, through the stars, to far galaxies travel,
> And of nebulous films the remotest unravel,
> He still could but learn, having fathomed infinity,
> That the great work of God was—the Master of Trinity.

p. 66, note 1. **Vestiges of Creation.** See the twelfth ed., 1884, with introd. by Alexander Ireland, who was one of Chambers's few confidants and his intermediary in dealing with the publisher. This interesting and venerable gentleman, Mr. Ireland, who lived to a great age in Manchester, had in his youth seen Scott, had twice been associated with the management of Emerson's circuit in England, and was full of recollections of the Carlyles : a living link also, as we see, with pre-Darwinian days.

p. 66, note 2. **Darwin.** *Life and Letters, including an autobiog. chapter*, ed. Francis Darwin, 3 vols., 1887. The relationship with Lyell is seen in the letters, and in Huxley's chapter in *Life.* Darwin's religious ideas are collected in vol. i., ch. viii. For a touch of his humour, see ii. 385 *sq.* (1862) in reference to the House of Lords : 'Primogeniture is most dreadfully opposed to selection ;

suppose the first-born bull was specially made by each farmer the begetter of his stock! On the other hand, as you say, the ablest men are continually raised to the peerage, and get crossed with the older Lord-breeds, and the Lords continually select the most beautiful and charming women from the lower ranks; so that a good deal of indirect selection improves the Lords.'

p. 67. **Wallace.** Most of his writings outside the sphere of zoology date after 1880. In some he defends spiritualism, in one the state ownership of land (1882); and he opposed vaccination. His speculative bent is seen in *Man's Place in the Universe* (1903), and two years later came his striking autobiography, *My Life.* Wallace's vitality and his range of interest and power are surprising, and he is one of the most vigorous warriors of the great age.

p. 70, note 1. **Spencer.** The bibliography, which is rather intricate owing to the number of recasts and transferences, is given by D. Duncan, *Life and Letters of H. S.*, 1908, and summarised in *D. N. B.*, Suppl. ii. (art. by H. S. R. Elliot; where see too reff. to Spencer literature). Duncan's biography supplements the *Autobiography* (1904) materially, and, while bringing out Spencer's minuter weaknesses, also shows him in a happier and more affectionate light than he does himself. W. H. Hudson's *Introd. to the Philosophy of H. S.*, 1895, is useful. F. Howard Collins, *Epitome of the Synthetic Philosophy* (1889), the authorised digest, is ample, accurate, and hard to read. The *Lives* of Huxley, Darwin, and George Eliot, etc., are full of personal references. There is no better critical summary of Spencer's thought than in H. Höffding, *Hist. of Mod. Philosophy*, Eng. tr., 1900, ii. 452-85; and for a criticism of what Benn regards his latent 'teleology,' see *Rationalism*, ii. 204-35. See too W. R. Sorley, *Camb. Eng. Lit.*, xiv. 27-32.

p. 70, note 2. **landmarks.** Details are given at length in *Autob.*, especially ii. 8-10, 166-70, the stages by which Spencer's governing idea dawned on him and reached completion being specified and dated; see too the reff. given by F. C. S. Schiller in *Ency. Brit.*, eleventh ed., xxv. 637, and the whole article. The programme of the synthetic philosophy, as at first schemed, is given at the beginning of *First Principles*, and in *Autob.*, ii. 479 ff. (App. A).

p. 71. **authority.** J. Arthur Thomson, *H.S.* (in 'English Men of Science' series), 1906, ch. viii. foll., describes the work (p. 93) as 'a biological classic, which, in its range and intensity, finds no parallel except in Haeckel's greatest and least known work, the *Generelle Morphologie*, which was published in 1866 about the same time as the *Principles.*' Prof. Thomson's review of Spencer, and that not merely on the scientific side, is grateful to the lay reader.

p. 72. **No contemptuous title.** *Essays*, ii. 199 (*Represent. Government*, 1857).

p. 74, note 1. **Matthew Arnold.** In *God and the Bible*, ch. v. (passage dropped in popular ed.) he jibes (quoting a line of Homer in contrast) at the 'great sentence.' Spencer's retort, given in text, is in *First Principles*, fifth ed. (1880), p. 570 (appendix). The 'sentence' comes at end of ch. xvii., and has often been cited, but may appear once more as an example of technical English: 'Evolution is an integration of matter and concomitant dissipation of motion; during which the matter passes from an indefinite, incoherent homogeneity to a definite, coherent heterogeneity; and during which the retained motion undergoes a parallel transformation.' Of course Matthew Arnold was wrong; the definition, right or not, is worded in the only way that can express the idea, as the reader of *First Principles* will see.

p. 74, note 2. **Comtism in England.** See too bibliographies in *Ency. Brit.* *s.v.* 'Comte,' and in *Camb. Hist. Eng. Lit.*, vol. xiv., ch. i. *s.vv.* 'Beesly, Bridges, Congreve, H. Martineau, Lewes.'—A small but typical case of Comte's influence can be read in the autobiographical ch. prefixed to W. M. Wilks Call's *Reverberations*, 1849 and 1876, a book of verse. Call was first 'disturbed' by reading Shelley and *Cain*, and then by 'the subtle Hume' and James Mill: was quieted awhile by reading Coleridge, and took Anglican orders; read Baur, and began to doubt Moses, and also the fact of eternal perdition; then, owing to Strauss and J. S. Mill, ceased to credit miracles; held fast for a time to a 'natural Christianity,' but lost even that 'residuary faith'; and at last found peace in the religion of humanity, as supplying 'an object to action, a rule of conduct, an intellectual rallying-point'; quitting the Church accordingly. Call is all the more representative for not being a very original person. His *Golden Histories*, 1871, contains the more than pretty poem *The Bird in the Bower*, the once popular *Manoli*, and also some translations (*e.g.* of the *Hymn to Demeter*).

p. 75, note 1. **Life of Goethe.** It has been reprinted in a cheap form, but ought to be edited and brought up to date; Prof. J. G. Robertson informs me that this has not yet been done; and the task awaits some such competent hand.

p. 75, note 2. **Huxley.** *Life and Letters*, by his son Leonard Huxley, 2 vols., 1900. The *Scientific Memoirs* are in four large vols. (and one supplementary), 1898 foll. Some portions of these appear, where of general interest, in the nine vols. of *Collected Essays*, 1893, which include the *Hume* (in *Eng. Men of Letters* originally), and wherein the subjects are re-grouped, not as in the original issues (*Lay Sermons*, etc.). Bibliography in *Life*, ii. 453-70. Many reff. in the Darwin and Spencer literature. The art. by Sir William T. Thiselton-Dyer in *Ency. Brit.*, eleventh ed., xiv. 17-20, contains instructive citations of Huxley's philosophical views.

p. 76. **give a push.** Spencer, *Autob.*, ii. 5. Compare the letter to Spencer, May 8, 1888 (*Life*, ii. 198-9): 'You and I, my dear friend, have had our innings, and carry our bats out while our side is winning. One could not reasonably ask for more.'

p. 78. **'agnostic.'** *Life*, i. 319-20; and *Agnosticism*, 1889, in *Coll. Essays*, v. 237-9. The term occurred to Huxley when he was at a loss, in the meetings of the 'Metaphysical Society,' founded in 1869, to define his attitude by a title.

p. 79, note 1. **the Bible.** In *Coll. Essays*, vol. iii.; originally in *Fort. Rev.*, 1870, *The School Boards*; and quoted in *Controverted Questions*, 1892, p. 51 See too *s.v.* 'Bible-reading in elementary schools,' in index to *Life*.

p. 79, note 2. **Goethe.** Huxley's translation was published in the first number of *Nature*, Nov. 1869. See *Life*, i. 326; and T. Bailey Saunders, *The Maxims and Reflections of Goethe*, 1893, preface, p. vi.

p. 80, note 1. **Eyre.** See the fierce letters in *Life*, ii. 279-83. See Mill, *Autobiog.*, pp. 298-9; and art. 'Eyre' in *D. N. B.*, Suppl. ii. vol. i. *ad fin.*; Eyre lived till 1901.

p. 80, note 2. **negro.** See too Emancipation—*Black and White*, 1865; 'Emancipate girls,' he says, when he passes to the question of the 'white'; but the result, he believes, is that 'women will find their place . . . Nature's old salique law will not be repealed.' Women will always be weighted: 'the duty of man is to see that not a grain is piled upon that load beyond what Nature imposes; that injustice is not added to inequality.'

p. 81. **orang.** In *Science and Morals*, 1886; in *Coll. Essays*, ix.; *Controverted Questions*, pp. 214-15.

p. 82. **Clifford.** *Lectures and Essays*, edited by Sir Leslie Stephen and Sir Frederick Pollock, 2 vols., 1901; memoir, in vol. i., by the latter; *q.v.* for an utterance of the 'natural religion' of this age and group of friends. Clifford, even more than his comrades, was fiercely and naïvely anti-clerical, in a style that led Matthew Arnold to say that Messrs. Moody and Sankey were, compared with him, 'masters of the philosophy of history.'

p. 84, note 1. **conservative thinkers.** For an attack on Stephen's 'naturalism,' or 'agnostic empiricism,' see A. J. Balfour, *Theism and Humanism*, 1915 (Gifford lectures), pp. 140-6; the general ground being that with the naturalist, as with the supernaturalist, 'his beliefs will always transcend his arguments.' So reasoned Newman earlier.

p. 84, note 2. **Henry Sidgwick.** See the *Memoir*, 1906, 'by A. S[idgwick] and E. M. S. [Mrs. Henry Sidgwick].'

p. 86. **æsthetic feelings.** *Theory of Practice*, 2 vols., 1870; paces of different rhythms (dactylic, etc.), i. 150 *sq.*; i. 170 *sq.*, Fancy, unlike imagination, does not try to 'find and express emotional truth,' but to 'exercise the faculty of comparison of images, which will certainly thus be coloured by emotion but will not be its adequate expression.' i. 291 *sq.*, in poetry 'the art of imaginative reasoning and emotion go hand in hand.' ii. 270, style: 'the more transient modifications of speech by trains of consciousness, the more flexible details within the limits of the general rules of inflexion and syntax' (this follows on a long and suggestive account of the logic and psychology of the parts of speech and of inflexions); see too the account of 'eros,' i. 196 *sq.*

p. 87. 'He appealed . . .' W. R. Sorley, *Camb. Hist. Eng. Lit.*, vol. xiv. (1916), p. 43.

p. 92. **Fortnightly Review.** See Lord Morley, *Recollections*, 1917, i., ch. vi.

p. 93. **Lewis.** *Letters*, ed. Sir G. F. Lewis, 1870. *Political Terms*, ed. Sir T. Raleigh, 1898. *Influence of Authority*, etc., new ed. 1875. The rest do not seem to have been reprinted. The best account of Lewis is that of W. Bagehot, in his *Biographical Studies* (1863). Lewis's *Origin of the Romance Languages*, 1835, and his *Survey of the Astronomy of the Ancients*, 1862, are proofs of his multifarious erudition. *Essay on the Government of Dependencies*, ed. C. P. Lucas, Oxford, 1891.

p. 94. **Roman ballad-poetry.** *Enquiry*, etc., i. 202-37; on Macaulay, pp. 217 ff., 'one of the last persons who should treat brilliant and striking passages in a prose history, glowing with poetical warmth, and diversified with poetical imagery, as proofs of a metrical original' (p. 221); see too on the *Lays*, pp. 236-7.

p. 95. **Buckle.** A. H. Huth, *Life and Writings of B.*, 1880. The *Hist. of Civilization* has been edited by J. M. Robertson, 1904. The *Misc. and Posth. Works*, ed. Helen Taylor, 3 vols., 1872, is mostly a commonplace-book, or rag-bag of notes and references, with a memoir.

p. 96, note 1. **Lecky.** *Memoir*, by Mrs. Lecky, 1909. *Historical and Political Essays*, posthumous, 1908. The standard ed. of the *Hist. of England*, etc., is now in 7 vols., and of the *Hist. of Ireland* in 5 vols. *Democracy and Liberty*, two vols., 1896.

p. 96, note 2. **Lecky and Buckle.** For exposure of the fallacy of averages, see *Rationalism*, introduction; *Memoir*, p. 59, for acknowledgement of debt; *id.*, p. 106, 'I quite think with Grote that the master-error of Buckle is his absurd underrating of the accidents of history'; also the paper 'Formative Influences,' in *Hist. and Pol. Essays* (a judicial and generous summary).

p. 96, note 3. **science of history.** See the whole passage, *Memoir*, p. 59; and the reference, *id.*, p. 54, note, to Comte in this connexion.

p. 97. **accident** in history. *Hist. of England*, i. 17-19. Lecky, however, defines 'accident' more broadly; 'instances in which a slight change in the disposition of circumstances, or in the action of individuals, would have altered the whole course of history' (*e.g.* the Jews might have been thus extirpated, Greece conquered by Xerxes, Rome by Hannibal; and the story of France would have been different if the Duke of Burgundy had succeeded Louis XIV.). This idea recurs in *The Political Value of History*, 1892, pp. 32-3: 'though there is a certain steady and orderly evolution that it is impossible in the long run to resist, yet individual action and even accident have borne a very great part in modifying the direction of history, as there are periods when the human mind is in such a state of pliancy that a small pressure can give it a bent which will last for generations. If Mohammed had been killed,' etc.

p. 99. **'judicious,'** etc. *Memoir*, p. 166.

p. 100. **recast** of *Leaders of Public Opinion in Ireland.* The work first appeared, almost unregarded, in 1861; then in purged and revised shape, in 1871; became suddenly popular before 1887, and was quoted, in its earlier discarded shape, by pleaders for Home Rule, to the author's annoyance; and was finally recast thoroughly in 1903 (2 vols.: see introduction for above details); the *Swift*, meanwhile, being detached and also revised, and now appearing in the *Prose Works of Swift* (Bohn ed.).

p. 102. **Maine.** See Sir M. E. Grant-Duff, *Brief Memoir* (with some of the Indian Speeches), 1892.

p. 104. **Bagehot.** *Works and Life*, ed. Mrs. Russell Barrington, 10 vols., 1914. The chief works are easily to be had in various edd.; but the collected ed. contains many smaller articles of interest, *e.g.* that on *The Ignorance of Man.* The memoir by R. H. Hutton, given in *Works*, vol. i., is admirable.

p. 109. **Macaulay.** The definitive (1908) ed. of (Sir) G. O. Trevelyan's *Life and Letters of Lord M.* (1876) contains the 'Marginal Notes,' also published separately. There are many passing allusions in the correspondence of Moore, Lockhart, Caroline Fox, etc. See, too, Viscountess Knutsford, *Life and Letters of Zachary M.*, 1900. The art. by Mark Pattison in *Ency. Brit.* (eds. 9 and 11) is of note: likewise the vol. by J. Cotter Morison, 1885 ('Eng. Men of Letters'), though somewhat superfine in criticism. To the well-known judgements by Bagehot in *Lit. Studies* and by Sir L. Stephen in *Hours in a Library*, should be added those by Frederic Harrison, *Studies in Early Victorian Lit.*, 1895, and G. Saintsbury, *Corrected Impressions*, 1895, and the excellent balanced lecture by Sir R. Jebb, 1900. Edd. of the works of Macaulay are numerous: that of the *Essays* by F. C. Montague, 3 vols., 1903, has valuable notes and introductions. C. H. Firth's illustrated ed. of the *History*, 6 vols., 1913-15, contains no commentary, but see below note to p. 126, note 2.

p. 110. **Carlyle on Macaulay.** I do not cite in text the letter of July 24, 1840, the most vicious of all, and the most amusing (M. will be 'a poor Holland House unbeliever, with spectacles instead of eyes, to the end of him'), because it was prompted by the mistaken belief that an article on Carlyle in the *Edinburgh*, really by Herman Merivale, was by Macaulay. (Froude, *C.'s Life in London*, ch. vii.) On being undeceived, he was 'heartily glad'—'of Macaulay I still have considerable hopes.'

p. 111. **Great Minute.** The essentials are quoted by Trevelyan, ch. vi.; but the whole should be made more accessible, and is given by W. F. B. Laurie, *Distinguished Anglo-Indians*, second series, 1888, pp. 170-84; see pp. 167-9, 184-5, for previous publication.

p. 112. **Mitchel.** See the whole passage (written in June 1848) in his *Jail Journal*, 'author's ed.' [1876], pp. 37-9.

p. 114. **Macaulay and religion.** For his conviction that there can be 'no progress' in theological inquiry, see not only the essay on Ranke, but *History*, ch. xvii., the pages on George Fox: 'In theology, the interval is small indeed between Aristotle and a child, between Archimedes and *a naked savage*' (italics mine). The next sentences may well glance at the secession of Newman: 'inquisitive and restless spirits take refuge from their own scepticism in the bosom of a church which pretends to infallibility, and, after questioning the existence of a Deity, *bring themselves to worship a wafer*' (italics mine). This is very like Mill's phrase in the *Liberty* about the man who 'spends a life in sophisticating with an intellect which he cannot silence.' See, too, letter of Nov. 13, 1840, in *Life*, ch. viii., where Macaulay says that he has 'no disposition to split hairs about' the Eucharist, but will write, preferably, about 'Wycherley and the other good-for-nothing fellows.' Macaulay was very much 'at peace' about the mysteries of the faith.

p. 126, note 1. **Acton.** See, in his *Correspondence* (1917), vol. i., p. 260, the whole letter of June 21, 1876, to Gladstone on Macaulay. M. 'is dishonest by display: of the Reformation he knew almost nothing, yet he so pillaged Ranke as to make believe that he was a rival authority on that age. Then how materialistic he is, his imagination especially,' etc.

p. 126, note 2. **riddled.** See art. in *D. N. B.* by Sir L. Stephen for list of the chief criticisms up to date. They include, besides those named in my text, John Paget's *New Examen*, 1861 (and his *Puzzles and Paradoxes*, 1874), which deals with Marlborough, Penn, Claverhouse, the picture of the Highlands, and the account of Glencoe; also the vindications of Penn by W. Hepworth Dixon in his *Life of P.*, 1851, and by W. E. Forster, *Observations*, etc., 1849. (Macaulay added notes dealing with these objections in his ed. of 1857.) F. C. Montague's commentary in his ed. of the *Essays* gives much matter for supplementing and judging Macaulay, *e.g.*, in the case of Hastings. C. H. Firth's paper in the *Scottish Hist. Rev.* for July 1918 on 'M.'s Treatment of Scottish History' is a sample of the treatment required by the whole *Hist. of England*, and is 'part of a series of lectures delivered at Oxford' on that work; these unfortunately are as yet unpublished. See too, on Macaulay's general use of evidence, Sir R. Lodge in Chambers's *Cyclop. of Eng. Lit.*, 1903, iii. 367-9; I have quoted from this art. in my text the phrase about 'extreme precision,' etc.

p. 130. **rhythm.** See Saintsbury, *Hist. of Eng. Prose Rhythm*, 1912, pp. 370-5, for a balanced statement; yet I would rate Macaulay higher on this count, and do not find him so monotonous. Prof. Saintsbury notes his fondness for trochaic endings of the clause; equally common is the habit of ending with a bang on a strong accent, often a monosyllable. Yet, within the clauses, the usual movement is smooth, though not too smooth, and is in what I have elsewhere labelled 'rising' and 'waved' rather than in 'falling' or 'level' rhythm (see a paper on 'English Prose Numbers' in *Essays and Studies by Members of the Eng. Association*, vol. iv., 1913). Formal analysis of chosen passages confirms this view. Sometimes a much freer and more poetic rhythm is attained, as in the celebrated 'purple patch' on Milton in *History*, ch. iii. (' A míghtier | póet, || tríed | at ónce | by paín, | dánger, | póverty, | óbloquy, | and blíndness, || méditated, || ùndistúrbed | by the obscéne | túmult | aróund him,' || etc.). The 37 'feet,' or accent-groups, of the complete sentence, contain almost every type of 'foot' that is possible in English, and the whole, in spite of the number of trochees and dactyls which it might be feared would check the flow, is wrought into an impeccable harmony.

p. 133. **Froude**. H. W. Paul, *Life*, 1905. No collected ed., and apparently no bibliography beyond the lists in *D. N. B.*, Suppl. i. and in *Camb. Eng. Lit.*, vols. xiii. and xiv. But most of the works, after the earliest, are easy to reach, the *History*, the *Short Studies*, *Oceana*, and the various Oxford lectures, being in popular form. For some of the Froude-Carlyle literature, see *ante*, note to p. 8.

p. 137. **Euripides**. See, in ch. xiv., sec. x. of text, on Browning's *Balaustion* and the revulsion in favour of Euripides; whose sceptical and satiric side Froude relishes, and three of whose plays he analyses with his graceful skill.

p. 140. **Froude and Freeman**. See Paul, *Life*, ch. v., for a summary of the disputes, and plea that Froude on the whole triumphed. A. Lang, *Hist. of Eng. Lit.*, 1902, pp. 651-3 (whence my quotation in text, pp. 140-1), remarks that Freeman 'did not know where to have him,' and gives other examples of inaccuracy. For the consensus of historians on this point, and for an excellent summary of Froude's qualities and defects as historian, see G. P. Gooch, *Hist. and Historians in the Nineteenth Cent.*, 1913, pp. 332-9.

p. 145. **Thirlwall**. *Letters, Lit. and Theological*, ed. J. J. S. Perowne and L. Stokes, 2 vols., 1881 (for my extract on Newman, see i. 260 ff.; on Morris, i. 292). *Letters to a Friend*, ed. A. P. Stanley, 1881. *Remains, Lit. and Theological*, ed. Perowne, 3 vols., 1877-80 (charges, essays, sermons). The *Hist. of Greece* remains in its revised ed., 1845-52.

p. 148. **Grote**. A condensed ed., containing the more valuable parts of the *History*, with notes and corrections and commentaries up to date, has been made by J. M. Mitchell and M. O. B. Caspari, 1907; see p. xiii on Grote's English predecessors; and the editors' lucid account, on which I have drawn, of the aspects in which Grote's work is and is not antiquated. For a contemporary appreciation and criticism, see E. A. Freeman's articles on *The Athenian Democracy*, 1856, and *Alexander the Great*, 1857, reprinted in his *Historical Essays*, second series, 1873. On Grote's share in *The Influence of Natural Religion*, by 'Philip Beauchamp,' see *ante*, note to p. 61 of text.

p. 149. **Finlay**. The complete work, with the author's last corrections, is *The History of Greece from the Conquest by the Romans to the Present Time, B.C. 146 to A.D. 1864*, ed. F. H. Tozer, 7 vols., 1877 (see the striking brief autobiography given in vol. i., and Finlay's reference to himself, vii. 272, n.).

The prefaces of 1843 and 1855 clearly explain Finlay's scope and purpose. See Tozer's account of the course, and intricate bibliography, of the book.

p. 150. **eye-witness.** See W. Alison Philips, in *Camb. Mod. Hist.*, x. 804, for ref. to the MSS. papers of Sir Richard Church in B. M., and Finlay's estimate thereof; and p. 806 for need of caution in reading all narratives of the event.

p. 151, note 1. **Christian ethics . . . national unity.** See *History*, i. 135 ff.

p. 151, note 2. **eschews rhythm and the graces.** A sentence like this is common: 'the power of systematic organis*ation*, as distinct from the pedantry of uniform centralis*ation*, was never more conspicuous than in the energy of the Othoman administr*ation*' (v. 11).

p. 151, note 3. **first Byzantine sovereigns.** iii. 9-10.

p. 151, note 4. . . . **tribute of Christian children.** *History*, v. 3; see also for the cast of Finlay's political philosophy, such passages as i. 121: 'It is impossible for man to exist in society without some religious feeling,' etc.; i. 191, 'there is nothing in the range of human affairs so completely democratic as taste; Sophocles addressed himself alike to the educated and the uneducated,' etc.; v. 132, 'the fermenting leaven of self-destruction which exists in all corporate bodies placed beyond the direct control of public opinion'; v. 36, 'fortunately it is the nature of despotism to accelerate the corruption even of those institutions which increase its power'; and iii. 165; v. 232; vii. 318, 'The best despot,' etc.

p. 152, note 1. **Thomas Arnold.** A. P. Stanley, *Life and Corr. of T. A.*, 2 vols., 1844 (bibliography in vol. ii.), many edd. Arnold's works are not collected. The *Misc. Works*, 1845, were edited by Stanley. The *Thucydides* and the *Hist. of Rome* live, and are easy to find. *The Second Punic War*, ed. W. T. Arnold, 1886, consists of chaps. xlii.-xlvii. of vol. iii. of the *History*, with some corrections from author's MS., additional notes, and valuable preface by the editor, as well as bibliography of the chief fresh authorities up to date. William Thomas Arnold (1852-1904), himself a writer of mark on the subject (*Roman System of Provincial Administration*, 1879, etc.; *Studies in Roman Imperialism*, ed. E. Fiddes, 1906) and a scholar-journalist of a rare type, working on the *Manchester Guardian*, was also an admirable editor of Keats and dramatic critic. His father, Thomas Arnold, junior, the younger son of the head master, wrote a *Manual of Eng. Literature* (1862) and edited the English works of Wiclif; Mrs. Humphry Ward, the novelist, was his daughter. Younger scions still of this race have the gift for letters; *vitai lampada tradunt*; but our limiting date of 1880, here again, has to be remembered.

p. 152, note 2. **ethics and politics.** See Arnold's inaugural lecture at Oxford, given in 1841, and printed in his *Introductory Lectures on Modern History*, 1845; where an appendix deals with his critics. Arnold clashes with Macaulay's Whig proposition, set out in his *Edinburgh* review (1839) of *Gladstone on Church and State*, that the chief aim of the state is 'the security of the persons and property of men.' Arnold insists on the larger moral and spiritual purpose, and works up to his theory of the 'perfect state and the perfect church' as identical. See the lecture, p. 10.

p. 157. **Stubbs.** *Letters*, ed. W. H. Hutton, 1904. The *Seventeen Lectures on the Study of Mediæval and Modern History* (1886) are of most general interest; many other series (*On European History*, *On Early Eng. History*, etc.), were collected and edited after Stubbs's lifetime by A. Hassall, who also reprinted (1902) the Introductions in the Rolls Series. The *Select Charters* have also been re-edited by H. W. C. Davis; for a summary of the value of the work, in the light of later research, see Gooch, *op. cit.*, pp. 342-5; and art. in *D. N. B.* (Suppl. ii.) by T. F. Tout.

p. 158. **philosophy of history**. See *Lectures on Early Eng. Hist.*, ed. Hassall, 1906, pp. 194 ff.

p. 159, note 1. **portraits.** See *Hist. Introd.* (Rolls), ed. Hassall, pp. 92 ff. (Henry II.); pp. 316-19 (Richard I.); pp. 439 ff. (John); and *Lect. on Europ. Hist.*, ed. Hassall, pp. 132 ff. (Charles V.), pp. 241 ff. (Henry IV.).

p. 159, note 2. **Freeman.** W. R. W. Stephens, *Life and Letters*, 2 vols., 1895; an excellent memoir, but most of the letters are of professional rather than general interest. See too F. York Powell, *Occasional Writings*, ed. O. Elton, 1906, ii. 27-37, for a personal sketch and estimate. For judgements by other historians, see Gooch, *History and Historians*, etc., 1913, pp. 346-52 ('The Oxford Historians'); and Sir A. W. Ward, *Camb. Hist. Eng. Lit.*, xiv. 69-74 (1916). Also an informing paper by Lord Bryce, *Studies in Contemp. Biography*, 1904, pp. 262-92, 'with a profound and minute knowledge of English history down to the fourteenth century, so far as his aversion to the employment of manuscript authorities would allow, and a scarcely inferior knowledge of foreign European history during the same period, with a less full but very sound knowledge down to the middle of the sixteenth century, and with a thorough mastery of pretty nearly all ancient history, his familiarity with later European history, and with the history of such outlying regions as India and America, was not much beyond that of the average educated man' (p. 280). Freeman's works, from their nature, can never be collected; a bibliography (excluding the *Sat. Rev.* and some archæological articles) is given in Stephens, vol. ii. *ad fin.*, and comprises over two hundred entries. To the works named in my text may be added the masterly *General Sketch of European History*, 1872.

p. 164. **Gardiner**. The 10 vols. of the *Hist. of England, 1603-1642*, were first issued together in 1883-4; I cite this ed. For life see art. by C. H. Firth in *Dict. Nat. Biog.*, Suppl. ii. The quotation from York Powell is from his *Life, Letters*, etc., ii. 42, 43; see the whole article; also G. P. Gooch, *op. cit.*, pp. 359-65. The remarks of Gardiner on the statesman and the historian occur in the preface to his tenth vol.

p. 166. **toleration.** See too viii. 165-6 ('the main condition of toleration was the absence of fear lest toleration should be used as a means of attack upon those who granted it'), and *id.*, p. 176, on the arguments of Vane in Massachusetts. In vol. x. (p. 12), 'the traditional belief of centuries, held alike by the zealot and the politician, was that religious liberty was but another name for anarchy'; and (pp. 34-7) the same text recurs with increasing emphasis as the civil war approaches.

p. 168, note 1. **Seeley**. See the admirable memorial sketch prefixed by G. W. Prothero to *The Growth of British Policy*, 2 vols., 1895; and, for estimates, Sir A. W. Ward, *op. cit.*, xiv. 90-3, and Gooch, *op. cit.*, pp. 369-74. Seeley's works are mostly easy of access, especially the histories: *The Expansion of England* has been often re-issued. His *Introduction to Political Science* (1896) is a reprint of lectures. The papers on 'Liberal Education in Universities' (1867) and on 'English in Schools' (1868), reprinted in *Lectures and Essays* (1870), should not be overlooked.

p. 168, note 2. **Ecce Homo.** Among many criticisms, see an acute but unsympathetic one in Benn, *Rationalism*, ii. 236-46.

p. 172. **many names.** Besides Gooch, *op. cit.*, and Ward, *op. cit.*, see, for a contemporary mention, Stubbs, *Seventeen Lectures*, etc. (1876), p. 64 ff., which names, beside the work of Freeman and Gardiner, that of J. S. Brewer on Henry VIII., of J. E. Thorold Rogers on the history of agriculture and prices, and the Oxford translation of Ranke ; and then (1884), p. 433 ff., the labours of James Gairdner on the early Tudors, and the first instalments of T. Hodgkin's *Italy and her Invaders* (1880, etc.), and of Creighton's *Hist. of the Papacy* ; also the Norse work of G. Vigfússon and F. York Powell (*Corp. Poet. Boreale*, 1883). 'All these and more came thronging,' and prove the unbroken continuity of historical studies ; but it is out of my plan, as well as beyond my powers, to deal with them. I have also omitted, as belonging more to learning than to letters, such work as Lord Stanhope's sober *War of the Succession in Spain*, 1832, and *Hist. of Eng. from the Peace of Utrecht*, 7 vols., 1836-54 ; Sir Archibald Alison's long popular *History of Europe, 1789-1815*, 10 vols., 1833-42 ; John Hill Burton's *History of Scotland*, 7 vols., 1867-70, and Patrick Fraser Tytler's earlier *Hist. of Scotland*, 9 vols., 1828-50 ; and the writings of W. Nassau Molesworth, Sir Spencer Walpole, and others.

p. 174. **Napier.** *Life*, by H. A. Bruce [Lord Aberdare], 2 vols., 1864. See i. 234 ff. for the inception of the *History* ; also i. 536 ff. ; ii. 40, telling how the account of Albuera was written 'during a rare interval of health, on a stormy day of March, as the author strode along the upland downs in Wiltshire, battling with an equinoctial gale' ; and ii. 200, a splendid outburst, uttered when Napier was ill and had been under narcotics : 'What am I now ? A bundle of pain and misery : and what will be the next step ? I suppose I shall be a little—a very little—better and happier than I am now; though low enough, I expect. Or will it be a large flat dreary plain of oblivion, without memory, without hope, without knowledge, without desire ? Well !—if so, I shall be *out*—that is all. And what am I that will be out ? Mere pain.'—Napier also published *English Battles and Sieges in the Peninsula*, consisting of extracts from the *History*, some of them compressed, and with some passages (including the Coruña fight and the character of Moore) 'entirely recomposed.'

p. 176, note 1. **Kinglake.** See W. Tuckwell, *A. W. K.*, 1902, which contains (pp. 22 ff.) clues to many allusions in *Eöthen*, and also new information as to Kinglake's friendship with Mme. Novikoff, pp. 90 ff. The 'cabinet' ed. of the *Invasion* appeared in 1887-8, and the prefaces to some of the vols. are new (*e.g.* the story of Nicholas Kiréeff, the Russian hero, in vol. i. ; see Tuckwell, pp. 90-1, on the circumstances). There are attacks on the first two vols. in both *Quart. Rev.* and *Ed. Rev.* for April 1863, the former the more lively and violent of the two. In defence, *Mr. Kinglake and the Quarterlys*, 'by an old reviewer,' namely Abraham Hayward, 1863, exposes many misinterpretations effectively. There is an abridgement of the *Invasion*, 'adapted for military students,' by Sir G. S. Clarke, 1899, with a separate atlas.

p. 176, note 2. **Quarterly.** These articles are assigned to Kinglake by Sir Leslie Stephen, in *D. N. B.*

p. 179. **Oxford Movement.** Authorship most voluminous ; see bibliography by S. L. Ollard in *C. E. L.*, xii. 453-63, where there are 40 'particular authors' named; with much of this matter I do not affect to cope. The corresponding chapter, *id.*, no. xii., by W. H. Hutton, is in excellent perspective, and I am indebted to it. The fullest history is one written from a conciliatory Roman standpoint: P. Thureau-Dangin, *La Renaissance catholique en Angleterre*, three parts, 1899, 1903, 1906, the record coming down to 1892; tr. W. Wilberforce, 2 vols., 1915. For older accounts by participants, see under T. Mozley, F. Oakeley, and Sir W. Palmer in Ollard's list. See my text on R. W. Church, *The Oxford Movement (1833-1845)*, 1891 (posthumous ed., enhanced from author's MSS., 1909). For a critical review and strictures, see the Congregationalist divine A. M. Fairbairn's *Catholicism, Roman and Anglican*, ed. 3, 1899 (reprinted articles, including his dispute with Newman). For a fair and learned summary of the views of theologians from Paley to Martineau see John Hunt, *Religious Thought in England in the XIXth Century*, 1896. J. H. Overton, *The Eng. Church in the XIXth Century, 1800-1833*, 1894, chap. vi., registers the chief theological works of that period.

p. 181. **Hurrell Froude.** *H. F., Memoranda and Comments*, 1904, by Miss L. I. Guiney, contains a reprint (with some conjectural editing) of his letters, and also a full *catena* of extracts from the High Church literature concerning his life and character. Froude left his mark on those about him in a measure which nothing from his pen can now explain—least of all the painful and trivial tone of self-scrutiny, as of an ascetical minor Rousseau, which marks the *Remains*.

p. 182. **Newman.** *Lists of works*: in *C. E. L.*, xii. 459-61 (S. L. Ollard, chief works only); in *D. N. B.*, by W. S. Lilly (not exhaustive); and Newman's own, in 1865 and later edd. of *Apologia* (up to 1864). *Works*, uniform (not complete) ed., 36 vols., 1868-81. *Characteristics from Writings*, ed. Lilly, 1874. *Biography*: the *Apologia*; *Letters and Corresp.. in the Eng. Church*, ed. Anne Mozley, 2 vols., 1891, including 'autobiographical memoir' down to 1832; *Life*, by Wilfrid Ward, 2 vols., 1912 (full, and fair, and much new matter); Thureau-Dangin, *N. Catholique*, etc., 1912. Shorter sketches by R. H. Hutton, 1891; Canon W. F. Barry, 1904; and H. Brémond, 1905 and 1906. The Lives and Memoirs of Manning, Pattison, Pusey, W. G. Ward, and Wiseman furnish varied material. Hostile judgements and criticisms are exemplified in F. W. Newman's *Contributions to the Early Life of Card. Newman*, 1891; in Sir L. Stephen, *N.'s Theory of Belief*, reprinted in *An Agnostic's Apology*, etc.; and in E. A. Abbott, *Philomythus*, 1891 (on miracles), and *The Anglican Career of Card. N.*, 2 vols., 1892. This last is a bitter, captious book for the prosecution, with elaborate references at every point, mingled with shrewd but seemingly unwilling passages of appreciation, and not questioning Newman's personal honesty, but making him out, on the whole, a sophist, rhetorician, and self-deceiver. The detail is more copious than convincing.

p. 186. **Essay on Development.** See, for special aspects of the argument (I quote ed. 2, 1846), pp. 7-24, where the rival (supposedly Anglican) canon of Christian truth, *quod semper, quod ubique, quod ab omnibus*, is found wanting; the interesting but confused recital, pp. 44 ff., of the various species of 'development' ('material,' 'physical,' 'political,' etc.); the definition, somewhat question-begging, of the 'corruption' of an idea as that which 'obscures' its essence, and 'disturbs' or 'reverses' its growth; p. 181, on antecedent probability; pp.

320 ff., the defence of the interpretation of Scripture in its 'mystical sense,' as 'her [the Church's] most subtle and powerful method of proof'—a method of which Newman does not trace the 'corruptions.' For a criticism from the learned Anglican point of view, see J. B. Mozley, *The Theory of Development*, 1847 ; and, from the agnostic side, Sir Leslie Stephen, *op. cit.* in last note.

p. 190. **Idea of a University.** For the whole episode see Ward, *Life*, i. 305-416. Newman's comment on the want of 'sagacity' of Pius IX. in his Irish policy is a model of the furious-icy-deferential style (p. 388). The first nine lectures were prior to the actual foundation ; they were called *On the Scope and Nature of University Education.* The true 'inaugural' was given on Nov. 3, 1854, on *Christianity and Letters.*

p. 192. **Pattison.** *Memoirs*, 1885, p. 210. The 'grand development,' he says, was 'sealed to Newman,' who could not read German. 'A. P. Stanley once said to me, "How different the fortunes of the Church of England might have been if Newman had been able to read German."' Archdeacon Hutton (*Camb. Eng. Lit.* xii. 254) ascribes this remark to J. A. Froude.

p. 193, note 1. **Kingsley.** I will quote here Charles Bonnier, *Monographie du Mensonge*, *Essai sur la Casuistique*, Liverpool, 1913, privately printed, p. 17 : 'Que fût-il arrivé pourtant si Newman avait rencontré un Bayle sur sa route ? On pourrait se figurer le grand ironiste . . . couvrant N. d'éloges et K. de condoléances ; appréciant les coups et les parades, criant à l'un "bien touché !" à l'autre "Maladroit !" Puis, à la fin de son article, dans une petite note (Bayle a la note terrible) il eût fait doucement remarquer au lecteur que les deux pugillistes s'étaient battus en l'air et n'avaient pas abordé une fois le point dangereux ; de là sortirait une réquisitoire, avec preuves à l'appui, contre la religion chrétienne. Il renverrait enfin les deux plaideurs dos-à-dos et condamnerait aux dépens l'Eglise—protestante aussi bien que catholique.' The whole passage, pp. 14-17, on Newman, Kingsley, Gladstone, and Manning, is instructive : 'Ce fut une véritable "danse du scalp" intellectuelle' (of the *Apologia*). See, too, W. R. Inge, *Outspoken Essays*, cited below in note to p. 197.

p. 193, note 2. **Apologia.** See the ed. by Wilfrid Ward, 1913, which gives full *apparatus criticus* for comparison of edd. ; the changes were made in the second, of 1865, after which the title *Apologia*, etc., was restored, though the omitted chapters on Kingsley were not.

p. 193, note 3. **letter.** Ward, *Life*, ii. 46. The remark on the need to 'say something sharp' is in this letter.

p. 196. **'My surmise.'** *Id.*, ii. 90 (and cp. ii. 491-2) ; the reference is to Sir Frederic Rogers, afterwards Lord Blachford, whose *Letters*, ed. G. E. Marindin, 1896, are full of interesting allusions to Newman (pp. 246-7, 'thrown away by the communion to which he has devoted himself' (1863) ; and p. 407, 'discussion in 1881 on lines familiar from *Grammar of Assent*—'instinct,' according to N., 'often a truer guide than what is logically cogent,' etc.

p. 197. **sophist.** I have, of course, asserted this in the text rather than argued it ; but may refer to the handling of Newman in Abbott's *Philomythus* and by Sir L. Stephen, *op. cit.* I think that his powers as a reasoner and writer are at their flimsiest, and that he verges on the grotesque, in his dealing with the miraculous ; and this is not because, as it happens, I disagree with him ; for I should never use such terms of Mozley's Bampton Lectures on the same subject. See, for an admirable analysis, the article on Newman in W. R. Inge, *Outspoken Essays*, 1919, pp. 172-204. Dean Inge brings out the intellectual isolation of Newman in the Roman Church, and treats his 'personalism' (in contrast with the scholastic rationalism) as forecasting, and in some sense affecting, the phenomenon of 'Modernism' (I have borrowed one or two points in my text from this exposition).

p. 202. **Faber.** For the secular *Poems*, see Faber's own selection, 1856; the *Life and Letters*, ed. J. E. Bowden, 1869, contain florid descriptions of travel in Greece, Turkey and Italy, and also some explosions of fanaticism: Protestantism is 'the devil's masterpiece,' and even the English Bible, though it 'lives on in the ear like a music that can never be forgotten,' is still 'an unhallowed power.' *Hymns*, first ed., 1848; collected, 1871. *Works* (prose and verse), 11 vols., 1914.

p. 203, note 1. **Trench.** *Poems*, new ed., two vols., 1885; among the earliest were *Sabbation*, *Honor Neale*, etc, 1838; and *Poems from Eastern Sources*, 1842. Trench has no very definite note of his own, but throws a wide net for his topics, drawing on Arabian, Persian, Spanish, and Italian themes; translates Goethe, and echoes Tennyson as well as Wordsworth.

p. 203, note 2. **Neale.** *Collected Poems, Sequences, and Carols*, 1914. The *Mediæval Hymns and Sequences* appeared in 1851.

p. 204. **W. G. Ward.** Full narrative of his career by his son Wilfrid Ward, in *W. G. W. and the Oxford Movement*, 1889, and in *W. G. W. and the Catholic Revival*, 1893. These volumes (like the same writer's *Life of Newman*), are prolix, but equitable in tone, and contribute much to the history both of the Anglican and the Roman movements, from the Roman standpoint. They are also full of vivid traits and stories of W. G. Ward. *The Philosophy of Theism*, 2 vols., 1884, is edited by the same hand; the essays are reprinted from the *Dublin Review*. See, in particular, i. 185 ff., 'Mr. Mill's Philosophical Position' (1874); 'Science, Prayer, Freewill, and Miracle,' ii. 158 ff. (1867); and ii. 244 ff. (1871), 'Certitude in Religious Assent.'

p. 206, note 1. **J. B. Mozley.** List of books and articles in *Essays Historical and Theological*, 2 vols., 1875, vol. ii. *ad fin.* I have seen the reprinted articles (many from *Christian Remembrancer*) and some others, but not all; the Oxford sermons (Bampton and others); the *Lectures and other Theological Papers*, 1883, which contain some of Mozley's close reasoning on original sin, the Eucharist, the Athanasian Creed (in which he defends the damnatory clauses *with conditions*), and other fundamentals. See, for an humorous and appreciative picture of the man, H. Scott Holland, *A Bundle of Memories* [1915], pp. 33-47; where the stages and divisions of Mozley's writing are indicated. Also *Letters*, edited by his sister Anne Mozley, 1885, especially for many reff. to Newman; and, for a hostile and blankly unintelligent view, Purcell, *Life of Card. Manning*, 1896, ii. 680-1 (the Cardinal's words on reading J. B. M.'s comments on himself in the said *Letters*).

p. 206, note 2. **Church.** *Life and Letters*, ed. Mary C. Church, 1895, with list of works, pp. 351-2. D. C. Lathbury, *Dean Church*, 1905. *Spenser* and *Bacon* in *Eng. Men of Letters*, and in *Misc. Works*, 5 vols., the others being *Dante and other Essays*, *St. Anselm*, and *Misc. Essays.* Church's descriptions in his letters of Italy and other countries where he travelled are of interest; also Canon Scott Holland's account of the man and his work as Dean, *Life*, pp.

205-35. Church's paper on *Sordello* (1887), and reprinted with *Dante*, should be named.

p. 208, note 1. **'noetics.'** On Whately, see my *Survey* (1912), ii. 393-4; he belongs to both periods, and has had to be bisected. Edward Copleston of Oriel (1776-1849), later Bishop of Llandaff, is often pointed to as the inspirer of Whately and the 'noetics'; but he hardly figures in letters, save for such writing as that named in *Survey* (1912), i. 393.

p. 208, note 2. **broad churchmen.** See the article (1856), by F. D. Maurice, prefacing the reprint (I quote third ed., 1874, introd. by E. H. Plumptre) of J. C. Hare's *Victory of Faith*; Maurice here disowns and disproves the appellation of a 'party' as applied to the Broad Church; they did not try, he says, to found an 'Anglo-German school.' For a pungent adverse analysis of the tenets of Hare, Maurice, and Jowett, from the evangelical standpoint, see J. H. Rigg, *Modern Anglican Theology*, 1857 (the 1880 ed. also contains a memoir of C. Kingsley). The phrase 'broad church' is said (see, too, Sir L. Stephen, *s.v.* 'Maurice' in *D. N. B.*) to derive from a sentence in an article of Stanley's in *Ed. Rev.*, 1850, on the Gorham dispute: the English Church being 'by the very condition of its being, not High nor Low, but Broad'; for this ref. see J. Tulloch, *Movements of Religious Thought in Britain during the XIXth Century*, 1885, p. 260 ff. This book is an unprejudiced historical sketch of the whole subject. Its accounts of J. C. Hare, Erskine of Linlathen, Carlyle, and Maurice, on their theological side, are admirable. See, too, the ch. by F. E. Hutchinson in *Camb. Hist. of Eng. Lit.*, xii. 279-99, on the 'Growth of liberal theology': an interesting account, from which I borrow the translation 'noetics'= 'intellectuals.'

p. 210. **Essays and Reviews.** For full account of this work and its historic importance (also of Colenso's ideas) see Benn, *Rationalism*, ch. xiii., 'The Deliverance of Criticism'; to him I am indebted for the 'epigram' quoted in text. Benn well vindicates the historic importance of the volume. An account of the sandstorm which it raised may be read in the *Life of Jowett* (see next note), ch. x.

p. 211. **Jowett.** E. Abbott and L. Campbell, *Life and Letters of B. J.*, 2 vols., 1897.

p. 212, note 1. **literary judgements.** See on Carlyle, *Life*, i. 417 (1866), a pendant to Carlyle's note on Jowett as 'a good-humoured little owlet of a man,' etc.; and on Browning, ii. 355 ('nowhere is he really affected by the great themes of poets, *love, or ambition, or enthusiasm*'—italics mine); there is, however, a high appreciation of *Easter Day*.

p. 212, note 2. **memorandum.** *Life*, ii. 310-14. See the whole passage, which I think gives Jowett's ideas and aspirations at their best and deepest.

p. 213. **Stanley.** See R. E. Prothero and G. G. Bradley, *Life and Corr. of A. P. S.*, 3 vols., 1893; this contains bibliography; also G. G. Bradley, *Recollections of Stanley*, 1883.

p. 214. **Pattison.** The *Essays* were collected by Henry Nettleship, 2 vols., 1889; they are a selection from Pattison's writings in periodicals, and also contain the fragment on Scaliger from MS. A volume of *Sermons* (1885) should be named. I recall his aged figure, about 1881, silently and sternly presiding over a meeting of the Oxford Browning Society; the topic of the evening was that poet's conception of Love.

p. 218. **Ruskin**. The great ed. of the *Works*, by Sir E. T. Cook and A. Wedderburn, 39 vols., 1903-12, includes correspondence, bibliographies, collation of text, extracts from MSS., much material before unprinted or unreprinted, a monumental index, over a thousand illustrations, and a running biographical commentary : the latter being the foundation of Cook's *Life of J. R.*, 2 vols., 1911 (see, too, his *Studies in R.*, 1890). W. G. Collingwood's *Life and Work of J. R.*, 1903, is also to be consulted. Most of Ruskin's works are easily accessible in various edd. The best of the many compact studies are those by Mrs. Meynell, 1900, and by Frederic Harrison ('Eng. Men of Letters,' 1902 ; to which add his *Tennyson, Ruskin*, etc., 1899). But some of the best exposition is in French : J. Milsand, *L'esthétique anglaise*, 1864 ; R. D. la Sizeranne, *R. et la religion de la beauté*, 1897, E. tr. 1900 ; and notably J. Bardoux, *Le mouvement idéaliste et social dans la litt. anglaise au XIXe siècle : John Ruskin* [1900]. On the artistic side, see (Sir) C. Waldstein [Walston], *The Work of R.*, 1894 ; and on the economic and political side, J. A. Hobson, *J. R., Social Reformer*, 1898, a lucid vindication. Many personal reff. in the Carlyle and Rossetti literature. The familiar *Selections*, in two series (various dates) were not made by Ruskin, who was a 'tacitly consenting' party ; they are, on their scale, excellent ; but, as a collection of 'beauties,' they give an overgorgeous air to Ruskin's average style.

p. 219. **Claude**, etc. For revisions see *Works*, vol. iii. (the standard ed. is always cited *infra*). I must be content to refer generally to its Index, vol. xxxix. Without this aid the student of Ruskin's ideas and their development, and of his 'contradictions,' is in a maze ; with it he has all available clues, carefully unravelled. See, then, under 'Claude,' 'Raphael,' etc., in the Index. I cannot possibly give all references, even to this Index, still less to particular passages, but have used it freely ; and if any point of mine calls for correction, the Index will help to convict me. It will also enable these notes to be fewer.

p. 221. **eyes**. See, in *Recreations and Reflections*, 1902 ('middles' from *Sat. Review* by various hands), 'Ruskin,' by D. S. MacColl, pp. 57-70 : 'He is a man subject to a rapt vision of delicate things such as the fibres of moss, the sculpturing and veining of rocks, the tracery of leaves, the lacework of foam, the changing fires of gems and clouds, vision compact of minute, tender, treasuring observation and of religious awe' (p. 61).

p. 222, note 1. **theory of Beauty**. See B. Bosanquet, *Hist. of Æsthetic*, 1892, pp. 447-54 : 'he, like Winckelmann, has given the mind a new organ for the appreciation of beauty.' The same critic, I venture to think, makes rather light of the 'popular criticism' that Ruskin 'turns æsthetic into ethic.'

p. 222, note 2. **bibliography** (1843-60). For the connexion of *Modern Painters* with Ruskin's other works of this period, and for a clear account of its real divisions (as distinct from volumes) and their relationship, see Cook, *Life*, vol. i.

p. 232. **style**. For material here see *Works*, Index, p. 491, *s.v.* 'Ruskin.' My quotations from Ruskin's own remarks about his style will easily be traced there.

p. 233, note 1. **Ruskin's English**. On this see Cook, *Life* ; and the same writer's *Literary Recreations*, 1918, pp. 34-54, an admirable summary ; also Frederic Harrison, *Tennyson, Ruskin, Mill*, etc., 1899, pp. 51-76, 'Ruskin as master of prose' (containing an interesting note on his use of 'musical consonance,' or echoed sound). On cadence, see Saintsbury, *Hist. of English Prose Rhythm*, pp. 392-400.

p. 233, note 2. **Authorised Version.** H. J. Brunhes, *Ruskin et la Bible*, Paris, 1901, gives some details of interest, especially as to the influence of the Prophets and the Gospels upon Ruskin's vision, first of nature and her meaning, and then of man and his destiny.

p. 237. **Adria.** Of course this ending itself *can* be read into a blank line; but it *should* not be, for the natural, prose cadence overpowers the sense of metre.

p. 239. **social welfare.** On this whole matter consult J. A. Hobson, *Ruskin, Social Reformer*, 1898: a close study, at most points sympathetic, of Ruskin's economic and social gospel; also the relevant chapters in Bardoux, *Le mouvement idéaliste*, etc., 1900.

p. 242. **Munera Pulveris.** For a full dissection of the book, with reff. to many passages elsewhere in illustration, see editor's preface in *Works*, vol. xvii.

p. 245. **wailing voice.** Dr. John Sampson reminds me that this trait is noticed by W. H. Mallock, *The New Republic*, 2 vols., 1877, where Ruskin figures as 'Mr. Herbert.' The book is worth looking at, for it contains not only parody of style, but satire on ideas.

p. 247. **Fors Clavigera.** See the sifting-out of its contents in editor's preface to vol. xxvii. of *Works*; which brings out (*inter alia*) the amount of space devoted to 'readings' in Scott, Montaigne, and other writers. See also remarks of F. Harrison, *J. R.*, pp. 179-96: 'its wonderful quality lies in the utterly unexpected and incalculable sequence of ideas,' etc.

p. 249, note 1. **criticism.** For the subject of this and the next chapter see above all Saintsbury, *Hist. of Criticism*, iii. 472-560.

p. 249, note 2. **Keble.** *Lectures on Poetry, 1832-1841*, tr. by E. K. Francis, 2 vols., 1912. See too Saintsbury, *Hist. of Criticism*, iii. (1904), 621-5 (App. I.); I know of no other satisfactory account.

p. 252. **Brimley.** *Essays by the late G. B.*, ed. W. G. Clark, 1858, with brief prefatory note. Except for the 'Tennyson,' 'which appeared in the *Cambridge Essays* for 1855,' all Brimley's work was unsigned, and came out in the *Spectator* or *Fraser's*. The short paper on 'Comte's Positive Philosophy' is mostly in an orthodox strain. That on Lytton's *My Novel* is a good specimen of a polite and pulverising review.

p. 254. **Matthew Arnold.** *Works*, 15 vols., 1903-4, have a full bibliography (xv. 343-99) by T. B. Smart, which shows what is and is not contained in them; also synoptical index to poems. Vols. xiii.-xv. are the *Letters, 1848-1888*, ed. G. W. E. Russell, 1898, 2 vols. Collected *Poetical Works*, one vol., 1890, etc. The *Poems of M. A., 1840-1867*, ed. Sir A. Quiller-Couch (1909), do not contain the few later pieces, but give the rest in order of date and with textual variants, also the prefaces to *Poems* of 1853 and 1854, and to *Merope* (see too the same author's essay in *Studies in Literature*, 1918, pp. 231-45). Most of prose works in popular reprints (sometimes abridged by author, e.g. *God and the Bible*, 1884) and various other edd. The *Reports on Elementary Schools, 1852-1882*, ed. Sir F. Sandford, 1869, and re-ed. F. S. Marvin, 1908, are not in any collection of the *Works*. *Notebooks of M. A.*, ed. Hon. Mrs. Wodehouse, 1902. Volumes entitled *M. A.*, mostly brief, by

G. Saintsbury, 1899, Herbert Paul, 1902, and G. W. E. Russell, 1904. For other criticism, see the pages by E. Dowden in *Chambers's Cyclop. of Eng. Lit.*, iii. 591-600; Swinburne, *Essays and Studies.*

p. 255. **Carlyle**, etc. *Letters*, March 25, 1881: 'I never much liked Carlyle. He seemed to me to be "carrying coals to Newcastle," as our proverb says; preaching earnestness to a nation which had plenty of it by nature, but was less abundantly supplied with several other useful things'; but see, for amends, the lecture on *Emerson*. As to Shelley, see p. 273 in my text. Charlotte Brontë, despite what is said in *Haworth Churchyard*, is hardly treated in *Letters*, April 14, 1853: 'Why is *Villette* disagreeable? Because the writer's mind contains nothing but hunger, rebellion, and rage, and therefore that is all she can in fact put into her book.' As to Tennyson, *Enoch Arden* is oddly preferred to *Tithonus*; see *Letters*, Sept. 22, 1864: 'I do not think T. a great and powerful spirit in any line as Goethe was in the line of modern thought, Wordsworth in that of contemplation, Byron, even, in that of passion.'

p. 259. **Empedocles.** Arnold makes little use of the famed conception of Love and Strife; but one of the passages where he comes nearest to the 'grand style' is suggested by the lines:—'There is an ordinance of Necessity, a time-honoured decree of the Gods, eternal and sealed fast by broad oaths, that whenever any of the dæmons whose portion is length of days have by sinning defiled their hands with bloodshed, or in compliance with Strife have committed the sin of false witness, they must wander for thrice ten thousand seasons away from the blessed, being born throughout the time in all manner of mortal shapes, as they pass in succession over the grievous pathways of life. For the might of the air drives them to the ocean, and the sea vomits them out on the soil of the earth, and the earth again into the beams of the tireless sun, and he flings them into the eddies of the air. So each one in turn receives them, but they loathe them all alike. Of such dæmons I, too, am one, an exile and a wanderer by God's will, obedient to the frenzy of Strife' (H. Diels, *Fragmente der Vorsokratiker*, ed. 3, i. 267. For this reference, and for essential parts of the above translation, I am indebted to my colleague Professor A. C. Pearson).

p. 261. **Rugby Chapel**, etc. Saintsbury, *Hist. of Eng. Prosody*, iii. 257.

p. 264. **Church of Brou.** See Sir E. T. Cook, *Literary Recreations*, 1918, pp. 294-6, on Arnold's attempt to correct the poem. He first separated (1877) the first two parts and called them *A Tomb Among the Mountains*; but afterwards repented, and put them back again.

p. 266. **Worsley.** He says too modestly that 'it is those who have little or no Greek that I desire to interest,' and compromises sensibly in the spelling of the names. His book seems now little known, but ought to be reprinted. Worsley's *Poems and Translations*, 1863, contain some neat turnings from Horace, and some more vivid ones from the Latin hymnodists; the original poems are often over-Tennysonian in style.

p. 272. **George Sand.** The familiar paper on her occurs in *Mixed Essays* (originally in *Fort. Rev.*, June 1877); but the brief one here referred to is only reprinted in *Works*, iv. 245-9 (originally in *Pall Mall Gazette*, Aug. 12, 1884).

p. 273. **Sainte-Beuve.** From the article in *Ency. Brit.*, ninth ed., xxi. 165 (1886). I rescue this passage, because it disappears (why?) in the eleventh ed. of the *Ency. Brit.*, xxiii. 1023 (1911), which reproduces the article (not included in *Works*, 1903-4).

p. 280. **Pater.** Uniform standard edition, various dates, ed. C. L. Shadwell; this includes the *Guardian* reviews, and apparently all of Pater's published work except *Æsthetic Poetry* (withdrawn after first ed. of *Appreciations*, 1889), and the preface to Mr. Shadwell's own translation, 1892, of Dante's *Purgatorio*, i-xxvii. There is a bibliography, often giving dates of composition, in the *Misc. Studies*, and further detail in the editor's preface to *Greek Studies*. The best biographical sketch, embodying corrections of various legends, is by A. C. Benson, 1907, in 'Eng. Men of Letters' series. T. Wright, *Life of W. P.*, 1907, gives a full chronicle. See, too, E. Gosse, *Critical Kit-kats*, 1896, and art. in *D. N. B.*

p. 295. **Leslie Stephen.** F. W. Maitland, *Life and Letters of L. S.*, 1906; and see art. in *D. N. B.*, Suppl. ii., by Sir Sidney Lee; and *Letters of George Meredith*, 1912. Meredith's letters to Stephen illustrate the stern courage, and the common points in the creed, of the two men. Vernon Whitford in *The Egoist* was sketched from Stephen (*Letters of G. M.*, ii. 331).

p. 297. **Dowden.** *Letters of E. Dowden*, ed. E. D. Dowden and H. M., 1914.

p. 299, note 1. **Furnivall.** See *F. J. F., a Volume of Personal Record*, 1911 (memoir by J. Munro, and 49 notes and recollections by as many hands). Also *An English Miscellany*, 1901, presented to Furnivall on his 75th birthday, and containing 49 contributions and bibliography.

p. 299, note 2. **Hutton.** See his *Essays, Theological and Literary*, 2 vols., 1871 and 1877.

p. 301. **J. C. Hare.** See note, p. 423, l. 8, *ante*, to p. 208 of text (on 'broad church'). The articles there referred to by Maurice and Stanley contain full accounts of Hare and his activities; his theology had a character of its own, and he belonged to no 'party.'

p. 303. **Enigmas of Life.** The 18th ed. (1891), which I have used, contains a memoir by Mrs. W. R. Greg. It is explained that Greg expressly forbore to discuss the questions of theism and the soul in set form, feeling that they do not admit of positive answer, and that each man may keep his own working theory on the matter. Among the more striking articles are those on 'The direction of human development,' on 'The significance of life,' *De Profundis*, and *Elsewhere*.

p. 305. **John Brown.** See his *Letters*, ed. by his son and D. W. Forrest, with introd. by Eliz. T. M'Laren, 1907 (includes letters from Ruskin, Thackeray, etc.); also *Dr. J. B.*, by John Taylor Brown (his cousin), 1903, ed. W. B. Dunlop. The title *Horæ Subsecivæ* is sometimes applied to the first series (1858), sometimes to all three; but the second and third have also special titles, namely *Locke and Sydenham*, and *John Leech and other Papers*, respectively. *Rab*, *Marjorie Fleming*, and some other single papers have been very often reprinted.

p. 307. **Butler.** *Life and Letters*, by H. Festing Jones, 2 vols., 1919; R. A. Streatfeild, *S. B., Records and Memorials*, 1903; art. in *D. N. B.*, Suppl. ii., by T. Seccombe. Bibliography in *Camb. Hist. Eng. Lit.*, xiii. 570-2. Most of the works easy of access in modern reprints. For Butler's own view of his more important ideas see his *Note-Books*, ed. Festing Jones, 1912, pp. 374-8; and *id.*, pp. 379-98, for his verses, including the memorable *Psalm of Montreal*, the Whitmanesque pieces *The Righteous Man* and *To Critics and Others*, and the version in Homeric Greek of some observations by Mrs. Gamp.

p. 308. **the modern biologist.** See, for a full conspectus, Marcus Hartog's introduction, pp. ix-xxxv, to *Unconscious Memory*, ed. of 1910. I have not touched in text on this favourite idea of Butler's, nor on his extension of the idea of a 'machine' or 'tool' (set forth in *Erewhon* and elsewhere), to the human organism and to its possible supplanters.

p. 313. **Ricardian views.** On Miss Martineau's economics see Cazamian, *Le Roman social en Angleterre*, pp. 96-110.

p. 315. **Burton.** Lady Burton, *Life of Captain Sir R. F. Burton*, 2 vols., 1898. T. Wright, *Life of Sir R. B.*, 2 vols., 1906, adds a great amount of material, and deals, *inter alia*, with the debated matter of Burton's borrowings (for his *Arabian Nights*) from John Payne, also the translator of Villon, Boccaccio, etc., and an original poet as well; Payne's translations in verse and prose are often beautiful and elegant.

p. 319. **Borrow.** Bibliography by G. F. Black, in *A Gypsy Bibliography* (Gypsy Lore Soc. Monographs, No. 1), 1914, pp. 21-5; and in Knapp, vol. ii. (including note of MSS.). W. I. Knapp, *Life, Writings, and Corresp. of G. B.*, 2 vols., 1889, gives a store of indispensable documents, and is not superseded. H. Jenkins, *Life of G. B.*, 1912, adds many more; a well written and ordered biography. and C. Shorter, *G. B. and his Circle*, 1913, furnishes yet more letters and illustrative material. Borrow's five original works, and the *Romano Lavo-Lil*, are in easily accessible edd.; on his translations see note below. The edd., in Methuen's 'Little Library,' of *Lavengro*, by F. Hindes Groome, 2 vols., 1901, and of *The Romany Rye*, by John Sampson, are valuable in point of gypsy lore and otherwise. The articles by T. Watts-Dunton in *Chambers's Cyclop. of Eng. Lit.*, 1903, iii. 429-35, and in *Athenæum*, 3 and 10 Sept. 1881, are noticeable; I have failed to see S. Jackson Pratt's *Gleanings in England, Wales, and Holland*, to which Watts-Dunton refers as probably studied by Borrow. See, too, T. Seccombe's ed. of *Isopel Berners* (*i.e.* the relevant chapters), 1901, also E. Thomas, *G. B.*, 1912. For a meritorious parody of Borrow's adventures on the English roads, see 'Borrowed Scenes,' in Sir A. Conan Doyle's *Danger, and other Stories*, 1918, pp. 127-44.

p. 320, note 1. **loomwork.** For examples see Sampson, *Rom. Rye*, introduction, tracing from contemporary evidence one of Borrow's itineraries, and marking some of his bold coincidences. So Jenkins, *op. cit.*, pp. 58-9, etc.: 'he never hesitated to change a date if it served his purpose, much as an artist will change the position of a tree in a landscape to suit the exigencies of composition.' F. Hindes Groome in his ed. of *Lavengro* gives compact examples of Borrow's 'lax adherence to fact,' such as his 'pretended visits to Iceland, Moultan, and Kiachta,' and his antedating by nine years (a point noted by Knapp) of the incident of the trotting stallion in *Lavengro*, ch. xvi. The notes by Sampson and Groome also illustrate Borrow's casual methods with the Romany language.

p. 320, note 2. **hardly explored.** I owe to Dr. J. Sampson a reference to Richard Bright, *Travels from Vienna through Lower Hungary*, 1818,—a still earlier account (and also Ford's remark, text, p. 321, about *Gil Blas*).

p. 320, note 3. **letters.** Printed by T. H. Darlow, *Letters of G. B. to the Brit. and For. Bible Soc.*, 1911; copies of them had previously been used by Jenkins, *Life*, chs. vi.-xx.; those written from Russia, chs. vi.-ix., are of much vigour and interest. Amongst the passages transcribed, often with small changes and insertions, from these letters into the *Bible in Spain*, are the first three chapters. For the next eight (iv.-xi.) any originals that may have existed are lost; the transcripts recommence fully in ch. xv., with Borrow's second arrival in Spain, but there are many additions. The vivid chaps. xxiii., xxiv. (from Astorga to Villafranca) are again copied; and so on. The new matter increases as the book goes on; but the scene (ch. xxxv.) in the Black Pass, quoted from in my text, p. 321, *ante*, is almost verbally reproduced (from the letter of Nov. 1, 1837, *Letters*, pp. 257-9); so is the night visit at Oviedo of the ten cavaliers (ch. xxxiii.); and so, too, is the strange incident of the Jew who warned Borrow of danger by pronouncing the Hebrew word for 'rabbit' (ch. xliv.; *Letters*, p. 346).

p. 321. **Richard Ford.** Ford was a shrewd and sympathetic adviser of Borrow (who was not conspicuous for gratitude) and critic of his work (see Jenkins, *Life of G. B.*, index *s.v.*). See *Letters of R. F., 1797-1858*, ed. R. E. Prothero, 1905. The *Handbook* (one of Murray's) is, as Mr. Prothero well says (p. 173), 'a most entertaining encyclopædia of Spanish history and antiquities, religion and art, life and manners'; and 'communicates to the reader a prodigious mass of information in the easiest possible manner.' There have been many edd.; that of 1845 is said to be the most vivid; and certainly it is hard to open on a page that is not full of life.

p. 324. **Galloway notes.** Partly printed by Knapp, *Life*, ii. 219-22; and in full, from the original material supplied by Knapp, in *The Gallovidian*, Dumfries, summer number, 1905, pp. 116-26, by Andrew M'Cormick (another reference which I owe to Dr. J. Sampson).

p. 327, note 1. **style.** See Shorter, *G. B. and his Circle*, p. 284, who quotes Borrow's remark (made to Whitwell Elwin): 'that his composition cost him a vast amount of labour, that his first drafts were diffuse and crude, and that he wrote his productions several times before he had condensed and polished them to his mind.' See too *id.*, p. 268, for Borrow's remark about 'Turkish,' quoted in my text, p. 328.

p. 327, note 2. **Gordon Hake.** Shorter, *op. cit.*, p. 391; reported by Watts-Dunton.

p. 328. **translations.** I have only been able to see the *Romantic Ballads*, reprinted by Jarrold, Norwich, 1913 (*Sir John* is there, pp. 40-3); and the *Targum*, also reprinted by Jarrold, London [1892], in one vol. with *The Talisman*, etc. Filicaja's *terzine* are translated (in the same metre) in *Targum*, pp. 98-100. *The Lay of Biarke*, *id.*, pp. 40-1, is an impudently lax reproduction of the Norse *Biarka-Mal*, and the scrap from *Beowulf* (*id.*, p. 39) is no better. The two passages from the *Iliad*, though fairly close, are in spavined and stumbling hexameters.

p. 331, note 1. **Tennyson.** *Bibliography*, by T. J. Wise, 2 vols., 1908; and Grolier Club, *Chronolog. List of Works*, New York, 1897 (and see *Camb. Hist. Eng. Lit.*, xiii. 473 ff.). A. E. Baker, *Concordance*, 1914. *Works*, ed. Hallam, Lord Tennyson, 9 vols., 1907-8, with the poet's notes. Many one-vol. and other edd. of *Works*. J. Churton Collins, *The Early Poems of T.*, 1900 (a valuable ed.), reprints discarded pieces, and collates up to the vol. of 1842 inclusive (save for *Poems by Two Brothers*, reprinted by the present Lord Tennyson, 1893). For *In Memoriam* see the standard commentary (without text) by A. C. Bradley, 1901. Many ed. of separate poems, by many hands. For biography see *Memoir*, 2 vols., 1897 (and one vol. 1899), by the present Lord Tennyson, the poet's son, and his *T. and his Friends*, 1911; also Lady Ritchie, *Records of T., Ruskin, Browning*, 1892; and the Carlyle, Browning, Fitzgerald, and Huxley literature. Many short lives and studies, *e.g.* by A. Lang, 1901; Sir A. Lyall, 1902; A. C. Benson, 1904. See too W. MacNeile Dixon, *A Primer of T.*, 1896; W. P. Ker, *T.: A Lecture*, 1909; and O. Elton, *T.*, in *Modern Studies*, 1907. On Prof. Lounsbury's illuminating work see notes *infra.*

p. 331, note 2. **Coleridge.** *Table Talk*, remark of April 24, 1833. He says that T. 'has begun to write verses without very well understanding what metre is,' and advises him to write 'for the next two or three years' only in 'one or two well-known and strictly-defined metres.' This sounds humorous in view of the sequel, but the force of it is clear if we turn to some of the poems that Tennyson suppressed. See Lounsbury, *Life and Times*, etc., pp. 343-4.

p. 333. **Poe.** For his appreciation of Tennyson, see reff. in Lounsbury, *Life and Times of T.*, pp. 461-2; the words *ventus textilis* come from *Democratic Review*, Dec. 1844 (as quoted through Herne Shepherd by Churton Collins, *Early Poems of T.*, p. 43); I have not seen these American periodicals.

p. 335. **Tennyson's reputation.** See *The Life and Times of Tennyson (from 1809 to 1850)*, by the late Prof. T. R. Lounsbury, 1915; a minute study of all the early criticisms, bad and otherwise, in well-known and other periodicals; with special reference to the doings of Wilson, Lockhart, Bulwer, etc., to the reception of Tennyson in America; and to the poet's own reception of his critics. J. S. Mill's praise in the *London Review*, July 1835, shines out among the rest (p. 346 ff.). Tennyson's changes of text were seldom due to the critics, pp. 400 ff.; also, pp. 500 ff., his public reputation, as distinct from his recognition by the elect, was quite gradual even after 1842. Prof. Lounsbury died before giving his work the last revision, which has been made by Mr. Wilbur L. Cross.

p. 339. **Boadicea.** Written 1859, published in *Cornhill*, Dec. 1863, among *Attempts at Classic Metres in Quantity*, and in the *Enoch Arden* vol. next year among *Experiments.* Meredith's *Phaéthôn*, first in *Fortnightly*, Sept. 1867, later in *Ballads and Poems of Tragic Life*, 1887. The technique of the measure in the two poems, though in both cases within the rules, has a different effect, Meredith's lines ending oftener on the stress, and being generally ruggeder.

p. 341. **The Princess.** See Lounsbury, *Life and Times of T.*, ch. xx. for brief account of the revision; and edd. of the poem by J. C. Collins, and by P. M. Wallace.

p. 344. **A living poet.** Mr. W. B. Yeats, in *Discoveries*, 1907, p. 12:

p. 347. **trance-experience.** See *Memoir*, 1899, pp. 815-16, where Tyndall reports Tennyson's account of an indescribable state 'into which he could throw himself by thinking intently of his own name.' He said: 'By God Almighty, there is no delusion in the matter! It is no nebulous ecstasy, but a state of transcendent wonder, associated with absolute clearness of mind.'

p. 349. **Rizpah.** See *Lit. Anecdotes of the Nineteenth Century*, 2 vols., 1896, ed. Sir W. R. Nicoll and T. J. Wise, ii. 441-2, where is quoted H. Martin, *Hist. of Brighton and its Environs*, Brighton, 1871, telling of an event dated 1792. One Rock was hanged for mail-robbing; and his 'aged mother,' we hear, 'night after night, in all weathers, and especially in tempestuous weather, visited' the gallows, brought home the bones as they fell, and 'in the dead silence of the night interred them, deposited in a chest, in the hallowed ground of Old Shoreham Church.'

p. 351. **Enid and Nimuë.** On all this, see an article on *The Building of the Idylls*, in *Lit. Anecdotes of the Nineteenth Century*, ii. 219-72, which gives much bibliographical and textual detail, and on which I draw freely. There seems to be no complete *apparatus criticus* yet of the text. See too S. H. Gurteen, *The Arthurian Epic*, 1895 ; and, for a close comparison of the *Idylls*, point by point, with originals, H. Littledale, *Essays on Lord Tennyson's Idylls of the King*, 1893.

p. 353. **prose argument of Balin.** In *Memoir*, 1899, pp. 529-34.

p. 360. **metres.** See Saintsbury, *Hist. of Eng. Prosody*, ii. 183-240, 'Tennyson and Browning.'

p. 361. **Charles Tennyson Turner.** Instalments of his sonnets were published in 1830, 1864, 1868, and 1873. These, with fifty more, were collected in 1880, with a biographical note by Hallam (afterwards Lord) Tennyson, and with a full and sympathetic essay by James Spedding. Variants are recorded, and also the MS. comments made by S. T. Coleridge in his copy of the 1830 volume.

p. 364, note 1. **Browning.** *Bibliography*: in (Sir) W. R. Nicoll and T. J. Wise, *Lit. Anecdotes of the XIXth Cent.*, 2 vols., 1895-6, i. 360-627 ; founded partly on lists by F. J. Furnivall in Browning Soc. *Papers*, pt. i. pp. 27-71 (1881). Shorter lists, *e.g.* in A. Symons, *Introd. to the Study of B.* (1886), new ed. of 1906, pp. 241-54. *Biography*: Mrs. Sutherland Orr, *Life and Letters of R. B.*, 1891 (new ed. 1908, revised by Sir F. G. Kenyon) ; *Life*, by W. Hall Griffin, completed by H. C. Minchin, 1910 (the fullest and latest). *Letters of R. B. and E. B. Barrett, 1845-6*, 2 vols., 1899 ; and see some *Letters* privately printed by T. J. Wise, 2 vols., 1895-6. See, too, Lady Ritchie [Miss Thackeray], *Records of Tennyson, Ruskin, and B.*, 1892. Many edd. of works ; *e.g.* in 10 vols., 1912 (centenary), with introductions by Sir F. G. Kenyon ; in 17 vols., 1888-94 ; in 2 vols., 1896 ; and other popular forms ; many selections. The best short guide is still that of Symons, *op. cit.* above, which treats of Browning's art as well as of his ideas ; see, too, Mrs. S. Orr, *Handbook to the Works of B.*, 1885, and E. Berdoe, *Browning Cyclopædia*, 1892. Amongst more continuous studies may be named those of P. Berger, *R. B.*, 1912 (*Grands Ecrivains étrangers*) ; Stopford A. Brooke, *The Poetry of B.*, 1902 ; G. K. Chesterton, *B.*, 1903 ; E. Dowden, *R. B.*, 1904 ; C. H. Herford, *B.*, 1905. The gifted early interpreter of the poet, J. T. Nettleship, should not be forgotten ; *Essays on B.'s Poetry*, 1868, enlarged 1890, as *R. B., Essays and Thoughts* (see especially analyses of *Sordello*, *Christmas Eve*, and of *Fifine*, etc. ; and classification of poems, pp. 321-5, ed. 1890).

p. 364, note 2. **explaining.** The *Papers* of the Browning Society, which was led by F. J. Furnivall, extend from 1881 to 1890, and contain, besides the bibliography named above, material still of much value. See (*e.g.*) 1885, A. Symons, 'Is B. dramatic ?' ; 1886, H. S. Pearson, 'B. as a landscape-painter' ; C. H. Herford, No. 37, on *Hohenstiel-Schwangau*.

p. 366. **Shelley.** Browning's *Introductory Essay* to *Letters of Percy Bysshe Shelley*, 1852, disappeared when the letters were found to be forged and the vol. was suppressed ; but was reprinted by the Browning Society and the Shelley Society, and latterly (1911) by Miss L. Winstanley, with introduction and notes (along with Sidney's *Defence of Poetry*) in the 'Belles-Lettres Series (Boston, U.S.A., and London). Its value is not impaired by the spuriousness of the letters. *Memorabilia* came in the vol. of 1855.

p. 367. **story of Sordello.** See J. T. Nettleship, *Essays on Browning*, ed. 1890, pp. 114-69 (originally 1868); and Browning Soc. *Papers*, 1889, No. 57, W. J. Alexander, *Analysis of S.*; also 1889, No. 62, W. M. Rossetti, on the historical Taurello Salinguerra.

p. 371. **Bells and Pomegranates.** See Exodus xxviii. 33, 34: 'And beneath upon the hem of it thou shalt make pomegranates of blue, and of purple, and of scarlet . . . and bells of gold between them round about: a golden bell and a pomegranate, a golden bell and a pomegranate, upon the hem of the robe round about.' Also preface to *B. and P.*, No. viii., 1846, quoted by Symons, *Introd. to B.*, 1906 ed., pp. 258-9: 'an endeavour towards something like an alteration, or mixture, of music with discoursing, sound with sense, poetry with thought; which looks too ambitious, thus expressed, so the symbol was preferred.' The bells 'of gold' can chime well and sweetly enough, but the pomegranates, the fruit of wisdom, have a seed which at times is hard and gritty.

p. 372, note 1. **Domett's** *Ranolf and Amohia* [Amohīa], 1872, is a long tale in verse, not lacking in poetry or entertainment, but compact of queerness, and thus far worthy of 'Waring.' Ranolf, in the intervals of wooing the Maori maiden and hearing native songs and legends, muses on science, and on various philosophic and theologic systems, which he turns into somewhat neat heroics. Can Browning be glanced at in the lines (p. 60),

> 'still high and clear forth stood
> For this inquirer's cheery thought and mood,
> God and the great predominance of Good,' etc.?

The passage of happiest colour is perhaps that on the cicada (p. 315), which has a Greek-idyllic kind of beauty.

p. 372, note 2. **Carducci.** See his lecture, *Jaufré Rudel: Poesia Antica e Moderna*, Bologna, 1888. Carducci gives the earliest allusion to Rudel, translations from his poems, and of extracts from Uhland and Heine. His own little romance is appended, *ad fin.*

p. 378. **Wiseman.** Griffin and Minchin, *Life of R. B.*, p. 202, whence I take quotation from *Rambler* (Jan. 1856).

p. 380. **Ring and the Book.** See above all Charles W. Hodell, *The Old Yellow Book: Source of Browning's 'The Ring and the Book'* (in complete photo-reproduction, with translation, essay, and notes), Carnegie Institution of Washington, 1908. The translations give all essential parts; the essay (on which I have drawn freely) contains valuable analyses of the documents and of Browning's use of them, which is most minutely worked out in the 'corpus of topical notes' and line-index, pp. 294-342. I have barely indicated Browning's immense assimilation of his 'case.' The Book is now in Balliol College Library. Mr. Hodell also prints the Casanatense pamphlet, not used by the poet, and reproduces the contemporary pen-sketch of the very Guido, said to have been done on the night before his execution (p. 274). The Casanatense tract is given in Griffin and Minchin, *Life*, pp. 309-27, 'App. B.'

p. 381. **Henry James.** *Notes on Novelists*, 1914, pp. 306-26, 'The Novel in *The Ring and the Book*' (originally an address given in 1912 on the anniversary of Browning's birthday). The imagined novel, for reasons, would make Caponsacchi 'the indicated centre of our situation or determinant of our form' (p. 322), and would end with a solitary interview between him and the Pope; '*there* is a scene, if we will.'

p. 385, note 1. **'cause célèbre.'** See Nicoll and Wise, *Lit. Anecdotes of XIXth Cent.*, i. 516-17, which gives the names, and Furnivall's note. Browning himself made the names public later.

p. 385, note 2. **Inn Album.** See *id.*, i. 533, for Furnivall's note (in *Notes and Queries*, March 25, 1876) on the actual facts and on Browning's modification of them.

p. 387. **Herakles.** In Browning 'Herakles,' 'Alkestis,' 'Aischulos,' and so on. In this purist spelling the poet (*Artemis Prologizes*, 1842) had just preceded Grote (*Hist. of Greece*, vols. i. and ii., 1846), and is more thoroughgoing; see too his preface to his *Agamemnon*, 1877. Unluckily the vowel-values, as given by an English speaker, still remain incorrect under this system; see Sir F. G. Kenyon on the point, *Works of B.*, 1912, vol. viii. pp. xi-xii. Besides, many of these names must be thought of as now actually English words like 'Plato' and 'Homer'; having often become so, of course, through the Latin. I therefore do not follow Browning's spellings save when quoting from him.

p. 392, note 1. **false accent.** For the normal anapæst he often substitutes as follows:—

And the stárs | of *night* béat | with emó | tion, and tíng | led and shót |
Oút in fíre | the *strong* paín | of *pént* knówl | edge; but Í | fáinted nót |.

Now the words in italics, if read naturally, *must* bear a full stress ('the stróng paín,' etc.); but then, if this value be given to them, the metre disappears; for 'Oút in fíre the stróng paín of pént knówledge' simply will not go into verse. So, to recover the metre, we are tempted to read these words with lighter stresses: 'the stròng paín | of pènt knówl | edge,' which is unnatural reading. The point may seem a fine one, but much of the discomfort and jar in Browning's utterance is due to it. Conversely, the metre requires a perhaps doubly false emphasis in 'fáinted nót' (or 'fàinted nót'), which is unnatural; the prose run is a 'dactyl,' *i.e.* 'fáinted not,' which murders the metre. So, in the line

And I stópped | hére; for hére, | in the dárk | ness, Sa′ul gro′aned,

the second foot is dubious, for the natural run requires the 'cretic' (′x′) which is over-harsh; while the variation (x″, 'bacchius') in the last foot is a superb one, and quite natural.

p. 392, note 2. **grammar.** Shadworth Hodgson, *Theory of Practice*, 1870, ii. 272 ff., says that his style shows 'the constant wrestling with the difficulties which the English language offers to the combination of brevity and rapidity with clearness and fulness of thought.' B. is always 'elliptically suppressing relatives, articles, prepositions, auxiliary verbs, and the "to" in infinitives; and thus having continually to trust to the context to show whether the word is a verb, noun, or participle. . . . This dependence of the syntactical construction upon the context . . . compels the reader to be constantly interpreting the parts by the whole instead of the whole by the parts, and constitutes, as it seems to me, at once the peculiar difficulty and the peculiar beauty of Mr. Browning's style.'

p. 394. **philosophised.** The course of Browning's speculations is shown well, though unsympathetically, by Benn, *Rationalism*, ii. 275-83. The whole chapter, 'Rationalism in politics and literature,' is noteworthy. Mr. Benn is concerned with ideas and not with art, and is pleasantly prone to consider all transitional and unsystematic minds as 'gelatinous,' but his analyses are of value.

p. 397. **Mrs. Browning.** *Letters*, ed. F. G. Kenyon, 2 vols., 1897 ; *Letters of R. Browning and E. B. Barrett*, 2 vols., 1899 ; *Letters of E. B. Browning to R. H. Horne*, 2 vols., 1877. J. K. Ingram, *E. B. Browning*, 1888 ('Eminent Women' series). *Complete Poems*, 2 vols., 1904 (also in one vol.). For bibliography see *Camb. Hist. Eng. Lit.*, xiii. 479-85 ; also Nicoll and Wise, *Lit. Anecd. of Nineteenth Cent.*, ii. 81-104 (for scarce issues).

p. 398. **Carlyle.** For Mrs. Browning's essay, 'disentangled' from MS., see Nicoll and Wise, *op. cit.*, ii. 109-22.

p. 401. **rhyming falsely.** See *Letters*, ed. Kenyon, i. 178, 182-3, for Mrs. Browning's defence.

p. 403. **Aurora Leigh.** For a sympathetic analysis of the ideas and temper of the poem see J. Texte, *Études de litt. européenne*, 1898, pp. 239-77, 'Elisabeth Browning et l'idéalisme contemporain.' It is 'un évangile de ce christianisme moderne qu'on nous promet,' etc. ; and this, again, is 'très-moderne, sans rien d'officiel, et sans autre Dieu, comme dit Taine, que "celui d'une âme ardente et féconde en qui la poésie devient une piété."'